Lecture Notes in Computer Science 4016

Commenced Publication in 1973
Founding and Former Series Editors:
Gerhard Goos, Juris Hartmanis, and Jan van Leeuwen

Editorial Board

David Hutchison
Lancaster University, UK
Takeo Kanade
Carnegie Mellon University, Pittsburgh, PA, USA
Josef Kittler
University of Surrey, Guildford, UK
Jon M. Kleinberg
Cornell University, Ithaca, NY, USA
Friedemann Mattern
ETH Zurich, Switzerland
John C. Mitchell
Stanford University, CA, USA
Moni Naor
Weizmann Institute of Science, Rehovot, Israel
Oscar Nierstrasz
University of Bern, Switzerland
C. Pandu Rangan
Indian Institute of Technology, Madras, India
Bernhard Steffen
University of Dortmund, Germany
Madhu Sudan
Massachusetts Institute of Technology, MA, USA
Demetri Terzopoulos
University of California, Los Angeles, CA, USA
Doug Tygar
University of California, Berkeley, CA, USA
Moshe Y. Vardi
Rice University, Houston, TX, USA
Gerhard Weikum
Max-Planck Institute of Computer Science, Saarbruecken, Germany

Jeffrey Xu Yu Masaru Kitsuregawa
Hong Va Leong (Eds.)

Advances in Web-Age Information Management

7th International Conference, WAIM 2006
Hong Kong, China, June 17-19, 2006
Proceedings

Volume Editors

Jeffrey Xu Yu
Chinese University of Hong Kong, Department of Systems Engineering and Engineering Management
Shatin, N.T., Hong Kong, China
E-mail: yu@se.cuhk.edu.hk

Masaru Kitsuregawa
University of Tokyo, Institute of Industrial Science
4-6-1 Komaba, Meguro-Ku, Tokyo 153-8505, Japan
E-mail: kitsure@tkl.iis.u-tokyo.ac.jp

Hong Va Leong
Hong Kong Polytechnic University, Department of Computing
Hung Hom, Kowloon, Hong Kong, China
E-mail: cshleong@comp.polyu.edu.hk

Library of Congress Control Number: 2006927069

CR Subject Classification (1998): H.2, H.3, H.4, I.2, H.5, C.2, J.1

LNCS Sublibrary: SL 3 – Information Systems and Application, incl. Internet/Web and HCI

ISSN 0302-9743
ISBN-10 3-540-35225-2 Springer Berlin Heidelberg New York
ISBN-13 978-3-540-35225-9 Springer Berlin Heidelberg New York

This work is subject to copyright. All rights are reserved, whether the whole or part of the material is concerned, specifically the rights of translation, reprinting, re-use of illustrations, recitation, broadcasting, reproduction on microfilms or in any other way, and storage in data banks. Duplication of this publication or parts thereof is permitted only under the provisions of the German Copyright Law of September 9, 1965, in its current version, and permission for use must always be obtained from Springer. Violations are liable to prosecution under the German Copyright Law.

Springer is a part of Springer Science+Business Media

springer.com

© Springer-Verlag Berlin Heidelberg 2006
Printed in Germany

Typesetting: Camera-ready by author, data conversion by Scientific Publishing Services, Chennai, India
Printed on acid-free paper SPIN: 11775300 06/3142 5 4 3 2 1 0

Preface

The rapid prevalence of Web applications requires new technologies for the design, implementation and management of Web-based information systems. WAIM 2006, following the past tradition of WAIM conferences, was an international forum for researchers, practitioners, developers and users to share and exchange cutting-edge ideas, results, experience, techniques and tools in connection with all aspects of Web data management. The conference drew together original research and industrial papers on the theory, design and implementation of Web-based information systems. As the seventh event in the increasingly popular series, WAIM 2006 made the move towards internationalization by migrating out of mainland China into Hong Kong, the Oriental Pearl, and the cultural junction and melting pot between the East and the West. It was successful in attracting outstanding researchers from all over the world to Hong Kong. These proceedings collected the technical papers selected for presentation at the 7th International Conference on Web-Age Information Management, held in Hong Kong, on June 17–19, 2006.

In response to the call for papers, the Program Committee received 290 full-paper submissions from North America, South America, Europe, Asia, and Oceania. Each submitted paper underwent a rigorous review by three independent referees, with detailed referee reports. Finally, 50 full research papers were accepted, from Australia, China, Germany, Hong Kong, Japan, Korea, Macau, New Zealand, Singapore, Spain, Taiwan, the UK and USA, representing a competitive acceptance rate of 17%. The contributed papers addressed a broad spectrum on Web-based information systems, ranging from data caching, data distribution, data indexing, data mining, data stream processing, information retrieval, query processing, temporal databases, XML and semistructured data, sensor networks, peer-to-peer, grid computing, Web services, and Web searching.

We were extremely excited with our strong Program Committee, comprising outstanding researchers in the WAIM research area. We would like to extend our sincere gratitude to the Program Committee members and external reviewers.

Last but not least, we would like to thank the sponsor, for their strong support of this conference, making its every success. Special thanks go to The Chinese University of Hong Kong, City University of Hong Kong, Hong Kong Baptist University, The Hong Kong Polytechnic University, The Hong Kong University of Science and Technology, The University of Hong Kong, Hong Kong Web Society, IEEE Hong Kong Section Computer Society Chapter, and Hong Kong Pei Hua Education Foundation.

June 2006

Jeffrey Xu Yu
Masaru Kitsuregawa
Hong Va Leong

Message from the Conference Co-chairs

It is our great pleasure to welcome you to WAIM 2006. At age 7, WAIM was ready to reach new heights. This year, WAIM featured a couple of new initiatives. We added two accompanying workshops, one co-chaired by Hong Va Leong and Reynold Cheng and the other co-chaired by Lei Chen and Yoshiharu Ishikawa. A project demo session, organized by Joseph Ng, was introduced so that conference participants could get their hands on the research prototypes and interact directly with the researchers who developed them.

With the help of a dedicated PC, Jeffrey Yu and Masaru Kitsuregawa put together an excellent technical program, including three inspiring keynote speeches by leading experts in the field. In addition to the paper sessions, we had a rich tutorial program, put together by Wang-Chien Lee and Frederick Lochovsky, and a panel that was carefully selected by Kamal Karlapalem and Qing Li to reflect timely research issues relevant to this region.

Besides the technical program, WAIM 2006 would not have been successful without the hard work of many members of the Organizing Committee. Hong Va Leong, the Publication Chair, was responsible for the negotiation and logistics for the publication of the proceedings you are reading. Xiaofeng Meng, Huan Liu and Arkady Zaslavsky helped to publicize WAIM 2006 in four key regions, Asia, USA, Australia and Europe.

We need to thank Joseph Fong for securing the sponsors for the conference and Vincent Ng for carefully managing the budget. Robert Luk and Ben Kao, the Local Arrangement Co-chairs, working with the office staff at the Hong Kong Polytechnic University, Department of Computing, arranged the conference site and social activities to give the conference participants an enjoyable experience during the conference and pleasant memories to bring home.

Last but not least, the six universities in Hong Kong and the Hong Kong Web Society provided both financial and moral support to WAIM 2006. Additional major funding was received from Hong Kong Pei Hua Education Foundation Limited and IEEE Hong Kong Section Computer Society Chapter. Their generosity is much appreciated.

June 2006 Dik Lun Lee and Wang Sang

Organization

WAIM 2006 was jointly organized by The Chinese University of Hong Kong, City University of Hong Kong, Hong Kong Baptist University, The Hong Kong Polytechnic University, The Hong Kong University of Science and Technology, and The University of Hong Kong, and was hosted by the Department of Computing, The Hong Kong Polytechnic University.

Organizing Committee

Honorary Conference Chair:	Keith Chan, The Hong Kong Polytechnic University, Hong Kong
Conference General Co-chairs:	Dik Lun Lee, Hong Kong University of Science and Technology, Hong Kong Shan Wang, Renmin University of China, China
Program Committee Co-chairs:	Jeffrey Xu Yu, Chinese University of Hong Kong, Hong Kong Masaru Kitsuregawa, University of Tokyo, Japan
Tutorial Co-chairs:	Wang-Chien Lee, Pennsylvania State University, USA Frederick H. Lochovsky, Hong Kong University of Science and Technology, Hong Kong
Panel Co-chairs:	Kamal Karlapalem, International Institute of Information Technology, India Qing Li, City University of Hong Kong, Hong Kong
Publication Chair:	Hong Va Leong, The Hong Kong Polytechnic University, Hong Kong
Publicity Co-chairs:	Xiaofeng Meng, Renmin University of China, China Huan Liu, Arizona State University, USA Arkady Zaslavsky, Monash University, Australia
Exhibition and Industrial Liaison Chair:	Joseph Fong, City University of Hong Kong, Hong Kong

Research Project Exhibition and Demonstration Chair:	Joseph Ng, Hong Kong Baptist University, Hong Kong
Local Arrangement Co-chairs:	Robert Luk, The Hong Kong Polytechnic University, Hong Kong Ben Kao, The University of Hong Kong, Hong Kong
Finance Chair:	Vincent Ng, The Hong Kong Polytechnic University, Hong Kong
Steering Committee Liaison:	Sean X. Wang, University of Vermont, USA

Program Committee

Toshiyuki Amagasa	University of Tsukuba, Japan
James Bailey	University of Melbourne, Australia
Sourav S. Bhowmick	Nanyang Technological University, Singapore
Stephane Bressan	National University of Singapore, Singapore
Ying Cai	Iowa State University, USA
Wojciech Cellary	The Poznan University of Economics, Poland
Chee Yong Chan	National University of Singapore, Singapore
Kevin Chang	University of Illinois at Urbana-Champaign, USA
Arbee L.P. Chen	National Tshing Hua University, Taiwan
Lei Chen	Hong Kong University of Science and Technology, Hong Kong
Reynold Cheng	The Hong Kong Polytechnic University, Hong Kong
Kak Wah Chiu	Dickson Computer Systems, Hong Kong
Chin-Wan Chung	KAIST, Korea
Gao Cong	University of Edinburgh, UK
Gill Dobbie	University of Auckland, New Zealand
Ling Feng	Twente University, The Netherlands
Ada Fu	Chinese University of Hong Kong, Hong Kong
Xiang Fu	Georgia Southwestern State University, USA
Stephane Grumbach Liama	The Sino-French IT Lab Institute of Automation, China
Takahiro Hara	Osaka University, Japan
Haibo Hu	Hong Kong University of Science and Technology, Hong Kong
Joshua Huang	University of Hong Kong, Hong Kong
Edward Hung	The Hong Kong Polytechnic University, Hong Kong
Haifeng Jiang	IBM Almaden Research Center, USA

Hyunchul Kang	Chung-Ang University, Korea
Ben Kao	University of Hong Kong, Hong Kong
Hiroyuki Kitagawa	University of Tsukuba, Japan
Yasushi Kiyoki	Keio University, Japan
Flip Korn	AT&T, USA
Chiang Lee	National Cheng-Kung University, Taiwan
Wookey Lee	Sungkyul University, Korea
YoonJoon Lee	KAIST, Korea
Chen Li	University of California, Irvine, USA
Ee Peng Lim	Nanyang Technological University, Singapore
Xuemin Lin	University of New South Wales, Australia
Chengfei Liu	Swinburne University of Technology, Australia
Guimei Liu	National University of Singapore, Singapore
Mengchi Liu	Carleton University, Canada
Tieyan Liu	Microsoft Research Asia, China
Frederick H. Lochovsky	Hong Kong University of Science and Technology, Hong Kong
Nikos Mamoulis	University of Hong Kong, Hong Kong
Weiyi Meng	Binghamton University, USA
Xiaofeng Meng	Renmin University of China, China
Mukesh K Mohania	IBM India Rearch Lab, India
Miyuki Nakano	University of Tokyo, Japan
Wilfred Ng	Hong Kong University of Science and Technology, Hong Kong
Beng Chin Ooi	National University of Singapore, Singapore
Jian Pei	Simon Fraser University, Canada
Zhiyong Peng	Wuhan University, China
Keun Ho Ryu	Chungbuk National University, Korea
Klaus-Dieter Schewe	Massey University, New Zealand
Heng Tao Shen	University of Queensland, Australia
Timothy K. Shih	Tamkang University, Taiwan
Dawei Song	Open University, UK
Kazutoshi Sumiya	University of Hyogo, Japan
Keishi Tajima	Kyoto University, Japan
Kian-Lee Tan	National University of Singapore, Singapore
Katsumi Tanaka	Kyoto University, Japan
Changjie Tang	Sichuan University, China
David Taniar	Monash University, Australia
Yufei Tao	City University of Hong Kong, Hong Kong
Masashi Toyoda	University of Tokyo, Japan
Anthony Tung	National University of Singapore, Singapore
Guoren Wang	Northeastern University, China
Haixun Wang	IBM T. J. Watson Research Center, USA
Ke Wang	Simon Fraser University, Canada
Min Wang	IBM T. J. Watson Research Center, USA
Wei Wang	Fudan University, China

Wei Wang	University of New South Wales, Australia
X. Sean Wang	University of Vermont, USA
Jirong Wen	Microsoft Research Asia, China
Raymond Wong	University of New South Wales, Australia
Jianliang Xu	Hong Kong Baptist University, Hong Kong
Chris Yang	Chinese University of Hong Kong, Hong Kong
Dongqing Yang	Peking University, China
Jun Yang	Duke University, USA
Yun Yang	Swinburne University of Technology, Australia
Masatoshi Yoshikawa	Nagoya University, Japan
Cui Yu	Monmouth University, USA
Ge Yu	Northeastern University, China
Arkady Zaslavsky	Monash University, Australia
Chengqi Zhang	University of Technology, Sydney, Australia
Yanchun Zhang	Victoria University, Australia
Baihua Zheng	Singapore Management University, Singapore
Aoying Zhou	Fudan University, China
Lizhu Zhou	Tsinghua University, China
Shuigeng Zhou	Fudan University, China
Xiaofang Zhou	University of Queensland, Australia
Manli Zhu	Institute for Infocomm Research, Singapore

Steering Committee

Guozhu Dong	Wright State University, USA
Masaru Kitsuregawa	University of Tokyo, Japan
Jianzhong Li	Harbin Institute of Technology, China
Xiaofeng Meng	Renmin University, China
Baile Shi	Fudan University, China
Jianwen Su	University of California at Santa Barbara, USA
Shan Wang	Remin University, China
X. Sean Wang	University of Vermont, USA
Ge Yu	Northeastern University, China
Aoying Zhou	Fudan University, China

External Reviewers

Sihem Amer-Yahia
Rebecca Lynn Braynard
Huiping Cao
Badrish Chandramouli
Bo Chen
Jinchuan Chen
Tao Cheng
Ding-Ying Chiu
Chung-Wen Cho
Shui-Lung Chuang
Yu-Chi Chung
Bin Cui

Manoranjan Dash
Susumu Date
Chun Feng
Guang Feng
Andrew Flahive
Chan Kai Fong
Bin Gao
Matthew Gebski
Byunghyun Ha
Rachid Hamadi
Gab-Soo Han
Wook-shin Han
Kenji Hatano
Bin He
Hao He
Qi He
Wai-Shing Ho
Ming-Qiang Hou
Kenneth Hsu
Ming Hua
Yuan-Ke Huang
Lucas Hui
Huan Huo
Nobuto Inoguchi
Yoshiharu Ishikawa
Arpit Jain
Mingfei Jiang
Govind Kabra
Odej Kao
Panagiotis Karras
Roland Kaschek
Seung Kim
Chui Chun Kit
Isao Kojima
Man Ki Mag Lau
Yuangui Lei
Hou U Leong
Chengkai Li
Chunsheng Li
Jianxin Li
Li Li
Xiaoguang Li
Xiang Lian
Seungkil Lim
Taesoo Lim
Lanturn Lin
Lienfa Lin
Tie-Yan Liu
Yen-Liang Liu
Yuting Liu
Xudong Luo
Yi Luo
Qiang Ma
Xiuli Ma
Robert Magai
Masahiro Mambo
Jiarui Ni
Zaiqing Nie
Bo Ning
Tao Qin
Wenwu Qu
Wenny Rahayu
Vasudha Ramnath
Weixiong Rao
Sourashis Roy
Jarogniew Rykowski
Takeshi Sagara
Akira Sato
Cheng Heng Seng
Vibhuti S. Sengar
Shuming Shi
Houtan Shirani-Mehr
Guojie Song
Ifang Su
Aixin Sun
Yu Suzuki
Takayuki Tamura
Nan Tang
Gu Tao
Norimasa Terada
Bernhard Thalheim
Alexei Tretiakov
Maria Vargas-Vera
Rares Vernica
Krzysztof Walczak
Bin Wang
Di Wang
En-Tzu Wang
Wojciech R. Wiza
Raymond Chi-Wing Wong

Junyi Xie
Linhao Xu
Liang Huai Yang
Qi Yang
Zaihan Yang
Ikjun Yeom
Cai Yi
Yiqun Lisa Yin
Man Lung Yiu
Tomoki Yoshihisa
Yaxin Yu
Yidong Yuan
Kun Yue
Shun-Neng Yung
Wanyu Zang
Xinghuo Zeng
Qing Zhang
Zhen Zhang
Qiankin Zhao
Qiankun Zhao
Xiaohui Zhao
Yuhai Zhao
Jiling Zhong
Bin Zhou
Jianhan Zhu
Sergiy Zlatkin

Sponsoring Institutions

The Chinese University of Hong Kong
City University of Hong Kong
Hong Kong Baptist University
The Hong Kong Polytechnic University
The Hong Kong University of Science and Technology
The University of Hong Kong
Hong Kong Web Society
Hong Kong Pei Hua Education Foundation
IEEE Hong Kong Section Computer Society Chapter

Table of Contents

Indexing

XML Query Processing

Information Retrieval I

Information Retrieval II

Sensor Networks and Grid Computing

Peer-to-Peer

Web Services

Web Searching

Caching and Moving Objects

Temporal Database

Clustering

Clustering and Classification

Data Mining

Data Stream Processing

XML and Semistructured Data

Data Distribution and Query Processing

Advanced Applications

On-Demand Index for Efficient Structural Joins

Kun-Lung Wu, Shyh-Kwei Chen, and Philip S. Yu

IBM T.J. Watson Research Center
{klwu, skchen, psyu}@us.ibm.com

Abstract. A structural join finds all occurrences of structural, or containment, relationship between two sets of XML node elements: ancestor and descendant. Prior approaches to structural joins mostly focus on maintaining offline indexes on disks or requiring the elements in both sets to be sorted. However, either one can be expensive. More important, not all node elements are beforehand indexed or sorted. We present an *on-demand, in-memory* indexing approach to performing structural joins. There is no need to sort the elements. We discover that there are similarities between the problems of structural joins and stabbing queries. However, previous work on stabbing queries, although efficient in search time, is not directly applicable to structural joins because of high storage costs. We develop two storage reduction techniques to alleviate the problem of high storage costs. Simulations show that our new method outperforms prior approaches.

1 Introduction

Structural joins, or containment joins, have been identified as important operations for finding structural relationships, such as ancestor-descendant, within XML documents [1, 3, 6, 13, 15]. Important for XML query processing, a structural join is a set-at-a-time operation that finds all the ancestor-descendant relationships between two different sets of node elements.

Many prior approaches to structural joins assume that each node element is first labeled as an interval [3, 6, 15], (*start, end*), a pair of numbers representing the start and end positions of the element in the document tree [4, 15], encoding the region of the node.[1] Structural joins are then performed on these intervals. In this paper, we similarly assume that node elements are labeled as intervals.

With region-encoded intervals, a structural join can be formally defined as follows. Given two input lists, A and D, where A contains intervals representing ancestor node elements and D contains intervals representing descendant node elements, a structural join is to report all pairs (a, d), where $a \in A$ and $d \in D$, such that $a.start < d.start < d.end < a.end$. In other words, a contains d.

Various approaches have been proposed to perform structural joins. Most of them assume (i) offline indexes are maintained on disks for both input sets [9, 15, 3, 6], or (ii) the elements in both input sets are sorted [8, 15, 1, 3, 6], or (iii) both. However, maintaining indexes on disks incurs both storage and CPU

[1] In general, *start* and *end* need not be the absolute positions of the element.

J.X. Yu, M. Kitsuregawa, and H.V. Leong (Eds.): WAIM 2006, LNCS 4016, pp. 1–12, 2006.
© Springer-Verlag Berlin Heidelberg 2006

costs for storing and updating the indexes, and sorting the elements is rather time consuming. More important, as pointed out in [13], not all elements in an XML document are indexed or sorted beforehand. In contrast, we describe an on-demand, in-memory indexing approach, which does not require node elements to be sorted. To the best of our knowledge, this is the first on-demand, in-memory indexing approach to efficient structural joins.

Because node elements are labeled as intervals, we discover that there are similarities between the problems of structural joins and stabbing queries [11]. A stabbing query problem is to find all the intervals that are stabbed by a point. A structural join problem is to find all the ancestor/descendant element pairs in an XML document. The two problems are similar if we treat all the ancestor elements as intervals and use the start points (or end points) of all the descendant elements to stab the ancestor intervals. Unfortunately, previous work on stabbing queries is not directly applicable to structural joins. For example, although efficient in search time, the state-of-the-art CEI (Containment-Encoded Interval) index [14] can incur a high storage cost for structural joins.

In this paper, we develop a new, on-demand, stabbing query-based index for structural joins, referred to as *StabQ-OD*. Besides keeping the advantage of fast search time, it considerably lessens the high-storage-cost problem by two storage reduction techniques: *unit-length grid elimination* and *domain range partitioning*. We found that the storage cost can be reduced by almost 50% by eliminating the unit-length grid intervals. Moreover, the entire domain range of the ancestor elements can be divided into multiple ampartitions. Structural joins can then be performed serially or in parallel on individual domain partitions.

In [1], an in-memory stack was used to facilitate structural joins of two ordered interval lists. It was the state-of-the-art non-indexed, main memory-based approach, but the elements in both input sets must be in a sorted order. In [3, 6], offline indexes were maintained on disks on the elements to help skip those without matches. A B^+-tree was proposed in [3] to skip descendants without matches. An XR-tree was proposed in [6] to skip both ancestors and descendants without matches. The XR-tree was the state-of-the-art approach that uses indexes to skip elements. However, some elements might not have pre-built indexes.

In [13], a relational DB-based approach to structural joins was proposed. Each XML node element was labeled with a number derived from embedding the XML document tree onto a perfect binary tree. After the labeling, structural joins are transformed into equi-joins and the traditional join operator of a relational DBMS can be called upon to perform the operations. There is no need to sort the elements or maintain indexes on disks. However, this is not a main memory-based approach like ours. In [12], a partition-based scheme was proposed for efficient processing of XML containment queries. However, it is not an index-based approach like ours. A staircase join was proposed in [5]. It is based on ordered encoding of XML documents and never builds indexes.

Finally, structural joins can also be applied to the problem of holistic twig joins [2, 7], which finds the occurrences of a much more complex structural path or twig in an XML document. It can be performed by first applying structural joins to individual sub-paths between two node elements and then combining the intermediate results. However, holistic joins are outside the scope of this paper. In this paper, we focus on structural joins between two sets of node elements.

The rest of the paper is organized as follows. Section 2 briefly summarizes the original CEI indexing scheme for stabbing queries. Section 3 describes the StabQ-OD schemes for structural joins. Section 4 shows our performance studies. Finally, Section 5 summarizes the paper.

2 CEI Indexing for Stabbing Queries

2.1 Containment-Encoded Intervals

Fig. 1 shows an example of containment-encoded intervals and their local ID labeling for CEI indexing. Assume the range of interest of an attribute A is $[0, r)$. First, the range is partitioned into r/L segments of length L, denoted as S_i, where $i = 0, 1, \cdots, (r/L - 1)$, $L = 2^k$, and k is an integer. Note that r is assumed to be a multiple of L. Segment S_i contains all the attribute values in $[iL, (i+1)L)$. Then, $2L - 1$ CEI's are defined for each segment.

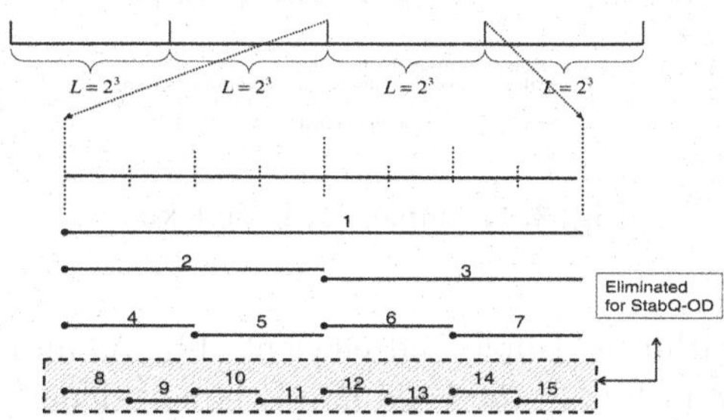

Fig. 1. Example of containment-encoded intervals and their ID labeling

These $2L-1$ CEI's have containment relationships among them. The labeling of CEI's is encoded with such relationships. The ID of a CEI has two parts: the segment ID and the local ID. For each segment, $1, 2, \cdots, 2L - 1$ are assigned to each of the $2L - 1$ CEI's as their local IDs. The local ID assignment follows the labeling of a perfect binary tree. Fig. 1 shows the assignment of local IDs to CEI's within a segment. The global unique ID for a CEI in segment S_i, where $i = 0, 1, \cdots, (r/L) - 1$, is simply computed as $l + 2iL$, where l is the local ID. The local ID of the parent of a CEI with local ID l is $\lfloor l/2 \rfloor$, and it can be efficiently computed by a logical right shift by 1 bit.

Note that CEI's can be alternatively viewed as multi-layered grid intervals. There are $k + 1$ layers, where $k = \log(L)$. The length of a grid interval at layer i is exactly twice that of a grid interval at layer $i + 1$, where $0 \leq i \leq k$. Layer-0 grid intervals have a length of L while layer-k grid intervals have a length of 1.

2.2 Insertion and Search Operations

To insert a query interval, it is first decomposed into one or more grid intervals, then its ID is inserted into the ID lists associated with the decomposed grid intervals [14]. Fig. 2 shows an example of CEI indexing. It shows the decomposition of four query intervals: $Q1, Q2, Q3$ and $Q4$ within a specific segment containing grid intervals of $c1, \cdots, c7$. $Q1$ completely covers the segment, and its ID is inserted into $c1$. $Q2$ lies within the segment and is decomposed into $c5$ and $c6$, the largest grid intervals that can be used. $Q3$ also resides within the segment, but its right endpoint coincides with a guiding post. As a result, we can use $c3$, instead of $c7$ and $c8$ for decomposition. Similarly, $c2$ is used to decompose $Q4$. As shown in Fig. 2, query IDs are inserted into the ID lists associated with the decomposed grid intervals.

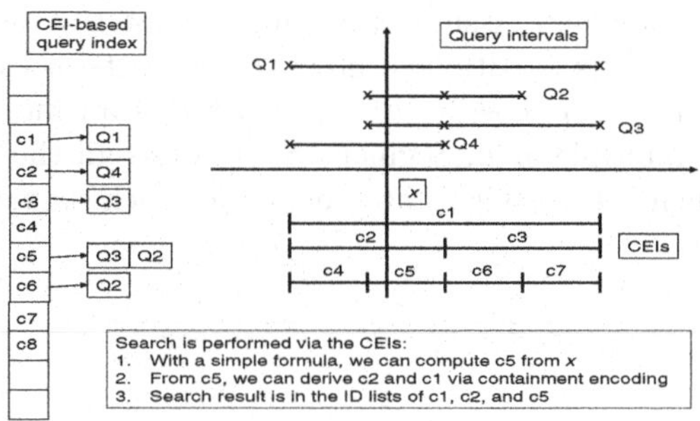

Fig. 2. Example of CEI indexing

The search algorithm is simple and efficient [14]. As an example, to search with a data value x in Fig. 2, the local ID of the unit-length grid interval that contains it is first computed. In this case it is $c5$. Then, from $c5$, the local IDs of all its ancestors that contain $c5$ can be efficiently computed via containment encoding. Namely, the parent of a grid interval with local ID l can be computed by a logical right shift by 1 bit of l. In this case, they are $c2$ and $c1$. As a result, the search result is contained in the 3 ID lists associated with $c1, c2$ and $c5$. We can verify from Fig. 2 that the result indeed contains $Q1, Q2, Q3$ and $Q4$.

3 On-Demand Indexing for Structural Joins

3.1 StabQ-SP

With each node element encoded with a pair of integers, (*start, end*), the structural relationship between two elements can be easily determined [6, 15, 1, 3]. For any two distinct elements u and v in a tree-structured document, the following holds [6]: (1) The region of u is either completely before or completely after that of v; or (2) the region of u either contains that of v or is contained by that of v. Namely, two intervals never partially overlap with each other.

With this complete containment property, the problem of structural joins of two sets of intervals can be transformed into one that searches the CEI index of the ancestor intervals with the start, or end, points of the descendant intervals.

Theorem 1. *A structural join of two sets of intervals, A and D, can be carried out by (a) constructing a CEI index with all the intervals in A, (b) using the start (or end) point of each interval d, where $d \in D$, to search the CEI index, and (c) constructing a join pair (a, d) for each $a \in A_d$, where A_d is the set of interval IDs from the search output in (b).*

Proof: Fig. 3 shows an example of structural joins viewed as stabbing the ancestor intervals with descendant start points. We draw each element interval as a horizontal line segment. Let A_d be the set of interval IDs stabbed by the vertical line at the start point of a descendant interval d. Because there is no partial overlapping between any two elements, each $a \in A_d$ must completely contain d. Since the result of searching the CEI index with the start point of a descendant interval d contains all the ancestor intervals that cover the point, such a search operation generates all the join output pairs involving d. Similar arguments can be made regarding the end point of a descendant interval. □

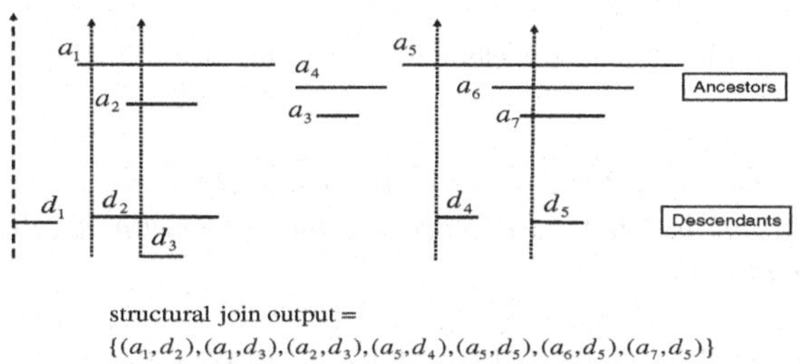

structural join output =
$\{(a_1,d_2),(a_1,d_3),(a_2,d_3),(a_5,d_4),(a_5,d_5),(a_6,d_5),(a_7,d_5)\}$

Fig. 3. Structural joins: stabbing ancestor intervals with descendant start points

Note that because of node element nesting, not uncommon in XML documents, we can use only the start or end point of a descendant element to search the CEI index of the ancestor elements for performing structural joins. For example, in Fig. 3, a_2 contains d_3, but not d_2.

3.2 StabQ-OD

Unit-Length Grid Elimination. The storage cost of the StabQ-SP can be too high, especially if the domain range r is large. From Fig. 2, the pointer array will be large if r is large.

Theorem 2. *For structural joins, the unit-length grid intervals can be completely eliminated.*

Proof: A unit-length grid interval can only appear at the left endpoint and/or the right endpoint of an ancestor element after decomposition [14]. Because node elements are encoded with a pair of integers, representing the start and end positions of the element in the document, no two elements can share the same endpoint and the minimal length of an descendant interval is 1. As a result, the start point of a descendant element would never stab at the portion of an ancestor element that corresponds to a unit-length grid interval. Hence, unit-length grid intervals can be eliminated. □

Note that the minimal ancestor element that can possibly contain a descendant element has a length of at least 3 (see Fig. 4). This is because (a) the length of any descendant element must be greater than or equal to 1 and (b) any pair of elements cannot share the same endpoint. Therefore, ancestor elements of length 1 or 2 can be ignored in index construction.

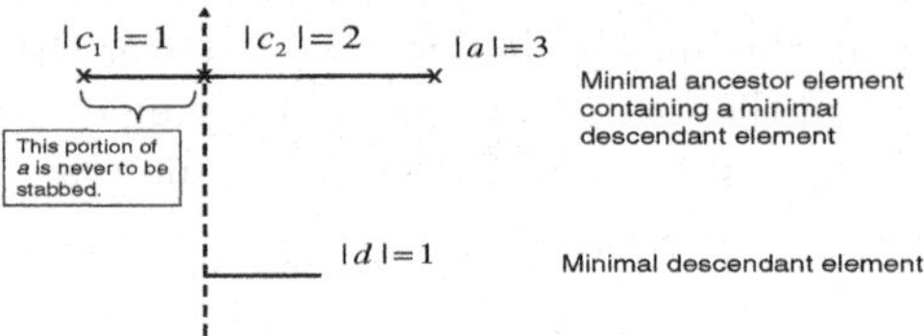

Fig. 4. The minimal ancestor element containing a minimal descendant element

Theorem 3. *For structural joins, any grid interval of length greater than or equal to 2 cannot be eliminated, even if the minimum length of a descendant element is greater than 2.*

Proof: This theorem can be proved by a counter example. Fig. 5 shows an example of a descendant element of length 4. It is contained by an ancestor element of length 6. However, the start point of the descendant element d stabs the ancestor element at the decomposed grid interval c_1, which is of length 2. Hence, we cannot eliminate grid intervals of length 2. □

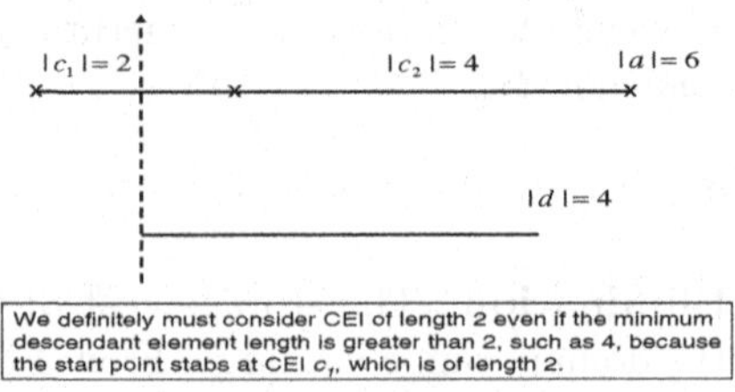

Fig. 5. Grid intervals of length 2 cannot be eliminated

Domain Range Partitioning. Even with unit-length grid intervals completely eliminated, the index storage cost of StabQ-OD can still be high. Containing lots of empty pointers, the pointer array can be replaced with a hash table. However, a hash computation can be too costly, compared with a direct array access.

Instead, we can divide the domain range into multiple partitions and perform structural joins serially or in parallel on individual domain partitions. For example, assume we divide the entire domain range $[0, r)$ into 2 partitions: $P_1 : [0, r/2)$ and $P_2 : [r/2, r)$. To perform a structural join between A and D, we can perform 2 in-memory scans of A and D. During the first scan, all the elements from A that overlap with P_1 are used to build a StabQ-OD index and all the starting points of elements in D that are less than $r/2$ are used to search the index to find the join output. The elements in A that are disjoint with P_1 are ignored; the elements in D with starting points outside P_1 are also ignored. During the second scan, the rest of the elements in A and D are processed.

Structural Join Algorithms with StabQ-OD. With Theorems 2 and 3, we now describe the structural join algorithm using the StabQ-OD with $P = 1$, where P denotes the number of domain range partitions. Fig. 6 shows the pseudo code for **StructuralJoin**, which takes two interval sets, A and D, as inputs and produces an output that contains all the (a, d) pairs where $a \in A$, $d \in D$ and a contains d. For each $a \in A$, it calls **Insertion** function with the element ID and its start and end points as the input parameters. This builds a CEI index for the ancestor set. After that, each descendant element is used to search the CEI index by calling **Search** with the start point as the input parameter. **Search** returns a set of ancestor elements that contain the descendant element. Each of the elements in the returned set can be used to form a join output pair.

```
StructuralJoin (A, D) {
  for (i = 0; i < |A|; i++)
    Insertion(a_i, a_i.start, a_i.end);
    // a_i ∈ A & a_i is the interval ID of an ancestor element
  Joined = φ;
  for (j = 0; j < |D|; j++) {
    A_{d_j} = Search(d_j.start);
    if (A_{d_j} ≠ NULL)
      for all a ∈ A_{d_j}, Joined = Joined ∪ {(a, d_j)};
  }
  return(Joined);
}
```

Fig. 6. Pseudo code for the structural join algorithm with StabQ-OD

Most of the **Insertion** and **Search** algorithms are similar to those for the original CEI indexing [14]. However, for the StabQ-OD, there is only L grid intervals for each segment, hence the global ID of a grid interval with a segment ID S_i and a local ID l is $S_iL + l$, instead of $2S_iL + l$. Because no unit-length grid intervals are used, the search algorithm finds the local ID of the grid interval of length 2 and more stabbed by a data point x.

4 Performance Evaluation

4.1 Simulation Studies

We implemented 5 algorithms for structural joins: the XR-tree [6], the XB-tree [2], the Stack [1], the StabQ-SP and the StabQ-OD. For the XR-tree and the XB-tree, we constructed in-memory indexes for both A and D lists. Once the indexes are built, the elements on the leaf nodes are in sorted order. Hence, we did not sort the elements again and no sorting time was included. However, for the Stack approach, we did. For the Stab-SP and StabQ-OD approaches, only a CEI index was built for the A list. We implemented the domain range partitioning in a single machine and performed the structural joins serially on each domain partition. The simulations were performed on an RS 6000 model 43P machine running AIX 5.1. We conducted structural joins on 8 XML workloads: 4 synthetic and 4 real (see Table 1 for the characteristics of these XML documents).

Table 1. XML workload characterization

XML workload	description	type	size (M)	ancestor/descendant	highly nested?	$\|A\|$ (M)	$\|D\|$ (M)	$\|output\|$ (M)
1	Departments	synthetic	146	employee/name	yes	1.433	2.174	4.844
2	Departments	synthetic	146	employee/email	yes	1.433	1.292	2.908
3	Conferences	synthetic	186	paper/author	no	1.017	3.389	3.050
4	Conferences	synthetic	186	paper/title	no	1.017	1.130	1.017
5	Treebank [10]	real	86	PP/NP	yes	0.136	0.435	0.281
6	Treebank [10]	real	86	VP/NP	yes	0.154	0.435	0.481
7	DBLP [10]	real	134	inproceedings/author	no	0.212	0.716	0.492
8	DBLP [10]	real	134	article/author	no	0.112	0.716	0.221

The synthetic XML documents were generated based on two DTDs used in [6]. Fig. 7 shows the two DTDs, one for departments and one for conferences. For the departments XML, we created two workloads, 1 and 2, and used `employee/name` and `employee/email`, respectively, as the ancestor and descendant pairs. The `employee` node elements can be highly nested in the document. For the conferences XML, we used `paper/author` and `paper/title` as the ancestor/descendant pairs for two different workloads, 3 and 4. The `paper` node elements are fairly flat for the conferences DTD.

For real XML documents, we used the DBLP and the Treebank XML documents downloaded from [10]. The Treebank XML contains English sentences, tagged with parts of speech. The nodes in this document are deeply recursive. For this XML, `PP/NP` and `VP/NP` were chosen as the ancestor and descendant

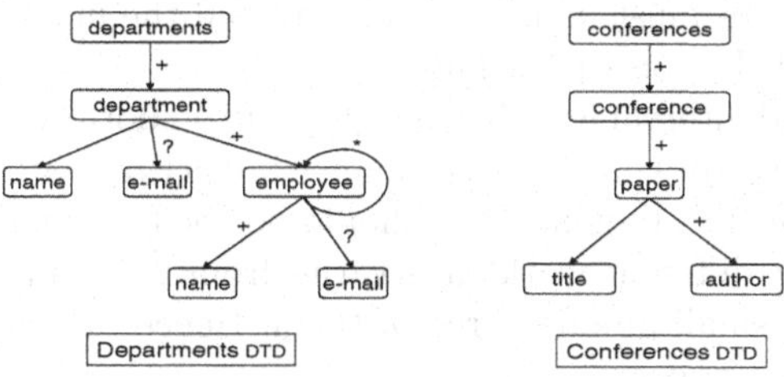

Fig. 7. The DTDs for synthetic data

pairs of two different workloads, 5 and 6. DBLP stands for Digital Bibliography Library Project. The DBLP XML document contains bibliographic information on major computer science journals and proceedings. For DBLP, we used `inproceedings/author` and `article/author` as the ancestor and descendant pairs for two different workloads, 7 and 8. The `inproceedings` and `article` node elements in the document are relatively flat, similar to the conferences DTD as shown in Fig. 7.

Note that some readers might not think that it is fair to include the index construction time for the prior approaches, such as the XR-trees, because they were not designed for on-demand indexing and the indexes can be pre-built offline. However, as we have discussed in Section 1, not all node elements would have the indexes built beforehand when the join operations are performed. In

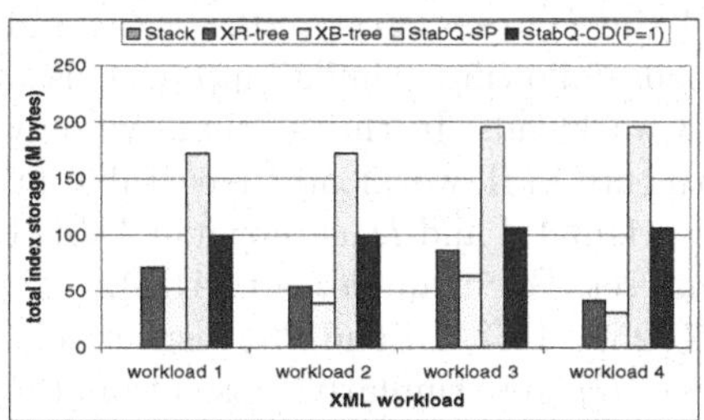

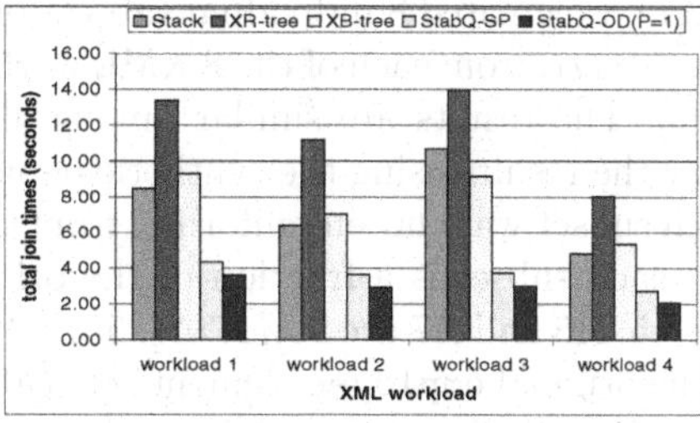

Fig. 8. Comparisons of structural join algorithms with synthetic XML workloads

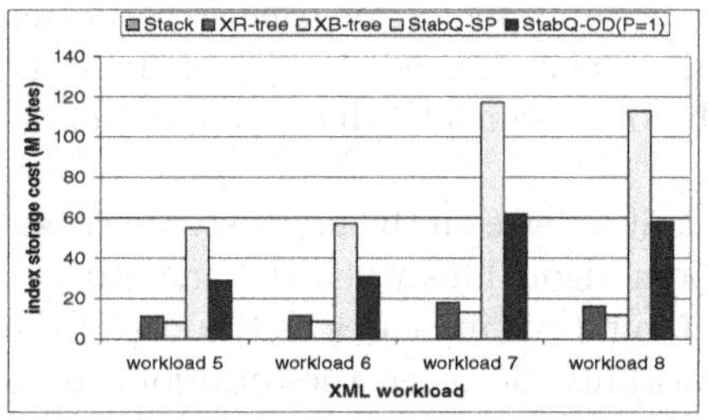

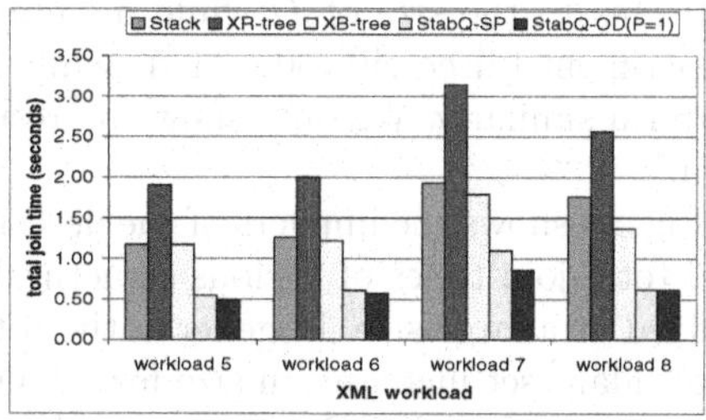

Fig. 9. Comparisons of structural join algorithms with real XML workloads

such cases, the indexes must be built on the fly and the index construction time must be counted in the total join time.

The maximal grid interval length L has impacts on both storage cost and total join time. Detailed studies on the performance impact of L are not provided here and can be found in [14]. In general, L should not be too small or too large. The optimal L for the 8 different workloads varies from 8, 16 and 32. However, the difference is rather small among three of them. Hence, we chose $L = 16$ for all of our studies in this paper.

4.2 Comparisons of Different Join Algorithms

Figs. 8 and 9 show the index storage costs and total join times of 5 different structural join algorithms using the 4 synthetic and real XML workloads, respectively. Here, we used a single domain range partition for the StabQ-OD, denoted as StabQ-OD(P=1). Each workload has a different join selectivity, as evidenced by the different output sizes among the workloads (see Table 1). For all workloads, the StabQ-OD substantially outperforms the XR-tree, the XB-tree and the Stack approaches in terms of total join time. The total join time of the StabQ-SP is comparable to that of the StabQ-OD. However, the storage cost of the StabQ-SP is almost twice as high as that of the StabQ-OD(P=1), which is also higher than those of the XR-tree and XB-tree. Note that there is no index storage cost for the Stack approach.

4.3 Impacts of Input Sizes and Domain Range Partitioning

In order to understand the sensitivity of the join algorithms to the sizes of A and D, we created 8 individual subsets of A and D, respectively, $A0, \cdots, A7$ and $D0 \cdots, D7$, from each of the 8 XML workloads, following a similar approach used in [6]. The results are similar among all 8 workloads. In this section, we only show the results using the synthetic departments XML workload 1 (see Table 1). Each subset was chosen uniformly from the original A and D as shown in Table 1 and each subset is a fraction of the original set. For example, $A0$, $A1, A2$, $A3$, $A4, A5$, $A6$ and $A7$ are 90%, 70%, 55%, 40%, 25%, 15%, 5% and 1%, respectively, of the original `employee` element set. $D0, \cdots, D7$ were similarly chosen from the original `name` element set. We conducted four different sets of experiments using these 16 subsets of A and D.

Experiments I and II were designed to show the sensitivity of these join algorithms to the size of D while maintaining the same A for each experiment. Experiment I used $A0$ (90% of A) while experiment II used $A6$ (5% of A). Both perform similarly. We only show the results of expriment I due to space limitation.

Fig. 10 shows the impacts of the descendant set size on the index storage costs and total join times of various structural join algorithms when the ancestor set is fixed at a large size. In general, the total join time increases as the size of the descendant set increases in size for all algorithms. However, the total join times of the three StabQ-OD schemes, with different domain range partitioning, are less sensitive to the increase in descendant set. For StabQ-OD, the index build

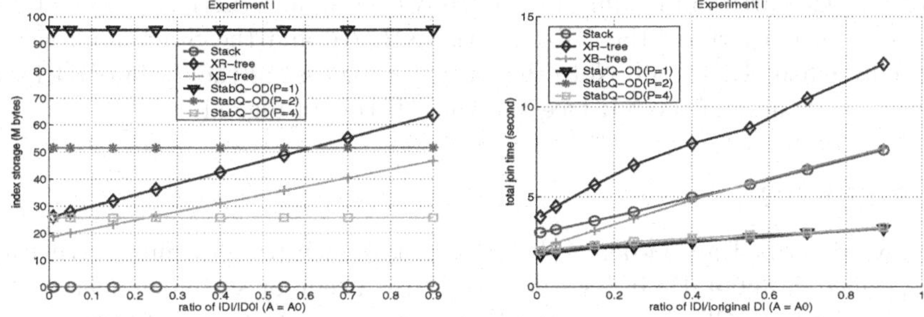

Fig. 10. Experiment I: impact of the descendant set size

time is the same for all the cases in this experiment since the same ancestor set is used. On the other hand, the XR-tree and the XB-tree need to construct on demand two complex indexes. The Stack approach needs to sort two input sets. Hence, their total join times are more positively correlated to the size of the descendant set. The XR-tree, the XB-tree and the Stack approaches are all outperformed by the three StabQ-OD schemes for all the cases. Moreover, the performance advantages of the StabQ-OD schemes over the XR-tree, the XB-tree and the Stack approaches increase as the descendant set increases in size.

Note that we performed the structural joins serially with domain range partitioning. Hence, the total join time is the entire elapsed time of the structural join times for all the domain partitions. However, the index storage cost is measured by the maximal index storage cost of individual partitions. As shown in Fig. 10, the index storage cost of StabQ-OD can be effectively reduced with domain range partitioning with $P = 4$. Moreover, the storage reduction is achieved without a noticeable increase in total join time.

Experiments III and IV show the sensitivity of the structural join algorithms to the size of A while using the same D for each experiment. Experiment III used $D0$ (90% of D) while experiment IV used $D6$ (5% of D). Again, we only show the results of expriment III due to space limitation.

Fig. 11 shows the impacts of different-sized ancestor sets when the descendant set is large. In this experiment, all three StabQ-OD schemes with different

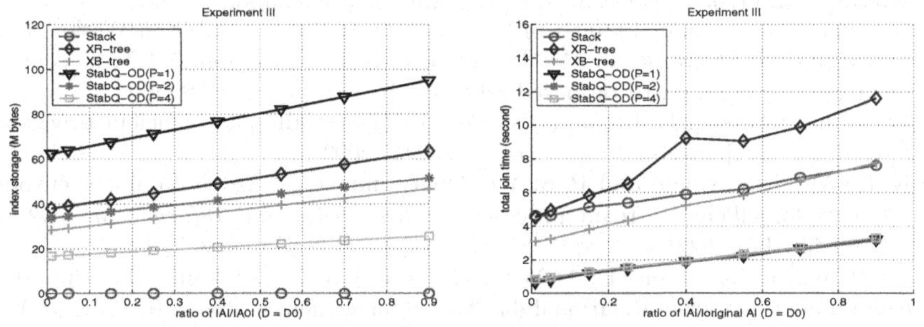

Fig. 11. Experiment III: impact of the ancestor set size

domain range partitioning almost completely overlap in terms of total join times and they all outperform the XR-tree, the XB-tree and the Stack approaches, especially when A is small. Note that the storage cost of the StabQ-OD(P=4) is lower than those of the XR-tree and the XB-tree in Fig. 11.

5 Summary

We have described an on-demand indexing approach to performing structural joins, called StabQ-OD. It incorporates the concept of stabbing query-based indexing, such as CEI indexing, with two storage reduction techniques: unit-length grid elimination and domain range partitioning. There is no need to sort the elements or maintain indexes on disks beforehand. Simulations show that (a) The StabQ-OD outperforms substantially prior techniques, such as the XR-tree, the XB-tree and the Stack approaches; (b) The two storage reduction techniques of the StabQ-OD approach are effective.

References

1. S. Al-Khlifa, H. V. Jagadish, N. Koudas, J. M. Patel, D. Srivastava, and Y. Wu. Structural joins: A primitive for efficient XML query pattern matching. In *Proc. of IEEE ICDE*, 2002.
2. N. Bruno, N. Koudas, and D. Srivastava. Holistic twig joins: Optimal XML pattern matching. In *Proc. of ACM SIGMOD*, 2002.
3. S.-Y. Chien, Z. Vagena, D. Zhang, V. J. Tsotras, and C. Zaniolo. Efficient structural joins on indexed XML documents. In *Proc. of VLDB*, 2002.
4. P. F. Dietz and D. D. Sleator. Two algorithms for maintaining order in a list. In *Proc. of ACM Conf. on Theory of Computing*, 1987.
5. T. Grust, M. van Keulen, and J. Teubner. Staircase join: Teach a relational DBMS to watch its (axis) steps. In *Proc. of VLDB*, 2003.
6. H. Jiang, H. Lu, W. Wang, and B. C. Ooi. XR-Tree: Indexing XML data for efficient structural joins. In *Proc. of IEEE ICDE*, 2003.
7. H. Jiang, W. Wang, H. Lu, and J. Yu. Holistic twig join on indexed XML documents. In *Proc. of VLDB*, 2003.
8. Q. Li and B. Moon. Indexing and querying XML data for regular path expressions. In *Proc. of VLDB*, 2001.
9. J. McHugh and J. Widom. Query optimization for XML. In *Proc. of VLDB*, 1999.
10. XML Data Repository. Dept. of Computer Science and Engineering, University of Washington, http://www.cs.washington.edu/research/xmldatasets.
11. H. Samet. *Design and Analysis of Spatial Data Structures*. Addison-Wesley, 1990.
12. Z. Vagena, M. M. Moro, and V. J. Tsotras. Efficient processing of XML containment queries using partition-based schemes. In *Proc. of IDEAS*, 2004.
13. W. Wang, H. Jiang, H. Lu, and J. X. Yu. PBiTree coding and efficient processing of containment joins. In *Proc. of IEEE ICDE*, 2003.
14. K.-L. Wu, S.-K. Chen, and P. S. Yu. Query indexing with containment-encoded intervals for efficient stream processing. *Knowledge and Information Systems*, 9(1):62–90, Jan. 2006.
15. C. Zhang, J. Naughton, D. DeWitt, Q. Luo, and G. Lohman. On supporting containment queries in Relational database management systems. In *Proc. of ACM SIGMOD*, 2001.

An Efficient Indexing Scheme for Moving Objects' Trajectories on Road Networks*

Jae-Woo Chang and Jung-Ho Um

Dept. of Computer Eng., Chonbuk National Univ., Chonju, Chonbuk 561-756, Korea
jwchang@chonbuk.ac.kr, jhum@dblab.chonbuk.ac.kr

Abstract. Even though moving objects usually move on spatial networks, there has been little research on trajectory indexing schemes for spatial networks, like road networks. In this paper, we propose an efficient indexing scheme for moving objects' trajectories on road networks. For this, we design a signature-based indexing scheme for efficiently dealing with the trajectories of current moving objects as well as for maintaining those of past moving objects. In addition, we provide both an insertion algorithm to store the initial information of moving objects' trajectories and one to store their segment information. We also provide a retrieval algorithm to find a set of moving objects whose trajectories match the segments of a query trajectory. Finally, we show that our indexing scheme achieves much better performance on trajectory retrieval than the leading trajectory indexing schemes, such as TB-tree and FNR-tree.

1 Introduction

Most of studies on spatial databases in the last two decades have considered Euclidean spaces, where the distance between two objects is determined by the ideal shortest path connecting them in the spaces [Se99]. However, in practice, objects can usually move on road networks, where the network distance is determined by the length of the real shortest path connecting two objects on the network. For example, a gas station nearest to a given point in Euclidean spaces may be more distant in a road network than another gas station. Therefore, the network distance is an important measure in spatial network databases (SNDB). Recently, there have been some studies on SNDB for emerging applications, such as location-based service (LBS) and Telematics [B02, PZM03, SJK03, SKS03]. First, Speicys et al. [SJK03] dealt with a computational data model for spatial network. Secondly, Shahabi et al. [SKS03] presented k-nearest neighbors (k-NN) query processing algorithms for SNDB. Finally, Papadias et al. [PZM03] designed a novel index structure for supporting query processing algorithms for SNDB.

Because moving objects usually move on spatial networks, instead of on Euclidean spaces, efficient index schemes are required to gain good retrieval performance on

* This work is financially supported by the Ministry of Education and Human Resources Development (MOE), the Ministry of Commerce, Industry and Energy (MOCIE) and the Ministry of Labor (MOLAB) though the fostering project of the Lab of Excellency.

J.X. Yu, M. Kitsuregawa, and H.V. Leong (Eds.): WAIM 2006, LNCS 4016, pp. 13 – 25, 2006.
© Springer-Verlag Berlin Heidelberg 2006

their trajectories. However, there has been little research on trajectory indexing schemes for spatial networks, like road networks. In this paper, we propose an efficient indexing scheme for moving objects' trajectories on road networks. For this, we design a signature-based indexing scheme for efficiently dealing with the trajectories of current moving objects as well as for maintaining those of past moving objects. In addition, we provide both an insertion algorithm to store the initial information of moving objects' trajectories and one to store their segment information. We also provide a retrieval algorithm to find a set of moving objects whose trajectories match the segments of a query trajectory. The rest of the paper is organized as follows. In Section 2, we introduce related work. In Section 3, we propose a signature-based indexing scheme for moving objects' trajectories. In Section 4, we provide the performance analysis of our indexing scheme. Finally, we draw our conclusions in Section 5.

2 Related Work

There has been little research on trajectory indexing schemes for spatial networks. So we overview both a predominant trajectory index structure for Euclidean spaces and a leading trajectory index structure for spatial networks. First, Pfoser et al. [PJT00] proposed a hybrid index structure which preserves trajectories as well as allows for R-tree typical range search in Euclidean spaces, called TB-tree (Trajectory-Bundle tree). The TB-tree has fast accesses to the trajectory information of moving objects, but it has a couple of problems in SNDB. Firstly, because moving objects move on a predefined spatial network in SNDB, the paths of moving objects are overlapped due to frequently used segments, like downtown streets. This leads to a large volume of overlap among the MBRs of internal nodes. Secondly, because the TB-tree constructs a three-dimensional MBR including time, the dead space for the moving object trajectory is highly increased in case of a long time movement. This leads to a large volume of overlap with other objects' trajectories. Meanwhile, Frentzos [F03] proposed a new indexing technique, called FNR-tree (Fixed Network R-tree), for objects constrained to move on fixed networks in two-dimensional space. The general idea of the FNR-tree is to construct a forest of 1-dimensional (1D) R-trees on top of a 2-dimensional (2D) R-tree. The 2D R-tree is used to index the spatial data of the network, e.g. roads consisting of line segments, while the 1D R-trees are used to index the time interval of each object movement inside a given link of the network. The FNR-tree outperforms the R-tree in most cases, but it has a critical drawback that the FNR-tree has to maintain a tremendously large number of R-trees, thus leading to a great amount of storage overhead to maintain it. This is because the FNR-tree constructs as large number of R-trees as the total number of segments in the networks.

3 Efficient Indexing Scheme for Moving Objects' Trajectories

In this section, we will describe our indexing scheme not only for current trajectories of moving objects, but also for their past trajectories. In addition, we will present both insertion and retrieval algorithms for the trajectories of moving objects.

3.1 Indexing Scheme for Current Trajectories of Moving Objects

For indexing road networks, the TB-tree may lead to a large volume of overlap among the MBRs of its internal nodes. The FNR-tree usually leads to a great amount of storage overhead to maintain a great number of R-trees. To solve their problems, we propose a new signature-based indexing scheme which can have fast accesses to moving object trajectories. Figure 1 shows the structure of our trajectory indexing scheme.

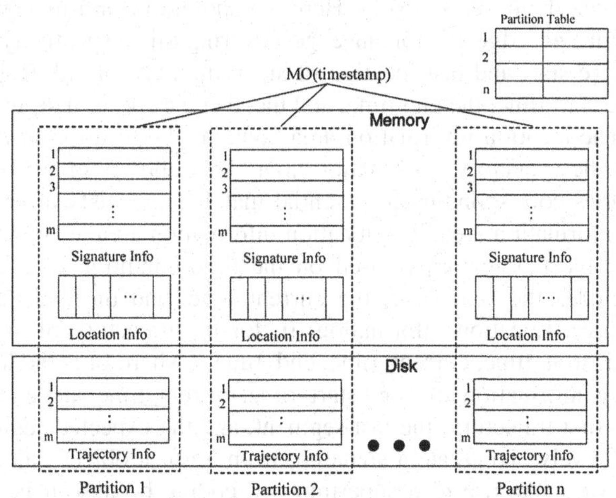

Fig. 1. Signature-based trajectory indexing scheme

The main idea of our trajectory indexing scheme is to create a signature of a moving object trajectory and maintain partitions which store the fixed number of moving object trajectories and their signatures together in the order of their start time. There are a couple of reasons for using partitions. First, because a partition is created and maintained depending on its start time, it is possible to efficiently retrieve the trajectories of moving objects on a given time. Next, because a partition can be accessed independently to answer a trajectory-based query, it is possible to achieve better retrieval performance by searching partitions in parallel. As a result, our trajectory indexing scheme has three advantages. First, our indexing scheme is not affected by the overlap of moving objects' paths and never causes the dead space problem because it is not a tree-based structure like TB-tree. Secondly, our indexing scheme well supports a complex query containing a partial trajectory condition since it generates signatures using a superimposed coding. Finally, our indexing scheme can achieve very good retrieval performance because it can be easily adapted to a parallel execution environment.

Our trajectory indexing scheme consists of a partition table and a set of partitions. A partition can be divided into three areas: trajectory information, location information, and signature information. A partition table maintains a set of partitions which store trajectories for current moving objects. The partition table is resided in the main memory due to its small size. To answer a user query, we find partitions to be accessed by searching the partition table. An entry Ei for a partition i is Ei = <p_start_time, p_end_time, p_expected_time, final_entry_no> where p_start_time, p_current_time, and p_end_time are the smallest start time, the largest current time, the largest end time of all the trajectories, respectively, and final_entry_no means the last entry number in a partition i. The trajectory information area maintains moving object trajectories which consist of a set of segments (or edges). A trajectory Ti for an object MOi is Ti =<MOi_{id}, #_past_seg, #_future_seg, #_mismatch, {sij,eid, start,end,ts,(te or v)}> where #_past_seg, #_future_seg, and #_mismatch are the number of past segments, expected future segments, and the number of mismatched segments between them, respectively. Here, sij and eid mean j-th segment of the trajectory for MOi and edge ID for an edge covering sij, respectively. Start and end mean the relative start and last location of sij in the edge of eid, respectively. ts, te, and v mean the start time, the end time, and the average speed of sij in the edge of eid, respectively. The location information area contains the location of an object trajectory stored in the trajectory information area. This allows for accessing the actual object trajectories corresponding to potential matches to satisfy a query trajectory in the signature information area. The location information area also allows for filtering out irrelevant object trajectories based on the time condition of a query trajectory because it includes the start time, the current time, and the end time for a set of object trajectories. Location information, Ii, for the trajectory of an object MOi is Ii = <MOi_{id}, Li, strat_time, current_time, end_time > where Li is the location for MOi in the trajectory information area and start_time, current_time, and end_time mean the time when the first trajectory, the last segment, and the expected segment for MOi is inserted, respectively. To create a signature from a given object trajectory in an efficient manner, we make use of a superimposed coding because it is very suitable to SNDB applications where the number of segments for an object trajectory is variable [ZMR98]. In case the total number of object trajectories is N and the average number of segments per object trajectory is r, optimal values for both the size of a signature in bits (S) and the number of bits to be set per segment (k) can be calculated as $\ln Fd = -(\ln 2)^2 * S/r$ and $k = S * \ln 2/r$ [FC84]. Here we assume that Fd (false drop probability that a trajectory signature seems to qualify, given that the corresponding object trajectory does not actually qualify) is 1/N. To achieve good retrieval performance, we store both the signature and the location information in the main memory.

3.2 Indexing Scheme for Past Trajectories of Moving Objects

To answer trajectory-based queries with a past time, it is necessary to efficiently search the trajectories of past moving objects which no longer move on road networks. The trajectories of moving objects can be divided into two groups: one being frequently used for answering queries based on current object trajectories (COTSS) and the other for answering queries based on past object trajectories (POTSS). Figure 2 shows an overall architecture of indexing schemes for moving object trajectories. When a current moving object trajectory in COTSS is no longer changed due to the completion of the object movement, the object trajectory should be moved from COTSS to POTSS. The signature and the location information areas of COTSS are resided in the main memory for fast retrieval, whereas all of three areas of POTSS are maintained in the secondary storage. To move current object trajectories from COTSS to POTSS, we should consider three requirements: retrieval of past object trajectories in an efficient way, accesses of the small number of partitions to answer a trajectory-based query, and construction of an efficient time-based index structure. To satisfy the first requirement, we make use of a bit-sliced method [ZMR98] for constructing a signature-based indexing scheme in POTSS, instead of using a bit-string method in COTSS. In the bit-sliced method, we create a fixed-length signature slice for each bit position in the original signature string. That is, we store a set of the first bit positions of all the trajectory signatures into the first slice, a set of the second bit positions into the second slice and so on. When the number of segments in a query trajectory is m and the number of bits assigned to a segment is k, the number of page I/O accesses for answering the query in the bit-sliced method is less than k*m. Therefore, when the number of segments in a query trajectory is small, our indexing scheme requires the small number of page I/O accesses due to the small number of signature slices needed for the query. Figure 2 shows the movement of a partition from COTSS to POTSS. The partitions from 1 to i-1 have been moved to POTSS and k partitions are newly created in COTSS due to the insertion of new moving object trajectories. Because all the trajectories of the partition i-1 have no longer changed, the partition i-1 has just moved from COTSS to POTSS.

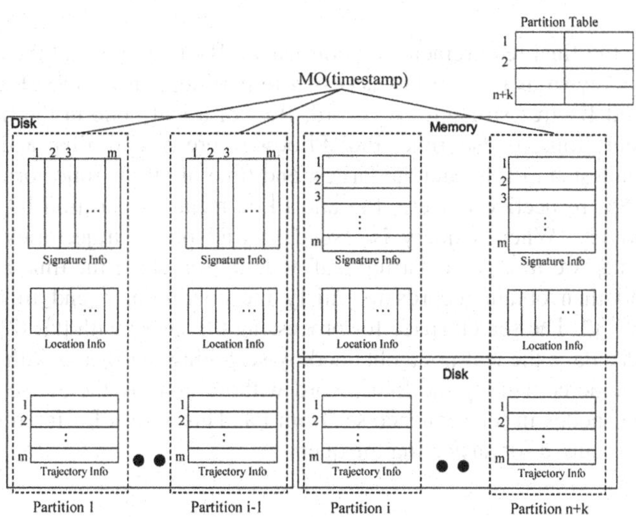

Fig. 2. Movement of partitions from COTSS to POTSS

To satisfy the second requirement, we maintain all the partitions in POTSS so that they can hold the condition that if start_time(partition i)<start_time(partition i+1), end_time(partition i) ≤end_time(partition i+1). If this condition is not satisfied among partitions in POTSS, query processing may be inefficient depending on the time window distribution of partitions in POTSS, even for queries with the same time window. For example, assuming that there are six partitions with their start and their end time as shown in Figure 3, three queries with the same time window can be answered by accessing two, four, and two partitions in POTSS, respectively. Actually, if all the trajectories of the partition i have completed their movements earlier than those of the partition i-1, the partition i should move from COTSS to POTSS earlier than the

partition i-1, leading to the dissatisfaction of the above condition. To prevent it, we require a strategy to store partitions such that if all the trajectories of the partition i are no longer changed, but those of the partition i-1 are changed, we exchange trajectories being changed in the partition i-1 with those having the smallest end time in the partition I and then move the partition i-1 from COTSS to POTSS.

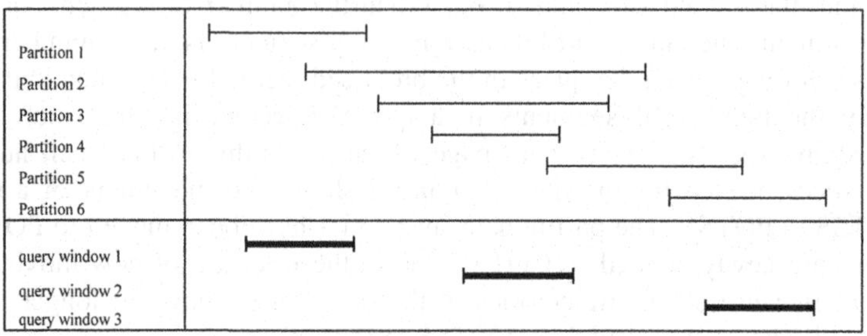

Fig. 3. Example of three queries with the same time window

To satisfy the final requirement, we construct a B+-tree by using the end time of a partition as a key so as to have fast accesses to partitions in POTSS. Figure 4 shows the time-based B+-tree structure. A record, Rec, of a leaf node in the time-based B-tree is <p_start_time, p_end_time, Pid, PLoc> where p_start_time and p_end_time mean the smallest start time and the largest end time of all the trajectories for a partition in POTSS, respectively. Here, Pid and PLoc mean its partition ID and its location, respectively. When a query is issued to find object trajectories with a time window [t1, t2], we first get a starting leaf node by searching the time-based B+-tree using t1, and then obtain records to satisfy the condition, p_end_time ≥ t1 AND p_start_time ≤ t2. The search space for processing the query with [t1, t2] ranges from Pa to Pb. Here Pa is the leaf node obtained by searching the B-tree with key = t1 and Pb is a leaf node containing the first record without holding the above condition by following leaf nodes in the sequence set from Pa. This allows for the minimum page I/O accesses required for answering the query.

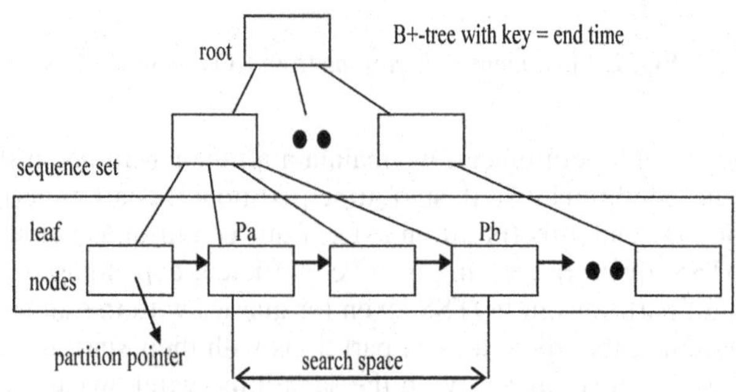

Fig. 4. Time-based B+-tree structure for partitions in POTSS

3.3 Insertion Algorithms for Trajectories of Moving Objects

The algorithms for inserting moving objects trajectories can be divided into an initial trajectory insertion algorithm and a segment insertion algorithm for its trajectory. For the initial trajectory insertion, we find the last partition in the partition table and obtain an available entry (NE) in the last partition. The initial trajectory insertion can be performed according to two cases; one with no expected future trajectories and the other with expected trajectories. First, for the insertion with no expected trajectories, we create a new expected future segment based on an edge where an object currently moves and store it into the NE entry of the trajectory information area in the last partition. Using the expected future segment created, we store start_time (StartT), current_time (CurrentT), and end_time (ExpectedET) into the NE entry of the location information area in the last partition. Here StartT and CurrentT are both assigned to the start time of the moving object and ExpectedET is assigned to NULL. Figure 5

```
Algorithm InsertFirst(MOid, TrajSegList)
/* TraSegList contains the information of a set of expected segments for
the trajectory of a moving object Moid */
    TrajSeg = the first segment of TrajSegList
    Generate a signature SigTS from TrajSeg
    StartT = CurrentT = ts of TrajSeg
      Obtain final_entry_no of the entry, in the partition table, for
      the last partition, LP
      NE = final_entry + 1 //NE=the next available entry in LP
      Obtain the location, Loc, of the entry NE in the trajectory info
      area for inserting object trajectory
        if(end field of TrajSeg=NULL){//no expected trajectory
        ExpectET = NULL
        Store <MOid,0,1,TrajSeg> into the entry NE, pointed by Loc, of
          the trajectory information area in LP}
    else { // expected trajectory exists
       #fseg = 1
       while (the next segment Sn of TrajSegList ≠ NULL) {
          #fseg = #fseg + 1
          Generate a signature SSn from Sn and SigTS = SigTS | SSn }
         Store <MOid,0,#fseg,TrajSegList> into the entry NE, pointed by
         Loc, of the trajectory info area in LP
         Compute ExpectET by using ts, start, and v of the last segment
         of TrajSegList
     } // end of else
    Store SigTS into the entry NE of the signature info area in LP
    Store <MOid,Loc,StartT,CurrentT,ExpectET> into the entry NE of the
    location information area in the LP
    Store <StartT,CurrentT,ExpectET,NE> into the entry for LP in the
    partition table
End InsertFirst
```

Fig. 5. Initial trajectory insertion algorithm for moving objects shows the initial trajectory insertion algorithm (i.e., InsertFirst). Secondly, for the initial trajectory insertion with expected ones, we insert a list of expected future segments (TrajSegList) into the NE entry of the trajectory information area in the last partition. In addition, we create a segment signature (SSn) from each of TrajSegList and generate a trajectory signature (SigTS) by using superimposing (Oring) all of the segment signatures. Using the TrajSegList, we store StartT, CurrentT, and ExpectedET into the NE entry of the location information area. ExpectedET is assigned to the expected end time of the last segment of the TrajSegList. Finally, we store the SigTS into the NE entry of the signature information area. We store <StartT, CurrentT, ExpectedET> into the last partition entry (LP) of the partition table.

For the segment insertion of a moving object trajectory, we find a partition storing its trajectory from the partition table by using the start time (ST) of the moving object.

```
Algorithm InsertSeg(MOid, TrajSeg, ST) /* TraSeg contains a segment for
the trajectory of a moving object Moid, to be stored with an object
trajectory's start time, ST*/
Generate a signature SigTS from TrajSeg
  Locate a partition P covering ST in partition table
  Locate an entry E covering ST for the moving object with MOid in
  the location information area and get its location, Loc, in the
  trajectory information area
  Obtain #actual_seg, #future_seg, and #mismatch of the trajectory
  info entry E (i.e., TE) for the MOid in P
  if(#future_seg = 0) { // no expected trajectory
      Insert TrajSeg into(#actual_seg+1)-th trajectory segment of TE
      Store SigTS into the entry E of the signature info area in P}
  else { // expected trajectory exists
      seg_pos = find_seg(TrajSeg,Loc)
      #actual_seg++, #future_seg = #future_seg - seg_pos
      case(seg_pos = 0) { // find no segment
          Insert TrajSeg into segment of TE and relocate the future
          traj segments backward
          Store SigTS into entry E of the signature info area in P }
      case(seg_pos = 1) //find the first segment
          Insert TrajSeg into (#actual_seg)-th trajectory segment of
          TE for exchanging the old segment
      case(seg_pos > 1) {//find the (seg_pos)-th segment
          #mismatch = #mismatch + seg_pos - 1
        Insert TrajSeg into (#actual_seg)-th segment of TE and relo-
      cate the future traj segments forward
          if(#mismatch/(#future_seg+#actual_seg) >  )
         regenerate_sig(Loc,SigTS,E,P)}// end of case
} // end of else
Update #actual_seg, #future_seg, and #mismatch of TE
CurrentT = te of TrajSeg
  Store CurrentT into the current_time of the entry E of the loca-
  tion information area in the partition P and store CurrentT into
  the p_current_time of the partition P entry in the partition table
End InsertSeg
```

Fig. 6. Segment insertion algorithm for moving object trajectories

In addition, we obtain the entry storing the trajectory information in the partition. Figure 6 shows the segment insertion algorithm (i.e., InsertSeg) for moving object trajectories. Here NE is the entry in the partition covering the object identified by MOid and Loc is the location of the NE entry in the trajectory information area. The segment insertion can be performed in two cases. First, for a segment insertion for trajectories with no expected future ones, we just store a new segment (TrajSeg) into the NE entry of the trajectory information area, being addressed by Loc. In addition, we generate a trajectory signature (SigTS) from the TrajSeg and store the SigTS into the NE entry of the signature information area. Then, we store <MOid,Loc, StartT,CurrentT,ExpectET> into the NE entry of the location information area. Secondly, for a segment insertion for trajectories with expected future ones, we can store a new segment according to three types of the discrepancy between a new segment and the expected segment of a trajectory. To check if a new segment accords with an expected trajectory's segment, we call a find-seg() function to find a segment coinciding with TrajSeg from the expected trajectory of the NE entry. First, in case of no segment coinciding with TrajSeg (seg_pos = 0), we perform the same procedure as the segment insertion algorithm with no expected future segments. In addition, we move the trajectory's expected segments backward by one and store the TrajSeg into the (#_actual_seg)-th segment of the NE entry. Secondly, in case where the segment coinciding with TrajSeg is the first one (seg_pos = 1), we store only the TrajSeg into the (#_actual_seg)-th segment of the NE entry because the TrajSeg is the same as the first expected segment of the trajectory. Otherwise (seg_pos > 1), we delete the (seg_pos-1) number of segments from the expected segments of the NE entry, store the TrajSeg into the (#_actual_seg)-th segment, and move all the expected segments forward by seg_pos-2. If the ratio of mismatched segments (#_mismatch) over all the segments of the trajectory is less than a threshold (τ), we store the trajectory signature (SigTS) generated from the TrajSeg into the NE entry of the signature information area. Otherwise, we regenerate SigTS from the trajectory information by calling a signature regeneration function (regenerate_sig). Finally, we update the values of #_actual_seg, #_future_seg, and #_mismatch in the NE entry, and we update the CurrentT of the NE entry in the location information area and that of the partition P's entry in the partition table.

3.4 Retrieval Algorithm for Trajectories of Moving Objects

The retrieval algorithm for moving object trajectories finds a set of objects whose trajectories match the segments of a query trajectory. Figure 7 shows the retrieval algorithm (i.e., Retrieve) for moving object trajectories. To find a set of partitions satisfying the time interval (TimeRange) represented by <lower, upper> of a given query (Q), we call a find_partition function to generate a list of partitions (partList) by searching both the partition table of COTSS and the B+-Tree of POTSS. The search cases can be determined by comparing the TimeRange (T) with the p_end_time (PEtime) of the last partition in POTSS as well as with the p_start_time (CStime) of the first partition in COTSS as follows.

1. If T.lower > PEtime, both T.lower and T.upper are ranged in COTSS
2. If T.upper ≤ PEtime AND T.upper < CStime, both T.lower and T.upper are ranged in POTSS

3. If T.upper≤PEtime AND T.upper ≥ CStime, both T.lower and T.upper are ranged in POTSS and T.upper is at least within in COTSS simultaneously
4. If T.lower≤PEtime AND T.upper>PEtime, T.lower is within POTSS while T.upper is in COTSS

For the first case, we perform the sequential search of the partition table in COTSS and find a list of partitions (partList) to satisfy the condition that if end_time≠NULL, end_time ≥ T.lower AND start_time ≤ T.upper and otherwise, current_time ≥ T.lower AND start_time ≤ T.upper. Because the partition table of COTSS is resident in a main memory, the cost for searching partition table is low. For the second case, we get a starting leaf node by searching the B+-tree of POTSS with key = lower and obtain the partList to satisfy the above condition by searching the next leaf nodes from the starting leaf node in the sequence set. For the third case, we get two lists of partitions to satisfy the TimeRange in both COTSS and POTSS, respectively. We obtain the partList by merging the two lists of partitions acquired from both POTSS and COTSS. For the last case, we get a starting leaf node by searching the B+-tree of POTSS with key = lower and obtain a list of partitions to satisfy the TimeRange and obtain a list of partitions to satisfy a condition p_start_time ≤ T.upper by searching

```
Algorithm Retrieve(QSegList, TimeRange, MOidList) /* MOidList is a set
of ids of moving objects containing a set of query segments, QsegList,
for a given range time, TimeRange */
Qsig = 0, #qseg = 0, partList = Ø
t1 = TimeRange.lower, t2 = TimeRange.upper
for each segment QSj of QsegList {
     Generate a signature QSSi from Qsj
     QSig = QSig | QSSj, #qseg = #qseg + 1 }
find_partition(TimeRange, partList)
for each partition Pn of partList {
     Obtain a set of candidate entries, CanList, examining the sig-
      natures of signature info area in Pn
     for each candidate entry Ek of CanList {
     Let s,e,c be start_time, end_time, current_time of the entry Ek
      of location information area
     if((s ≤ t2) AND (e ≥ t1 OR c ≥ t1)){
      #matches = 0
      Obtain the first segment ESi of the entry Ek of the trajectory
      info area, TEk and obtain the first segment QSj of QsegList
      while(ESi ≠ NULL and QSj ≠ NULL) {
      if(match(Esi, QSj)=FALSE)
           Obtain the next segment ESi of TEk
      else { #matches = #matches + 1
           Obtain the first segment ESi of Tek }
      if(#matches=#qseg)MOidList=MOidList ∪ {TEk's MOid}
      } } } //end of while //end of if //end of for- CanList
} // end of for - partList
End Retrieve
```

Fig. 7. Retrieval algorithm for moving object trajectories the partition table of COTSS. We obtain the partList by merging the partitions acquired from POTSS and those from COTSS. Next, we generate a query signature (QSig) from a query trajectory's segments. For each partition of the partList, we search the signatures in the signature information area and acquire a list of candidates (CanList). For the entries corresponding to the candidates, we determine if their start_time, end_time, and current_time satisfy the condition. Finally, we determine if the query trajectory matches the object trajectories corresponding to the entries. If it matches object trajectories, we insert the object 's ID into a result list (MoidList).

4 Performance Analysis

We implement our trajectory indexing scheme under Pentium-IV 2.0GHz CPU with 1GB main memory, running Window 2003. For our experiment, we use a road network consisting of 170,000 nodes and 220,000 edges [WMA]. For simplicity, we consider bidirectional edges; however, this does not affect our performance results. We also generate 50,000 moving objects randomly on the road network by using Brinkhoff's algorithm [B2]. For performance analysis, we compare our indexing scheme with the TB-tree and the FNR tree in terms of insertion time and retrieval time for moving object trajectories. Table 1 shows the insertion performance to store one moving object trajectory. It is shown from the result that our indexing scheme preserves nearly the same insertion performance as TB-tree, but the FNR tree provides about two orders of magnitude worse insertion performance than TB-tree. This is because the FNR-tree constructs a tremendously great number of R-trees, i.e., each per a segment in the road network.

Table 1. Ttrajectory insertion performance

	TB-tree	FNR-tree	Our indexing scheme
Trajectory insertion time(sec)	1.232	401	1.606

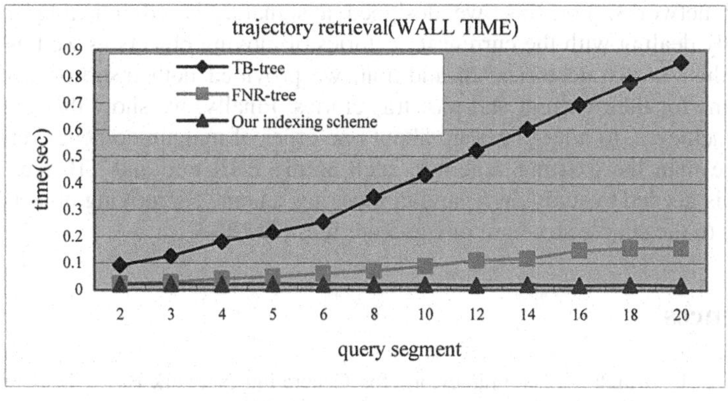

Fig. 8. Trajectory retrieval performance

We measure retrieval time for answering queries whose trajectory contains 2 to 20 segments. Figure 8 shows the trajectory retrieval performance. It is shown from the result that our indexing scheme requires about 20 ms while the FNR-tee and the TB-tree needs 25ms and 93ms, respectively, when the number of segments in a query is 2. It is shown that our indexing scheme outperforms the existing schemes when the number of segments in a query trajectory is small. On the contrary, the TB-tree achieves bad retrieval performance due to a large extent of overlap in its internal nodes even when the number of segments in a query trajectory is small. As the number of segments in queries increase, the retrieval time is increased in both the FNR-tree and the TB-tree; however, our indexing scheme requires constant retrieval time. The reason is why our indexing scheme creates a query signature combining all the segments in a query and it searches for potentially relevant trajectories of moving objects once by using the query signature as a filter. When the number of segments in a query is 20, it is shown that our indexing scheme requires about 20 ms while the FNR-tree and the TB-tree needs 150ms and 850ms, respectively. Thus our indexing scheme achieves about one order of magnitude better retrieval performance than the existing schemes. This is because our indexing scheme constructs an efficient signature-based indexing structure by using a superimposed coding technique. On the contrary, the TB-tree builds a MBR for each segment in a query and performs a range search for each MBR. Because the number of range searches increases in proportion to the number of segments, the TB-tree dramatically degrades on trajectory retrieval performance when the number of segments is great. Similarly, the FNR-tree should search for an R-tree for each segment in a query. Because it gains accesses to as the large number of R-trees as the number of segments in the query, the FNR-tree degrades on trajectory retrieval performance as the number of segments is increased.

5 Conclusions

Even though moving objects usually moves on spatial networks, there has been little research on trajectory indexing schemes for spatial networks, like road networks. Therefore, we proposed an efficient indexing scheme for moving objects' trajectories on road networks. For this, we designed a signature-based indexing scheme for efficiently dealing with the current trajectories of moving objects as well as for maintaining their past trajectories. In addition, we provided both insertion and retrieval algorithms for their current and past trajectories. Finally, we show that our indexing scheme achieves, to a large extent, about one order of magnitude better retrieval performance than the existing schemes, such as the FNR-tree and TB-tree. As future work, it is needed to study on a parallel indexing scheme for moving objects' trajectories, due to the simple structure of signature files [ZMR98].

References

[B02] T. Brinkhoff, "A Framework for Generating Network-Based Moving Objects," GeoInformatica, Vol. 6, No. 2, pp 153-180, 2002.

[F03] R. Frentzos, "Indexing Moving Objects on Fixed Networks," Proc. of Int'l Conf on Spatial and Temporal Databases (SSTD), pp 289-305, 2003.

[FC84] C. Faloutsos and S. Christodoulakis, "Signature Files: An Access Method for Documents and Its Analytical performance Evaluation," ACM Tran. on Office Information Systems, Vol. 2, No. 4, pp 267-288, 1984.

[PJT00] D. Pfoser, C.S. Jensen, and Y. Theodoridis, "Novel Approach to the Indexing of Moving Object Trajectories," Proc. of VLDB, pp 395-406, 2000.

[PZM03] S. Papadias, J. Zhang, N. Mamoulis, and Y. Tao, "Query Processing in Spatial Network Databases," Proc. of VLDB, pp, 802-813, 2003.

[Se99] S. Shekhar et al., "Spatial Databases - Accomplishments and Research Needs," IEEE Tran. on Knowledge and Data Engineering, Vol. 11, No. 1, pp 45-55, 1999.

[SKS03] C. Shahabi, M.R. Kolahdouzan, M. Sharifzadeh, "A Road Network Embedding Technique for K-Nearest Neighbor Search in Moving Object Databases," GeoInformatica, Vol. 7, No. 3,, pp 255-273, 2003.

[SJK03] L. Speicys, C.S. Jensen, and A. Kligys, "Computational Data Modeling for Network-Constrained Moving Objects," Proc. of ACM GIS, pp 118-125, 2003.

[WMA] http://www.maproom.psu.edu/dcw/

[ZMR98] J. Zobel, A. Moffat, and K. Ramamohanarao, "Inverted Files Versus Signature Files for Text Indexing," ACM Tran. on Database Systems, Vol. 23, No. 4, pp 453-490, 1998.

Spatial Index Compression for Location-Based Services Based on a MBR Semi-approximation Scheme*

Jongwan Kim, SeokJin Im, Sang-Won Kang, and Chong-Sun Hwang

Department of Computer Science and Engineering, Korea University, Seoul, Korea
wany@korea.ac.kr, {seokjin, swkang, hwang}@disys.korea.ac.kr

Abstract. The increased need for spatial data for location-based services or geographical information systems (GISs) in mobile computing has led to more research on spatial indexing, such as R-tree. The R-tree variants approximate spatial data to a minimal bounding rectangle (MBR). Most studies are based on adding or changing various options in R-tree, while a few studies have focused on increasing search performance via MBR compression. This study proposes a novel MBR compression scheme that uses semi-approximation (SA) MBRs and SAR-tree. Since SA decreases the size of MBR keys, halves QMBR enlargement, and increases node utilization, it improves the overall search performance. This scheme decreases quantized space more than existing quantization schemes do, and increases the utilization of each disk allocation unit. This study mathematically analyzes the number of node accesses and evaluates the performance of SAR-tree using real location data. The results show that the proposed index performs better than existing MBR compression schemes.

1 Introduction

Location is an intuitive, but important, class of location-based services. Advances in mobile devices and wireless communication technologies have enabled location-based services (LBSs) that deliver location information to mobile users. Typical spatial data management of LBS system is depicted in Figure 1 [1]; examples of such services include finding a hospital or hotel, obtaining local maps, or acting as a tour guide [2]. Client queries are sent to a server, which searches for target objects in a spatial database and returns the search results to the mobile client. At this point, we are interested in the server side index and query processing of location information that is comprised of 2D positions, such as hospital or hotel locations. A LBS server has an index stored in a spatial database to process queries, such as R-tree.

A spatial database system needs a server with considerable memory, and extended processing power, to manage spatial objects. In order to process spatial queries more effectively, appropriate spatial indexes and query processing schemes are required. Most of the spatial data indexing schemes assume a region ranging from the smallest value to the biggest value. The objects in each relevant region try to search the spatial

* This work was supported by the Korea Research Foundation Grant funded by the Korea Government(MOEHRD) (KRF-2005-041-D00665).

J.X. Yu, M. Kitsuregawa, and H.V. Leong (Eds.): WAIM 2006, LNCS 4016, pp. 26 – 35, 2006.
© Springer-Verlag Berlin Heidelberg 2006

data effectively by indexing using a minimum-bounding rectangle (MBR). However, a disk-based spatial database system is limited in terms of its index size. Particularly, when the disk allocation unit is fixed in the operating system, if the index is large, more blocks must be read and the throughput consequently decreases. If the key size is small, a block can contain more keys and consequently fewer blocks are read.

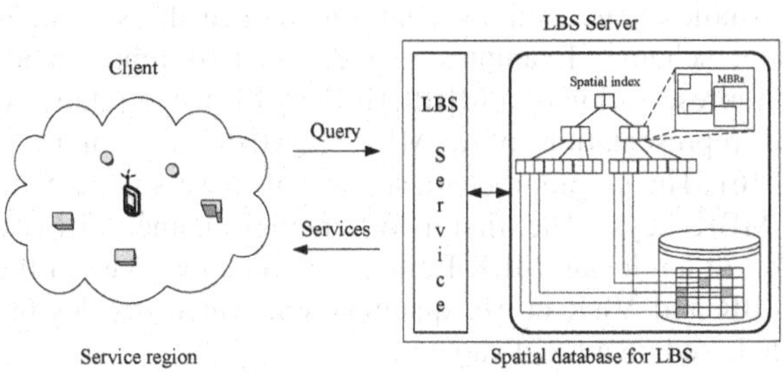

Fig. 1. LBS system architecture and spatial data management

For spatial indexes, especially for R-tree managing two-dimensional data, MBR keys for each dimension account for approximately 80% [3] of the index. Therefore, if the keys are compressed, the number of entries stored in one node increases and search performance improves accordingly. As the entries in a node increase, the overall height of the index is reduced, decreasing disk I/O. With this method, the index saves space. As spatial data have increased over the last few years, studies on spatial data indexes have progressed, especially for R-tree-based indexes. Nevertheless, few studies have attempted to improve performance by reducing the size of the index.

In this paper, we propose a novel spatial indexing scheme and structure, which processes effectively geographical data queries for location-based services. That is, we propose a semi-approximation R-tree (SAR-tree) that indexes spatial data and introduces a semi-approximation MBR (SA) scheme. The basic concept is to compress the MBRs in the spatial index. By decreasing the size of MBR keys, SA halves QMBR enlargement, increases node utilization, and improves overall search performance. This is the first effort, to the best of our knowledge, to take into account the semi-approximation MBR compression that decreases QMBR by 50% in two-dimensional data.

This paper describes three definitions: the relative coordinates of a MBR, semi-approximated MBR using quantization, and the false-overlap region (FOR). We analyzed the performance of SAR-tree by analyzing the number of node accesses in two-dimensional space mathematically and using real location data. The results of the experiment show that the proposed index performs better than existing MBR compression methods.

In the remainder of this paper, Section 2 summarizes MBR compression schemes. Section 3 describes the SA scheme proposed here and includes some definitions. The SA scheme and SAR-tree are implemented in Section 4. Using a variety of experimental results based on real data, Section 5 shows that the SAR-tree performs better than existing MBR compression schemes. Finally, Section 6 concludes the paper with a brief discussion of future work.

2 MBR Compression Schemes

Spatial objects can be expressed by using coordinates to represent the objects, which are expressed as MBRs consisting of the bottom-left and top-right coordinates (Fig. 2) [4]. Since these keys take up most of the index structure, reducing the size of entries by compression enables more entries to be stored in a node.

A number of studies have examined how to reduce the size of indexes using a MBR compression scheme. Examples include relative representation of a MBR (RMBR), hybrid representation of a MBR (HMBR) [3] using relative coordinates in a MBR, quantized representation of a MBR (QMBR) [5], and virtual bounding rectangle (VBR) [6]. The common characteristic of these studies is that they reduce the number of MBR keys. The first two schemes, namely RMBR and HMBR, calculate the offset of a relevant MBR from a specific coordinate of the search region. By contrast, QMBR and VBR utilize quantization, which divides the search region using a grid shape based on a fixed value.

RMBR compresses keys by calculating the relative offset for the MBR stored in each entry with reference to the MBR of one node. Typically, a MBR coordinate is stored in 4 bytes so that a MBR occupies 16 bytes of storage, as R0 in Figure 2. By using a relative offset to store the MBR key of each entry contained in a node, 8 bytes of space can be saved. If the end coordinate of R1 is calculated using the relative offset from the starting coordinate, the storage space of a coordinate is reduced to 2 bytes, further improving node utilization (Fig. 3). HMBR calculates the height and width relative to the starting point of the same MBR, without relating the relative coordinates of the MBR with reference to the entire search space (Fig. 4).

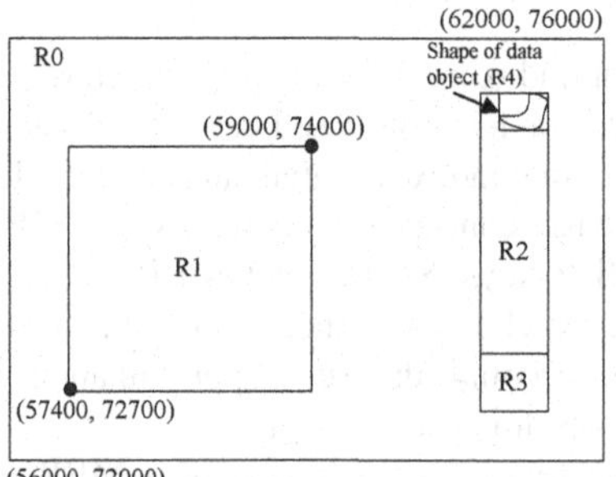

Fig. 2. Minimum bounding rectangles of objects

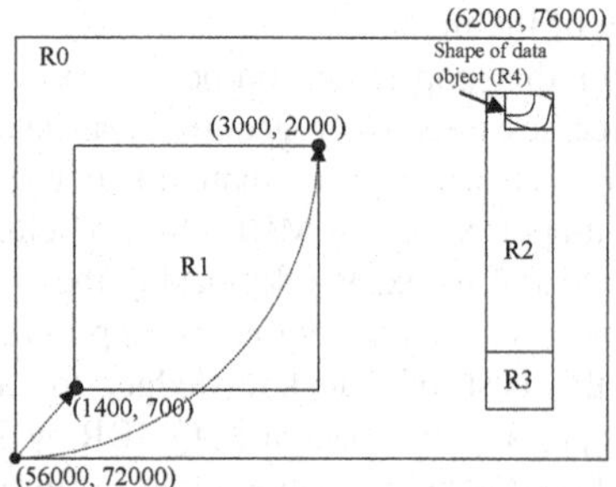

Fig. 3. Relative representation of a MBR

Dividing the search space by a constant integer and compressing keys by using the space in *n*-number quantization can save more space than RMBR or HMBR, and this scheme is referred to as QMBR. We can limit a MBR to a very small value if we replace keys with the number of quantization units by enlarging the MBR in the directions of the x- and y-axes so that it can correspond to the quantization level q. Figure 5 shows the result in which the x- and y-axes are quantized by 16×11 on each axis. If a quantization level is smaller than 256, each coordinate is stored in 1 byte.

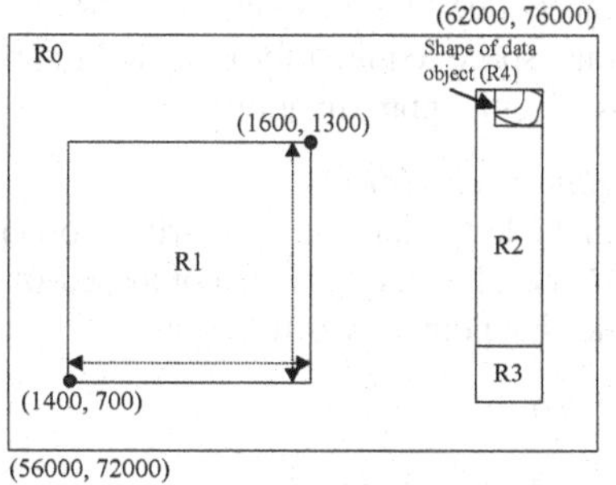

Fig. 4. Hybrid representation of a MBR

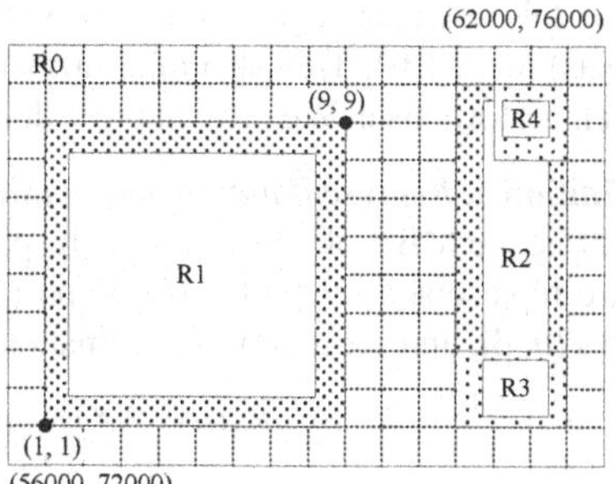

Fig. 5. Quantized representation of MBRs

The concept of VBR, proposed in A-tree [6], reduces the number of units required to store key values by quantizing the search region, as with QMBR. In other words, it constructs a VBR by enlarging the MBR to the closest quantization unit. Unfortunately, these QMBR variants make the MBR larger and thereby enlarge the search region, causing the relevant region to be larger than the real MBR, when searching for objects. As a result, overlap with other MBRs occurs and the number of node accesses increases, degrading the overall search performance.

Although the results in Figures 1, 2, and 3 show that the keys are stored after compression, RMBR and HMBR need 8 and 6 bytes of storage space, respectively. In the case of QMBR, overlapping due to enlargement of the MBR occurs, affecting search performance. RMBR and HMBR enable keys to be stored in fewer bytes by calculating the relative offsets of the keys from the starting coordinates of the search region. In RMBR, a key value stored in 16 bytes is reduced to 8 bytes, while it is further reduced to 6 bytes in HMBR. Nevertheless, HMBR has the disadvantage that the keys to be stored are 4 bytes larger than those for QMBR. Table 1 is a summary of the compression schemes.

Table 1. Summary of MBR compression schemes

Scheme	Approximation	Size	Description
MBR	Two points of a rectangle	16	No compression
RMBR	Relative coordinates	8	MBR size/2 bytes
HMBR	End point=(height, width)	6	Start point=RMBR
QMBR	Quantization of a space	4	MBR enlarges

3 Semi-approximated Representation of MBRs

Since an n-dimensional rectangle, such as a MBR, can be viewed as a $2n$-dimensional point [7], point compression saves index space and increases search performance. Four points represent a 2-D rectangle. In the semi-approximation MBR scheme, each node has a MBR that comprises all entries stored in that node. The MBR of a 2-D space is represented by two endpoints (α, β), where $\alpha = (\alpha.x, \alpha.y)$ and $\beta = (\beta.x, \beta.y)$. The aim of the SA scheme is to represent α as a relative value, and to quantize β in order to halve the size of the false-overlap region (a region without objects due to the expanded MBRs of real objects) in QMBR. This also minimizes the storage space required for keys and improves search performance. We present three definitions of semi-approximation.

Definition 1. *Representation of the relative coordinates of a MBR*
Let M be the MBR of an entire search space; then the lower-left and upper-right corners of M are represented by ($M.lx$, $M.ly$) and ($M.rx$, $M.ry$). The entry, R1, is composed of two points (α, β), and the relative coordinate for the starting point α is as follows:

$$R_M(\alpha) = (|M.lx - \alpha.x|,\ |M.ly - \alpha.y|) \ . \tag{1}$$

Definition 2. *Semi-approximation of a MBR in quantization*
Let (M_s, M_e) be the two points of M using Definition 1, and q be the quantized level, then β is defined as follows, where Q_e is the endpoint of a quantized MBR:

$$Q_e(\beta) = \begin{cases} 1 & ,(\beta = M_s) \\ \lceil ((\beta - M_s)/(M_e - M_s)) \times q \rceil & ,otherwise \ . \end{cases} \tag{2}$$

The endpoint β is transformed into Q_e according to the quantized level, which minimizes the storage space required in bits. The quantized levels, 2^n (n = 0, 1, 2, …, 8), are represented by 1 byte. Since β is determined by the quantized level q, it can be represented by a bit string. In other words, the binary representation is $(Q_e)_2$ and the length of the bit string is $\log_2 q$. The endpoint is stored as $(Q_e - 1)_2$. For example, if $Q_e(\beta.x) = 15$ and $Q_e(\beta.y) = 12$, the bit string is 11101011, the concatenation of the two binary codes. As a result, the R1 keys require only 5 bytes of storage.

Definition 3. *False-overlap region (FOR)*
Let *quantized_MBR* be the region enlarged in quantization; then the search region is enlarged by expanding a MBR to the closest quantization unit. If the enlarged region is defined as FOR, which causes MBRs to overlap, it is defined as follows:

$$FOR = Quantized\_MBR - MBR \ . \tag{3}$$

The SA scheme appears only in the areas of the expanded space (Fig. 6, false-overlap region). The region is half that in the QMBR scheme. The coordinate space also decreases to a minimum of 5 bytes. Although high levels of quantization increase the number of bits, thereby increasing the stored bytes of keys, the SA scheme still maintains its advantage over other methods.

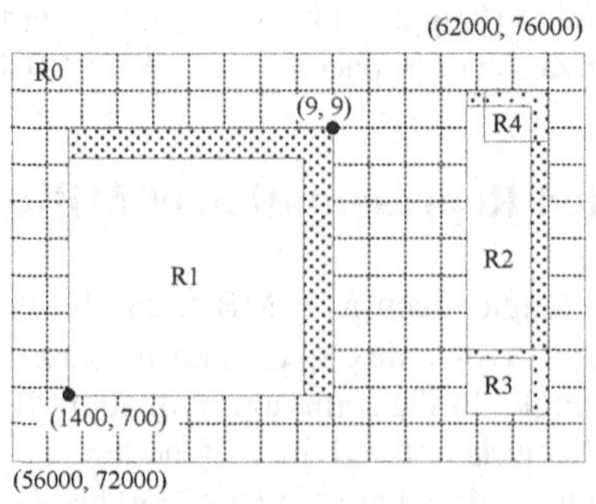

Fig. 6. Semi-approximation of MBRs

4 Implementation of Semi-approximation

A SAR-tree is a height-balanced tree based on R-tree. The differences between SAR-tree and R-tree are insertion and searching. In this section, we discuss the index structure and algorithms of SAR-tree. The SAR-tree comprises the MBRs (MBR_M) based on the minimum approximation of the objects that represent the entire region of node entries as well as a pair of (ptr, SA(MBR)) entries with information on sub-node pointers and the expanded MBR. As shown in Figure 7, a node has up to a maximum m number of entries, and a flag that distinguishes whether the node is a leaf or internal node.

The root node calculates the SA(MBR) of the entire space, and does not possess information on the node MBR. The real MBR of an entry is calculated from the SA(MBR), the parent MBR, and the sub-MBR. That is, the child SA(MBR)s in a node can be calculated from the parent MBR in the same node and the child MBRs. Accurate information on each entry is used to prune the nodes.

# of entries

MBR_M	flag	#	ptr	$SA(R_1)$	ptr	$SA(R_2)$	...	ptr	$SA(R_m)$

Fig. 7. Node structure in SAR-tree

Since the SAR-tree algorithm is based on R-tree, this section discusses only the differences between the two trees. The major differences concern insertion and searching. To insert an object, SAR-tree searches down from the root node to the leaf node, calculates the object SA(MBR), and compares it to the entry for insertion.

Algorithm 1. *Object insertion*
Input: Node n, Object o, QuantizationLevel q

```
Insert(n, o, q){
 if first time
    Invoke SemiApp_makeMBR(entire_space, o,
    q_level);
 if(n==root) Compare o.MBR to MBR of entire space;
    n=root.ptr;
 if(n==leaf node)
    Insert o into the node and check overflow;
    Return to upper;
 Else Compare SA(o.MBR) with all entries;
    n=Entry.ptr;
 Insert(n, o, q);
}
```

Another difference is that SAR-tree compares the quantized endpoint of query region Q with the SA key of each entry. Quantization is processed using the function *SemiApp_makeMBR* (Algorithm 2). An advantage of so doing is that the two coordinates, the query region Q and an entry, can be compared even though the SA (MBR) is not restored to the original coordinate.

Algorithm 2. *Semi approximation of MBRs*
Input: entireSpace M, object O, quantization q_level

```
SemiApp_makeMBR(M, O, q_level){
   SA_s=abs(M_s-O_s);
      /* In detail, SA.lx=abs(M.lx-O.lx); */
      /* SA.ly=abs(M.ly-O.ly); */
   If(O_e==M_s) SA_e=1;
   Else SA_e=Ceiling(q_level*(O_e-M_s)/(M_e-M_s));
   Return SA(O.MBR) to upper; /* SA(O.MBR)=SA_s+SA_e */
}
```

5 Performance Evaluation

Search performance can be improved by increasing node size or compressing MBR keys. In this section, we mathematically analyze the number of node accesses, and evaluate the performance of SAR-tree using a real data set.

5.1 Analysis of the Number of Node Accesses

A mathematical analysis of the number of node accesses in R-tree is outlined in [5]. All nodes are assumed to have MBRs of equal height. Let h denote the hight and M_h denote the number of nodes at the hight h. Then, M_h is equal to the result of Equation (4). Defining the average region of a node as a_h in a tree with height h, a_h of each node is $1/M_h$. The probability that a node of height h will overlap a given query region is $(\sqrt[d]{s}+\sqrt[d]{a_h})^d$. Let d be a dimension and s be the size of the query region, then the overlapping region of nodes with a height of h and the query region is $M_h(\sqrt[d]{s}+\sqrt[d]{a_h})^d$; this is represented as follows, where N is the total number of data and f is the average fan-out of the leaf nodes:

$$\left(1+\sqrt[d]{\left\lceil\frac{N}{f^h}\right\rceil}\cdot s\right)^d. \tag{4}$$

The total number of node accesses from the root to the leaf nodes in R-tree consists of the summation of the nodes at each height, as represented by Equation (5).

$$1+\sum_{h=1}^{\lceil\log_f N\rceil-1}\left(1+\sqrt[d]{\left\lceil\frac{N}{f^h}\right\rceil}\cdot s\right)^d. \tag{5}$$

When the quantized level q is applied, each node has a quantized cell of q^d. Since access to the nodes in QMBR is first conducted at nodes of height h, followed by the sub-nodes, the probability is $(\sqrt[d]{s}+\sqrt[d]{a_h}/q+\sqrt[d]{a_{h-1}}+\sqrt[d]{a_h}/q)^d$. Since this applies to all of the nodes from the root to the leaf nodes, the total number of node accesses is as shown in Equation (6). The QMBR scheme accesses more nodes than the MBR scheme because the MBRs are bigger than the real MBRs owing to quantization.

$$1+\sum_{h=1}^{\lceil\log_f N\rceil-1}\left(1+\sqrt[d]{\left\lceil\frac{N}{f^h}\right\rceil}\cdot s+\sqrt[d]{\left\lceil\frac{N}{f^{h+1}}\right\rceil}\cdot s/q\right)^d. \tag{6}$$

Equation (6) denotes the expanded sides of a MBR, and is modified into Equation (7) to reduce the expansion by half. This is similar to the pattern shown in Figure 8(b).

$$1+\sum_{h=1}^{\lceil \log_f N \rceil - 1}\left(\left(1+\sqrt[d]{\left\lceil \frac{N}{f^h} \right\rceil}\cdot s+\sqrt[d]{\left\lceil \frac{N}{f^{h+1}} \right\rceil}\cdot s/q\right)/2\right)^d . \tag{7}$$

This assumes 1,000,000 objects, a query range of 0.01%, a pointer for each entry of 4 bytes, and that the MBR size of each entry is 16 bytes. The keys in 2-D space are set at 8, 6, 4, and 5, for RMBR, HMBR, QMBR, and SA, respectively. In real quantization, the false-overlap region is a slightly smaller space than in the results of the formula.

5.2 Environment for the Experiment

To measure the practical impacts of our method, we compared SAR-tree with the MBR, RMBR, HMBR, and QMBR schemes. The MBR scheme was performed using R-tree, which is a 2-D index. Existing compression scheme algorithms and SAR-tree were implemented by modifying R-tree. We used a Pentium-IV 2.6-GHz CPU with 1 GB of memory, running on Windows XP Professional.

This experiment used the SEQUOIA dataset, which contains the locations of 62,556 Californian Giant Sequoia groves [8], and was performed using Visual C++. To eliminate the influence of background processes in Windows, we applied the CSIM simulator [9]. Table 2 outlines the parameters in this experiment.

Table 2. Experimental parameters

Parameters	Values
Node size (bytes)	128, 256, 512, 1024
Query range (%)	5, 10, 15, 20, 25, 30
Buffer size (bytes)	4 K
Quantization level	0, 8, 16, 64, 128, 256
Initial Fan-out	200
Data set	62,556 location points

5.3 Experimental Results

Measurement of performance in terms of processing queries was conducted for a range query, and the proportion of the query region in the entire search space was set at a range of 5 to 30%. We generated 10,000 different query rectangles of the same size, and accumulated the results. As shown in Figure 8(a), the number of node accesses was lower for compressed MBRs than for non-compressed MBRs in all query regions. This is attributable to the increased fan-out of each node due to the decrease in MBR keys. Consequently, the number of node accesses also decreases.

The quantization levels of both QMBR and SA were set at 16. Since QMBR stores one coordinate of even the lowest level in 2 bytes, levels were set at equivalence. RMBR and HMBR performed better than QMBR due to the false-overlap region in QMBR. The increased size of nodes allows more node entries. As shown in

Figure 8(b), SA allows more entries than does the HMBR scheme, which requires 6 bytes for keys; thus, SA has a lower number of node accesses.

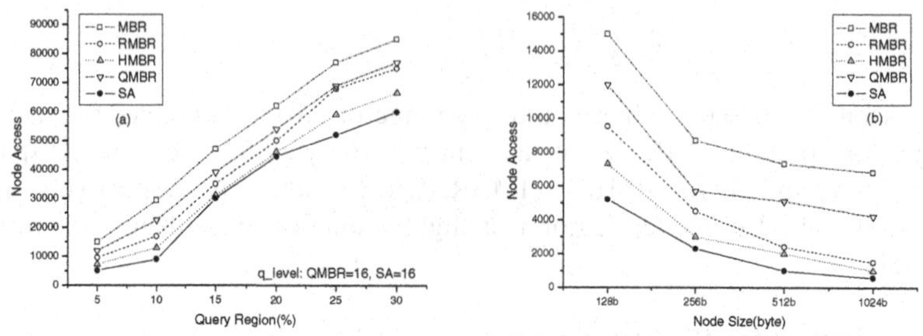

Fig. 8. Number of node accesses of query region (a), node size (b)

As shown in Figure 9, search times reflect the node access patterns. As the node size grows, the search time is quickly minimized. The performance using the QMBR scheme is worse than for the other compression methods due to the increased search region. Performance is better using the RMBR and HMBR schemes owing to the increased number of entries due to reduced key size. It is important to note that although the size of QMBR keys is reduced to 4 bytes, the false-overlap region owing to enlargement by quantization causes backtracking. Thus, the search time increases. Figure 10 shows the accumulated number of node accesses in QMBR and SA with adjustment of the size of quantization. Using the QMBR scheme, the number reduces slowly, but using SA it decreases radically at q=16, when the key is stored in 5 bytes, and gradually increases thereafter. Access is much less frequent than in the QMBR scheme.

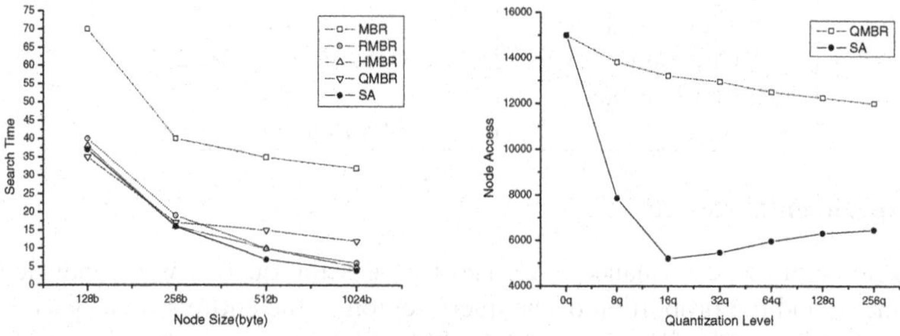

Fig. 9. Search time according to node size **Fig. 10.** Number of node accesses by q level

6 Conclusions and Further Work

We introduced a new scheme, SA, which applies the MBR compression scheme when implementing indexes for spatial data in a spatial database system. In conventional spatial index structures, indexes using MBR compression have rarely been implemented. Existing compression schemes reduce the storage space required for keys in comparison with the original MBRs. Nevertheless, our scheme reduces storage further and improves search performance by halving the enlargement region of QMBR.

In this paper, we proposed SAR-tree, a new spatial index to reduce the size of MBRs by using SA. The performance was evaluated and compared with existing compression schemes by implementing an algorithm in both the SA schemes and SAR-tree. In the experiment, the number of node accesses in SAR-tree, measured by changing the query region, the size of the nodes, and the quantization level, were distinct from those of the existing R-tree. The scheme also performed better than HMBR, although the difference was small. The evaluation in terms of quantized levels compared our method with QMBR using quantization. The methods differed sharply at level 16 due to the difference in the enlargement space in QMBR. The processing time for queries was equivalent to the number of node accesses, and QMBR also differed markedly from other schemes.

The results showed that SAR-tree performed better than both the two-dimensional index R-tree and existing compression schemes, although the difference was small. In a structure in which the keys account for most of the index, compressing the keys reduces the height of the tree, as well as the size of the index, thereby reducing the search time. Therefore, we should consider the case in which we have to restore the compressed keys to their original values, a process that is also minimized using the algorithm proposed here. The scheme proposed in this paper can be used to improve performance in areas that need a fast search, while having constraints on memory size or computation capability, such as in mobile devices. Accordingly, we plan to study performance improvement in those areas.

References

1. J. Schiller, A. Voisard, Location-Based Services. Elsevier, Morgan Kaufmann, San Francisco (2004)
2. S.Y. Wu, K.T. Wu: Dynamic Data Management for Location Based Services in Mobile Environments. IDEAS (2003) 180-191
3. J.D. Kim, S.H. Moon, J.O. Choi: A Spatial Index Using MBR Compression and Hashing Technique for Mobile Map Service. Lecture Notes in Computer Science, Vol. 3453. Springer-Verlag, Berlin Heidelberg New York (2005) 625-636
4. A. Guttman: R-trees: A Dynamic Index Structure for Spatial Searching. ACM SIGMOD Int. Conf. on Management of Data (1984) 47-57
5. K.H. Kim, S.K. Cha, K.J. Kwon: Optimizing Multidimensional Index trees for Main Memory Access. Int. Conf. on ACM SIGMD (2001) 139-150
6. Y. Sakurai, M. Yoshikawa, S. Uemura, H. Kojima: Spatial indexing of high-dimensional data based on relative approximation. VLDB J. (2002) 93-108
7. J. Goldstein, R. Ramakrishnan, U. Shaft: Compressing Relations and Indexes. Proceedings of IEEE Conference on Data Engineering (1998) 370-379
8. The R-tree Portal: http://www.rtreeportal.org
9. H. Schwetman: CSIM19: A Powerful Tool for Building System Models. Proceedings of the 2001 Winter Simulation Conference (2001) 250-255

KCAM: Concentrating on Structural Similarity for XML Fragments*

Lingbo Kong[1], Shiwei Tang[1,2], Dongqing Yang[1], Tengjiao Wang[1], and Jun Gao[1]

[1] Department of Computer Science and Technology, Peking University, Beijing, China, 100871
{lbkong, ydq, tjwang, gaojun}@db.pku.edu.cn
[2] National Laboratory on Machine Perception, Peking University, Beijing, China, 100871
tsw@pku.edu.cn

Abstract. This paper proposes a new method, KCAM, to measure the structural similarity of XML fragments satisfying given keywords. Its name is derived directly after the key structure in this method, Keyword Common Ancestor Matrix. One KCAM for one XML fragment is a $k \times k$ upper triangle matrix. Each element $a_{i,j}$ stores the level information of the SLCA (Smallest Lowest Common Ancestor) node corresponding to the keywords k_i, k_j. The matrix distance between KCAMs, denoted as $KDist(\cdot,\cdot)$, can be used as the approximate structural similarity. KCAM is independent of label information in fragments. It is powerful to distinguish the structural difference between XML fragments.

1 Introduction

XML is rapidly emerging as the *de facto* standard for data representation and exchange on Web applications, such as Digital Library, Web service, and Electronic business. Fig. 1(a) is one example XML data. In order to allow common users to retrieve information conveniently from XML data, it is attractive to adapt keyword search into XML data processing. During this procedure, the similarity measuring mechanism for retrieved XML fragments is a popular issue. It is the core of many operations, such as Top-K or K-NN techniques.

The most popular concept for similarity measuring is edit distance. Regretfully its CPU and I/O cost is too high. So many approximate measures are developed, such as (i) Extended $TF*IDF$ (Including ELIXIR [7], BIR [5], Timber [10], Path coefficient method [8], XRank [11], XPRES [3], MLP [13]), (ii) Path bag model [12], (iii) Structural $TF*IDF$ ([6,9,14–16]). They all borrow the concept of "term" unit from traditional IR, but in different unit forms. Ex-

* Supported by Project 2005AA4Z307 under the National High-tech Research and Development of China, Project 60503037 under National Natural Science Foundation of China (NSFC), Project 4062018 under Beijing Natural Science Foundation (BNSF).

J.X. Yu, M. Kitsuregawa, and H.V. Leong (Eds.): WAIM 2006, LNCS 4016, pp. 36–48, 2006.
© Springer-Verlag Berlin Heidelberg 2006

cept methods in (i), most of them are sensitive to the labels or node positions, which makes them not able to retrieve the fragments with same structure but different labels. Even methods in (i) are not genuinely interested at the structural similarity, except MLP. Further they all do not consider the correlation between nodes. We will illustrate this in more details at Section 2.2.

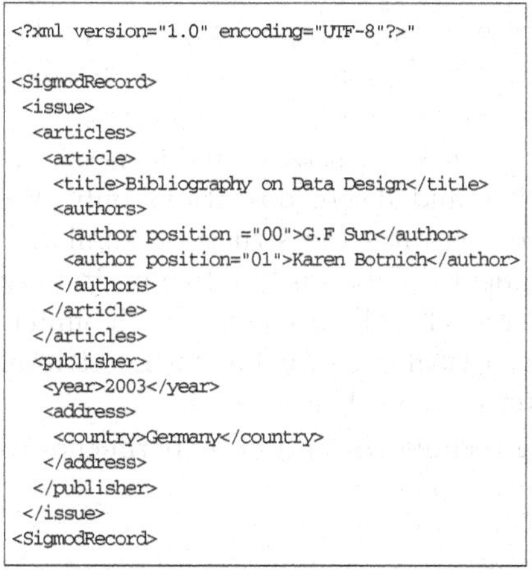

```
<?xml version="1.0" encoding="UTF-8"?>"

<SigmodRecord>
 <issue>
  <articles>
   <article>
    <title>Bibliography on Data Design</title>
    <authors>
     <author position ="00">G.F Sun</author>
     <author position="01">Karen Botnich</author>
    </authors>
   </article>
  </articles>
  <publisher>
   <year>2003</year>
   <address>
    <country>Germany</country>
   </address>
  </publisher>
 </issue>
<SigmodRecord>
```

(a) Part of SigmodRecord.xml

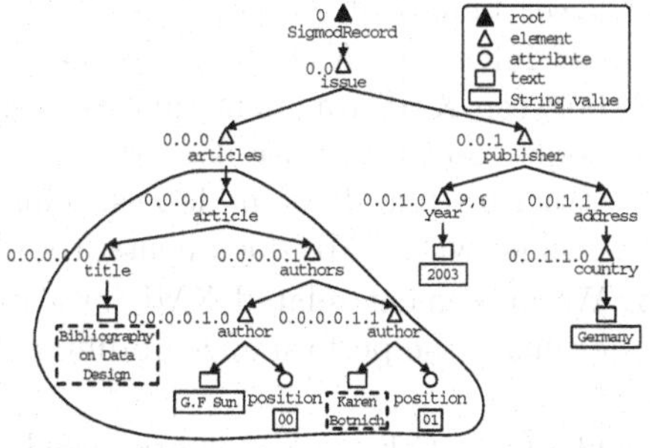

(b) The XML tree for SRecord.xml with Dewey codes and XML fragment for keywords "Botnich Bibliography" (Circled). The integer sequences at the left of nodes are the Dewey codes [1].

Fig. 1. The XML document and its tree model

In this paper we propose a new method, Keyword Common Ancestor Matrix (KCAM in short), to cope with the structural similarity measuring of XML fragments satisfying given keywords. It incorporates the concept of SLCA (See Section 2.1) to capture the structural correlation between keywords, which concentrates on the structural similarity and is independent of labels. One KCAM for one XML fragment is a $k \times k$ upper triangle matrix. Each element $a_{i,j}$ stores the level information of the SLCA node corresponding to the keywords k_i, k_j. By mapping XML fragments into matrices, KCAM can naturally borrow the distance theory developed for matrix. This makes it have precise mathematical illustration. It is powerful to distinguish structural difference between XML fragments than those in extended $TF*IDF$ and path coefficient method. The reason is that the latter can only utilize the depth of nodes to evaluate the weight of retrieved fragments, and do not consider the correlation structure between keywords. Moreover, since it is independent of the labels and node positions, KCAM can retrieve more interesting results, such as fragments with same structure but different labels, while most current techniques are helpless for this kind of interest. Finally it is easy to combine KCAM with other approximate skills. For instance, if we are more interested in some fragments with special semantic (dominated by some particular labels), we can put a filtering level (such as technique from path bag model) before KCAM processing.

The contributions of this paper can be illustrated as follows:

1. We propose a new mechanism KCAM, named after Keyword Common Ancestor Matrix, to capture the structural feature of XML fragments satisfying given keywords. Based on the matrix theory, we also propose experiential distance equation between two XML fragments, T_1 and T_2, based on KCAM. We denote it as $KDist(T_1, T_2)$.
2. We investigate the properties of KCAM, such as distance uniqueness, the lower bound of edit distance with insert and delete operations only. We can infer that $KDist(T_1, T_2)$ mainly concentrates the structural similarity between XML fragments and is independent of labels or relative position of nodes. So we can use it to retrieve interested XML fragments with similar structure but different labels. This is particular useful for XML retrieval dealing with XML documents from heterogeneous background.
3. We implement related XML processing techniques, and do experiments to evaluate the performance of different techniques.

The rest of this paper is organized as follows. Section 2 retrospects related researches focusing on SLCA and structural similarity measuring for hierarchical XML data. We propose KCAM method for XML keyword searching in Section 3. Section 4 illustrates the experiment result. Finally, Section 5 concludes this paper and sheds light on future work.

2 Preliminaries and Related Work

Keyword search [4] is popular when trying to convenience retrieving interesting information from XML data. Among the techniques for keyword processing, retrieving XML fragments satisfying given keywords is the primary issue. [2] conclude this as SLCA problem, in which Dewey encoding [1] is the popular XML indexing scheme. The other important issue is the similarity measuring for retrieved XML fragments.

Before the review, we first illustrate three XML fragments for keywords $\{ k_1, k_2, k_3, k_4, k_5\}$ in Fig. 2 here. The intention is to help readers intuitively understand the difference of our KCAM and other methods at later discussion by real instances. The three fragments have same label domain, "{a, b, c, d }". The fragment in Fig. 2(a) is the source one. We achieve fragment in Fig. 2(b) by exchanging the position of 'k1' and 'k4' of Fig. 2(a). We can directly infer that two fragments of Fig. 2(a) and Fig. 2(b) are different in structure while having same text distribution similarity. When we exchange the position of 'k2' and 'k3'

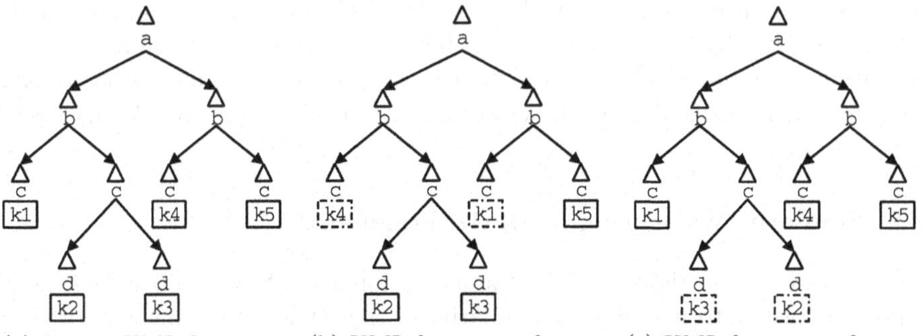

(a) Source XML fragment (b) XML fragment after exchanging K1 and K4 (c) XML fragment after exchanging K2 and K3

Fig. 2. Three XML fragments. The latter two are the variants after exchanging the sequence of some two elements.

in Fig. 2(a), we get the Fig. 2(c). The two fragments of Fig. 2(a) and Fig. 2(c) in fact are same in structure and text distribution similarity.

2.1 SLCA Problem

Retrieving XML fragments for given keywords is the preliminary task for XML keyword searching. In order to guarantee the quality of target fragments, finding the SLCA nodes is the first step, defined as follows.

Definition 1 (SLCA problem). *Given one labeled directed tree, $G = (V_G, E_G, r, A)$, and a sequence of keywords $W = \{k_1, k_2, \ldots, k_k\}$, the SLCA problem is to find all nodes which are the roots of all tightest XML fragments $S = \{s_1, s_2, \ldots, s_n\}$ corresponding to W from G. The tightest XML fragment s_i ($1 \leq i \leq n$) has following properties.*

1. *Each s_i must include W;*
2. *There is no any subtree in s_i which includes W;*

The circled part in Fig. 1(b) is the tightest fragments for keywords "Bibliography Botnich". The "article" node with Dewey code "0.0.0.0" is the SLCA node. We can see that the Dewey code for this SLCA node is just the common longest prefix of Dewey codes corresponding to "title" and "author01" nodes. This obviously benefits from the property of Dewey encoding which adopts the node path information into the Dewey codes [1].

When we investigate the linked edges from "title" node to "author01" node across their SLCA node, we can clearly see that the relative position of SLCA node can be used to illustrate the correlation of those two nodes. We can understand this by following analogy. The linked edges can be mapped as one string "title.article...author01", in which each position between two dots means there is one linked node. When we change the position of "article" as "title..article..author01", it means different structure according to the mapping idea. So the relative position of SLCA node with corresponding nodes can be used to capture the structural difference between XML fragments. This fact enlightens us to adopt SLCA information in structural similarity measuring among XML fragments satisfying given keywords. The result is our KCAM discussed in Section 3.

2.2 Similarity Measuring for XML Fragments

After retrieving the tightest XML fragments following SLCA processing, next important task is to measure the similarity of the retrieved fragments. For now researchers have developed a lot of methods, and most of them are intimate with $TF * IDF$ concept [4] from traditional Information Retrieval theory, in which there are two key skills. The first one is the "term" unit idea. All keyword queries and documents are represented using these terms. The second is the distance measure for vector space. The methods of similarity measures developed for XML fragments can be categorized in three classes, Extended $TF * IDF$, Path bag model, and Structural $TF * IDF$ as follows.

- Extended $TF * IDF$ methods model the problem of XML fragment similarity as multi-variant regression problem based on the text distributions on leaf nodes. They first calculate the text distribution similarity using the concept of $TF * IDF$ on leaf nodes. Then they use the hierarchical information of XML fragment to calculate the final value, which corresponds to the common ancestor node of those leaf nodes. This kind of measures only use hierarchical information to realize the regression, and cannot distinguish fragments through the structural difference. So the three fragments always are same according to this kind of measures.
- Path bag model uses node label path distribution vector to simulate the distance between XML fragments. They do not consider the correlation structure between nodes, so they take for granted that the two XML fragments in Fig. 2(a) and Fig. 2(b) are same. [8] also introduces XPath model with "node position" information trying to absorb the branch information. Nevertheless this also leads to bad situation, i.e., it becomes "position" sensitive, which will see Fig. 2(a) and Fig. 2(c) different. Obviously this method is sensitive with labels, so that it is helpless for fragments with same structure but different labels.
- Structural $TF * IDF$ method absorbs the "term" concept of $TF * IDF$. But "term" here changes to the "*Twig* unit". So the key task of this method is to determine the *Twig* unit vector space, which is proved to be complicated. [14] itself also admits this and resort to path based approximation, which has similar drawback like Path bag model. Researches in [15, 16, 9] have similar ideas. They are sensitive with labels and node position.

We can see that the prominent limitation of current work is their sensitivity with labels and relative node position. The essence of this limitation is induced by the structural simulation using label strings. To sum up, it is necessary to develop new similarity method mainly concentrating on structural feature of

XML fragments. The new method should be independent of the labels and node position. It should also be easy to combine with other skills so as to satisfy users when they are interested in fragments with special labels. Our KCAM here is one example, we will discuss it in detail at Section 3.

Before that, we introduce ID edit distance as the standard to illustrate the structural similarity between XML fragments, which is independent of node labels.

Edit Distance with Insert and Delete Operations Only. In order to formally illustrate the structural similarity between two XML fragments satisfying given keywords, we propose ID edit distance following the edit distance definition.

Definition 2 (ID edit distance). *The edit distance between two XML fragments, T_1 and T_2, satisfying given keywords W, is denoted as $EDist_{I,D}(T_1, T_2)$. It is the minimum cost of all ID edit sequences that transform T_1 to T_2 or vice versa. An ID edit sequence consists only of insertions or deletions of nodes: $EDist_{I,D}(T_1, T_2) = min\{c(S)|S$ is an ID edit sequences transforming T_1 to $T_2\}$.*

Intuitively we have $EDist_{I,D}(T_1, T_2) \leq EDist(T_1, T_2)$, where $EDist(T_1, T_2)$ is the popular edit distance with additional Relabeling. We can see that $ED_{I,D}(T_1, T_2)$ mainly concentrates on the structure information.

3 KCAM: Keyword Common Ancestor Matrix

3.1 KCAM Concept

	K1	K2	K3	K4	K5
K1	3	2	2	1	1
K2		4	3	1	1
K3			4	1	1
K4				3	2
K5					3

(a) KCAM for Source XML fragment in Figure 2(a)

	K1	K2	K3	K4	K5
K1	3	1	1	1	2
K2		4	3	2	1
K3			4	2	1
K4				3	1
K5					3

(b) KCAM for XML fragment in Figure 2(b)

	K1	K2	K3	K4	K5
K1	3	2	2	1	1
K2		4	3	1	1
K3			4	1	1
K4				3	2
K5					3

(c) KCAM for XML fragment in Figure 2(c)

Fig. 3. Three KCAM instances for XML fragments in Figure 2

Though the relative position of SLCA node with two nodes can illuminate the structural information, it is deficient to use mapped strings to calculate the structural difference. The reason is that it is sensitive to labels and relative positions of related nodes as demonstrated in Section 2.2. For seeing this, we propose KCAM as follows to capture the structural information.

Definition 3 (KCAM). *Given a sequence of keywords* $W = \{ k_1, k_2, \ldots, k_k\}$, *the KCAM A for one XML tightest fragment* s_i *according to* W *is one* $k \times k$ *upper triangular matrix whose element* $a_{i,j}$ $(1 \leq i \leq k, i \leq j \leq k)$ *is determined by following equations:*

$$a_{i,j} = \begin{cases} \text{Level of keyword } k_i & i = j \\ \text{Level of the SLCA node of keywords } k_i \text{ and } k_j & i \neq j \end{cases} \quad (1)$$

The matrices for fragments in Fig. 2 are listed in Fig. 3. And we can see that the KCAM for given fragment is unique when the order of keywords W is appointed. This is not a problem for similarity measuring using KCAM because we can build KCAMs for all XML fragments in the same order. Since we can build unique matrix for every fragment satisfied W, we can directly use the norm equations developed in matrix theory. We prefer to use the popular *Frobenius* norm because it not only has simple computation but also covers the whole elements.

$$||A||_F = \sqrt{\sum_{i=1}^{k}\sum_{j=i}^{k} |a_{i,j}|^2} \quad (2)$$

Using the matrix distance induced from *Frobenius* norm, we have following Theorem 1 which guarantees the uniqueness of distance based on KCAM.

Theorem 1. *Here is some keywords,* W, *we have two keyword sequences* W_1 *and* W_2. *According to two given fragments,* T_1 *and* T_2, *there are two KCAMs corresponding to* W_1 *and* W_2, *denoted as* A_{T_1,W_1}, A_{T_1,W_2} *for* T_1, *and* A_{T_2,W_1} *and* A_{T_2,W_2} *for* T_2 *according to* T_2.

They must satisfy following equation:

$$||A_{T1,W_1} - A_{T_2,W_1}||_F = ||A_{T_1,W_2} - A_{T_2,W_2}||_F \quad (3)$$

Proof (Sketch). The SLCA node of any two keyword nodes, k_i *and* k_j, *is definite and unique. its level information is independent of the order of keyword sequence. So the element corresponding to* k_i *and* k_j *is unique. According to the linear transformation for matrix in 'Linear Algebra' theory, two KCAMs from two keyword sequence for same tree with fixed keywords can be interconverted. So the distance of* T_1 *and* T_2 *under* W_1 *is equal to the distance of* T_1 *and* T_2 *under* W_2. *The Equation (3) is tenable.* □

3.2 Structural Distance Based on KCAM

Based on KCAM concept and matrix distance above, we conclude KCAM distance between given XML fragments satisfying some keywords as Definition 4.

Definition 4 (KCAM Distance). *Given a sequence of keywords* $W = \{ k1, k_2, \ldots, k_k\}$, *there are two XML fragments* T_1 *and* T_2 *satisfying* W. *According to Definition 3 we can construct two KCAMs corresponding to* T_1 *and* T_2 *as* A_{T1} *and* A_{T_2}. *The KCAM distance* $KDist(T_1, T_2)$ *between* T_1 *and* T_2 *is defined as follows:*

$$\text{KDist}(T_1, T_2) = \frac{||A_{T_1} - A_{T_2}||_F}{k-1} \tag{4}$$

The $(k-1)$ is used as factorial coefficient.

We have following theorem which shows $KDist$ is one lower bound of $EDit_{I,D}$.

Theorem 2. *Here is one keyword sequence W with k words ($k \geq 2$ by default), and two XML fragments satisfying W, T_1 and T_2. The edit distance with only Insert and Delete operations is denoted as $EDist_{I,D}(T_1, T_2)$. The KCAM distance is marked as $KDist(T_1, T_2)$. They have following relationship:*

$$\text{KDist}(T_1, T_2) \leq \text{EDist}_{I,D}(T_1, T_2) \tag{5}$$

Proof (Sketch). We only discuss the influence when we insert one node into T_1 so as to transform T_1 to T_2. The largest influence occurs when the insertion involves maximum leaf nodes, such as changing Fig. 4(a) into Fig. 4(b) with inserting one new node (Black triangle). The difference matrix according to KCAM concept is illustrated in Fig. 4(c). We have $\sqrt{5 * (5-1)/2}$ where '5' is the number of keywords. When we continue to insert n nodes of this kind for largest influence, the $EDist_{I,D}$ is n. The $KDist$ for this situation is as follows.

$$KDist = \frac{\sqrt{\frac{k(k-1)}{2} n^2}}{k-1} = \sqrt{\frac{1}{2} \frac{k}{k-1} n^2}$$

The ratio of $KDist$ and $EDist_{I,D}$ is $\sqrt{\frac{1}{2}\frac{k}{k-1}}$. Since $k \geq 2$, the ratio must be less than or equal with 1. So we get the Equation. (5). □

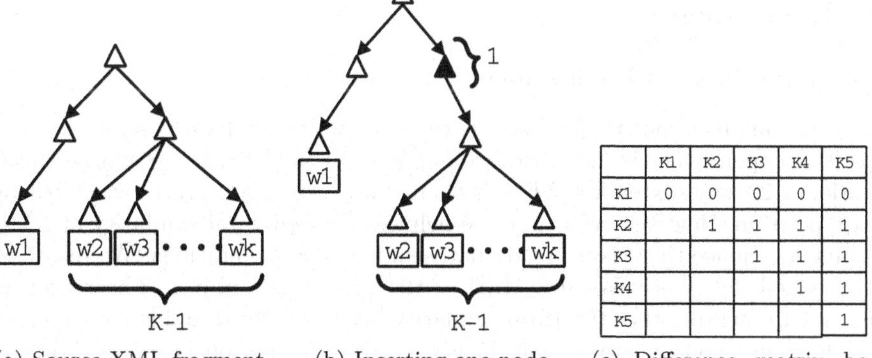

	K1	K2	K3	K4	K5
K1	0	0	0	0	0
K2		1	1	1	1
K3			1	1	1
K4				1	1
K5					1

(a) Source XML fragment (b) Inserting one node (c) Difference matrix between 4(a) and 4(b)

Fig. 4. Demonstration for the largest influence when inserting one node

Based on the definition of $KDist(T_1, T_2)$, we can see the distance between Fig. 2(a) and Fig. 2(b) is $\sqrt{6}/4 \approx 0.612$. The distance between Fig. 2(a) and Fig. 2(c) is 0. Clearly we can use KCAM to distinguish Fig. 2(a) and Fig. 2(b), and at the same time we will not classify Fig. 2(a) and Fig. 2(c) as same.

From illustration above, we can see that KCAM mainly concentrates the structural differences between XML fragments. Based on the mathematical description, it is straightforward to design and implement corresponding algorithms. We do not illustrate the pseudo code of KCAM method here for room reason. The only thing reminding here is that when continuing to implement the KCAM method, we suggest to use vector w.r.t the upper triangle matrix rather than the matrix itself to calculate $KDist$. The conversion from one upper triangle matrix to its vector is to "flatten" the matrix according to matrix theory, illustrated as following:

$$\begin{pmatrix} a_{1,1} & a_{1,2} & \cdots & a_{1,k} \\ & a_{2,2} & \cdots & a_{2,k} \\ & & \vdots & \vdots \\ & & & a_{k,k} \end{pmatrix} \Longrightarrow (a_{1,1}, \cdots, a_{1,k}, a_{2,2}, \cdots, a_{2,k}, \cdots, a_{k,k}) \qquad (6)$$

Our KCAM mechanism has similar properties with MLP scheme proposed in [13]. MLP also has the ability to simulate the structural similarity, but is different from other methods in Extended $TF * IDF$, which essentially care the weight of keywords in retrieved fragments. MLP is also independent of labels and node position. Different from level information of our SLCA nodes, it uses the maximum length among all pathes from the node to its leaves. So MLP cannot distinguish the difference of fragments in Fig. 3(a) and Fig. 3(b). Finally, MLP can also be combined with other label filtering skill when users are interested more at specific domain.

4 Experiments

4.1 Experimental Environment

Since the main property of KCAM is to evaluate the structural similarity, the motif of experiments is unwound around this. Regretfully as we can see from Section 2.2, only Extended $TF * IDF$ methods are not sensitive to label or node position. However even they are helpless for structural similarity of XML fragments. Hence there is no ready datasets for experimentations. We resort to synthesized data here. We use MLP as the comparison object. The reason is that it can measure the structural similarity like our KCAM and is independent of labels and node position. We do not do experiments on other methods in Extended $TF * IDF$, because they have similar computation like MLP.

The synthesized data is constructed similarly with the fragments in Fig. 2. We first build several template fragments like Fig. 3(a), and then increase the number of fragments by randomly shuffling the keyword position and inserting

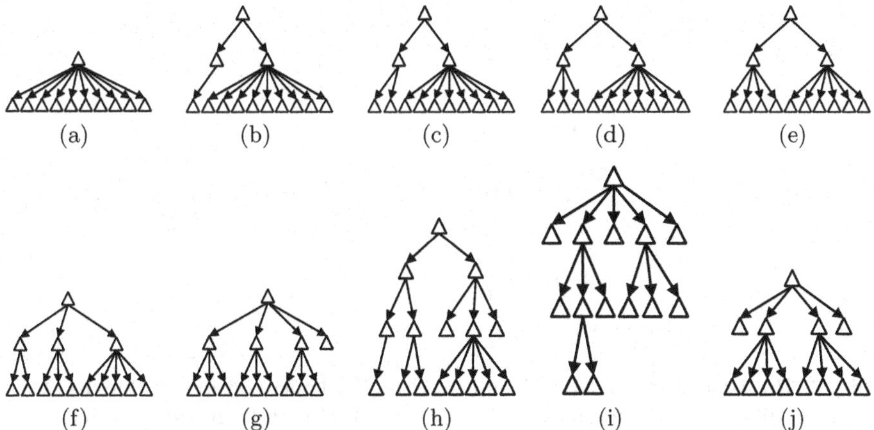

Fig. 5. Ten templates for experimental XML fragments

new node. There are four parameters to control the fragments. One is keyword number (10 in our experiment). The second is the number of template fragments. We select 10 kinds, see Fig. 5. The third is the times of randomly insertion. We set it as 20. The last one is the exchange times among keywords for each template fragments and their variants after insertion. The number of exchange is 20. Finally we get $10 \times 20 \times 40 = 8000$ fragments.

After getting synthesized dataset, we do two kinds of experiments. The first one is for structural sensitivity. After specified fixed keyword number (for example, 4), we construct 10 groups of fragments, each of which has 30 XML fragments randomly selected from the synthesized data and all have fixed keywords. Then we run our KCAM and MLP on them, and compare their precision. The result is show in Fig. 6. The second is for the computation performance. We separate the dataset into 5 groups, from 500 to 2500. We run all methods on each group, and illustrate the running time of each method. We also do experiments to investigate the situations when changing the number of keywords. We pick up one fragment randomly as the structure of keywords. Its result is shown as Fig. 7.

All experiments are run on a Dell Dimension 8100 computer with 1.4GHz Pentium IV processor and 256MB of physical memory. The Operating System is Windows 2000 Professional. We use JAVA as the programming language. The JDK is Java 2 SDK Standard Edition Version 1.4.1. We execute each test 6 times with the performance result of the first run discarded.

4.2 Experiment Result

Fig. 6 is the result for precision comparison of KCAM and MLP. When the number of keywords is specified, we run MLP and KCAM on the sampled XML fragments. After we obtain the precision of KCAM and MLP, we get the ratio of the two precision values corresponding to the two methods. From Fig. 6 we can

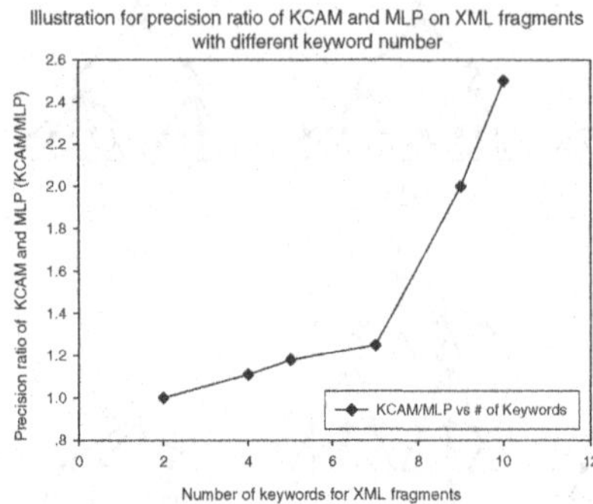

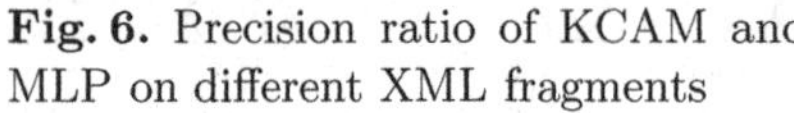

Fig. 6. Precision ratio of KCAM and MLP on different XML fragments

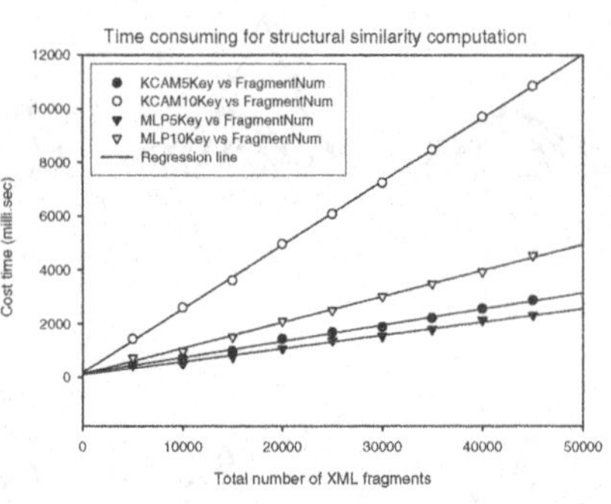

Fig. 7. Time consuming for KCAM and MLP with fragment scale increasing

see that the KCAM/MLP precision ratio is adjacent when the keyword number is small. While the ratio become larger when the keyword number increases. This evolution verifies our KCAM method is more sensitive with the structural changes than MLP method.

Fig. 7 illustrates the runtime performance result of the two methods. We first construct two kinds of synthesized data corresponding to 5 and 10 keywords with different number of fragments from 5000 to 45000. Then we run KCAM and MLP respectively on the datasets. "KCAM5Key" and "KCAM10Key" mean that there are 5 and 10 keywords in all fragments when running KCAM. "MLP5Key" and "MLP10Key" mean that there are 5 and 10 keywords in all fragments when running MLP. From Fig. 7 we can see that when the number of keywords is small, KCAM has comparatively performance with MLP even there are 45000 fragments. When there is many keywords, the performance of KCAM becomes lower than MLP, and the gap becomes larger and larger as fragment number increases.

Though the performance of KCAM is lower than MLP from Fig. 7, KCAM's merit is still obvious according to Fig. 6, that is KCAM has more power to distinguish the structural difference. Besides, we notice that the largest cost of KCAM performance is lower than 12000 millisecond. This shows that the computation of KCAM is still efficient and has pragmatic value for real application.

5 Conclusion and Future Work

In this paper, we propose an effective structural similarity measure for XML fragments satisfying given keywords. We name it as keyword common ancestor matrix, KCAM for short. KCAM is a $k \times k$ upper triangle matrix w.r.t one XML fragment. Element $a_{i,j}$ $(i \neq j)$ stores the level information of SLCA node corresponding to keywords k_i and k_j. Based on distance theory of matrix space, we deduce the structural distance between any XML fragments satisfying given k keywords, $KDist(\cdot,\cdot)$. It is independent of label and node position, while most of current similarity measures for XML fragments are restricted by this. It is exciting that we can retrieve fragments from heterogeneous XML databases even they are substantially different on labels. By the way, it is convenient to combine KCAM with other semantic filtering techniques so as to confine fragments in specific domain.

Our future work will concentrate on investigating techniques in one mechanism which can support XML keyword search and XML query processing (XPath, XQuery) together.

References

1. I. Tatarinov, S. D. Viglas. Storing and Querying Ordered XML Using a Relational Database System. ACM SIGMOD'2002.
2. Y. Xu, Y. Papakonstantinou. Efficient Keyword Search for Smallest LCAs in XML Databases. SIGMOD. 2005.
3. F. Weigel, H. Meuss, K. U. Schulz, F. Bry. *Content and Structure in Indexing and Ranking XML. WebDB.* 2004
4. Baeza-Yates, R., & Ribeiro-Neto, B. (1999). *Modern Information Retrieval*: Pearson Education Limited.
5. Wolff, J. E., Flörke, H., & Cremers, A. B. (2000). *Searching and browsing collections of structural information. In Proceedings of IEEE Advances in Digital Libraries (ADL 2000)*, 141–150.
6. Schlieder, T., & Meuss, H. (2000). *Result ranking for structured queries against xml documents. DELOS Workshop: Information Seeking, Searching and Querying in Digital Libraries.*
7. Chinenyanga, T., & Kushmerick, N. (2001). *Expressive and Efficient Ranked Querying of XML Data. WebDB.*
8. Kotsakis, E. (2002). *Structured Information Retrieval in XML documents. Proceedings of the 2002 ACM symposium on Applied computing*, 663–667.
9. Guha, S., et al. (2002, June 3-6). *Approximate XML Joins. Proceedings of the 2002 ACM SIGMOD International Conference on Management of Data (SIGMOD).*
10. Yu, C., Qi, H., & Jagadish, H. V. (2002). *Integration of IR into an XML Database. INEX Workshop*, 162–169.
11. Guo, L., Shao, F., Botev, C., & Shanmugasundaram, J. (2003, June 9-12). *XRANK: Ranked Keyword Search over XML Documents. SIGMOD 2003.*
12. Joshi, S., Agrawal, N., Krishnapuram, R., & Negi, S. (2003, August 24-27). *A Bag of Paths Model for Measuring Structural Similarity in Web Documents. SIGKDD'03.*
13. Kailing, K., Kriegel, H., Schönauer, S., & Seidl, T. (2004, March 14-18). *Efficient Similarity Search for Hierarchical Data in Large Databases. Advances in Database Technology - EDBT 2004, 9th International Conference on Extending Database Technology*, **ISBN 3-540-21200-0**, 676–693.
14. Amer-Yahia, S., et al. (2005, August 30 - September 2). *Structure and Content Scoring for XML. Proceedings of the 31st International Conference on Very Large Data Bases (VLDB)*, 361–372.

15. Yang, R., Kalnis, P., & Tung, A. K. (2005, June 13-16). *Similarity Evaluation on Tree-structured Data. ACM SIGMOD Conference.*
16. Augsten, N., Böhlen, M. H., & Gamper, J. (2005, August 30 - September 2). *Approximate Matching of Hierarchical Data Using pq-Grams. Proceedings of the 31st International Conference on Very Large Data Bases (VLDB)*, 301–312.

A New Structure for Accelerating XPath Location Steps

Yaokai Feng and Akifumi Makinouchi

Graduate School of Information Science and Electrical Engineering,
Kyushu University, Hakozaki 6-10-1, Fukuoka City, Japan
{fengyk, akifumi}@is.kyushu-u.ac.jp

Abstract. Multidimensional indices have been successfully introduced to the field of querying on XML data. Using R*-tree, T. Grust proposed an interesting method to support all XPath axes. In that method, each node of an XML document is labeled with a five-dimensional descriptor. All the nodes of the XML document are mapped to a point set in a five-dimensional space. T. Grust made it clear that each of the XPath axes can be implemented by a range query in the above five-dimensional space. Thus, R*-tree can be used to improve the query performance for XPath axes. However, according to our investigations, most of the range queries for the XPath axes are partially-dimensional range queries. That is, the number of query dimensions in each of the range queries is less than five, although the R*-tree is built in the five-dimensional space. If the existing multidimensional indices are used for such range queries, then a great deal of information that is irrelevant to the queries also has to be read from disk. Based on this observation, a new multidimensional index structure (called Adaptive R*-tree) is proposed in this paper to support the XPath axes more efficiently.

1 Introduction

As XML has been so successful in being adopted as a universal data exchange format, particularly in he World Wide Web, the problem of managing and querying XML documents poses interesting challenges to database researchers. Although XML documents could have rather complex internal structures, they share the same data type underlying the XML paradigm: ordered tree. Tree nodes represent document elements, attributes or text data, while edges represent the element-subelement (or parent-child) relationship.

To retrieve such tree-shaped data, several XML query languages have been proposed in the literature. Examples include XPath [2] and XQuery [3]. XQuery is being standardized as a major XML query language. The main building block of XQuery is XPath, which addresses part of XML documents for retrieval [16]. For example, "*paragraph//section*" is to find all sections that are contained in each paragraph. Here, the double slash "//" represents the *ancestor-descendant* relationship. A single slash "/" in an XPath represents a *parent-child* relationship, for example "*section/figure*".

J.X. Yu, M. Kitsuregawa, and H.V. Leong (Eds.): WAIM 2006, LNCS 4016, pp. 49–60, 2006.
© Springer-Verlag Berlin Heidelberg 2006

In line with the tree-centric nature of XML, XPath provides operators to describe path traversals in a tree-shaped document. Path traversals evaluate to a collection of subtrees (forests), which may then, recursively, be subject to further traversal. Starting from a so-called context node, an XPath query traverses its input document using a number of location steps. For each step, an axis describes which document nodes (and the subtrees below these nodes) form the intermediate result forest for this step. The XPath specification [2] lists a family of 13 axes (among these the children and descendant-or-self axes, probably more widely known by their abbreviations / and //, respectively).

Generally speaking, XPath expressions specify a tree traversal via two parameters: (1) a context node (not necessarily for the root) which is the starting point of the traversal, (2) and a sequence of location steps syntactically separated by /, evaluated from left to right. Given a context node, a step's axis (only one step of a regular XPath expressions) establishes a subset of document nodes. This set of nodes, or forest, provides the context nodes for the next step which is evaluated for each node of the forest in turn. The results are unioned together and sorted in document order. To illustrate the semantics of the XPath axes, Figure 1 depicts the result forests for three steps along different axes taken from context node e (note that the preceding axis does not include the ancestors of the context node). Table 1 lists all XPath axes.

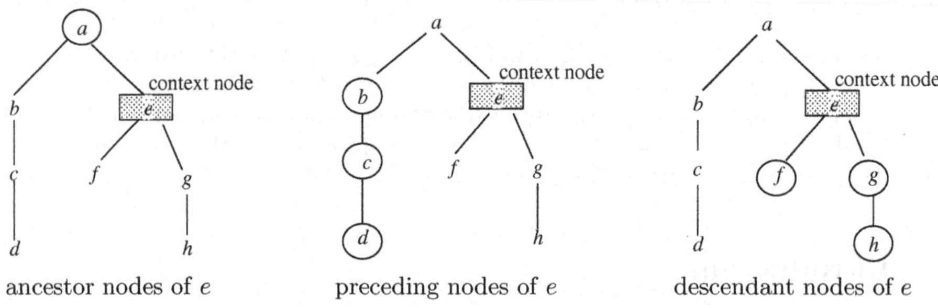

Fig. 1. Results of three XPath axes, circled nodes are elements of the result

It is important and basic work to efficiently implement XPath axes on XML documents. In work [1], R*-tree has been successfully applied to implementing XPath axes and the method proposed in [1] is able to support all XPath axes. In [1], each node of an XML document is labeled with a five-dimensional tuple. All the nodes of the XML document are mapped to a point set in a five-dimensional space. T. Grust made it clear that each of the XPath axes can be implemented by a range query on the above five-dimensional space. Thus, R*-tree is helpful to improving the query performance of the range queries of XPath axes. This method has been proved efficient in [1]. However, according to our investigations, most of the range queries for the XPath axes are partially-dimensional range queries (i.e., the number of query dimensions in each of the range queries is less than five, although the R*-tree is built in five-dimensional space). If the existing

Table 1. All axes and their semantics

Axis	Result
child	Direct element child nodes of the context node
descendant	All descendant nodes of the context node
descendant-or-self	Like descendant, plus the context node
parent	Direct parent node of the context node
ancestor	All ancestor nodes of the context node
ancestor-or-self	Like ancestor, plus the context node
following	Nodes following the context node in document order
preceding	Nodes preceding the context node in document order
following-sibling	Like following, same parent as the context node
preceding-sibling	Like preceding, same parent as the context node
attribute	Attribute nodes of the context node
self	Context node itself
namespace	Namespace nodes of the context node

multidimensional indices (such as R*-tree, which is used in [1]) are used for such range queries, then a great deal of information that is irrelevant to the queries also has to be read from disk, which heavily degrades the query performance. Based on this observation, in this study, a new multidimensional index structure (called Adaptive R*-tree) is proposed to support XPath axes more efficiently. The discussions and experiments with various datasets indicate that Adaptive R*-tree is better suited to XML documents, especially large documents.

In the remainder of this paper, Section 2 is some related works and our observation is presented in Section 3. Section 4 presents the proposed method, a new index structure for XPath axes, including its structure and algorithm. The experiment results are presented in Section 5. Section 6 concludes this paper and point out the future works.

2 Related Work

The concept of regular path expressions dominates this field of research by far [4, 5, 6, 7]. The work [4] presented an index over the prefix-encoding of the paths in an XML document tree (in a prefix-encoding, each leaf l of the document tree is prefixed by the sequence of element tags encountered during a path traversal from the document root to l). Since tag sequences obviously share common prefixes in such a scheme, a variant of the Patricia-tree is used to support lookups. Clearly, the index structure is tailored to respond to path queries that originate in the document root. Paths that do not have the root as the context node need multiple index lookups or require a post-processing phase (as does a restore of the document order in the result forest). In [4], so-called refined paths are proposed to remedy this drawback. Refined paths, however, have to be preselected before index loading time.

The T-index structure, proposed by Milo and Suciu in [6], maintains (approximate) equivalence classes of document nodes which are indistinguishable with respect to a given path template. In general, a T-index does not represent the whole document tree but only those document parts relevant to a specific path template. The more permissive and the larger the path template, the larger the resulting index size. This allows to trade space for generality, however, a specific T-index supports only those path traversals matching its path template (as reported in [6], an effective applicability test for a T-index is known for a restricted class of queries only).

There is other related work that is not directly targeted at the construction of index structures for XML. In [8], the authors discuss relational support for containment queries. Especially the multi-predicate merge join (MPMGJN) presented in [8] would provide an almost perfect infrastructure for the XPath accelerator. MPMGJN join supports multiple equality and inequality tests. The authors report an order of magnitude speed-up in comparison to standard join algorithms.

The work [1] successfully adopts multidimensional index structure in processing XML queries. It proposes an XPath accelerator that can completely live inside a relational database system, i.e., it is a relational storage structure in the sense of [10]. The implementation of the proposal in [1] benefits from advanced index technology, esp. the R-tree, that has by now found its way into mainstream relational database systems. It has been developed with a close eye on the XPath semantics and is thus able to support all XPath axes.

The main contributions of [1] are that (1) it proposed a five-dimensional descriptor (labeling schema) for each node of the XML document, (2) it made it clear that, using this labeling schema, each of the 13 XPath axes can be mapped to a range query in the five-dimensional descriptor-space, and (3) the range queries for XPath axes were implemented using R*-tree.

In this paper, based on the work [1], we will (1) present our observations on the range queries of XPath axes, and (2) according to the features of these range queries, present a new index structure (instead of R*-tree) to further improve the query performance of XPath axes. Since our work is based on [1], the key idea of [1] is described as follows.

2.1 Labeling Schema and Mapping XPath Axes to Range Queries

Each node v of an XML document is represented by the following five-dimensional descriptor:

$$desc(v) = < pre(v), post(v), par(v), att(v), name(v) >,$$

where $pre(v)$ and $post(v)$ are the preorder and the postorder of v, respectively. $par(v)$ is the preorder of parent node of v. $att(v)$ is a Boolean value indicating whether v is attribute node or not. The last one, $name(v)$ is the name of v. In this way, all the nodes in an XML document can be mapped to a set of points in the five-dimensional *descriptor space* (or say *labeling space*).

As others have noted [5, 8, 11], one can use $pre(v)$ and $post(v)$ to efficiently characterize the descendants v' of v. We have that

$$v' \text{ is a descendant of } v \iff pre(v') > pre(v) \wedge post(v') < post(v) \quad (1)$$

In the same way, we have that

$$v' \text{ is a ancestor of } v \iff pre(v') < pre(v) \wedge post(v') > post(v) \quad (2)$$

$$v' \text{ is a preceding node of } v \iff pre(v') < pre(v) \wedge post(v') < post(v) \quad (3)$$

$$v' \text{ is a following node of } v \iff pre(v') > pre(v) \wedge post(v') > post(v) \quad (4)$$

According to the above four equations, we can see that the four XPath axes of *descendant*, *ancestor*, *preceding* and following can be mapped to range queries in the two-dimensional space of *preorder/postorder*, which is shown in Fig. 2. With the help of the other items in the five-dimensional descriptor, the other XPath axes also can be mapped to range queries. Table 2 presents the ranges of all the XPath axes. Like [1], the two axes of *self* and *namespace* are omitted since they are so simple.

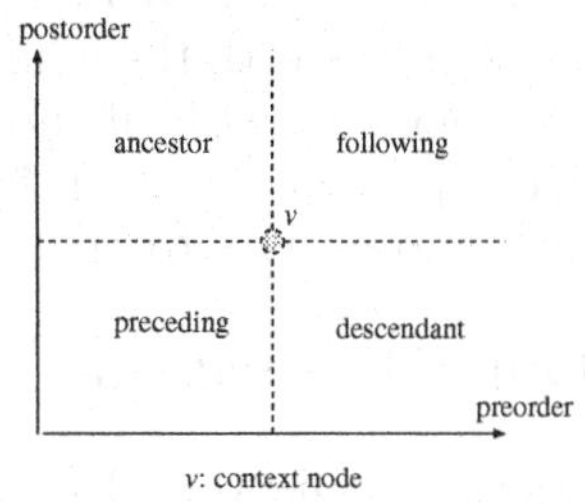

Fig. 2. Four XPath axes in two-dimensional space

2.2 Implementation of Range Queries Using R*-Tree

Since all of the XPath axes can be mapped to range queries in the five-dimensional descriptor-space, R*-tree (used in [1]) seems helpful to improving the range query performance. Because we will propose a new structure to further improve the range query performance, R*-tree is briefly recalled here.

R*-tree [12] is a hierarchy of nested multidimensional MBRs. Each non-leaf node of the R*-tree contains an array of entries, each of which consists of a pointer and an MBR. The pointer refers to one child node of this node and the MBR is the minimum bounding rectangle of the child node referred to by the pointer. Each leaf node of the R*-tree contains an array of entries, each of which consists of an object identifier and the object itself (for point-object datasets) or

Table 2. XPath axes and their ranges in descriptor space (v is the context node)

XPath Axes	ranges in descriptor-space				
	pre	*post*	*par*	*att*	*name*
child			$pre(v)$	*false*	*
descendant	$(pre(v), \infty)$	$[0, post(v))$		*false*	*
descendant-or-self	$[pre(v), \infty)$	$[0, post(v)]$		*false*	*
parent	$[par(v), par(v)]$				*
ancestor	$[0, pre(v))$	$(post(v), \infty)$			*
ancestor-or-self	$[0, pre(v)]$	$[post(v), \infty)$			*
following	$(pre(v), \infty)$	$(post(v), \infty)$		*false*	*
preceding	$[0, pre(v))$	$[0, post(v))$		*false*	*
following-sibling	$(pre(v), \infty)$	$(post(v), \infty)$	$par(v)$	*false*	*
preceding-sibling	$[0, pre(v))$	$[0, post(v))$	$par(v)$	*false*	*
attribute			$pre(v)$	*true*	*

its MBR (for extended object datasets). In the present paper, object and tuple are used interchangeably. In the R*-tree, the root node corresponds to the entire index space and each of the other nodes represents a sub-space (i.e., the MBR of all of the objects contained in this region) of the space formed by its parent node. Note that, each MBR in R*-tree nodes is denoted by two points. One is the lowest vertex with the minimum coordinate in each axis and the other is the upper-most vertex with the maximum coordinate in each axis. When R*-tree is used for a range query, all of the nodes intersecting the query range are accessed and their entries have to be checked.

3 Our Observations

From the above-mentioned Table 2, we can observe that most of the query ranges of XPath axes only use partial items of the five-dimensional descriptor. For example, *child* axis only uses *par* and *att*; *parent* axis only uses *pre*. In this paper, the range queries that only use partial (rather than all) dimensions of the entire space are called partially-dimensional range queries (denoted as PD range queries). Contrarily, the range queries that use all dimensions of the entire space are called all-dimensional range queries (denoted as AD range queries).

We want to note that all the existing multidimensional indices are designed to evaluate AD queries. This is because all of the objects are clustered in the leaf nodes according to their information in all index dimensions and every node contains information of its entries in all of the index dimensions. Actually, they can also evaluate PD range queries as follows. Using one n-dimensional index in the entire n-dimensional index space, one PD range query using d ($d < n$) query dimensions can be evaluated by simply extending the query range in each of the $(n - d)$ irrelevant index dimensions to the entire data range.

However, a disadvantage of using all-dimensional indices for PD range queries is that each node of the index contains n-dimensional information, but only d-dimensional information is necessary for a PD range query using only d ($d < n$) dimensions. This means that a great deal of unnecessary information, i.e., the information in the irrelevant dimensions, also has to be read from disk, which degrades the query performance. In other words, the irrelevant information in the index nodes decreases capacity (fanout) of each node. Directing to this disadvantage and considering that most of the query ranges of XPath axes are PD range queries, a new index structure for indexing XML data is proposed in this paper.

4 New Structure: AR*-Tree

According to the features of the range queries of XPath axes, a new index structure, called Adaptive R*-tree (denoted as AR*-tree), is proposed to improve the performance of such range queries.

4.1 Structure

The key concept of AR*-tree is to divide each of the n-dimensional R*-tree nodes into n one-dimensional nodes (these n one-dimensional nodes are called a *node-group*), each of which holds information in only one dimension, while each node of R*-tree holds information in all of the dimensions of the index space. Like each node in R*-tree, each node-group in AR*-tree corresponds to an n-dimensional subspace in the index space. Every entry of nodes in each index node-group corresponds to an edge of the corresponding subspace, while each entry of one R*-tree index node corresponds to a subspace.

Figure 3 shows the structure difference between R*-tree nodes and AR*-tree node-group. All of the entries with the same index in the n nodes of this node-group form a complete n-dimensional MBR in the index space. Whereas every entry in R*-tree nodes includes MBR information in all of the dimensions, each entry in the nodes of AR*-tree includes only one-dimensional information. The term entry of node-group, which refers to the set of entries having the same index distributed in all the different nodes of one node-group, is used hereinafter. One entry of each index node-group corresponds to a complete MBR in the index space. In Fig. 3, all of the entries in an ellipse form an complete entry of the node-group, which is a complete MBR in the entire index space.

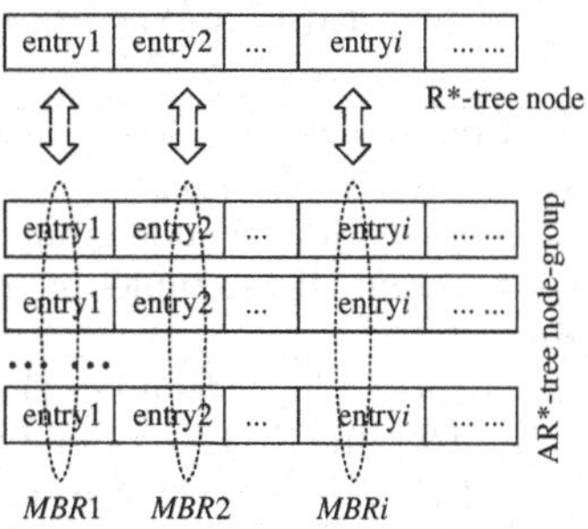

Fig. 3. Node structures of R*-tree and AR*-tree

The question then arises as to whether the total number of nodes in AR*-tree becomes n times that in R*-tree, because each node of R*-tree has been divided into n nodes. However, this is not the case because the maximum number of entries in each node of AR*-tree is up to approximately n times that in R*-tree since the dimensionality of each node in AR*-tree becomes 1. The structure of AR*-tree guarantees that it can be applied to PD range queries with any combinations of the query dimensions and that only the relevant one-dimensional nodes are visited.

The main advantage of AR*-tree over R*-tree (all-dimensional index) is that, for PD range queries, only the relevant nodes of the accessed node-groups need be visited and the other nodes, even if they are in the same node-groups, can be skipped. In R*-tree, information in all of the index dimensions is contained in each R*-tree node, but only information in the query dimensions are necessary for PD range queries, which means that a great deal of irrelevant information has to be loaded from disk and this certainly degrades the search performance, especially for large datasets.

4.2 Algorithms of AR*-Tree

The insert algorithm of AR*-tree is a naive extensions of the counterparts of R*-tree. After the new tuple reaches the leaf node-group, it is divided and stored in different nodes of the leaf node-group according to dimension. If some node-group must be split, then all of its nodes have to be split at the same time and the split may be up propagated. After a delete operation, if the node-group under-flowed, then all of its nodes should be deleted at the same time and all of its entries are inserted to the AR*-tree again. That is, all of the nodes in each node-group must be born simultaneously and die simultaneously.

A range query algorithm for AR*-tree, which can be used for AD range queries and PD range queries, is shown in Table 3.

Table 3. Algorithm for range queries on AR*-tree

```
Procedure RangeQuery (rect, node-group)
Input:    rect: query range
     node-group: initial node-group of the query
Output: result: all the tuples in rect
Begin
For each entry e in node-group Do
     If e INTERSECT rect in all the query dimensions Then
        If (node-group is not at leaf) Then
          RangeQuery (rect, e.child); //e.child means the child node-group of e
        Else result ← e
EndFor
End
```

Staring with the root node-group, each entry of the current node-group needs to be checked to determine whether its MBR intersects the query range. If its MBR intersects the query range, and the current node-group is not at the leaf level, then this algorithm is invoked recursively with the corresponding child node-group. Note that, when each entry *e* of the current node-group is checked, (1) not all of the nodes in the current node-group have to be accessed (such irrelevant nodes are skipped), and (2) even, not all of the nodes in the relevant dimensions (query dimensions) have to be visited. That is, further checks are not necessary after the current entry is found not to intersect the query range in some dimension.

5 Experiments

5.1 Experiment Process

The process of our experiments is shown in Fig. 4.

XML Documents. The XML documents used in our experiments are generated by XMLgen [17], an easily accessible XML generator, which is developed for the Xmark benchmark project [14]. Using XMLgen, three documents shown in Table 4 were generated and used. In this table, XMLgen factor were given as a size factor to control document sizes.

Figure 5 is the distribution of the nodes in the 5.5 MB XML document. Because Figure 5 (a) contains a total of 103,135 nodes, it could not be seen

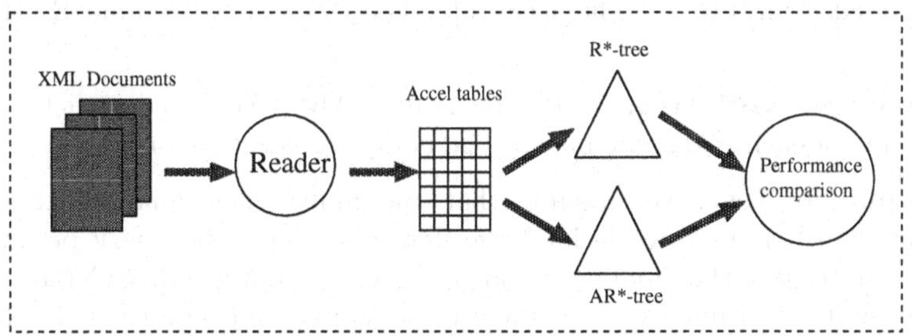

Fig. 4. Process of experiments

Table 4. XML documents used in the experiments

Document size [MB]	Number of nodes	XMLgen factor
5.5	103135	0.05
11.1	206130	0.10
22.4	413108	0.20

clearly. Figure 5 (b) is a partial enlargement, in which there are nearly 200 nodes of this XML document. The X axis represents preorder and the Y axis postorder.

Reader. Based on Libxml2 [15] which is an XML C parser and toolkit, we built a loader to obtain one accel table for each XML document, which is used to build the indices. Because the XML documents have a total of 77 different node names, all of the possible node names are encoded from 0 to 76 in order to be dealt with by R*-tree and AR*-tree.

Accel Table. Each tuple of accel table is the five-dimensional descriptor of one node of an XML document. As mentioned above, all of the node names

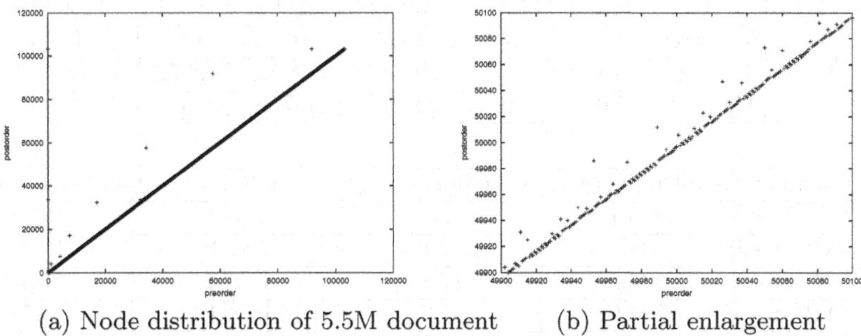

(a) Node distribution of 5.5M document (b) Partial enlargement

Fig. 5. Node distribution on preorder/postorder plane

are encoded from 0 to 76. The accel table is directly used to build R*-tree and AR*-tree.

R*-Tree and AR*-Tree. An R*-tree and an AR*-tree are constructed for the accel table of each XML document. The node size is set to 4096 bytes.

Performance Test. We assume that the multidimensional index is disk-resident, which is reasonable for large datasets. Thus, the query performance is tested in term of the number of node accesses. Except the three XPath axes of self, attribute, and namespace (they are too simple and performance difference between R*-tree and AR*-tree could not be shown clearly), the query performance of all the other 10 XPath axes are tested using R*-tree and AR*-tree, respectively. By comparing the query performance of XPath axes on R*-tree and AR*-tree, we will see which of R*-tree and AR*-tree is better suited to XPath axes.

5.2 Experiment Result

The experiment result is shown in Tables 5. The context nodes for different XML documents are chosen independently. That is, the same XPath axis is possibly tested with different context nodes for different data documents. Certainly, for the sake of comparison, all the tests on R*-tree and AR*-tree for the same XML documents used the same context nodes.

From the above experiment, we can obtain the following observation. Except the XPath axes of ancestor (including ancestor-or-self) and preceding-sibling, for which the advantage of AR*-tree is not shown very clearly, AR*-tree performs clearly better than R*-tree for the other seven XPath axes. As mentioned in Section 1, the query performance of XPath axes is very important because that the main building block of XQuery is XPath and XPath expressions consists

Table 5. Experiment result

XML document		parent	ancestor	descendent	following	preceding	child
5.5M	R*-tree	10.3	13.3	749.0	1420.0	1186.2	484.6
	AR*-tree	4.4	12.9	582.1	1095.2	973.4	116.0
11.1M	R*-tree	11.6	17.8	1507.2	2700.3	1641.3	1200.3
	AR*-tree	6.4	14.5	1163.0	2072.2	1321.0	230.4
22.4M	R*-tree	11.6	13.3	2995.6	5705.6	2972.0	1848.0
	AR*-tree	7.0	12.4	2304.6	4375.1	2323.6	439.9

XML document		following-sibling	preceding-sibling	descendent-or-self	ancestor-or-self
5.5M	R*-tree	485.1	22.6	749.0	13.3
	AR*-tree	338.3	21.1	582.1	12.9
11.1M	R*-tree	493.2	17.8	1507.2	17.8
	AR*-tree	353.0	17.7	1163.0	14.5
22.4M	R*-tree	1030.5	21.9	2995.6	13.3
	AR*-tree	680.4	18.0	2304.6	12.4

of a sequence of XPath axis operations, which are evaluated from left to right. Moreover, each step of an XPath expression (one XPath axis operation) often obtain a great number of intermediate results, which means that the evaluation of one XPath expression may need a great number of XPath axis operations. Thus, any improvement on the query performance of XPath axes will be significant.

6 Conclusion and Future Work

Multidimensional indices have been successfully introduced to the field of querying on XML data. And, the query performance of XPath axes is very important because they are the main building blocks of XQuery. The evaluation of one XPath expression may need a great number of XPath axis operations since each step of an XPath expression (one XPath axis operation) often obtain a great number of intermediate results. Thus, any improvement on the query performance of XPath axes will be significant. The existing methods that introduced multidimensional indices to implementing XPath axes apply all-dimensional indices (e.g., R*-tree in [1]). In this paper, a new multidimensional index structure, called AR*-tree, was proposed and discussed. The discussion and experiments using various XML documents showed that the proposed method has a clear performance advantage for XPath axes compared with R*-tree, a famous and popular all-dimensional index structure. As one of future works, the performance of AR*-tree for XPath axes will be examined using some other kinds of XML documents.

Acknowledgment

This research was supported in part by the Japan Society for the Promotion of Science through Grants-in-Aid for Scientific Research 17650031 and 16200005. In addition, the authors would like to thank Mr. Satoshi Tani, who conducted the experiments, and to thank Prof. Kunihiko Kaneko for his helpful comments.

References

1. T. Grust: Accelerating XPath Location Steps. Proc. ACM SIGMOD International Conference, pages 109-120, 2002.
2. A. Berglund, S. Boag, D. Chamberlin, M. F. Fernandez, et.al.: XML Path Language (XPath) 2.0. Technical Report W3C Working Draft, Version 2.0, World Wide Web Consortium, December 2001. http ://www. w3. org/TR/xpath20/.
3. S. Boag, D. Chamberlin, M. F. Fernandez,et.al.: XQuery 1.0: An XML query language. In W3C Working Draft 16 August 2002, http://www.w3.org/TR/xquery/, 2002.
4. B. F. Cooper, N. Sample, M. J.Franklin, G. R. Hjaltason, and M. Shadmon: A Fast Index for Semistructured Data. Proc. the 27th International Conference on Very Large Data Bases (VLDB), pages 341-360, 2001.

5. Q. Li and B. Moon: Indexing and Querying XML Data for Regular Path Expressions. Proc. the 27th International Conference on Very Large Data Bases (VLDB), pages 361-370, 2001.
6. D. Suciu and T. Milo: Index Structures for Path Expressions. Proc. the 7th International Conference on Database Theory (ICDT), LNCS 1540, pages 277-295 Springer Verlag, 1999.
7. R. Goldman and J. Widom: DataGuides: Enabling Query Formulation and Optimization in Semistructured Databases. Proc. the 23rd International Conference on Very Large Databases (VLDB), pages 436-445, 1997
8. C. Zhang, J. Naughton, D. DeWitt, Q. Luo, and G. Lohman: On Supporting Containment Queries in Relational Database Management Systems. Proc. ACM SIGMOD International Conference on Management of Data, pages 425-436, 2001.
9. H. P. Kriegel, M. Potke, and T. Seidl: Managing Intervals efficiently in Object-Relational Databases. Proc. the 26th International Conference on Very Large Databases (VLDB), pages 407-418, 2000.
10. H. P. Kriegel, M. P. otke, and T. Seidl: Managing Intervals Efficiently in Object-Relational Databases. Proc. the 26th International Conference on Very Large Databases (VLDB), pages 407-418, 2000.
11. P. F. Dietz and D. D. Sleator: Two Algorithms for Maintaining Order in a List. Proc. the 19th Annual ACM Symposium on Theory of Computing (STOC), pages 365-372, 1987. ACM Press.
12. N. Beckmann, and H. Kriegel: The R*-tree: An Efficient and Robust Access Method for Points and Rectangles. Proc. ACM SIGMOD Intl. Conf., pp.322-331, 1990.
13. G.R.l Hjaltason and H. Samet: Distance Browsing in Spatial Database. ACM Transactions on Database Systems, Vol.24, No.2, pages 265-318, 1999.
14. A. R. Schmidt, F. Waas, M. L. Kersten, D. Florescu, I. Manolescu, M. J. Carey, and R. Busse: The XML Benchmark Project. Technical Report INSR0103, CWI, Amsterdam, The Netherlands, April 2001.
15. http://xmlsoft.org/
16. H. Jiang, H. Lu, W. Wang, B. C. Ooi: XR-Tree: Indexing XML Data for Efficient Structural Joins. Proc. International Conference on Data Engineering (ICDE), page 253-263, 2003.
17. http://monetdb.cwi.nl/xml/downloads.html

Efficient Evaluation of Multiple Queries on Streamed XML Fragments

Huan Huo, Rui Zhou, Guoren Wang, Xiaoyun Hui,
Chuan Xiao, and Yongqian Yu

Institute of Computer System, Northeastern University, Shenyang, China
wanggr@mail.neu.edu.cn

Abstract. With the prevalence of Web applications, expediting multiple queries over streaming XML has become a core challenge due to one-pass processing and limited resources. Recently proposed Hole-Filler model is low consuming for XML fragments transmission and evaluation; however existing work addressed the multiple query problem over XML tuple streams instead of XML fragment streams. By taking advantage of schema information for XML, this paper proposes a model of tid+ tree to construct multiple queries over XML fragments and to prune off duplicate and dependent operations. Based on tid+ tree, it then proposes a notion of FQ-Index as the core in M-XFPro to index both multiple queries and XML fragments for processing multiple XPath queries involving simple path and twig path patterns. We illustrate the effectiveness of the techniques developed with a detailed set of experiments.

1 Introduction

The recent emergence of XML [1] as a *de facto* standard for information representation and data exchange over the web has led to an increased interest in using more expressive subscription/filtering mechanisms that exploit both the structure and the content of XML documents. Evaluating XML queries, such as XPath [2] and XQuery [3], is thus widely studied both in traditional database management systems and in stream model for web applications. Figure 1 gives an XML document and its DOM tree, which acts as an example of our work.

Recently, many research works [4,5,6,7,8,9,10] focus on answering queries on streamed XML data, which has to be analyzed in real-time and by one pass. In the push-based model [5,4], XML streams are broadcasted to multiple clients, which must evaluate continuous, sophisticated queries (as opposed to simple, single path specifications) with limited memory capacity and processing power. In the pull-based model [6,7,8,9,10], such as publish-subscribe or event notification systems, XML streams are disseminated to subscribers, but a larger number of registered queries pose heavy workload on the server. Hence, expediting multiple queries on XML streams is the core technical challenge.

In order to reduce processing overhead, *Hole-Filler* model is proposed in [11]. In the model, a hole represents a placeholder into which another rooted subtree (a fragment), called a filler, could be positioned to complete the tree. In this

J.X. Yu, M. Kitsuregawa, and H.V. Leong (Eds.): WAIM 2006, LNCS 4016, pp. 61–72, 2006.
© Springer-Verlag Berlin Heidelberg 2006

way, infinite XML streams turn out to be a sequence of XML fragments, and queries on parts of XML data require less memory and processing time, without having to wait for the entire XML document to be received and materialized. Furthermore, changes to XML data may pose less overhead by sending only fragments corresponding to the changes, instead of sending the entire document.

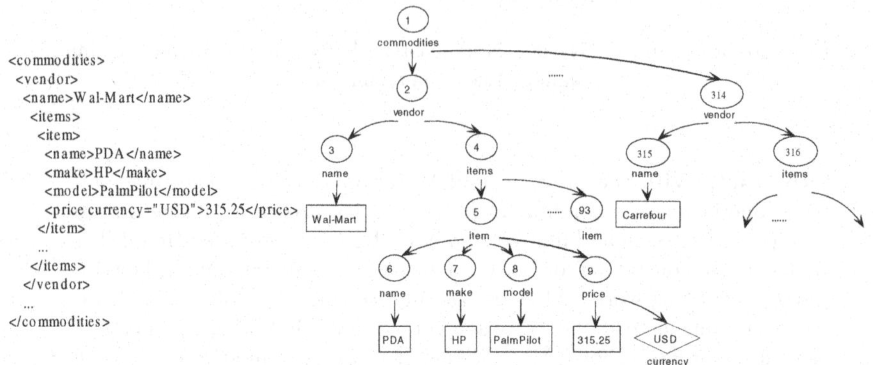

Fig. 1. An XML Document and its DOM Tree

However, to the best of our knowledge, there is no work for evaluating multiple queries on streamed XML fragments so far. In XFrag [4] and XFPro [12], XML fragments can only be evaluated under simple, single queries. While other research work [6, 7, 8, 9, 10] consider problems on a stream of XML tuples, not XML fragments, and can not avoid "redundant" operations caused by fragments.

In this paper, we present an efficient framework and a set of techniques for processing multiple XPath queries over streamed XML fragments. As compared to the existing work on supporting XPath/XQuery over streamed XML fragments, we make the following contributions: (i)we propose techniques for enabling the transformation from multiple XPath expressions to optimized query plan. We model the query expressions using *tid+ tree* and apply a series of pruning policies, which enable further analysis and optimizations by eliminating the "redundant" path evaluations. (ii)based on tid+ tree, we present a novel index structure, termed FQ-Index, which supports the efficient processing of multiple queries (including simple path queries and twig path queries) for streamed XML fragments by indexing both the queries and the fragments. (iii)based on FQ-Index, we address the main algorithms of query evaluation in M-XFPro, which is able to both reduce the memory cost as well as avoid redundant matchings by recording only query related fragments. Note that, we assume the query ends cannot reconstruct the entire XML data before processing the queries.

The rest of this paper is organized as follows. Section 2 introduces *Hole-Filler* model as the base for our XML fragments. Section 3 gives a detailed statement of our multiple query processing framework. Section 4 shows experimental results from our implementation and reflects the processing efficiency of our framework. Our conclusions are contained in Section 5.

2 Model for Streamed Fragmented XML Data

In our approach, we adopt the hole-filler model [11] to correlate XML fragments with each other. We assume that XML stream begins with finite XML documents and runs on as and when new elements are added into the documents or updates occur upon the existing elements.

Given an XML document tree $T_d = (V_d, E_d, \Sigma_d, root_d, Did)$, a filler $T_f = (V_f, E_f, \Sigma_f, root_f, fid, tsid)$ is a subtree of XML document associating a fid and a $tsid$, where V_f, E_f, Σ_f is the subset of node set V_d, edge set E_d and element type set Σ_d respectively, and $root_f$ $(\in V_f)$is the root element of the subtree; a hole H is an empty node $v(\in V_d)$ assigned with a unique hid and a $tsid$, into which a filler with the same fid value could be positioned to complete the tree. Note that the filler can in turn have holes in it, which will be filled by other fillers. We can reconstruct the original XML document by substituting holes with the corresponding fillers at the destination as it was in the source. In this paper, we assume that XML documents have been fragmented already. Fragmenting algorithm is stated in [13] and omitted here. Figure 2 gives two fragments of the document in Figure 1.

```
Fragment 1:
<commodities filler id="0" tsid="1">
  <vendor>
    <name>Wal-Mart</name>
      <items>
        <stream: hole id="10" tsid="5" />
        <stream: hole id="20" tsid="5" />
        ...
  </vendor>
  ....
</commodities>

Fragment 2:
<stream: filler id="10" tsid="5">
  <item>
    <name>PDA</name>
    <make>HP</make>
    <model>PalmPilot</model>
    <price currency="USD">315.25</price>
  </item>
</stream: filler>
```

Fig. 2. XML Document Fragments

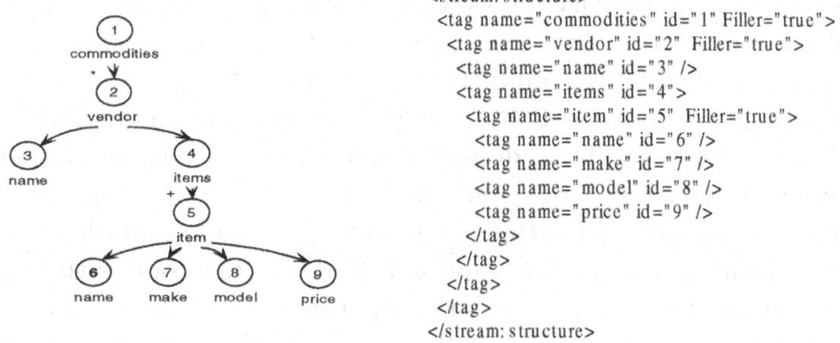

Fig. 3. Tag Structure of Hole-Filler Model

In order to summarize the structure of XML fragments, *tag structure* [11] is exploited to provide structural information (including fragmentation information) for XML and capture all the valid paths. A tag structure $TS = (V_t, E_t,$

$root_t, \Sigma_t, TYPE_t)$ is itself structurally a valid XML fragment with the highest priority, where V_t is a set of tag nodes in XML document, E_t is a set of edges, Σ_t is a set of *tsids* identifying the tag nodes in XML document, and $TYPE_t$ is a set of tag node type. Tag structure can be generated according to XML Schema or DTD, and also can be obtained when fragmenting an XML document without DTD. The DTD and the corresponding tag structure of the XML document (given in Figure 1) are depicted in Figure 3.

3 M-XFPro Query Handling

Based on the Hole-Filler model, we have proposed M-XFPro, a system aimed at providing efficient evaluation for multiple queries over streamed XML fragments. In this section, we first introduce *tid+ tree* for rewriting the queries for XML fragments, and describe the pruning policies to eliminate "redundant" path evaluations. Then we present our novel FQ-Index for processing streamed XML fragments based on optimized *tid+ tree*. We present the main matching algorithms for query handling with FQ-Index at last.

3.1 Tid+ Tree Construction

In our earlier framework [12], we propose *tid tree* to represent the structural patterns in an XPath query. Each navigation step in an XPath is mapped to a tree node labelled with a tag code, which encodes the tsid and "TYPE" together. For "$Filler = true$", we set the end of the tag code with "1", otherwise we set it with "0". As for tsid, we separate it from the "TYPE" code by a dot. By checking the end of the code, we can easily tell subroot nodes (i.e. the root of a filler) from subelement nodes (i.e. the node that locates in a filler but is not the root of the subtree).

We expand the concept of *tid tree* into *tid+ tree* to represent multiple query expressions and enable further analysis and optimizations on query operations.

Given a collection of XPath expressions $P = \{p_1, p_2, \cdots, p_n\}$, we map multiple queries into a single tree, noted as *tid+ tree*, by defining $root_t$ as a special root node, which allows for conjunctive conditions at the root level. Parent-child relationship is represented by a single arrow, while ancestor-descendant relationship is represented by a double arrow. And the output of each query q_i is depicted by a single arrow and marked with the ID of q_i. In order to distinguish between the nodes that represent a tag code and the nodes that represent an atomic predicate, we represent nodes of tag code with circles and values of predicate with rectangles. The operators (such as $<$, $>$, $\geq$, $\leq$, $=$) and boolean connectors are represented with diamonds. Note that the common prefixes of all the queries are shared.

Figure 4 shows an example of such a tid+ tree, representing three queries on the XML document described in Section 1, where *Query 1* and *Query 2* share the common prefix "*/commondities/vendor*" (i.e./1.1/1.2). Since "*name*" in *Query 2* corresponds to two tsids in the tag structure, we enumerate all the possible tsids in the tid+ tree such that *Query 2* has two output arrows.

Since tid+ tree is the base for FQ-Index to install multiple XPath expressions into the indexing structure, the optimization of tid+ tree impacts both the space and performance of the index. We now introduce two kinds of optimizations on tid+ tree to eliminate the redundant operations as early as possible.

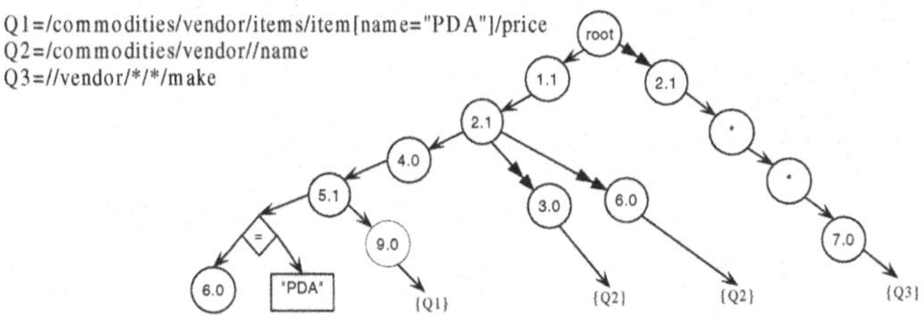

Fig. 4. Tid+ Tree

Duplication Pruning. Given an XPath p, we define a simple subexpression s of p if s is equal to the path of the tag nodes along a path $< v_1, v_2, \cdots v_n >$ in the tid tree of p, such that each v_i is the parent node of $v_{i+1} (1 \leq i < n)$ and the label of each v_i (except perhaps for v_1) is prefixed only by "/".

Definition 1. *Given a collection of XPath expressions $P = \{p_1, p_2, \cdots, p_n\}$, subexpression s is a common subexpression if more than one tid tree of p_i contains s. If a common subexpression is also a simple subexpression, we define it as a simple common subexpression. A common subexpression s is defined as a* maximal common subexpression *if no other longer common subexpression in the tid+ tree of P contains s.*

Common subexpressions degrades the performance significantly, especially when the workload has many similar queries. Since the common prefixes of all the queries are shared in tid+ tree, we consider optimizing tid+ tree by grouping all the common subexpressions in the structure navigation.

In order to extract the common subexpressions, we have to find out the structural relationship shared among the queries. By taking advantage of tag structure, we can replace "//" in tid+ tree with the corresponding structure consisting of "/" and expand "*" in tid+ tree to specify query execution. As for twig pattern query, we add the subroot nodes involved in the branch expression into the tid+ tree if the testing node and the branch expression belong to different fragments. In this way, common subexpressions turn out to be simple common subexpressions, and all the possible duplicated expressions can be pruned off.

Figure 5(a) presents the tid+ tree in Figure 4 after eliminating "//" and "*" based on tag structure, where the dashed regions enclose the subexpression (i.e. /1.1/2.1/4.0/5.1) shared by *Query 2* and *Query 3* while the solid regions enclose the subexpression (i.e. /1.1/2.1/4.0) shared by *Query 1*, *Query 2* and *Query 3*. Since tid node 5.1 in *Query 1* has a predicate, which is not included in the other two queries, we treat the tid node 5.1 in *Query 1* as a different node and exclude it in the common subexpression. Note that Figure 5(a) captures all the maximal common subexpressions among the queries. The optimized tid+ tree after pruning off the duplicated subexpressions is presented in Figure 5(b).

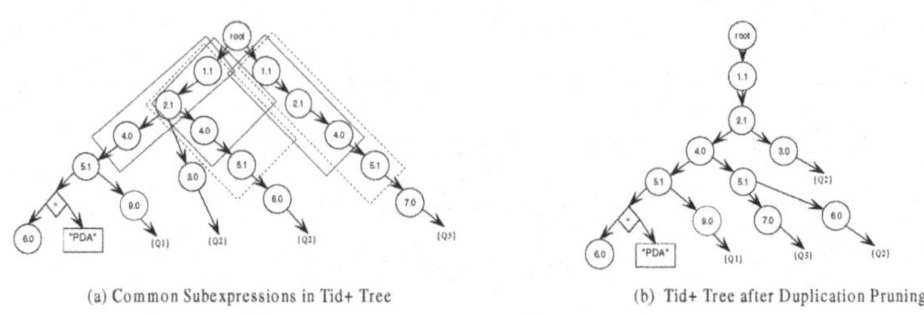

(a) Common Subexpressions in Tid+ Tree

(b) Tid+ Tree after Duplication Pruning

Fig. 5. Duplication Pruning on Tid+ Tree

Dependence Pruning. Before we describe the dependence pruning policy for tid+ tree, we first introduce some definitions of operation dependence.

Definition 2. *Given any pair of nodes in a tid+ tree* $< n_1,n_2 >$*, if the query result of* n_2 *is valid only if the query result of* n_1 *is valid,* n_2 *is defined as dependent on* n_1*. We use a directed edge* $e = (n_1, n_2)$ *to imply the dependence between* n_1 *and* n_2*.*

Definition 3. *Given any pair of nodes in a tid+ tree* $< n_1,n_2 >$*, we say that* n_2 *is subsumption dependent on* n_1 *if: (i)* n_2 *is dependent on* n_1*, and (ii) the query result of* n_2 *is a subset of the query result of* n_1*.*

In streaming XML fragment model, operation dependence usually occurs when the query results to preceding query node and successive query node are in the same fragment(here we are not considering predicates), since the fragments with the same tsid share the same structure so that any fragment matching the preceding node also matches the successive one. In most cases, the dependence operation can be eliminated by removing the successive query nodes.

When the query node involve predicates, if the result set of predicate p_2 is a subset of that of predicate p_1, we refer to p_2 as subsumption dependent on p_1. Subsumption-free queries are intuitively queries that do not contain "redundancies". Some queries can be rewritten to be subsumption-free, by eliminating redundant portions.

Much of our analysis focuses on pruning off operation dependencies on tid nodes caused by fragmentation to eliminate "redundant" structural evaluations. Since tag structure guarantees that the fragments with the same tsid share the same structure, we keep all the subroot nodes and delete the subelement nodes which have no predicates and are not the leaf nodes in tid+ tree. According to tag code, subroot nodes ended with "1" are kept in the tid+ tree while subelement nodes ended with "0" and without predicate nodes in their children are removed. Thus the original tid+ tree becomes an optimized tid+ tree.

Figure 6(a) shows the operation dependence in the optimized tid+ tree in Figure 5(b), where tid node 4 depends on tid node 2 and is referred to as a dependent node. We use dashed arrows to represent operation dependencies, and dashed rectangles for dependent nodes. Figure 6(b) shows the optimized tid+ tree after pruning off the operation dependencies.

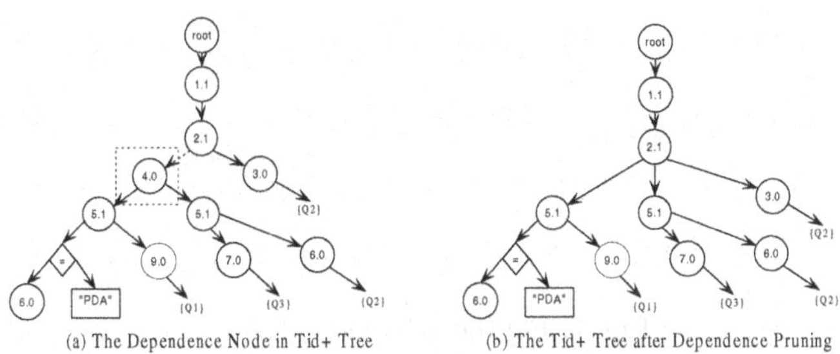

(a) The Dependence Node in Tid+ Tree (b) The Tid+ Tree after Dependence Pruning

Fig. 6. Dependence Pruning on Tid+ Tree

3.2 FQ-Index Scheme

Our FQ-Index is a hybrid index structure, which indexes both the queries and fragments on the basis of optimized tid+ tree. An FQ-Index consists of two key components: (1) a query index (denoted by QI), constructed by tid+ tree to facilitate the detection of query matchings in the input XML fragments; and (2) a filler table (denoted by FT), which stores the information about each XML fragment. Both of the components share a hash table for subroot nodes in tid+ tree. We now describe each of these two components in detail.

Query Index. Query index is generated from optimized tid+ tree before processing to keep track of the query steps that are supposed to match next. Let $P = \{p_1, p_2, \ldots, p_n\}$ denote the set of XPath expressions, and $T = \{t_1, t_2, \ldots, t_n\}$ denote the subroot nodes in optimized tid+ tree. Query index QI of P for each t_i is a 4-tuple list. Each item in the query list for t_i is a 4-tuple (*query id set, predecessor, successor, predicate*), denoted as *q-tuple*, where:

- *Query id set* represents the queries in set P that share the same predicate, predecessor and successor.
- *Predecessor* refers to the tag code of the fragment in tid+ tree corresponding to the parent node of q_i. (*Predecessor* = NULL if q_i is a root node.)
- *Successor* refers to the tag code of the fragment in tid+ tree corresponding to the child node of q_i. (*Successor* = NULL if q_i is the end of the query.)
- *Predicate* is the branch expression of twig path queries in tid+ tree.

Predecessor and successor in each item keep track of the query steps, while predicate keeps the reference of branch expressions. With the help of query id set, we can avoid duplicate evaluations shared by multiple queries. Since subroot nodes indicate the tsids of the fragments involved in the queries, we can directly access the relative query steps by the corresponding entry of the hash table when a fragment arrives. Figure 7 presents the query index converted from the optimized tid+ tree(*"all"* represents all of the queries in set P) in Figure 6(b).

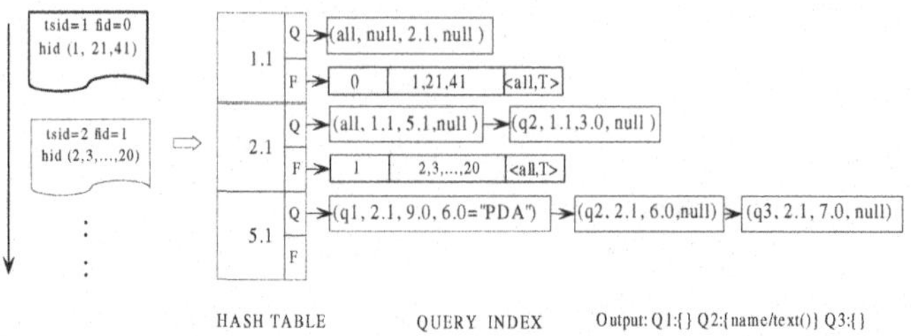

Fig. 7. FQ-Index of Tid+ Tree

Filler Table. As fragments in the original document may arrive in any order and query expressions may contain predicates at any level in the XML tree, it is necessary to keep track of the parent-child links between the various fragments. We maintain the fragments' information in filler table at each entry of the hash table when processing arrived fragments. Since the structural information corresponds to a small part of the actual data in the XML fragment, the rest of which is not relevant in producing the result, we discard the fragments corresponding to intermediate steps to save space cost.

The filler table FT contains one row for each fragment. Each row in FT is denoted as a *f-tuple* $(fillerid, \{holeid\}, \{< q_i, tag >\})$, in which tag can be set to $true$, $false$, undecided ($\perp$), or a result fragment corresponding to q_i in set P. While the former three values are possible in intermediate steps that do not produce a result, the latter is possible in the terminal steps in the tid+ tree branch. Figure 7 shows the construction of filler table.

With the hash table, the filler table and the query index cooperate together as FQ-Index. Taking advantage of the query index, we can quickly inquire the parent fragment by matching the same *holeid* in the *predecessor's* FT. In this way, filler table enhances the performance by only maintaining the information of fragments that will contribute to the results. Thus FQ-Index efficiently supports the online evaluation of multiple queries over streamed XML fragments, including both simple path queries and twig pattern queries.

3.3 Query Handling

In this section, we address the main algorithms of query evaluation in M-XFPro. The basic idea of the matching algorithms is as follows. We use the query index QI to detect the occurrence of matching tsids as the input fragments stream in, since before we record the structrual information of a fragment, it needs to verify if the preceding operation has excluded its parent fragment due to either predicate failure or due to exclusion of its ancestor.

For example, *Query 1: /commodities/vendor[name= "Wal-Mart"]//item* [*make* = "*HP*"] is a twig pattern query with two atomic predicates, while *Query 2: /commodities/vendor[name= "Price-Mart"]//item[make= "IBM"]* is a similar query just with different predicates. When the "commodities" fragment with tsid "1", filler id "0" and hole ids "1, 21, 41" arrives, the FT to the entry 1 is updated as $(0, \{1, 2, 41\}, \{< all, T >\})$. Note that, the "commodities" filler can be discarded as it is no more needed to produce the result and the hole filler association is already captured. This results in memory conservation on the fly. When the "vendor" fragment with tsid "2", fillerid "1", holeid "$2, 3, \cdots, 20$" and "name=Wal-Mart" arrives, the FT to the entry 2 is updated as $(1, \{2, 3, \cdots, 20\}, \{< q2, T >, < q3, F >\})$. When the "item" fragment with fillerid "2" arrives, only after determine that the filler matches the predicate of *Query 1* [*make* = "HP''], the fragment can be regarded as the query result of *Query 1*. Taking advantage of QI, it won't be mixed up with the result of *Query 2* [*make* = "IBM''] since the *Predecessor* has excluded its parent fragments.

Algorithm 1. startElement()

```
if ( isFragmentStart()==true ) then
   fid=getFid(); tsid=getTsid();
   if ( hashFindEntry(tsid)!=null) then
      fillQueryFT(tsid,createFTuple(fid));
      // generate an f-tuple and fill it into the corresponding queries' lists in FT;
   end if
end if
if ( isHoleTag()==true ) then
   hid=getHid(); tsid=getTsid();
   addQueryFT(tsid,hid);
   // find the entry by tsid and fill hid into the corresponding f-tuple;
else if ( isElementTag()==true ) then
   tsid=getTsid();
   if ( isQueryRelatedTag()==true ) then
      relevantTag==true;
   end if
end if
```

We implement the callback functions startElement() and endElement() of SAX interface when parsing each XML fragment. In algorithm 1, if an element is a subroot node, the information of the corresponding fragment in which it falls will be captured and loaded into FT. Similar operation is performed when encountering the element representing a hole. The variable *relevantTag* will be set to *true* if the element is query related. In algorithm 2, parent fragment and predicate fragment of the filler containing the element are inquired, and *tag* value of the corresponding f-tuple is set to *true* in case both kinds of the above fragments are valid. Child fragments need to be trigged as well, for some early arrived fragments may be set to "$\perp$" and waiting for their parent fragments.

Algorithm 2. endElement()

```
if ( isFragmentEnd()==true ) then
  // ft is the corresponding f-tuple of the current fragment
  if ( findParentFTuple(ft)!=null ) then
    ft.parentValue=parentFTuple(ft).parentValue;
  end if
  if ( findTwigPredicate(ft)!=null ) then
    ft.conditionValue=conditionFTuple(ft).conditionValue;
  end if
  if ( findChildFTupleList(ft)!=null ) then
    for each child f-tuple ftc of ft do
      ftc.parentValue=ft.parentValue && ft.conditionValue;
    end for
  end if
end if
```

4 Performance Evaluation

In this section, we present the results of performance evaluation of various algorithms over queries with different types, depths and document sizes on the same platform. We consider the following algorithms: (1) M-XFPro, (2)Du-XFPro, i.e. M-XFPro based on tid+ tree without dependence pruning, (3)De-XFPro, i.e. M-XFPro based on tid+ tree without duplication pruning. All the experiments are run on a PC with 2.6GHz CPU, 512M memory. Data sets are generated by the xmlgen program [14]. We have written an XML fragmenter that fragments an XML document into filler fragments to produce an XML stream, based on the tag structure defining the fragmentation layout. And we implemented a query generator that takes the DTD as input and creates sets of XPath queries of different types and depths.

In figure 8(a) three kinds of processing strategies over various query numbers are tested and compared. The numbers of queries in each set are 1,2,10 respectively. From the result, we can conclude that dependence pruning and duplication pruning in M-XFPro play an important role in efficiently evaluating multiple queries. In the following experiments, we fix the query number and test other properties of the queries. Figure 8(b) shows the performance on different types of queries: (1)simple path queries only involving "/", denoted as Q_1 (2)simple path queries involving "*" or "//", denoted as Q_2 (3)twig pattern queries with value predicates, denoted as Q_3. We can see that for any query type, M-XFPro outperforms its counterparts, and query types do not bring in exceptions, i.e. query performance doesn't vary much on different query types. For simplicity, but without losing generality, we only test twig queries in the next two set of experiments. Figure 8(c) shows the impacts of various query depths. Considering the depth of the XML documents generated by xmlgen, we design three query sets of depth 3, 5 and 7 respectively. As is shown in the figure, when the depth increases, the processing time of De-XFPro and Du-XFPro increases due to the increased path steps. While with duplication and dependence pruning, M-XFPro greatly reduces path steps, furthermore time cost of deep queries is much less than short queries, since fragment processing is much faster. Figure 8(d) shows the influence of different document size: 5M, 10M and 15M.

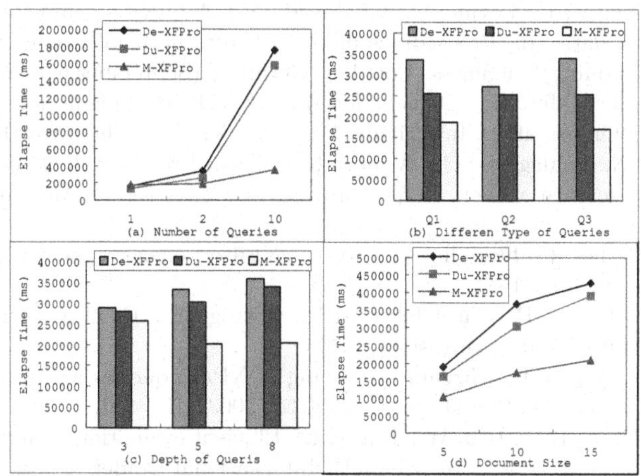

Fig. 8. Experimental Results

5 Conclusions

In this paper, we have proposed a framework and a set of techniques for processing multiple XPath queries over streamed XML fragments. We first model the multiple queries into tid+ tree, which helps to transform queries on element nodes to queries on XML fragments and serves as the base for analyzing "redundant" operations caused by common subexpression and operation dependence. Based on optimized tid+ tree after duplication pruning and dependence pruning, FQ-Index is proposed to index both the queries and fragments by sharing a hash table for tid nodes, which supports not only simple path queries, but also twig pattern queries. Our experimental results over multiple XPath expressions with different properties have clearly demonstrated the benefits of our approach.

Acknowledgments. This research was partially supported by the National Natural Science Foundation of China (Grant No. 60273079 and 60573089) and Specialized Research Fund for the Doctoral Program of Higher Education (SRFDP).

References

1. W3C Recommendation: Extensible Markup Language (XML) 1.0 (Second Edition). (2000) http://www.w3.org/TR/REC-xml.
2. W3C Working Draft: XML Path Languages (XPath), ver 2.0. (2001) Tech. Report WD-xpath20-20011220, W3C, 2001, http://www.w3.org/TR/WD-xpath20-20011220.

3. W3C working draft: XQuery 1.0: An XML Query Language. (2001) Technical Report WD-xquery-20010607, World Wide Web Consortium.
4. Bose, S., Fegaras, L.: XFrag: A query processing framework for fragmented XML data. In: Eighth International Workshop on the Web and Databases (WebDB 2005), Baltimore, Maryland (June 16–17,2005)
5. Bose, S., Fegaras, L., Levine, D., Chaluvadi, V.: A query algebra for fragmented XML stream data. In: Proceedings of the 9th International Conference on Data Base Programming Languages, Potsdan, Germany (September 6–8, 2003)
6. Altmel, M., Franklin, M.: Efficient filtering of XML documents for selective dissemination of information. In Abbadi, A.E., Brodie, M.L., Chakravarthy, S., Dayal, U., Kamel, N., Schlageter, G., Whang, K.Y., eds.: Proceedings of the 26th International Conference on Very Large Data Bases, Cario, Egypt, Morgan Kaufmann (2000) 53–63
7. Diao, Y., Fischer, P., Franklin, M., To, R.: YFilter: efficient and scalable filtering of XML documents. [15]
8. Chan, C.Y., Felber, P., Garofalakis, M.N., Rastogi, R.: Efficient fltering of XML documents with XPath expressions. [15]
9. Gupta, A.K., Suciu, D.: Stream processing of XPath queries with predicates. In: SIGMOD Conference, San Diego, CA, ACM (2003) 419–430
10. Lee, M.L., Chua, B.C., Hsu, W., Tan, K.L.: Efficient evaluation of multiple queries on streaming XML data. In: Eleventh International Conference on Information and Knowledge Management, McLean, Virginia, USA (November 4–9, 2002)
11. Fegaras, L., Levine, D., Bose, S., Chaluvadi, V.: Query processing of streamed XML data. In: Eleventh International Conference on Information and Knowledge Management (CIKM 2002), McLean, Virginia, USA (November 4–9, 2002)
12. Huo, H., Wang, G., Hui, X., Zhou, R., Ning, B., Xiao, C.: Efficient query processing for streamed XML fragments. In: The 11th International Conference on Database Systems for Advanced Applications, Singapore (April 12–15,2006)
13. Huo, H., Hui, X., Wang, G.: Document fragmentation for XML streams based on hole-filler model. In: 2005 China National Computer Conference, Wu Han, China (October 13–15,2005)
14. Diaz, A.L., Lovell, D.: XML Generator. (1999) http://www.alphaworks.ibm.com/tech/xmlgenerator.
15. Proceedings of the the 2002 International Conference on Data Engineering. In: ICDE Conference, San Jose, California, USA (2002)

Automated Extraction of Hit Numbers from Search Result Pages

Yanyan Ling[1], Xiaofeng Meng[1], and Weiyi Meng[2]

[1] School of Information, Renmin University of China, China
{lingyy, xfmeng}@ruc.edu.cn
[2] Dept. of Computer Science, SUNY at Binghamton, Binghamton, NY 13902, USA
meng@cs.binghamton.edu

Abstract. When a query is submitted to a search engine, the search engine returns a dynamically generated result page that contains the number of hits (i.e., the number of matching results) for the query. Hit number is a very useful piece of information in many important applications such as obtaining document frequencies of terms, estimating the sizes of search engines and generating search engine summaries. In this paper, we propose a novel technique for automatically identifying the hit number for any search engine and any query. This technique consists of three steps: first segment each result page into a set of blocks, then identify the block(s) that contain the hit number using a machine learning approach, and finally extract the hit number from the identified block(s) by comparing the patterns in multiple blocks from the same search engine. Experimental results indicate that this technique is highly accurate.

1 Introduction

Today the Web has become the largest data repository and more and more information on the Web can be accessed from search engines and Web databases (WDBs). Ordinary users can retrieve information from search engines and WDBs by submitting queries to their search interfaces. As we observed, besides the wanted results, most web sites also return a number (we call it hit number) indicating how many results are found for this query. Fig.1shows an example obtained by submitting a query "game" to Ikotomi, which is a web site providing online technical documents. In the result page, besides the results, we also get knowledge from the hit number on how many matching records there are in Ikotomi's database (in our example, it is 1400). Furthermore, by comparing the hit numbers of different web sites providing similar information, such as documents on java, a rank can be assigned to each one showing their capabilities. And based on them, interesting applications of integrating or utilizing these web sites can be implemented, such as giving user suggestions according to his/her queries. For example, when a user wants to find technical documents using key word "java, the system can suggest to him/her the web site having the largest database about Java, which probably returns results he/she wants. Therefore, there is a need for the technique for automatic discovery of this hit number from any search result web pages.

Much useful information about a search engine can be derived from the hit numbers. First, for a single-term query t submitted to a search engine S, the hit number

J.X. Yu, M. Kitsuregawa, and H.V. Leong (Eds.): WAIM 2006, LNCS 4016, pp. 73–84, 2006.
© Springer-Verlag Berlin Heidelberg 2006

is in fact the document frequency of t in the document collection indexed by S. As we know, document frequency information is critical in some applications, such as metasearch engines that utilize document frequency of each term to compute the importance/usefulness of terms in representing and differentiating different document databases. Second, the hit numbers can be used to estimate the size of search engines. Third, hit numbers can be used to classify search engines. For example, the method proposed in [4] uses the hit numbers of probe queries, which represent specific categories (e.g. sports), to compute the coverage and specificity of each search engine and then classify it into an appropriate category of a concept hierarchy. These applications suggest that, we need an automatic hit number extraction technique to be devised. Despite the importance to obtain the hit numbers automatically, this problem has not been seriously studied before to the best of our knowledge.

Intuitively, we may think that most hit numbers are placed in a special block in the result web pages (we call it the hit number block, HNB for short)."1400 results found, top 500 are sorted by relevance" is the HNB in Fig.1. Sometimes by using some simple patterns, HNBs may be identified and the hit numbers can be extracted. This naive solution does solve this problem in some cases, but, unfortunately, when we want to extend it and devise a general method, it broke. Our study shows that it is quite difficult to accurately and automatically extract hit numbers from general search result web pages because HNBs vary from one web site to another. In other words, there are numerous formats and patterns, which will be studied in Section 2 in detail. So, the main problem studied in this paper is to automatically find hit numbers in returned result web pages of search engines or web databases, and our contributions are: (1) we report a detailed study on various cases of HNBs; (2) we propose a novel method for solving the hit number extraction problem by applying machine learning techniques; and (3) we evaluate on our method experimentally and the experimental results show that our approach is highly effective.

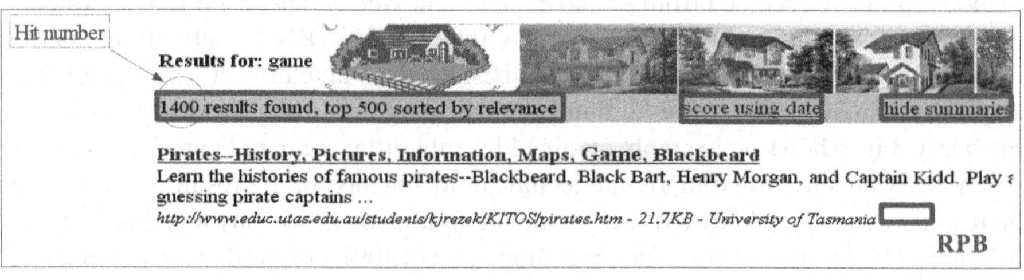

Fig. 1. A Result Page obtained from Ikotomi

The rest of the paper is organized as follows. In Section 2, we report our survey of the diverse patterns of hit number presentations by different systems. From this survey, we can see that the hit number extraction problem is not trivial. In Section 3, a result page is represented as a set of blocks and we discuss how to identify the HNBs among all blocks based on its special features including layout features, visual features and semantic features. In Section 4, we propose an approach to extract the hit numbers from the HNBs. In Section 5, we report our experimental results based on 500 real result pages from various search engines and WDBs. We review related works in Section 6. We conclude the paper in Section 7.

2 Diversity of Hit Number Patterns

In this Section we show our investigation on various hit number patterns based on observing numerous real life Web sites. Below, we summarize our investigation: first we introduce some intuitive patterns used by web page authors; second we show many diverse cases which cannot easily be covered by naive pattern recognition techniques. Finally, in support of our strategy, we will also discuss the reason why intuitive approaches actually cannot solve the hit number extraction problem.

2.1 Intuitive Patterns of Hit Numbers

Web page authors frequently report the hit numbers of specific queries using a literal structure containing the word "of". Table 1 shows some examples of this kind. Generally speaking, this pattern consists of more than one number, which is usually in the order "X V Y U Z", where "X" and "Y" are two numbers forming a range, "V" is preposition such as "-", "to" and "through", "U" contains a variation of the "of" structure such as "of about" and "out of", and "Z" is the hit number we want. Based on our investigation, 41.7% (167 out of 400) result pages contain hit numbers in this pattern. And as we also observed, designers of search engines prefer this kind of pattern, and there are also some variations (e.g. the fourth example in Table 1 contains four numbers, in which the fourth one denotes the query processing time).

Table 1. Most common pattern

(1) Jobs 1 to 50 of more than 1000
(2) Now displaying vehicles 1 - 4 of total 4
(3) Results 1 through 10 of about 19,000,000
(4) Hits 1-10 (out of about 1,259,425 total matching pages) in 0.51 seconds

Table 2. Active voice pattern

(1) Your search resulted in 1 business that matched
(2) Your single word search for tax found 202 names - top 150 listed
(3) Your search for "life" returned 230 of 33793 records
(4) Your search produced 26 records

Table 3. Passive voice pattern

(1) 32 documents match your query
(2) 24 objects returned
(3) 3 occurrence(s) found for "troy"
(4) 54 unique top-ten pages selected from 48,809,621 matching results

Table 4. Diverse cases

(1) Document count: apple (30)
(2) There are 6 institutions
(3) For: "WEB" Total Hits: 40
(4) 2 Total Resources Below:
(5) Page: 1 2 3 4 5 of 100 or more hits

Our survey also shows that the designers of search engines and web databases also like another type of pattern to show hit numbers. For example, Table 2 and Table 3 give out some examples retrieved from web databases and search engines. In general, there are two kinds of patterns. One embeds hit numbers in active voice structures (Table 2 shows examples of this kind). As we can see, the hit numbers usually follow a verb, such as "return", "result in", and "produce". Among the 400 we surveyed, 122 or 30.5% are in this pattern, and some variations also exist, such as the 3rd example in Table 2, which contain extra numbers. The other pattern embeds hit numbers in passive voice structures (Table 3 shows some examples of this kind). It is similar to the active voice case with differences. The hit numbers appear before verbs, as we can see in the examples in Table 3. 13.3% (53 out of 400) web pages we surveyed are in this pattern and there are also variations.

Though most of the web pages (85.5% in all) are covered by intuitive patterns we have discussed. Naively developing programs based on them do not lead to an effective solution. Two reasons are as follows: (1) there are still 14.5% pages that are not covered by these patterns; (2) variations for each pattern make it difficult to use only basic patterns. Thus, we need a general, robust and automated solution.

2.2 Diverse Cases of Hit Numbers

The remaining 14.5% web pages introduce diverse cases on embedding hit numbers. In our survey, we found out some formats that are beyond our imaginations. Table 4 displays some diverse cases. As one can see, some do not have any verbs (1st example), some do not have complete sentences (1st, 3rd, and 4th examples). The appearance location of hit numbers also varies, such as at the beginning of a sentence (4th example), the middle of a sentence (2nd example), and the end of a sentence (1st and 3rd examples). One of the worst cases is the 5th example, where it does not show the accurate hit number at all (it uses the word "more"). Instead it displays numbers like 1, 2, 3, 4, 5, and 100, which can easily cause most solutions to fail.

In summary, due to the diversity and unpredictability of the patterns used to present hit numbers by different search systems, traditional pattern recognition strategies are unlikely to work well for solving the hit number extraction problem. In this paper, we explore the special features in the web context such as visual features and layout features, to solve this problem.

2.3 The Problem of an Intuitive Solution

Before we introduce our solution, in this subsection we would like to discuss an intuitive solution by giving the reasons why it is not general enough, which also provides a clearer picture on how complex this problem is.

One may think that the hit numbers can be easily detected since they often appear at the beginning of the result pages and have distinguishing colors to attract users' attention. In fact, this is not true in general. Sometimes the hit number appears before the data records while other times after them. Due to the different sizes of data regions and advertising regions of different result pages, the absolute positions of hit numbers on result pages are uncertain. Also, only a small percentage of result pages use special colors to display hit numbers.

Therefore, based on all these analyses above, we take all the helpful cues into consideration because none of them is a decisive factor. In our method, all these helpful information are utilized to achieve high performance. Generally speaking, the basic idea of our approach is that we first split web pages into blocks (we will explain it below) and select the ones that probably contain hit numbers, and then we check all these blocks in the hope of finding hit numbers. Thus our method consists of following two main steps - Hit Number Block discovery and Hit Number extraction.

3 Hit Number Block Discovery

As we have stated, the mission of this step is to split web pages into blocks and then select the ones that probably contain hit numbers. In our strategy, a block in web pages is just a group of adjacent words, in which no more than 3 consecutive white spaces are allowed. By ignoring tags in web pages, result web page can be split into many blocks according to this definition, and we call them result page blocks (RPB for short). In Fig.1, the contents in thick-lined boxes are examples of RPBs. After a result web page is split into a set of RPBs, the next step is to identify HNB(s), which probably contain hit numbers.

3.1 Splitting Web Page and Preprocessing RPBs

Splitting web page into RPBs is easy and straightforward. By viewing web pages as a token sequence, RPBs can be derived according to their definition, where in our work, a token can be a HTML tag, a single word, or consecutive white spaces. As the techniques used for splitting are fairly simple, we do not discuss them here.

Next we do basic preprocessing on obtained RPBs. Two kinds of RPBs will be removed from the set as they definitely do not contain hit numbers. One is RPBs that do not contain any digit, which are definitely not hit number block. The other is RPBs that do contain digit(s) but these digit(s) cannot be hit numbers. For example, Such RPBs contain only float numbers (they can be easily identified by their formats), or numbers for prices (they have a common prefix such as "$"), and numbers for date (they usually are concatenated by special characters, such as "/"). After preprocessing, for a given result web page, the RPBs that contain possible hit numbers are identified. The remaining steps only need to identify whether they contain hit numbers or not. In our solution, a machine learning method is employed to perform this.

3.2 HNB Identification by Decision Tree

Many features of web pages, which can be discovered by simply observing example web pages, could be utilized to identify hit number blocks. However, not all of these features are significant. Some of them are critical in identifying hit number block while some are not. Thus we need a mechanism to discover and select significant features. Thus in our work we apply the C4.5 learning technique to induce a decision tree, which is implemented based on Weka [6].Then we can do identifications based on induced decision tree. In overall picture, the steps of our strategy are as follows.

1. We select some example web pages, and manually identify HNBs from RPBs. The results will be recorded in a log file.
2. For each example web page, values of various web page features of each block are checked and calculated. The results will also be logged.
3. We apply C4.5 algorithm to induce a decision tree with selected examples. Each condition in decision tree is represented in the form whether a specific web page feature is fulfilled.

4. Finally we evaluate the induced decision tree with training set and possibly refine it.

In our work, for each RPB, almost 50 web features are checked and calculated. As we investigated, some features have discrete values, such as where specific word exists, but most of them have continuous values, such as various offsets. Therefore we prefer the C4.5 algorithm to ID3 for its ability to handle continuous values. The most important part, which is also our contribution, is to identify various web page features. Next we will discuss each of them in detail.

3.3 Web Page Features

This subsection describes various web page features used in inducing decision tree for identifying HNBs. You will see that for each RPB, various features can be utilized to do identification. In particular, human beings also rely on these features to separate HNB from other parts of the web page. They can be visual cues, text characteristics, and even frequent words. In the following paragraphs we will describe them one by one. Before doing that, we would like to introduce an illustrative example first, which is shown in Fig.2. As we can see, there is a hit number block "3577 stories and blog posts contain the term health" in the broken-line box, and let us mark it as B.

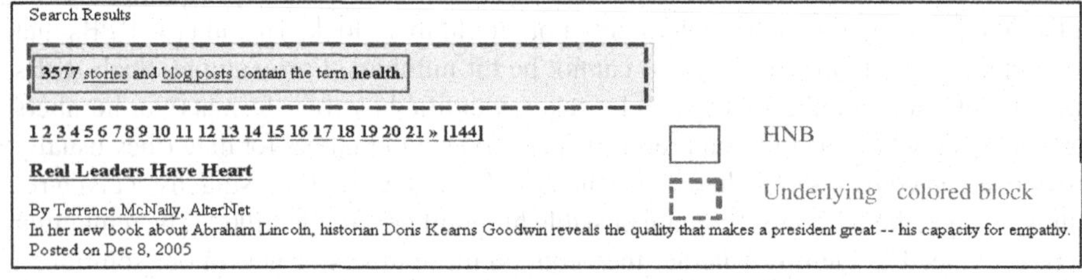

Fig. 2. A Result Page obtained from AlterNet

Layout Related Features. Firstly, we observe that HNB is not randomly placed on a result page and the HNB is usually small in size. Thus the absolute position of each RPB in the result page is taken into consideration, such as *BlockOfsetX*, *BlockOfsetY*, *BlockWidth*, *BlockHeight*. For example, the distance between the left border of B and the left border of the page along the X-axis is 14 pixels (*B.BlockOfsetX* = 14 pixels).

Secondly, considering the result page structure, we find that HNB(s) usually occur either near the beginning or the end of the data region. Hence, the relative distance between HNB(s) and data regions should also be taken into consideration, such as *DataRegionOfsetX*, *DataRegionOfsetY*, *DataRegionWidth*, *DataRegionHeight*, *RelativeY1*, *RelativeY1Ra*, *RelativeY2* and *RelativeY2Ra*. Many works deal with the problem of data region identification. [5] proposed a technique which is able to mine both contiguous and noncontiguous data records. [5] proposed a novel partial alignment technique based on tree matching and extract data region very accurately. In general, we cannot dismiss RPBs within the data region,because none of the current techniques on data region identification is perfect.So we will calculate the above features for each candidate RPB. For example, B is closer to the top border of the data region, and the distance between the bottom border of RPB and the top border of the data region along the Y-axis is 38 pixels (*B.RelativeY1* = 38 pixels).

Finally, sometimes the HNBs are emphasized with a background block with outstanding color to attract people. Then some layout features of the background block are taken into consideration, such as *BoxOfsetX*, *BoxOfsetY*, *BoxWidth* and *BoxHeight*. If no background block exists, the 4 features are set to zero. For example, the height of the background block of B is 42 pixels (*B. BoxHeight* = 42 pixels).

Color Related Features. This class of features is based on our observation that HNBs on a result page usually have special appearances distinguishable from other RPBs. The designers of Web pages often make the HNB salient with outstanding background color and foreground color, in order to emphasize it and attract users' attention. Therefore, some color related features are taken into consideration, such as *BackgroundColor*, *ForeColor*, *BodyBackgroundColor*, *ColorCount* and *IsHighlight*. For example, the color behind the content of B in Fig.2 is gray (*B. BackgroundColor*=gray). In addition, 2 different font colors are used in B (*B.ColorCount*=2).

Characters Related Features. Firstly, we observed that numbers occurred in HNB(s) may have their own features distinguishable from the numbers in other RPBs. Some features such as *DigitalCount*, *CharacterCount*, *DigitPercent*, *NumberCount*, *WordCount* and *NumberPercent* are taken into considerations. For example, the amount of numbers appeared in the RPB (*NumberCount*) is usually within a range. In Fig.2 *B.NumberCount*=1 ("3577") and *B.NumberPercent*=11% while *NumberPercent* denotes the ratio of the *NumberCount* and the total amount of words in the RPB.

Secondly, we observed that seldom words were hyperlinked within a HNB and some words were overstriked in order to emphasize them and attract the users' attention. Therefore, *LinkCount* and *BoldCount* may also help in identifying HNB. For example, *B.BoldCount*=2 while 2 words are overstriked ("3577" and "health").

Semantic Related Features. This class of features is based on our observation that some frequent words play an important role in HNB identification. These words will be called clue words. A survey is conducted to identify the frequent terms in a set of more than 400 HNBs from different result pages. Top-n words were selected (here n is set to 20). A fraction of the results is listed in Table 5. Though such terms would often appear in HNBs, their appearances alone are not enough to accurately identify HNBs. First, such words may also appear in other RPBs. For example, "of" appears in "Page 1 of 20". Second, some HNBs do not have any of these frequent words. For example, none of the frequent words appear in "There are 6 institutions" even though this block is a real HNB.

$$Frequency = \frac{occurrences \quad of \quad HNBs}{total \quad number \quad of \quad HNBs}$$

For each frequent word w, we use *B.Count (w)* to denote the number of times the word occurs in block B. For 20 frequent words, 20 such Counts will be collected as

20 features for each block. In addition, we use *CountTotal* to denote the summation of these Counts for each block. Overall, there are 21 (20+1) features involved in this class. For example, *B.Count(Term)* denotes how many times the word "term" occur in B and we have *B.Count(Term)* = 1.

Table 5. Frequent Terms

Terms	Frequency	Terms	Frequency
-	47%	search	17%
result	38%	return	16%
of	34%	document	11%
for	19%	you	11%
match	18%	found	9%
show	17%		

4 Hit Number Extraction from HNB

After the HNBs are found, the next step is to extract the hit numbers from them. Intuitively, we may think that the largest number in a HNB is the hit number. However this simple heuristic rule is not valid in general. For example, there is an example "Found 72 of 1,434 searched" we find when doing investigations. It is clear that the hit number is "72", which is not the largest number ("1,434").

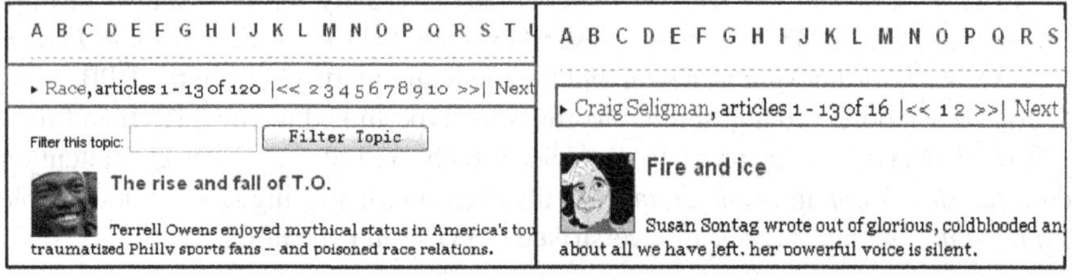

Fig. 3. Example obtained from Salon(www.dir.salon.com)

On the other hand, one may discover that for a given web site, different result pages returned by submitting different queries share similar template. For example, consider the HNBs, where one is "1-10 of 4,199 results for java" and the other is "1-10 of 7,509 results for database". By comparing them, we find out that only hit numbers (4,199 vs. 7,590) and query keywords (java vs. database) are different. It seems a solution can be devised based on comparing changed numbers. Unfortunately, it is also not general enough. Let us check a complex example in Fig.3. By comparing "Race, articles 1- 13 of 120 << 2 3 4 5 6 7 8 9 10 >> Next" with "Craig Seligman, articles 1- 13 of 16 << 1 2>> Next", we can see that more than one number changed and the idea of simply comparing changed numbers does not work.

With the above observations in mind, we learn that simple pattern-matching algorithm is not general enough to identify hit numbers. A hybrid algorithm combining

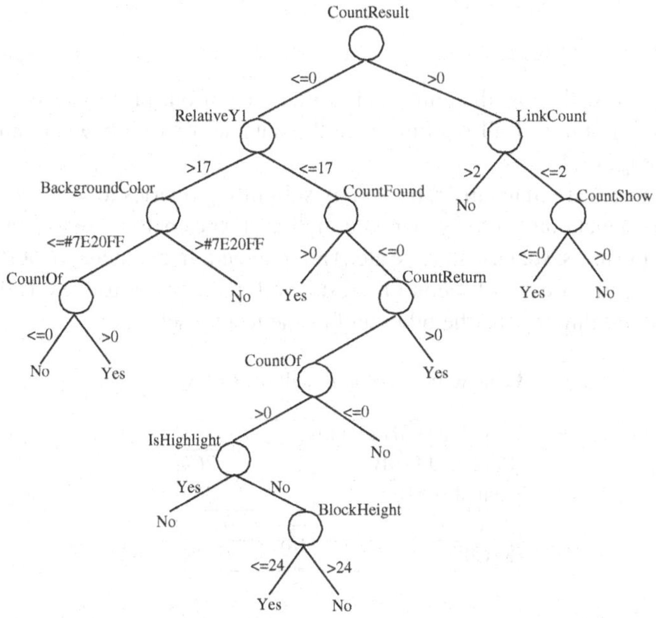

Fig. 4. Induced Decision Tree, which is induced with 50 features

characteristics observed so far should be invented. Thus in our work, we propose a novel algorithm which identifies the hit number step by step.

The input of our algorithm consists of two or more HNBs retrieved by submitting different query keywords to the same web site. And the output is the hit numbers (if there is one). Our algorithm consists of the following steps:

1. Identify number sequence and remove it from HNBs: A number sequence is a sequence of integer numbers, such as "2 3 4 5 6 7 8 9 10" in the left portion and "1 2" in the right portion in Fig.3. Number sequences could not be hit numbers.
2. Identify range pattern and remove it from HNBs: A range pattern consists of two integers with a connector in between, where the connector can be "-", "to", and "through". For example, "1-13" is a range pattern. Range patterns do not contain hit numbers.
3. Identify all non-numbers and remove them from HNBs: The words or characters strings that are all non-numbers in HNBs will be removed. For the two HNBs in Fig.3, the static contents include "articles", "of", "<<", ">>", and "Next".
4. Identify query keyword(s) that is a number and remove them from HNBs: They are the key words which may be numbers submitted to retrieve the result pages. The reason for doing this is to remove possible numbers used in queries.
5. Identify hit number by comparing HNBs: At this time, each number in HNB could be the hit number and we simply choose the largest one.

The basic idea behind our algorithm is to gradually identify impossible cases. It is easy to implement as well as effective. Next we will show experiments to support it.

5 Empirical Evaluation

5.1 Data Set

In this section we will show the empirical evaluations of our prototype system for hit number extraction. First of all we introduce the data set of web pages obtained from real-life Web pages.

These web pages are manually retrieved by submitting queries to Web sites listed in www.completeplanet.com. To be general enough, web sites belonging to a broad range (news, media, business, society, science etc..) are selected. In all, there are 500 web sites in our data set, and for each of them, one result web page was retrieved. Half of them are used as the training set and the other half as the testing set.

Table 6. Evaluation Result on Test Set

Possible HNB Found	271
Predicted HNB	264
Actual HNB	269
Precision	$\frac{264}{271} = 97.4\%$
Recall	$\frac{264}{269} = 98.1\%$

Each result web page in the entire data set is broken into RPBs, and we manually mark out HNBs. Remember that we remove RPBs that cannot be HNBs (Section 3.1), however, the number of RPBs (including Non-HNBs and HNBs) is lager than the number of web pages. In general, some web pages may contain more than one HNB for different purposes. Therefore, we generated a training set containing 272 positive examples (HNB) and 352 negative examples (non-HNB). Similar work is also done on the testing set where 269 positive instances (HNB) and 376 negative instances (non-HNB) are identified. The training set will be used for inducing decision tree and the testing set will be used in empirical evaluation.

5.2 Evaluatation of the HNB Discovery Algorithm

Fig.4 shows the decision tree induced from web page features described in Section 3.3. 9 out of 50 features are selected and associated with nodes in the decision tree. Feature selection is automatically implemented by this classification algorithm. All 50 features were weighted and ranked individually and the top 9 highest weighted features were selected, which work very well on random selected HNB discovery in our experiments.

Then we do classification by using the reduced decision tree on our testing set. In order to measure the performance, recall and precision are defined. They are defined as

$$Recall = \frac{|PredictedHNB \cap ActualHNB|}{|ActualHNB|} \quad Precision = \frac{|PredictedHNB \cap ActualHNB|}{|PredictedHNB|}$$

where ActualHNB is the set of real HNBs in the testing set (it is manually obtained), and PredicatedHNB is the set of HNBs discovered by our method.

Table 6 shows the evaluation result on the testing set. In fact, there are 269 actual HNBs, which is known when we preparing this set. Our algorithm found 271 HNBs, in which 264 of them are real HNBs (we manually checked them). Therefore, the precision is 98.1 % and the recall is 97.4%. As we can see, our method is highly effective.

5.3 Evaluation of the Hit Number Extraction Algorithm

After HNBs are identified, we proceed to evaluate our hit number extraction algorithm on them. In the previous step we obtained 264 HNBs, and, remember that in the training step, we also obtained 277 HNBs. So in all there are 541 HNBs. After the execution, our algorithm identified 536 right hit numbers (we also manually checked them). Therefore the accuracy is 99.1%, which clearly shows that our algorithm is highly effective.

6 Related Work

Discovering hit numbers from search result pages of search engines and WDBs can be considered as a special case of automated data extraction for specific information from web pages. There are lots of works focusing on extracting specific information from text documents and web pages of different domains. For example, there are works which automatically identify human names or extracting individual product information, such as price [3]. The closest work to ours is [1], which tried to detect and extract postal addresses from web pages. But we are not aware of any prior work on automatic hit number extraction. In terms of techniques used, we adopted and adapted two kinds of techniques proposed in literature in our solution. One is classification by inducing a decision tree. The work reported in [2] induced a decision tree for automatically discovering search interfaces from a set of HTML forms. Similar classification techniques are also used in our work. The other is utilizing visual cues in web pages. As reported in [7], by utilizing specific visual cues, such as shape of HTML block, layout position, data records can be automatically extracted from result web pages returned by search engines. However, in our work, by inducing a decision tree from many visual features of various representations of hit numbers, the above two techniques are combined together to form a novel and effective method to identify and extract specific pieces of data, which in our case are hit numbers.

7 Conclusion and Future Work

In this paper, we proposed an automatic approach to extract hit numbers from the result pages returned from search engines and WDBs. As mentioned in the introduction, automatic hit number extraction is important in several important applications. This approach consists of three steps. The first step segments a result page into a set of RPBs. The second step applies a machine learning technique to discover HNB(s) from the RPBs based on an extensive list of features. The third step identifies hit numbers from HNBs based on comparing the patterns among multiple HNBs from the same site. Experiments show our approach is highly effective with its accuracy close to perfection.

In the future, we plan to consider hit number extraction from result pages containing multiple data regions. Each region may have its own hit number and the presence of multiple data regions may pose new complications to this problem.

Acknowledgments

This research was partially supported by the grants from the Natural Science Foundation of China under grant number 60573091, 60273018; China National Basic Research and Development Program's Semantic Grid Project (No. 2003CB317000); the Key Project of Ministry of Education of China under Grant No.03044 ; Program for New Century Excellent Talents in University (NCET) and NSF IIS-0414981.

References

1. Lin Can, Zhang Qian, Xiaofeng Meng, and Wenyin Lin. Postal address detection from web documents. In *WIRI*, pages 40–45. IEEE Computer Society, 2005.
2. Jared Cope, Nick Craswell, and David Hawking. Automated discovery of search interfaces on the web. In Klaus-Dieter Schewe and Xiaofang Zhou, editors, *ADC*, volume 17 of *CRPIT*, pages 181–189. Australian Computer Society, 2003.
3. Robert B. Doorenbos, Oren Etzioni, and Daniel S. Weld. A scalable comparison-shopping agent for the world-wide web. In *Agents*, pages 39–48, 1997.
4. Panagiotis G. Ipeirotis, Luis Gravano, and Mehran Sahami. Probe, count, and classify: Categorizing hidden web databases. In *SIGMOD Conference*, 2001.
5. Bing Liu, Robert L. Grossman, and Yanhong Zhai. Mining web pages for data records. *IEEE Intelligent Systems*, 19(6):49–55, 2004.
6. Ian H. Witten and Eibe Frank. *Data Mining: Practical machine learning tools and techniques (2nd edition)*. Morgan Kaufmann, San Francisco, 2005.
7. Hongkun Zhao, Weiyi Meng, Zonghuan Wu, Vijay Raghavan, and Clement T. Yu. Fully automatic wrapper generation for search engines. In Allan Ellis and Tatsuya Hagino, editors, *WWW*, pages 66–75. ACM, 2005.

Keyword Extraction Using Support Vector Machine

Kuo Zhang, Hui Xu, Jie Tang, and Juanzi Li

Department of Computer Science and Technology, Tsinghua University
Beijing, P.R.China, 100084
{zkuo99, xuhui99, j-tang02}@mails.tsinghua.edu.cn,
ljz@keg.cs.tsinghua.edu.cn

Abstract. This paper is concerned with keyword extraction. By keyword extraction, we mean extracting a subset of words/phrases from a document that can describe the 'meaning' of the document. Keywords are of benefit to many text mining applications. However, a large number of documents do not have keywords and thus it is necessary to assign keywords before enjoying the benefit from it. Several research efforts have been done on keyword extraction. These methods make use of the 'global context information', which makes the performance of extraction restricted. A thorough and systematic investigation on the issue is thus needed. In this paper, we propose to make use of not only 'global context information', but also 'local context information' for extracting keywords from documents. As far as we know, utilizing both 'global context information' and 'local context information' in keyword extraction has not been sufficiently investigated previously. Methods for performing the tasks on the basis of Support Vector Machines have also been proposed in this paper. Features in the model have been defined. Experimental results indicate that the proposed SVM based method can significantly outperform the baseline methods for keyword extraction. The proposed method has been applied to document classification, a typical text mining processing. Experimental results show that the accuracy of document classification can be significantly improved by using the keyword extraction method.

1 Introduction

Keywords summarize a document concisely and give a high-level description of the document's content. Keywords provide rich semantic information for many text mining applications, for example: document classification, document clustering, document retrieval, topic search, and document analysis.

Unfortunately, a large portion of documents (on internet and intranet) still do not have keywords assigned. In order to enjoy the benefit of keywords, it is necessary to extract keywords from the documents. This is exactly the problem addressed in this paper.

Existing methods on keyword extraction have been done mainly by using a predefined controlled-vocabulary, which cannot process the unknown words/phrases. In natural language processing, base Noun Phrase (baseNP) finding and key-term recognition have been studied. But the extracted baseNPs are not necessary to be keywords

J.X. Yu, M. Kitsuregawa, and H.V. Leong (Eds.): WAIM 2006, LNCS 4016, pp. 85–96, 2006.
© Springer-Verlag Berlin Heidelberg 2006

of the document. Recently, several methods are proposed to extract keywords by utilizing the 'global context information'. The global information includes term frequency, term inverted document frequency, etc. This kind of global information ignores the term's local context information and makes the extraction performance limited. In the research community, no previous study has so far sufficiently investigated the problem by making use of not only the 'global context information', but also the 'local context information', to the best of our knowledge.

Three questions arise for keyword extraction: (1) how to formalize the problem (since it involves many different understandings of the 'keyword'), (2) how to solve the problem in a principled approach, and (3) how to make an implementation.

(1) We formalize keyword extraction as a classification problem, in which the words/phrases in a document can be classified into three groups: 'good keyword', 'indifferent keyword', and 'bad keyword'. We give a specification of keyword in this paper.

(2) We propose to conduct keyword extraction by a classification approach. In the approach, we select the candidate keywords by tri-grams, and then define the features by both 'global context information' and 'local context information'. We then accomplish the keyword extraction by a classification model that is trained in advance.

(3) We propose a unified statistical learning approach to the tasks, based on Support Vector Machines (SVMs).

We tried to collect data from as many sources as possible for experiments. Our experimental results indicate that the proposed SVM based method performs significantly better than the baseline method for keyword extraction. We also applied our method to document classification. Experimental results indicate that our method can indeed enhance the accuracy of document classification. We observed improvements ranging from 7.79% to 22.12% on document classification in terms of F1-Measure.

The rest of the paper is organized as follows. In section 2, we introduce related work. In section 3, we formalize the problem of keyword extraction. In section 4, we describe our approach to the problem and in section 5, we explain one possible implementation. Section 6 gives our experimental results. We make concluding remarks in section 7.

2 Related Work

2.1 Keyword Extraction

Keyword extraction is the task of selecting a small set of words/phrases from a document that can describe the meaning of the document. It is an important area in text mining [Hulth2004].

For example, Turney has developed a system, called GenEx, for keyword extraction based on a set of parameterized heuristic rules that can be tuned by using a genetic algorithm [Turney2000]. The system optimizes the rules' parameters from the training documents.

Eibe Frank et al propose a key phrase extraction algorithm, called KEA, based on Naïve Bayes machine learning approach [Frank1999, Witten1999]. They have employed the extracted keywords to learn a model and have applied the model for finding keywords from new documents. They have defined the features in the model by utilizing the global context information, i.e. term frequency and first occurrence of the word/phrase.

Tang et al also apply Bayesian decision theory to the task of keyword extraction [Tang2004]. They make use of word linkage information and define two 'local context' features. See also [Azcarraga2002, Hulth2004, Matsuo2004, Zhu2003].

Our method exploits both global context and local context information. We translate the problem of keyword extraction to a binary classification problem, and use SVM algorithm as the classifier.

2.2 Keyword Assignment

Keyword assignment is aimed to assign keywords from a predefined controlled-vocabulary to documents.

For example, Dumaisn et al propose a method for finding a mapping from documents to the categories that are defined as keywords in a controlled-vocabulary [Dumais1998]. They make use of machine learning method to learn classifiers from a set of training documents. A new document then is processed by each of the classifiers and is assigned to those categories with higher probability. Keyword assignment has been limited by the predefined controlled-vocabulary, which cannot process the unknown words/phrases.

2.3 Key-Term Recognition

Term extraction is a task in which base noun phrases (base NP) are extracted from documents [Xun2000]. The extracted terms can be used as features of documents for document mining applications such as document categorization and document clustering. It is different from keyword extraction in two aspects. First of all, the goals are different. Term extraction is aimed to extract base noun phrases that can be used as features of documents for other mining applications, while keyword extraction is aimed to extract the most meaningful words/phrases that can be used to describe the documents. In this way, a keyword can be a base NP; however, a base NP is not necessary a keyword. Secondly, the number of extracted words/phrases can be significantly different. Keywords extracted from a document should be as few as possible if only they can make the user easily distinguish the document from the others, while term extraction can extract many words/phrases. See also [Brill1999].

2.4 Text Summarization

Text summarization is another type of similar work to keyword extraction. Informally, the goal of text summarization is to take a textual document as input, extract content from it, and present the most 'meaningful' content to users in a condensed form and in a manner sensitive to the user's or application's needs [Mani2001]. Extracted content by text summarization can be paragraph(s) or sentences(s). Therefore, text summarization differs in nature from keyword extraction.

Zha, for instance, proposes a summarization method by first clustering sentences of a document (or a set of documents) into topical groups and then, within each topical group, selecting the key phrases and sentences by their saliency scores [Zha2002]. See also [Berger2000, DUC, Mani1999].

3 Keyword Extraction

Keywords extracted from a document play an important role in describing the meaning of that document. For example, in a simple application, a user wants to find an expertise report in a certain field from a document collection. He can quickly judge whether or not a document is what he wants by using only keywords of that document. In more sophisticated application, the user can group documents by using keywords. Keywords can be also useful for text mining applications, for example: document classification and document clustering. In section 6, we will demonstrate that keywords indeed improve the accuracy of document classification.

Now we formally define the keyword extraction problem that we are solving. Given a document *D* with a bag of words $w_1, w_2, \ldots, w_N$, we need to find a small set of keywords. Here, the word is the smallest language unit in our problem, and a keyword can be either a word or a word sequence (i.e. phrase). This also means that the keywords extracted should occur in the document.

Judging whether a word/phrase is keyword in an objective way is hard. However, we can still provide relatively objective guidelines for judgment. We call it the specification in this paper. It is indispensable for development and evaluation of keyword extraction.

In the specification, we create three categories for keywords which represent their goodness as keywords: 'good keyword', 'indifferent keyword' and 'bad keyword'.

A good keyword must contain the general notion of the document, and several important properties of the document. From a good keyword, one can understand the basic meaning of the document. Furthermore, a good keyword should be easily searchable and understandable by humans and it should be specific enough to allow the user to distinguish between documents with similar contents.

A bad keyword neither describes the general notion nor properties of the document. It can be difficult to be understood by human. One cannot get the meaning of the document by reading a bad keyword.

An indifferent keyword is one that between good and bad keyword.

4 Our Approach

We formalize keyword extraction as a classification problem. We take 'good keyword', 'indifferent keyword', and 'bad keyword' as classes, words/phrases manually labeled with the three classes in the 'training documents' as training examples, words/phrases in the 'test documents' as test examples, so that keyword extraction can be automatically accomplished by predicting the class of each test example.

We perform keyword extraction in two passes of processing: learning, and keyword extraction.

In learning, we construct the classification model that can predict the class of each word/phrase. In the classification model, we view each word/phrase as an example. For each example, we define a set of features and assign a label. The label represents whether the word/phrase is a 'good keyword', 'indifferent keyword', or 'bad keyword'. We use the labeled data to train the classification models in advance.

In keyword extraction, the input is a document. We extract a bag of words/phrases from that document. Then, for each word/phrase in that document, we employ the learned classification models to predict whether it is 'good keyword', 'indifferent keyword', or 'bad keyword'. We next view the words/phrases that are predicted as 'good keywords' as keywords.

In this paper, we will focus our implementation on how to classify a word/phrase as 'keyword' or not, and re-formalize the problem as a two-classification problem. However, to determine whether a word/phrase is 'good keyword', 'indifferent keyword', or 'bad keyword' is still one of our near future work.

5 Implementation

We consider one implementation of our approach. We make use of SVM (Support Vector Machines) as the classification model [Vapnik1995].

Let us first consider a two class classification problem. Let $\{(x_1, y_1), \ldots, (x_N, y_N)\}$ be a training data set, in which x_i denotes an example (a feature vector) and $y_i \in \{-1,+1\}$ denotes a classification label. In learning, one attempts to find an optimal separating hyper-plane that maximally separates the two classes of training examples (more precisely, maximizes the margin between the two classes of examples). The hyper-plane corresponds to a classifier (linear SVM). It is theoretically guaranteed that the linear classifier obtained in this way has small generalization errors. Linear SVM can be further extended into non-linear SVMs by using kernel functions such as Gaussian and polynomial kernels.

We use SVM-light, which is available at http://svmlight.joachims.org/. We choose polynomial kernel, because our preliminary experimental results show that it works best for our current task. We use the default values for the parameters in SVM-light. When there are more than two classes, we adopt the "one class versus all others" approach, i.e., take one class as positive and the other classes as negative.

5.1 Process

The input is a document. The implementation carries out extraction in the following steps.

(1) Preprocessing. For a document, we conduct the sentence split, word tokenization and POS (part-of-speech) tagging by using GATE [Cunningham2002]. We next employ Linker [Sleator1991] to analyze the dependency relationships between words in each sentence. After that, we employ tri-gram to create candidate phrases, and then filter the phrases whose frequencies are below a predefined threshold. We also exclude the common words in the stop-words list. We conduct a gentle stemming by using WordNet [Miller1990]. Specifically, we only stem the plural noun, gerund, and passive infinitive by their dictionary form. Finally, we obtain a set of 'keyword candidate' for the later processing.

(2) Feature extraction. The input is a bag of words/phrases in a document. We make use of both local context information and global context information of a word/phrase in a document to define its features (see following section for a detailed

definition of the features). The output is the feature vectors, and each vector corresponds to a word/phrase.

(3) Learning. The input is a collection of feature vector by step (2). We construct a SVM model that can identify the keyword. In the SVM model, we view a word/phrase as an example, the words/phrases labeled with 'keyword' as positive examples, and the other words/phrases as negative examples. We use the labeled data to train the SVM model in advance.

(4) Extraction. The input is a document. We employ the preprocessing and the feature extraction on it, and obtain a set of feature vectors. We then predict whether or not a word/phrase is a keyword by using the SVM model from step (3). Finally, the output is the extracted keywords for that document.

The key issue here is how to define *features* for effectively performing the extraction task.

5.2 Features in the Model

We make use of both 'global context information' and 'local context information' features to represent our data. Each word/phrase is represented by a set of its local context features and the document global context features.

(1) Global Context Features

TFIDF Feature. The feature is calculated by TF*IDF, where TF is the Term Frequency in the document and IDF is the Inverted Document Frequency, i.e. $log((N+1)/(n+1))$. N is the total number of the documents in the document collection. n is the number of documents in which the current word/phrase occurs.

First Occurrence Feature. The feature represents the percentage of words/phrases occurring before the current word/phrase to the total number of words in the document. Its value ranges between 0 and 1.

Position Features. Three features respectively represent whether or not the current word/phrase occurs in document title, abstract (if there exists), and section title (if there exists). The words/phrases occurring in the document title, abstract and section title have higher probabilities of being keywords.

(2) Local Context Features

Local context features have not been investigated previously for the task of keyword extraction.

POS Feature. The feature represents the POS of the current word. A keyword usually is a noun word/phrase. For phrase, we define a unified POS: "PHRASE".

Linkage Features. In the preprocessing step, the dependency relationships between words are recognized. We give two linkage definitions: Linkage Authority and Linkage Hub. Linkage Authority denotes how many words that modify the word. The more the word is modified by, the higher authority it has. Linkage Hub denotes how many words that are modified by the word. The more the word modifies, the higher hub it has.

The two linkages are defined as follows:

$$wl_h = \frac{freq(w_i, \forall)}{count(\forall, \forall)} \times -\log \frac{df(w_i, \forall)}{N}$$

$$wl_a = \frac{freq(\forall, w_i)}{count(\forall, \forall)} \times -\log \frac{df(\forall, w_i)}{N}$$

Where:

wl_h and wl_a represent the modifying relationship and the modified relationship respectively.

$freq(w_i, \forall)$ is the number of words that w_i is modifying in a given document.

$df(w_i, \forall)$ is the number of documents containing the modifier relation $freq(w_i, \forall)$ in the global corpora.

$count(\forall, \forall)$ is the number of total modifier relationships.

N is the size of the global corpora.

The value wl_h and wl_a are located between 0 and 1. $\log(df(\forall, w_i)/N)$ is the log of probability that this word appears in any document of the corpora.

Contextual TFIDF Feature. Contextual TFIDF is the sum of the TFIDF of words in the 'context' of the current word/phrase, which represents the contextual TFIDF. We view words in the same sentence as the current word as its contextual words.

6 Experimental Results

Data Sets and Evaluation Measures

Data Sets. We tried to collect documents for experiments from as many sources as possible. We randomly chose in total 350 documents from four sources and created four data sets. ACM is from the proceedings of conference from 2002 to 2004 in ACM digital library (http://portal.acm.org/portal.cfm). CiteSeer is from CiteSeer website (http://citeseer.ist.psu.edu/cs). Reuter is from the distribution 1.0 of Reuter text collection (http://www.research.att.com/~lewis/ reuters21578.html). Web Doc is downloaded arbitrarily from the Internet.

Table 1 shows the statistics on the data sets. The columns present respectively the data set, its description and the number of documents in it.

Among the four datasets, some research papers already have author assigned keywords, but some of the keywords do not conform to our specification (defined in

Table1. Statistics of the datasets in experiments

Dataset	Description	Total Number
ACM	From ACM Digital Library, proceedings of conferences hold during 2002~2004	200
CiteSeer	From CiteSeer	65
Reuter	Distribution 1.0 of Reuter text collection	50
Web Doc	Downloaded arbitrarily from internet	35

section 3). Moreover, the other documents do not have keywords. Human annotators conducted annotation on all the documents. Keywords of research papers were updated according to the specification, and keywords in the other documents were labeled. Specifically, five graduates in our laboratory were asked to conduct the annotation for all the documents. The number of annotated keywords ranges from 4 to 10. The average of annotated keywords is 9.69 per document. Finally, for each document, intersection of keywords assigned by different annotators is taken as the 'correct' keywords. In this way, each document has six 'correct' keywords averagely.

Evaluation Measures. In all the experiments on extraction, we conducted evaluations in terms of precision, recall and F1-Measure. The evaluation measures are defined as follows:

Precision: $P = A / (A + B)$

Recall: $R = A / (A + C)$

F1-Measure: $F1 = 2PR / (P + R)$

where A, B, C and D denote number of instances.

Table 2. Contingence table on results of detection and extraction

	Is Target	**Is Not Target**
Detected	A	B
Non Detected	C	D

In all evaluations, we view a keywords assigned by humans as a 'target'. If a method can extract the target, we say that it makes a correct decision; otherwise, we say that it makes a mistake. Precision, recall, and F1-Measure are calculated on the basis of the result.

Baseline Method. We use TFIDF as the baseline to extract the keyword (many text mining applications use this method for bag-of-word feature selection). Specifically, for a document, we selected six words/phrases with the higher TFIDF as keywords.
We also carried out the comparison of our method and the KEA algorithm [Frank1999, Witten1999]. KEA algorithm has been proposed by Eibe Frank et al. It uses TFIDF and first occurrence as features and uses Naïve Bayes for learning and extraction. We downloaded the KEA algorithm from http://www.nzdl.org/Kea/index.html#download, and applied it to the four datasets.

Finally, we conducted the experiments of using only global features and using all the features we defined in our model (including global and local features). We carried out the comparison of the results by our methods with the two kinds of features.

Keyword Extraction

Experiment. We evaluated the performances of our keyword extraction methods on the four data sets.

We performed comparisons with the baseline methods and the KEA algorithm. We also evaluated our method with only the global context features and with all the features we defined.

Because the average number of keywords annotated manually is six, we select six keywords in the baseline method and KEA method. In our approach, we select the words as keywords that are classified as positive examples by the SVM model.

Table 3 shows the five cross-validation results on the four data sets. In the table, Global, Local respectively denotes the global context features and local context features. The second column indicates the average number of keywords extracted.

Table 3. Evaluation of Keyword Extraction (%)

	Average Number	Precision	Recall	F1-Measure
Baseline Method	6	12.70	13.11	12.90
KEA	6	32.39(+19.69)	29.09(+15.98)	30.65(+17.75)
Our Method (Global)	5.88	70.75(+58.05)	42.87(+29.76)	53.39(+40.49)
Our Method (Global)+(Local)	7.75	67.43(+54.73)	53.87(+40.76)	59.90(+47.00)

We see that our method can significantly outperform the baseline method and the KEA algorithm. Our method by using global context features and local context features also outperforms that by using only global context features. We conducted sign tests on the results. The p values are significantly smaller than 0.01, indicating that the improvements are statistically significant.

Discussions

(1) Improvements over baseline method. The TFIDF based extraction method results in a poor performance (only 12.90% in terms of **F1**-Measure). When using only global context features, we can obtain greatly improvement +40.09% in terms of F1-Measure. Furthermore, by combining the global context features and local context features, we can again obtain improvement +47.00% in terms of F1-Measure.
(2) Improvements over KEA algorithm. When using only global context features, we can obtain greatly improvement +22.47% in terms of F1-Measure over KEA algorithm. Furthermore, by combining the global context features and local context features, we can again obtain improvement +29.25% in terms of F1-Measure.
(3) Effectiveness of local context features. Our method using both global context features and local context feature outperforms that using only global context features (+6.51% in terms of F1-Measure). In the latter method more keywords were assigned as keywords than that in our method with only global features. With the local features, we observed significant improvement (+11.00%) in terms of recall. We also note that the precision drops a little. This is because of inevitable mistaken assignments.
(4) Error analysis. We conducted error analysis on the results.

For the method using global context features only, 80% of the errors were from those extracted words that have high scores in global context features but are not 'keyword'. 20% of the errors were due to the 'ambiguity' of the extracted keywords. Those 'ambiguity' words/phrases represent some kind of the meaning of the given document. But it is difficult to classify them to 'keyword' or not. Maybe they should correspond to the 'indifferent keyword' in our specification.

For the method combining both global and local context features, 25% of the errors were from those words having high scores in global context features but not 'keyword'. This was due to the effect of local context features. 75% of the errors were due to the 'ambiguity' of the extracted keywords.

(5) No free lunch. As the proverb says, "Every coin has its two sides". Although the local context features can improve the performance of the keyword extraction, their computation costs are heavy, especially on linker analysis. The linker analysis on the four data sets cost nearly 22 hours.

(6) Difficult task. It is difficult to accurately extract keywords from documents. That is because in some cases judging whether a word/phrase is keyword or not is difficult, even for human.

Document Classification

Experiment. In order to evaluate the effectiveness of our keyword extraction method, we have applied it to document classification. Document classification is a task in which we aim to assign documents of a corpus to a fixed set of categories. We chose Naïve Bayes as the classification method. For each document, the extracted keywords are viewed as features and are assigned with higher weights.

Table 4. Performance of document classification (%)

Category	Method	Precision	Recall	F1-Measure
alt.atheism	Bayes	65.71	91.09	76.35
	+Keyword	81.51(+18.5)	96.04(+4.95)	88.18(+11.83)
comp.graphics	Bayes	27.17	68.32	38.88
	+Keyword	50.00(+22.83)	78.22(+9.9)	61.00(+22.12)
comp.os.ms-windows.misc	Bayes	28.25	86.14	42.55
	+Keyword	43.96(+15.71)	90.10(+3.96)	59.09(+16.54)
comp.sys.ibm.pc.hardware	Bayes	29.23	75.25	42.10
	+Keyword	39.90(+10.67)	82.18(+6.93)	53.72(+11.62)
comp.sys.mac.hardware	Bayes	27.65	85.15	41.74
	+Keyword	38.99(+11.34)	84.16(-0.99)	53.29(+11.55)
comp.windows.x	Bayes	51.72	44.55	47.87
	+Keyword	64.04(+12.32)	56.44(+11.89)	60.00(+12.13)
misc.forsale	Bayes	31.60	84.16	45.95
	+Keyword	40.95(+9.35)	85.15(+0.99)	55.30(+9.35)
rec.autos	Bayes	33.33	92.08	48.94
	+Keyword	50.00(+16.67)	96.04(+3.96)	65.76(+16.82)
rec.motorcycles	Bayes	39.83	93.07	55.79
	+Keyword	47.76(+7.93)	95.05(+1.98)	63.58(+7.79)
rec.sport.baseball	Bayes	50.54	93.07	65.51
	+Keyword	60.63(+10.09)	96.04(+2.97)	74.33(+8.82)
Average	Bayes	38.50	81.29	50.57
	+Keyword	51.77(+13.27)	85.94(+4.65)	63.43(+12.86)

The data set used for classification is 20 newsgroups, which is downloaded from CMU Text Learning Group Data Archives (http://www-2.cs.cmu.edu/afs/cs.cmu.edu/project/theo-20/www/data/news20.html). Among the collection, ten categories were used in the evaluation. The bag-of-word (BOW) features are extracted as features. Both stemming and stop-word removal were applied in the processing of feature extraction.

We carried out the experiments as follows. In the first experiment, we used all the BOW features to evaluate the classification performance. In the other experiment, we conducted the keyword extraction, viewed them as features, and doubled the weight of the extracted keywords.

Table 4 shows the five cross-validation results on the ten categories. In the table, the first column lists ten categories. Bayes, Keyword respectively denotes the Naïve Bayes classification on the original data and on the data with extracted keywords.

From table 4, we see that by using keyword extraction, a significant improvement can be obtained on the task of document classification (ranging from 7.79% to 22.12% in terms of F1-Measure). We observed improvements on precision (+13.27%), recall (+4.65%), and F1-Measure (+12.86%) on average. The results indicate that our method of keyword extraction is effective. The results are also consistent with the result obtained in the experiment of keyword extraction.

We also applied the extracted keywords to document classification by using SVM as the document classification method. However, no significant improvement obtained. The reason maybe lies in that SVM has already achieved the start-of-art result on the task of document classification.

7 Conclusion

In this paper, we have investigated the problem of keyword extraction. We have defined the problem as that of extracting words/phrases in the document. We have proposed a classification approach to the task. Using Support Vector Machines, we have been able to make an implementation of the approach. Experimental results show that our approach can significantly outperform baseline methods for keyword extraction. When applying it to document classification, we observed a significant improvement on extraction accuracy.

As future work, we plan to make further improvement on the accuracy. We also want to apply the keyword extraction method to other text mining applications.

References

[Azcarraga2002] Azcarraga, A; Yap, T. J.; and Chua, T. S. Comparing Keyword Extraction Techniques for WEBSOM Text Archives, International Journal of Artificial Intelligence Tools, 11(2):219 - 232.

[Berger2000] Berger, A. L.; and Mittal, V. O. OCELOT: A System for Summarizing Web Pages. In Proceedings of the 23rd ACM SIGIR Conference, 144 - 151.

[Brill1999] Brill, E.; and Ngai, G. Man vs. machine: A case study in baseNP learning. In Proceedings of the 18th International Conference on Computational Linguistics, 65-72.

[Cunningham2002] Cunningham, H.; Maynard, D.; Bontcheva, K.; and Tablan, V. GATE: A Framework and Graphical Development Environment for Robust NLP Tools and Applications. In Proceedings of the 40th Anniversary Meeting of the Association for Computational Linguistics. Philadelphia.

[DUC] Document Understanding Conference. http://www-nlpir.nist.gov/projects/duc/.

[Dumais1998] Dumais, S.T.; Platt, J; Heckerman, D.; and Sahami, M. Inductive Learning Algorithms and Representations for Text Categorization. In Proceedings of the 7th International Conference on Information and Knowledge Management, 148-155.

[Frank1999] Frank, E.; Paynter, G. W.; and Witten, I. H. Domain-Specific Keyphrase Extraction. In Proceedings of the 16th International Joint Conference on Artificial Intelligence, 668-673, Stockholm, Sweden, Morgan Kaufmann.

[Hulth2004] Hulth, A. Combining Machine Learning and Natural Language Processing for Automatic Keyword Extraction. Ph.D. diss., Dept. of Computer and Systems Sciences, Stockholm University.

[Mani1999] Mani, I.; and Maybury, M. T. Advances in Automatic Text Summarization. The MIT Press.

[Mani2001] Mani, I. Automatic Summarization. John Benjamins Pub Co.

[Matsuo04] Matsuo, Y.; and Ishizuka. M. Keyword Extraction from a Single Document using Word Co-occurrence Statistical Information, Int'l Journal on Artificial Intelligence Tools, 13(1):157-169.

[Miller1990] Miller, G.; Beckwith, R.; Fellbaum, C.; Gross, D.; and Miller, K.J. Wordnet: An On-line Lexical Database. International Journal of Lexicography, 3(4):235--312.

[Sleator1991] Sleator, D.; and Temperley, D. Parsing English with a Link Grammar. Technical Report, CMU-CS-91-196, Dept. of Computer Science, Carnegie Mellon University.

[Tang2004] Tang, J.; Li, J.Z.; Wang, K.H.; and Cai, Y.R. Loss Minimization based Keyword Distillation. In Proceedings of 6th Asia-Pacific Web Conference, 572-577. Springer, LNCS 3007, ISBN 3-540-21371-6.

[Turney2000] Turney, P.D. Learning Algorithms for Keyphrase Extraction. Information Retrieval, 2(4):303–336.

[Vapnik1995] Vladimir N. Vapnik. The Nature of Statistical Learning Theory. Springer.

[Witten1999] Witten, I. H.; and Paynter, G. W. et al. 1999. KEA: Practical Automatic Keyphrase Extraction. In Proceedings of 4th ACM Conference on Digital Libraries, 254-255. Berkeley, CA.

[Xun2000] Xun, E.; Huang, C.; and Zhou, M. A Unified Statistical Model for the Identification of English baseNP. In Proceedings of the 38th Annual Meeting of the Association for Computational Linguistics. Hong Kong.

[Zha2002] Zha, H. Generic Summarization and Keyphrase Extraction Using Mutual Reinforcement Principle and Sentence Clustering. In Proceedings of the 25th ACM SIGIR Conference, 113-120.

[Zhu2003] Zhu, M.; Cai, Z.; and Cai, Q. Automatic Keywords Extraction of Chinese Document Using Small World Structure. In Proceeding of the international conference on Natural Language Processing and Knowledge Engineering.

LSM: Language Sense Model for Information Retrieval

Shenghua Bao, Lei Zhang, Erdong Chen, Min Long, Rui Li, and Yong Yu

APEX Data and Knowledge Management Lab,
Department of Computer Science & Engineering,
Shanghai Jiao Tong University, Shanghai, P.R.China, 200230
{shhbao, zhanglei, edchen, mlong, rli, yyu}@apex.sjtu.edu.cn

Abstract. A lot of work has been done on drawing word senses into retrieval to deal with the word sense ambiguity problem, but most of them achieved negative results. In this paper, we first implement a WSD system for nouns and verbs, then the language sense model (LSM) for information retrieval is proposed. The LSM combines the terms and senses of a document seamlessly through an EM algorithm. Retrieval on TREC collections shows that the LSM outperforms both the vector space model (BM25) and the traditional language model significantly for both medium and long queries (7.53%-16.90%). Based on the experiments, we can also empirically draw the conclusion that the fine-grained senses will improve the retrieval performance when they are properly used.

1 Introduction

Word sense disambiguation (WSD) has been studied for a long time in natural language processing. In the field of information retrieval (IR), word sense ambiguity is regarded as one of the main causes which affect the retrieval performance for two reasons:

- **Polysemy:** One word may have different meanings under different contexts.
- **Synonymy:** Different words may have the same meaning.

This encouraged various of work to integrate the WSD into IR. However, most of them achieved negative results, e.g. [1, 2, 3]. At the same time, the potential causes for the poor results were intensively studied, which can be categorized as follows:

- **Fine-grained Sense:** The words might be resolved to senses which are too specific for IR[4].
- **Poor WSD Results:** The low accuracy of the WSD system affects the final performance of the sense based IR system a lot[5].
- **Cannot Fall Back:** The pure sense based IR system can not fall back to the term based IR system. The term based IR system does not suffer from the ambiguity problem severely due to word collocation, and word senses' skewed distribution[6]. So It is not easy for a pure sense based IR system to exceed the term based IR system.

An example which successfully solved the three problems above would be Kim's work in 2004 which improved retrieval performance significantly[7]. Firstly, it achieved

J.X. Yu, M. Kitsuregawa, and H.V. Leong (Eds.): WAIM 2006, LNCS 4016, pp. 97–108, 2006.
© Springer-Verlag Berlin Heidelberg 2006

the high WSD accuracy by using the coarse-grained senses which consisted of 25 root senses in WORDNET[1]. Secondly, it combined the root senses and the document terms through a revised vector space model. It successfully integrated the coarse-grained senses and terms. However, there are still some questions to be further addressed,

- Will the integration of fine-grained senses and terms work as well?
- Is there any other model to integrate the terms and senses besides the vector space model?

To answer these questions, we first implement a WSD system using the fine-grained senses in WORDNET. In our WSD system, only nouns and verbs are disambiguated because the nouns and verbs play important roles in IR and they are much easier to disambiguate with a comparatively higher accuracy.

Then, the fine-grained senses are utilized based on the language model[8]. Firstly, the language model on term representation (LMTR) and sense representation (LMSR) are studied. Then, a novel model, language sense model (LSM) for information retrieval, is proposed which utilizes both sense and term representations. The experimental results on the TREC collections shows that the LMSR can not bring any improvement. However, the LSM outperforms both vector space model and traditional language model for medium and long queries significantly (7.53% - 16.90%).

The rest of the paper is organized as follows. In Section 2, some related work is discussed . In Section 3, the process and evaluation of WSD are presented. The discussion of the LSM is given in Section 4. The experiment results of the LSM are given in Section 5. Finally, we make a conclusion and give some future work in Section 6.

2 Related Work

In this section, the related work is surveyed in two aspects. One relates to the previous efforts on WSD for IR while the other to the previous work on language models.

2.1 Word Sense Disambiguation for Information Retrieval

Most of the early work which integrated WSD into IR resulted in no improvement. A complete review of the integration of WSD and IR prior to the year 2000 can be found in the work of Sanderson [9]. In this section, we review some recent work which reported significant improvements by integrating WSD into IR.

In 2003, Stokoe represented documents and queries with sense vectors and retrieved the relevant documents using the traditional vector space model[10].Their experiments on TREC WT10G data collection empirically showed that their WSD system could significantly improve the retrieval performance. However, it was problematic that the absolute precision of the baseline and the proposed system were too low to investigate the effect of sense-based retrieval. Compared with Stokoe's work, the LSM improves the retrieval performance significantly when the baseline's absolute precision is comparatively much higher. More importantly, in the LSM, the terms and senses are integrated to achieve a better performance.

[1] http://wordnet.princeton.edu/

In 2004, Kim et al proposed the root sense tagging approach for information retrieval by integrating the root sense tags into the vector space model[7]. As proposed in Section 1, Kim solved the three existing problems successfully. Different from Kim's work, the LSM utilizes fine-grained senses, and combines the terms and senses in the language model.

2.2 Language Model

For many years, the primary consumers of statistical language models were speech recognition systems [11]. In 1998, Ponte and Croft [8] proposed a smoothed version of the document unigram model to assign a score to a query, which can be thought of as the probability that the query was generated from the document model. Since then, there emerged a great amount of research work related to language model. Most of them tried to solve the following two problems:

- **Data Sparseness:** Many smoothing methods were suggested to re-evaluate the probabilities of generating the query terms that did not appear in the document. Song and Croft proposed the good-turing smoothing based on terms' power law distribution [12]. Zhai et al proposed the two-stage smoothing for language model[13]. In addition, cluster based smoothing methods were proposed and achieved significant improvement[14, 15]. In the LSM, the existing smoothing methods can be applied easily on both terms and senses to solve the data sparseness problem.
- **Term Dependency:** The unigram language model made an improper assumption that all terms were generated independently. Plenty of work has been done to model the proper dependencies between the query terms. Srikanth et al proposed the concept language model, where the query was viewed as a sequence of concepts and each concept as a sequence of terms[16]. Gao et al introduced the dependence language model by integrating the linkage of query terms as a hidden variable[17]. Recently, Cao et al exploited the word relations of WORDNET and co-occurrences and then integrated them into language models[18]. In the LSM, the query independent assumption can be relaxed to a certain extent as the terms and senses in the LSM depend strongly on each other.

3 Word Sense Disambiguation

Word Sense Disambiguation (WSD), which is a classical problem in Natural Language Processing (NLP), aims to improve the accuracy, namely the number of words correctly disambiguated. Our approach is based on the Co-occurrence, SEMCOR [2], and WORDNET. In order to achieve the high disambiguation accuracy, only the nouns and verbs on both the queries and the documents are disambiguated. Most of the methods are based on popular and effective techniques in [19, 7, 20].

SEMCOR2.0 is distributed with WORDNET2.0, an online thesaurus created at Princeton University. WORDNET2.0 consists of 90,000 terms and collocates organized into Synsets. Each Synset contains words which are synonymous with each other, while

[2] http://multisemcor.itc.it/semcor.php

the links between Synsets represent hypernymy and hyponomy relationships to form a WORDNET hierarchical semantic network. SEMCOR2.0 is a manually sense tagged subset of the Brown Corpus consisting of 352 documents split into three data sets. The tag set used in SEMCOR consists of the unique sense identifiers used within WORDNET.

At first, three pre-processing procedures are implemented. Firstly, each word is tagged with part-of-speech (POS) by Brill's tagger[3]. Secondly, ANNIE TAGGER[4] performs on the text to remove named entities from the WSD candidate set. In the experiment, only three types of named entities: LOC (location), PER (person) and ORG (organization) are extracted. Thirdly, each monosemous word is identified with the unique sense it owns. In the following three subsections, we will introduce the main methods of the WSD system.

Our WSD system makes use of mutual information (MI) of the adjacent words in the text. Besides, WORDNET and SEMCOR information is integrated into the following procedures to identify the senses of the candidate words. We get context clues from the SEMCOR of the occurrence of the collocation. If, in all the occurrences of the collocation, the word has only one sense, and the number of the occurrences is larger than a given threshold (≥ 2 in our experiment), then we identify the word with the sense. We identify the sense of a word by comparing the original context of the word and the context set of the word's senses at WORDNET and SEMCOR . The following nouns will be added to the context set of the sense: the words in the sense at WORDNET, the first shortest noun phrase from the definition of the sense at WORDNET, all the nouns which occur within a window size (20 words in our experiment) with respect to the sense in SEMCOR.

Our WSD system also integrates the hierarchical information of the synsets in WORDNET. In WORDNET, all the words with the same POS are organized into hierarchies, each synset is a part of a hierarchy. Taking the noun as an example, there are 25 root senses. For two words t_1 and t_2 within a window size, if the hierarchical distance between a sense of the word t_1 and the word t_2 is equal to or less than 1, the system identifies the two words with their corresponding senses.

We trained our method on the first 300 documents of SEMCOR, and tested it on the last 52 documents. The accuracy of noun is 78.12% and accuracy of verb is 60.58%, the overall accuracy of WSD system is 72.40%, which is much higher than the previous WSD sytem applied to IR.

4 Integrating Sense into Language Model

In this section, we talk about how to utilize the fine-grained word senses. In Section 4.1, the language model for term and sense representations is proposed. Then, the smoothing methods are discussed and a new hierarchical smoothing method is proposed. Finally, in Section 4.2, the LSM and the correspondingly parameter estimation methods are proposed to integrate the term and sense representations.

[3] http://www.cs.jhu.edu/ brill/

[4] http://gate.ac.uk/ie/annie.html

4.1 Language Model and Smoothing Methods

Language Model for Term and Sense Representations. In this paper, each document has two different representations: namely term representation and sense representation, as shown in Figure 1. Two examples from TREC Fbis corpus are given in the right.

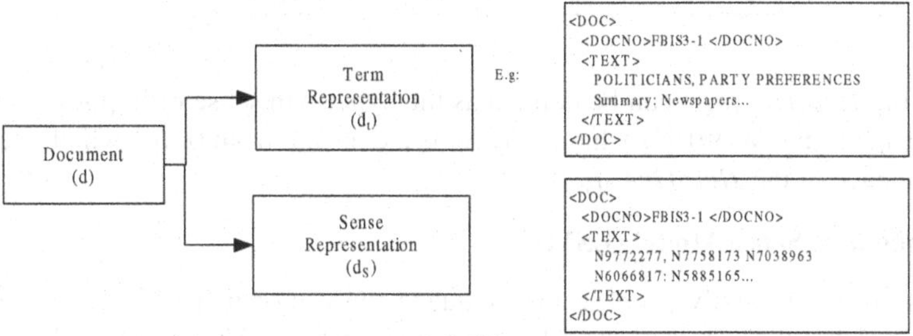

Fig. 1. Document Representations

The language model on term representations (LMTR) is the traditional approach. It first generates a model d_t for each document d. Given a query $q_t = q_{t1}q_{t2}\dots q_{tm}$, the documents are ranked according to the probability the model could generate. In this paper, the urigram language model is adopted and the equation could be represented as follows:

$$P(q_t|d_t) = \prod_{i=1}^{m} P(q_{ti}|d_t) \tag{1}$$

Where q_t and d_t means the term representations of query q and document d respectively. q_{ti} means the ith term of the query q_t and m is the length of the query q_t.

The language model on sense representations (LMSR) is similar to the one on term representations. It first generates a sense model d_s for each document d using the sense representation, and then estimates the probability of d_s generating the sense query $q_s = q_{s1}q_{s2}\dots q_{sm}$. The corresponding equation can be shown as follows.

$$P(q_s|d_s) = \prod_{i=1}^{m} P(q_{si}|d_s) \tag{2}$$

Smoothing Methods. The smoothing method plays an important role in language model due to the data sparseness problem. An empirical study of smoothing methods for the language model can be found at [21]. Table 1 shows three of them which are popularly used in language model for information retrieval [13].

The three smoothing approaches can be applied to the LMTR and the LMSR. For the LMSR, we developed a new smoothing method, namely hierarchical smoothing, based on the WORDNET hierarchy as follows:

$$P^h(q_s|d_s) = \prod_{i=1}^{m} (1-\lambda_h)P(q_{si}|d_s) + \lambda_h P(Relative(q_{si})|d_s)) \tag{3}$$

Table 1. Smoothing Methods of Language Model for Information Retrieval

Smoothing Methods	Formula
Jelinek-Mercer	$(1-\alpha)P(w\|d)+\alpha P(w\|C)$
Dirichlet	$\frac{c(w;d)+\mu P(w\|C)}{\sum_w c(w;d)+\mu}$
Absolute discount	$\frac{max(c(w;d)-\delta,0)}{\sum_w c(w;d)}+\frac{\delta\|d\|_u}{\|d\|}P(w\|C)$

Here the $Relative(q_{si})$ can be defined as the hypernym sense or hyponym sense of the sense q_{si} in the WordNet hierarchy.λ_h is a constant from 0 to 1 which measures the confidence of the $Relative(q_{si})$.

4.2 Language Sense Model (LSM)

In this section, we firstly propose the language sense model (LSM) for information retrieval which utilizes both term and sense representations. Then the model parameter estimation is discussed.

Model Description. Figure 2 shows the framework of the LSM. In the LSM, the model generates the probability of a given query from both document's term representation and sense representation. The sense representation d_s can be further extended to d_h and d_r which stand for sense's hypernym sense and root sense respectively. In this paper, we choose the d_s to be integrated with d_t as we want to study the effects of the fine-grained senses in information retrieval. So the LSM can be shown as Equation 4:

$$P(q|d)=\prod_{i=1}^{m}((1-\lambda)P(q_{ti}|d_t)+\lambda P(q_{si}|d_s)) \tag{4}$$

where $P(q_{ti}|d_t)$ and $P(q_{si}|d_s)$ means the probability of generating the ith query term q_i from term representation and sense representation respectively. Note that not all the

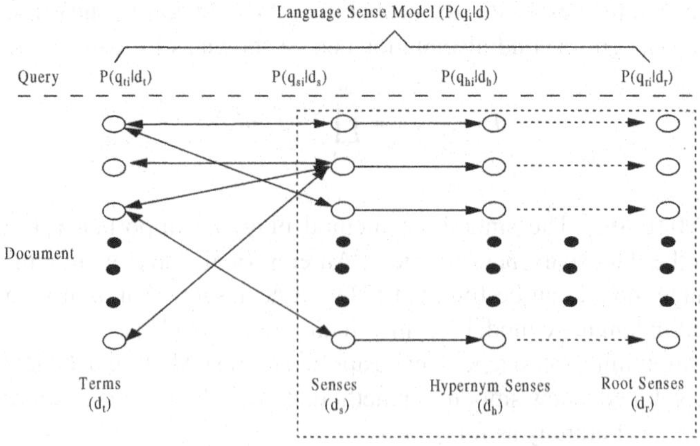

Fig. 2. Language Sense Model for Information Retrieval

terms in q_t can be disambiguated as the WSD is only conducted on the nouns and verbs. A default value will be given to the q_{si} if q_{ti} can not be disambiguated.

To solve the data sparseness problem, the existing smoothing method (as shown in Table 1) can be integrated into the LSM. An integration example of Jelinek-Mercer smoothing into LSM can be shown as follows:

$$P(q|d) = \prod_{i=1}^{m}(1-\alpha)[(1-\lambda)P(q_{ti}|d_t)+\lambda P(q_{si}|d_s)]+\alpha[(1-\lambda)P(q_{ti}|C_t)+\lambda P(q_{si}|C_s)] \tag{5}$$

Other than the traditional smoothing methods, the hierarchical smoothing can also be integrated by replacing $P(q_{si}|d_s)$ and $P(q_{si}|C_s)$ in Equation 5 with $P^h(q_{si}|d_s)$ and $P^h(q_{si}|C_s)$ defined in Equation 3 as follows:

$$P(q|d)=\prod_{i=1}^{m}(1-\alpha)[(1-\lambda)P(q_{ti}|d_t)+\lambda P^h(q_{si}|d_s)]+\alpha[(1-\lambda)P(q_{ti}|C_t)+\lambda P^h(q_{si}|C_s)] \tag{6}$$

Parameter Estimation. To compute the query generating probability from the LSM, there are three components to be estimated: $P(q_{ti}|d_t)$, $P(q_{si}|d_s)$ and the combination parameter λ.

$P(q_{ti}|d_t)$, $P(q_{si}|d_s)$ can be estimated as the maximally likelihood of the term representation and sense representation generating the corresponding query term. Given a query, we estimate the optimal weights λ^* which could maximize the likelihood of the queries. This method is similar to Zhai's method in estimating the parameter of the two stage model[13] and Cao's method in estimating the combination in NSLM [18] . Let λ^* be the optimal weight, taking the formula 5 as an example, we have:

$$\lambda^* = \arg\max_{\lambda} \log \left\{ \begin{array}{c} (1-\alpha)\sum_{i=1}^{N} \pi_i \prod_{j=1}^{m}[(1-\lambda)P(q_{tj}|d_{ti}) + \lambda P(q_{sj}|d_{si})] \\ +\alpha \sum_{i=1}^{N} \pi_i \prod_{j=1}^{m}[(1-\lambda)P(q_{tj}|C_t) + \lambda P(q_{sj}|C_s)] \end{array} \right\} \tag{7}$$

where N is the number of documents in the dataset, and m is the length of query q. $\{\pi_i\}_{i=1}^{N}$ acts as the prior probability with which to choose the document to generate the query. With this setting, the EM formulae to update the parameter can be shown as follows:

$$\pi_i^{(r+1)} = \frac{\pi_i^{(r)} \prod_{j=1}^{m}[(1-\lambda^{(r)})P(q_{tj}|d_{ti}) + \lambda^{(r)}P(q_{sj}|d_{si})]}{\sum_{i=1}^{N} \pi_i^{(r)} \prod_{j=1}^{m}[(1-\lambda^{(r)})P(q_{tj}|d_{ti}) + \lambda^{(r)}P(q_{sj}|d_{si})]} \tag{8}$$

and

$$\lambda^{(r+1)} = \frac{1}{m}\sum_{j=1}^{m} \frac{(1-\alpha)\sum_{i=1}^{N} \pi_i^{(r)}\lambda^{(r)}P(q_{sj}|d_{si}) + \alpha\lambda^{(r)}P(q_{sj}|C_s)}{\begin{array}{c}(1-\alpha)\sum_{i=1}^{N} \pi_i^{(r)}[(1-\lambda^{(r)})P(q_{tj}|d_{ti}) + \lambda^{(r)}P(q_{sj}|d_{si})]+ \\ \alpha[(1-\lambda^{(r)})P(q_{tj}|C_t) + \lambda^{(r)}P(q_{sj}|C_s)]\end{array}} \tag{9}$$

The EM algorithm will be terminated if the log-likelihood of the query changes within a threshold. In the experiment, we initialized the π_i with uniform distribution. In fact,

It allows to initialize the π_i with randomized value too because the EM algorithm guarantees the convergence with a local optimization. The EM update formula for Dirichlet and Absolute Discount smoothing can be inferred similarly. Note that there are no training data and testing data. The EM algorithm estimates the optimal λ for each query directly without training on sample data. The λ for each query is generated independently.

5 System Evaluation and Analysis

5.1 Experiment Setup

The whole TREC FBIS collection is used in our experiment. At first, all the nouns and verbs of queries and documents of TREC FBIS corpus were disambiguated with the methods proposed in Section 3. In order to evaluate the LSM's performance on different length queries, we generated three types of queries, shown as in Table 2. The queries are extracted from the TREC-5 routing topic which consists of 50 queries with 40 titles, 50 descriptions and 50 narratives.

Table 2. Short Queries, Medium Queries and Long Queries Extracted from the TREC-5 Routing Task

Query Type	Query Count	Average Length(Term/Sense)	Extracted From
Short query	40	3.60 / 2.3	Title
Medium query	50	21.86 / 10.34	Tilte, Description
Long query	50	78.34 / 31.04	Title, Description,Narrative

The LSM system is built based on the Lemur 3.1. The Vector Space Model is based on the BM25 formula whose term frequency component is implemented as follows [22]:

$$TF(t,d) = \frac{k * f(t,d)}{k * ((1-b) + b * doclen/avgdoclen) + f(t,d)} \quad (10)$$

where f(t,d) means the term count of t in document d. In the experiment, k and b are set to 1 and 0.3 respectively.

In the following experiment, the standard mean average precision(MAP) and the total retrieved relevant document number (Recall) are used to evaluate the retrieval performance.

5.2 Evaluation of LMTR and LMSR

The results of language models on term and sense representations are compared on different queries and different smoothing methods, shown as Table 3. From the table, we can see that the language model on term representation (LMTR) performs much better than language model on sense representation (LMSR) in both precision and recall. Noting that some terms in the term representation cannot be disambiguated, we generated a mixed document representation, where the undisambiguated terms are reserved in the

Table 3. Comparison of LMTR and LMSR

Query Type	Smoothing Methods	LMTR (MAP/Recall)	LMSR (MAP/Recall)	Improved MAP	Improved Recall
Short Query	Jelinek-Mercer	0.1041 1692	0.0646 1388	-61.15%	-17.97%
	Dirichlet	0.1247 1859	0.0773 1569	-61.32%	-15.60%
	Absolute Discount	0.1133 1726	0.0736 1435	-53.94%	-16.86%
Medium Query	Jelinek-Mercer	0.1228 2329	0.0892 1887	-37.67%	-18.99%
	Dirichlet	0.1339 2357	0.1005 2126	-33.23%	-9.80%
	Absolute Discount	0.1150 2203	0.0961 1920	-19.67%	-12.85%
Long Query	Jelinek-Mercer	0.1649 2707	0.1222 2262	-34.94%	-16.07%
	Dirichlet	0.1630 2603	0.1337 2473	-21.91%	-4.99%
	Absolute Discount	0.1363 2431	0.1141 2142	-19.46%	-11.89%

Table 4. Comparison of LMTR and LSM

Query Type	Smoothing Methods	LMTR (MAP/Recall)	LSM (MAP/Recall)	Improved MAP	Improved Recall	Sign MAP
Short Query	Jelinek-Mercer	0.1041 1692	0.1060 1677	1.90%	-0.89%	0.1695
	Dirichlet	0.1247 1859	0.1310 1897	5.06%	2.04%	0.1688
	Absolute Discount	0.1133 1726	0.1208 1769	6.59%	2.49%	0.1693
	Vector Space Model	0.1161 2042	⋄ 0.1310 1897	12.83%	-7.10%	0.0506
Medium Query	Jelinek-Mercer	0.1228 2329	0.1344 2356	9.46%	1.16%	0.0805
	Dirichlet	0.1339 2357	0.1478 2492	10.36%	5.72%	* 0.0272
	Absolute Discount	0.1150 2203	0.1344 2326	16.90%	5.58%	* 0.0179
	Vector Space Model	0.1112 2391	⋄ 0.1478 2492	32.91%	4.22%	* 0.0223
Long Query	Jelinek-Mercer	0.1649 2707	0.1792 2784	8.68%	2.84%	* 0.0381
	Dirichlet	0.1630 2603	0.1752 2719	7.53%	4.46%	* 0.0388
	Absolute Discount	0.1363 2431	0.1516 2526	11.26%	3.90%	* 0.0487
	Vector Space Model	0.0907 2531	⋄ 0.1752 2719	93.16%	7.42%	* 0.0001

sense representation. However, we got the conclusion again that the LMTR performs much better than the language model on mixed representations.

The hierarchical smoothing for LMSR is also tested with two kinds of $Relative(q_{si})$, namely hypernym sense and hyponym sense. However, the result of LMSR remains almost unchanged. So in the next section, the experiments of the LSM is conducted without hierarchical smoothing.

5.3 Evaluation of Language Sense Model

The results of the LMTR and LSM are compared with different queries and different smoothing methods as shown in Table 4, where a diamond (⋄) means the LSM using the Dirichlet smoothing. From the "Improved Map" column, we can see that the LSM outperforms both the traditional language model and vector space model (BM25) on all queries. From the "Improved Recall" column, we can see that the LSM improved the recall on the medium and long queries as well. The 11-point precision/recall curves for the LSM using the Jelinek-Mercer, Dirichlet and Absolute Discount smoothing are

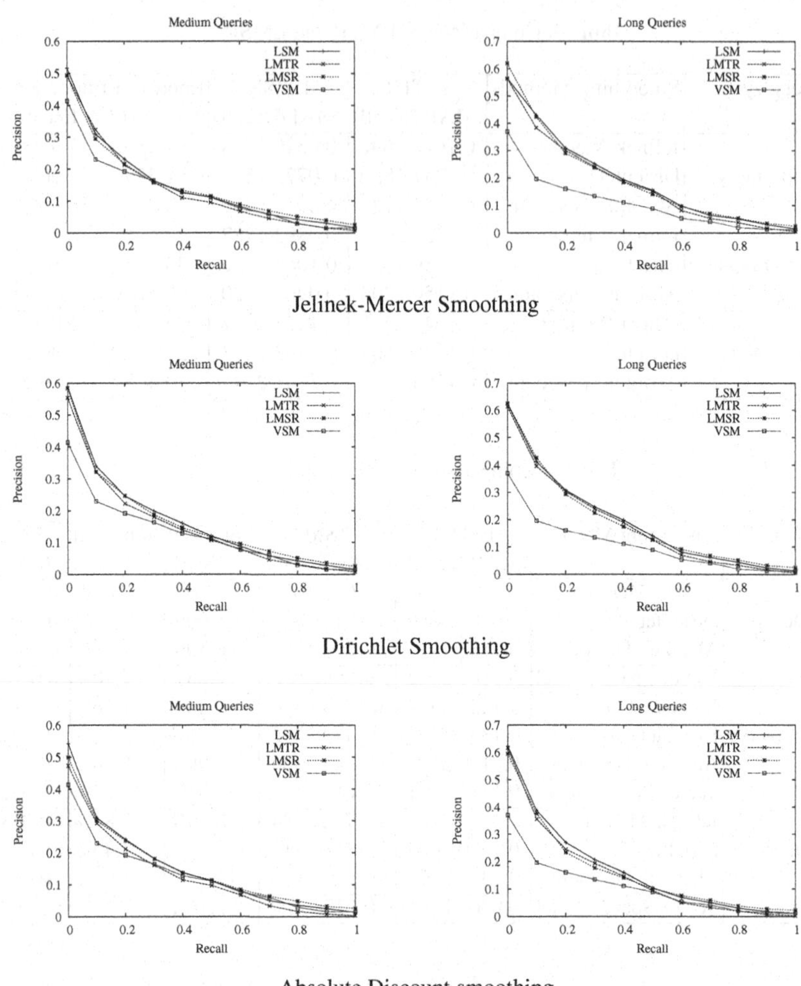

Fig. 3. 11-point precision/recall curves for the LSM, LMTR, LMSR and VSM on Medium and Long Queries

shown in Figure 3. In each figure, the four curves from the up-right to bottom-left are LSM, LMTR, LMSR and VSM respectively. To understand whether these improvements are statistically significant, we performed t-tests on MAP. The p-values are shown in the "Sign" column of Table 4 where an asterisk (*) means significant improvement (< 0.05). From the result, we can see that the LSM improves significantly on both medium and long queries, however, not significantly on short queries. It's reasonable because that:

- There are less nouns and verbs to be disambiguated for short queries (see Table 2).
- It's much harder to disambiguate the short queries because of the sparse context.

6 Conclusion and Future Work

In the work, we implement a WSD system which is designed for nouns and verbs only. Then the language model on sense representations (LMSR) and language sense model (LSM) are proposed. The LSM integrated the fine-grained disambiguated senses and terms seamlessly through an EM algorithm. The experiments show that the LSM outperforms both vector space model (BM25) and traditional language models significantly on both medium and long queries (7.53%-16.90%) with various smoothing methods. From this study, we can also empirically draw that the fine-grained senses will help the information retrieval if they are properly utilized.

In the future, we will study the hierarchical smoothing using more WORDNET relations. In addition, we will further evaluate the LSM on more corpus and study how the accuracy of WSD affects the LSM.

References

1. Voorhees, E.M.: Using wordnet to disambiguate word senses for text retrieval. In Korfhage, R., Rasmussen, E.M., Willett, P., eds.: Proceedings of the 16th Annual International ACM-SIGIR Conference on Research and Development in Information Retrieval. Pittsburgh, PA, USA, June 27 - July 1, 1993, ACM (1993) 171–180
2. Wallis, P.: Information retrieval based on paraphrase. (1993)
3. Sussna, M.: Word sense disambiguation for free-text indexing using a massive semantic network. In: CIKM '93: Proceedings of the second international conference on Information and knowledge management, ACM Press (1993) 67–74
4. Gonzalo, J., Verdejo, F., Chugur, I., Cigarran, J.: Indexing with WordNet synsets can improve text retrieval. In: Proceedings of the COLING/ACL '98 Workshop on Usage of WordNet for NLP, Montreal, Canada (1998) 38–44
5. Sanderson, M.: Word sense disambiguation and information retrieval. In: Proceedings of the 17th annual international ACM SIGIR conference on Research and development in information retrieval, Dublin, Ireland (1994) 142–151
6. Krovetz, R.: Viewing Morphology as an Inference Process,. In: Proceedings of the Sixteenth Annual International ACM SIGIR Conference on Research and Development in Information Retrieval. (1993) 191–203
7. Kim, S.B., Seo, H.C., Rim, H.C.: Information retrieval using word senses: root sense tagging approach. In: SIGIR '04: Proceedings of the 27th annual international conference on Research and development in information retrieval, ACM Press (2004) 258–265
8. Ponte, J.M., Croft, W.B.: A language modeling approach to information retrieval. In: Research and Development in Information Retrieval. (1998) 275–281
9. Sanderson, M.: Retrieval with good sense. Information Retrieval **2** (2000) 47–67
10. Stokoe, C., Oakes, M.P., Tait, T.: Word sense disambiguation in information retrieval revisited. In: Proceedings of the 26th Annual International ACM SIGIR Conference on Research and Development in Information Retrieval. Text representation (2003) 159–166
11. Rosenfeld, R.: Two decades of statistical language modeling: Where do we go from here (2000)
12. Song, F., Croft, W.B.: A general language model for information retrieval. In: Proceedings of the eighth international conference on Information and knowledge management. (1999) 316 – 321

13. Zhai, C., Lafferty, J.: A study of smoothing methods for language models applied to information retrieval. ACM Transactions on Information Systems **22** (2004) 179–214
14. Kurland, O., Lee, L.: Corpus structure, language models, and ad hoc information. In: Proceedings of the 27th International ACM SIGIR conference conference. (2004) 194–201
15. Xu, J., Croft, W.: Cluster-based retrieval using language models. In: Proceedings of the 27th International ACM SIGIR conference conference. (2004)
16. Srikanth, M., Srihari, R.K.: Exploiting syntactic structure of queries in a language modeling approach to ir. In: Proceedings of the 2003 ACM CIKM International Conference on Information and Knowledge Management, New Orleans, Louisiana,USA, ACM (2003) 476–483
17. Gao, J., Nie, J.Y., Wu, G., Cao, G.: Dependence language model for information retrieval. In: Proceedings of the 27th annual international conference on Research and development in information retrieval. (2004)
18. Cao, G., Nie, J.Y., Bai, J.: Integrating word relationships into language models. In: Proceedings of 17th ACM SIGIR conference. (2005) 298–305
19. Mihalcea, R.F., Moldovan, D.I.: A highly accurate bootstrapping algorithm for word sense disambiguation. International Journal on Artificial Intelligence Tools **10** (2001) 5–21
20. Liu, S., Liu, F., Yu, C., Meng, W.: An effective approach to document retrieval via utilizing wordnet and recognizing phrases. In: SIGIR '04: Proceedings of the 27th annual international ACM SIGIR conference on Research and development in information retrieval, New York, NY, USA, ACM Press (2004) 266–272
21. Chen, S.F., Goodman, J.: An empirical study of smoothing techniques for language modeling. In Joshi, A., Palmer, M., eds.: Proceedings of the Thirty-Fourth Annual Meeting of the Association for Computational Linguistics, San Francisco, Morgan Kaufmann Publishers (1996) 310–318
22. Robertson, S.E., Walker, S., Hancock-Beaulieu, M., Gull, A., Lau, M.: Okapi at TREC. In: Text REtrieval Conference. (1992) 21–30

Succinct and Informative Cluster Descriptions for Document Repositories*

Lijun Chen and Guozhu Dong

Wright State University, Dayton, OH 45435, USA
{lichen, gdong}@cs.wright.edu

Abstract. Large document repositories need to be organized, summarized and labeled in order to be used effectively. Previous clustering studies focused on organizing, and paid little attention to producing cluster labels. Without informative labels, users need to browse many documents to get a sense of what the clusters contain. Human labeling of clusters is not viable when clustering is performed on demand or for very few users. It is desirable to automatically generate informative cluster descriptions (CDs), in order to give users a high-level sense about the clusters, and to help repository managers to produce the final cluster labels.

This paper studies CDs in the form of small term sets for document clusters, and investigates how to measure the quality or fidelity of CDs and how to construct high quality CDs. We propose to use a CD-based classification for simulating how to interpret CDs, and to use the F-score of the classification to measure CD quality. Since directly searching good CDs using F-score is too expensive, we consider a surrogate quality measure, the CDD measure, which combines three factors: *coverage*, *disjointness*, and *diversity*. We give a search strategy for constructing CDs, namely a layer-based replacement method called PagodaCD . Experimental results show that the algorithm is efficient and can produce high quality CDs. CDs produced by PagodaCD also exhibit a monotone quality behavior.

1 Introduction

Large document repositories need to be organized, summarized and labeled in order to be used effectively. Cluster labels are essential for users to efficiently get a high-level sense of what the clusters contain, and for use as conceptual "handles" to the clusters. Without such labels, users will need to browse many documents in the clusters to get that sense. Human labeling of clusters is not viable when clustering is performed on demand or for few users. It is desirable to automatically generate cluster labels, or succinct and informative cluster descriptions (CDs), so that users can get that sense about the clusters by just examining the CDs. Such CDs can also be used as hints for producing final cluster labels by humans.

---

* This work was partially supported by a grant from AFRL. Lijun Chen was also partially supported by a DAGSI scholarship.

J.X. Yu, M. Kitsuregawa, and H.V. Leong (Eds.): WAIM 2006, LNCS 4016, pp. 109–121, 2006.
© Springer-Verlag Berlin Heidelberg 2006

Much research has been done on document clustering. However, previous clustering algorithms mainly focused on cluster formation, and paid little attention to producing CDs. Even when CDs were generated [1, 2, 3, 4, 5], they were often just by-products of the clustering process: [1, 2, 3] use the most frequent terms as CDs, [6, 7, 4] use "descriptive" or centroid-like terms as CDs, [4] use "discriminating" terms as CDs, and [5] use terms and their frequency distributions as CDs. Except [5], these approaches did not treat CDs as primary product to generate. Furthermore, none of them addressed the diversity factor on the terms in CDs, and the quality of CDs has not been thoroughly addressed, to the best of our knowledge. While there are approaches that produce a short summary for multiple documents by extracting some key phases or sentences [8, 9, 10], our study is focused on succinct and informative CDs consisting of a set of terms. We believe that such CDs is more useful for cluster labeling.

We propose a CD-based classification for simulating how to interpret CDs; the corresponding classifier only uses the CDs and their associated interpretation in making classification decisions. We then propose to use the F-score of the classification to measure CD quality. This classification approach also allows us to resolve cluster competition in the interpretation process.

Using F-score directly to search for high quality CDs is too expensive. We need some "surrogate" measures of F-score for efficient search. In this paper we consider the CDD measure which combines the three factors of *coverage*, *disjointness* between terms across CDs for different clusters, and *diversity* among terms within the CD of one cluster. Notice that diversity measures overlap among terms in the CD of one cluster, whereas disjointness measures overlap among terms in CDs of different clusters. We will argue that diversity is important in capturing the different flavors of a given cluster. Diversity has not been considered explicitly in previous work on CD construction.

We give a search algorithm, namely PagodaCD, for constructing CDs. PagodaCD is a layered improvement-based replacement algorithm, and it uses the CDD surrogate quality measure. We also preselect a set of candidate terms to reduce computation cost. Experimental evaluation on subsets of the Reuters collection shows that the PagodaCD algorithm is efficient, and it can produce high quality CDs. CDs produced by PagodaCD also has the monotone quality behavior, giving higher quality CDs when more terms are in the CDs.

Organizationally, Section 2 discusses related works. Section 3 defines cluster description. Section 4 introduces our CD quality evaluation methodology. Section 5 discusses the CDD surrogate measure. Section 6 presents the PagodaCD search algorithm. Section 7 describes our experimental evaluation. Section 8 concludes.

2 Related Works

Roughly speaking, we study CD in the form of small term sets for document clusters, and address the issues of how to measure the quality of CDs and how to construct high quality CDs. Related works can be categorized as follows:

Frequent-terms as CDs. Reference [3] uses frequent terms to represent clusters for browsing. References [1,2] use frequent term-sets to *produce* a hierarchy of clusters and those frequent terms can be considered as CDs.

Descriptive or Centroid-like CDs. In [7,4], each cluster is described by a *descriptive* CD, consisting of a set of terms whose corresponding values in the centroid vector[1] are above a user-given threshold. Reference [6] describes a cluster by k objects located near the center of the cluster.

Discriminating CDs. The *Cluto* clustering toolkit [4] also generates *discriminating* CDs, which are selected from those terms that are "more prevalent in the cluster compared to the rest of the objects"(here objects mean documents).

***COBWEB* CDs.** In *COBWEB* [5], a conceptual clustering algorithm, each cluster is summarized by a list of attributes and associated probabilities.

Notice that these term-based approaches did not address the diversity factor on the terms in CDs. The quality of CDs as cluster labels has not been thoroughly addressed, to the best of our knowledge.

Others. There are approaches that try to produce a short summary for multiple documents by extracting some key phases or sentences [8, 9, 10]. In contrasts, our study is focused on succinct and informative CDs consisting of a set of terms. Some of the other approaches extract information from documents based on certain pre-defined templates [11]. The filled templates can be considered as some kind of CDs. This approach involves the use of NLP and Information Extraction (IE) techniques, which is different from our term-based approach.

There are also other approaches to describing clusters for non-textual data. [12] uses "bounding boxes" plus some statistics to represent clusters; [13] uses multiple representatives in a cluster to represent the cluster; *CLIQUE* [14] generates CDs in the form of DNF expressions.

3 Cluster Description

Let D be a given collection of documents. A document is a set of terms and is not treated as a bag or sequence. A *clustering*[2] $\mathcal{K}$ consists of a number L of clusters, $C_1, C_2, ..., C_L$, of all the documents in D. Roughly speaking, a CD is intended to be used as a succinct cluster label. Formally, we have:

Definition 1. A *cluster description* (CD) for a cluster C is a set of k terms. A *clustering description* for a clustering $\mathcal{K}$ consists of L cluster descriptions $CD_1, ..., CD_L$, one for each cluster C_i. □

To allow easy interpretation, k should be a fairly small number. Constraints can be imposed on the terms in a CD. For example, we can require a CD to contain

---

[1] The centroid vector for a collection of documents S is commonly defined as $\frac{1}{|S|}\sum_{d \in S} d$, assuming that each document d is represented as a TF-IDF vector.

[2] Clustering is used as a noun here.

only terms that occur in its cluster. While we consider document clusters only here, one can also consider CDs for non-document clusters.

Although previous studies also considered using sets of terms as CDs, as discussed in Section 2, they have not considered the following important issues: (i) how to interpret CDs, (ii) how to measure the quality of CDs, and (iii) how to produce high-quality CDs. We will address those issues in the rest of the paper.

4 CD Interpretation and Quality

To be useful as descriptive "labels" to clusters, CDs should allow users to get a rough picture of the contents of the clusters; they should get such a picture by looking at the CDs (but not the actual contents of the clusters) and mentally interpreting them in some natural manner. The interpretation can be viewed as a mapping from CDs to the interpreted clusters; the interpreted clusters contain what users believe are in the clusters. The amount of difference between the interpreted and the original clusters can then measure the quality of the CDs. We formalize the interpretation process and consider the CD quality below.

4.1 Interpretation Via CD-Based Classification

Suppose the original clusters are $C_1, ..., C_L$, and their corresponding CDs are $CD_1, ..., CD_L$. The interpretation can be illustrated in Figure 1. The initial clusters are only provided to show the entire picture; users do not need to examine them during interpretation.

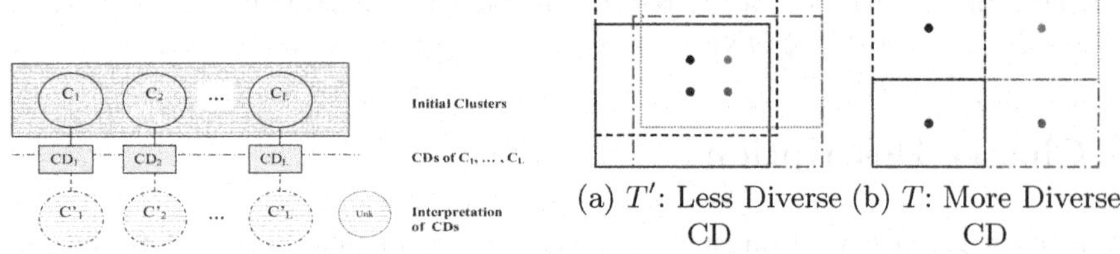

(a) T': Less Diverse CD (b) T: More Diverse CD

Fig. 1. Clusters, CDs and interpreted clusters

Fig. 2. Importance of Diversity

CD interpretation can be formalized in different ways. We believe that a natural way is the following: a user combines his/her understanding or interpretation of the individual terms in the CDs to form a rough picture of the clusters' contents. We capture user interpretation of individual terms as follows.

Definition 2. The *interpretation* of a term t w.r.t. an underlying universe S of documents, denoted as $\mathsf{INT}_S(t)$, is the set of documents in S containing the term t: $\mathsf{INT}_S(t) = \{d \mid d \in S \text{ such that } t \in d\}$. We will omit S when S is the collection D of all documents under consideration. □

While $\mathsf{INT}_S(t)$ is semantically the same as the concepts of tid-set, cover or SAT previously used in the literature, we use the notation of INT to emphasize that these sets are the basis of users' perception of the terms. Notice that one can also consider other factors such as synonyms of terms when defining $\mathsf{INT}_S(t)$.

When interpreting CDs, users form virtual or interpreted clusters by assigning documents to clusters based on their intuition and some "rough mental reckoning". Since a term t can occur in different clusters, there is competition in the interpretation of t with respect to the "right" cluster. On the other hand, since a document d can contain terms from CDs of multiple clusters, there can be competition regarding which cluster to assign d to: if d contains a term $t_1 \in CD_1$ and a term $t_2 \in CD_2$, then competition occurs since t_1 indicates that d should belong to C_1 and t_2 indicates that d should belong to C_2.

We combine the interpretation of the terms in CDs and resolve the competition to form interpretations for all clusters by using the *CD-based classification* approach. Here, we use the terms in the CDs as a classifier to classify documents into interpreted clusters as follows:

Algorithm 1. The CD-based classification

1. For each document d and each cluster C_i, let $\mathsf{Score}(d, C_i)$ *be defined*[3] *as* $\frac{|\cup_{t \in d \cap CD_i} \mathsf{INT}_{C_i}(t)|}{|C_i|}$. *Each document d' in* $\mathsf{INT}_{C_i}(t)$ *gives a signal regarding the membership of d in C_i, where $t \in d \cap CD_i$. By using the union of INTs, this score uses the signal contained in any given document d' exactly once.*

2. A document d is assigned to the interpreted cluster C_i' if d has the highest score at cluster C_i (i.e., $\mathsf{Score}(d, C_i) = max\{\mathsf{Score}(d, C_j) \mid 1 \le j \le L\}$*). If the highest score is zero, then d is assigned to the unknown cluster. We break ties by assigning d to the first cluster (in some fixed order) having the highest score.* □

Collectively, the interpreted clusters $C_1', ..., C_L'$ will be referred to as the *interpretation* of the CDs using the *CD-based classification* approach. While Score combines terms using roughly the OR, other logical connectives can also be used.

Table 1. The interpreted clusters using CD-based classification

CD_1 = {a, c}	CD_2 = {g, i}
d_{11}: a b c d	d_{21}: e g h i
d_{12}: a c e f	d_{22}: c i j

(a) Two given clusters and their CDs

C_1'	C_2'
d_{11}: a b c d	d_{21}: e g h i
d_{12}: a c e f	
d_{22}: c i j	

(b) The interpreted clusters

Example 1. We now use the example given in Table 1 to illustrate. Suppose we are given two clusters $C_1 = \{d_{11}, d_{12}\}$ and $C_2 = \{d_{21}, d_{22}\}$, and two CDs $CD_1 = \{a, c\}$ and $CD_2 = \{g, i\}$ (See (a)). To evaluate the quality of the given CDs, we apply our *CD-based classification* approach to those documents. The interpreted

[3] We use $|S|$ to denote the cardinality of a set S.

clusters formed by this process are shown in (b). Consider document d_{22}. It contains c in CD_1 and i in CD_2. Both d_{11} and d_{12} contain c, so $score(d_{22}, C_1) = |\{d_{11}, d_{12}\}|/2 = 1$. Only d_{22} contains c or i, so $score(d_{22}, C_2) = |\{d_{22}\}|/2 = 0.5$. Since $score(d_{22}, C_1) > score(d_{22}, C_2)$, we assign it to C'_1. Note that the scores are calculated based on the contents of the original clustering. □

4.2 F-Score as Measure of Quality

We measure the quality of CDs by using the amount of difference between the original and the interpreted clustering. We measure the difference using F-score [15], also called *F-measure.*

Suppose the original clustering is $\mathcal{K} = \{C_1, ..., C_L\}$, the corresponding CDs are $CD_1, ..., CD_L$, and the interpreted clustering of the CDs is $\mathcal{K}' = \{C'_1, ..., C'_L\}$. For each i, the F-score for C'_i and C_i, denoted by $F(C'_i, C_i)$, is defined as $F(C'_i, C_i) = \frac{2*P(C'_i,C_i)*R(C'_i,C_i)}{P(C'_i,C_i)+R(C'_i,C_i)}$, where $P(C'_i, C_i) = |C'_i \cap C_i|/|C_i|$ is the *precision*, $R(C'_i, C_i) = |C'_i \cap C_i|/|C'_i|$ is the *recall.* The overall difference between the interpreted clustering and the original clustering is defined as the weighted average of the F-score of the component clusters: $F(\mathcal{K}', \mathcal{K}) = \sum_{i=1}^{L} \frac{|C'_i|}{|D|} F(C'_i, C_i)$, where $D = \cup_{i=1}^{L} C_i$. We use $F(\mathcal{K}', \mathcal{K})$ as our measure of CD quality.

5 Surrogate CD Quality Measures for Efficient Search

Using F-score to directly search for good CDs is too expensive (The detailed analysis is omitted due to the space limitation). So we need to give efficient surrogate quality measures for use in the search process. In this section, we introduce one such measure, namely the CDD measure, which combines the three factors of *coverage*, *disjointness*, and *diversity.*

Intuitively, *coverage* is used to encourage the selection of terms with high frequency (matching large number of documents) in a given cluster, *disjointness* is used to discourage the selection of terms with high inter-cluster overlap, and *diversity* is used to discourage the selection of terms with high intra-cluster overlap. Consequently, the three factors help us to capture the quality measure discussed in Section 4.

5.1 Three Factors

We now discuss the three factors of *coverage*, *disjointness*, and *diversity.* While the *disjointness* is defined on CDs for one clustering, the other two are on CDs for one cluster.

To describe the contents of the clusters well, a CD must cover the cluster well: A good CD for a cluster C is a term set T where $\mathsf{Cov}_C(T)$ is large.

Definition 3. *The* coverage *of a* $CD = T$ *for a cluster* C *measures how well a term set* T *covers* C*, and is defined by* $\mathsf{Cov}_C(T) = \frac{|\bigcup_{t \in T} \mathsf{INT}_C(t)|}{|C|}$. □

To avoid the adverse impact of competition, the CDs for different clusters should have minimal competition against each other: good CDs for a clustering $C_1, ...,$ C_L is a set of CDs such that $\mathsf{Dis}(CD_1, ..., CD_L)$ is large.

Definition 4. *Let $CD_1, ..., CD_L$ be a CD for a given clustering $C_1, ..., C_L$.* Disjointness *measures overlap between terms in different CDs, and is defined by* $\mathsf{Dis}(CD_1, ..., CD_L) = \frac{1}{\sum_{1 \le i,j \le L,\ i \ne j} |\mathsf{INT}_{C_j}(CD_i)|+1}$. □

The terms in a good CD should be as different as possible (less overlap among INTs): A good CD for a cluster C is a term set T such that $\mathsf{Div}_C(T)$ is large.

Definition 5. *The* diversity *of a $CD = T$ for a cluster C measures overlap among terms of T, and is defined by* $\mathsf{Div}_C(T) = \frac{1}{\sum_{t,t' \in T,\ t \ne t'} |\mathsf{INT}_C(t) \cap \mathsf{INT}_C(t')|+1}$.

To see why $\mathsf{Div}_C(T)$ is important, consider the cluster C depicted in Figure 2. Suppose $T = \{t_1, t_2, t_3, t_4\}$ and $T' = \{t'_1, t'_2, t'_3, t'_4\}$ are two candidate term sets. Suppose the unions of their INTs are the same, i.e. $\cup_{i=1}^{4} \mathsf{INT}_C(t_i) = \cup_{i=1}^{4} \mathsf{INT}_C(t'_i)$. Suppose further that overlap in (Figure 2.a) is much larger than overlap in (Figure 2.b). Metaphorically speaking, a term t can be viewed as the centroid of $\mathsf{INT}_C(t)$. The centroids are much closer to each other in Figure 2.a than in Figure 2.b. As a consequence, it is much harder to synthesize the whole picture of the entire cluster using T' than using T.

In general, when the centroids are close to each other, it is hard to synthesize the whole picture of the entire cluster; in contrast, when they are more widely and evenly distributed, they can be combined to offer better picture of the whole cluster. The importance of diversity can also be seen from an analogy: diversity is important [16] for the performance of classifier ensembles [17, 18], and the terms in a CD play a similar role for the collective interpretation of the CD as the committee-member classifiers in the collective classification.

5.2 The CDD Measure

We now define the CDD surrogate measure in terms of the three factors. For use in the search process, we are interested in comparing two CDs, a new and an old, to determine the quality improvement offered by the new over the old. We will first define improvement for the factors, and then combine them to form improvement of the CDD measure.

Let $C_1, ..., C_L$ be a given clustering. Let $CD_1^o, ..., CD_L^o$ and $CD_1^n, ..., CD_L^n$ be two (an old and a new) CDs for the clustering. We require that the new be obtained from the old by modifying[4] just one of the CD_i^o's, keeping the others unchanged; let CD_j^o be the CD_i^o that is modified.

The *improvement* of the factors are defined as:

$$\delta(\mathsf{Cov}) = \frac{\mathsf{Cov}_{C_j}(CD_j^n) - \mathsf{Cov}_{C_j}(CD_j^o)}{\mathsf{Cov}_{C_j}(CD_j^o)}, \quad \delta(\mathsf{Dis}) = \frac{\mathsf{Dis}(CD_1^n, ..., CD_L^n) - \mathsf{Dis}(CD_1^o, ..., CD_L^o)}{\mathsf{Dis}(CD_1^o, ..., CD_L^o)},$$

$$\delta(\mathsf{Div}) = \frac{\mathsf{Div}_{C_j}(CD_j^n) - \mathsf{Div}_{C_j}(CD_j^o)}{\mathsf{Div}_{C_j}(CD_j^o)}.$$

Observe that $\delta(\mathsf{Cov})$ and $\delta(\mathsf{Div})$ are defined in terms of the cluster CD being modified, whereas $\delta(\mathsf{Dis})$ is defined in terms of the entire clustering CDs.

---

[4] Later we will consider adding or replacing one term only in our search.

The *CDD measure* is defined in terms of the three factors. For the old CD $CD_1^o, ..., CD_L^o$ and new CD $CD_1^n, ..., CD_L^n$, the *CDD improvement* is defined by

$$\Delta\mathsf{CDD} = \begin{cases} \delta(\mathsf{Cov}) + \delta(\mathsf{Dis}) + \delta(\mathsf{Div}), & \text{if } min(\delta(\mathsf{Cov}), \delta(\mathsf{Dis}), \delta(\mathsf{Div})) \geq 0 \\ 0, & \text{otherwise.} \end{cases}$$

Observe that in the formula we took the sum of the individual improvements for the three factors and insisted that each improvement is non-negative. We can also replace "sum" by "multiply", or drop the non-negative improvement requirement; however, experiments show that these do not perform as well.

When combining multiple factors to form a quality measure, trade-off among the factors occurs. In the above formula each factor carries a constant and equal weight; one may also use different and adaptive weights.

6 The PagodaCD Algorithm

We now consider how to efficiently construct succinct and informative CDs. We will present the PagodaCD Algorithm, which is a layer-based replacement algorithm using the CDD surrogate quality measure.

A natural but naive approach to searching good CDs is to repeatedly perform the best single-term replacement among all clusters and candidate terms, until no good replacement can be found. Our experiments indicated that this method suffers from two drawbacks: it is still quite expensive, and it does not necessarily produce better CDs when the CD size increases. These drawbacks motivate us to introduce the PagodaCD Algorithm.

Roughly speaking, our PagodaCD Algorithm divides the search process into multiple major steps, working in a layered manner. Each major step corresponds to the iterative selection of some k_s new terms for each CD_i; it does not replace terms selected at earlier steps. This process is level by level, and in each level all clusters are considered together. This is why the algorithm is called PagodaCD.

Algorithm 2. The PagodaCD Algorithm

Inputs: *Clusters* $C_1, ..., C_L$; *k (CD size); baseSize, incSize, minImp;*
Outputs: *CDs*
Method:

1. *For each* i, *set* CD_i *to* $\emptyset$, *and let* CP_i *consist of the most frequent* $50 + k$ *terms occurring in cluster* C_i;
2. IterReplace($\overline{CP}$,$\overline{CD}$,$minImp$,$baseSize$); // $\overline{CP}$ *and* $\overline{CD}$ *are vectors*
3. *For* $j = 1$ *to* $\frac{k-baseSize}{incSize}$ *do* IterReplace($\overline{CP}$,$\overline{CD}$,$minImp$,$incSize$);
4. *Return* $(CD_1, ..., CD_L)$ □

Parameter $baseSize$ is the number of terms to be obtained for each CD_i in the first major step, and $incSize$ is the number of terms to be added for each CD_i in each subsequent major step. Parameter $minImp$ is a user given minimum quality improvement threshold.

The IterReplace procedure is used to select $stepSize$ new terms for each CD_i, while keeping the terms selected in previous levels unchanged. It first selects the most frequent $stepSize$ unused terms from the candidate term pools (CDTL), and then use the CDD measure to repeatedly select the best replacement terms. For each iteration, it finds the best replacement term among all clusters and all terms for the current major step. This is repeated until no replacement term with significant quality improvement is found.

Method 1. IterReplace($\overline{CP}$, $\overline{CD}$, $minImp$, $stepSize$)

1. *For each i, let* $CDTL_i = \{$*the most frequent* $stepSize$ *of terms in* $CP_i - CD_i\}$, *and let* $CD_i = CD_i \cup CDTL_i$;
2. *Repeat until no replacement is found:*
   - *For each i, term* $t^o \in CDTL_i$ *and term* $t^n \in CP_i - CD_i$, *compute* $\Delta CDD_i(t^o, t^n)$ *for the hypothetical replacement of* t^o *in* CD_i *by* t^n. *Suppose the best replacement among all possible* (t^o, t^n) *pairs for i is* $\Delta CDD_i(t^o_i, t^n_i)$, *achieved at* t^o_i *and* t^n_i.
   - *Let* C_j *be the cluster with the largest* ΔCDD_i, *i.e.* $\Delta CDD_j(t^o_j, t^n_j) = \max_i \Delta CDD_i(t^o_i, t^n_i)$.

   If $\Delta CDD_j(t^o_j, t^n_j) > minImp$, *then (a) let* CD^n_j *(respectively* $CDTL_j$*) be the result of replacing* t^o_j *in* CD_j *(respectively* $CDTL_j$*) with* t^n_j, *(b) replace* CD_j *by* CD^n_j, *and (c) keep the other* CD_i *unchanged.* □

Notice that PagodaCD uses IterReplace to do the replacement only in a local one-layer-at-a-time manner. This leads to both faster computation and the monotone-quality behavior (getting higher F-scores when CDs become larger). Due to the space limitation, we omit the complexity analysis here.

We conclude this section with some remarks on preselection of candidate terms. For large document collections, the number of unique terms can be very large. Constructing CDs from all those terms is expensive. Moreover, some terms will not contribute much to quality CDs, especially when some terms only been appeared in few documents. To address these concerns, it is desirable to select and use only a subset of terms for constructing the CDs. In this paper, we preselect a number of the most frequent terms for each C_i as candidate terms. Notice that the choice of the number of candidate terms involves a trade-off between quality and efficiency. Here, we choose to have that number be $\gamma = 50 + k$, where k is the desired description size (or CD size) for each cluster.

7 Experimental Evaluation

In this section, we present an empirical evaluation of various CD construction algorithms, including ours. The goals of the experiments are (1) to demonstrate the superior quality of CDs produced by our algorithms than those produced by other algorithms, and (2) to validate the claims that *coverage*, *disjointness* and *diversity* are important factors for constructing succinct and informative CDs.

7.1 Experiment Setup

In this paper, we only consider CDs and assume that a clustering is given by other algorithms. We used the *Cluto* [4] toolkit to generate the clusterings; the clustering algorithm we used is *repeated bisecting*, which was shown to outperform the basic k-means and UPGMA algorithms [19]. Below, all data sets are divided into 10 clusters, unless indicated otherwise.

We evaluate the following CD construction approaches, in addition to PagodaCD. The "Descriptive CD" and "Discriminating CD" were described in Section 2, and were generated using the *Cluto* package. The "Frequency-based CD" were simply the most frequent terms from each cluster. Finally, the "COBWEB-like CD" approach is also considered, which uses the utility category [20, 5, 21] as the search criterion and uses our PagodaCD strategy to search.

7.2 Data Sets

Our experiments were performed on the Reuters-21578 [22] documents collection. The collection contains 21578 news articles, distributed in 22 files. We constructed five subsets, *Reuter2k*, *Reuter4k*, *Reuter6k*, *Reuter8k* and *Reuter10k*, containing 2k, 4k, 6k, 8k and 10k documents respectively, in the following manner: The 22 files were first concatenated in the order given. We then eliminated those documents contain little or no meaningful textual content. Finally, we got the desired number of documents from the concatenation starting from the beginning, i.e. *Reuter2k* contains the first 2000 documents from the concatenation, *Reuter4k* the first 4000 documents, and so on. All documents were preprocessed by removing stop-words and stemming, following common procedures in document processing.

7.3 CD Quality

PagodaCD vs. Existing Approaches. We compare the CD quality of our approach with other existing approaches. Figure 3 shows the average F-score of different approaches for different CD-Sizes in the Reuter8k data set. We can see that PagodaCD outperforms the *Descriptive* approach, which is the best among others, by at least 15% relative (or 8% absolute) percent for all description sizes. Figure 4 shows the average F-score of different approaches in Reuter2k, 4k, 6k, 8k and 10k data sets, with the description size fixed at 8. Again, the PagodaCD Algorithm outperforms the *Descriptive* approach by at least 10% relative (or 7% absolute) percent. For other data sets and description sizes, the performance comparison is similar.

Interestingly, when the description size increases, the average F-score of CDs produced by PagodaCD and *COBWEB-like CD* also increases. However, this is not true for other approaches. Figure 3 indicates that the F-score of other approaches jumps up and down, and it even deteriorates in some cases when the description size increases.

Table 2 shows some description terms produced by different approaches in Reuter4k when the description size is 4. We selected 2 clusters from total of 10

Table 2. CDs by different approaches when CD-Size = 4 in Reuter4k

Approaches	Cluster 4	Cluster 7
PagodaCD	bank pct financ billion	offer dlr stock share
Descriptive CD	bank rate stg debt	share offer stock common
Discriminating CD	bank net shr loss	share net shr offer
Frequency-based CD	bank said pct rate	share dlr inc compani
COBWEB-like CD	funaro reschedul imf citibank	registr redeem subordin debentur

clusters to save space. Although terms are in their root or abbreviated form, we can still sense that cluster 4 is about "large-scale" bank financing and cluster 7 is about stocks. This will be more obvious to domain experts. PagodaCD and *Descriptive* CDs give us better sense about these topics. For *Discriminating* CDs, there are duplicated terms in both clusters, namely *net* and *shr*. For *Frequency-based* CD, *inc* and *compani* in cluster7 give redundant information.

Impact of Clustering Quality on CD Quality. Clustering quality has big impact on CD quality. High clustering quality means that documents in a cluster are very similar to each other, but are very different from those in other clusters. It turns out that CDs constructed from high quality clusterings tend to have high quality, and those constructed from low quality clustering tend to have low quality. To demonstrate the effect of clustering quality, we produced different clusterings (5, 10, 15, 20-way) from Reuter4k. We measured the clustering quality by the weighted sum of the difference between the internal similarity and external similarity of each cluster. Interestingly, the clustering quality deteriorates when the number of clusters increases for this dataset. Figure 5 indicates that CD quality also deteriorates when clustering quality deteriorates.

7.4 Importance of the Three Factors

Experiments confirmed that the three factors of *coverage*, *disjointness* and *diversity* are very important for constructing informative CDs. Indeed, if we leave any of them out, the CD quality is not as good as when all three are used. Figures 6 and 7 show the importance of different factors in terms of relative loss or gain

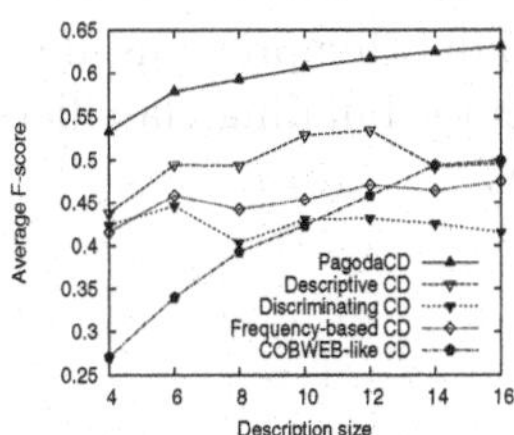

Fig. 3. F-score vs CD-Size in Reuter8k

Fig. 4. F-score vs data sets when CD-Size = 8

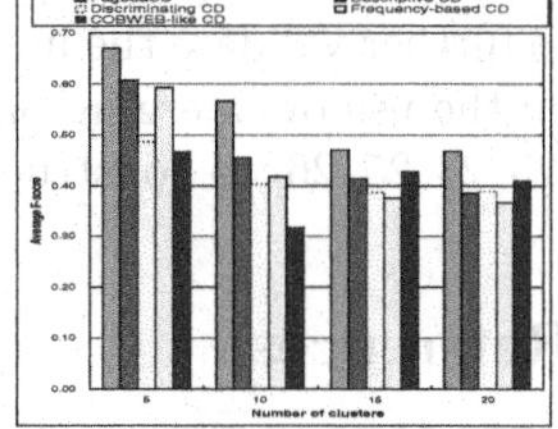

Fig. 5. F-score vs. number of clusters in Reuter4k

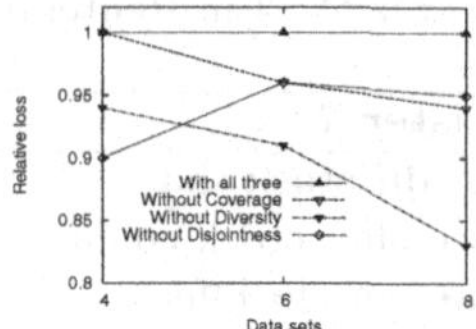

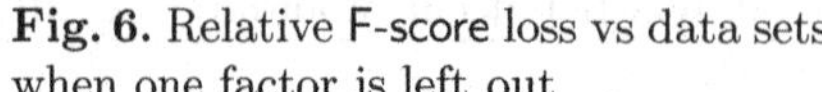

Fig. 6. Relative F-score loss vs data sets when one factor is left out

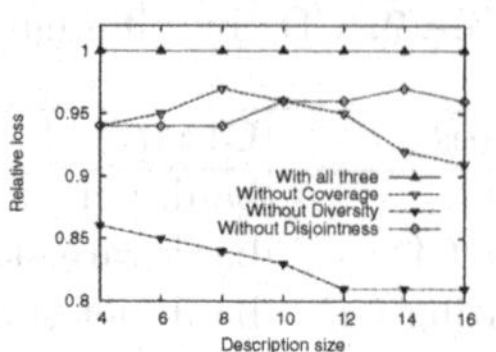

Fig. 7. Relative loss vs CD-Sizes when one factor is left out in Reuter8k

of average F-score . Because the candidate terms are frequent terms, *coverage* is less important than *diversity*. In other experiments we observed that, when *coverage* is less important, the other two factors, especially *diversity*, are very important.

8 Concluding Remarks

We argued that constructing succinct and informative CDs is an important component of clustering process, especially for managing large document repositories. We believe that succinct and informative CDs can help users quickly get a high-level sense of what the clusters contain, and hence help users use and "digest" the clusters more effectively.

We discussed and formalized how to interpret the CDs and how to resolve perception competition. We introduced a CD-based classification approach to systematically evaluate CD quality. We identified a surrogate quality measure for efficiently constructing informative CDs. We gave a layer-based replacement search method called PagodaCD for constructing CDs. Experimental results demonstrated that our method can produce high quality CDs efficiently, and CDs produced by PagodaCD also exhibits a monotone quality behavior.

For future research, we would like to do the following: (1) performing clustering and constructing informative CDs at the same time in order to get high quality CDs and clusterings, (2) giving the three factors different weights in different situation, and considering new surrogate quality measures, (3) considering synonyms and taxonomy in forming CDs, (4) involving human evaluation efforts to further validate the understandability of CDs, and (5) adapting previous ideas on the use of emerging patterns and contrasting patterns for building classifiers [23, 24, 25, 26] to construct succinct and informative CDs.

References

1. Beil, F., Ester, M., Xu, X.: Frequent term-based text clustering. In: Proc. 8th Int. Conf. on Knowledge Discovery and Data Mining (KDD). (2002)
2. Fung, B.C., Wang, K., Ester, M.: Hierarchical document clustering using frequent itemsets. In: Proc. of SIAM Int. Conf. on Data Mining. (2003)

3. Hearst, M.A., Karger, D.R., Pedersen, J.O.: Scatter/gather as a tool for the navigation of retrieval results. In: Working Notes of AAAI Fall Symp. (1995)
4. Karypis, G.: Cluto: A clustering toolkit (release 2.1.1) (2003)
5. Fisher, D.H.: Knowledge acquisition via incremental conceptual clustering. Machine Learning **2** (1987) 139–172
6. Gordon, A.: Classification, 2nd ed. Chapman & Hall (1999)
7. Hotho, A., Stumme, G.: Conceptual clustering of text clusters. In: Proceedings of FGML Workshop. (2002) 37–45
8. Hovy, E., Lin, C. Y.: Automated text summarization in summarist (1997)
9. DUC: Document understand conferences. http://duc.nist.gov/ (2005)
10. Maybury, M.T., Mani, I.: Automatic summarization. Tutorial on ACL (2001)
11. Mooney, R.J., Bunescu, R.: Mining knowledge from text using information extraction. SIGKDD *explorations 7, 1, pp. 3-10.* (2005)
12. Zhang, T., Ramakrishnan, R., Livny, M.: BIRCH: an efficient data clustering method for very large databases. In: Proc. ACM-SIGMOD. (1996) 103–114
13. Guha, S., Rastogi, R., Shim, K.: CURE: An efficient clustering algorithm for large databases. In: SIGMOD. (1998) 73–84
14. Agrawal, R., Gehrke, J., Gunopulos, D., Raghavan, P.: Automatic subspace clustering of high dimensional data for data mining applications. In: Proc of the ACM SIGMOD int'l conference on management of data. (1998) 94–105
15. van Rijsbergen, C.J.: Information Retireval. Butterworths, London (1979)
16. Cunningham, P., Carney, J.: Diversity versus quality in classification ensembles based on feat ure selection. In: ECML. (2000) 109–116
17. Shapire, R.: The strength of weak learnability. ML **5(2)** (1990) 197–227
18. Breiman, L.: Bagging predictors. Machine Learning **24(2)** (1996) 123–140
19. Steinbach, M., Karypis, G., Kumar, V.: A comparison of document clustering techniques. In: Proceedings of KDD Workshop on Text Mining. (2000)
20. Biswas, G., Weinberg, J.B., Fisher, D.H.: ITERATE: A conceptual clustering algorithm for data mining. IEEE Tran. **28C** (1998) 219–230
21. Gluck, M.A., Corter, J.E.: Information, uncertainty, and the utility of categories. In: Proc of the Seventh Annual Conference of the Cognitive Science Society. (1985)
22. Lewis, D.D.: Reuters-21578 text categorixation test collection (1997)
23. Dong, G., Li, J.: Efficient mining of emerging patterns: Discovering trends and differences. In: Proc. of the 5th ACM SIGKDD. (1999)
24. Dong, G., Zhang, X., Wong, L., Li, J.: CAEP: Classification by aggregating emerging patterns. In: Discovery Science. (1999) 30–42
25. Li, W., Han, J., Pei, J.: CMAR: Accurate and efficient classification based on multiple class-association rules. In: ICDM. (2001) 369–376
26. Han, J., Fu, Y.: Exploration of the power of attribute-oriented induction in data mining. In Fayyad, U., Piatetsky-Shapiro, G., Smyth, P., Uthurusamy, R., eds.: Advances in Knowledge Discovery and Data Mining. (1996) 399–421

LRD: Latent Relation Discovery for Vector Space Expansion and Information Retrieval

Alexandre Gonçalves[1], Jianhan Zhu[2], Dawei Song[2], Victoria Uren[2], and Roberto Pacheco[1,3]

[1] Stela Institute, Florianópolis, Brazil
{a.l.goncalves, pacheco}@stela.org.br

[2] Knowledge Media Institute, The Open University, Milton Keynes, United Kingdom
{j.zhu, d.song, v.s.uren}@open.ac.uk

[3] Department of Computing and Statistics, Federal University of Santa Catarina, Florianópolis, Brazil
rpacheco@inf.ufsc.br

Abstract. In this paper, we propose a text mining method called LRD (latent relation discovery), which extends the traditional vector space model of document representation in order to improve information retrieval (IR) on documents and document clustering. Our LRD method extracts terms and entities, such as person, organization, or project names, and discovers relationships between them by taking into account their co-occurrence in textual corpora. Given a target entity, LRD discovers other entities closely related to the target effectively and efficiently. With respect to such relatedness, a measure of relation strength between entities is defined. LRD uses relation strength to enhance the vector space model, and uses the enhanced vector space model for query based IR on documents and clustering documents in order to discover complex relationships among terms and entities. Our experiments on a standard dataset for query based IR shows that our LRD method performed significantly better than traditional vector space model and other five standard statistical methods for vector expansion.

1 Introduction

Textual corpora, such as web pages on a departmental website and blogs of a group of people, often mention named entities which are related to each other, and their relatedness is often shown by their co-occurrence in the same documents and their occurring close to each other in these documents, e.g., one document mentions Thomas works on project X in one sentence, and another document mentions Jack works on X in one paragraph. Given an entity, we can use either standard statistical measures such as mutual information [12] or our own CORDER method [11] to find related entities in a textual corpus. Given a document, suppose there are a number of entities originally occurring in the document, however, entities which are related to these original entities may not necessarily also occur in the document, e.g., Thomas and Jack both work on X but one document only mentions Thomas works on X.

Therefore, we propose to enhance the content description of a document with entities, which are not in the document but are closely related to existing entities in a document. By doing so, we can enrich what is missing but in fact very relevant to the

J.X. Yu, M. Kitsuregawa, and H.V. Leong (Eds.): WAIM 2006, LNCS 4016, pp. 122–133, 2006.
© Springer-Verlag Berlin Heidelberg 2006

document, e.g., since Thomas and Jack both work on X, we add Jack to one document which only mentions Thomas works on X.

In terms of information retrieval (IR), vector space models are traditionally used to index a document with terms and words occurring in the document for term-based querying and document clustering. Thus, we propose to enhance the vector of a document with entities and terms (CORDER and statistical methods are applied to terms in the same manner as entities) which are not in the document but are closely related to existing entities and terms in the document. Since humans' term-based queries are often an approximation of the kind of information they are looking for, these enhanced vectors can often lead to improved quality of returned documents, e.g., one document, which has Thomas and Jack as original dimensions and project X as an enhanced dimension, will match the query "X", and the user may find this document useful since it provides detailed information about Thomas and Jack, two members of X.

In this paper, we propose a text mining method called LRD (latent relation discovery) which can automatically process a textual corpus for unearthing relationships among entities and terms, and use these relationships to enhance traditional vector space model for IR and document clustering.

We propose a relevance measure for a pair of co-occurring entities by taking into account both their co-occurrence and distance. The relevance measure measures the degree of relatedness and is referred to as relation strength between them. Given a target entity, we aim to find its related entities and rank them by their relation strengths to the target entity.

LRD is based on our own CORDER algorithm [11]. LRD can be viewed as an unsupervised machine learning method, i.e., the method does not need either richly annotated corpora required by supervised learning methods or instances of relations as initial seeds for weakly supervised learning methods.

LRD identifies entities which are relevant to a given target entity based on its co-occurrence and distance with other entities in a textual corpus. Given a document, entities, which are not in the document but are relevant to entities originally in the document, are used to enhance the vector representation of the document. The enhanced vector space model has led to improved IR on these documents and document clustering over the traditional vector space model. Since richer contexts are encoded in enhanced vectors, a document A, which is judged as not relevant to a query Q or another document B in the traditional vector space, however can be judged as relevant to the query Q or document B in the enhanced vector space. We have evaluated LRD in terms of F measure, a combination of precision and recall, in IR and compared with five other standard methods, and LRD has significantly outperformed all of them and the original vector space model.

The rest of the paper is organized as follows. We present related work in Section 2. Our LRD method is presented in Section 3. The experimental results are reported in Section 4. Finally, we conclude the paper and discuss future work in Section 5.

2 Related Work

Co-occurrence based methods have been widely applied, for instance, in the identification of collocations and information retrieval. Such methods aim to correlate textual structures in order to unearth latent relationships. One of these approaches is *Latent*

Semantic Indexing (LSI) [3], which automatically discovers latent relationships among documents and terms through *Singular Vector Decomposition* (SVD). LSI has been applied mainly in the information retrieval area, and also used to discover highly related terms [4]. Furthermore, LSI can reduce the dimensionality without undermining precision in information retrieval systems. However the method is time-consuming when applied to a large corpus [7].

Other related methods which can be applied in this context are *t* test, chi-squared, *z* score, and mutual information (MI) [12]. Criticisms of these methods are that probabilities are assumed to be approximately normally distributed in *t* test, Z score is only applicable when the variance is known, *t* test and χ^2 test do not work well with low frequency events, and mutual information does not deal properly with data sparseness. Unlike these methods, LRD can deal with data sparseness and scales well to a large corpus since LRD treats each document as an atomic unit and any change requires only unitary reprocessing (the details of LRD is presented in Section 3).

In the line of document clustering, Hotho and Stumme [6] have made use of Formal Concept Analysis using background knowledge by mapping words to some concept in Wordnet in order to improve the clustering process. Also, Hotho et al. [5] proposed a model called COSA (Concept Selection and Aggregation) which uses ontologies for restricting the set of document features through aggregations. Another approach is based on analogy, aiming to produce, through alignment, pairs of definitions that share the same headword term, and promotes replacements in pairs without major changes in the meaning [1]. In previous work, we [9] presented a model that extracts relevant terms from researchers' curricula vitae integrated with ontology aiming to promote support to clustering. The problem with this approach lies in its ontology dependency. Our LRD method analyzes co-occurrences through textual corpora in order to establish the relation strength among entities which in turn improves IR and document clustering tasks.

In essence, our proposed LRD method is similar to those co-occurrence based approaches which aim to enhance context representation. However, by combining relation strength, which establishes latent relationships between entities, with the vector space model, our LRD method has achieved better results.

3 Proposed Approach

3.1 Overview

Our LRD model maps entities and their relationships extracted from documents. Entities are named entities extracted from documents using a *Named Entity Recognition* (NER) tool called ESpotter [10] and terms in the document. We calculate the relation strength between every pair of entities[1] by taking into account the pair's co-occurrences in these documents. We represent each document as a vector of entities, and construct an entity-by-document matrix. Given a document and its vector, the most relevant entities to those originally in the vector are identified to expand the document vector. We use these expanded vectors for query based information retrieval and document clustering.

[1] Entities refer to both named entities recognized by ESpotter and terms in the document.

3.2 Entity Extraction

Named Entity[2] Recognition (NER) is a well studied area [2]. We have used ESpotter [10], a NER system based on standard NER techniques and adapted to various domains on the Web by taking into account domain knowledge. ESpotter recognizes Named Entities (NEs) of various types. Users can configure ESpotter to recognize new types of entities using new lexicon entries and patterns. Domain knowledge, taken from sources such as ontologies, is represented as lexicon entries (e.g., the project names in an organization).

3.3 Relation Strength

Given a target entity (*E1*) which occurs in various documents, there are a number of entities which co-occur with it in these documents. We propose a latent relation discovery algorithm which ranks co-occurring NEs based on relation strength. Thus, NEs which have strong relations with a target NE can be identified. Our approach takes into account three aspects as follows:

Co-occurrence: Two entities are considered to co-occur if they appear in the same text fragment, which can be a document or a text window. For simplicity, in this section, we use document as the unit to count entity co-occurrence. The effect of different granularities of text fragments will be discussed later in Section 4. Generally, if one entity is closely related to another entity, they tend to co-occur often. To normalize the relatedness between two entities, *E1* and *E2*, the relative frequency [8] of co-occurrence is defined as follows.

$$\hat{p}(E1,E2)=\frac{Num(E1,E2)}{N} \tag{1}$$

where *Num*(*E*1,*E*2) is the number of co-occurring documents for *E1* and *E2*, and *N* is the total number of documents in a corpus.

Distance. Two NEs which are closely related tend to occur close to each other. If two NEs, *E1* and *E2*, occur only once in a document, the distance between *E1* and *E2* is the difference between the word offsets of *E1* and *E2*. When *E1* or *E2* occur multiple times in the document, given *E1* as the target, the mean distance between *E1* and *E2* in the *i*th document, $m_i(E1, E2)$ is defined as follows.

$$m_i(E1,E2)=\frac{\sum_{j=1}^{f_i(E1)}\min(E1_j,E2)}{f_i(E1)} \tag{2}$$

where $f_i(E1)$ is the number of occurrences of *E1* in the *i*th document, $min(E1_j, E2)$ is the minimum distance between the *j*th occurrence of *E1*, $E1_j$, and *E2*. Generally, $m_i(E1, E2)$ is not equal to $m_i(E2, E1)$.

Relation Strength: Given an entity, *E1*, the relation strength between two entities *E1* and *E2* takes into account their co-occurrence, mean distance, and frequency in co-

[2] In this paper, named entities are proper names consisting of words or collocations extracted from documents and labeled as a particular class, i.e., person or organization.

occurred documents as defined in Equation 3. The greater the mean distance is, the smaller the relation strength. Generally, the relation strength between *E1* and *E2* is asymmetric depending on whether *E1* or *E2* is the target.

$$R(E1,E2)=\hat{p}(E1,E2)\times\sum_i\left(\frac{f(Freq_i(E1))\times f(Freq_i(E2))}{m_i(E1,E2)}\right), \qquad (3)$$

where $f(Freq_i(E1)) = tfidf_i(E1)$, $f(Freq_i(E2)) = tfidf_i(E2)$, and $Freq_i(E1)$ and $Freq_i(E2)$ are the numbers of occurrences of *E1* and *E2* in the *i*th document, respectively. The term frequency and inverted document frequency measure *tfidf* is defined as $tfidf_i(j) = tf_i(j) * \log_2\left(N/df_j\right)$, where $tf_i(j)= f_i(j)/\ max(f_j(k))$ is the frequency $f_i(j)$ of entity *j* in the *i*th document normalized by the maximum frequency of any entity in the *i*th document, *N* is the number of documents in the corpus, and df_j is the number of documents that contain the entity *j*.

3.4 Vector Expansion

In vector composition, we intend to enhance the vector space by co-occurred entities. After entity extraction, we calculate the relation strength between every pair of entities using Equation 3. For example, in Table 1, an entity-by-document is constructed from 3 documents (D1, D2, and D3) and 7 entities.

Table 1. Example of a document-to-entity matrix and frequencies in the matrix are normalized using *tfidf* in the matrix on the right (D1-N, D2-N and D3-N)

Entities	D1	D2	D3	D1-N	D2-N	D3-N
E1	4	2	0	0.5850	0.5850	0
E2	2	0	3	0.2925	0	0.5850
E3	3	2	0	0.4387	0.5850	0
E4	1	1	0	0.1462	0.2925	0
E5	0	2	0	0	1.5850	0
E6	0	0	2	0	0	1.0566
E7	1	0	2	0.1462	0	0.3900

We create a table consisting of pairs of related entities. Each row in the table consists of a document ID, a source and a target entity co-occurring in the document with their frequencies, the frequency of their co-occurrences, and their intra-document distance. As an example, Table 2 shows pairs of related entities in document 1, their frequencies and the distance between them calculated using Equation 2 and the intra-document relation strength calculated using the second part of Equation 3 (i.e., $(f(Freq_i(E1))\times f(Freq_i(E2)))/m_i(E1,E2)$). Similarly, we can get the table for co-occurred entities in document 2 and 3.

Given a pair of entities, we can calculate their relation strength shown in Table 3. For example, the relation strength between target entity (TE) E1 and source entity (SE) *E*3,is computed using Equation 3 as *R(E1,E3)*=2/3*(0.4938+0.5850)=0.7192. Relation strength is used to recompose the vector space. For example, in Table 1, the vector of document 1 does not contain *E*5 and *E*6. However, judging by relation

Table 2. Example of co-occurred entities in documents

Doc	Source Entity (SE)	SE tf	Target Entity (TE)	TE tf	Distance	Intra-doc relation strength
1	E1	4	E2	2	2.0000	0.4387
1	E1	4	E3	3	2.0731	0.4938
1	E1	4	E4	1	2.3634	0.3094
1	E1	4	E7	1	2.8540	0.2562
1	E2	2	E3	3	2.3412	0.3123
1	E2	2	E4	1	2.6887	0.1632
1	E2	2	E7	1	3.0805	0.1424
1	E3	3	E4	1	2.2642	0.2584
1	E3	3	E7	1	2.5654	0.2280
1	E4	1	E7	1	3.8074	0.0768

Table 3. Example of relation strengths between co-occurred entities

SE/TE	E1	E2	E3	E4	E5	E6	E7
E1	N/A	0.1462	0.7192	0.4788	0.2590	0	0.0854
E2	0.1136	N/A	0.1041	0.0544	0	0.2609	0.3290
E3	0.6528	0.0364	N/A	0.3898	0.3155	0	0.0760
E4	0.3675	0.1754	0.2568	N/A	0.1847	0	0.0256
E5	0.3687	0	0.4876	0.2512	N/A	0	0
E6	0	0.1856	0	0	0	N/A	0.1423
E7	0.1569	0.4587	0.1233	0.0489	0	0.1423	N/A

strength, the most relevant entity to *E3* not in the vector of document 1 is *E5* and to *E2* not in the vector of document 1 is *E6*, with relation strength 0.3155 and 0.2609, respectively. Since *E3* and *E2* are dimensions in the vector of document 1, *E5* and *E6* are considered to be added to the vector of document 1. Generally, for each entity originally in a document vector as the target, we add each of the top *n* entities related to the target and not in the document vector (ranked by their relation strengths), E_{new}, to the document vector. The weight of E_{new}, $w(E_{new})$, is defined as follows.

$$w(E_{new}) = \sum_{i=1}^{num(E_{new},D)} R(E_{new}, E_i) \times w(E_i) \tag{4}$$

where $R(E_{new}, E_i)$ is the relation strength between E_{new} and E_i, which is originally in the vector of document *D*, $w(E_i)$ is the weight of E_i in document *D*, and $num(E_{new}, D)$ is the total number of entities originally in the document vector having E_{new} in the top *n* most relevant entities in terms of relation strength.

In Table 4, we set *n*=1. We add *E5* (No. 1 entity not in document vector (N1NDV) of SEs: E1, E3, E4) and *E6* (N1NDV of SE: E2) to document one, *E2* (N1NDV of SE: E1, E4) and *E7* (N1NDV of SE: E3) to document two, and *E3* (N1NDV of SE: E1, E2, E7) to document three. For example, the weight of *E5* in *D1* is: 0.5850*0.2590+0.4387*0.3155+0.1462*0.1847 = 0.3169.

3.5 Query-Based Information Retrieval and Document Clustering

We calculate a cosine coefficient between the expanded vector of each document and the vector of a term-based query and use the cosine coefficients to rank documents with respect to the query. We setup a threshold on the cosine coefficient to trade precision against recall in retrieving these documents.

We apply a clustering algorithm to generate patterns for in-depth analysis of how documents and entities are inter-connected. Unlike the traditional k-means algorithm which is based on the parameter k (number of clusters), we use an approach based on a radius parameter (r) to control the cluster formation.

Table 4. Example of an entity-by-document matrix enhanced by related entities

Entities	D1	D2	D3
E1	0.5850	0.5850	0.1462
E2	0.2925	0.1368	0.5850
E3	0.4387	0.5850	0.2143
E4	0.1462	0.2925	0
E5	0.3169	1.5850	0
E6	0.0763	0	1.0566
E7	0.1462	0.0445	0.3900

The algorithm starts with selecting a vector (either randomly or the one most separated from the others) and forms the first cluster. By repeating the process, the next vector is selected and compared with the first cluster by applying the cosine measure defined as follows.

$$\cos\theta = \frac{\sum_{i=1}^{n}\left(t_i * q_i\right)}{\sqrt{\sum_{k=1}^{n}\left(t_k\right)^2} * \sqrt{\sum_{j=1}^{n}\left(q_j\right)^2}}, \tag{5}$$

where t_i and t_k are the normalized frequencies of the ith and kth entities in the vector t, and q_i and q_j are the normalized frequencies of the ith and jth entities in the vector q.

If the similarity between a vector and a cluster centroid subtracted from 1 is greater than the r parameter, the vector forms a new cluster. Otherwise, it is assigned to the cluster and we recalculate the centroids of the clusters. Experiments using a range of values of r from 0.2 to 0.7 were carried out and the best results were achieved with $r = 0.3$. During the next iterations, if the vector moves from one cluster to another, the centroid updating is carried out in both the new cluster to which the vector has been added and the old cluster from which the vector has been removed.

The clustering process stops when it reaches convergence, which is determined by the total average difference between the current and previous epoch. Our experiments on different datasets have shown that epochs between 2 and 10 are required. After the clustering, we get clusters consisting of vectors and cluster centroid average.

4 Empirical Evaluation

We have evaluated our proposed relation strength model (LRD) in term of F measure, which combines precision and recall, by comparing with five standard statistical methods (LSI and four other methods based on a relation strength model for vector expansion) in information retrieval. In order to automate the evaluation process, the Glasgow Information Retrieval benchmark dataset called CISI[3] containing 1,460

[3] http://www.dcs.gla.ac.uk/idom/ir_resources/test_collections/cisi/

documents and 112 queries has been used. Terms in the documents and entities extracted from documents using ESpotter are used during the correlation and vector expansion processes.

4.1 Relation Strength Models

We have compared LRD with four standard statistical methods in relation strength calculation. These relation strengths are used for vector expansion. The four methods, i.e., mutual information (MI), improved MI, phi-squared, and Z score are presented as follows.

Mutual Information (MI) compares the probability of two entities, *x* and *y* or any other linguistic unit, such as named entities, appearing together against the probability that they appear independently. The higher the MI value, the greater the degree of relevance between two entities. MI is defined as follows.

$$I(x, y) = \log_2 \frac{P(x, y)}{P(x)P(y)}, \tag{6}$$

where $P(x,y)$ is the probability that x and y co-occur in a text fragment (which can be a document, or a text window), and $P(x)$ and $P(y)$ are the probabilities that x and y occur individually.

We have also applied Vechtomova et al.'s improved MI (VMI) method [13]. The standard MI is symmetrical, i.e. $I(x,y) = I(y,x)$, as joint probabilities are symmetrical, $P(x,y) = P(y,x)$. Unlike traditional MI, VMI is asymmetrical. An average window size calculated from all windows around term x is used to estimate the probability of occurrence of y in the windows around x. VMI is defined as follows.

$$I_v(x, y) = \log_2 \frac{P_v(x, y)}{P(x)P(y)} = \log_2 \frac{\dfrac{f(x, y)}{Nv_x}}{\dfrac{f(x)f(y)}{N^2}}, \tag{7}$$

where $f(x,y)$ is the joint frequency of x and y in the corpus, $f(x)$ and $f(y)$ are frequencies of independent occurrence of x and y in the corpus, v_x is the average window size around x in the corpus, and N is the corpus size.

Phi-squared (ϕ^2) makes use of a contingency table as follows:

	w_2	$\overline{w_2}$
w_1	a	b
$\overline{w_1}$	c	d

where cell a indicates the number of times entities w_1 and w_2 co-occur in a window. Cell b indicates the number of times w_1 occurs but w_2 does not. Cell c indicates the number of times w_2 occurs but w_1 does not. Finally, cell d indicates the number of times neither entity occurs, that is, $d = \frac{N}{S} - a - b - c,$ where N is the size of the corpus and S the size of the text window. ϕ^2 measure between w_1 and w_2 is defined as:

$$\phi^2 = \frac{(ad - bc)^2}{(a+b)(a+c)(b+d)(c+d)}, \tag{8}$$

where $0 \le \phi^2 \le 1$. Unlike MI which typically favors entities with low frequency, ϕ^2 can be used as an alternative, since it tends to favor high frequency ones.

Z score has been used by Vechtomova et al. [13] for query expansion. Z score is defined as follows.

$$Z(x,y) = \frac{O-E}{\sqrt{E}} = \frac{f(x,y) - \frac{v_x f(x) f(y)}{N}}{\sqrt{\frac{v_x f(x) f(y)}{N}}}, \tag{9}$$

where $f(x,y)$ is the joint frequency of x and y in the corpus, $f(x)$ and $f(y)$ are frequencies of independent occurrence of x and y in the corpus, v_x is the average window size around x in the corpus and N is the corpus size.

4.2 Experimental Results of Vector Space Model for Information Retrieval

By expanding document vectors and applying different relation strength methods we intend to establish a way to automatically evaluate our proposed method. In this sense we have compared LRD, Phi-squared, MI, VMI and Z score in order to find out entities and terms closely related to the original entities and terms in the vector. For each method, the original vector is expanded using the method by taking into account different text windows and expansion factors.

Given a document vector, it is expanded using the method presented in Section 3 with different text windows and *n* factors (the *n* most related entities to each original entity in a document vector, which do no occur in an original vector as dimensions, are added to the vector). We have used the text window of 20, 50, 100 and 200, and the whole document (i.e., two entities are considered as co-occurring as long as they occur in a same document). For the *n* factor, values of 1, 5, 10, 20, 30, 40 and 50 most relevant entities are used to expand the vector space. The same vector expansion process using each of the relation strength methods is applied to the corpus using different text window and *n* factor.

We have applied each relation strength method to the 1,460 documents in the CISI dataset. The constructed vector space by each method using different text window and *n* factor is used for information retrieval. We randomly selected 20 queries from the 112 queries in CISI. Given a query, we calculate a cosine coefficient between the vector of each document and the vector of the query to rank these documents against the query.

Given a query, we set a threshold on the cosine coefficient and only documents having cosine coefficient with the query above the threshold are taken into account in our precision and recall calculation. Given a query, the precision (*P*) of our answer is the number of relevant documents returned divided by the total number of returned documents, and recall (*R*) is the number of relevant documents returned divided by the total number of relevant documents as the gold standard in CISI. We define the *F* measure as $F = \frac{2 \times P \times R}{P+R}$. In our experiments, we set the cosine similarity threshold as

0.54 which maximizes F measure on most queries. Given a relation strength method with different window size and *n* factor, we average the *F* measure for each of the 20 answers to get the total F measure and the results are shown in Table 5.

Table 5. The average F measure for LSI and 5 methods with seven expansion factor (*n*) values and five text window settings, the highest *F* measure for each window setting is in bold and shaded cell

F-measure (%)		*n*=1	5	10	20	30	40	50
No window	**LRD**	16.5	18.4	18.1	18.7	**19.3**	18.9	17.8
	Phi-squared	12.9	11.5	10.8	10.8	10.9	11.3	12.1
	MI	9.3	6.6	6.3	5.9	5.8	5.7	5.9
	VMI	10.5	6.6	6.1	5.8	5.8	5.9	5.9
	Z Score	14.7	12.8	13.0	11.8	11.0	10.0	10.0
	LSI	15.3	16.1	15.7	16.1	16.6	15.2	14.9
Size =20	**LRD**	16.9	18.3	18.7	18.9	**19.0**	18.7	18.6
	Phi-squared	15.3	12.9	13.1	10.7	12.0	11.7	11.1
	MI	10.3	6.6	6.2	5.9	5.8	6.0	5.9
	VMI	10.6	6.7	6.2	5.9	5.8	6.0	5.9
	Z Score	14.4	14.3	14.4	14.9	14.5	15.6	15.3
Size =50	**LRD**	16.8	18.4	18.2	18.8	**18.9**	18.9	18.7
	Phi-squared	13.3	10.6	9.7	9.6	9.3	10.8	9.9
	MI	10.3	6.7	6.2	5.9	5.8	5.9	5.9
	VMI	10.5	6.7	6.1	5.8	5.8	6.0	5.9
	Z Score	14.5	14.5	14.0	15.6	15.2	17.1	16.1
Size =100	**LRD**	16.5	18.4	18.1	18.6	**19.2**	18.8	17.7
	Phi-squared	13.8	10.4	7.9	8.1	7.1	6.6	6.3
	MI	9.4	6.7	6.3	5.9	5.8	5.7	5.9
	VMI	9.6	6.6	6.1	5.8	5.8	5.9	5.9
	Z Score	14.5	14.6	13.9	15.2	15.4	17.4	16.8
Size =200	**LRD**	16.5	18.3	18.1	18.7	**19.2**	18.8	17.8
	Phi-squared	14.2	13.0	12.0	8.7	7.7	7.6	7.2
	MI	9.3	6.6	6.2	5.9	5.8	5.7	5.9
	VMI	10.5	6.6	6.1	5.8	5.8	5.9	5.9
	Z Score	14.5	14.6	13.9	15.2	15.4	16.7	16.6

The average *F* measure for the original vector space model, i.e., without vector expansion and text window, is 9.2% and provides a baseline for our comparison. As shown in Table 5, LSI, which is only evaluated based on the use of whole documents rather than text windows, is also included. For LSI and the other five methods which work on different window settings, LRD consistently performs the best. The highest *F* measure is 19.3% using LRD with no window and *n*=30. The second best performing method is LSI with highest *F* measure 16.6% with *n*=30. The third best performing method is Z score with highest F measure 17.4% with window size 100 and *n*=40. MI and VMI have similar performance.

In terms of the influence of *n* factor on these methods, when *n* factor increases, the *F* measure of LSI keeps roughly the same. For a given window setting, when *n* factor increases, the *F* measures of LRD and *Z* score increase (for the *F* measure of LRD, the biggest increases is from *n*=1 to *n*=5 and the increase from *n*=5 becomes very small even some small decreases), the *F* measure of phi-squared, MI and VMI decrease. Since the baseline is 9.2%, we can see that vector expansion with LRD, LSI, phi-squared and *Z* score have a positive effect on information retrieval and with the other methods have a negative effect on information retrieval. LRD has achieved the best performance for all window sizes when $n = 30$, and larger n values will not bring benefit to the performance and on the contrary bring computational cost.

In terms of the effect of window size on average F measure, LRD and Z score are not very sensitive to the varying window sizes, and consistently perform better than the other methods. Phi-squared, MI, and VMI achieve better F measures with smaller window sizes than those with larger window sizes.

5 Conclusions and Future Work

We present a co-occurrence based approach, namely LRD (Latent relation Discovery), which associates entities using relation strengths among them. We propose to use inter-entity relation strength to enhance the traditional vector representation of documents in order to provide additional meaning and improve query based information retrieval on these documents. Our initial experiments using the CISI dataset have shown that LRD can dramatically improve the F measure of information retrieval over the traditional vector space model, and significantly outperformed five standard methods for vector expansion. Our experiments on the CISI dataset show that LRD's running time increases linearly with the size of documents and the number of documents it examines. It can incrementally evaluate existing relations and establish new relations by taking into account new documents. Thus, LRD can scale well to a large corpus.

Our future work is five-fold. First, we are working on refining the LRD model in order to improve the metrics used to establish the relation strengths between entities and improve the clustering method. Second, we propose clustering documents based on the enhanced vector space models produced by our LRD method, however, the evaluation and interpretation of these clusters is neither an easy nor an intuitive task. We are carrying out work on using various techniques to evaluate these clusters. Our work underway is the visualization of these clusters in order to show complex patterns of inter-connected entities in clustered documents for easy comparison between these clusters produced by different vector space models. Third, we are evaluating our enhanced vector space models for information retrieval and clustering on large scale TREC collections such as TIPSTER. Fourth, dimensionality reduction is another direction and needs to be studied in order to improve the performance of our method. Finally, entities and their relations constitute a social network of communities of practice. We are working on using the social network to help analyze and understand the behavior of these communities.

References

1. Castillo, G., Sierra, G., and McNaught, J. An improved algorithm for semantic clustering. In Proc. of 1st International Symposium on Information and Communication Technologies, ACM International Conference Proceeding Series, Dublin, Ireland, 2003, 304-309.
2. Cunningham, H. GATE: a General Architecture for Text Engineering. Computers and the Humanities, vol. 36, issue 2, 2002, 223-254.

3. Deerwester, S. C., Dumais, S. T., Landauer, T. K., Furnas, G. W., and Harshman, R. A. Indexing by latent semantic analysis. Journal of the American Society of Information Science, vol. 41, issue 6, 1990, 391-407.
4. Ding, C. H. Q. A probabilistic model for dimensionality reduction in information retrieval and filtering. In Proc. of the 1st SIAM Computational Information Retrieval Workshop, Raleigh, NC, 2000.
5. Hotho, A., Maedche, A., and Staab, S. Text clustering based on good aggregations. In Proc. of the 2001 IEEE International Conference on Data Mining, IEEE Computer Society, San Jose, CA, 2001, 607-608.
6. Hotho, A., and Stumme, G. Conceptual clustering of text clusters. In Proc. of the Fachgruppentreffen Maschinelles Lernen (FGML), Hannover, Germany, 2002, 37-45.
7. Ikehara, S., Murakami, J., Kimoto, Y., and Araki, T. Vector space model based on semantic attributes of words. In Proc. of the Pacific Association for Computational Linguistics (PACLING), Kitakyushu, Japan, 2001.
8. Resnik, P. Semantic similarity in a taxonomy: An information-based measure and its application to problems of ambiguity in natural language. Journal of Artificial Intelligence Research: An International Electronic and Print Journal, vol. 11, 1999, 95-130.
9. Gonçalves, A., Uren, V., Kern, V. and Pacheco, R. Mining Knowledge from Textual Databases: An Approach using Ontology-based Context Vectors. In Proc. of the International Conference on Artificial Intelligence and Applications (AIA 2005), Innsbruck, Austria, 2005, 66-71.
10. Zhu, J., Uren, V., and Motta, E. ESpotter: Adaptive Named Entity Recognition for Web Browsing. In Proc. of the 3rd Conference on Professional Knowledge Management (WM 2005), pp.518-529, Springer LNAI, 2005.
11. Zhu, J., Gonçalves, A., Uren, V., Motta, E., and Pacheco, R. (2005). Mining Web Data for Competency Management. In Proc. of Web Intelligence (WI 2005), France, 2005, pp. 94-100, IEEE Computer Society.
12. Church, K., and Hanks, P. Word association norms, mutual information, and lexicography. Computational Linguistics, vol. 16, issue 1, 1990, 22-29.
13. Vechtomova, O., Robertson, S., and Jones, S. Query expansion with long-span collocates. Information Retrieval. vol. 6, issue 2, 2003, 251-273.

Web Image Retrieval Refinement by Visual Contents

Zhiguo Gong, Qian Liu, and Jingbai Zhang

Faculty of Science and Technology
University of Macau
P.O.Box 3001 Macao, PRC
{zggong, ma46620, ma46597}@umac.mo

Abstract. For Web image retrieval, two basic methods can be used for representing and indexing Web images. One is based on the associate text around the Web images; and the other utilizes visual features of images, such as color, texture, shape, as the descriptions of Web images. However, those two methods are often applied independently in practice. In fact, both have their limitations to support Web image retrieval. This paper proposes a novel model called 'multiplied refinement', which is more applicable to combination of those two basic methods. Our experiments compare three integration models, including multiplied refinement model, linear refinement model and expansion model, and show that the proposed model yields very good performance.

1 Introduction

With the explosive increase of the Web, Web images, with huge amount and comprehensiveness in meaning, are becoming one of the most indispensable information representation types on the Web. Comparing with Web pages, it is, however, much difficult to find a model to support efficient and effective Web image retrieval. The main reason is due to the facts that (1) The Web images are used freely in the Web pages, and no standard exists for the relationships between the texts and embedded images in the same Web pages; (2) Web images are quite comprehensive in meaning, and they are created by different persons for different purposes; (3) the qualities of the Web images vary greatly. For those reasons, we can not either use the traditional database models (relational model), or visual-content-based model alone for the Web image retrieval. Those challenges make web image retrieval become an attractive research area. For a web image, two sources can be used as its content descriptions: high level or semantic content, such as what the image means, and visual content, such as color, texture, and shape of the objects. Accordingly, two basic approaches are exploited in the web image retrieval: text-based and visual content-based.

Semantic content-Based or text-based web image retrieval(TBIR)[1, 2] utilizes semantic content and is based on the assumption that the associated text can describe the semantics of Web images. Therefore, the associated text is used to index the images. Such systems, such as google and yahoo, try to correlate

J.X. Yu, M. Kitsuregawa, and H.V. Leong (Eds.): WAIM 2006, LNCS 4016, pp. 134–145, 2006.
© Springer-Verlag Berlin Heidelberg 2006

associated terms to the embedded images with respect to their importance and relative positions to the image. However, many words, though close to the image, are irrelevant to its semantics. Further more, many noise images exist, such as logos, banners, buttons, which generate many noises to the result. In contrast to the text-based method, the other method is visual content-based web image retrieval(CBIR) [3,4,5,6,7,8]. The method assumes that images of the same kind are related to each other in visual features, such as color and texture, and it uses visual content features to support image retrieval. As a matter of the fact, visual content-based image search systems can only provide satisfied performances if all the images are for the same semantic. However, in the context of Web, large percent of noise images will be in the result. That is, visual feature-based method alone can not work well for Web image retrieval.

To improve the performance, in recent years, the hybrid method[9,10] is used. The basic idea of the hybrid model is to combine text-based ranking with content-based ranking using linear composition model. However, the linear combining model does not take into account of the co-support of those two rankings and great margin of their performance. In this paper we propose a novel model called 'multiplied refinement' for the integration of these two basic models to overcome the limitations of that model. In our solution, the user can start his image search with words or concepts, then he can refine his search with visual features by sample images by multiplied refinement model. Our experiments reveal that the multiplied refinement model is better than both the linear refinement model and expansion model.

The rest of the report will be organized as follows. Sect. 2 introduces some related work. Sect. 3 presents the architecture of web image retrieval and the technologies of its components: text-based image retrieval and visual content image retrieval. Sect. 4 describes different integration models of visual content-based and text-based. Sect. 5 compares their performances and Sect. 6 gives our conclusion.

2 Related Work

There are two basic approaches to support Web image retrieval, including TBIR and CBIR. TBIR creates text-based image indices using the associate texts of the Web images. And in general, a term's relevance to a Web image is based on its locations in the Web document. One of the early researches of TBIR was reported by Chua et al.[1] and Chang and Lee[11]. Sanderson and Dunlop[12] attempted at modeling the semantic of a Web image as a bag of words extracted from both the owner page of the image and the source pages which link to the owner page. Shen et al.[13] modeled surrounding texts, including image's title, image's caption, page's title and image's alt, into corresponding chainnets with different weights. However, it is hard to support fast access to the Web images.

On the other hand, CBIR is also attractive. It utilizes visual contents of images, such as color, texture and shape. Kato[14] was among the first to model visual contents of images. Shortly, John and Chang[5] provided image retrieval based on color set. More recently, Yanai[15] incorporated visual features such as color and region signatures to model visual contents of images. However, the performance of this method is low and inadequate. To address this problem, Aslandogan and Yu[16] relied on special features to look for human images on the web.

However, Both approaches are pros. and cons.. Therefore, some researches are based on the integration of TBIR and CBIR. Chen et al.[17] and Zhuang et al.[9] utilized expansion model with linear combination of the two approaches. But low precision of CBIR affects the performance.

3 The Technologies of Image Retrieval

Image retrieval includes two basic components, CBIR and TBIR. Its architecture is shown in Fig. 1. There are two basic technologies, including semantic

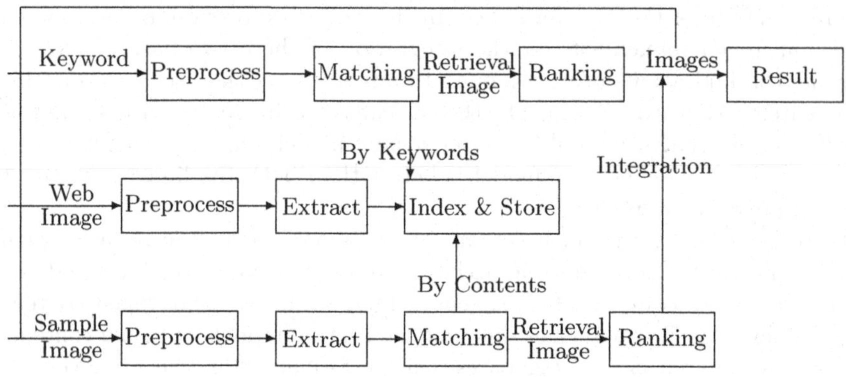

Fig. 1. The Architecture of the System

extractions and visual feature representations of Web images. In this section, we introduce those two technologies in our model.

3.1 Text-Based Image Retrieval

TBIR is to annotate Web images using their associate texts. Then, the techniques for traditional text retrieval can be employed for the Web image retrieval. In order to do so, it is time to determine what parts of the associate texts are used for the extraction and what are the impacts of different parts to the semantics of the images.

Semantic Source. To obtain semantic representation, semantic source (scope of the associated text) must be traced. Based on the relationship between the HTML documents and their containing web images, several parts of the text should be taken into account: image's title, image's alt, image's caption, page's title [2, 13] and other nearest surrounding texts[2]. There are also some other sources, such as HTML meta data. But these sources may provide false information, which is unrelated to the image and causes some confusion. At length, the five parts, including image's title(STT), image's alt(STA), image's caption(STC), page's title(STP) and nearest surrounding text(STS), fall into better choices.

Semantic Representation. There are several common models to represent the semantics of Web images, including term oriented representation model[2] and ChainNet model[13]. The term oriented model assumes each terms in the associate text are independent with each other and calculates terms' contributions to the images with respect to their locations in the text. That is, different words may have different weights according to the type of its semantic source text. A variable of TFIDF model[2] is used in our system for the calculation of the semantic relevances of terms t_k in any type of text blocks ST_l with respect to image i_j as follows:

$$ntf(t_k)|_{ST_l} = \frac{tf(t_k)|_{ST_l}}{|ST_l|} \quad (1)$$

In (1), $tf(t_k)|_{ST_l}$ is the frequency of term t in text block ST_l which is any of STT, STA, STC, STP or STS. $|ST_l|$ is the size of block ST_l. Thus, the total semantic relevance of term t_k for image i_j is defined as:

$$ttf(t_k)|_{i_j} = \sum_{k=1}^{L} w_l * ntf(t_k)|_{ST_l} \quad (2)$$

In (2), L is the total number of the text blocks extracted from the associate text of the image, and w_l is the weight of ST_l, which is defined according to how much that semantic text block contributes to the image i_j in semantics and $\sum_{k=1}^{L} w_l = 1$. The experiment in [2] shows this method provides satisfactory performance.

3.2 Visual Content-Based Image Retrieval

Besides TBIR, visual content-based model is popularly used in traditional image database search. For CBIR, there are several necessary components,including identifying the available visual content features, adopting effective feature representation, automatically extracting the visual features and choosing the discriminating function for the visual features. Now, visual contents include color, texture, objects' shape and spatial frequency, which can be the information of the whole images or the region after partitioning the whole image into several regions. Because segmentation of image is still an open research, the whole image's information is used in this paper.

Color Extraction. Color is the basic and most straight-forward characteristic of the image and most extensively used in CBIR. There are several important issues for color extraction, including appropriate color space and effective color representation. Generally, there are many different color spaces, such as RGB,

CMY, HSL. Among those spaces, HSL represents color by three variables: hue, lightness and saturation, and is more similar to human vision system principles. More importantly, HSL is its tractability, perceptually uniform, and possible and easy transformation from popular RGB space to HSL space.

There are several choices for color representation: color histogram, color coherence vector[22], color correlogram, color moments and color set[8]. Global color histogram is effective and easy to compute and robust to translation, rotation and scale. In global color histogram, each bin represents the number of pixels which has the same color. For an image, there may be plenty of bins which makes for a tremendous increase in the cost of computing the similarity of two images and also leads to inefficient index. Thus, it is necessary to preprocess images and quantization is an effective way.

Texture Extraction. Texture is an innate property of all surfaces and refers to visual patterns of homogeneity. It is discriminable and important structure of the image. There are three basic approaches to extract texture: spectral approaches, structural approaches and statistical approaches. In recent years, wavelet, as one of structural approaches, is popular used in image processing. Based on wavelet transform, the useful information is the statistics of coefficients in each frequency in wavelet transform processing, and mean and variance of the energy distribution of the coefficients for each frequency at each decomposition are used to construct the vector. This representation of texture vector is:

$$\overrightarrow{fvt} = \{\frac{\mu_{11}}{\delta_{\mu_{11}}}, \frac{\sigma_{11}}{\delta_{\sigma_{11}}}, \frac{\mu_{12}}{\delta_{\mu_{12}}}, \frac{\sigma_{12}}{\delta_{\sigma_{12}}}, \dots, \frac{\mu_{ij}}{\delta_{\mu_{ij}}}, \frac{\sigma_{ij}}{\delta_{\sigma_{ij}}}, \dots, \frac{\mu_{NM}}{\delta_{\sigma_{NM}}}, \frac{\sigma_{NM}}{\delta_{\sigma_{NM}}}\} \tag{3}$$

In (3), N is the level of the transform and M is the number of frequencies of each level, and that number is four denoting one approximation frequency and three detail frequencies. μ_{ij} and σ_{ij} is respectively the mean and variance of the frequency j in level i. $\delta_{\sigma_{ij}}$ and $\delta_{\mu_{ij}}$ are standard deviations of σ_{ij} and μ_{ij} respectively in the entire database.

Dissimilarity Functions. Jan Puzicha et al.[18] summarize dissimilarity functions and propose four categories, including heuristic histogram distances, non-parametric test distances, information-theoretic distances and ground distances. Among the functions of those kinds, Euclidean distance is the effective and common dissimilarity function. In fact, Euclidean distance is effective and easy to calculate. The calculation of Euclidean distance, for vector v_1 and v_2, whose form is $\{b_1, b_2 \dots, b_L\}$, is:

$$d = \sum_{l=1}^{L} (v_1.b_l - v_2.b_l)^2 \tag{4}$$

In (4), L is the dimensions of vector. In our methods, those two vectors can be color histogram vector and texture vector.

4 Integration Models of Visual Content-Based Image Retrieval and Text-Based Image Retrieval

In our prototype system, an image query can be q=(q_t, q_i), where q_t is the query description for TBIR and q_i is the sample images for CBIR. In the case of q_i=NULL(users do not provide), the query is TBIR. if q_t is NULL, it is CBIR. If users provide both q_t and q_i at the same time, that is the combined image retrieval, which has a common situation where after the retrieval with q=(q_t, NULL), q_i is selected from the result for CBIR. There, the structure of retrieval results for TBIR and CBIR are defined as follows:

$$\begin{aligned} RS_{\text{TBIR}} &= \{(i_1, R_1), (i_2, R_2) \ldots (i_j, R_j) \ldots (i_N, R_N)\} \\ RS_{\text{CBIR}} &= \{(i_1, S_1), (i_2, S_2) \ldots (i_j, S_j) \ldots (i_N, S_N)\} \end{aligned} \tag{5}$$

In 5, supposed the image collection $\{i_1, i_2 \ldots i_N\}$ has totally N images. RS_{TBIR} is the resultant set of TBIR, RS_{CBIR} is the resultant set of CBIR. Item (i_j, R_j) means the relevance between image i_j and some keyword is R_j, and item (i_j, S_j) means the similarity between image i_j and some sample image is S_j. Before integration, RS_{TBIR} can prune the images with R_j less than some threshold, generally, that value is 0 and we call the rest prune-RS_{TBIR}, and RS_{CBIR} also prune the image with S_j less than some threshold for the low performance of CBIR and we call the rest prune-RS_{CBIR}. Therefore, the integrated set may be composed of three parts, including common items which is in both prune-RS_{TBIR} and prune-RS_{CBIR}, TBIR-only items which is in prune-RS_{TBIR} but not in prune-RS_{CBIR}, and CBIR-only items which is in prune-RS_{CBIR} but not in prune-RS_{TBIR}. In our prototype system, the retrieval result set is $\{i_1, i_2 \ldots i_M\}$ with M images. If that set includes those three parts, that is, the integrated set is (RS_{TBIR}, RS_{CBIR}), and then ranks items again based on integrated relevance, that model is *expansion model.* If only common items and TBIR-only items is in that set, and prunes CBIR-only items, that is, the integrated set is still (RS_{TBIR}) but the sequence of their items may be changed based on integrated relevance, that model is *refinement model.* Each model can use different integrated method to obtain the integrated relevance, such as *linear method and multiplied method.* It is linear combined method, if the integrated relevance is produced by the formula $RS_{\text{new}} = \alpha * R_j + \beta * S_j$, where RS_{new} is new integrated relevance, and α and β are coefficients and α+β=1. Without more words, in that linear formula, S_j of TBIR-only items and R_j of CBIR-only items are 0. And if the formula, $RS_{\text{new}} = R_j * (1 + S_j)^{\gamma}$, where RS_{new} and γ is coefficient, is used to compute the integrated relevance, it is multiplied combined method. In that multiplied formula, the similarity S_j is added by 1 to avoid the relevance based on TBIR multiplied by zero for TBIR-only items. Therefore, there are three available models: linear expansion model, linear refinement model and multiplied refinement model.

Linear expansion model is reported by Chen et al.[17] and Zhuang et al.[9]. However, expansion model makes the same disposal for common items and others. As we know, the precision of those two parts varies greatly and more greatly in CBIR. However, that model treats TBIR and CBIR equally, that is, items with same value of their contribution in TBIR and CBIR is handled with same importance. In fact, CBIR often produces many irrelevant results because of the comprehensive semantics of Web images. In other words, even though an image is much similar to the sample image in visual features, it may have a far distance in semantics. To overcome the limitation, Guojun Lu and Ben Williams[10] provided the linear refinement model to integrate CBIR into TBIR. And different from the expansion model, CBIR-only items are pruned. Refinement model makes different disposal of common items and CBIR-only items. However, linear expansion model and linear refinement model make integration based on linear method, which is not sensitive to the co-support of retrieval sets of CBIR and TBIR. More importantly, linear method disregards the speciality for two image retrieval sets: the correlation between the terms and images which is more apparent in refinement.

In detail, in the refinement, image retrieval starts with the query q=(q_t, NULL), then users can refine their retrieval with visual features by sample Web images with the query q=(NULL,q_i). From this process, we know that the relevance of the keywords to some resultant image obtained by keywords is original, and more importantly, the refinement by CBIR means that under the situation some sample image is completely semantic to the keyword and other images possess different similarity between them and the sample image, what is the new relevance of the keywords to some resultant image. Without question, the correlation of keywords and images is implied and new relevance can be obtained by multiplying original relevance by the similarity of the sample image and other resultant images. That is the novel multiplied refinement model and that model overcomes the limitation of expansion model and linear method. To evaluate the performance of different models, the prototype system is implemented, which is similar to Fig. 1.

In the prototype system, TBIR extracts the associated text in STT, STA, STC, STP and STS, and calculates the relevance based on the variation of TFIDF model. In CBIR, color and texture are utilized. In detail, color histogram and statistic of the wavelet transform are used as the feature vectors. For color histogram, HSL color space is better choice and quantization method is used to get color histogram, that is, hue is divided into eighteen levels, saturation and lightness are divided into three levels respectively, and grey color is scaled into four levels. Therefore, the color vector is 166-dimension(18*3*3+4). For texture, Daubechies wavelet transform is used. As we know, four frequencies are obtained after one time wavelet transform: one is composed of approximation coefficients(LL) and three are composed of detail coefficients, including horizontal coefficients(LH), vertical coefficients(HL) and diagonal coefficients(HH). And wavelet transform can be continued further based on the data of those four frequencies. There are two popular methods for that continuing wavelet transform: pyramid-structured wavelet transform(PWT), which only decomposes LL, and tree-structured wavelet transform(TWT), in which all frequencies will be decomposed. For PWT, some information is lost and for TWT, the decomposition of

HH is unstable. Therefore, the composite method is to decompose the frequencies except HH in each level of the transform again. The mean and variance of each frequencies in each level are utilized as components of the feature vector. The prototype system makes use of wavelet transform four times and produces 320-dimension(2*4*(1+3+9+27)) texture vector.

5 Performance Evaluation

In our prototype system, more than 12000 web images from 50000 web pages are gathered after noise images, such as icons, banners, logos and any image with size less than 5k, removed. In the experiments, 20 terms with their 60 relevant images are used to obtain the optimal parameters and 10 terms with their 20 relevant images are used for testing. In the prototype system, the performance is evaluated by average precision (AP) objective in (6),

$$AP_{jk} = \frac{1}{R_{jk}} \sum_{k=1}^{R_{jk}} \frac{k}{N_k} \tag{6}$$

where R_{jk} is the number of relevant images in the result and N_k is the number of the results when there are up to k revelant results.

The first step is to determine the parameters for each integration. There are five parameters, two for linear expansion model, two for linear refinement model and one for our novel model. Based on the prototype system, Tables 1 can be obtained. Tables 1 are for linear expansion model, linear refinement model and multiplied refinement model. For the left table, the smaller the parameter, β, for the similarity of visual contents is, the better the integration's precision is, which is due to its low precision and single-independence of linear method, that

Table 1. Coefficients of Different Models

Linear Expansion Model

β	α	AP
0	1	0.428571
β:0-0.1 α:0.9-1	α:0.98	0.429175
	α:0.96	0.429375
	α:0.94	*0.430828*
	α:0.92	0.429134
0.1	0.9	0.428252
0.2	0.8	0.4003912
0.3	0.7	0.391616
0.4	0.6	0.380326
0.5	0.5	0.374529
0.6	0.4	0.323
0.7	0.3	0.290917
0.8	0.2	0.263213
0.9	0.1	0.197241

Linear Refinement Model

β	α	AP
0	1	0.428571
0.1	0.9	0.429186
0.2	0.8	0.429308
0.3	0.7	0.430311
0.4	0.6	0.432207
0.5	0.5	0.43651
β:0.5-0.6	α:0.44	0.437063
α:0.4-0.5	α:0.42	0.438132
0.6	*0.4*	*0.438*
β:0.6-0.7	α:0.38	0.438625
α:0.3-0.4	α:0.36	0.438209
0.7	0.3	0.434484
0.8	0.2	0.430433
0.9	0.1	0.435272

Multiplied Refinement Model

γ		AP
0		0.428571
1		0.436518
2		0.442337
3		0.443291
3 to 4	3.4	0.44434
	3.6	0.444258
	3.8	0.445431
4		0.447749
4 to 5	*4.2*	*0.448586*
	4.4	0.447794
	4.6	0.447237
5		0.446812
6		0.446704
7		0.445797

is, the images with larger value in each collection may be contribute more largely to resultant ranking than common items with smaller value in both collections. In our prototype system, better β is 0.06 for its maximum AP 0.430820. For the middle table, β for the similarity of visual contents is actually for common items for refinement model prunes CBIR-only items before. Therefore, better value of β is larger than that of linear expansion model. In our prototype system, better β is 0.6 for its maximum AP 0.438. From the comparison of linear expansion model and linear refinement model, the precision of common items and of CBIR-only items in CBIR vary largely through better value of β. For the right table, 4.2 for γ is optimal with maximum AP 0.448586.

The next experiment is to compare the performance of different models and the result in Fig. 2 can be obtained. Figure 2 shows that all models improve

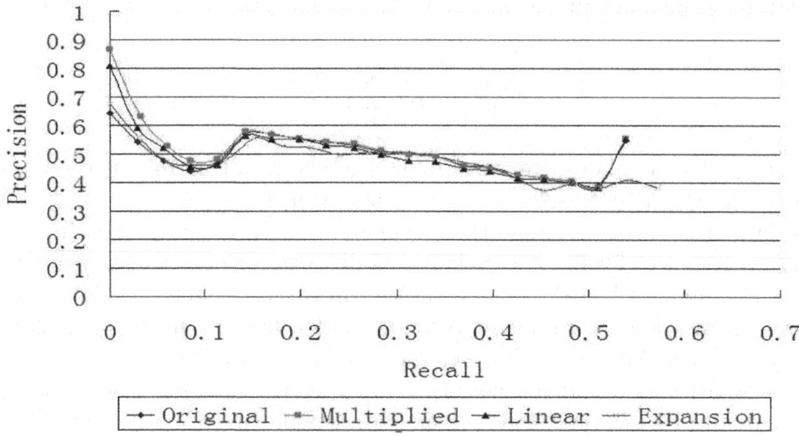

Fig. 2. Comparison between Different Models

the performance. In Fig. 2, original retrieval's AP is 0.428571, its maximum recall is 0,53856 and the AP before the recall with 0.113381 is 0.444375. Linear expansion model, at the beginning of the recall, gives a little improvement. Out of question, this model can obtain higher recall, 0.572158. In our prototype system, its AP is 0.430828, its maximum recall is 0.572158 and the AP before the recall with 0.113381 is 0.457954. The expansion model is more effective when TBIR has less recall. For each refinement, the maximum has no change. Therefore, it is more effective when TBIR has higher recall but less AP. In our prototype system, linear refinement model provides better improvement. Its AP is 0.439073 and the AP before the recall with 0.113381 is 0.525908. More importantly, multiplied refinement model provides best improvement. Its AP is 0.450086 and the AP before the recall with 0.113381 is 0.551451. From Fig. 2, the notable improvement cannot be shown. But the remarkable improvement is the beginning of the retrieval. As we know, users most focus on the first K items of each retrieval. Therefore, those items are most important and the improvement of those items is more interesting and useful. From our experiment, the APs of original retrieval, Linear expansion model, linear refinement model and multiplied refinement model before the recall with 0.113381 are 0.444375, 0.457954, 0.525908 and 0.551451, respectively. From those values, we know all model make satisfied improvement and the improvement of multiplied refinement model is the best.

To make clear comparison of different integration model , More statistics is provided in Table 2, where 'O', 'M', 'L' and 'E' represent original retrieval, the retrieval of multiplied refinement model, the retrieval of linear refinement model and the retrieval of linear expansion model, respectively. Table 2 shows

Table 2. Examples for Comparison between Different Models

Keyword	Top 16 Images				Top 48 Images				Top 96 Images			
	O	M	L	E	O	M	L	E	O	M	L	E
dv	8	12	9	9	37	36	36	36	46	49	48	51
notebook	8	11	10	10	19	25	24	19	26	34	21	24
game	5	9	7	7	30	40	37	36	56	55	53	41

that each integration model can produce better performance before the top 48 images. At the 100 images, the variation is small, even if some original result may be better because of the noise of the integration. Among those integration, our novel multiplied refinement model show best performance because it overcomes the limitation of expansion model and linear method.

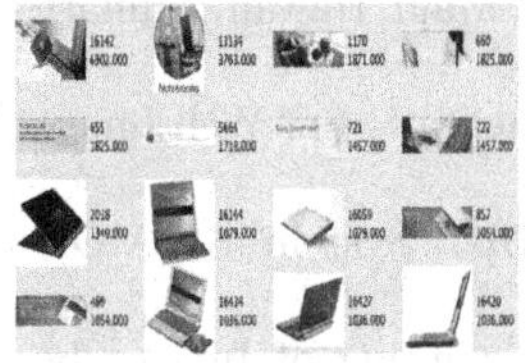

Fig. 3. Original Result of "Notebook"

Fig. 4. Original Result of "DV"

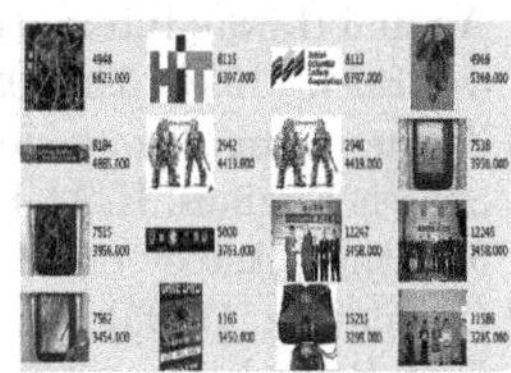

Fig. 5. Original Result of "Game"

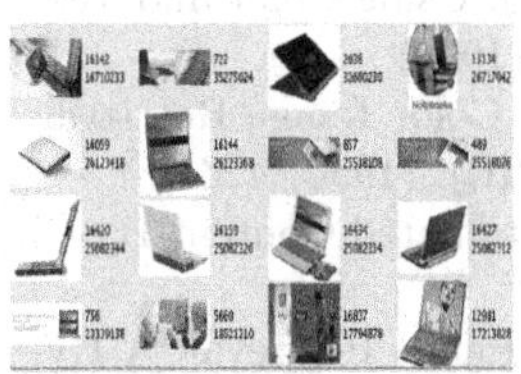

Fig. 6. Refined Result of "Notebook"

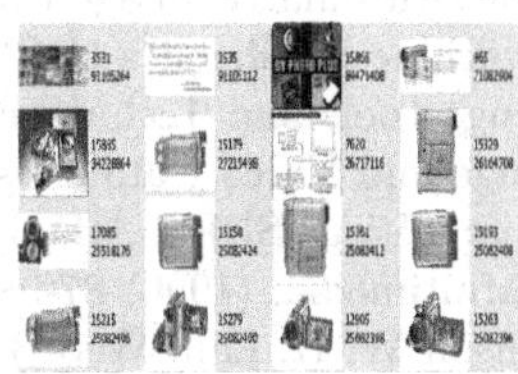

Fig. 7. Refined Result of "DV"

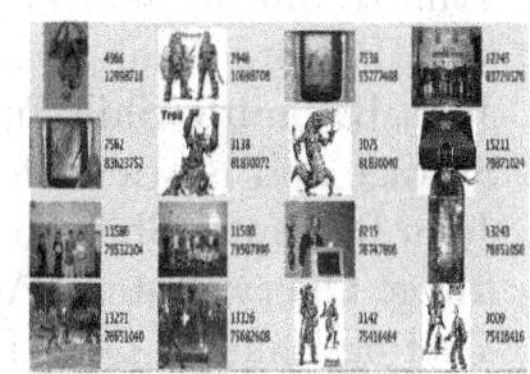

Fig. 8. Refined Result of "Game"

For the detail of the performance of multiplied refinement model, we give some examples where there are top 16 images of search results to show. The result of text-based retrieval of *notebook, dv and game* is respectively in Fig. 3, Fig. 4 and Fig. 5. In our novel refinement model, Fig. 6, Fig. 7 and Fig. 8 are obtained after refinement. Without more words, the refinement produces better performance. Take the images of "DV", there are 12 related images compared to 8 images before refinement.

6 Conclusion

Much attention [9, 10] has been devoted to Web image retrieval. And two basic approaches for image retrieval are TBIR and CBIR, which utilize the associated text and visual features, respectively. Each can be utilized independently but has its limitations. Therefore, different integration models are tried. Expansion model and refinement model are two common models, and multiplied method and linear method are two common methods. Therefore, the available models include linear expansion model, linear refinement model and multiplied refinement model. However, expansion model doesn't consider low precision of CBIR and linear method disregards the correlation of TBIR and CBIR. Therefore, this report has proposed a novel model—multiplied refinement model to integrate CBIR into TBIR to overcome those limitations and the performance is better than others.

References

1. Chua T. S et al: A Concept-based Image Retrieval System. Proceedings of 27th Annual Hawaii International Conference on System Science, Maui, Hawaii, January 4-7 1994. (1994) 590-598
2. Zhiguo Gong, Leong Hou U, Chan Wa Cheang: An Implementation of Web Image Search Engines. ICADL. (2004) 355-367
3. Jonathan Ashley et al: The Query By Image Content (QBIC) System. SIGMOD Conference. (1995) 475
4. Ediz Saykol, Ugur Güdükbay,Özgür Ulusoy: Integrated Querying of Images by Color, Shape, and Texture Content of Salient Objects. ADVIS. (2004) 363-371
5. John R. Smith, Shih-Fu Chang: Single Color Extraction and Image Query. ICIP-95. (1995)
6. John R. Smith, Shih-Fu Chang: Automated Image Retrieval Using Color and Texture. Pattern Analysis and Machine Intelligence (PAMI). (1996)
7. John R. Smith, Shih-Fu Chang: Tools and Techniques for Color Image Retrieval. Storage and Retrieval for Image and Video Databases (SPIE). (1996) 426-437
8. John R. Smith, Shih-Fu Chang: TVisualSEEk: A Fully Automated Content-Based Image Query System. ACM Multimedia. (1996) 87-98
9. Yueting Zhuang, Qing Li,Rynson W. H. Lau: Web-Based Image Retrieval: A Hybrid Approach. Computer Graphics International. (2001) 62-72
10. Guojun Lu, Ben Williams: An Integrated WWW Image Retrieval System. http://ausweb.scu.edu.au/aw99/papers/lu/paper.html. (1999)

11. C. C. Chang, S. Y. Lee: Retrieval of similar pictures on pictorial databases. Pattern Recogn. **24** (1991) 675–681
12. V. Harmandas, Mark Sanderson, Mark D. Dunlop: Image Retrieval by Hypertext Links. SIGIR. (1997) 296-303
13. Heng Tao Shen, Beng Chin Ooi, Kian-Lee Tan: Giving meanings to WWW images. MULTIMEDIA '00: Proceedings of the eighth ACM international conference on Multimedia. (2000) 39–47
14. Kato T: Database Architecture for Content-Based Image Retrieval. Proceedings of Society of the Photo-Optical Instrumentation Engineers: Image Storage and Retrieval, 1662. 1992. San Jose, California, USA, SPIE. (1992)
15. Keiji Yanai: Generic image classification using visual knowledge on the web. ACM Multimedia. (2003) 167-176
16. Y. Alp Aslandogan, Clement T. Yu: Multiple evidence combination in image retrieval: diogenes searches for people on the Web. SIGIR. (2000) 88-95
17. Zheng Chen et al: Web mining for Web image retrieval. JASIST. **52** (2001) 831-839
18. Jan Puzicha et al: Empirical Evaluation of Dissimilarity Measures for Color and Texture. ICCV. (1999) 1165-1172
19. Petra Nass: The Wavelet Transform. http://www.eso.org/projects/esomidas/doc/user/98NOV/volb/node308.html. (1999)
20. M. K. Mandal, T. Aboulnasr: Fast wavelet histogram techniques for image indexing. Comput. Vis. Image Underst. **75** (1999) 1077-3142
21. Wikipedia: HSL color space. http://en.wikipedia.org/wiki/HLS_color_space.
22. Greg Pass, Ramin Zabih, Justin Miller: Comparing Images Using Color. ACM Multimedia. (1996) 65-73

An Effective Approach for Hiding Sensitive Knowledge in Data Publishing

Zhihui Wang, Bing Liu, Wei Wang, Haofeng Zhou, and Baile Shi

Department of Computing and Information Technology,
Fudan University, Shanghai, China
{041021056, 031021057, weiwang1, haofzhou, bshi}@fudan.edu.cn

Abstract. Recent efforts have been made to address the problem of privacy preservation in data publishing. However, they mainly focus on preserving data privacy. In this paper, we address another aspect of privacy preservation in data publishing, where some of the knowledge implied by a dataset are regarded as private or sensitive information. In particular, we consider that the data are stored in a transaction database, and the knowledge is represented in the form of patterns. We present a data sanitization algorithm, called *SanDB*, for effectively protecting a set of sensitive patterns, meanwhile attempting to minimize the impact of data sanitization on the non-sensitive patterns. The experimental results show that *SanDB* can achieve significant improvement over the best approach presented in the literature.

1 Introduction

With the wide application of computer and the Internet, data publishing is easier than before. However, privacy concerns have limited the data publishing. Recent efforts have been made to address the problem of privacy preservation in data publishing. But they mainly focus on preserving data privacy, i.e., preventing the disclosure of raw data.

Some studies consider to limit the disclosure of raw data, meanwhile attempting to minimize the impact on knowledge minable from the published database. These studies maintain the data privacy by perturbing raw data with some kind of random noise. At the same time, they allow to reconstruct the data distribution at an aggregate level, and thus retain the accuracy of mining results [2, 9, 11]. Other studies [7, 8] aim at preventing from re-identification of individuals or entities when the published data contains sensitive information of individuals or entities. These studies mainly preserve the anonymity of individuals or entities by applying generalizations and suppressions on *quasi-identifiers* in raw data, before the data are published.

In this paper, we address another aspect of privacy preservation in data publishing. That is, we consider some of the knowledge implied by a dataset as sensitive information, instead of data themselves. These sensitive knowledge need be hidden before publishing the dataset. For example, consider a data owner publishes his data on the Internet. A malicious user may acquire the sensitive

J.X. Yu, M. Kitsuregawa, and H.V. Leong (Eds.): WAIM 2006, LNCS 4016, pp. 146–157, 2006.
© Springer-Verlag Berlin Heidelberg 2006

knowledge by mining the published data, while the data owners do not want to open those knowledge to the public.

In particular, we consider that the data are stored in a transaction database, and the knowledge is represented in the form of patterns. Some of the patterns contain sensitive information, which cannot be disclosed. We propose an effective approach, called *SanDB*, for protecting the sensitive patterns during data publishing. *SanDB* hides sensitive patterns by a procedure of data sanitization. We assign a threshold for each sensitive pattern, and let the data owner control the degree of sensitive pattern protection. At the same time, we attempt to minimize the impact on non-sensitive patterns in the published dataset. The experimental results show that our approach is much more effective than previous research.

The remainder of this paper is organized as follows. We introduce related work in Section 2, and define the problem of our research in Section 3. Then, we present a special data structure, called *Weak Pattern Tree* (or *WPTree* in short) in Section 4, and describe the details of our *SanDB* algorithm in Section 5. With the help of *WPTree*, *SanDB* can fast identify appropriate transactions and items, sanitize them from database, thus hide sensitive knowledge. Finally, we conclude our work in Section 7.

2 Related Work

Studies closely related to our work can be classified into two categories: sanitization-based approaches and obscurity-based approaches.

Sanitization-based approaches prevent the disclosure of sensitive rules through removing or adding data items in raw data. Data sanitization was first proposed by Atallah [3]. They proved that finding an optimal solution for data sanitization was NP-Hard by reducing the data sanitization problem to the hitting-set problem. Dasseni [4] addressed the problem of hiding association rules by sanitizing the data to modify the support and confidence of rules. Oliveira and Zaïane [10, 12] further proposed some better heuristics of data sanitization for protecting from the discovery of sensitive frequent itemsets. Their best algorithm is called *SWA*, which sanitizes a transaction database by removing items from transactions. These removed items have higher frequencies in the set of sensitive frequent itemsets.

Obscurity-based approaches were proposed by Saygin [5, 6]. Instead of removing or adding data items, obscurity-based approaches selectively replace the values of data items with unknowns to obscure the sensitive rules, thus to hide sensitive rules from the published data. The rationale underlying obscurity-base approaches is to increase the uncertainty of the supports and confidences of sensitive rules. However, obscurity-based approaches may have the risk of disclosing sensitive knowledge. A malicious attacker may reconstruct the raw data from the published data, then obtain sensitive rules by mining on the data reconstructed.

3 Problem Statement

3.1 Basic Concepts

Let $I = \{i_1, i_2, ..., i_n\}$ be a set of literals, called items. A transaction $T = (T_{id}, T_{items})$, where T_{id} is the unique identifier associated with the transaction T, and T_{items} is a set of items from I, i.e., $T_{items} \subseteq I$. A transaction database D is a set of transactions.

An *itemset* X is a subset of items I, $X \subseteq I$. If there are k items in X, we say that the length of itemset X is k, or X is a *k-itemset*. A transaction T contains itemset X if and only if $X \subseteq T_{items}$. The *support* of itemset X is the percentage of transactions in database D that contain X, denoted $SUPP_X$. For facility, we write an itemset $p = \{i_1, i_2, \cdots, i_n\}$ in the form of $p = i_1 i_2 \cdots i_n$. Particularly, an itemset is also called *pattern* in this paper.

3.2 The Problem

We consider some of the knowledge implied by a dataset as sensitive information in this paper. These sensitive knowledge need be hidden before publishing the dataset. At the same time, there are some important non-sensitive knowledge we may want to release in the published dataset.

Particularly, we consider the data are stored in a transaction database, and the knowledge is represented in the form of patterns. Our problem is stated as follows. Let D be a transaction database, P_S and P_K are two sets of patterns in D. When publishing D, we need hide P_S and release P_K. Specifically, we transform D to D' by data sanitization, and release database D', meanwhile attempting to minimize the impact on $SUPP_q(q \in P_K)$.

For each $p \in P_S$, we provide a threshold σ_p, which is controlled by the data owner. Let $SUPP_p$ and $SUPP'_p$ be p's support in D and D', respectively. When $SUPP'_p \leq (\sigma_p \times SUPP_p)$, we say p is hidden from D'. The threshold σ_p expresses the degree of sensitive knowledge hiding. When $\sigma_p = 0\%$, the pattern p is completely hidden from D'. When $\sigma_p = 100\%$, p is not any longer required to be hidden.

For facilitating our discussion, we call P_S *sensitive pattern set*, P_K *released pattern set*, and σ_p *disclosure threshold of pattern* p. We assume that P_S, P_K and σ_p are identified by domain experts, according to the requirements of specific applications. Furthermore, we assume that P_S and P_K are disjoint. That is, $\nexists p, p \in (P_S \cap P_K)$.

We focus on a special form of data sanitization in this paper. That is, we get the published database D' by removing some items from transactions in D. Intuitively, for hiding $\forall p \in P_S$, we only need consider the transactions containing p (called *sensitive transactions*), and remove from them the items also contained in p (called *sensitive items*). We give the formal definitions of *sensitive transactions* and *sensitive items* below.

Definition 1 (Sensitive transaction). *Let T be a transaction in D. If $p \in P_S$ and $p \subseteq T_{items}$, then T is a sensitive transaction of p. The set of p's all sensitive* *transactions is called sensitive transaction set of* p*, denoted* TS_p*. The size of* TS_p *is* $SUPP_p$*.*

Definition 2 (Sensitive item). *Let* $p \in P_S$*, and* $T \in TS_p$*. For item* $s \in p$*, if* $s \in T_{items}$*, then* s *is a sensitive item of* p *in* T*.*

The goal of our research is to hide $\forall p \in P_S$, meanwhile attempting to minimize the impact on $SUPP_q (q \in P_K)$ after data sanitization. Therefore, it is important to identify appropriate sensitive transactions, and remove appropriate sensitive items from them. We show this with an example given below.

Example 1. In Fig. 1, we have a transaction database D shown at the left hand, P_S and P_K at the right hand. Let $p_1 = bc, p_2 = be$, and $\sigma_{p_1} = \sigma_{p_2} = 50\%$. The sensitive transaction sets of p_1 and p_2 are $\{T_6, T_8\}$ and $\{T_5, T_8\}$, respectively. A good choice is to remove item b from T_8. That hides both p_1 and p_2, and there is no impact on $SUPP_q$, where $q \in P_K$.

T_{id}	T_{items}
T_1	a f g
T_2	e f g
T_3	a c e f g
T_4	a b d
T_5	b d e
T_6	a b c
T_7	d e f g
T_8	b c e

$$P_S = \{bc, be\}$$
$$P_K = \{ab, ac, af, ag, bd, ce, de, ef, eg, fg, afg, efg\}$$

Fig. 1. An Example of Data Sanitization

Before giving the details of our approach, we first introduce a special data structure, called *Weak Pattern Tree*, or *WPTree* in short. We use it to organize the patterns, and thus fast identify appropriate sensitive transactions and items.

4 Weak Pattern Tree

4.1 Definition

Given a transaction database D, our approach hides a sensitive pattern by removing its sensitive items from the transactions in D. For example, let $p = xy$ be a sensitive pattern. We hide p by removing item x or y from p's sensitive transactions in D. An observation is that except for p, only the supports of the patterns containing x or y may be affected. We call them *weak patterns.* The formal definition of *weak pattern* is given below.

Definition 3 (Weak pattern). *Let* p *be a pattern in* D*. If* $\exists p' \in P_S$ *and* $p \cap p' \neq \emptyset$*, we say that* p *is a weak pattern.*

Theorem 1. *Given sensitive pattern set P_S, database D is sanitized by removing sensitive items of $p \in P_S$. Let D' be the result database, $SUPP_p$ and $SUPP'_p$ be p's support in D and D' respectively. If p is not a weak pattern, then $SUPP_p = SUPP'_p$.*

Proof. Since p is not a weak pattern, then $\forall p' \in P_S, p \cap p' = \emptyset$. Therefore, p does not contain any sensitive item. The data sanitization considered only removes sensitive items from D. Thus, $SUPP_p = SUPP'_p$. □

According to Theorem 1, we only need consider weak patterns when sanitizing D. For $q \in P_K$, if q is not a weak pattern, we filter it from P_K. Notice that $\forall p \in P_S$ is a weak pattern. Furthermore, we can determine a set of weak patterns just according to P_S. We use a data structure, called *weak pattern tree*, to organize the weak patterns. The definition of *weak pattern tree* is given below.

For facility, we order the set of items I ascendingly, denoted I_O. $\forall i, j \in I_O, i \prec j$ if and only if (1) i is a sensitive item, and j is not; or (2) Both i and j are sensitive or non-sensitive items, and $i \prec j$ in ascending lexicographic order.

Definition 4 (Weak Pattern Tree (WPTree)). *Each node in a WPTree is labelled by an item. The root of a WPTree is labelled by a special item $\varnothing$. The children of a WPTree node are sorted in the order of I_O. Each WPTree node N represents a weak pattern p_N, where items are in the order of I_O. The weak pattern p_N can be obtained by concatenating the label items of nodes along the path from root to node N (except for item $\varnothing$).*

Definition 5 (S-node, R-node). *Let N be a WPTree node. If the path from root to node N represents a sensitive pattern, we say that node N is a sensitive node, or S-node in short. Similarly, if the path from root to node N represents a released pattern, we say that node N is a released node, or R-node in short.*

WPTree has some nice properties, which can help us to prune the tree during traversing a WPTree. We give the properties below, and describe how to prune a WPTree during tree traverse in Section 5.2.

Property 1. Let N_i be a WPTree node (labelled by item i). If a WPTree node N_j (labelled by item j) is a descendant of N_i, then $i \prec j$.

Property 2. Let N_i be a WPTree node (labelled by item i). If a WPTree node N_j (labelled by item j) has the same parent as N_i, and N_j is one of the right siblings of N_i, then $i \prec j$.

For facilitating the traverse of WPTree, we augment each node with *parent-link*. The parent-link of a node points to its parent. With parent-link, we can easily get the weak pattern represented by a WPTree node. If a WPTree node is labelled by a sensitive item, we also argument it with *node-link*.The node-link points to next node labelled by the same sensitive item. For a WPTree, we keep a header table of node-links, denoted $HLink$. Each entry of the header table has two fields: a sensitive item, and a node-link to the first WPTree node labelled by that item. For an item i, its entry in the header table is denoted as $HLink_i$.

4.2 Constructing Weak Pattern Tree

Given sensitive pattern set P_S and released pattern set P_K, the algorithm for constructing weak pattern tree is shown in Fig. 2.

Algorithm: Construct_WPTree
Input: sensitive pattern set P_S, released pattern set P_K
Output: WPTree rooted at N_R, and its node-links' head table $HLink$

```
filter non-weak patterns from P_K;
construct root node N_R, labelled by ∅;
construct HLink with an entry for each sensitive item;
N = N_R;
FOR each p = (i_1, i_2, ··· , i_n) ∈ (P_S ∪ P_K) DO
    sort items in p in the order of I_O;
    FOR i = i_1 TO i_n DO
        IF ∃ node N's child N_i, labelled by item i THEN N = N_i;
        ELSE
            create a new node N'_i, labelled by item i;
            let N'_i be a child of N;
            IF i is a sensitive item THEN add N'_i into HLink_i;
            N = N'_i;
        ENDIF
    ENDFOR
    IF p ∈ P_S THEN N is a S-node;
    IF p ∈ P_K THEN N is a R-node;
ENDFOR
```

Fig. 2. Algorithm for Constructing WPTree

In algorithm *Construct_WPTree*, we first filter non-weak patterns from P_K, since they are not impacted by our data sanitization. Then, we initialize the WPTree by constructing a root node labelled by $\varnothing$, and an empty head table of node-links. The patterns $p = (i_1, i_2, \cdots, i_n) \in (P_S \cup P_K)$ are added into WPTree one by one. For an item $i \in p$, if we cannot find its corresponding WPTree node, we then create a new node N'_i, and add N'_i as a child of the current WPTree node. If item i is a sensitive item, we also insert N'_i into the node-link $HLink_i$. Finally, if $p \in P_S$ (or $p \in P_K$), the WPTree node corresponding to item i_n is a S-node (or R-node).

Example 2. Continue with Example 1. Consider the database D, sensitive pattern set P_S and released pattern set P_K in Fig. 1. The weak pattern set is $\{ab, ac, bc, bd, be, ce, de, ef, eg, efg\}$, and $I_O = (b, c, e, a, d, f, g)$ in ascending order. Its weak pattern tree is shown in Fig. 3. The black nodes in the tree are S-nodes, and the square nodes are R-nodes.

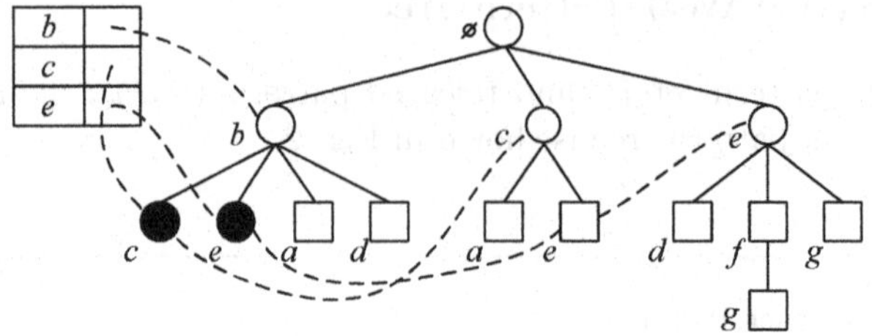

Fig. 3. Weak Pattern Tree with Node-Links

5 The Sanitization Algorithm

For hiding $\forall p \in P_S$, we first find its sensitive transaction set TS_p, then remove appropriate sensitive items from transactions in TS_p, thus decrease $SUPP_p$ below disclosure threshold σ_p. The key steps of our algorithm are described below.

5.1 Finding Sensitive Transaction Set

Given a transaction database D with a finite set of items $I = \{i_1, i_2, \cdots, i_n\}$, we read each transaction from D, and represent it in the form of n-dimensional vector. Suppose there are m transactions in D, then D can be represented in a $m \times n$ matrix, denoted Mat_D. If an item i_j appears in a transaction T_k, then $Mat_D[k, j] = 1$. Otherwise, $Mat_D[k, j] = 0$. For example, for the transaction database in Fig. 1, its matrix representation is shown in Fig. 4.

	a	b	c	d	e	f	g
T_1	1	0	0	0	0	1	1
T_2	0	0	0	0	1	1	1
T_3	1	0	1	0	0	1	1
T_4	1	1	0	1	0	0	0
T_5	0	1	0	1	1	0	0
T_6	1	1	1	0	0	0	0
T_7	0	0	0	1	1	1	1
T_8	0	1	1	0	1	0	0

Fig. 4. The Matrix Representation of Transaction Database

The matrix representation of transaction database can facilitate us to find the sensitive transaction set of a pattern $p \in P_S$. Consider a sensitive pattern $p = (i_j, i_{j+1}, \cdots, i_k)$, its sensitive transactions can be obtained by intersecting together the column vectors $V_j, V_{j+1}, \cdots, V_k$ corresponding to items $i_j, i_{j+1}, \cdots, i_k$. In the result vector V_R, if $\exists l, V_R[l] = 1$, then T_l is a sensitive transaction of p. Thus, the sensitive transaction set of p is $TS_p = \{T_l | V_R[l] = 1\}$.

5.2 Identifying Victim Item

When the length of a sensitive pattern p is larger than one, there are more than one sensitive items in transaction $T \in TS_p$. For sanitizing T, it is enough to remove only one of the sensitive items from T. We call that item *victim item*.

In order to identify victim item, we assign a score for each sensitive item of p in T. The definition of *item score* is given below.

Definition 6 (Gain, Loss, and Item score). *Let $p \in P_S$, and $T \in TS_p$. For a sensitive item i of p in T, its gain is the size of $S_i = \{p_1 | p_1 \in P_S, p_1 \subseteq T_{items}, \text{and } i \in p_1\}$, denoted $G_i = |S_i|$; its loss is the size of $S'_i = \{p_2 | p_2 \in P_K, p_2 \subseteq T_{items}, \text{and } i \in p_2\}$, denoted $L_i = |S'_i|$. The score of item i is $Score_i = G_i/(L_i + 1)$. The sensitive item with the highest score is T's victim item for p.*

Algorithm: Identify_VItem
Input: WPTree (rooted at N_R) with head table $HLink$, sensitive pattern p, transaction $T(T \in TS_p, T_{items} = (i_1, \cdots, i_n)$ sorted in order of I_O)
Output: victim item i_v, and its score $Score_v$

```
i_v = ∅; Score_v = 0;
FOR i_m = i_1 to i_n DO
    IF i_m is a sensitive item of p THEN
        G_m = L_m = 0;
        N_m = HLink_m's first node;
        WHILE N_m ≠ NULL DO
            get pattern p_m represented by node N_m;
            IF p_m ⊆ T_items THEN call Calc_GainLoss(N_m, T, G_m, L_m);
            N_m = HLink_m's next node;
        ENDWHILE
        calculate item i_m's Score_m = G_m/(L_m + 1);
        IF Score_v < Score_m THEN i_v = i_m; Score_v = Score_m;
    ENDIF
ENDFOR
```

Fig. 5. Algorithm for Identifying Victim Item

The algorithm for identifying victim item is shown in Fig. 5. Given sensitive pattern p, and $T \in TS_p$ sorted in the order of I_O, algorithm *Identify_VItem* calculates the score of each sensitive item in T, and chooses the one with the highest score as T's victim item for p. For a sensitive item i_m, we locate WPTree node N_m labelled by i_m with node-link $HLink_m$, and use the parent-link to get the pattern p_m represented by N_m. If $p_m \subseteq T_{items}$, we then calculate i_m's gain and loss by calling algorithm *Calc_GainLoss*, which is shown in Fig. 6.

In algorithm *Calc_GainLoss*, if N_m is a S-node, we increase the gain by one. Otherwise, if N_m is a R-node, we increase the loss by one. Then, we recursively traverse the sub-WPTree rooted at node N_m, and accumulate the values of gain and loss. When traversing the WPTree, we do tree pruning according to

```
Algorithm: Calc_GainLoss
Input:   WPTree node N_m(labelled by item i_m),
         transaction T(T_items = (i_1, ··· , i_n) sorted in order of I_O)
Output: gain G, loss L (G and L are passed by reference)
1:   IF i_m ∈ T_items THEN
2:      IF N_m is a S-node THEN G = G + 1;
3:      IF N_m is a R-node THEN L = L + 1;
4:      IF i_m = i_n THEN RETURN;
5:      N_s = N_m's first child; (N_s labelled by item i_s)
6:      WHILE (N_s ≠ NULL) AND (i_s ⪯ i_n) DO
7:         Calc_GainLoss(N_s, T, G, L);
8:         N_s = N_m's next child;
9:      ENDWHILE
10:  ENDIF
```

Fig. 6. Algorithm for Calculation of Gain and Loss

WPTree's properties in Section 4. At line 4 of algorithm *Calc_GainLoss*, we prune a WPTree node's children according to Property 1. At line 6, we prune a WPTree node's right siblings according to Property 2.

5.3 The SanDB Algorithm

For hiding a pattern $p \in P_S$, it is often unnecessary to sanitize all the transactions in TS_p. Given disclosure threshold σ_p, we just need meet $SUPP'_p \leq (\sigma_p \times SUPP_p)$, where $SUPP_p$ and $SUPP'_p$ are p's support in D and D', respectively. Sanitizing more transactions may have greater impact on the support of $q \in P_K$.

Particularly, we select transactions from TS_p according to *transaction score*, and remove the corresponding victim item in a chosen transaction. The definition of *transaction score* is given below.

Definition 7 (Transaction score). *Let $p \in P_S$, $T \in TS_p$, and i_v be T's victim item for p. The score of transaction T is the score of item i_v, that is, $Score_T = Score_v$.*

In practice, a database may have so many transactions that the whole database cannot be held in memory. Therefore, our algorithm reads k transactions each time. We call k *transaction buffer size*. The details of our *SanDB* Algorithm is shown in Fig. 7.

SanDB first constructs a WPTree according to P_S and P_K, then reads k transactions from D each time, and represents the k transactions in a matrix. For each pattern $p \in P_S$, we find its current sensitive transaction set TS_p^k in the k transactions, and calculate the victim item and the score for each transaction $T \in TS_p^k$. Notice that even for a same pattern p, different transactions in TS_p^k may have different victim items. We then sanitize $(1 - \sigma_p) \times |TS_p^k|$ transactions from TS_p^k in the descending order of transaction score. Finally, we write the k transactions into D'.

Algorithm: SanDB

Input: transaction database D, sensitive pattern set P_S, disclosure threshold σ_p for $p \in P_S$, released pattern set P_K

Output: published database D'

call Construct_WPTree(P_S, P_K), get WPTree rooted at N_R;

FOR each k transactions in D DO

  read them from D, and represent in a matrix;

  FOR each $p \in P_S$ DO

    find p's current sensitive transaction set TS_p^k;

    FOR each transaction $T \in TS_p^k$ DO

      sort T_{items} in the order of I_O;

      call Identify_VItem(N_R, p, T), get T's victim item i_v;

      $Score_T = Score_v$;

    ENDFOR

    sort TS_p^k in the descending order of transaction score;

    FOR $i = 1$ to $(1 - \sigma_p) \times |TS_p^k|$ DO

      remove victim item from the i-th transaction T_i of TS_p^k;

    ENDFOR

  ENDFOR

  write the k transactions into D';

ENDFOR

Fig. 7. Algorithm for Database Sanitization

6 Experimental Results

In this section, we evaluate the performance of our algorithm *SanDB*, and compare it with *SWA*. Because as reported in [10], *SWA* is better than other algorithms in previous related work. *SWA* chooses an item with higher frequency in sensitive patterns as victim, and sanitizes sensitive transactions in ascending order of transaction size. All the experiments are performed on a 733MHz Intel Pentium III PC with 512MB main memory, running Red Hat Linux 9.0.

We use a synthetic dataset, T40I10D100K, which is generated by IBM data generator. The generation procedure is described in [1]. In the synthetic dataset, there are 1000 different items, and $100K$ transactions. The average size of transactions is 40 items. We choose 10 patterns from T40I10D100K as sensitive pattern set P_S, and measure the effectiveness of algorithms by varying transaction buffer size k, disclosure threshold σ_p, and the size of released pattern set P_K. We choose P_K by applying *Apriori* [1] on T40I10D100K with some minimum support threshold τ, and $\forall p \in (P_S \cap P_K)$ is removed from P_K.

The effectiveness of algorithm is measured as follows. We first use *SanDB* or *SWA* to transform the synthetic dataset into the published database D'. Then, we mine on D' by *Apriori* with the same τ as the one for generating P_K. The mined result is denoted P'_K, and $\forall p \in P_S \cap P'_K$ is removed from P'_K. We measure algorithm's effectiveness with the metric $PattLoss = |\{p | p \in P_K, p \notin P'_K\}|$,

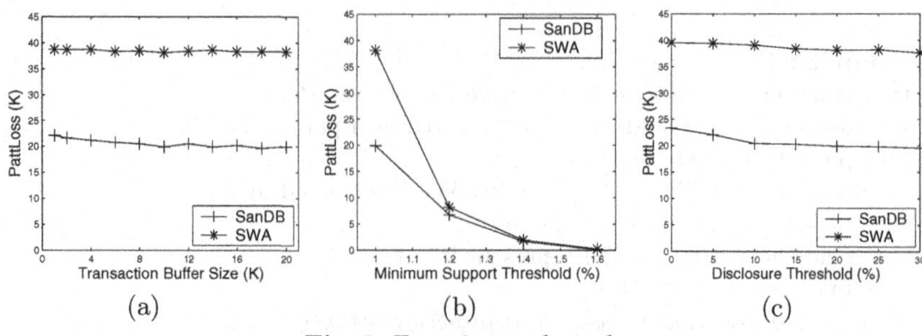

(a) (b) (c)

Fig. 8. Experimental results

i.e., the number of patterns in P_K but not in P'_K. An algorithm with smaller *PattLoss* is more effective.

In the first set of experiments, we measure the effectiveness of *SanDB* and *SWA* with different transaction buffer size k. We fix disclosure threshold $\sigma_p = 20\%$ for each $p \in P_S$. The released pattern set P_K is generated by applying *Apriori* on T40I10D100K with minimum support threshold $\tau = 1\%$. There are 65236 patterns in P_K. We vary transaction buffer size from 1000 to 20000, and measure *PattLoss* for *SanDB* and *SWA*, respectively. The results are shown in Fig. 8(a). As it can be seen, the *PattLoss* of *SanDB* is roughly half of that of *SWA* in various settings of transaction buffer size.

In Fig. 8(b), we report the experimental results when varying the size of released pattern set. The disclosure threshold is fixed as $\sigma_p = 20\%$ for each $p \in P_S$. The transaction buffer size $k = 10000$. We generate different sizes of released pattern sets by applying *Apriori* on T40I10D100K with different τ. Specifically, we set $\tau = 1\%, 1.2\%, 1.4\%, 1.6\%$, and the corresponding sizes of released pattern sets are $65236, 19412, 8293, 4591$, respectively. As the size of released pattern set decreases, the *PattLoss* is reduced for both *SanDB* and *SWA*. However, for a large released pattern set, the performance of *SanDB* is much better than that of *SWA*.

The effect of disclosure threshold on *PattLoss* is shown in Fig. 8(c). In this set of experiments, we fix the transaction buffer size $k = 10000$. The released pattern set P_K is generated by applying *Apriori* with $\tau = 1\%$. The size of P_K is 65236, fixed in this set of experiments. We let all $p \in P_S$ have a same disclosure threshold σ_p, but vary the value of σ_p from 0% to 30% in different experiments. A smaller disclosure threshold means higher degree of sensitive knowledge protection. That is, more sensitive transactions need be sanitized. Particularly, for sensitive pattern p with $\sigma_p = 0\%$, p will be completely hidden from the published dataset. The experimental results in Fig. 8(c) show that the *PattLoss* of *SanDB* is dramatically less than that of *SWA* for each settings of disclosure threshold.

7 Conclusion

In this paper, we address the problem of privacy preservation in data publishing, where some of the knowledge implied by a dataset are regarded as private or sensitive information. In particular, we consider that the data are stored in a transaction database, and the knowledge is represented in the form of patterns. We have presented an effective data sanitization algorithm, called *SanDB*, for hiding a set of sensitive patterns, meanwhile attempting to minimize the impact on the released patterns in data publishing. The experimental results have shown that *SanDB* can achieve significant improvement over the best approach presented in the literature.

References

1. Rakesh Agrawal, Ramakrishnan Srikant: Fast Algorithms for Mining Association Rules in Large Databases. VLDB 1994: 487-499
2. Shariq Rizvi, Jayant R. Haritsa: Maintaining Data Privacy in Association Rule Mining. VLDB 2002: 682-693
3. M. Atallah, E. Bertino, A. Elmagarmid, M. Ibrahim, V. Verykios: Disclosure Limitation of Sensitive Rules. KDEX 1999: 45-52
4. Elena Dasseni, Vassilios S. Verykios, Ahmed K. Elmagarmid, Elisa Bertino: Hiding Association Rules by Using Confidence and Support. Information Hiding 2001: 369-383
5. Yücel Saygin, Vassilios S. Verykios, Chris Clifton: Using Unknowns to Prevent Discovery of Association Rules. SIGMOD Record 30(4): 45-54 (2001)
6. Yücel Saygin, Vassilios S. Verykios, Ahmed K. Elmagarmid: Privacy Preserving Association Rule Mining. RIDE 2002: 151-158
7. Gagan Aggarwal, Tomás Feder, Krishnaram Kenthapadi, Rajeev Motwani, Rina Panigrahy, Dilys Thomas, An Zhu: Anonymizing Tables. ICDT 2005: 246-258
8. Kristen LeFevre, David J. DeWitt, Raghu Ramakrishnan: Incognito: Efficient Full-Domain K-Anonymity. SIGMOD Conference 2005: 49-60
9. Shipra Agrawal, Jayant R. Haritsa: A Framework for High-Accuracy Privacy-Preserving Mining. ICDE 2005: 193-204
10. Stanley R. M. Oliveira, Osmar R. Zaïane: Protecting Sensitive Knowledge By Data Sanitization. ICDM 2003: 613-616
11. Rakesh Agrawal, Ramakrishnan Srikant: Privacy-Preserving Data Mining. SIGMOD Conference 2000: 439-450
12. Stanley R. M. Oliveira, Osmar R. Zaïane: Privacy Preserving Frequent Itemset Mining. IEEE ICDM Workshop on Privacy, Security and Data Mining, 2002

Tracking Network-Constrained Moving Objects with Group Updates

Jidong Chen, Xiaofeng Meng, Benzhao Li, and Caifeng Lai

School of Information, Renmin University of China,
Beijing, 100872, China
{chenjd, xfmeng, bzli, laicf}@ruc.edu.cn

Abstract. Advances in wireless sensors and position technologies such as GPS enable location-based services that rely on the tracking of continuously changing positions of moving objects. The key issue in tracking techniques is how to minimize the number of updates, while providing accurate locations for query results. In this paper, for tracking network-constrained moving objects, we first propose a simulation-based prediction model with more accurate location prediction for objects movements in a traffic road network, which lowers the update frequency and assures the location precision. Then, according to their predicted future functions, objects are grouped and only the central object in each group reports its location to the server. The group update strategy further reduces the total number of objects reporting their locations. A simulation study has been conducted and proved that the group update policy based on the simulation prediction is superior to traditional update policies with fewer updates and higher location precision.

1 Introduction

The continued advances in wireless sensors and position technologies such as GPS enable new data management applications such as traffic management and location-based services that monitor continuously changing positions of moving objects [2, 7]. In these applications, large amounts locations can be sampled by sensors or GPS periodically, then sent from moving clients to the server and stored in a database. Therefore, continuously maintaining in a database current locations of moving objects namely tracking technique becomes a fundamental component of these applications [1, 2, 9, 10]. The key issue is how to minimize the number of updates, while providing precise locations for query results.

The number of updates from moving objects to the server database depends on both the update frequency and the number of objects to be updated. To reduce the location updates, most existing works are proposed to lower the update frequency by a prediction method [1, 9, 10]. They usually use the linear prediction which represents objects locations as linear functions of time. The objects do not report their locations to the server unless their actual positions exceed the predicted positions to a certain threshold. This provides a general principle for the location update policies in a moving object database system.

J.X. Yu, M. Kitsuregawa, and H.V. Leong (Eds.): WAIM 2006, LNCS 4016, pp. 158–169, 2006.
© Springer-Verlag Berlin Heidelberg 2006

However, few research works focus on improving the update performance from the aspect of reducing the number of objects to be updated. We observe that in many applications, objects naturally move in clusters, including vehicles in a congested road network, packed goods transmitted in a batch, animal and bird migrations. It is possible that the nearby objects are grouped and only one object in the group reports its location to the server to represent all objects within it. Considering real life applications, we focus on objects moving on a road network. Figure 1 gives an example of grouping vehicles on a part of road network. Due to the grouping of vehicles in each road segment, the total location updates sent to the server are reduced from 9 to 5.

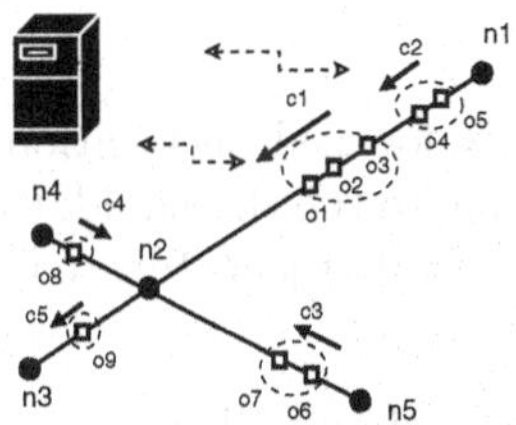

Fig. 1. Group location updates

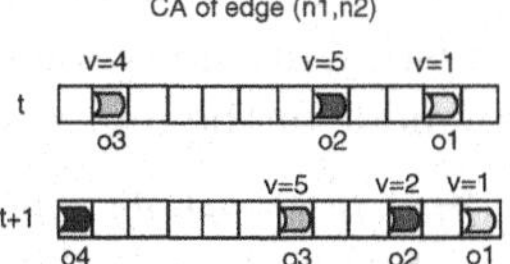

Fig. 2. A transition of the CA on an edge

The idea of grouping objects for location updates is similar to the GBL proposed in [6], but the GBL groups objects by their current locations and predicted locations after a time parameter τ. In fact, it obtains the predicted locations also by the linear prediction model assuming the linear movement with current velocity. However, in the urban road network, due to complex traffic conditions, cars may update their velocities frequently even for each timestamp. In this case, the linear prediction used in the GBL and other location update methods is inapplicable because the inaccurate predicted locations result in frequent location updates and lots of group management. In this paper, for the purpose of improving the performance of tracking for network-constrained moving objects, we focus on the both two factors affecting location updates and propose our solutions. One is a better prediction model to lower update frequency, and the other is a group update strategy to reduce the total number of objects reporting their locations. The accurate prediction model also reduces the maintenance of the groups and assures the location precision for querying.

Therefore, we first propose a simulation-based prediction (SP) model which captures traffic features in constrained networks. Specifically, we model road networks by graphs of cellular automata, which are also used to simulate vehicles future trajectories in discrete points in accordance with the surrounding traffic conditions. To refine the accuracy, we simulate two future trajectories to obtain the predicted movement function, which correspond to the fastest and slowest possible movements. We then propose a group location update strategy based on the SP model (GSP) to minimize location updates. In the GSP, for each edge in the road network, the objects with their predicted movement functions similar are grouped or clustered and only the object nearest to its group center needs to report the location of the whole group. Within a certain precision, the locations of other objects can be approximated to their group location. Finally, through the experimental evaluations, we show that the GSP strategy has more efficient update performance as well as higher location precision.

The rest of the paper is organized as follows. Section 2 surveys related work by classifying the existing tracking techniques. In Section 3, a road network modeled as a graph of cellular automata is represented and our simulation-based prediction model is proposed. Section 4 describes our group update strategy. Section 5 contains an experimental analysis, and finally Section 6 concludes.

2 Related Work

Research on tracking of moving objects has mainly focused on location update policies. Existing methods can be classified according to the threshold, the route, the update mode or the representation and prediction of objects future positions.

Updates differ in threshold and route
Wolfson et al.[9] first proposed the dead-reckoning update policies to reduce the update cost. According to the threshold, they are divided into three policies, namely the Speed Dead Reckoning (SDR) having a fixed threshold for all location updates, the Adaptive Dead Reckoning (ADR) having different thresholds to different location updates and the Disconnection Detection Reckoning (DTDR) having the continuously decreasing threshold since last location update. The policies also assume that the destination and motion plan of the moving objects is known a priori. In other words, the route is fixed and known. In [4], Gowrisankar and Nittel propose a dead-reckoning policy that uses angular and linear deviations. They also assume that moving objects travel on predefined routes. Lam et al. propose two location update mechanisms for further considering the effect of the continuous query results on the threshold [7]. The idea is that the moving objects covered by the answers of the queries have a lower threshold, leading to a higher location accuracy. Zhou et al. [11] also take the precision of query results as a result of a negotiated threshold by the Aqua location updating scheme proposed.

Updates differ in representation and prediction of future positions
Wolfson and Yin [10] consider tracking with accuracy guarantees. They introduce the deviation update policy for this purpose and compare it with the distance policy. The difference between the two polices lies in the representation of future positions respectively with the linear function in the former and constant function in the latter. Based on experiments with artificial data generated to resemble real movement data, they conclude that the distance policy is outperformed by the deviation policy. Similarly, Civilis et al. [1, 2] propose three update policies: a point policy, a vector policy, and a segment-based policy, which differ in how they predict the future positions of a moving object. In fact, the first and third policy are the good representatives of the policies in [10]. They further improve the update policies in [2], by exploiting the better road-network representation and

acceleration profiles with routes. It should also be noted that Ding and Guting [3] have recently discussed the use of what is essentially segment-based tracking based on their proposed data model for the management of road-network constrained moving objects. In paper [8], the non-linear models such as the acceleration are used to represent the trajectory which is affected by the abnormal traffic such as traffic incident.

Updates based on individual object and their group
Most existing update techniques are developed to process individual updates efficiently [1, 2, 9, 10]. To reduce the expensive uplink updates from the objects to the location server, Lam et al. [6] propose a group-based scheme in which moving objects are grouped so that the group leader will send location update on behalf of the whole group. A group-based location update scheme for personal communication network is also proposed in [5]. The aim is to reduce location registrations by grouping a set of mobile objects at their serving VLRs.

Our work improves the tracking technique from the aspect of prediction model and update mode, and focuses on the accuracy of the predicted positions of the objects in urban road networks. Based on their predicted movement functions, we groups objects to further reduce their location updates. To the best of our knowledge, there exists no proposal for tracking of moving objects that combines the simulation based prediction and grouping of objects by exploiting the movement features of objects in traffic systems.

3 Data Model and Trajectory Prediction

We model a road network with a graph of cellular automata (GCA), where the nodes of the graph represent road intersections and the edges represent road segments with no intersections. Each edge consists of a cellular automaton (CA), which is represented, in a discrete mode, as a finite sequence of cells. The CA model was used in this context by [12].

In the GCA, a moving object is represented as a symbol attached to the cell and it can move several cells ahead at each time unit. Intuitively, the velocity is the number of cells an object can traverse during a time unit. Let i be an object moving along an edge. Let $v(i)$ be its velocity, $x(i)$ its position, $gap(i)$ the number of empty cells ahead (forward gap), and $P_d(i)$ a randomized slowdown rate which specifies the probability it slows down. We assume that V_{max} is the maximum velocity of moving objects. The position and velocity of each object might change at each transition of the GCA according to the rules below (adapted from [12]):

1. if $v(i) < V_{max}$ and $v(i) < gap(i)$ then $v(i) \leftarrow v(i) + 1$
2. if $v(i) > gap(i)$ then $v(i) \leftarrow gap(i)$
3. if $v(i) > 0$ and $random() < P_d(i)$ then $v(i) \leftarrow v(i) - 1$
4. if $(x(i) + v(i)) \leq l$ then $x(i) \leftarrow x(i) + v(i)$

The first rule represents linear acceleration until the object reaches the maximum speed V_{max}. The second rule ensures that if there is another object in front of the current object, it will slow down in order to avoid collision. In the third rule, the $P_d(i)$ models erratic movement behavior. Finally, the new position of object i is given by the fourth rule as the sum of the previous position with the new velocity if it is in the CA. Figure 2 shows a transition of the cellular automaton of edge (n_1, n_2) in Figure 1 in two consecutive timestamps. We can see that at time t, the speed of the object o_1 is smaller than the gap (i.e. the number of cells between the object o_1 and o_2). On the other hand, the object o_2 will reduce its speed to the size of the gap. According to the fourth rule, the objects move to the corresponding positions based on their speeds at time $t+1$.

We use GCAs not only to model road networks, but also to simulate the movements of moving objects by the transitions of the GCA. Based on the GCA, a *Simulation-based Prediction (SP)* model to anticipate future trajectories of moving objects is proposed. The SP model treats the objects simulated results as their predicted positions. Then, by the linear regression, a compact and simple linear function that reflects future movement of a moving object can be obtained. To refine the accuracy, based on different assumptions on the traffic conditions we simulate two future trajectories to obtain its predicted movement function. Figure 3 and Figure 4 show the comparison of the SP model and the linear prediction (LP) model. We can see from Figure 3 that the LP model cannot predict accurately the future trajectories of objects due to the frequent changes of the object velocity in traffic road networks.

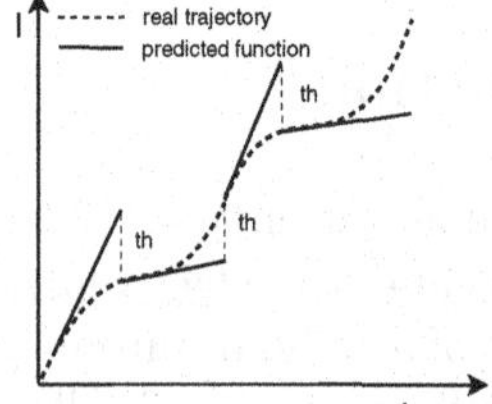

Fig. 3. The *Linear* Prediction

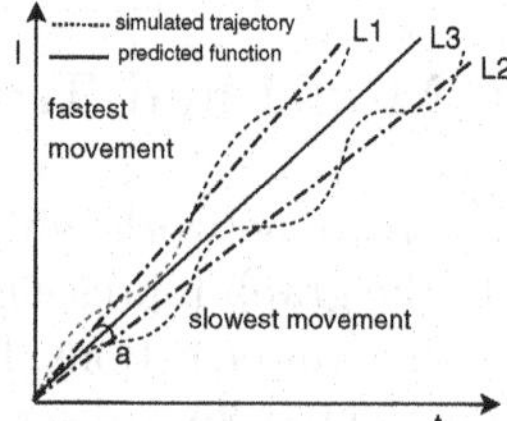

Fig. 4. The *Simulation Based* Prediction

Most existing work uses the CA model for traffic flow simulation in which the parameter $P_d(i)$ is treated as a random variable to reflect the stochastic, dynamic nature of traffic system. However, we extend this model for predicting the future trajectories of objects by setting $P_d(i)$ to values that model different traffic conditions. For example, laminar traffic can be simulated with $P_d(i)$ set to 0 or a small value, and the congestion can be simulated with a larger $P_d(i)$. By giving $P_d(i)$ two values, we can derive two future trajectories, which describe, respectively, the fastest and slowest movements of objects. In other words, the object future locations are most probably bounded by these two trajectories. The value of $P_d(i)$ can be obtained by the experiences or by sampling from the given dataset. Our experiments show one of methods to choose the value of $P_d(i)$. It is proved that 0 and 0.1 are realistic values of $P_d(i)$ in our cases.

For getting the future predicted function of an object from the simulated discrete points, we regress the discrete positions to a linear function by the

Least Square Estimation (LSE) in Statistics. It can be calculated efficiently with low data storage cost. Let the discrete simulated points be $(t_0, l_0), (t_1, l_1), ...,$ $(t_i, l_i), ..., (t_{n-1}, l_{n-1})(i \geq 0, n > 0)$, where t_i is the time at $i+1$ timestamp, l_i is the relative distance of the moving object in an edge at timestamp t_i, n is the total time units for the simulation, a linear function of time variable t can be obtained as follows:

$$l = a_0 + a_1 t \tag{1}$$

where the slope a_1 and the intercept a_0 can be calculated in Statistics

$$a_1 = \frac{n \sum_{i=0}^{n-1} t_i l_i - \sum_{i=0}^{n-1} t_i \sum_{i=0}^{n-1} l_i}{n \sum_{i=0}^{n-1} t_i^2 - (\sum_{i=0}^{n-1} t_i)^2} \tag{2}$$

$$a_0 = \frac{1}{n} \sum_{i=0}^{n-1} l_i - \frac{a_1}{n} \sum_{i=0}^{n-1} t_i \tag{3}$$

After regressing the two simulated future trajectories to two linear function denoting L_1 and L_2 in Figure 4, we can compute the middle straight line L_3, the bisector of the angle a between L_1 and L_2 as the final predicted function $L(t)$.

Through the SP model, we obtain a compact and simple linear prediction function for the moving object. However, this is different from the linear prediction in that the simulation-based prediction method not only considers the speed and direction of each moving object, but also takes correlation of objects as well as the stochastic behavior of the traffic into account. The experimental results also show it is a more accurate and effective prediction approach.

4 Group Location Update Strategy

As the number of updates from moving objects to the server database depends on both the update frequency and the number of objects updated, we propose a group location update strategy based on the SP model (GSP) to minimize location updates. In the GSP, for each edge in a road network, the objects are grouped or clustered by the similarity of their predicted future movement function and their locations are represented and reported by the group (Figure 1). It means that the nearby objects with similar movement during the future period on the same edge are grouped and only the object nearest to its group center needs to report the location of the whole group. Within a certain precision, the locations of other objects can be approximated to their group location.

The idea of grouping objects for location updates is similar to the GBL proposed in [6]. The main differences are that the GSP groups the objects by their future movement function predicted from the SP model instead of their current locations and predicted locations after a time parameter τ obtained by current velocity. Grouping by objects predicted movement function can insure the validity of the groups. The accurate prediction from the SP model can also reduce the maintenance of the groups. Due to the constraint of the road network, each group in the GSP has its lifetime in accordance to the edge. A group only exists on one edge and will be dissolved when objects within it leave the edge. Furthermore, unlike the GBL in which objects have to send a lots of messages to each other and compute the costly similarities for grouping and leader selection, the GSP executes the grouping on the server after predicting. This alleviates the resource consumption of moving clients and overloads of wireless communication.

The similarity of two objects simulated future trajectories in the SP model has to be computed by comparing a lot of feature points on the trajectories. A straightforward method is to select some of the simulated points to sum their distance difference. However, the computation cost for simulated trajectories is very high. For simplicity and low cost, we group objects by comparing their final predicted linear functions. Therefore, the movement similarity of two objects on the same edge can be determined by their predicted linear functions and the length of the edge. Specifically, if both the distance of their initial locations and their distance when one of the objects arrives the end of the edge are less than the given threshold (corresponding to the update threshold ε), we group the two objects together. These distances can be easily computed by their predicted functions. Figure 5 shows the predicted movement functions (represented as $L1, L2, L3, L4, L5$) of the objects o_1, o_2, o_3, o_4, o_5 on the edge (n_1, n_2) from Figure 1. le is the length of the edge and $t1, t2, t3, t4$ are respectively the time when the objects o_1, o_2, o_3, o_4 arrive the end of the edge. Given the threshold is 7, for objects o_1, o_2, the location difference between them at initiate time and t_1 are not larger than 7, therefore, they are clustered in one group c_1. We then compare the movement similarities of o_3 and o_1 as well as o_3 and o_2. The location differences are all not larger than 7, so o_3 can be inserted to c_1. Although at the initiate time, o_3 and o_4 are very close with the distance less than 7, they move far away each other in the future and their distance exceeds 7 when o_3 arrives the end of the edge. They cannot be grouped in one cluster. In the same way, o_4 and o_5 form the group c_2. Therefore, given a threshold, there are three cases of the objects predicted linear function when they are grouped together on one edge. These cases can be seen in the Figure 5 respectively labeled by a ($L2$ and $L3$ with objects moving close), b ($L1$ and $L3$ with objects moving far away) and c ($L1$ and $L2$ with one object exceeding another one).

In a road network, we group objects on the same edge. When objects move out of the edge, they may change direction independently. So we dissolve this group

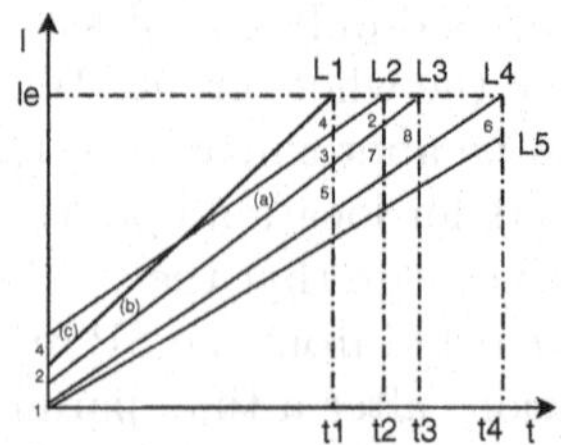

Fig. 5. Grouping objects by their predicted functions

and regroup the objects in adjacent edges. Each group has its lifetime from the group formation to all objects within it leaving the edge. For each edge, with the objects predicted functions, groups are formed by clustering together sets of objects not only close to each other at a current time, but also likely to move together for a while on one edge. We select the object closest to the center of its group both the current time and some period in future on the edge to represent the group. The central object represents its group and is responsible for reporting the group location to the server. For reselecting the central object, according to objects predicted future functions, we can choose the objects close to the center of the group during its lifetime as the candidates of the central object. We can also identify when the central object will move away from the group center and choose another candidate as a new central object. A joining from a moving object to a group must be executed as follows. The system first finds the nearby groups according to the edge the object lies and then compares the movement similarity of the object and the group by their predicted functions. If the object cannot join to the nearby groups, a new group will be created with only one member. When a moving object leaves a group, the central object of the group needs to be reselected. However, for the object leaving an edge, to reduce the central object reselection of its group, we just delete it from its group and do not change the central object until the central object leaves the edge.

Algorithm 1. GroupUpdate($objID, pos, vel, edgeID, grpID$)

```
input  : objID, edgeID and grpID are respectively the identifier of the object
         to be updated, its edge and group, pos, vel are its position and velocity
Simulate two future trajectories of objID with different P_d by the CA;
Compute the future predicted function l(t) of objID;
if objID does not enter the new edge then
    if objID is the central object of grpID then
        Update the current position pos and predicted function l(t) of grpID;
        Send the predicted function l(t) of grpID to the client of objID;
    end
else
    if GetObjNum(grpID) > 1 then
        Deletes objID from its original group grpID;
        if objID is the central object of grpID then
            Reselect the central object of grpID, update and send its group info;
        end
    else Dissolve the group grpID;
    Find the nearest group grp_1 for objID on edgeID;
    Compute the time t_e when objID leaves edgeID by l(t) and edgeID length;
    if Both distances between objID and grp_1 at initiate time and t_e ≤ ε then
        Insert objID into grp_1 and send grp_1 identifier to the client of objID;
        Reselect the central object of grp_1, update and send its group info;
    else  Create a new group grp_2 only having objID and send its group info;
end
```

In the GSP, the grouping method assures the compactness and movement similarity of the objects within a group. Given the precision threshold ε, the objects locations in a group may be approximated by the location of the group (i.e. location of its central object). Only the location update from the central object of the group to the location server is necessary. After the server makes predictions for objects in a road network and initiates their groups, the client of the central object measures and monitors the deviation between its current location and predicted location and reports its location to the server. Other objects do not report their locations unless they enter the new edge. The prediction and grouping of objects are executed in the server and the group information (including the edge id, the central object id, its predicted function and a set of objects within the group) is also stored in the database of the server. The update algorithm in the server is described in Algorithm 1.

5 Performance Evaluation

In this section, we experimentally measure the performance of the *point-based*, *segment-based* [1], and our *GSP* update policies. We also evaluate the simulation based prediction (SP) method used in the *GSP* update policy with the simulation parameter P_d and prediction accuracy compared to the linear prediction (LP) method. We implemented the three update policies in Java and carried out experiments on a Pentium 4, 2.4G PC with 256MB RAM running Windows XP.

5.1 Datasets

The datasets of our experiments are generated by Thomas Brinkhoff Network-based Generator of Moving Objects [13], which is used as a popular benchmark in many related work. The generator takes a map of a real road network as input and may simulate the moving behaviors of various kinds of moving objects in real world. Our experiment is based on the real map of Oldenburg city with 7035 segments. For modeling the road network, we associate those adjacent but not crossed segments together to form edges of the graph. After that, the total number of edges is 2980 and their average length is 184. We set the generator the parameter "maximum time" to be 20, "maximum speed" 50 and the number of initial moving objects 100000. The generator places these objects at random positions on the road network, and updates their locations at each time-stamp. The positions of the objects are given in two dimensional X-Y coordinates. We transform them to the form of (`edgeid`, `pos`), where `edgeid` denotes the edge identifier and `pos` denotes the object relative position.

5.2 Update Performance

For evaluating update performance and accuracy, we consider two metrics, namely, the number of updates (for 100000 moving objects during 20 time-stamps) and average error of the location of each object at each times-tamp as following.

$$average\_error = \frac{1}{mn}\sum_{j=0}^{n-1}\sum_{i=0}^{m-1}|l_{ij} - l_{rij}| \tag{4}$$

where l_{ij} is the predicted location of mo_j or approximated location by its group at the timestamp t_i, l_{rij} is the real location of mo_j at timestamp t_i, m is total update time-stamps and n is the number of moving objects.

Figure 6 and 7 show the update number and average error of three update policies respectively with different update thresholds. We observe that with increase of the threshold, the update number will decrease and the average error will increase in any one of these three policies. This is because the larger the threshold is, the larger the allowable deviation between the predicted location and its real location, and the less updates it causes. However, the GSP update policy outperforms the other two policies for fewer number of update and average error. Specifically, the GSP only causes 30%-40% updates of segment-based policy and 15%-25% of point-based policy, while improves the location accuracy with lower average error. This owns to the accurate prediction of the SP method and the technique of grouping moving objects. For the GSP policy, larger threshold results in more objects in one group and therefore fewer group updates and higher location average error. In addition, notice that the largest performance improvement of the GSP policy over other policies is for smaller thresholds. For thresholds below 10, the GSP policy is nearly three times better than the segment-based policy and four times than the point-based policy.

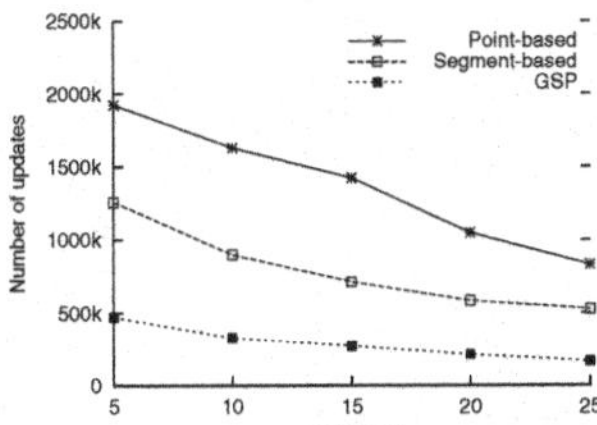

Fig. 6. Number of Updates

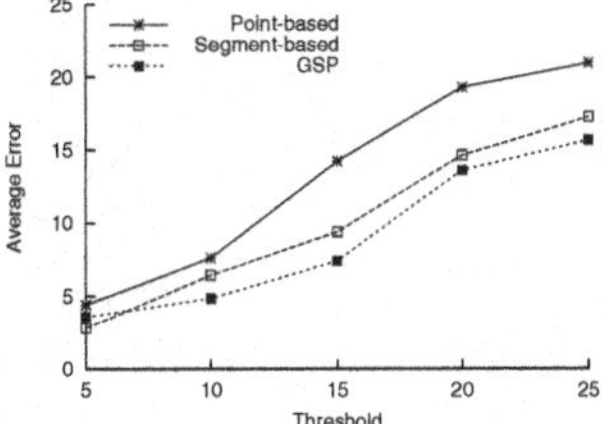

Fig. 7. Average Error of Updates

5.3 Prediction Performance

The Slowdown Rate P_d. We study the effect of the choices of different P_d, which determines two predicted trajectories corresponding to the fastest and slowest movements. We use P_d from 0 to 0.5 and measure the prediction accuracy by the average error and overflow rate. The overflow rate represents the probability of the predicted positions exceeding the actual positions. The purpose of this metric is to find the closest two trajectories binding the actual one as future trajectories. In this way, we choose the P_d with both the lower average error and overflow rate, which can also be treated as one of methods to set the proper values of P_d in a given dataset. Figure 8 and Figure 9 show the prediction accuracy of the SP method with different P_d. We can see that when P_d is set to 0 and 0.1, both the average error and overflow rate are lower than others. Therefore, we use them in the experiments to obtain better prediction results.

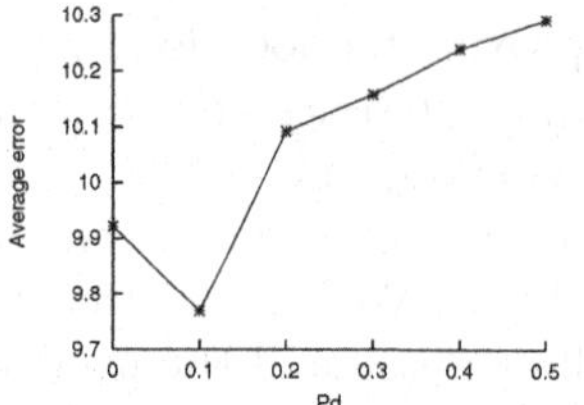

Fig. 8. Average Error with Different P_d

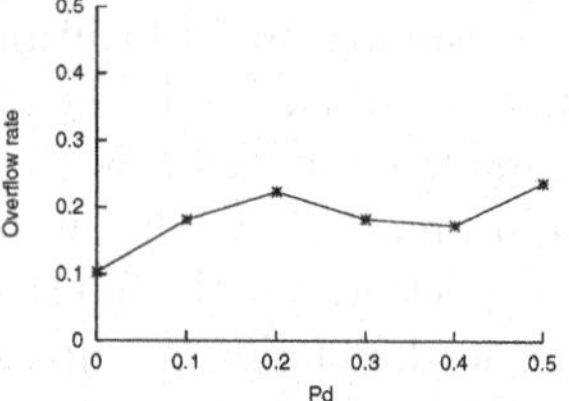

Fig. 9. Overflow Rate with Different P_d

Prediction Accuracy and Cost. Finally, we compare the prediction accuracy of the SP method with the LP method. We measure the average error for predicted locations (without grouping) with different thresholds. From Figure 10, we observe that the average error will increase when the threshold increases. This is tenable in both the LP and SP method. However, the SP method predicts more accurately than the LP method with any threshold. For the costs of SP method, as its time complexity depends on many factors, we compute average CPU time when simulating and predicting the movements of one object along the edge with length 1000. The results show that the average cost of one prediction is about 0.25ms. This is acceptable even for large number of moving objects.

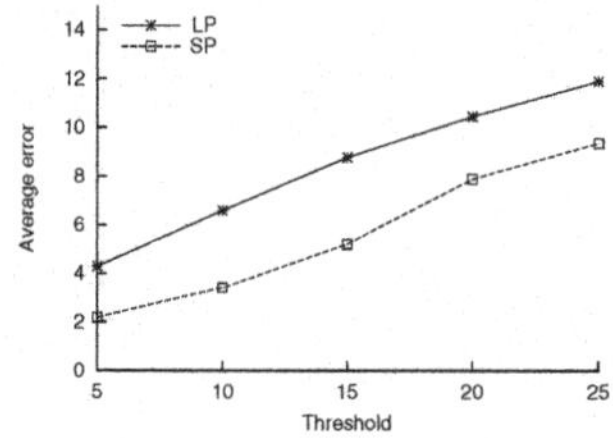

Fig. 10. Comparison of Prediction Accuracy

6 Conclusion

Motivated by the features of vehicles movements in traffic networks, this paper presents new techniques to track network-constrained moving objects. Our contribution is twofold. First we propose a prediction model, based on simulation, which predicts with a great accuracy the future trajectories of moving objects. This lowers location update frequency in tracking. Then, based on the prediction, we propose a group update strategy which further reduces location updates and minimizes the cost of wireless communication. The experiments show that the update strategy has much higher performance and location accuracy.

Acknowledgments

This work was partially supported by the grants from the Natural Science Foundation of China with grant number 60573091, 60273018; China National Basic Research and Development Program's Semantic Grid Project (No.2003CB317000); the Key Project of Ministry of Education of China under Grant No.03044; Program for New Century Excellent Talents in University(NCET); Program for Creative PhD Thesis in University.

References

1. A. Civilis, C. S. Jensen, J. Nenortaite, S. Pakalnis. Efficient Tracking of Moving Objects with Precision Guarantees. In MobiQuitous 2004: 164-173.
2. A. Civilis, C. S. Jensen, S. Pakalnis. Techniques for Efficient Road-Network-Based Tracking of Moving Objects. In IEEE Trans. Knowl. Data Eng. 17(5): 698-712 (2005).
3. Z. Ding, R. H. Guting. Managing Moving Objects on Dynamic Transportation Networks. In SSDBM 2004: 287-296.
4. H. Gowrisankar, S. Nittel. Reducing Uncertainty In Location Prediction Of Moving Objects In Road Networks. In GIScience 2002: 228-242.
5. Y. Huh, C. Kim. Group-Based Location Management Scheme in Personal Communication Networks. In ICOIN 2002: 81-90.
6. G. H. K. Lam, H. V. Leong, S. C. Chan. GBL: Group-Based Location Updating in Mobile Environment. In DASFAA 2004: 762-774.
7. K. Y. Lam, O. Ulusoy, T. S. H. Lee, E. Chan, and G. Li, An Efficient Method for Generating Location Updates for Processing of Location-Dependent Continuous Queries. In DASFAA 2001: 218-225.
8. G. Trajcevski, O. Wolfson, B. Xu, Peter Nelson: Real-Time Traffic Updates in Moving Objects Databases. In DEXA 2002: 698-704.
9. O. Wolfson, A. P. Sistla, S. Camberlain, Y. Yesha. Updating and Querying Databases that Track Mobile Units. In Distributed and Parallel Databases 7(3): 257-387 (1999).
10. O. Wolfson and H. Yin. Accuracy and Resource Consumption in Tracking and Location Prediction. In SSTD 2003: 325-343.
11. J. Zhou, H. V. Leong, Q. Lu, K. C. Lee. Aqua: An Adaptive QUery-Aware Location Updating Scheme for Mobile Objects. In DASFAA 2005: 612-624.
12. K. Nagel and M. Schreckenberg, A Cellular Automaton Model for Free Traffic, In physique I, 1992, 2: 2221-2229.
13. T. Brinkhoff. A Framework for Generating Network-based Moving Objects, In GeoInformatica 6(2): 153-180 (2002).

Dynamic Configuring Service on Semantic Grid

Qing Zhu

Department of Computer Science, Information School,
Renmin University of China,
Beijing, 100872, P.R.China
zq@ruc.edu.cn

Abstract. Dynamic configuring service composition can automatically leverage distributed service components and resources to compose an optimal configuration according to the requirements on Semantic Grid. One major challenge is how to comprehend service-specific semantics and how to generate workflow to reuse common service composition functionalities. Current ontological specifications for semantically describing properties of Grid services are limited to their static interface description. In this paper, we present an automaton [1, 2] model in which service providers express their service-specific knowledge in the form of a service template and create composition plan that is used by a synthesizer to perform dynamic configuring composition automatically. Our main contribution is to formally describe dynamic processing of composition, to take QoS-driven composition goal into account to find best quality composition on Semantic Grid.

1 Introduction

The Semantic Grid [3] is an Internet decoupling interconnection environment that can effectively organize, share, cluster, fuse, and manage globally distributed versatile resources based on the interconnection semantics. Semantic Grid services will allow the semi-automatic or automatic annotation, discovery, selection, composition, and execution of inter-organization service logic. It can make the Internet become a global common platform when semantic web re-organizations and individuals communicate among each other to carry out various activities and to provide value-added services. In order to fully harness the power of web services, their functionality must be re-combined to create process workflow on Grid. Semantics can play an important role in all stages of process lifecycle.

Service composition not only enables the reuse of existing services, but provides an attractive way for dynamic production and customized delivery of service contents on Semantic Grid. One promising challenge for developing such services is dynamic composition. Instead of statically integrating components [4] while the service is developed, dynamic services dynamically combine available components and resources into optimized service configurations at the invocation time, when a user request is received. This allows the service composition process to take the semantic requirement and the system characteristics into consideration.

J.X. Yu, M. Kitsuregawa, and H.V. Leong (Eds.): WAIM 2006, LNCS 4016, pp. 170–181, 2006.
© Springer-Verlag Berlin Heidelberg 2006

How can one describe the service composition on semantic Grid? Ontology [5] is a formal, explicit specification of a shared conceptualization. We can describe the ontology of a program by defining a set of representational terms and knowledge about a domain. Definitions associate the names of entities in the universe of classes, relations, functions or other objects with human-readable text describing what the names mean and formal axioms that constrain the interpretation and well-formed use of these terms. A set of grid services that share the same ontology will be able to communicate about a domain of knowledge. In this paper we address the problem of automatic composition description and synthesis of web services sharing knowledge based on Semantic Grid.

The rest of the paper is organized as follows. Section 2 describes an overview of dynamic composition model. Section 3 presents the design, configurations and operation of synthesizer. Section 4 presents key technology of physical mapping. Section 5 presents simulation and evaluation. Section 6 discusses related work. Finally, the paper concludes with future work in Section 7.

2 System Architecture

Dynamic service composition [6], generally, consists of two main steps [7]. The first one, sometimes called composition synthesis, describes the process of automatically computing a specification of how to coordinate the components to answer a service request. The second step, often referred to as orchestration, defines the actual run-time coordination of service executions, considering also data and control flow among services.

2.1 Model of Service Composition

We propose GSC (Grid service composition) architecture for dynamic configuration of services to achieve flexibility of sharing knowledge on semantic Grid. The service specification defines the components required by a service and describes how components are interrelated after user requesting. Resource discovery identifies the location and capabilities of processing resources to build a resource graph describing the physical topology. Service mapping translates the service specification onto the physical resource graph while taking into account all service-specific constraints. The service allocation task reserves and configures appropriate physical resources as determined by the service mapping process. Once the service has been deployed, service deployment is the final task that executes all required components to provide an operational service composition for users. Our main contribution is to formally describe dynamic processing of composition and mapping process on Semantic Grid, to validate the feasibility and adaptability of such an approach.

The GSC architecture is implemented as a distributed middleware infrastructure deployed in wide-area networks, which can automatically map the user's composite service requests into an instantiated distributed application service in semantic web. The GSC architecture includes a semantic interpreter and a resource synthesizer, which consistent of interpreter module and facility module.

A semantic interpreter realizes operational description of the domain knowledge and executes a template submitted by a developer to compose a service configuration for each user request. A resource synthesizer is across different services and contains discovery, mapping, allocation, and deployment modules (Fig. 1). The synthesizer provides the basic building components to build new services through composition and provides common, reusable service composition functionalities, component selection algorithms and mechanisms for accessing the support infrastructure.

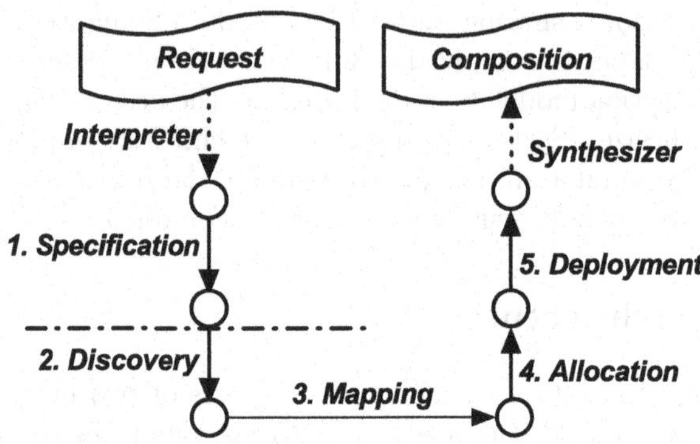

Fig. 1. Service Composition System Architecture

In dynamic composition model, the synthesizer identifies relevant services, explicitly states their interactions and creates a composition plan. Composition plans are created at runtime based on dynamically defined composition objectives, their semantic descriptions, constraints, and available services and resources. This model can support self-configuring behaviors, changeful interaction patterns and can be synthesized on-demand at design time. A key contribution is an dynamic composition model based on service-specific knowledge and automata model in which service providers express their service-specific knowledge.

From the view of the point, service specification is the foundation of service composition which can describe semantic explanation of user requisition and create requiting goal. It is the key problem that consists automatically of new process work-flow of Grid service by using available web services. This paper focuses on the service specification and composition plan part.

2.2 Overview of the Approach

Service composition is a process of binding execution of two or more services. Dynamic composition is defined the integration of generating services automatically. That means that a new web service achieves a given goal by interacting with some of the available web services. More specifically, we take a declarative description of the program that realizes the service. Given the process description of n available services (S1, ···, Sn), we encode each of them in a state automata (ΣS1, $\cdots$, ΣSn), State automata provide a sort of operational semantics to process models. Each of them describes the corresponding web service as state-based dynamic automata, that can evolve changing state, and that can be partially controlled and tested.

From the view of Fig.2, the new composed service ΣS that is the process of state transition has to be generated by the state automata (ΣS1, $\cdots$, ΣSn). Each of ΣSi constitutes the environment to operate by receiving and sending service requests (S1, $\cdots$, Sn). They constitute the planner in a planning [8] domain where the planner has to plan for a goal. In our case, the planning domain is a state automata Σ that combines (ΣS1, $\cdots$, ΣSn) and Goal G (G1, $\cdots$, Gn). The Composition Goal G imposes some requirements on the desired behavior of the planning domain. The planner generates a plan Γ by given Σ and G to satisfy the goal G and interacts with the external services S1, $\cdots$, Sn. The plan encodes the new service S that has to be generated, which dynamically receives and sends invocations from/to the external services (S1, $\cdots$, Sn), tests their behaviors, and behaves depending on responses received from the external services. G is encoded as an automaton that, depending on the testing and on its internal state, executes different actions.

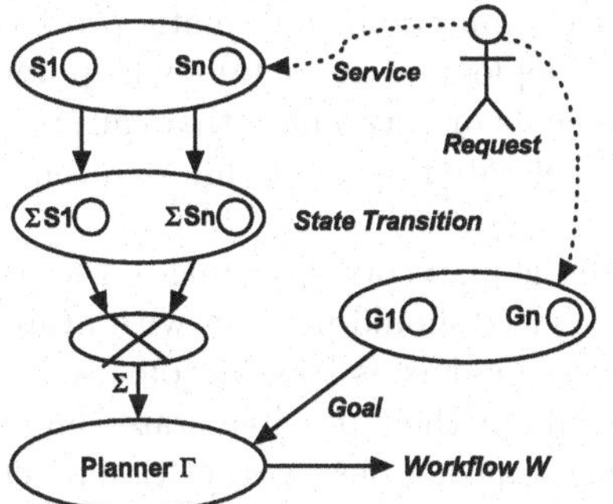

Fig. 2. Dynamic Service Composition Model

$((S) \rightarrow (\sum S)) \otimes (G) \Rightarrow (W)$,
$S = (S_1, ..., S_n)$ Services of Request
$\sum S = (\sum S_1, ..., \sum S_n)$ State automata
$G = (G_1, ..., G_n)$ Service Goal
$W = (W_1, ..., W_n)$ Process Workflow
" $\rightarrow$ ": State Transition
" $\otimes$ ": Composite Plan and Goal
" $\Rightarrow$ ": Create Process Workflow

Fig. 3. Service Composition Function

Formally, this combination is a synchronous product, which allows the n services to evolve independently and in parallel. They can be described as Fig 3. In the rest of the paper, we will describe step by step the automated composition task introduced above through the following example.

3 Specification of Service Composition

In this section, we present how a real-world application benefit from placing processing functions into the physical resources using the state automata. We demonstrate how the application can conveniently express their processing requirements using state transition, how our service composition software maps these requirements onto available resources, and how processing modules and forwarding state interior to the physical resources are finally configured.

3.1 Model of Service Composition

There is an example for the travel industry. Consumers can now acquire service compositions from a diversity of Web sites including online agencies and airlines. With the spread of service online of travel industry, a new technology of ontology has surfaced for the leisure travel industry. For the development of dynamic integrating solutions it is necessary to look in detailed at the service components needed to enhance the online vacation planning experience.

By transitioning service in most applications, dynamic service synthesizer can better select composition offerings, pricing and merchandizing to consumer demand. The cumulative effort of various companies and international organizations, including air, car, cruise, rail, hotel, travel agencies, tour operators and technology providers, has produced a fairly complete set of available services for the travel industry.

3.2 Formal Specification

The development of such service Grid can be used to bring together autonomous and heterogeneous Grid services, processes, applications, data, and components residing in distributed environments. Semantics allow rich descriptions of Grid services and processes that can be used by computers for automatic processing in various tourism related applications. The deployment of ontology help understand a well-defined set of common data elements or vocabulary that can support communication across multiple channels, accelerate the flow of information, and meet travel industry and customer needs.

The problem is to automatically generate the plan corresponding to the travel industry service, when the travel industry service should interact with available services: S1, S2, $\cdots$, Sn. We interpret process models as state automata, which describe dynamic systems that can be in one of their possible states and can evolve to new states as a result of performing some actions. A transition function describes how the execution of an action leads from one state to possibly many different states. System's evolutions can be tested through QoS [9] describing the visible part of the system state.

Definition 1. *Service composition is modeled using nondeterministic state automaton* $\Sigma = (S, A, Q, I, F, \xi, \lambda)$, *where*

(1) S *is a finite set of states.* $I \subseteq S$ *is the set of initial states;* $F \subseteq S$ *is the set of final states; we require* $I \neq \emptyset$ *and* $F \neq \emptyset$.

(2) A *is the set of actions.*

(3) Q *is the set of Quality of Service.*

(4) ξ: $S \times A \rightarrow 2^S$ *is the transition function; it associates to each current state* $s \in S$ *and to each action* $a \in A$ *the set* $\xi(s, a) \subseteq S$ *of next states.*

(5) λ: $S \rightarrow Q$ *is the testing function of Quality of Service.*

Each action may result in several different outcomes and the transition function returns sets of states, so state automata are nondeterministic. Non-deterministic state automata are needed since the system cannot often know a priori-level which outcome will actually take place, whether it will receive a confirmation or a cancelation from an available service. Moreover, our state automata are partially testing QoS of user requirement to transfer to next states.

3.3 QoS-Driven Composition Goals

QoS-driven composition goals express requirements for the service to be automatically generated according to user providing and character of system. They should represent conditions on the temporary evolution of services, and requirements of different strengths and preference conditions, by addressing the QoS-driven composition of Semantic Grid services.

When we create a composite service and subsequently execute it following a user request, the number of component services involved in this composite service may be large, and the number of Grid services from which these component services are selected is likely to be even larger. On the other hand, the QoS of the resulting composite service executions is a determinant factor to ensure customer satisfaction, service goal. Different users may have different requirements and preferences regarding QoS. For example, a user may require minimizing the execution duration while satisfying certain constraints in terms of price and reputation, while another user may give more importance to the price than to the execution duration. A QoS-driven approach to service composition is therefore needed, which maximizes the QoS of composite service executions by taking into account the constraints and preferences of the users.

A multi-dimensional QoS model [10] is a broad concept that includes a number of non-functional properties such as price, duration, availability, succeed-rate, and reputation. These properties apply both to alone Grid services and to new composite Grid services. In order to reason about QoS properties in Grid services, the QoS model is needed to captures the descriptions of these from a user requirement. It can be formally defined as follow:

QoS = (Q1, $\cdots$, Qn), for example: Q1 = Q.price, Q2 = Q.duration, Q3 = Q.availability, Q4 = Q.succeed-rate, Q5 = Q.reputation; QoS = (Q1, $\cdots$, Qn) $\Rightarrow$ Goal G = (G1, G2, $\cdots$, Gn), Where: "$\Rightarrow$" expresses create composition goal.

3.4 Automated Composition

The composition goal and the planning domain Σ decide the planner (see Fig 2). The planning domain Σ represents all the ways in which the services represented by (ΣS1, $\cdots$, ΣSn) can evolve. Formally, this combination is a synchronous product, $\Sigma = \Sigma S1 \times \cdots \times \Sigma Sn$. The dynamic service composition is created by finding a domain plan that satisfies the composition goal G on Semantic Grid. We are interested in complex plans that may encode sequential, conditional and iterative behaviors. The plan can represent the flow of interactions of the synthesized composed service and the required QoS over the other services. We therefore model a plan as an automaton.

Definition 2. *A plan for planning domain* $\Sigma = (S, A, Q, I, F, \xi, \lambda)$, *is a tuple* $\Gamma = (P, p0, \beta, \delta)$, *where*

(1) P is the set of plan contexts. p0 ∈ P is the initial context.

(2) $\beta : P \times Q \rightarrow A$ is the action function; it associates to a plan context p ∈ P and an quality of service q ∈ Q, an action a ∈ A, a = β(p, q) to be executed .

(3) δ: $P \times Q \rightarrow P$ is the context evolutions function, it associates to a plan context p ∈ P and an quality of service q ∈ Q, a new plan context p' ∈ P, p' = δ(p, q).

The contexts of the plan have been chosen from a composition goal by taking into account the semantic knowledge during the previous execution steps. Actions defined by action function β to be executed by the testing quality of service and on the context. Once an action is executed, the context evolutions function δ updates the plan context. Functions β and δ are partial deterministic since a plan may be obtained from a composition goal and the contexts correspond to the sub-formulas of the goal.

3.5 Dynamic Configuration Composition

Dynamic configuration composition describes the state of the domain and the plan and can be executed by abstract described and physical mapping. The execution of a plan over a domain can be described in terms of transitions between configurations on semantic grid.

Definition 3. *A configuration for domain $\Sigma = (S, A, Q, I, F, \xi, \lambda)$ and plan $\Gamma = (P, p0, \beta, \delta)$, is a pair (s; p) such that s ∈ S and p ∈ P. Configuration (s; p) may evolve into configuration (s', p'), written (s, p) → (s', p'), if s' ∈ ξ(s; β(p, δ(s))) and p' = δ(p, λ(s)). Configuration (s; p) is initial if s ∈ I and p = p'.*

As we know, a dynamic configuration is a snapshot of the domain controlled by the plan. A "non-deterministic" finite automation has the power to be in several states at once. This ability is often expressed as an ability to "guess" something about its input. We may have an infinite number of different executions of a plan due to the non-determinism in the domain. But we can convert "non-deterministic" finite automation to "deterministic" finite automation. So we can provide a finite presentation of these executions with execution workflow configurations as states.

Definition 4. *The execution structure corresponding to domain Σ and plan Γ is the execution structure $\Sigma_\Gamma = (W, W_0, R)$ where:*

(1) W is the set of configurations, $W = S \times P$;

(2) $W_0 \subseteq W$ is the initial configurations;

(3) $R \subseteq S \times P \rightarrow W$ is the transitions between configurations.

The execution workflow Σ_Γ represents the evolutions of the domain Σ controlled by the plan Γ and must satisfy the composition goal G (see Fig. 2).

If $((S)\rightarrow(\Sigma S)) \otimes (G) \Rightarrow (W)$, we say that Γ is a valid plan for G on Σ.

3.6 Mapping Procession

Dynamic composition techniques automate the entire composition process by using AI planning or similar technology. The synthesizer addresses the automated composition problem by GSC framework which uses generic procedures and semantically marked up services to guide composition. The synthesizer acts as a gateway to Grid services and is responsible for selecting and invoking the services. We assume the existence of a mapping procedure. In the absence of one, mapping cannot proceed. Additionally, if the synthesizer cannot match a service, execution will fail. An important component of automated composition is the discovery of the services required.

An abstract configuration is a graph consisting of nodes representing the abstract components and links representing the connections between the components. While the synthesizer needs to use the knowledge in the template to decide what components and connections to use, the structures for the graph can be reused across services to handle abstract configurations.

For instance, a search for travel service is done in parallel with a flight, a car and an accommodation booking. After the searching and booking operations complete, the distance from the hotel to the accommodation is computed, and either a car or a hotel rental service is invoked, in Fig.2.

As an example, the travel industry service should interact with three available services: s0, s1, s2, and s3; s0=flight, s1=car, s2=hotel, s3=cruise, which are described as OWL-S process models and translated to state transition systems. Where: a1=s0 $\rightarrow$ s1, a2=s1 $\rightarrow$ s2, a3=s2 $\rightarrow$ s3; q0: QoS of flight-service, q1: QoS of car-service, q2: QoS of hotel-service, q3: QoS of cruise-service. The problem is to automatically generate the plan p0={providing flight-service}, p1 = {providing car-service}, p2 = {providing hotel-service}, p3 = {providing cruise-service} corresponding to the travel industry service. Finally, Σ_Γ creates configuration workflow: (s0, p0) $\rightarrow$ (s1, p1) $\rightarrow$ (s2, p2) $\rightarrow$ (s3, p3). We express process models as state automata, which describe dynamic systems that can be in one of their possible states (some of which are marked as initial states) and can evolve to new states as a result of performing some actions. A transition function describes how (the execution of) an action leads from one state to possibly many different states. System's evolutions can be tested through Quality of Service (QoS) describing the visible part of the system state. A Quality of Service (QoS) defines the user associated to each state of the domain. Specifically, we introduce the mapping of service composition. Mapping of service composition includes four parts.

Firstly, state automaton Σ = (S, A, Q, I, F, ξ, λ), where, user's require services S = {s0, s1, s2, s3}; state transfer action A = {a0, a1, a2, a3, a4}; QoS Q=q1 and q2 and q3, provide resources for S; Start State I = {S0}, Final State F = {S3}; Mapping of transition function: s1=ξ(s0, a1), s2=ξ(s0, a0), s2=ξ(s1, a2), s3=ξ(s2, a3), s3=ξ(s1, a4), a $\in$ A, s $\in$ S, Mapping of testing QoS q0= λ(s0), q1= λ(s1), q2= λ(s2), q3= λ(s3), $s_i \in$ S, $q_i \in$ Q.

Secondly, plan is a four-tuple Γ = (P, p0, β, δ) for planning domain Σ = (S, A, Q, I, F, ξ, λ); where (1) P = {p0, p1, p2, p3} is the set of plan contexts. p0

$\in$ P is the initial context. (2) Mapping of providing resources and testing QoS: a1 = β(p0, q0), a2 = β(p1, q1), a3 = β(p2, q2) are the action function to be executed; it associates to a plan context p and an quality of service q_i. Mapping of the context evolutions function: p1 = δ(p0, q0), p2 =δ(p1, q1), p3 =δ(p2, q2), it associates to a plan context p $\in$ P and an quality of service $q_i \in$ Q, a new plan context P={p0, p1, p2, p3}.

Thirdly, a configuration for domain Σ = (S, A, Q, I, F, ξ, λ) and plan Γ = (P, p0, β, δ), is a pair (s, p) such that s $\in$ S and p $\in$ P. Configuration (s, p) may evolve into configuration (s', p'), written (s, p) $\rightarrow$ (s', p'), if s' $\in \xi$(s, β(p, λ(s)))= ξ(s, β(p, q))= ξ(s, a) and p' =δ(p, λ(s))= δ(p, q). Configuration (s0, p0) is initial if s0 $\in$ I and p' = p0.

Finally, the execution structure is Σ_Γ = (W, W_0, R), where W is the set of configurations; w=(s, p), $W_0 \subseteq$ W =S $\times$ P are the initial configurations, R $\subseteq$ S $\times$ P $\rightarrow$ W are the transitions between configurations. Thus, configuration workflow: W = {w0, w1, w2, w3} = {(s0, p0), (s1, p1), (s2, p2), (s3, p3)}; s_i'=R(s), p_i'=R(p). (s_i', p_i'), i=1, 2, 3, $\cdots$, n, consists the sets of configuration from (s, p).

4 Physical Mapping

To enable flexible services on semantic grid, there is a need for synthesizer on top of physical processing capabilities that facilitates the deployment and configuration of available services. The synthesizer can be seen as a distributed system component that automates the configuration of Grid resources to form services that applications use. The system accepts processing demands from applications of template, discovers available processing resources, maps those processing requirements onto Grid resources, and configures the appropriate state on Grid nodes.

Given an abstract configuration, the synthesizer generates a physical configuration specifying which physical component should be selected for each abstract component such that a Goal is optimized. The GSC uses a dynamic adaptable algorithm to match each service in the abstract mapping with an instance of an executable service available on the network. Let us first describe formally the problem and discuss the algorithms for solving them.

To state the mapping problems more formally, we use the following notation. We are given a directed graph, M = (S, A), with a transmission cost co(a), for each link a $\in$ A, and a service cost unit co(s), for each node s $\in$ S. Let the source be defined by Σ and the destination by Γ, In graphs, we denote transmission costs on the links and the unit for processing costs within the node. For now we assume that all services require a cost of 1, that is, the cost for processing a service corresponds to co(s). This convenience will allow us to express the mapping problem as a shortest-path problem.

5 Simulation and Evaluation

In this section, we illustrate our approach by using a scenario from the travel domain and provide some preliminary results of performance evaluation experiments. All the main components are implemented as Grid services. We use existing Semantic Web tools and reasoning mechanisms to provide the basic representation and reasoning technology. Services are described using OWL-S.

To analyze data of templates are correlated with the signal using fast correlation by a technique known as matching. This simulation uses approximately 50 separate services connected together to form a process workflow. The GSC generates a process model referring to the services by their logical mapping. These are then matched to actual simulations available on the network by physical mapping. The purpose of our experiments is two-fold: to assess plan generation times and success rates. We ran our experiments on a Windows machine with a 1.4GHz Intel processor and 512Kb RAM.

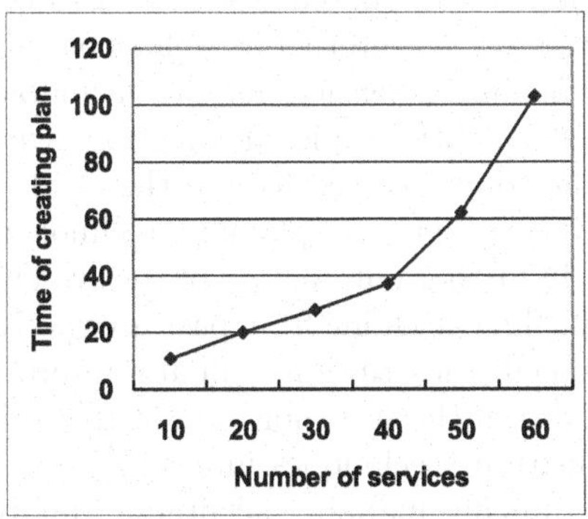

Fig. 4. Times of Creating Plan

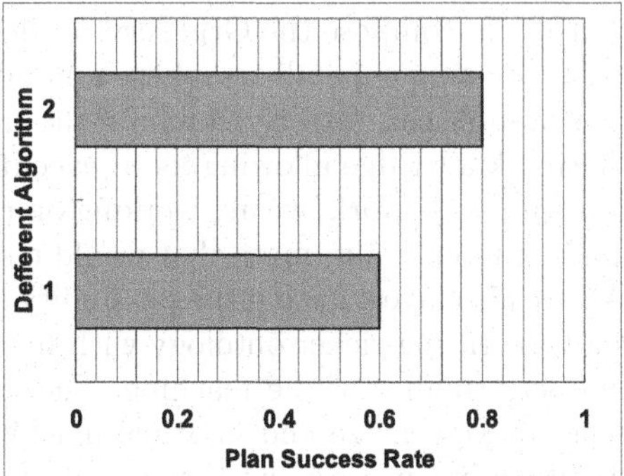

Fig. 5. Success Rates of Creating Plan

We first evaluate the time for generating process workflows (see Fig. 4). There is an exponential relationship between the number of services in a plan and the time required to match and compose an executable graph. We also looked at the workflow generation success rates (see Fig. 5). We compared our framework with a simple automated back-tracking composition algorithm. We used the same process ontology and composition requests for both of these techniques. Based on 50 requests, the results show that our framework had a success rate of 80% while the back-tracking algorithm had a success rate of about 60%. This confirms our expectation that our adaptive framework has a higher probability of successfully generating workflows.

6 Related Work

In the research area of e-service, there are service composition methods and tools of using automata. Finite state automata [2] are proposed as conceptual model for e-services, taking time constraints into account, and using a new web service transition language that integrates well with standard languages in order to completely specify e-Services. The work in [11] illustrates that e-services are modeled by automata whose alphabet represents a set of activities or tasks to be performed (namely, activity automata), automated design is the problem of "delegating" activities of the composite e-service to existing e-services so that each word accepted by the composite e-service can be accepted by those e-services collectively with each accepting a subsequence. Their approach focus on description, our approach, however, focus on understanding semantic to formally describe dynamic processing of composition, to take QoS-driven composition goal into account to find best quality composition on Semantic Grid.

7 Conclusion and Future Work

In this work, we have shown how to use semantic descriptions to aid in the composition of Grid services. We have developed a simulated system and shown that it can compose the Grid services deployed on the internet as well as providing processing capabilities where a number of similar services may be available. Our system can directly combine the user's semantic service descriptions with sharing knowledge allowing us to execute the composed services on the Grid.

As a future work, we are working on the incorporation of planning technology in the inference automata that would result in further automation of the system. We are also investigating the possibility of machine learning from past user activity. Generating richer ontology with more specific descriptions will also improve the performance of the machine. The key idea is the incorporation of multiple types of knowledge and multiple machine learning techniques into all stages of the mapping process, with the goal of maximizing mapping accuracy. Finally, we are going to implement the design of the synthesizer to select an appropriate optimization algorithm according to a developer's service-specific between optimality of component selection and optimization cost in our prototype.

Acknowledgements

This work is supported by National Natural Science Foundation of China under Grant No. 60473069, and the project of China Grid (No. CNGI-04-15-7A).

References

1. J. Hopcroft and J. Ullman. Introduction to Automata Theory, Languages, and Computation. Second Edition, Addison Wesley, 2001.
2. D. Berardi, F. De Rosa, L. De Santis, M. Mecella: Finite State Automata as Conceptual Model for E-Services. Proceedings of the 7th World Conference on Integrated Design and Process Technology (IDPT 2003), Special Session on Modeling and Developing Process-Centric Virtual Enterprises with Web-Services (VIEWS 2003).
3. H. Zhuge, Semantic Grid: Scientific Issues, Infrastructure, and Methodology, Communica-tions of the ACM. 48 (4) (2005)117-119.
4. D. Berardi, D. Calvanese, G. De Giacomo, R. Hull, M. Mecella: Automatic Composition of Transition-based Semantic Web Services with Messaging. In Proceedings of the 31st Inter-national Conference on Very Large Data Bases (VLDB 2005) (Trondheim, Norway, 2005).

5. I. B. Arpinar, R. Zhang, B. Aleman, and A. Maduko, Ontology-Driven Web Services Com-position. IEEE E-Commerce Technology, July 6-9, 2004, San Diego, CA.
6. S. Majithia, D. W. Walker and W. A. Gray, A framework for automated service composi-tion in service-oriented architecture, in 1st European Semantic Web Symposium, 2004.
7. D. Berardi, D. Calvanese, G. D. Giacomo, M. Lenzerini, and M. Mecella, Automatic com-position of e-services that export their behavior. In Proc. 1st Int. Conf. on Service Oriented Computing (ICSOC), volume 2910 of LNCS, pages 43-58, 2003.
8. M. Carman, L. Serafini, and P. Traverso, Web service composition as planning, in proceed-ings of ICAPS03 International Conference on Automated Planning and Scheduling, Trento, Italy, June 9-13 2003.
9. X. Gu, K. Nahrstedt, R. N. Chang, and C. Ward, QoS-Assured Service Composition in Managed Service Overlay Networks. Proc. of IEEE 23nd International Conference on Dis-tributed Computing Systems (ICDCS 2003), Providence, RI, May 2003.
10. Hanhua Chen, Hai Jin, Xiaoming Ning, Q-SAC: Toward QoS Optimized Service Auto-matic Composition, Proceedings of 5th IEEE/ACM International Symposium on Cluster Computing and the Grid (CCGrid05), May, 2005.
11. Z. Dang, O. H. Ibarra, and J. Su. Composability of Infinite-State Activity Automata, Proceedings of the 15th Annual International Symposium on Algorithms and Computation (ISAAC), 2004.

Object Placement and Caching Strategies on AN.P2P*

Su Mu[1], Chi-Hung Chi[2], Lin Liu[2], and HongGuang Wang[2]

[1] School of Computing, National University of Singapore, Singapore
[2] School of Software, Tsinghua University, Beijing, China
chichihung@mail.tsinghua.edu.cn

Abstract. This paper discusses the object placement and caching strategies on the AN.P2P, which is an Application Networking infrastructure to implement pervasive content delivery on the peer-to-peer networks. In general, the AN.P2P allows the peer to send the content's original object with the associated content adaptation workflow to other peers. The recipient peer can reuse the original object to generate different content presentations. In order to achieve reasonable performance, this paper proposes several object placement schemes and caching strategies. Our simulation results show that these methods could effectively improve the system performance in terms of query hops, computation cost and retrieval latency.

1 Introduction

In recent years, the peer-to-peer (P2P) systems have witnessed more heterogeneous presentation requirements than before because of the emergence of diverse devices. However, legacy P2P file sharing facilities [5,6,11,16,17] cannot deal with these requirements effectively without necessary system support to content adaptation and service customization. For instance, a PC based peer shared a piece of high quality media content. However, a smart phone based peer cannot render this content unless it is adapted to a lower quality version. This necessitates the architectural change in tandem.

Our previous work [20] on Application Networking (App.Net) was to implement pervasive content delivery for heterogeneous requirements. Its key idea was rooted from the observation that despite the heterogeneous requirements for object presentations, the processes to generate the presentations are homogeneous. In general, the App.Net enables the delivery of content's original or intermediate object with an associated workflow. The recipient node can thus reuse these objects to generate different presentations by performing the tasks in the workflow. In particular, our work [21] on AN.P2P attempted to apply the Application Networking mechanism onto the P2P file sharing systems. We have shown that the AN.P2P could help to reduce the average search size because of the reuse of original object and the associated workflow.

However, integrating the Application Networking mechanism into a practical P2P system is not a trivial exercise. It involves multiple aspects as performance

* This research is supported by the funding 2004CB719400 of China.

J.X. Yu, M. Kitsuregawa, and H.V. Leong (Eds.): WAIM 2006, LNCS 4016, pp. 182 – 192, 2006.
© Springer-Verlag Berlin Heidelberg 2006

optimization, service security, application reuse, and so on. The work of this paper focused on improving overall performance on AN.P2P through dedicated object placement methods and the revised caching strategies. In particular, we proposed two placement schemes to populate objects and their associated workflow, in order to improve the query efficiency and to reduce the mean retrieval delay. Our simulation showed that these methods could help to improve the overall system performance.

2 Summary of Previous Work

In general, the Application Networking mechanism [20] allows the content provider associate a piece of content adaptation logic to the published content. Instead of encapsulating the logic into a single application module, we specified the logic as a ***workflow*** composed by multiple tasks, each of which can be instantiated by an application module. We have defined a standard interface, called ANlet, for mobile applications. Given application modules that implement the ANlet interface, the Application Networking nodes can dynamically load them locally and remotely. In particular, we defined a callback function in ANlet, as given by equation (1).

AppNetContent modResponse (queryMsg msg, AppNetContent content); (1)

The function has two input parameters: the query message and available content object. The query message contains the presentation profile of the client and AppNetContent contains both the content object and the attributes of the object. Therefore, the ANlet can generate the appropriated output ANP2PContent according to the input parameters.

Hence, if we input the original object to a workflow, it can output the final presentation of the input object by performing the adaptation tasks. In particular, we believe the workflow structure can facilitate the progressive application deployment in that the fundamental applications are loaded first, while the remaining ones are loaded later on demand. Moreover, the workflow can get the intermediate objects of the original object. Our simulation results will show that caching these intermediate objects can help to reduce the average computation time by avoiding repeated content adaptation.

Upon receiving a request, the content host can send the original or intermediate object and the associated workflow to the requestor. The recipient can thus reuse the retrieved object to generate appropriate content presentations by performing the workflow associated with the response object. In addition, a workflow normally specifies a list of URLs, which can provide the relevant application modules. In case of no available local application module to instantiate a task, the node can download a mobile application from remote site according the URL specified by the workflow. Due to dynamic application loading, we can achieve reasonable system scalability in the open Internet environment.

In particular, our recent work on AN.P2P [21] implemented an Application Networking platform on P2P networks. The AN.P2P can reside on any P2P substrate and is not mandatory to install on each peer within the network. When an AN.P2P peer serves an ordinary peer, it will send a particular presentation of the content as if the AN.P2P is transparent to the ordinary peers. In contrast, when an AN.P2P peer serves another AN.P2P peer, it can send either the original object and the workflow or a final presentation. We believe this back compatibility feature could ease the adoption of AN.P2P into existed P2P networks.

Our preliminary simulation results have shown that using AN.P2P, we can achieve better system performance in terms of query hops and response transmission cost. It suggested that the AN.P2P has the potential benefits to deliver content in P2P networks with heterogeneous presentation requirements.

However, to derive a feasible AN.P2P infrastructure, we need to consider more aspects, such as the effects of different object placement methods, the cost of content adaptation, the trade-off between the computation delay and the transmission delay. These gaps motivated the study of this paper.

3 Object Placement Schemes

Generally, the AN.P2P aims to improve the overall system performance by placing the replica of objects and their workflow within the network. We defined two object placement schemes in the AN.P2P, as shown in figure 1.

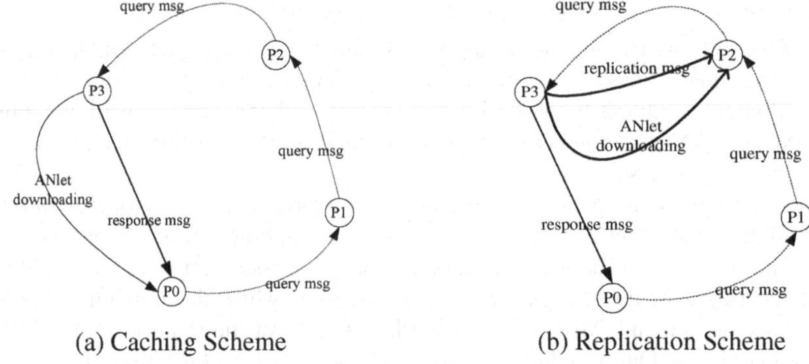

(a) Caching Scheme (b) Replication Scheme

Fig. 1. Object placement schemes

In this paper, we call the peer that publishes the content as the home peer (e.g. P_3 in figure 1), the peer that issues a query as the requesting peer (e.g. P_0), all peers that forward the query as the intermediate peers (e.g. P_1 and P_2), and the peer that serves the query as the target peer. The target peer can be the home peer itself or another peer with a replica of the content. We supposed the requesting peer could insert the user's presentation profile into the query message when it issues a query.

The caching scheme piggybacks the placement instruction within the response message, as shown in figure 1(a). Upon receiving a query message, the home peer can send either the final presentation of the queried content or its original object and the associated workflow to the requesting peer using a response message. The decision is made according to specific system policy.

After receiving the response message, the requesting peer will treat the response object as the final presentation of the queried content if there is no workflow within the response message. Then the requesting peer will render it to the user directly.

However, if the requesting peer detects there is a workflow within the response message, it will attempt to instantiate the workflow by downloading relevant ANlet modules. After that, the requesting peer feeds the received object to the workflow tasks, which will generate the appropriate content presentation according to the user profile in the query message. At the same time, the requesting peer will store the response message and the downloaded ANlets in its local cache. When it receives a later query for the same content, the peer can serve it directly. Similar to the home peer, the intermediate peer can either send the final presentation or the original object and the workflow to the new requesting peer.

In contrast, the replication scheme performs content placement using a dedicated replication message, as shown in figure 1(b). Upon receiving a query message, the home peer generates the final presentation of the queried content according to the user profile in the query message. Then it sends the generated content presentation to the requesting peer directly using a response message.

At the same time, the home peer can select a particular intermediate peer and send it a replica of the original object with the workflow. Upon receiving the replication message, the intermediate peer will store it in its local cache. When this peer receives a new query for the same content, it will load the cached object, instantiate the associated workflow using the downloaded ANlets, and generate the final presentation to the new requesting peer. Similarly, this peer can select another peer to replicate the object and workflow.

In summary, the replication scheme enables the AN.P2P to select an optimal peer to place the replica at the cost of dedicated replication message. On the other side, the caching scheme naturally populates content to the requesting peers at the cost of the forfeit of selective content placement.

In practice, the caching scheme and the replication scheme can coexist with each other. However, our later simulation will evaluate them separately to study their respective effect to the overall system performance.

In our simulation based on Pastry, the target peer will attempt to replicate the object to the intermediate peer at the previous hop of the current query path. Our simulation results will show that this last-hop replication strategy is much more efficient than a random placement on the structured P2P networks, such as Pastry, Chord and DKS.

4 Cache Design

Figure 2 shows the general architecture of an AN.P2P peer. The user interacts with a particular file sharing software utility, which performs interaction with the end user, retrieves content from the network to the local file directory, and shares the files within the directory to other peers. In addition, the software utility is responsible to provide the user presentation profile to the back-end AN.P2P platform. The profile is specified as a list of name and value pairs, including the user device type, display size, processing capabilities, and so on. We intended to leverage on existing techniques, such as CC/PP [4], to specify the user profile.

The AN.P2P platform resides between the software utility and the P2P network. It issues queries according to the user action, forwards bypassing messages, receives responded or replicated objects, and delivers the retrieved content to the software utility.

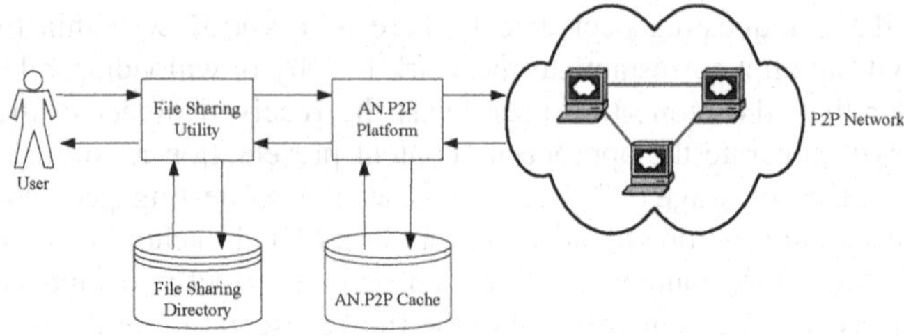

Fig. 2. Architecture of an AN.P2P peer

In particular, each AN.P2P maintains a local cache to store the response message or the replication message. We have designed an XML format to encapsulate both the content object and the workflow specification into a single message.

In AN.P2P cache, the content id is not sufficient to identify a cached item since multiple versions of the same content may coexist. Hence, we use the union of content id and a list of attribute entries to identify an object. Each attribute entry is specified as a name and value pair.

When the peer lookups its cache, it first checks if there exist cached items with the requested content id. If found, the peer cache then matches each profile entry in the query message against the corresponding attribute entry of the cached item. If all entries are compatible, it is a cache hit and the cache can use this item to serve the query, with possible content adaptation by the associated workflow. Otherwise, it is a cache miss.

If there is a profile entry in the query message but no corresponding attribute entry of the cached item, the cache treats it as a compatible match since the content provider cannot predict all possible entries inserted by the client. Therefore, our matching strategy attempts to achieve the best-effort content availability while avoiding conflicting attributes.

In particular, we defined two types of entries. One type is the "string" entry, whose value is a character string. For instance, the language attribute of a document is of string type (e.g. lang="eng"). To match a string type attribute, the two strings in comparison should be exactly same. The second type is the "range" entry, whose value is a numerical range. To match a query message to the cached item, the numerical range in the query message should be within the range defined by the attribute of the cached item. For instance, the quality attribute of a music clip defines the range of (0, 0.8). This item can be used to a query with quality profile (0, 0.4), but cannot be used to a query for full quality music (0, 1).

5 Performance Evaluation

5.1 Background

Recently, P2P file sharing is infamous for copyright infringement, as evident in the rampant piracy in P2P media-sharing applications. Hence, digital rights management on P2P has become an urgent requirement by the media-recording industry.

Iwata and Abe [9] proposed several P2P based DRM models. In general, when authoring content, the media object will be encapsulated by a secured container. The secured object is distributed in the network and any peer can download it freely. In order to render the content, the recipient's media player needs to retrieve a license that supplies the key to disclose the secured object. Pioneer implementations have paved the way for this new paradigm, such as Altnet [1]. However, integrating DRM into P2P systems is not a trivial exercise. It involves multiple functions as identification, tracking and sharing of music with those of licensing, monitoring and payment [12,13]. Our case study in this paper considered two particular problems: (i) watermarking to trace user and (ii) transcoding on secured object.

First, traditional DRM system normally traces the user of content by watermarking the content before it is secured on the original server. However, this method cannot be applied to the P2P network, since the intermediate peers are not authorized to watermark the secured object. Secondly, media transcoding to the secured objects would be infeasible on intermediate peers without explicit system support. If all watermarking and adaptation are performed on the home peer of the content, the system will regress to the server-client model.

To tentatively address the problems above, we implemented a sample workflow to deliver media objects with DRM copyright protection. The home peer attaches its secured object with this workflow composed by two ANlets, as shown in figure 3. Each of them contains the key to disclose the associated object, transform it, and write it back securely using the key. The first ANlet is a *media trimmer* that transforms original media object to appropriate lower quality versions according to the type of the recipient device. The second ANlet inserts watermark into the object according to the certification presented by the user. After receiving the response object, the recipient media player will attempt to obtain the license and render the media. In addition, the protection of key in ANlet and the peer authentication are beyond the scope of this paper. We intend to leverage existing research results on mobile code safety [7,19] and distributed authentication methods [15].

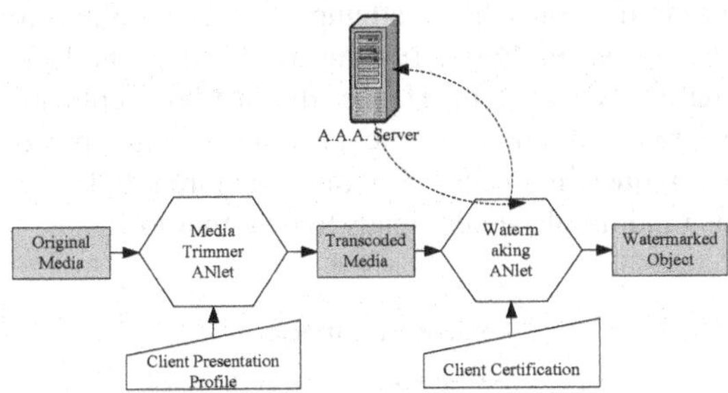

Fig. 3. Emulated peer-to-peer DRM workflow

5.2 Simulation Results

Our simulation emulated two P2P DRM scenarios. The first one is the End-user scenario, where the P2P network is composed directly by end users who want to retrieve and share media content on the network. In the simulation, we authored 10000 media contents on a Pastry network with 1024 peers. We assume each peer is resided on PC, PDA or mobile phone. The percentages for the number of these devices are 50%, 20% and 30% respectively. The PC renders the original media, the PDA renders 0.6 quality of original media, and the mobile phones can only render 0.3 quality of original media. Finally, we treated the PC as the high-end peers who are capable to execute ANlets. Hence, the AN.P2P schemes only deploy workflow to these PC peers, while treating PDA and phone peers as ordinary peers.

The other scenario is the Media-library scenario, where whole network is a hybrid structure. In particular, the end user will connect to a particular local media library to search and retrieve media content, while several media libraries will form a Pastry network to share media content between each other. In the simulation, we assumed there are 16 media libraries located in different places to share 10000 media contents in total. Similarly, we assume the end users connected to each library are resided on PC (50%), PDA (20%) or mobile phone (30%). Since all library peers are installed on powerful servers, the AN.P2P schemes can place object and workflow to all of them.

In both simulations, we assume the sizes of the original media objects follow the Pareto [3] distribution with α=1.25 and k=3MB, and the user requests follow the Zipf-like [2] distribution with λ=0.7. The simulation results will be presented in the following sections respectively.

5.2.1 Placement Schemes

Our first experiment evaluated the effect of the caching and replication placement schemes. Figure 4 presents the network cache hit ratio of the two placement schemes under different cache size. In particular, we defined there is a network cache hit when a query is resolved from an intermediate peer instead of the home peer of the queried content. Hence, the network cache hit ratio can represent the percentage of queries that are resolved from replicas distributed within the network.

It is noticeable that the replication scheme greatly outperforms the caching scheme. The hit ratio of the replication scheme increases considerably when we enlarge the cache size, in contrast to the trivial enhancement under the caching scheme. This is because our last-hop replication scheme attempts to place replicas to the previous hop along query path. Based on the Pastry routing mechanism, the last hop peer tends to receive more queries for the content. Hence, the last-hop replication would achieve higher cache reuse rate. In contrast, the caching scheme places replicas to the randomly generated requesting peers. On the structured P2P network, the replica reuse rate under this random placement tends to be rather low.

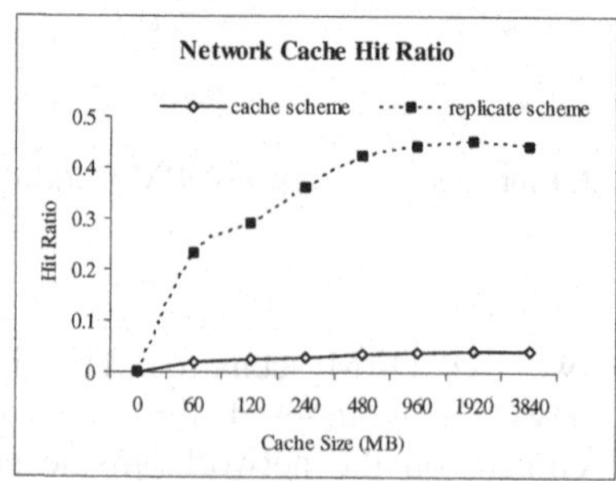

Fig. 4. Network cache hit ratio under different placement schemes

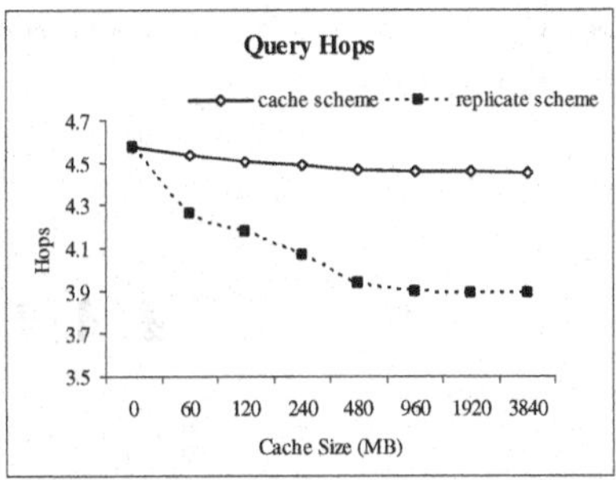

Fig. 5. Query hops under different placement schemes

Moreover, figure 5 presents the average query hops under the two placement schemes. In our simulation, the number of query hops is defined as the number of peers passed until the query is resolved. In general, less query hops implies higher searching efficiency and smaller query delay. The result shows that the replication scheme outperforms the caching scheme, because the former can achieve much higher replica reuse than the latter.

Because our simulation is based on the structured P2P network, the absolute reduction of query hops may not be much significant. However, if applying the AN.P2P to unstructured P2P networks, such as Gnutella, the reduction of searching size would be much more considerable.

Figure 6 presents the reduction of direct distance under the two placement schemes. We define the direct distance as the geographic distance between the requesting peer and the target peer. The curves within the figure represent the reduction ratio of direct distance after applying a placement scheme, compared to no scheme applied. The figure shows that the replication scheme can reduce the average distance by 10% with the increase of cache size. However, the caching scheme only achieves insignificant improvement (less than 2%). The result suggests that under the replication scheme, requesting peers are more likely to retrieve contents from nearby peers.

Figure 7 presents the retrieval latency under the two placement schemes. Figure 7(a) shows that the replication scheme achieves much lower overall retrieval latency than the caching scheme, while figure 7(b) gives the detailed computation and transmission latencies.

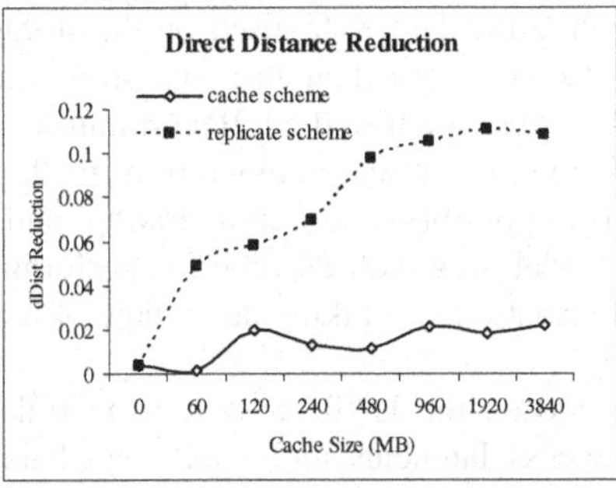

Fig. 6. Distance reduction under different placement schemes

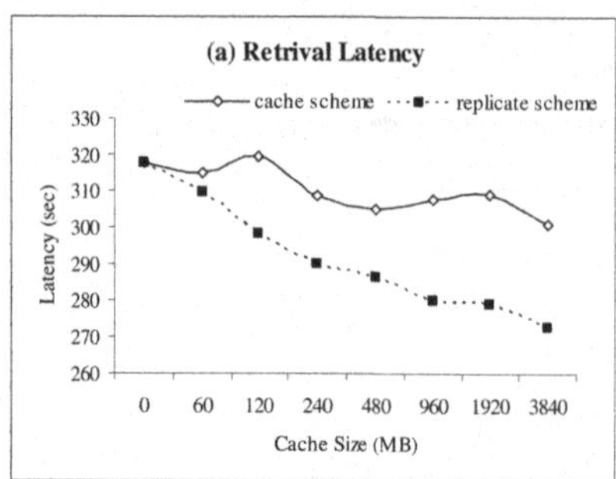

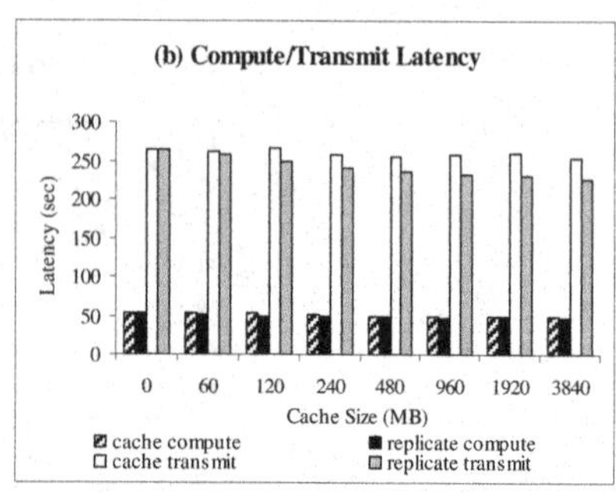

Fig. 7. Delays under different placement schemes

6 Related Work

There have been many P2P file sharing systems in use or under development. Early systems are based on either the central index server such as Napster [16], or the unstructured substrate such as Gnutella [6] and KaZaA [11]. These systems were primarily intended for the large-scale of data files; while persistence and reliable content location were not guaranteed or necessary in those environments.

Many later researchers proposed other systems built upon key-based routing (KBR) overlays. Typical examples are the PAST [17] and CFS [5]. They both aimed to provide a large-scale peer-to-peer persistent storage utility, based on Pastry [18] and Chord [22] respectively. In particular, the CFS storage is block-oriented. Each block is stored on multiple nodes with adjacent Chord node ids and popular blocks can be cached at additional nodes. Though the block based file structure causes additional overhead as each file data and metadata block must be located using a separate Chord lookup, CFS allows fine-grained block storage and permits parallel block retrievals, which benefits large files.

Based on the fundamental P2P file sharing systems above, recent researchers have proposed many augmented application and studies, including the Top-K replication, Squirrel web cache, replica enumeration, and LAR. Top-K [14] and Squirrel [10] are two similar systems. They targeted to implement the peer-to-peer based community storage. The key idea was to enable the end user to share their local caches, to form an efficient and scalable P2P file sharing systems. In particular, the Squirrel aimed to cache the Web objects, while the Top-K focused on the storage of large media files. Moreover, Kangasharju also provided their in-depth study on fundamental issues of Top-K replication and file replacement in the P2P community.

Waldvogel [23] designed a replica enumeration method, which allowed for controlled replication. The possibility of enumerating and addressing individual replicas allows dynamic updates as well as superior performance without burdening the network with state information, yet taking advantage of locality information when available.

Gopalakrishnan [8] proposed the LAR, a system neutral replication protocol. It aimed to maintain low access latencies and good load balance even under highly skewed demand. Instead of creating replicas on all nodes on a source-destination path, LAR relied on server load measurement to choose the replication points precisely. In addition, LAR augmented the routing process with lightweight "hints" that effectively shortcut the original routing and direct queries towards new replicas. However, LAR did not address the server joining and leaving problems. Hence, the effect of the network structure change on the LAR performance is not clear yet.

7 Conclusion

The work of this paper was to improve the overall performance of AN.P2P through dedicated content placement schemes and caching strategies. Our simulation results based on an emulated P2P based DRM system suggests that the proposed methods could help to achieve higher overall performance. In particular, the replication scheme could effectively place the object replica onto peers within a structured network. Our performance evaluation was restricted on structured P2P network. A thorough evaluation on both structured and unstructured P2P networks can help to infer complete understanding on various strategies. Moreover, our simulation was based on synthetic workload. We are looking forward to deploying the AN.P2P onto real P2P networks, which could help us study the Application Networking mechanism in more details.

References

1. Altnet. [online]. http://www.altnet.com
2. L. Breslau, P. Cao, L. Fan, G. Phillips, S. Shenker, "Web Caching and Zipf-like Distributions: Evidence and Implications", Proceedings of INFOCOM, 1999.
3. M. E. Crovella, A. Bestavros, "Self-Similarity in World Wide Web Traffic: Evidence and Possible Causes", Proceedings of the ACM International Conference on Measurement and Modeling of Computer Systems, 1996.
4. Composite Capabilities/Preferences Profile . http://www.w3.org/Mobile/CCPP.
5. F. Dabek, , M. F. Kaashoek, D. Karger, "Wide-area Cooperative Storage with CFS", Proceedings of Symposium of Operation System Principles, 2001.
6. Gnutella, http://www.gnutella.com
7. G. McGraw, E.W. Felten, "Securing Java: Getting Down to Business with Mobile code", Wiley, 1999.
8. V. Gopalakrishnan, B. Silaghi, B. Bhattacharjee, P. Kelenher, "Adaptive Replication in Peer-to-Peer Systems", Proceedings of 24th Inter. Conf. on Distributed Computing System, 2004.
9. T. Iwata, T. Abe, K. Ueda, H. Sunaga, "A DRM System Suitable for P2P Content Delivery and the Study on its Implementation", Proceeding of the 9th Asia-Pacific Conf. on Comm., Vol.2, 21-24, pp.806-811, 2003.
10. S. Iyer, A. Rowstron, P. Drusche, "Squirrel: A Decentralized Peer-to-peer Web Cache", Proceedings of the 21st ACM Symposium on Principles of Distributed Computing, July 2002.
11. KaZaA, http://www.kazaa.com
12. W. Ku, C-H. Chi, "Survey on the technological aspects of Digital Rights Management", Proceedings of the 7th Information Security Conference, 2004.

13. T. Kalker, D. Epema, P. Hartel, I. Lagendijk, M. v. Steen, "Music2Share – Copyright-compliant Music Sharing in P2P Systems", Proceedings of the IEEE, vol.92(6):961-970, June 2004.
14. J. Kangasharju, K. W. Ross, D. A. Turner, "Adaptive Content Management in Structured P2P Communities", Proceedings of 21st ACM Symposium on Principles of Distributed Computing, 2002.
15. J. Li, M. Yarvis, P. Reiher, "Securing distributed adaptation", Proceeding of Computer Networks, Vol. 38, pp. 347-371, 2002.
16. Napster. http://www.napster.com.
17. A. Rowstron, P. Druschel, "Storage Management and Caching in PAST, a Large-scale, Persistent Peer-to-peer Storage Utility", Proceedings of ACM Symposium on Operating Systems Principles, Nov. 2001.
18. A. Rowstron, P. Druschel, "Pastry: Scalable, Decentralized Object Location and Routing for Large-scale Peer-to-peer Systems", Proceedings of the 18th IFIP/ACM International Conference of Distributed Systems Platforms, Nov. 2001.
19. A. D. Rubin, E.E. Greer, "Mobile Code Security", IEEE Internet Computing, Nov. 1998.
20. M. Su, C-H. Chi, "Architecture and Performance of Application Networking for Pervasive Content Delivery", Proceedings of 21st International Conference on Data Engineering, Tokyo, 2005.
21. M. Su, C-H. Chi, "Application Networking on Peer-to-peer Networks", Proceedings of the 14th International World Wide Web Conference, Japan, 2005.
22. I. Stoica, R. Morris, D. Karger, M. F. Kaashoek, H. Balakrishnan, "Chord: A Scalable Peer-to-peer Lookup Service for Internet Applications", Proceedings of the 2001 ACM SIGCOMM Conference, 2001.
23. M. Waldvogel, P. Hurley, D. Bauer, "Dynamic Replica Management in Distributed Hash Tables", IBM Research Report, July 2003.

Role-Based Peer-to-Peer Model: Capture Global Pseudonymity for Privacy Protection

Zude Li, Guoqiang Zhan, and Xiaojun Ye

Institute of Information System and Engineering,
School of Software, Tsinghua University, Beijing, China. 100084
{li-zd04, zhan-gq03}@mails.tsinghua.edu.cn, yexj@mail.tsinghua.edu.cn

Abstract. Peer-to-peer (P2P) resource dissemination has raised some security concerns for privacy protection and intellectual property rights protection along resource dissemination over the network. To solve these challenges, we propose the Role-Based P2P model, in which the *role* notion is functioned as the bridge component between users and resources to enforce secure resource dissemination together with relative constraints. The property rights attached to resource and user's private identity information are both protected as promise by taking each local role as a permission set in local centralized network and each global role as a user's pseudonym in global decentralized network. Furthermore, we propose the access control algorithm to describe how to handle access requests by the role policy in the role-based *hybrid* P2P model. In addition, we illustrate the *intra* and *inter* access schemas as two kinds of access processes. The model is feasible as its role structure and the connection with user and resource in open environment are consistent with the application objectives. The model is extensible, as the role structure can be also available for Purpose-Based Privacy Protection technologies.

Keywords: Peer-to-Peer, Privacy Protection, Role, Pseudonymity.

1 Introduction

The notion of *peer-to-peer* (P2P) refers to a class of systems and applications that employ distributed resources to perform a critical function in a decentralized manner [8]. Currently the growth of availability of powerful networked computers and decentralizing trends of large-scale software development are to form the perfect playground for P2P research and product development [21], which result in many namable systems and applications, such as FreeNet [3], Napster[1], PAST [9], Gnutella[2], Seti@Home[3], etc. Since there is no general agreement about what *is* and what *is not* P2P [17], here we only extract some striking features to describe its general meaning as follows: (1) Sharing of digital resources by direct

[1] Napster system introduction, www.napster.com
[2] Gnutella. The Gnutella web site: http://gnutella.wego.com
[3] The seti@home project web site. http://setiathome.ssl.berkeley.edu

J.X. Yu, M. Kitsuregawa, and H.V. Leong (Eds.): WAIM 2006, LNCS 4016, pp. 193–204, 2006.
© Springer-Verlag Berlin Heidelberg 2006

exchange; (2) Fault-tolerant (variable connectivity and transmission) and self-organizing [10, 14, 17]; (3) Decentralized computing with independent addressing system on operational computers.The advantages of P2P systems are obvious, cost sharing/reduction, improved scalability/reliability, resource aggregation and interoperability, increased autonomy and anonymity (a privacy feature [20]) [8].

Resource dissemination is an important P2P application category on the network, which allows personal computers to function in a coordinated manner as a distributed storage medium by contributing, searching, and obtaining digital resource [17, 22]. However, it also raises some security concerns for privacy protection, intellectual property rights protection along resource dissemination in P2P environment. For example, in some applications, different users in the P2P network may need different identity control policies when they try to access different resources, which can be exactly expressed by access control models. But whether or how to enforce access control mechanisms on P2P network is still an open problem [4], as many P2P systems just focus on enough information sharing but not authentication and authorization on resource dissemination.

We argue that a feasible access control policy or mechanism is indispensable for property rights protection in generic *hybrid* P2P resource dissemination applications [22, 17]. In addition, privacy protection on user attracts more and more human attention. In generic P2P applications, a troubling contradiction is that the user's identity should be hid as user's private information in a resource dissemination transaction while it is needed to be known by another user for the trust relationship establishment between two sides, which is a critical factor for successful resource dissemination beside property rights allowance. The user pseudonymity is a requirement for privacy protection [5, 1, 20, 2], which should refer to that user's identity should be hid in the access transaction to the system. Further, the relative user's behaviors should also be protected as the unobservability requirement for privacy protection [20, 2].

With advantages of neutral-policy, self-organization, and ease administration, Role-Based Access Control (RBAC) forms to a popular access control policy deployed in a large number of applications for secure resource access [18, 7]. The role notion in RBAC application is a system entity as the bridge of privilege management and information flow between user and resource. So we introduce it into generic P2P modelling for effective control on resource dissemination for property rights protection, as well as privacy protection through its *pseudonym* function in global decentralized P2P environment.

We propose the Role-Based P2P model to capture all of the above requirements (access control, property rights protection, privacy protection on user's identity and behaviors) in *hybrid* resource dissemination P2P applications, which is the main contribution of the paper. The model can be used for integrating several centralized RBAC applications to be a decentralized *hybrid* P2P system by taking global role as the connection among diverse (local) role structures. At the same time, global role can be seen as user's pseudonym over the global network that is consistent with the pseudonymity requirement of privacy protection on user's identity. In each local environment, the initial role hierarchies, user-role assignment, and role-permission assignment relations are maintained without change, while the local access decision module can collaborate with others to provide more resource sharing and dissemination opportunities.

The rest of this paper is organized as follows: Section 2 identifies the *hybrid* P2P model based on the taxonomy of P2P, the security challenges and the requirement for role policies and relative constraints in RBAC. Section 3 focuses on the role-based *hybrid* P2P integrating *hybrid* P2P model with RBAC mechanism. Finally, Section 4 gives a short conclusion of the whole paper.

2 Preliminaries

As proposed in the literature [17], we can classify P2P model into two categories: *pure* P2P and *hybrid* P2P model.

- *Pure* P2P refers to a completely decentralized P2P system, in which all nodes are fully equivalent in terms of functionality and tasks they perform. The Gnutella system is a typical *pure* P2P application instance;
- *Hybrid* P2P refers to a P2P system with limited nonequivalent nodes, such as *super nodes*, *host peers*), etc., which are designed as local reference monitors. Napster, seti@Home and Kazaa[4] are typical instances.

The essential difference between *pure* and *hybrid* P2P is the degree of *centralization*. In fact, there are three classifications for the centralization difference: fully (globally) centralized, partially (locally) centralized, non-centralized (completely decentralized). The first one refers to *non*-P2P systems, such as general RBAC systems, which is not in the scope of this paper, but the second refers to *hybrid* P2P and the third refers to *pure* P2P. In general, a *hybrid* P2P has more advantages than a pure one, such as its better flexibility, and effective resource dissemination among peers with respect to access control and privacy protection. And especially, all requirements and security mechanisms for the *pure* model should be described and specified for the *hybrid* one. So we take the *hybrid* P2P model as the generic base for convenient discussion in this paper.

As the *hybrid* P2P model definition described, there are some limited nonequivalent peers in *hybrid* P2P applications. So in our *hybrid* P2P model, we classify *peers* into three types according to their different privileges and domains: *host peer*, *user peer* and *resource peer*.

- *Host peer* refers to a local supernode with a control domain similar to a central server-side reference monitor of RBAC application, including user authentication, user-role assignment based on role's predefined permissions (later discussed more), active paths of resource dissemination, etc.;
- *User peer* refers to a user end-point, such as client-side automatic access requesting software, or explore-frame operation set, which presents the corresponding a user's identity and status when it is activated;

[4] Kazaa. The Kazaa web site. http://www. kazaa.com

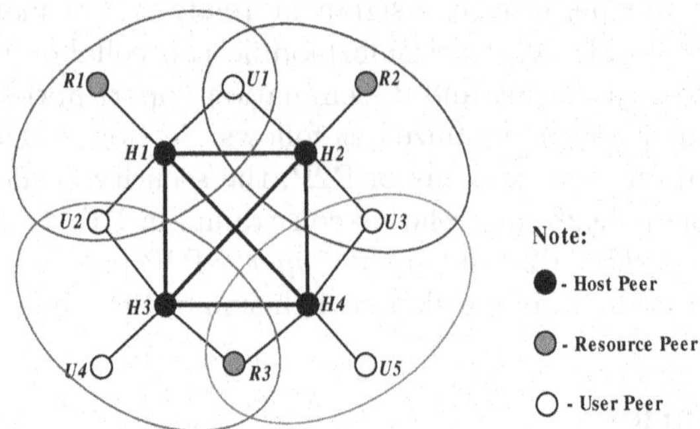

Fig. 1. The topology of a *hybrid* P2P model with four *intra*-P2P networks

– *Resource peer* refers to a storage warehouse in end-point storage medium to store digital resource for P2P dissemination applications.

It should be noted that user peer and resource peer can be integrated together in one end-point, which can both store and disseminate resource to other peers as well as access to resource in others.

A typical *hybrid* P2P network topology is demonstrated in *Fig.1.* It is obvious that there are different relations between user and resource, or among users in the *hybrid* P2P application. In some narrow domains consisting of several peers, users may be familiar with each other, including the name, role, habit, and behavior in the system. So user's identity is unnecessary to be hid in such a narrow environment. But users may require the system to protect (hide) their identities during the resource dissemination transaction with others out of the local environment. To distinguish the above different requirements while keep the role mechanism still feasible for such a complicated *hybrid* P2P application, we firstly identify two basic networks induced by the *hybrid* P2P model topology as the base for the solution, and then take *local* and *global* role structures to handle the difference, where the detail is discussed in the next section.

Definition 1 (inter-P2P network). An inter-P2P network (also named host peer network) refers to a subnetwork of the whole P2P topology consisting of all active host peers and their connections.

We define that a peer is *active* if it is on-line on the current time point. An active host peer takes the function of a reference monitor over the access requests to the outer resource from inner users and the requests to the inner resource from outer users. The *inter*-P2P network is a full complete graph, since there is always a connection edge(path) that have been existed or can be existed between any two active host peers.

Definition 2 (intra-P2P network). An intra-P2P network (also named local centralized network) is a subnetwork of a hybrid P2P topology consisting of one active host peer, several user and resource peers that connect to the host peer.

The *intra*-P2P network represents a narrow control domain which is independent from the outer peers. In such a domain, inner resource can be accessed and disseminated to inner users through the authentication and authorization mechanism on the host peer, which is worked as a local reference monitor in this domain. In general, we just define just one monitor in an *intra*-P2P network (it is helpful for control consistency). Overall, the network is similar to a centralized access control topology.

In any *hybrid* P2P network model, there is one and only one induced *inter*-P2P network, but several induced *intra*-P2P networks. As in *Fig.1*, there are four *intra*-P2P networks in the model (marked by four circles). In such a *hybrid* P2P model, it is obvious that any two host peers connect mutually in the *inter*-P2P network, and any user/resource peer connects with an active host peer in at least one *local intra*-P2P network.

To capture the different requirements above, the role mechanism is indispensable to a successful *hybrid* P2P resource dissemination application. There are several reasons supporting this view.

- Role is semantic constraint integration expressing a set of permissions, which can used for appropriate digital rights protection along resource dissemination over network;
- Role mechanism can be extended for user identity and behavior information protection. Since an active role is a de facto user's pseudonym in application, the user identity need not be disclosed and the behaviors also cannot map to the identity.

In short, the extended role mechanism is indispensable for a privacy-preserving *hybrid* P2P application. Before the elaborate solution on their integration, we first introduce the general RBAC model that contains role mechanism as the "bridge" function between users and permissions.

RBAC is a centralized policy by taking a reference monitor (with server function) to control all subjects' requests for resource, which is concerned more with access to functions and information than strictly with access to information in many applications [18, 7]. Role in RBAC is a bridge of information flow and permission management between subject and object. Core concepts of the general RBAC model include roles (and its hierarchy structure), users, permissions, user-role assignments, role-permission assignments, static/dynamic separation of duty (SSD/DSD) [6, 7].

RBAC is preferred within limited centralized control domain, and it is impossible to efficiently handle access requests from a large number of users within decentralized environment only by itself [11].

In our P2P modelling process, we should utilize RBAC's advantages, such as high efficiency for narrow centralized access control decision, while avoid its disadvantages including low performance for large-scale decentralized control.

To achieve the goal in a *hybrid* P2P model, we design the *local* and *global* role mechanisms for resource access decision in *intra*-P2P network and *inter*-P2P network, respectively. In *intra*-P2P environment, the role structure, user-role assignment, and role-permission assignment are maintained similar to general

RBAC application. While in the *inter*-P2P environment, we take global role as a conversion balance among these roles in different local networks. Such a mechanism is contained in our proposed Role-Based *hybrid* P2P model.

3 Secure Role-Based Hybrid P2P Model

The above *hybrid* P2P model is just a framework abstracting generic P2P applications. Based on it, we define the Role-Based Hybrid P2P model to achieve the objectives proposed above, including digital rights protection through authorization and authentication, user's identity and behavior protection.

It uses the local role mechanism and the relative constraints in the local intra-P2P environment to build the quasi-RBAC reference monitor in the host peer domain, while it creates a global role structure to balance the access permission conversion among different local networks.

- It is an extended *hybrid* P2P model that can be available for most comprehensive resource dissemination applications;
- It is a dual-technology model providing maximal resource dissemination under an appropriate access control mechanism;
- It is a privacy-aware model, in which the pseudonymity feature is satisfied as user's identity is replaced by relative global roles, while the unobservability feature is also achieved as user's behaviors cannot map to user itself. Further, with this model, some other privacy protection techniques can be formed directly, such as Purpose-Based Access Control (PBAC) [12, 13].

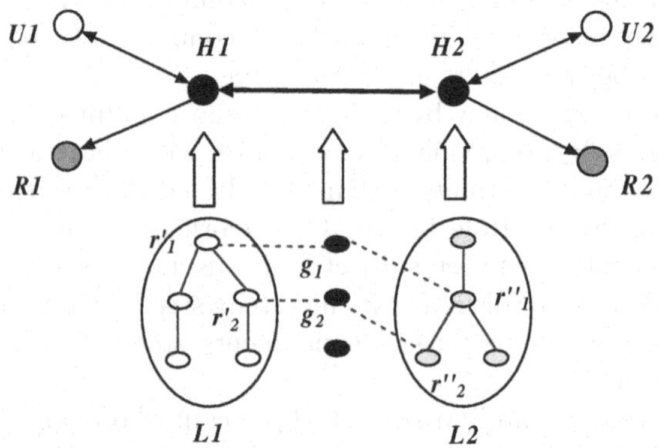

Fig. 2. A simple Role-Based Hybrid P2P model application

Fig.2 illustrates an application with the model. Node $H1$ (or $H2$), $R1$ (or $R2$), and $U1$ (or $U2$) refer to the host peer, resource peer, and user peer in intra-P2P network $L1$ (or $L2$). The role structures in $L1$ and $L2$ are different, such as r'_1 and r'_2 in the former structure and r''_1 and r''_2 in the latter one. In $L1$ (or $L2$), $U1$ (or $U2$) can successfully access to resources in $R1$ (or $R2$) through activating an appropriate role satisfying relative constraints in $H1$ (or $H2$). For accessing to resource out of the local environment, as the model defined, we set several global roles to balance the access permission conversion between the two role structures. For instance, we take g_1 as the conversion between r'_1 and r''_2, and g_2 between r'_2 and r''_2. It means if a user in $L1$ can activate r'_1 (or r'_2), he/she can also activate r''_1 (or r''_2) in $L2$ and successfully access to some resources in $R2$ that can be accessed by local users who can activate r''_1 (or r''_2). Users in $L2$ can do similarly. Overall, with the model, resource dissemination and sharing have been extended obviously while the relative digital rights protection and user identity protection are handled appropriately.

To specify the elaborate access control mechanism with role structure and some relations on the abstract *hybrid* model, we should firstly clarify the *local* and *global* notions for user, resource and role identification in various situations:

– A user is a *local* user within his/her belonged *intra*-P2P network, but is identified as a *global* one by peers in other indirect connected *intra*-P2P networks;
– A resource is a *local* resource within the *intra*-P2P network, but is identified as a *global* one by peers in other indirect connected *intra*-P2P networks;
– A *local* role refers to a role defined in a local centralized host peer as the bridge between local user and local resource, but a *global* role refers to a role as permission or function connection way of role hierarchy structure among host peers, which is activated automatically when a user accesses a resource dominated in different *intra*-P2P networks.

A *global* roles should be equivalent on access rights with a corresponding *local* role. For the whole P2P application with this model, the unique global administration task is to define *global* roles and their comparable relations with *local* roles in all *intra*-P2P networks. How to accomplish this work will be discussed later. Further, we describe the access trace from user to the resource by an *active path* defined as follows.

Definition 3 (Active Path). An *active path*, denoted as <ActiveHostPeerID, ActiveResourcePeerID, ResourceID>, is a dissemination channel which is available for resource dissemination from an active resource peer to an active user peer in the current P2P network status, where AcitiveHostPeerID, AcitiveResourcePeerID, ResourceID denotes the identity of an active host peer, an active resource peer, and a special resource respectively.

The preconditions for a resource can be disseminated to a user is that existing an active path towards the resource, and secondly, the user should be powerful (with enough rights) to access that resource, or in another word, the user can activate a role of appropriate permissions to do it. Now we define elements in our model formally.

- Resource(*Re*)={<*ResourceID*>}, which is dominated in the user peer side to list all resources (both *local* and *global*) in the network;
- Resource-RoleSet(*RR*)={<*ResourceID, RoleSet*>}. It is dominated in the resource peer side to list qualified *local*/ *global* roles for access corresponding resources inside;

- Resource-HostPeer(*RHP*)={<*ResourceIDHostPeerIDSet*>}, which is dominated in the host peer side to list which local/global resource that is possessed in which a local centralized environment represented by its unique host peer;
- Resource-ResourcePeer(*RRP*)={<*ResourceID,ResourcePeerID*>}, which is dominated in the host peer side to list which local resource is possessed in which local resource peers;
- User-Role(*UR*)={<*UserID,LocalRole,GlobalRole*>}, which is dominated in the host peer side to list which *local* roles and their equivalent *global* roles can be acquired by a user;
- Role-Hierarchy(*RH*)={<*Role,Role*>}, which denotes the role hierarchy structure in P2P resource dissemination applications. $< R_i,\ R_j > \in RH$ $(i \neq j)$, $(R_i \geq R_j)$, which indicates permissions of R_j are all contained in R_i.
- Static-Separation-of-Duty(*SSD*)={<*Role,Role*>}, which denotes mutual exclusive roles that cannot be possessed by same roles. $< R_i,\ R_j > \in SSD$ $(i{\neq}j)$, indicates R_i and R_j cannot be possessed by a role.

We can specify the relative RBAC security constraints by the above *UR*, *RH* and *SSD* within P2P network peers, and the expressive capability by our specification is equivalent to the original constraints in general RBAC models. We describe the security constraints within the above formula as follows:

Constraint 1. $\forall < u,\ r_i >, < u,\ r_j > \in UR$[5]$, < r_i,\ r_j > \notin SSD$.

Constraint 2. $< r_i,\ r_j > \in SSD,\ < r_j,\ r_k > \in RH \Rightarrow\ < r_i,\ r_k > \in SSD$.

Constraint 3. $\forall < u,\ r_i >, < u,\ r_j > \in UR,\ < r_i,\ r_j > \notin RH$.

Constraint 4. For roles activated by users to access to resource peers should be listed in *UR*.

Access Control Algorithm Running the Model. Now we propose the access control algorithm to describe the detail resource dissemination mechanism in the Role-Based Hybrid P2P model for general access control, property rights protection, and the user's pseudonym feature as follows:

1. A user peer submits request to direct-connected host peers for resource denoted by resourceID listed in *Re*;
2. A host peer receives the request and may do the following steps:
   (a) acquires the corresponding *local* role set and its equivalent *global* role set for this user from *UR*;
   (b) acquires the corresponding host peer set from *RHP* and judges whether the current host peer is contained in the set;
      - if the current host peer is in the set,
         • if the corresponding resource peer with respect to the resource in *RRP* is active, then returns the *local* role and the active path (the active resource peer) to the user peer;

[5] Here r_i, r_j are *local* or *global* roles.

    - or refuses the user's request by returning null and reporting that there are no active resource peers containing the resource;
  - or, broadcasts the resourceID into other host peers in the set and
    - if existing an active host peer which is in the set and the resource is listed in *RRP*, then
      - if the corresponding resource peer with respect to the resource in *RRP* is active, then returns the *local* and the corresponding *global* role, and the active path (the active host and the resource peer) to the user peer;
      - or, refuses the user's request by returning null and reporting that there are no active resource peers containing the resource.
    - or, refuses the user's request by returning null and reporting that there are no active host peers in the set available.

3. The user may do the following step according to the result from host peers:
   - if the result is the active path of the needed resource, then builds the connection according to the active path and activates a proper role (*local* role for local resource peer or *global* role for *global* resource peer) to send the access request to the active resource peer.
     - if the role is in the role set listed in *RR* in the resource peer with respect to the resource, the resource peer directly disseminates the resource to the user.
     - or, the resource peer refuses the request and reports the role's inability property to the user peer.
   - or, terminates the access process.

Through the algorithm, we can get two schemas of resource access process, the first is the access policy in an *intra*-P2P network, or called the *intra schema*, and the second is the access to resource among indirect connected *intra*-P2P networks, or called the *inter schema*.

Intra Schema. This schema is the simple one, where resource dissemination is limited in an *intra*-P2P network with *local* roles (without *global* roles). In *Fig.*3_I, user peer U_1 wants to require resource r_1, we can demonstrate the process within

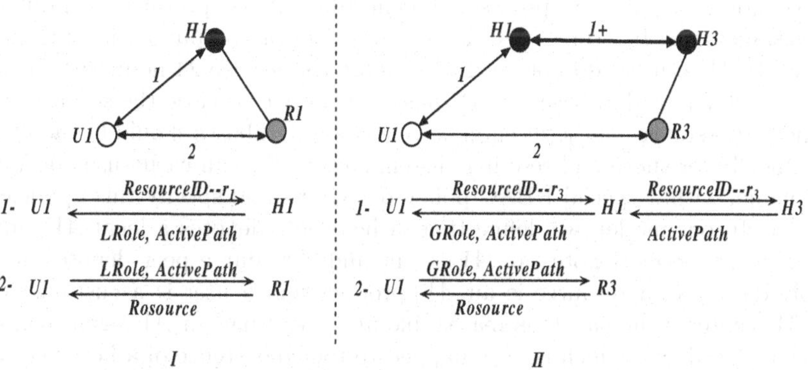

Fig. 3. *I*: the *intra* schema; *II*: the *inter* schema

this schema as follows: (1) U_1 sends the resource identity denoted by r_1 to the direct-connected active host peer H_1; (2) H_1 returns an active *local* role properly and an active path towards the resource peer R_1 containing r_1; (3) U_1 builds a connection to R_1 for r_1 dissemination; (4) R_1 directly sends r_1 to U_1.

Inter Schema. This schema is the complex one, where resource dissemination is propagated to global network with both *local* and *global* roles. In $Fig.3_{II}$, user peer U_1 wants to require resource r_3, we can demonstrate the process within this schema as follows: (1) U_1 sends the resource identity denoted by r_3 to the direct-connected active host peer H_1; (2) H_1 sends r_3 to any active host peers; (3) the host peer H_3 returns H_1 an active path towards to the resource peer R_3 containing r_3; (4) H_1 retransmits it with an active *global* role properly to U_1; (5) U_1 builds a connection to R_3 for r_3 dissemination by the *global* role; (6) R_3 directly sends r_3 to U_1.

Case Study *1*: Distributed Dissemination Control (DCON). DCON means that the distributor or rights holder can control recipients' access to the digital information [11], In another word, it is a security policy of controlling digital resource access before and after distribution [15, 16]. Through Internet, DCON can be applied as large as possible by taking local networks as *intra*-P2P networks and taking routers as host peers in P2P resource dissemination application model with RBAC policy. The special constraints in the real application, which should be implemented in P2P system, include: (1) different resources need different restriction levels for intellectual property rights protection, which can be expressed by role (with its hierarchy structure) mechanism; (2) it is allowed that customers in the DCON application are anonymous, which can be implemented by special technics on user peer identity in the P2P system; (3) resource property right should be materialized by users' some contributions such as money, contracts or other payments, which is implemented by a special e-payment system dominated in host peers. In conclusion, a DCON application can be modelled by a *hybrid* P2P network model with a special RBAC policy.

Case Study *2*: Audio/Video (AV) Supply Application. Building a distributed AV supply application on P2P network requires that, (1) different AV agents should acquire and process different kinds of AV products; (2) different AV products can be stored in different databases or computers in different regions; (3) AV centers do not need to support the service 24 hours for 7 days a week; (4) different databases or AV agents can open or close the service freely. So the active statues of these centers, agents, and databases should be monitored dynamically for successful resource dissemination. We can easily use our *hybrid* P2P model with a special RBAC policy to express and specify this application practice. In our model, we define that, a host peer denotes a local AV supply center, a user peer denotes an AV agent and a resource peer denotes an AV supply database, a resource is an AV product and a user is a customer or a sub-AV center principal. It is reasonable in reality that an AV agent contains some AV products, which is also mapped to the coexistence of a host peer or a user peer and some resource. From the above mapping specification, we can infer that the detail access process in this *AV* resource dissemination application can be simulated by the access control algorithm in our model.

Administration. The administration of our *hybrid* P2P model with RBAC policy mainly should dominate in host peers to manage all access control decisions and active status modification, since host peers contains the RBAC policy management to handle all requests from users and to be the access bridge for resource dissemination from resource peers to user peers. For administrating host peers in our model, we propose that it be preferred to set a *central administrator* (a software of automatization capability preferred) to manage the whole P2P system's work. It is feasible and effective since there is only one induced *inter*-P2P network in every P2P network model, where access elements in every host peer and transmission connections among them can be monitored efficiently by a central administrator. The corresponding tasks are: (1) automatically maintains *Re* list in user peer side, and makes sure that resourceIDs listed in *Re* can cover all existed or newly emerged resource identities; (2) automatically maintains *RR* list in resource peer side according to role setting and local resource status changes; (3) automatically maintains *RHP*, *RRP* in host peer side dynamically, and makes sure the active path can be built successfully according to the current P2P network status; (4) automatically maintains *UR*, *RH*, *SSD* in host peer side, and makes sure constraints for RBAC policy can be effective in time. Further, the dynamical status of P2P network should be monitored in real time. Any interaction can arise the modification of the whole P2P network.

4 Conclusion

This paper propose a *hybrid* P2P model with RBAC policy and constraints to effectively manage resource dissemination within the *hybrid* P2P environment. The access control algorithm provided describes how to handle access requests by RBAC policy and constraints within P2P network environment. The two access schemas (*intra* and *inter*) are to express the algorithm in detail. We propose the item *active path* for a role activated by a user to access to a resource by satisfying RBAC constraints on role cardinality, role hierarchy, static separation of duty. The advantages of our model include flexibility, scalability, and security.

In the above, we give the way of building a *hybrid* P2P model with RBAC policy and a novel access control algorithm to guide the real resource dissemination application on P2P network. The administration part proposed briefly in the end of the paper describes the functions of an excellent administrator, which should be specified in more detail in the following P2P modeling research.

References

1. Anna Lysyanskaya and Ronald L.Rivest and etc.: Pseudonym Systems, theory.lcs.mit.edu/ rivest/ LysyanskayaRivestSahaiWolf-PseudonymSystems.pdf
2. Anonymity, Unlinkability, Unovervability, Pseudonymity and Identity Management–A Consolidated Proposal for Terminology, Http://dud.inf.tu-dresden.de/

3. Clarke,I. et al.: Protecting Free Expression Online with Freenet. IEEE Internet Computing 6(1). January-February. (2002) 40-49
4. Daswani, N., Garcia-Molina, H., Yang, B.: Open Problems in Data-Sharing Peer-to-Peer Systems. In Proceedings of the 9th International Conference on Database Theory. Siena, Italy. (2003)
5. Daniel Cvrček and *Václav* Matyáš Jr.: Pseudonymity in The Light of Evidence-Based Trust, Twelfth International Workshop on Security Protocols, In Authentic Privacy, Berlin, DE, Springer, 109-116 (2002)
6. David Ferraiolo and Richard Kuhn: Role-Based Access Controls. Proceedings of the 15th National Computer Security Conference Vol. II. (1992) 554-563
7. David. Ferraiolo, Rsvi Sandhu, Serban Gavrila, D. Richard Kuhn and Ramaswamy Chandramouli: Proposed NIST Standard for Role-Based AccessControl, ACM Transactions on Information and System Security, Vol.4, No.3, (2001) 224-274
8. Dejan S. Milojicic, Vana Kalogeraki, and Rajan Lukose, er al. : Peer-to-peer Computing. HP Laboratories, HPL-2002-57, March 8th (2002)
9. Druschel P., Rowstorn, A.: PAST: A Large-Scale, Persistent Peer-to-Peer Storage Utility, HotOS VIII, Schloss Elmau, Germany, May (2001)
10. Graham, R.L.: Traditional and Non-Traditional Applications. Peer-to-Peer Networks. Lecture. http://www.ida.liu.se/ TDTS43/tdts43-10-peer-topeer.pdf. (2001)
11. Jaehong Park, Ravi Sandhu and James Schifalacqua: Security Architectures for Controlled Digital Information Dissemination. IEEE. (2000)
12. Ji-won Byun, Elisa Bertino and Ninghui Li: Purpose-Based Access Control Of Complex Data For Privacy Protection, SACMAT'05, Sweden, Jun, (2005)
13. Ji-won Byun, Elisa Bertino and Ninghui Li: Purpose-Based Access Control For Privacy Protection In Rrelational Database Systems, Technical Report 2004-52, Purdue University, (2004)
14. Peer-to-Peer Working Group. http://www.p2pwg.org. (2001)
15. Roshan K.Thomas and Ravi Sandhu: Towards Multi-dimensional Characterization of Dissemination Control, Proceedings of the 5th IEEE International Workshop on Policies for Distributed Systems and Networks (POLICY'04), (2004)
16. Renato Lannella and Peter Higgs: Driving Content Management with Digital Rights Management, IPR systems whitepaper series, (2003)
17. Stephanos, Dreoutsellis Theotokis, and Diomidis Spinellis: A Survey of Peer-to-Peer Content Distributioon technologies. ACM Computing Survey, Vol.36, No.4, December (2004) 335-371
18. Ravi Sandhu, et al.: Role-based Access Control Models, IEEE Computer, Vol.29, No.2, (1996) 38-47
19. Serban I. Gavrila and John F.Barkley: Formal Sepcification for Role Based Access Control User/Role and Role/Role Relationship Management. 3rd ACM Workshop on Role-Based Access Fairfax VA, (1998) 81-91
20. The Common Criteria Project Sponsoring Organisations: Common Criteria for Information Technology Security Evaluation, part 2, draft version 3 and version 2.1-2.3, August, (2005)
21. Todd Sundsted: A New-Fangled Name, but An Old and Useful Approach to Computing Level: Introductory. http://www-128.ibm.com/developerworks/library/j-p2p/index.html. (2001)
22. Yu Zhang, Xianxian Li, et al.: Access Control in Peer-to-Peer Collaborative Systems. Distributed Computing Systems Workshops, 25th IEEE International Conference June (2005) 835-840

A Reputation Management Scheme Based on Global Trust Model for Peer-to-Peer Virtual Communities*

Jingtao Li, Xueping Wang, Bing Liu, Qian Wang, and Gendu Zhang

School of Information Science & Engineering, Fudan University, Shanghai, 200433, China
{lijt, wangxp}@fudan.edu.cn

Abstract. Peer-to-peer virtual communities are often established dynamically with peers that are unrelated and unknown to each other. Peers have to manage the risk involved with the transactions without prior knowledge about each other's reputation. ***SimiTrust***, a reputation management scheme, is proposed for P2P virtual communities. A unique global trust value, computed by aggregating similarity-weighted recommendations of the peers who have interacted with him and reflecting the degree that the community as a whole trusts a peer, is assigned to each peer in the community. Different from previous global-trust based schemes, SimiTrust does not need any pre-trusted peers to ensure algorithm convergence and invalidates the assumption that the peers with high trust value will give the honest recommendation. Theoretical analyses and experiments show that the scheme is still robust under more general conditions where malicious peers cooperate in an attempt to deliberately subvert the system, converges more quickly and decreases the number of inauthentic files downloaded more effectively than previous schemes.

1 Introduction

Inauthentic file attacks by anonymous malicious peers are common on today's popular Peer-to-Peer (P2P) file-sharing communities. For example, malicious peer u provides a fake resource with the same name as the real resource peer v is looking for. The actual file could be a Trojan Horse program or a virus like the well-known VBS.Gnutella worm [3]. The recent measurement study of KaZaA [1] shows that pollution is indeed pervasive in file sharing, with more than 50% of the copies of many popular recent songs being polluted [2].

One way to address this uncertainty problem is to develop strategies for establishing reputation systems that can assist peers in assessing the level of trust they should place on the quality of resources they are receiving (e.g. [4, 7, 8, 9, 12]). Most existing reputation management systems require a central server for storing and disseminating the reputation information, and it does not accord with the open and distributed nature of these P2P systems. So the very core of the reputation mechanism in a P2P community is to build a distributed reputation management system that is efficient, scalable, and secure in both trust computation and trust data storage and dissemination. The main challenge of building such a reputation mechanism is how to effec-

* This work is supported by the National Natural Science Foundation of China (No. 60373021).

J.X. Yu, M. Kitsuregawa, and H.V. Leong (Eds.): WAIM 2006, LNCS 4016, pp. 205–216, 2006.
© Springer-Verlag Berlin Heidelberg 2006

tively cope with various malicious collectives of peers who know one another and attempt to collectively subvert the system by providing fake or misleading ratings about other peers [8, 9].

We present such a scheme, called **SimiTrust** (the degree a peer trusts another peer's recommendations depends on the **simi**larity between these two peers in our model), for reputation management in P2P virtual communities. The scheme includes a mathematical model for quantifying the trustworthiness and a distributed algorithm to implement the model over a structured P2P overlay network. The paper has a number of contributions. First, each peer *i* is assigned a unique trust value by aggregating similarity-weighted recommendations of the peers in the community who has interacted with peer *i*, and an iterative method is given to compute this trust value in our model (section 3); Second, the SimiTrust algorithm is presented to implement the iterative method in a decentralized way (section 4&5); Finally, A series of simulation-based experiments show that the SimiTrust scheme is robust and efficient to cope with various malicious collectives in Section 6.

2 Related Work

The reputation management systems can be classified into two major categories; those based on micro-payment [7, 12] and those based on recommendation [4, 8, 9].

In the eBay Feedback System [4] which is a reputation system currently in use, buyers and sellers can rate each other based on their past transactions with each other. It can be regarded as a recommendation-based local trust model. We call it local trust model in that a peer's knowledge about the other peers' trust value only depends on the recommendations of a few peers (or a few neighbors of the peers) in the community; that is, it only reflects the peer's local view. Li Xiong [8] presents an elaborate local trust model with five important parameters and a general trust metric combining these parameters for evaluating the trustworthiness of a peer in a P2P community.

Sepandar D. Kamvar et al proposed the eigentrust [9] algorithm for P2P file-sharing networks and ranked the eigentrust as a global trust model wherein each peer *i* is assigned a unique global trust value that reflects the experiences of all peers in the network with peer *i*. However, its basic assumption that the peers with high trust value will give the honest recommendations is questionable. A threat model (threat model DM in section 6.6) has been given to show that this assumption will not hold under it [9]. We also argue that the pre-trusted peers (the few peers born with higher trust value than the other peers, which are used to ensure the convergence of the eigentrust algorithm) may not be available in all cases and we give a more general approach in this paper.

In our approach, each peer *i* uses the similarity of rating behavior between peer *i* and peer *j* to weight the recommendations of peer *j*; That is, the more similar between *i* and *j*, the higher credibility of *j*'s recommendations. The credibility of *j*'s recommendation depends not only on the trust value of *j*, but also on the similarity between *i* and *j*. Further more, we do not need any pre-trusted peers to ensure the convergence of our algorithm. A series of simulation-based experiments show that our scheme is still robust under more general conditions (even under threat model DM) and also converges more quickly and decreases the number of inauthentic file downloads more effectively than the eigentrust.

3 The Trust Model

In this section, we present a general trust metric and describe the formulas which we use to compute the trust value for each peer in a P2P virtual community. For the abstraction of the model, we do not consider the dynamics of the P2P system in this section. The community consists of n peers and no peer joins or leaves. The dynamic issues such as peer joining/leaving will be discussed in the following two sections when we consider the distributed implementation of the trust model.

3.1 Problem Formulation

Each peer i rates another peer j with which it tries to make transactions by rating each transaction as either positive or negative, depending on whether i was able to accomplish a transaction with j or not. The sum of the ratings of all of i's interactions with j is called a **local trust value** S_{ij}. $S_{ij}=G_{ij}-F_{ij}$ wherein G_{ij} denotes the number of positive transactions which i has made with j and F_{ij} denotes the number of negative transactions. For example, in a P2P file-sharing community, peer i set $G_{ij}=G_{ij}+1$, if i has downloaded a file from j and the file is validated by i.

Definition 1. A **normalized local trust value** L_{ij} is defined as follows:

$$L_{ij}=\frac{\max(S_{ij},0)}{\sum_{j}\max(S_{ij},0)}\ . \tag{1}$$

L_{ij} is a real value between 0 and 1, and $\sum_{j}L_{ij}=1$. If $\sum_{j}\max(S_{ij},0)=0$, we define $L_{ij}=T_i/n$ where T_i is peer i's global trust value which will be given in Definition 3. We choose to normalize the local trust values in this manner because it ensures the convergence of the iterative method for global trust value computation that we describe below. And any peer can not assign local trust value larger than 1 to another peer to boost his trust value. For the same reason, we let L_{ii}=0 for each peer i. L_{ij} reflects the peer i's local view on the credibility of the peer j with whom he has directly interacted. And L_{ij} is used as the recommendation of i in the rest of the paper. Our goal is to get a global view of the whole system on the peer j by summarizing the recommendations of j's friends and by asking friends of friends.

One critical step in our model is to compute the similarity between rating opinions of peers and then to weight the peers' recommendations by that value. The basic idea in similarity computation between the rating opinion of peer i and that of peer j is to first define the rating opinion vector of a peer and then to apply a similarity computation technique to determine the similarity. There are a number of different ways to compute the similarity between vectors [6]. Here we use such a method, called cosine-based similarity. The similarity between them is measured by computing the cosine of the angle between these two vectors.

Definition 2. For any peer i and peer j, **the similarity** between peers i and j, denoted by C_{ij}, is given by

$$C_{ij} = \frac{B_i * B_j}{\|B_i\| \cdot \|B_j\|} , \tag{2}$$

where " * " denotes the dot-product of the two vectors. Here B_i denotes the **rating opinion vector** of peer i, defined as $B_i = [B_{i1}, B_{i2}, ..., B_{in}]$ where $B_{ik}(k=1, ...,n)$ is the rating opinion of peer i on peer k. B_{ik} is defined as follows:

If $i \neq k$, and $G_{ik}+F_{ik}= 0$, then $B_{ik}= 0$;

$$\text{if } i \neq k, \text{ and } G_{ik}+F_{ik} > 0, \text{ then } B_{ik} = \begin{cases} G_{ik} / (G_{ik} + F_{ik}) & G_{ik} \geq F_{ik} \\ -F_{ik} / (G_{ik} + F_{ik}) & G_{ik} < F_{ik} \end{cases} . \tag{3}$$

For each peer i, we let $B_{ii} = 1 + \varepsilon$ where ε is an arbitrarily small positive constant.

Definition 3. A **global trust value vector**, $T = [T_1, T_2, ... , T_n]^T$, is given by

$$T_i = \sum_{k \in U_i} (L_{ki} \cdot C_{ki} \cdot T_k) , \tag{4}$$

where " ^{T} " denotes the transposition of a vector or a matrix and T_i denotes the unique **global trust value** of peer i, which reflects a view of the community as a whole on peer i and serves as peer i's reputation score in the community. And U_i denotes the set of those who have interacted with i and have recommended i, given by:

$U_i = \{j \mid$ peer j has interacted with peer i, and rated i by a recommendation, $L_{ji}\}$;

The global trust value of peer i is the sum of the weighted recommendations of the peers that have interacted with i in a single iteration. The recommendation of peer k (L_{ki}) is weighted by the similarity (C_{ki}) between peer k and peer i, and weighted by the global trust value of peer k (T_k). After several iterations (notice that the global trust value of every peer k, $k \in U_i$, is also computed by (4)) of asking friends of friends by using the above formula, T_i reflects a view of the entire community.

The credibility of the recommendations of a peer is different from that of the peer itself, especially under some threat models (e.g. threat model DM in section 6.6). We weight the recommendations of peer k by the similarity between k and i. That means, when considering the credibility of the recommendations, a peer trusts more on the peers whose rating opinions are similar to him rather than those with high global trust values. Therefore the DM peers (in section 6.6) who act as normal peers in the community and try to increase malicious peers' global trust value can not take effect when our scheme is activated.

This can be written in matrix notation as

$$T = R^T T , \tag{5}$$

where R denotes a **recommendation matrix**. The element of the ith row and jth column of R, R_{ij}, is given by

$$R_{ij} = L_{ij} \cdot C_{ij} . \tag{6}$$

3.2 An Iterative Method for Global Trust Value Computation

We can easily derive an iterative method to get the solution of the linear equation (5):

$$T^{(k+1)} = R^T \cdot T^{(k)} \quad . \qquad (7)$$

We will prove the convergence of the iterative method given in (7) since the matrix norm of the iterative matrix, R^T, is less than 1.

Theorem 1. For any $T^{(0)} \in \Re^n$, the sequence { $T^{(k)}$ }, k=1…∞, generated by (7) converges to $T \in \Re^n$ (the solution to (7)). ($\Re^n$ denotes n-dimensional real space).

Proof. The iteration is sufficient for convergence if $\|R^T\|<1$ for some induced matrix norm [10].

Now $\|R^T\|_1 = \max_i \sum_j |L_{ij} \cdot C_{ij}| \le \max_{i,j} |C_{ij}| \cdot \max_i \sum_j L_{ij} \le \max_{i,j} |C_{ij}|$. Because $L_{ij} = L_{ii} = 0$ for each $i=j$, we have $L_{ij} \cdot C_{ij} = L_{ii} \cdot C_{ii} = 0$. Thus, we have $\max_{i,j} |C_{ij}| \le \max_{i,j(i \ne j)} |C_{ij}|$. And C_{ij} is the cosine of the angle between two vectors, B_i and B_j. Because there is at least one element, B_{ii} (B_{ii}=1+ε), in B_i differs from that, B_{ji} ($|B_{ji}| \le 1$), in B_j , we have $|C_{ij}|<1$ for any i and j, $i \ne j$. Therefore we have $\max_{i,j(i \ne j)} |C_{ij}| < 1$, so that $\|R^T\|_1 < 1$.

So we proved the convergence of the iterative method given in (7).

4 The Decentralized Trust Data Management Scheme

Decentralized and secure trust data management, i.e., how to efficiently and securely store and look up trust data that are needed to compute the trust value of a peer, is important in implementing a P2P trust model such as SimiTrust. We achieve these in two steps: First, having another, deterministically chosen peer in the network take over a peer's calculation job on his own trust value, becoming this peer's **trust value manager**. This can be done by using DHT (Distributed Hash Table) such as Chord to map peers to their trust value managers. Second, adding redundancy to the calculations through having each calculation being performed by several peers in parallel. Each peer can be queried for the results of his calculations, and the final result of a calculation is determined by a majority vote among the collaborating peers. The detailed methods are not given here due to space constraints.

Each peer is assigned several trust value managers and each peer also serves as a trust value manager for some other peers to store and calculate trust values. A trust value manager of peer i, M_i, shall have the following duties: (1) Storing the trust data of peer i such as G_{ij}, F_{ij}, L_{ij}, etc.; (2) Verifying the consistency of the stored data (i.e., comparing the G'_{ij}, newly submitted by peer i, to G_{ij}, now stored by M_i, if $G'_{ij}-G_{ij}>1$, it is very possible that peer i has submitted the malicious data); (3) Computing the global trust value of peer i; (4) Submitting the trust value, rating opinion vector, etc. of peer i as responses to search requests of other peers in the community.

5 The SimiTrust Algorithm

The SimiTrust algorithm is proposed in this section to implement the iterative method given in section 3.2 in a decentralized way. After introducing the trust value manager mechanism, a peer's global trust value is computed by his trust value managers based on the trust data that are collected about the peer.

5.1 Algorithm Description

Here we describe the SimiTrust algorithm to compute a global trust value vector. Before the description, we introduce the following two primitives which will be used in the algorithm:

Submit $(ID_i, (ID_j, ID_k), Value1, Value2)$ submitting *Value1* and *Value2* to the trust value managers of peer *i*. We use the *Value1* and *Value2* to refer to the normalized local trust value, L_{jk}, that peer *j* place in *k* and rating opinion vector of peer *j*, as the meaning will be clear from context;

Query (ID_j, T_j, L_{ji}, B_j) querying the global trust value, recommendation, and rating opinion vector of peer *j* from *j*'s trust value managers.

The algorithm consists of two components: the Algorithm1 and Algorithm2 as shown in pseudo-code in Table 1 and Table 2 respectively. Each peer *i* plays two roles: an ordinary peer who rates, or rated by, other peers, and a trust value manager of certain peers. As an ordinary peer, peer *i* uses the Algorithm1; as a trust value manager of peer *u*, *i* uses the Algorithm2.

Table 1. Pseudo-code for the Algorithm1

Algorithm 1. // peer *i*, as an ordinary peer.

UpdateAndSubmitTrustdata( )
// submits its rating (G_{ij}, F_{ij}) after a transaction with *j*.
{
  If (a good transaction) $G_{ij} \leftarrow G_{ij}+1$;
  else $F_{ij} \leftarrow F_{ij}+1$;
  $Submit(ID_i, (ID_i, ID_j), G_{ij}, F_{ij})$;
  // submits G_{ij} and F_{ij} to M_i, and triggers the UpdateLocaltrust( ) in M_i.
}

There are two ways to trigger *CalcGlobaltrust( )*: it will be triggered as soon as peer *i* receives a *submit( )* primitive from one of the peers who have interacted with *u*; or peer *i* sets up a threshold, and it is triggered when the number of the received *submit( )* primitives reaches the threshold.

5.2 The Overhead of the Algorithm

After each transaction, peer *i* only needs one message to submit its rating to its trust value manager in the Alogrithm1. *CalcGlobaltrust( )* only needs to ask, for one round, the peers who have interacted with peer *u* for their global trust values, recommendations and rating opinion vectors in the Algorithm2. Therefore the message complexity of our algorithm is $O(n)$ which is less than that $(O(n^2))$ of the eigentrust.

The complexity of the algorithm is also bounded in that the algorithm converges fast: For a community of 500 peers, the algorithm has converged after less than 6

Table 2. Pseudo-code for the Algorithm2

```
Algorithm 2.   // peer i, as a trust value manager of peer u.
UpdateLocaltrust( )    // updates L_uv and B_uv after receiving the Submit( ) from u.
{
    Verify the consistency of G_uv and F_uv;
    Compute S_uv, L_uv, B_uv;
    Submit (ID_v, (ID_u, ID_v ), L_uv, null);
    // submits L_uv to M_v, and triggers the procedure to put ID_u into the set U_v.
}
CalcGlobaltrust( )                    // calculates the global trust value of peer u.
{
    for ( every j∈U_u ( j≠u) )
    {
        Query (ID_j, T_j, L_ju, B_j );
        C_ju ← (B_j * B_u) / (||B_j||·||B_u||) ;    // calculates the similarity between u and j.
        T_u ← T_u + L_ju · C_ju · T_j ;
    }
    return T_u;
}
```

iterations, i.e., the computed global trust values do not change significantly any more after a low number of iterations. In the simulation of our algorithm, this corresponds to less than 6 query cycles of updated trust values among peers (see Section 6 for more detail).

Since either trust value store or computation processes in a decentralized manner, every peer only needs to have the knowledge of its neighbors to maintain the underlying structured P2P network and to store and compute the trust values of certain peers as a trust value manager. As a trust value manager of peer u, peer i only needs to keep the most recent trust data items about peer u (e.g. the ratings to u in recent 100 transactions) using an FIFO-like cache replacement policy. These data items should be refreshed so the values reflect the latest behavior of peer u. To get the reputation of the peer j from which he try to make a transaction, a peer i only needs to send a massage to ask j's trust value manager for j's global trust value.

6 Experiments

In this section, we will assess the performance of our scheme as compared to the eigentrust algorithm and to a P2P community where no reputation system is implemented, called random peer selection scheme. We call it random since peers randomly select a peer to make a transaction in such a community. We shall demonstrate the schemes' performance under a variety of threat models.

6.1 Simulation Setup

As a test bed for our experiments, we use the ***Query Cycle Simulator*** [11], which simulates a typical peer-to-peer file-sharing community. The global trust values in this community are used to bias download sources.

Each simulation is divided into query cycles. In each query cycle, any given peer in the community could be issuing a query, inactive, or down and not responding to queries. After issuing a query, a peer waits for incoming responses from the peers that have the file he is looking for, selects a peer, whose global trust value is the highest among those responding, as the download source, and downloads the file. The last two steps are repeated until the peer receives a complete, authentic copy of the file. After each query cycle, the global trust value computation is triggered and the numbers of authentic and inauthentic downloads observed by each peer are calculated. Then the simulation comes into the next query cycle. Each experiment is run several times and the results of the runs are averaged.

We set up a community consisting of 500 peers, 10 of which are pre-trusted peers for the eigentrust, and we do not need any pre-trusted peer to ensure the convergence of our algorithm. All peers divided into normal, good peers (peers who are participating in the community in order to share files) and malicious peers (peers who are participating in the community in order to spread bogus files and undermine its performance). The proportion of malicious peers will be given in the description of each experiment. When they join the community, malicious peers connect to the 6 most highly-connected peers in the community in order to receive as many queries traveling though the community as possible. And the good peers only connect to 3 neighbors. The pre-trusted peers also have 6 neighbors in the eigentrust. The initial distribution of the global trust values is a uniform probability distribution over all n peers, that is $T_i^{(0)}=1/n$ (i=1, … , n). The other detailed settings are described in [11].

6.2 Threat Models

We will consider two strategies of malicious peers to cause inauthentic uploads even when a reputation management scheme is activated, since the main challenge of building a reputation mechanism in a P2P environment is how to effectively cope with various malicious collectives of peers who know one another and attempt to collectively subvert the system.

Threat Model IM: Individual malicious peers, called IM peers, always provide an inauthentic file when selected as a download source and they always set their local trust values to $S_{ij}= F_{ij} - G_{ij}$, valuing inauthentic file downloads instead of authentic file downloads and assigning high local trust values to malicious peers from whom they try to download files.

Threat Model DM: Two groups of malicious peers (IM and DM) are present in the community. DM peers provide only authentic files and uses the reputation they gained to boost the trust values of IM peers that only provides inauthentic files. DM peers, answer 0.05% of the most popular queries and provide a good file when used as a download source for all queries that they answer. DM peers can get high global trust values in this way, and then DM peers assign trust values of 1 to all the IM peers in the community and trust values of 0 to the other peers. Precisely, if IMs and DMs respectively denote the set of IM peers and the set of DM peers in the community, each peer $u \in$DMs sets $L_{uv} = 1/\|IMs\|$ if peer $v \in$IMs.

6.3 Performance Indices

We are interested in evaluating the performance of the SimiTrust scheme and in comparing it with the two mentioned schemes. To facilitate our comparison, we consider the following metrics:

Proportion of Authentic Downloads (PAD), the ratio of the number of authentic downloads to the number of all downloads viewed by all good peers, is defined as

$$PAD = \frac{\sum_i \sum_j G_{ij}}{\sum_i \sum_j (G_{ij} + F_{ij})} \text{ (for all } i\text{, peer } i \text{ is a good peer).} \tag{8}$$

PAD is calculated for all good peers at the end of each experiment. This metric directly measures the effectiveness of the reputation management schemes. In an ideal P2P community where no malicious peers present, we have PAD=1.

Convergence Time is defined as the least number of query cycles required to make the number of inauthentic downloads in the community, defined as $\sum_i \sum_j F_{ij}$, approach to 0. If an algorithm for reputation management does work, the good peers can be differentiated from the malicious peers by their global trust values after a few query cycles; that is, the good peers can get the higher trust value than the malicious peers though every peer has the same initial global trust value. The inauthentic downloads in the community then approach to 0 because peers always choose the peer whose trust value is the highest among the peers responding their queries as the downloading source. The less query cycles required to eliminate the inauthentic downloads in the community, the faster an algorithm converges.

6.4 IM Experiments and Discussion

IM experiments are carried out in the presence of IM peers. Fig. 1 shows the number of inauthentic file downloads measured for each query cycle when the simulation of the P2P community proceeds from one query cycle to the next. We have IM peers make up 40% of all peers in the community. Using random peer selection scheme, malicious peers succeed in inflicting many inauthentic downloads in the community. Yet, if our scheme is activated, the inauthentic files downloaded are almost eliminated after the 5th cycle. **The Convergence Time**, 5, is less than that when using the eigentrust. That means malicious peers can not get the high global trust values when our scheme is activated, and because of their low trust values, malicious peers are rarely chosen as download sources which minimizes the number of inauthentic file downloads in the community.

In the next experiment, we have between 0% and 50% of the peers in the community be malicious peers, increasing this percentage in steps of 10% for each run of the experiment. The results of the number of inauthentic downloads of each query cycle are similar to that showed in Fig. 1 (using our scheme, inauthentic downloads are almost eliminated after 3-6 cycles). Fig. 2 plots the proportion of authentic downloads (PAD) against the percentage of IM peers in the community. The PAD is higher than 80% even if IM peers make up a half of the peers in the community when our scheme is activated.

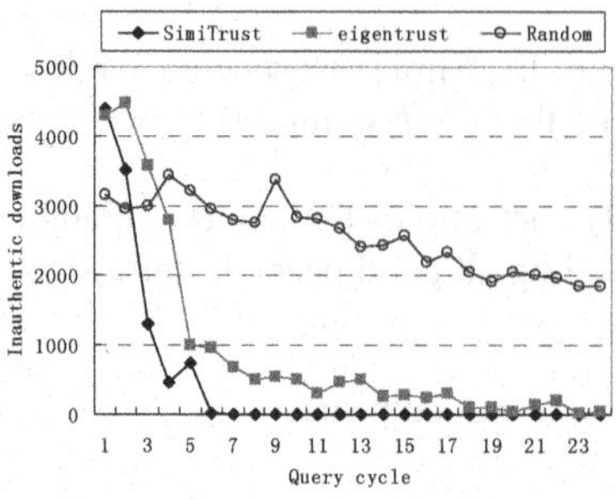

Fig. 1. The number of inauthentic downloads measured for each query cycle when the simulation proceeds

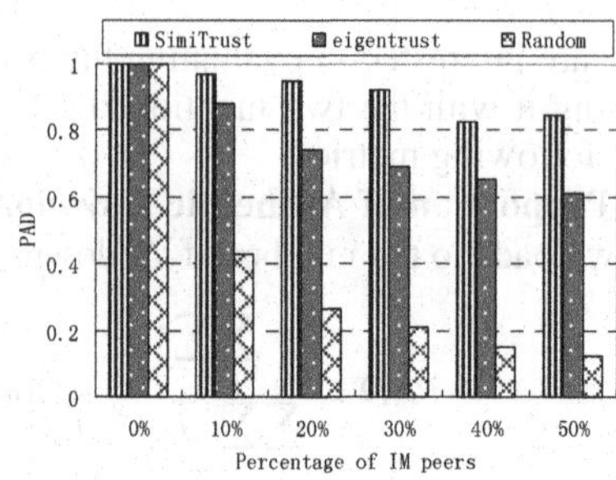

Fig. 2. The PAD against the percentage of IM peers

6.5 DM Experiments and Discussion

We assume that malicious peers are so intelligent that IM and DM peers can collaborate to subvert the reputation system in the DM experiments. Some experiments were also made in the analysis of the eigentrust [9], but the results are not good enough. Our experiments show that the eigentrust algorithm does not converge under threat model DM; that is, the good peers can not be differentiated from the malicious peers

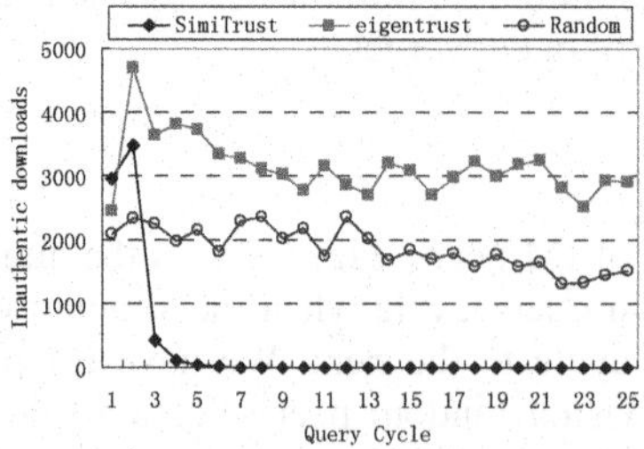

Fig. 3. The number of inauthentic downloads measured for each query cycle when the simulation proceeds. We have malicious peers make up 40% of all the peers in the community and DM peers make up 10% of all the malicious peers. When the eigentrust is activated, there are a considerable number of inauthentic downloads in the community, even more than that when using the random scheme, and that number does not tend to decrease.

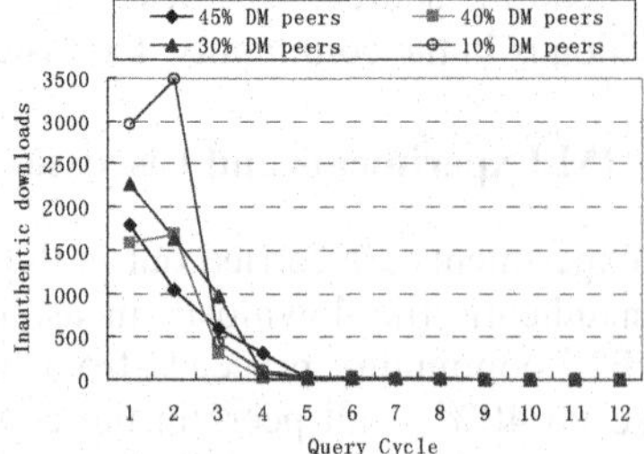

Fig. 4. The influence of the different percentage of DM peers on the performance of the SimiTrust. The y-axis plots the number of inauthentic downloads measured for each query cycle when the simulation proceeds. We have malicious peers make up 40% of the peers in the community and DM peers make up between 0% and 45% of all the malicious peers.

by their global trust values, even if there are only a few DM peers (less than 4% of all the peers) in the community. The fundamental reason is that DM peers have high global trust values, but they give untrue recommendations. The eigentrust algorithm does not distinguish the credibility of peers from that of the recommendations given by peers, and we use the similarity between peers to weight their recommendations so that the recommendations of DM peers can be screened. Therefore the performance of our scheme is still robust under this threat model. Fig. 3 shows the number of inauthentic downloads measured for each query cycle when the simulation proceeds from one query cycle to the next.

When we have more DM peers in the community, the eigentrust does not converge yet. We designed the next experiment to see how the increase of the percentage of DM peers in the community can influence the performance of the SimiTrust. Fig. 4 shows the number of inauthentic files downloaded in each query cycle when the simulation proceeds. We observe an interesting phenomenon that the more DM peers present, the less inauthentic file downloads occur. Malicious peers operating under threat model DM need to pay cost for uploading inauthentic files: DM peers have to provide some share of authentic files, which is undesirable for them. Suppressed by our scheme, malicious peers can not increase inauthentic uploads, but they contribute a considerable share of authentic files.

7 Conclusion

We have presented SimiTrust, a reputation management scheme for quantifying and comparing the trustworthiness of peers in a P2P virtual community. Each peer is assigned a global trust value which reflects the experience of the community as a whole with the peer. The global trust value for a peer is computed by calculating the similarity-weighted recommendations of the peers who have interacted with him, taking into consideration the entire community's history with the peer. In experiments, these trust values are used to bias downloads and this method is successful to reduce the number inauthentic files in a P2P file-sharing community under a variety of threat scenarios. The effectiveness of our scheme has shown to get the advantage over that of the eigentrust, especially under threat model DM.

References

1. Kazaa, http://www.kazaa.com/.
2. J. Liang, R. Kumar, Y. Xi, K. Ross, Pollution in p2p file sharing systems, Proceedings of IEEE Infocom 2005. (2005) http://photon.poly.edu/~jliang/ pollution.pdf.
3. VBS.GnutellaWorm, http://securityresponse.symantec.com/avcenter/venc/data/vbs.gnutella.html.
4. eBay Feedback Forum, http://pages.ebay.com/services/forum/feedback.html?ssPageName=STRK.
5. S. Saroiu, P.K. Gummadi, S.D. Gribble, A Measurement Study of Peer-to-Peer File Sharing Systems, Proceedings of Multimedia Computing and Networking 2002 (MMCN'02), Proceedings of SPIE, Vol 4673. (2002) 156–170.

6. B. Sarwar, G. Karypis, J. Konstan, J. Riedl, Item-Based collaborative filtering recommendation algorithms, Proceedings of the 10th International World Wide Web Conference. ACM Press. (2001) 285–295.
7. M. Gupta, P. Judge, M. Ammar, A Reputation System for Peer-to-Peer Networks, Proceedings of 13th ACM Workshop on Network and Operating Systems Support for Digital Audio and Video (NOSSDAV'03). ACM Press. (2003) 144–152.
8. L. Xiong, L. Liu, PeerTrust: Supporting Reputation-Based Trust for Peer-to-Peer Electronic Communities, IEEE TRANSACTIONS ON KNOWLEDGE AND DATA ENGINEERING 16(7). IEEE Press. 843–857.
9. S.D. Kamvar, M.T. Schlosser, The eigentrust algorithm for reputation management in P2P networks, Proceedings of the 12th international conference on World Wide Web. ACM Press. (2003) 640–651.
10. WM. Shi, HF. Yang, YS. Wu, X. Sun, Numerical Analysis, 2nd edition, Beijing. BEIJING INSTITUTE OF TECHNOLOGY PRESS. (2004) 91–93.
11. M.T. Schlosser, T.E. Condie, S.D. Kamvar, Simulating a File-Sharing P2P Network, Proceedings of First Workshop on Semantics in P2P and Grid Computing. (2003) 69–80.
12. P. Golle, K. Leyton-Brown, I. Mironov, Incentives for Sharing in Peer-to-Peer Networks, Proceedings of the 3rd ACM conference on Electronic Commerce. (2001) 264-267.

QoS-Aware Web Services Composition Using Transactional Composition Operator

An Liu[1,2,3], Liusheng Huang[1,2], and Qing Li[2,3]

[1] Department of Computer Science and Technology
University of Science & Technology of China, Hefei, China
[2] Joint Research Lab of Excellence
CityU-USTC Advanced Research Institute, Suzhou, China
[3] Department of Computer Science
City University of Hong Kong, Hong Kong, China
liuan@ustc.edu, lshuang@ustc.edu.cn, itqli@cityu.edu.hk

Abstract. As composite web services are often long lasting, loosely coupled, and cross application and administrative boundaries, transactional support is required. Most of the work has so far focused on relaxing some ACID properties of the traditional transaction model, with little being done on investigating how the transaction can influence the quality of service (QoS) of a composite web service. In this paper, a composition model is proposed to evaluate the quality of service (QoS) of a composite service with various transactional requirements. The proposed model is based on a transactional composition operator, which extends the traditional workflow patterns and integrates transactional properties. Using a recursive approach, the QoS of a composite service can easily be calculated, in spite of transactional requirements given by service providers or end users.

1 Introduction

As the use of web services grows, it becomes increasingly popular for organizations to introduce new value-added services (composite services) by composing some pre-existing web services (component services). Such a composite service is often long-running, loosely coupled, and cross application and administrative boundaries, thus requiring transactional support. Recently, much work has been proposed to address the requirements of different kinds of transactions, such as Business Transaction Protocol (BTP) [1], Web Services Transactions specifications [2], and Web Services Transaction Management (WS-TXM) [3]. These efforts focus on how to relax some ACID properties to ensure a reliable composition. However, improper transaction usage in the web service composition may degrade the quality of service (QoS), due to the inherent loss of concurrency of the two-phase commit protocol (2PC) which is used to guarantee the ACID property [4]. Therefore, how the transaction will influence the QoS of a composite web service has been largely overlooked, which nevertheless is a relevant and challenging problem.

On the other hand, QoS management in service composition has also received increasing attention recently. It is not sufficient to only consider the functional require-

J.X. Yu, M. Kitsuregawa, and H.V. Leong (Eds.): WAIM 2006, LNCS 4016, pp. 217–228, 2006.
© Springer-Verlag Berlin Heidelberg 2006

ments and interface signatures of service. The nonfunctional characteristics, particularly, quality of service, should also be taken into account. Most of the relevant work focused on the dynamic runtime selection of component services and execution paths based on a set of quality criteria. Little attention, however, has been paid to the QoS of a composite service in design-time. We argue that the consideration of QoS in design time is as important as in runtime, and can complement the existing work in service composition with QoS management.

In this paper we propose a model for the composition of web services with various transactional requirements. Based on this model, we can easily evaluate the QoS of the composite service using a recursive approach. The kernel of the proposed model is transactional composition operator, which extends the workflow patterns [5] introduced in the workflow community.

The rest of the paper is organized as follows. Section 2 presents related work on QoS management in web services and transactional web service composition. Section 3 introduces a motivating example that will be used throughout the reminder of the paper. Our transactional composition operator is presented in section 4. Section 5 explains how to determine the QoS of a composite service based on the transactional composition operator. Section 6 concludes the paper.

2 Related Work

QoS issues in web service have been widely investigated in the web service research community. We only mention here some representative proposals or ones most relevant to our work. D.A. Menasce described QoS from the perspective of service provider and service consumer, and discussed calculation of throughput, one of the QoS criteria of a service. He also mentioned that the transaction might degrade the QoS of a service, however, none further analysis was given [4]. In another paper, he discussed the QoS based on the composite web services flow and pointed out that not only the selection of component service but also the different composite flow would influence the QoS [6]. The composite flow is actually a kind of workflow patterns [5], which have been compiled from an analysis of various workflow languages.

One of the challenging problems in QoS Management in service composition is the runtime selection of component service. Zeng et al. considered it as a global optimization problem and solved it using linear programming methods [7]. However, this kind of work does not consider the influence caused by the abstract process at design time, which, according to [6], is an equally important issue of concern.

The most relevant work to ours is the one proposed by Jaeger et al. in [8]. The authors first defined a set of composition patterns which are derived from workflow patterns, and then analyzed these patterns from five QoS dimensions. However, as we will see in section 3, these composition patterns are unable to express the transaction requirements which can change the QoS of composite services. Another related work by Cardoso et al. focused on QoS for workflows [9]. In that work, a predictive QoS model is proposed to compute the QoS for workflows automatically based on elementary task QoS attributes. Like [8], no consideration is given on the influence caused by transactions.

Recently, some work has been proposed to model the transactional properties in web service composition. Vidyasankar and Vossen presented a multi-level service composition model which could specify transactional properties at all levels [10]. Four kinds termination were used to define atomicity for basic activities. Termination of composite activity was built on the combination of its component activities' terminations. Based on these terminations, some theorems were used to induce the transactional properties of composite services. Similar work has been done by Fauvet et al. in [11]. They divided services into three groups, each with a different transactional property. The characteristics of their work lay in a service composition operator which could specify atomicity constraints. However, the composition operator only supported parallel execution of services. Obviously, it is insufficient to express complex composite service with various transactional requirements.

3 Scenario

As a motivating example, consider an international conference scenario, where researchers around the world are going to attend the conference hold in city A and participate in some additional entertainment during the meeting. The conference organizers provide a web service to help attendants arrange the whole tour. The service (S) performs two primary tasks. One is accommodation arrangement, the other is entertainment arrangement. The former contains three sub-tasks. First, some flight tickets should be purchased. We assume that two flight booking service (FB1 and FB2) are used, each of them is provided by certain airways. Then a hotel booking service (HB) is used to reserve a hotel room and, finally, to book a taxi is through a taxi booking service (TB). The function of entertainment arrangement is realized by two alternative services named sightseeing service (SI) and shopping service (SH), which help to purchase some entrance tickets and arrange a bus to send attendants to a shopping mall that has sales promotion, respectively. Note that, the notion "service" here is abstract, that is, it only describes functionality, and no binding information for execution is given. For the sake of concise description, we shall use "service" to refer to both abstract service and concrete service in this paper. However, the particular kind can be easily determined according to its context.

This scenario is carried out by a composite service as illustrated in Figure 1. Rectangles represent web services, and ovals represent workflow patterns in which AND-s, XOR-s, AND-j, XOR-j, and Disc are abbreviations for AND-split, XOR-split, AND-join, XOR-join, and Discriminator, respectively.

While the composite service in Figure 1 seems to be fine, consider such a case where some attendants want to purchase ten tickets at certain particular time. Unfortunately, there are only six tickets available through service FB1 and two tickets available through service FB2. Although both of FB1 and FB2 may be completed successfully, the composite service will fail because it does not satisfy the global constraint given by the user. Consequently, there is no need to invoke services HB and TB, and the service SH or SI may be cancelled. Similarly, some attendants may require that a taxi is necessary if the reserved hotel is far from the conference hall, and if no taxi available, they would rather book another hotel by themselves through other web services. Therefore, if service TB fails, service HB needs to be cancelled or compensated. However, the composite service can still succeed if no error occurs in services SH and SI.

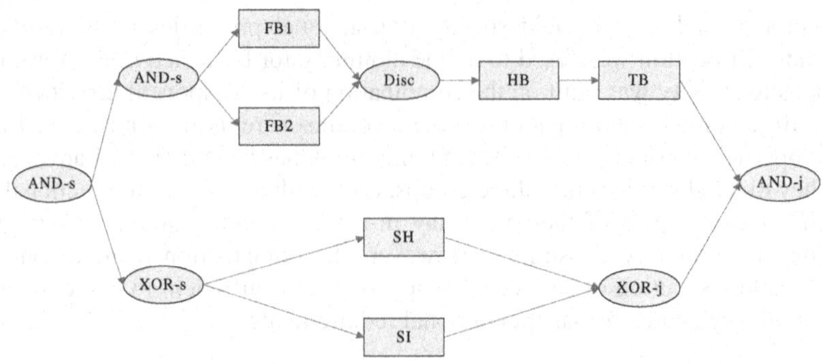

Fig. 1. A composite service for conference arrangement based on workflow patterns

To guarantee the correctness and reliability of the composite service under different requirements, it is insufficient to use workflow patterns only; instead, transactional support needs to be added in. In next section, a transactional composition operator is introduced to solve this problem.

4 Composition Model

This section presents a composition model for web services with various transactional requirements. In section 4.1, we extend the workflow patterns to composition patterns. In section 4.2, we introduce dependency to solve the different transactional requirements. Based on these, we propose a transactional composition operator and show how it works in the last subsection.

4.1 Pattern Evolution

Web service composition requires interactions between component services, which are driven by explicit process models. Currently, lots of process modeling languages including BPEL [12] have been proposed to capture the logic of a composite service, and some of them are still evolving. Rather than choosing a particular modeling language, we think it is better to adopt an abstract model to describe the composition, so that in case these languages are revised or disappear, the abstract model could be adapted to the changes more easily [8].

Although Van der Aalst's workflow patterns have excellent expressive power, they are not suitable for recursive analysis of a composite service. Instead, we need to first adapt them for recursive analysis which will be discussed in section 4.3. Note that, this point of view is similar to that of composition pattern [8], but ours results are different from theirs, especially in parallel cases. We will still use the term "composition pattern" here to reflect its accurate meaning.

The comprehensive list of our composition patterns is given in Table 1, where CP1 denotes a sequence case, and CP2 to CP8 are all parallel cases.

Let us first consider the sequence case. There are two workflow patterns aiming at linear sequence: sequence (WP1) and interleaved parallel routing (WP17). The former is ordered, and the latter is out-of-order and does not allow two activities in the sequence to be active at the same time. CP1 is the same as WP1. WP17 can be implemented by WP1 and dependencies between activities (services). The dependency is one part of our transactional composition operator, which will be introduced in next sub-section.

Table 1. Composition Patterns (CP) and Corresponding Workflow Patterns (WP)

CP	WP	CP	WP
CP1	WP1	CP5	WP4 + WP5
CP2	WP2 + WP3	CP6	WP6 + WP5
CP3	WP2 + WP5	CP7	WP6 + WP7
CP4	WP2 + WP9	CP8	WP6 + WP9

The parallel cases are more complex. The common structure of our composition patterns consists of one split workflow pattern and one join workflow pattern. There are three kinds of split patterns and five kinds of join patterns. The WP8 (OR-join) can be implemented by multiple parallel WP1 [5], so we do not consider it in pattern combination. It is a fact that some split patterns and some join patterns are incompatible, such as WP4+WP3. We also note that some combinations could be implied by other combinations, for example, WP2+WP7 is implied by WP2+WP3. Taking this into consideration, we have seven valid composition patterns for the parallel cases.

There are still ten workflow patterns that are not involved in our composition pattern. These workflow patterns either are not relevant to composition or could be implemented by above patterns and dependencies. Note that, arbitrary cycles (WP10) are left out here for two reasons: firstly, some modeling languages do not allow it (e.g., BPEL only supports structured cycles); secondly, the number of loops can not be determined during the design time. This pattern will be a possible direction of our future work when these modeling languages are standardized.

4.2 Dependency Between Services

As described in the above scenario and last sub-section, workflow patterns and composition patterns can not express complex transactional requirements. Generally, these transactional requirements can be mapped into a set of dependencies between these activities (services). The concept "dependency" has been widely investigated in database and workflow research communities [13-15]. It describes various relationships between transactions (activities), and can ensure the correct and reliable execution. We use here some simplified dependency instances discussed in [13] to revisit the scenario.

Firstly, let us consider one of the problems remains in the context of only using workflow patterns. Recall that if service TB fails, service HB must be cancelled or compensated. Thus we have an abort-dependency [13] from HB to TB.

Secondly, assume the conference organizers have such a plan: concerning the entertainment part of the conference, attendants can either go sightseeing or go shopping, but not both. Thus there is an exclusion-dependency [13] from service SI to SH, and vice versa. Note that, this dependency is implied by WP4.

Generally, transactional requirements in a composite service can always be described by dependencies between services. However, it is difficult and inconvenient to use these complicated dependencies directly. On the other hand, patterns provide a high level but limited expressive power. Therefore, it is natural to combine them together. In principle, we should use composition patterns to cover as many the required dependencies as possible, even though there are some dependencies that can not be covered by patterns.

4.3 Transactional Composition Model

Let us continue our conference scenario. Suppose the attendants want to purchase ten tickets, but there are only eight tickets available, then the service fails. Unfortunately, this kind of requirements still can not be captured by the combination of composition patterns and dependencies. In fact, we will need a global constraint to express such requirements. For example, we may have: {avl(FB1)+avl(FB2)≥10}, where function avl(S) returns the number of tickets service S can provide.

Summarizing above discussions, we give below the definition of a transactional composition operator.

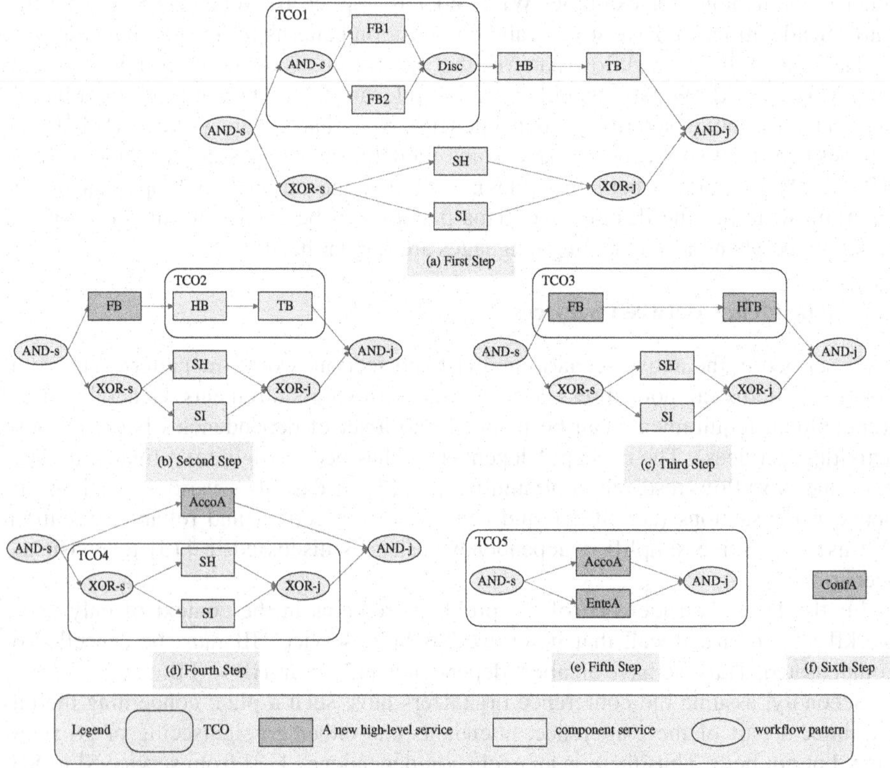

Fig. 2. Recursive composition using transactional composition operator (TCO)

Definition 1 - Transactional composition operator (TCO). A TCO is defined as a 3-tuple (CP, DL, GCE), where:

· CP is a kind of composition patterns.
· DL is a list of dependencies.
· GCE is a global constraint expression.

When we use a composition pattern to combine a set of component services, we get a new high-level abstract service, which encapsulates the control flow, and transactional requirements existing in these services.

To illustrate how to use the transactional composition operator (TCO) to recursively aggregate services, let us consider the conference trip scenario further, by making the requirements step by step. Assume an attendant wants to first purchase ten tickets, and next he only takes the flight tickets and ignores hotel room booking if no taxi is made available. He has no special preferences on the entertainment arrangement. The recursive aggregation process is as illustrated in Figure 2.

As shown in Figure 2, we use TCO one at a time. After using five TCOs, we get a top-level service named ConfA which provides all expected functions. The specific TCO used in each step is given in Table 2, where each row stands for a TCO, and each column stands for one value of the TCO. $S_1 \xrightarrow{a} S_2$ means that there is an abort-dependency from S1 to S2. Φ means there is no dependency or global constraint.

Table 2. TCO for conference trip composition

TCO	CP	DL	GCE
TCO1	CP4	Φ	avl(FB1)+avl(FB2) ≥10
TCO2	CP1	$HB \xrightarrow{a} TB$	Φ
TCO3	CP1	Φ	Φ
TCO4	CP5	Φ	Φ
TCO5	CP2	$EnteA \xrightarrow{a} AccoA$	Φ

Based on this stepwise approach, every service has been associated with a TCO. For example, service ConfA has associated with TCO5. For uniformity, let an elementary service have also a TCO, namely, TCO_Φ which has as value (Φ, Φ, Φ). We can now easily evaluate the QoS of a composite service. In section 5, both the transactional properties and the QoS of services are to be discussed, as we aim at QoS under different transactional requirements.

5 QoS Analysis

This section introduces how to evaluate the QoS of composite services based on the TCO. In section 5.1, we discuss transactional properties of services. In section 5.2, we present two algorithms to evaluate the QoS of a composite service.

Various quality criteria have been proposed to evaluate the QoS of composite services [4,7,8,9]. In the study of this paper, we consider only two: execution cost and response time. The execution cost is the cost to execute a service. The response time is the time a service needs to process a request.

5.1 Transactional Properties of Composite Services

There are many classifications concerning the transactional properties, such as compensatable, retriable, and pivot [16], atomic, quasi-atomic, and non-atomic [17]. We adopt and adapt here the terms atomic, quasi-atomic, and non-atomic to label transactional properties of a web service. A service is said to be atomic if it has no effect at all when it aborts. A service is said to be quasi-atomic if it needs compensation to undo its effect when it aborts. A service is said to be non-atomic if its effect cannot be eliminated once completed. In terms of QoS, atomic services have no execution cost when they need to be aborted. On the contrary, quasi-atomic services have to incur additional cost, namely, penalty.

The transactional property of a composite service is determined by its component services. If all component services are atomic, the composite service is atomic. If there is at least one quasi-atomic component service and no non-atomic ones, the composite service is quasi-atomic. Only if there is a non-atomic component service, the composite service is non-atomic.

Consider such a case where a composite service needs to abort. If it is atomic, there is no additional execution cost since all its component services are atomic, and if it is quasi-atomic, the additional execution cost comes from the quasi-atomic component services. Note that in the database field, when a transaction needs to abort, which operation should do first and which operation should do next is strictly defined, usually the operation sequence is determined by logs. However, in web services environments, this restriction is much more relaxed because of the inherent autonomy of web services. Therefore, we assume that there are no strict requirements on operation sequence when an abortion is needed.

5.2 QoS of Composite Services

When evaluating the QoS of a composite service, two actions, i.e. start and abort, should be considered individually. We first discuss the case where no abortion or compensation is needed.

The QoS of each composition pattern is given in Table 3. Assume each pattern involves following services: $s_1,s_2,\ldots,s_n$. T_i and c_i represent the response time and execution cost of s_i, respectively, where $i=1,2,\ldots,n$. For CP5, s_i will be invoked with probability p_i. For CP6 to CP8, they all use WP6, which makes the analysis more complex. WP6 means at least one of n services will be invoked, that is, there are 2^n-1 kinds of choices. Once a choice is made, CP6, CP7 and CP8 could be simplified into CP3, CP2, and CP4, respectively. We use function $Time^{CP}(s_1,\cdots,s_n)$ and $Cost^{CP}(s_1,\cdots,s_n)$ to calculate the response time and execution cost of CP involving n services that will be executed, respectively. Assume that the choice $(s_{k_1}, s_{k_2},\ldots, s_{k_j})$ is made with probability p, where $1\le j\le n$, and $1\le k_1<k_2<\cdots<k_j\le n$, then we have corresponding expressions for CP6 to CP8 (see Table 3).

Table 3. QoS of composition patterns (CP)

CP	Response Time	Execution Cost
CP1	$\max\{t_i\}$	$\sum_{i=1}^{n} c_i$
CP2	$\sum_{i=1}^{n} t_i$	$\sum_{i=1}^{n} c_i$
CP3	$\min\{t_i\}$	$\sum_{i=1}^{n} c_i$
CP4	$\min\{t_i\}$	$\sum_{i=1}^{n} c_i$
CP5	$\sum_{i=1}^{n} p_i \cdot t_i$	$\sum_{i=1}^{n} p_i \cdot c_i$
CP6	$\sum p \cdot Time^{CP3}(s_{k_1}, s_{k_2}, \ldots, s_{k_j})$	$\sum p \cdot Cost^{CP3}(s_{k_1}, s_{k_2}, \ldots, s_{k_j})$
CP7	$\sum p \cdot Time^{CP2}(s_{k_1}, s_{k_2}, \ldots, s_{k_j})$	$\sum p \cdot Cost^{CP2}(s_{k_1}, s_{k_2}, \ldots, s_{k_j})$
CP8	$\sum p \cdot Time^{CP4}(s_{k_1}, s_{k_2}, \ldots, s_{k_j})$	$\sum p \cdot Cost^{CP4}(s_{k_1}, s_{k_2}, \ldots, s_{k_j})$

Based on above analysis, let us consider TCO from the QoS point of view. GCE only describes some transactional constraints on TCO. It is the DL (list of dependencies) that leads to additional actions to ensure transactional requirements. These actions may bring additional execution cost and response time. Therefore, the QoS value of a TCO consists of two parts: one is from CP, and the other is from DL.

Now, consider what will happen on QoS if a dependency in DL requires a service to abort. The detailed abortion process is as discussed in section 5.1. From the discussion, we know the structure of the composite service, that is, composition pattern, is not important: it only sends asynchronous messages to its component services to tell them to abort. Therefore, the total response time equals to the maximal component service's response time, and the total execution cost is the sum of every quasi-atomic component service's penalty.

Summarizing the above discussions, we present two algorithms for QoS evaluation immediately below.

Algorithm 1. Evaluating the QoS of a service
Input: s - a service which has been associated with a TCO
Output: qos - an instance of the 2-tuple(time, cost)
Function getQoS()
Begin

```
qos.time = 0; qos.cost = 0; tco = s.TCO;
if (tco.CP ==Φ) { //elementary service
qos.time = s.time; qos.cost = s.cost;
}
else { //composite service, then recursively invoke function getQoS()
  // assume tco.CP involves n services that will be executed
  qos.time = qos.time + Time^tco.CP(s1, s2, …, sn);
  qos.cost = qos.cost + Cost^tco.CP(s1, s2, …, sn);
  for each service sk which needs to start according to tco.DL {
    newQos = getQoS(sk);
```

```
11    qos.time = qos.time + newQos.time; qos.cost = qos.cost + newQos.cost;
12  }
13  for each service s_j which needs to abort according to tco.DL {
14    penalty = getPenalty (s_j);
15    qos.time = qos.time + penalty.time; qos.cost = qos.cost + penalty.cost;
16  }
17 }//end if
18 return qos;
End
```

Algorithm 2. Evaluating the penalty when aborting a service
Input: s - a service needs to abort
Output: penalty: an instance of the 2-tuple(time, cost)
Function getPenalty()
Begin

```
01 penalty.time = 0; penalty.cost = 0;
02 if (s.TCO.CP ==Φ) { //elementary service
03   if (s is atomic) penalty.time = s.time;
04   else if (s is quasi-atomic) {penalty.time = s.time; penalty.cost = s.cost;}
05   else exception handling;
06 }
07 else { //assume the composite service involves n component services:
08   for (i = 1; i++; i <= n) {
09     penalty_i = getPenalty(s_i);
10     penalty.cost = penalty.cost + penalty_i.cost;
11   }
12   penalty.time = max{penalty_1.time,..., penalty_n.time};
13 }
14 return penalty;
End
```

Algorithms 1 and 2 both use a depth-first approach. Lines 07-08 and 09-16 of algorithm 1 evaluate QoS value caused by CP and DL, respectively. Lines 02-06 of algorithm 2 calculate the penalty when aborting an elementary service, according to its transactional properties. Lines 07-13 of algorithm 2 deal with the composite service. Note that, these algorithms only give the upper bound on the QoS values of a composite service. Because there is no loop pattern in the composite service, thus every component service will be invoked or cancelled at most once. Therefore, the time complexity of these two algorithms are both O(n).

Table 4. QoS for each component service

Service	Response Time	Execution Cost	Penalty.cost
FB1	1.5	3	1.5
FB2	1	4	2
HB	2	1.5	1
TB	2.5	2	0
SH	2.5	2	1
SI	1.5	1	0

Table 5. QoS for each composite service at all different levels

Service	Response Time	Execution Cost	Penalty.cost
FB	1.5	7	3.5
HTB	6.5	4.5	1
AccoA	8	11.5	4.5
EnteA	2	1.5	0.5
ConfA	12	13.5	5

Consider here a numeric example based on above scenario. Table 4 shows the response time, execution cost, and penalty.cost for each component service. Assume that the penalty.time equals to (normal) response time and every branch of CP5 is selected with equal probability. Table 5 shows the QoS values for composite services at different levels (See Figure 2).

6 Conclusion and Future Work

Transaction is generally used to ensure correct and reliable execution; however, it does influence the QoS of a composite service. In this paper, we have presented a composition model which captures both control flow and transactional requirements. The model aims at easily evaluating the QoS of a composite service with various transactional requirements. Based on the transactional composition operator (TCO), two algorithms are designed for the purpose of evaluating the QoS of composite services. Our model builds on TCO, which extends the classic workflow patterns, and thus is quite flexible.

One relevant issue is dynamic service selection in web service composition. This kind of work focuses on improving QoS of a composite service at runtime. Our work is complementary to such work since we focus on QoS improvement at design-time. Currently, our work of this paper only analyzed the transactional effects on QoS. How to design transactions to ensure not only correct execution but also optimal QoS remains a challenging problem, which is to be addressed in our subsequent research.

Acknowledgements

The research described here is supported by the National Basic Research Fund of China ("973" Program) under Grant No.2003CB317006, and has been benefited from various discussions among the group members of the Joint Research Lab between CityU and USTC in their advanced research institute in Suzhou (China), particularly Mr. Zhe Shan, Lin Baoping, and Liu Hai.

References

1. M. Potts, B. Cox and B. Pope, Business Transaction Protocol Primer, OASIS Committee Supporting Document, Available: http://www.oasis-open.org/committees/business-transactions/documents/primer/Primerhtml/BTP

2. Web Services Transactions specifications, Available: http://www-128.ibm.com/developerworks/library/specification/ws-tx/
3. D. Bunting et al., Web Services Transaction Management (WS-TXM) Version 1.0, July 28, 2003
4. D.A. Menasce, QoS Issues in Web Services, IEEE Internet Computing, 2002.6(6): pp. 72-75.
5. W.M.P. van der Aalst et al., Workflow Patterns, Distributed and Parallel Databases, 2003, vol.14, pp. 5-51.
6. D.A. Menasce, Composing Web Services: A QoS View, IEEE Internet Computing, 2004.8(6): pp. 88-90.
7. L. Zeng et al., Quality Driven Web Services Composition, in Proceedings of 12th International Conference on World Wide Web, 2003, ACM Press: Budapest, Hungary.
8. M.C. Jaeger et al., QoS Aggregation for Web Service Composition using Workflow Patterns, in Proceedings of 8th International Enterprise Distributed Object Computing Conference, 2004.
9. J. Cardoso et al, Modeling Quality of Service for Workflows and Web Service Processes, Technical Report#02-002 v2, LSDIS Lab, Computer Science, University of Georgia, December 2002.
10. K. Vidyasankar and G. Vossen, A Multi-Level Model for Web Service Composition, in Proceedings of 2nd IEEE International Conference on Web Services, 2004.
11. M.-C. Fauvet et al., Handling Transactional Properties in Web Service Composition, in Proceedings of 6th International Conference on Web Information Systems Engineering, 2005.
12. Business Process Execution Language for Web Services Version 1.1, Available: http://www-128.ibm.com/developerworks/library/specification/ws-bpel/
13. P.K. Chrysanthis and K. Ramamritham, A Formalism for Extended Transaction Models, in Proceedings of 17th International Conference on Very Large Data Bases, 1991, Morgan Kaufmann Publishers Inc.
14. P.K. Chrysanthis and K. Ramamritham, ACTA: A Framework for Specifying and Reasoning about Transaction Structure and Behavior, in Proceedings of 1990 ACM SIGMOD International Conference on Management of Data, 1990, ACM Press: Atlantic City, New Jersey, United States.
15. D. Georgakopoulos, M. Hornick and A. Sheth, An Overview of Workflow Management: From Process Modeling to Workflow Automation Infrastructure, Distributed and Parallel Databases, 1995, vol.3, pp. 119-153.
16. S. Mehrotra et al., A Transaction Model for Multidatabase Systems, in Proceedings of 12th International Conference on Distributed Computing Systems, 1992.
17. C. Hagen and G. Alonso, Exception Handling in Workflow Management Systems, IEEE Transactions on Software Engineering, 2000.26(10): pp. 943-958

Optimizing the Profit of On-Demand Multimedia Service Via a Server-Dependent Queuing System

Pei-chun Lin

Department of Transportation and Communication Management Science,
National Cheng Kung University,
1, University Road, Tainan 701, Taiwan
peichun@mail.ncku.edu.tw

Abstract. This study presents a profit maximization model that adopts the number of requests for image or voice transferring services on a network as decision variables for when to switch a second server on and off based on the costs of using a second server and of users waiting. A Markovian queue with a number of servers depending upon queue length and finite capacity is discussed. The data of interarrival time and service times of requests are collected by observing a queuing system. An empirical Bayesian method is then applied to estimate the traffic intensity of the system, which denotes the need for host computers. The mean number of transfer requests in the system and the queue length of transfer requests are calculated as the characteristic values of the system.

1 Introduction

A server, such as a web server, is a host computer linked to a network, such as the Internet, which provides data in response to requests by client computers (Fig. 1.). For instance, clients in an on-demand video server environment make requests for a movies to a centralized video server. Client requests may peak at particular hours in the day, causing congestion of data across the connection, or delaying the transfer requests, resulting in client dissatisfaction. To shorten the wait time, the number of servers must be increased which also increases the cost of providing services. However, servers are idle and resources are wasted when the demand declines, incurring unnecessary cost. Determining how to allocate servers efficiently to reduce unnecessary facility cost, idle cost, and the cost of losing transfer requests, while catering for varia-tions in demand, is a crucial issue for computer host managers.

The primary objective of this study is to establish an evaluation model for planning server requirements to optimize the profit of providing video or audio on demand. Decision makers may determine the service requirement and the number of servers needed according to the regular flow rate for requesting images or sounds across the network and on the expected service rate. An objective and effective model is necessary to operate systems optimally. This research implements the empirical Bayesian approach to estimate the network requests

J.X. Yu, M. Kitsuregawa, and H.V. Leong (Eds.): WAIM 2006, LNCS 4016, pp. 229–239, 2006.
© Springer-Verlag Berlin Heidelberg 2006

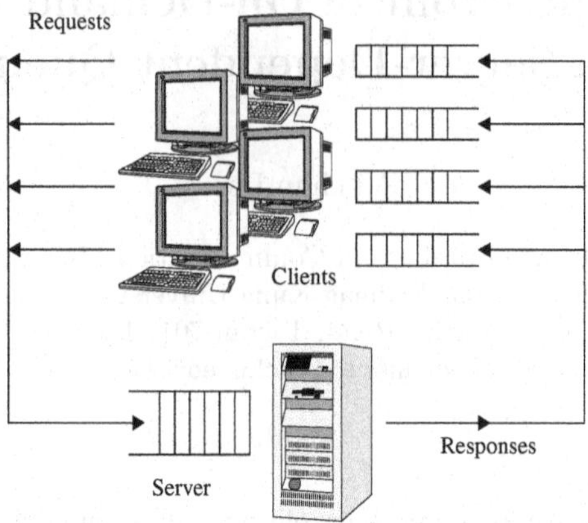

Fig. 1. Host computer connected to a network (Source: [6])

requirement based on the actual queuing operation, then constructs a server-dependent queuing system. The controllable system switches a second server on whenever the number of transfer requests in the system reaches a threshold, and switches it off whenever the number of transfer requests in system falls below another threshold. This study has the following specific goals:

1. Consider the randomness of transfer requests arrival and service time and utilize the empirical Bayesian approach to estimate the required numbers of transfer requests.
2. Construct a server-dependent $M/M/2/L$ queuing system, that initiates another server whenever the queue length in front of the first server reaches length N, and closes the second server whenever the queue length in front of first server falls to length Q. Additionally, the system characteristics, such as the expected number of transfer requests in system, and the probability of server being idle, should be analyzed.
3. Build a model to maximize the expected profit of providing services based on the cost of utilizing the second server and waiting for transfer requests, using N and Q as decision variables.

2 Related Literatures

This section first describes the reason for using traffic intensity to define the amount of transfer requests requirement, then describes the system characteristics and the development of a server-dependent queuing system and discusses the related references.

2.1 Traffic Intensity vs. the Amount of Transfer Requested

The definition of traffic intensity ρ is given by the ratio of arrival rate over service rate, and it is an important reference of queuing system, representing the utilization or proportion of the server being occupied. This study utilizes traffic intensity to indicate the number of transfer requests required. A higher traffic intensity means a higher transfer requests arrival rate or a lower service rate. The transfer requests arrival rate is great than or equal to the service rate when $\rho \geq 1$. A system with a single server is clearly insufficient to cope with the amount of service requirement, and eventually blown up [14]. Queues are caused by the uncertainty of the speed at which transfer requests arrive and the variation of service time. The waiting time is zero only when transfer requests arrive at a fixed interval and the service time is a constant. In reality, transfer requests arrive at random intervals, and the time needed to serve a transfer request is also random. To avoid the assumption that the transfer requests arrival rate and the service rate are known, this research applies the empirical Bayes-ian method to estimate the traffic intensity of a queuing system, which can satisfy the actual randomness and uncertainty and ensure that the proposed model is reasonable.

2.2 Server-Dependent Queues

Whitt [13] investigated how performance scaling in the standard $M/M/n$ queue with growing congestion-dependent customer demand. Assuming growing congestion dependent demand, service efficiency can be attained even if the potential demand is highly uncertain, because the actual arrival rate is adjusted according to the congestion. Zhang et al. [16] presented a nonlinear integer optimization model to determine the number of machines at each tier in a multi-tier server network, and utilized a result from an open queuing network model on the average response time. The optimization model minimizes the weighted sum of number of servers while fulfilling the average response time constraint. Jennings et al. [5] proposed a procedure to determine how many servers are needed, as a function of time, in a nonstationary stochastic service system. Singh [7] developed a server-dependent queue that provided a new service facility whenever the queue in front of the server reaches a certain length. Garg et al. [3] extended Singh's concept to develop an $M/M/2$ queue with several homogeneous or heterogeneous servers depending on the queue length. The service rate for the first and the second server are different in a two-server heterogeneous system. Garg et al. also proposed that the second server should be used at queue length N to maximum profit. Yamashiro [15] revised the model of Garg et al. [3] and assumed that a queue with finite capacity was applicable ($M/M/2/L$). Dai [2] proposed the finite capacity $M/M/3/L$ queuing system where the number of servers varies according to the queue length. Bansal et al. [1] investigated the cost factors for activating the second server.

Most of previous research concentrated on switching the second server on when the queue length reached N. Some approaches are set up so that the first server is not initiated until the queue reach length N. Researchers such as Wang et al. [10] considered the server with unexpected failure to derive the non-reliable $M/M/1/L$ system; Wang et al. [9] drew Erlang distribution into the non-reliable server in a finite and infinite $M/H_2/1$ queuing system. Hsie [4] proposed an $M/M/1$ system that turned the server off to reduce idling cost when it had no one to serve. The above studies all used the optimal queue length N as the decision variable to determine when to turn on the first server, and constructed the objective function for the minimum expected cost.

Wang et al. [11] and Dai [2] incorporated cost into the objective function. Their studies quantified the waiting cost of transfer requests, and addressed the cost of activating the second server, and its idle cost for building the model of the minimum expected cost. However, Yamashiro [15], Wang et al. [9], Garg et al. [3] and Dai [2] did not describe how to obtain the traffic intensity. This study estimates the traffic intensity by the empirical Bayesian approach. Additionally, the proposed system is set up so that the first server is always operating, thus fitting most conditions. This study also adopts the queue length as decision variables to switch on/off the second server.

3 Research Method

This investigation applied the empirical Bayesian approach to estimate the demand for service. A server-dependent queuing system using the queue length to activate and close the second server was constructed to maximize the expected profit for a decision maker. In part 1, the required amount of service was estimated using numerical data from simulation and observation, and the traffic intensity estimated with the empirical Bayesian approach proposed by Thiruvaiyaru [8]. The probability for each state was then calculated for an $M/M/2/L$ server-dependent queuing system in Part 2. Finally, the parameters of cost were considered, and the results of Parts 1 and 2 were combined to solve the optimal queue lengths N for starting a second server, and Q for switching it off. The method was first introduced to estimate traffic intensity using the empirical Bayesian approach and obtain observational data.

3.1 Empirical Bayesian Estimator of Traffic Intensity

Thiruvaiyaru [8] considered there are H independent $M/M/1$ queues in which the interarrival times $\{U_{ik},\ i = 1 \dots n\}$ of the first n transfer request, and the service times $\{V_{jk},\ j = 1 \dots m\}$ of the first m transfer requests are observed for $k = 1 \dots H$. The arrival rate λ_k , and $\{U_{ik},\ k = 1 \dots H\ \}$ are i.i.d exponential (λ_k) random variables, where

$$f_{\mathbf{U}_k}(u_k|\lambda_k) = \lambda_k^n exp\{-\lambda_k \sum_{i=1}^{n} u_{ik}\} \tag{1}$$

where $\mathbf{U}_k = (U_{ik}, i = 1 \dots n)'$.

Additionally, the service rate μ_k , and $\{V_{jk},\ j = 1 \dots m\}$ are i.i.d. exponential (μ_k) random variables, given by

$$f_{\mathbf{V}_k}(v_k|\mu_k) = \mu_k^m exp\{-\mu_k \sum_{j=1}^{m} v_{ik}\} \tag{2}$$

where $\mathbf{V}_k = (V_{jk}, j = 1 \dots m)'$.

The arrival rates $\{\lambda_1 \dots \lambda_n\}$ are assumed to be i.i.d. $Gamma(\alpha_1, \beta_1)$ (prior distribution) and the service rates $\{\mu_1 \dots \mu_m\}$ are assumed to be i.i.d. $Gamma(\alpha_2, \beta_2)$ (prior distribution). Additionally, the two sequences $\{\lambda_1 \dots \lambda_n\}$ and $\{\mu_1 \dots \mu_m\}$ are assumed to be independent of each other. The empirical Bayesian estimator is derived as

$$\hat{\rho} = \frac{(n + \hat{\alpha_1})(\sum_{j=1}^{m} v_j + \hat{\beta_2})}{(m + \hat{\alpha_2} - 1)(\sum_{i=1}^{n} u_i + \hat{\beta_1})} \tag{3}$$

where $\hat{\alpha_1}$, $\hat{\alpha_2}$, $\hat{\beta_1}$, and $\hat{\beta_2}$ denote the one-step maximum likelihood estimators of α_1, α_2, β_1, and β_2 respectively. First, let $\hat{\eta}_l = (\hat{\alpha}_l, \hat{\beta}_l)'$, $l = 1, 2$ be the one-step maximum likelihood estimators of $\eta_l = (\alpha_l, \beta_l)'$, $l = 1, 2$. Let $m_{11} = \sum_{k=1}^{H} \sum_{i=1}^{n} \frac{U_{ik}}{Hn}$ and $m_{21} = \sum_{k=1}^{H} \sum_{i=1}^{n} \frac{U_{ik}^2}{Hn}$, to calculate $m_{11} = \beta_1/(\alpha_1 - 1)$ and $m_{21} = 2\beta_1^2/(\alpha_1 - 1)(\alpha_1 - 2)$. The moment estimator $(\tilde{\alpha}_1, \tilde{\beta}_1)$ of (α_1, β_1) is given by

$$\tilde{\alpha}_1 = 2(m_{21} - m_{11}^2)/(m_{21} - 2m_{11}^2) . \tag{4}$$

$$\tilde{\beta}_1 = m_{11}m_{21})/(m_{21} - 2m_{11}^2) . \tag{5}$$

Again, let $m_{12} = \sum_{k=1}^{H} \sum_{j=1}^{m} \frac{V_{jk}}{Hm}$ and $m_{22} = \sum_{k=1}^{H} \sum_{j=1}^{m} \frac{V_{jk}^2}{Hm}$, the moment estimator of (α_2, β_2) are

$$\tilde{\alpha}_2 = 2(m_{22} - m_{12}^2)/(m_{22} - 2m_{12}^2) . \tag{6}$$

$$\tilde{\beta}_2 = m_{22}m_{12})/(m_{22} - 2m_{12}^2) . \tag{7}$$

Then, the one-step maximum likelihood estimators of $\eta_l = (\alpha_l, \beta_l)'$, $l = 1, 2$ are given by

$$\hat{\eta}_l = \tilde{\eta}_l - W_l^{-1}(\tilde{\eta}) \cdot S_l(\tilde{\eta}), l = 1, 2 . \tag{8}$$

where the marginal likelihood function is

$$\begin{aligned} L &= f(x_1, ..., x_n) = \prod_{k=1}^{H} f(\mathbf{U}_k) f(\mathbf{V}_k) \\ &= \prod_{k=1}^{H} \left[\frac{\beta_1^{\alpha_1}}{\Gamma(\alpha_1)} \cdot \frac{\Gamma(\alpha_1 + n)}{(\Sigma_{i=1}^{n} u_{ik} + \beta_1)^{\alpha_1 + n}} \cdot \frac{\beta_2^{\alpha_2}}{\Gamma(\alpha_2)} \cdot \frac{\Gamma(\alpha_2 + m)}{(\Sigma_{j=1}^{m} v_{jk} + \beta_2)^{m + \alpha_2}} \right] \end{aligned} \tag{9}$$

and

$$\eta_l = (\alpha_l, \beta_1)', S_l(\tilde{\eta}) = \left[\frac{\partial \ln L}{\partial \alpha_l}, \frac{\partial \ln L}{\partial \beta_l} \right]'_{\eta_l = \tilde{\eta}_l}, l = 1, 2 . \tag{10}$$

and

$$W_l(\tilde{\eta}) = \begin{bmatrix} \frac{\partial^2 \ln L}{\partial \alpha_l^2} & \frac{\partial^2 \ln L}{\partial \alpha_l \partial \beta_l} \\ \frac{\partial^2 \ln L}{\partial \alpha_l \partial \beta_l} & \frac{\partial^2 \ln L}{\partial \beta_l^2} \end{bmatrix}_{\eta_l = \tilde{\eta}_l}, l = 1, 2 . \tag{11}$$

3.2 Server-Dependent $M/M/2/L$ Queuing System

The major objective of this section is to establish a server-dependent M/M/2/L queuing system with finite capacity L. This system is set up so that the first server is al-ways on. When the number of transfer requests reaches N, the second sever is acti-vated to release the congestion in the system; when the number of transfer requests in systems falls to Q, then the system is no longer congested, and the second server can be switched off to cut cost. The number of waiting line is only 1, as demonstrated in Fig. 2.

The assumptions, parameters and variables used in the model are defined as follows.

Assumptions

1. The service rule is FCFS.
2. The interarrival time of transfer requests is exponentially distributed with unknown parameters.
3. The service time for each transfer request is exponentially distributed with unknown parameters.
4. The service system can provide a maximum of two servers, but at least one server remains active to serve transfer requests.
5. The system has finite capacity L, where $L \gg N$.
6. The service rates of the two servers are identical.
7. $1 < \rho < 2$.

Definition of symbols

λ: arrival rate of transfer requests;
μ: service rate of server;
ρ: traffic intensity $= \lambda \setminus \mu$;
i: number of servers in service, $i = 1, 2$;
j: number of transfer requests in system, $j = 0, \ldots, L$;
$P(1, j)$: the steady-state probability that only one server is in service when the number of transfer requests in system is j, where $j = 0,\ 1,\ 2,\ \ldots,\ Q,\ Q+1,\ \ldots,\ N-1$;
$P(2, j)$: the steady-state probability that only one server is in service when the number of transfer requests in system is j, where $j = Q+1,\ Q+2, \ldots,\ N,\ N+1,\ \ldots,\ N-1, L$.

This study build a server-dependent $M/M/2/L$ system based on the above assumptions and symbols. Figure 3 depicts the rate diagram of the birth and death process. To solve the birth-death flow balance equations based on Fig. 3, this study begins by expressing each $P(1, j)$ and $P(2, j)$ in terms of $P(1, 0)$. The steady-state probability of no transfer request in the system, given by $P(1, 0)$, is solved as follows:

$$P(1,0) = \left\{ \frac{1}{1-\rho} - \frac{\rho^N \{(2-\rho)(N-Q) + \rho(1-\rho)(\frac{\rho}{2})^{L-N}[1-(\frac{\rho}{2})^{N-Q}]\}}{(2-\rho)^2(1-\rho^{N-Q})} \right\}^{-1} \tag{12}$$

Then (12) can then be utilized to determine $P(1, j)$, $P(2, j)$. Each term of $P(1, j)$, $P(2, j)$ is a function of the traffic intensity ρ, and the decision variables N, Q. The cost parameters can now be adopted to formulate an NLP to maximize the expected profit resulting from waiting for transfer requests and server operation.

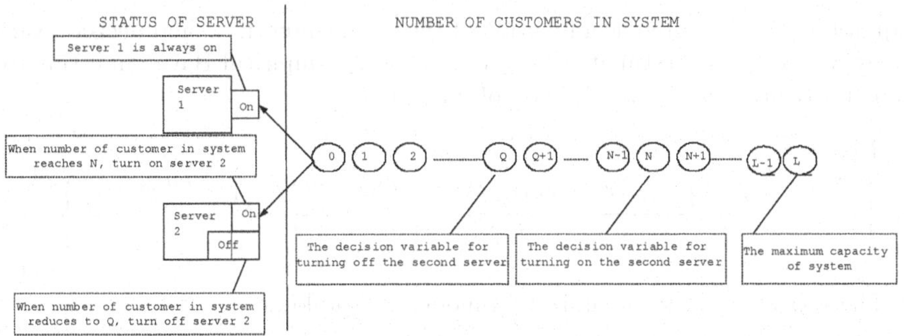

Fig. 2. Server-dependent queuing system with single waiting line

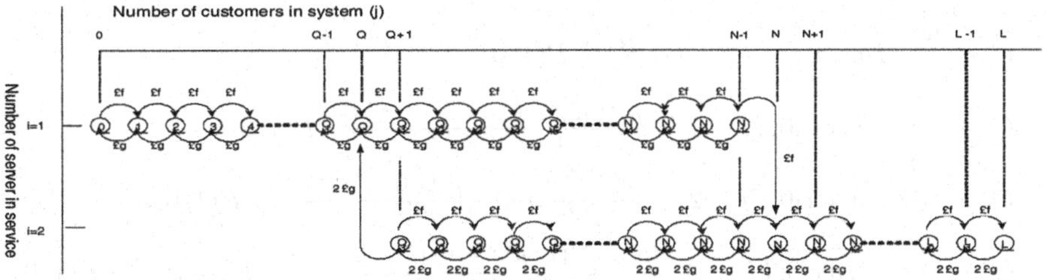

Fig. 3. Rate diagram for $M/M/2/L$ queuing system

3.3 Formulation of Objective Function

An objective function is then built to minimize the expected cost of the $M/M/2/L$ controllable queuing system. The definitions of parameters are as follows:
R: expected subscription revenue per day;
C_s: fulltime operating cost for second server per day;
C_i: fulltime idle cost for second server per day;
C_L: penalty cost for system being fully loaded per day;
C_e: cost for system being empty per day;
C_{on}: start up cost for turning the second server on per day;
C_{off}: shut down cost for turning the second server off per day;
C_w: the average waiting cost for each transfer request per day,

The expected profit per day is then given by

$$\begin{aligned}\pi(N,Q\,|\rho) &= R - C_s \cdot \sum_{Q+1}^{L} P(2,j) - C_w \cdot \sum_{j=0}^{N-1} Max[0,(j-1)] \cdot P(1,j)\\ &-C_w \cdot \sum_{j=Q+1}^{L} Max[0,(j-2)] \cdot P(2,j) - C_i \cdot \sum_{j=0}^{N-1} P(1,j) - C_{on} \cdot P(2,N)\\ &-C_{off} \cdot P(1,Q) - C_e \cdot P(1,0) - C_L \cdot P(2,L)\end{aligned} \tag{13}$$

Equation (13) is written as a function of the traffic intensity ρ and decision variables N and Q. ρ is estimated by substituting an empirical Bayesian estimator and substituting $\hat{\rho}^{EB}$ into (13) to obtain $\hat{P}(1,0)$:

$$\hat{P}(1,0) = \left\{\frac{1}{1-\hat{\rho}^{EB}} - \frac{(\hat{\rho}^{EB})^N\left((2-\hat{\rho}^{EB})(N-Q)+\hat{\rho}^{EB}(1-\hat{\rho}^{EB})(\frac{\hat{\rho}^{EB}}{2})^{L-N}\left(1-(\frac{\hat{\rho}^{EB}}{2})^{N-Q}\right)\right)}{(2-\hat{\rho}^{EB})^2(1-(\hat{\rho}^{EB})^{N-Q})}\right\}^{-1} \tag{14}$$

The expected profit maximization model is as follows:

$$\begin{aligned}Maximize(N,Q\,|\hat{\rho}^{EB}) &= R - C_s \cdot \sum_{j=Q+1}^{N} \frac{(\hat{\rho}^{EB})^N \cdot (1-\hat{\rho}^{EB}) \cdot [1-(\frac{\hat{\rho}^{EB}}{2})^{j-Q}]}{(2-\hat{\rho}^{EB}) \cdot [1-(\hat{\rho}^{EB})^{N-Q}]} \cdot \hat{P}(1,0)\\ &-C_s \cdot \sum_{j=N+1}^{L} \frac{(\hat{\rho}^{EB})^N \cdot (1-\hat{\rho}^{EB}) \cdot [1-(\frac{\hat{\rho}^{EB}}{2})^{N-Q}] \cdot (\frac{\hat{\rho}^{EB}}{2})^{j-N}}{(2-\hat{\rho}^{EB}) \cdot [1-(\hat{\rho}^{EB})^{N-Q}]} \cdot \hat{P}(1,0)\\ &-C_w \cdot \sum_{j=0}^{Q} Max[0,(j-1)] \cdot (\hat{\rho}^{EB})^j \cdot \hat{P}(1,0)\\ &-C_w \cdot \sum_{j=Q+1}^{N-1} Max[0,(j-1)] \cdot \frac{\hat{\rho}^{EB} \cdot [(\hat{\rho}^{EB})^{j-1}-(\hat{\rho}^{EB})^{N-1}]}{[1-(\hat{\rho}^{EB})]^{N-Q}} \cdot \hat{P}(1,0)\\ &-C_w \cdot \sum_{j=Q+1}^{N} Max[0,(j-2)] \cdot \frac{(\hat{\rho}^{EB})^N \cdot (1-\hat{\rho}^{EB}) \cdot [1-(\hat{\rho}^{EB}/2)^{j-Q}]}{(2-\hat{\rho}^{EB}) \cdot (1-(\hat{\rho}^{EB})^{N-Q})} \cdot \hat{P}(1,0)\\ &-C_w \cdot \sum_{j=N+1}^{L} Max[0,(j-2)] \cdot \frac{(\hat{\rho}^{EB})^N \cdot (1-\hat{\rho}^{EB}) \cdot [1-(\hat{\rho}^{EB}/2)^{N-Q}]}{(2-\hat{\rho}^{EB}) \cdot (1-(\hat{\rho}^{EB})^{N-Q})} \cdot (\frac{\hat{\rho}^{EB}}{2})^{j-N} \cdot \hat{P}(1,0)\\ &-C_i \cdot \left[\sum_{j=1}^{Q} (\hat{\rho}^{EB})^j \cdot \hat{P}(1,0) + \sum_{j=Q+1}^{N-1} \frac{\hat{\rho}^{EB} \cdot [(\hat{\rho}^{EB})^{j-1}-(\hat{\rho}^{EB})^{N-1}]}{[1-(\hat{\rho}^{EB})]^{N-Q}} \cdot \hat{P}(1,0)\right]\\ &-C_{on} \cdot \frac{(\hat{\rho}^{EB})^N \cdot (1-\hat{\rho}^{EB}) \cdot [1-(\hat{\rho}^{EB}/2)^{N-Q}]}{(2-\hat{\rho}^{EB}) \cdot (1-(\hat{\rho}^{EB})^{N-Q})} \cdot \hat{P}(1,0)\\ &-C_{off} \cdot (\hat{\rho}^{EB})^Q \cdot \hat{P}(1,0)\\ &-C_e \cdot \hat{P}(1,0) + C_L \cdot \frac{(\hat{\rho}^{EB})^N \cdot (1-\hat{\rho}^{EB}) \cdot [1-(\hat{\rho}^{EB}/2)^{N-Q}]}{(2-\hat{\rho}^{EB}) \cdot (1-(\hat{\rho}^{EB})^{N-Q})} \cdot (\frac{\hat{\rho}^{EB}}{2})^{L-N} \cdot \hat{P}(1,0)\end{aligned} \tag{15}$$

The above NLP is hard to solve analytically to prove that its feasible region is a convex set possessing the optimal $N*$ and $Q*$ and globally maximizing the expected profit. Therefore, this study applied a numerical method to explore how changes in the NLP's parameters change the optimal solution.

4 Sensitivity Analysis

This section illustrates some results obtained in previous sections with a hypothetical queuing experiment. The Monte Carlo simulation was first conducted to generate random data for five queues and the one-step maximum likelihood estimator $(\hat{\alpha}_1, \hat{\beta}_1)$ = (58.19542203,11.31472722), $(\hat{\alpha}_2, \hat{\beta}_2)$ = (28.31890446, 6.954543058). The empirical Bayesian estimator of traffic intensity was calculated to $\hat{\rho}^{EB}$ =1.294695872. A numerical analysis was performed to identify the influence of individual parameter and discover the following rules:

1. When there is no start up and shut down cost for the second server, in order to attain the maximum profit the second server should be turned on and off fre-quently.
2. The second server does not readily provide service as the fulltime operating cost for second server increases.
3. The second server should be kept busy most of the time when its fulltime idle cost rises.
4. The service system can provide a maximum of two servers, but at least one server remains active to serve transfer requests.
5. As long as the average waiting cost for each transfer request increases, the system should not keep transfer requests to wait, so the second server should be turned on as soon as possible.
6. The variation of penalty cost for system being fully loaded and empty reveal does not significantly affect the minimum cost. However, the penalty cost for system being fully empty does significantly change optimal $N*$ and $Q*$ significantly.
7. If the second server offered service at no cost, then it would be turned on as soon as possible. However, the startup cost and shut-down cost would prevent the sec-ond server from being turned on and off at will.
8. The greater the traffic intensity, the sooner the second server should be turned on to ease the congestion.

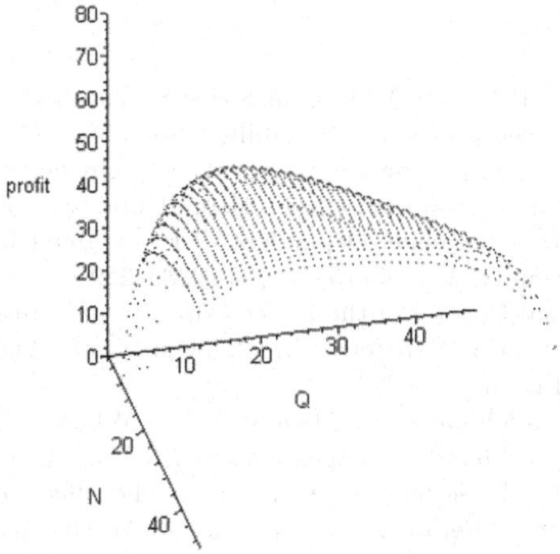

Fig. 4. The expected profit vs. the queue lengths N for starting a second server, and Q for switching it off

9. The system capacity L does not affect the optimal solution when it is sufficiently large.

Figure 4 depicts the relationship among the expected profit, the queue lengths N for starting a second server, and Q for switching it off.

5 Conclusions

This study built a server dependent queuing system by applying the empirical Bayesian approach to estimate the demand for service. An NLP model of maximum ex-pected profit for a decision maker was then constructed by utilizing the queue lengths as decision variables for when to activate and deactivate the second server. The optimal value of N and Q to maximize profit was obtained from the relationship among the costs of initializing the second server, switching it on and off, and waiting by transfer requests. A sensitivity analysis was undertaken to discover the effect of changes in the NLP's parameters $(R;C_s;C_i;C_L;C_e;C_{on};C_{off};C_w)$ on the optimal solution. The numerical analysis reveals the following conclusions:

1. Increasing the fulltime operating cost of the second server and the penalty cost of an empty system causes $N*$ and $Q*$ to rise;
2. Increasing the fulltime idle cost for the second server, the average waiting cost for each transfer request, and the penalty cost for system being fully loaded would decrease $N*$ and $Q*$;
3. Increasing the startup and shut-down cost for turning the second server on and off would cause larger $N*$ to increase but decrease $Q*$. The results of the evaluation model present a reference for service facility requirement planning.

References

1. Bansal, K.K., Garg, R.L.: An Additional Space Special Service Facility Heterogeneous Queue. Microelectronics and Reliability, Vol. 35(4). (1994) 725–730
2. Dai, K.Y.: Queue-Dependent Servers in an M/M/3 Queueing System with Finite Capacity. Master Thesis, National Chung Hsing University. Taiwan. (1999)
3. Garg, R.L., Singh, P.: Queue Dependent Servers Queueing System. Microelectronics and Reliability, Vol. 33(15). (1993) 2289–2295
4. Hsieh, W.F.: Optimal Control of the Finite Capacity and Infinite Capacity with a Removable Service Station Subject to Breakdown. Master Thesis, National Chung Hsing University. Taiwan. (1993)
5. Jennings, O.B., Mandelbaum, A., Massey, W.A., Whitt, W.: Server Staffing to Meet Time-Varying Demand. Management Science, Vol. 42 1383–1394 (1996)
6. Nahum, E.M., Rosu, M., Seshan, S., Almeida, J.: The Effects of Wide-Area Conditions on WWW Server Performance. In Proc. ACM SIGMETRICS. Cambridge, MA, (2001)
7. Singh, V.P.: Two-server Markovian Queues with Balking. Heterogeneous vs. Homogeneous Servers. Operations Research, Vol. 18(1), 145–59 (1970)

8. Thiruvaiyaru, D., Basawa, I.V.: Empirical Bayes Estimation for Queueing Systems and Networks. Queueing Systems, Vol. 11, 179–202 (1992)
9. Wang, K.H., Huang, H.M.: Optimal Control of a Removable Server in an M/Ek/1 Queueing System with Finite Capacity. Microelectronics and Reliability, Vol. 35(7), 1023–1030 (1995)
10. Wang, K.H., Hsieh, W.F.: Optimal Control of a Removable and Non-reliable Server in a Markovian Queueing Systems with Finite Capacity. Microelectron. Reliab., Vol. 35(2), 189–196 (1995)
11. Wang, K.H., Chang, K.W., Sivazlian, B.D.: Optimal Control of a Removable and Non-reliable Server in an Infinite and a Finite M/H2/1 queueing sys-tem. Applied Mathematical Modelling, Vol. 23(8), 651–666 (1999)
12. Wang, Y.L.: Optimal Control of an M/M/2 Queueing System with Finite Capacity Operating Under the Triadic (0,Q,N,M) Policy. Master Thesis, National Chung Hsing University. Taiwan. (2001)
13. Whitt W.: How Multiserver Queues Scale with Growing Congestion-Dependent Demand. Operations Research, Vol. 51(4), 531–542 (2003)
14. Winston, W.L.: Operations Research. 3rd edition, Duxbury, Indiana University (1994)
15. Yamashiro, M.: A System Where the Number of Servers Changes Depending on the Queue Length. Microelectronics and Reliability, Vol. 36(3), 389–391 (1996)
16. Zhang, A., Santos, P., Beyer, D., Tang, H.: Optimal server resource alloca-tion using an open queueing network model of response time. Technical Report HPL-2002-301, HP Labs. (2002)

Service Matchmaking Based on Semantics and Interface Dependencies

Shuiguang Deng, Jian Wu, Ying Li, and Zhaohui Wu

College of Computer Science, Zhejiang University, Hangzhou 310027, China
{dengsg, wujian2000, cnliying, wzh}@zju.edu.cn

Abstract. Most of the current service matchmaking algorithms are based on one presupposition, in which all inputs of a service are indispensable to each output of that service. However, this presupposition does not always hold. This paper analyses this presupposition and argues that it exerts a negative influence on the recall rate and precision to current matchmaking algorithms. A formal service model is then introduced, which extends the service profile of OWL-S. A new service matchmaking algorithm based on the model and semantics is proposed. Compared with other algorithms, the proposed one takes interface dependencies into consideration while performing matchmaking. This algorithm has been applied in a service composition framework called DartFlow. Our experimental data show that this novel service matchmaking outperforms others in terms of the recall rate and precision.

1 Introduction

Web service technologies provide a new way for business enterprises to communicate with their partners and customers. The number of services presented on the open Internet is growing at an explosive speed, which subsequently brings great challenges to the accurate, efficient and automatic retrieval of target services for consumers. Much work aspires to solve this challenge. Among those efforts, SWS (Semantic Web Service) is regarded as the most promising technology to retrieve services in an accurate and automatic way. Relying on related languages and inference engines, it aims at providing machine understandable descriptions of what services do and how they achieve their goals [1]. Based on it, many service matchmaking algorithms are proposed [2-6].

However, most of the service matchmaking algorithms are based on the presupposition, in which each output fully depends on all the inputs in a service. In other words, it is imperative for service consumers to provide all the inputs of the service in order to get even one output of the service. This requirement leads to some unwanted situations. If those algorithms are used, some deserved target services are not returned only because the number of each service's input is less than the one specified in the service request, even other information is the same. Consider such a matchmaking scenario between a service *S* and a service request *R*, where *S* has three inputs (*a*, *b* and *c*) and two outputs (o and *p*), and *R* specifies two inputs (*a* and *b*) and one output (*o*). Most of the existing algorithms do not return *S* to *R*, as *R* cannot provide all of the inputs to invoke *S*. This case indicates that the current algorithms take it for granted

J.X. Yu, M. Kitsuregawa, and H.V. Leong (Eds.): WAIM 2006, LNCS 4016, pp. 240–251, 2006.
© Springer-Verlag Berlin Heidelberg 2006

that all the inputs (*a*, *b* and *c*) are indispensable to get the output (*o*). But for service providers, in fact, this presupposition is not always consistent with their original intention. In the above scenario, the actual intention of the service provider is that *o* depends on only *a* and *b*, and *p* depends on only *b* and *c*. Hence service consumers can only provide *a* and *b* when they invoke *S* to get *o*. Accordingly, *S* is certainly one target service for *R*.

The presupposition is accepted by the existing service matchmaking algorithms because the current service specification languages, such as WSDL and OWL-S, do not provide such a mechanism to depict and publish interface dependency information inside a service. We argue that interface dependencies should be added to the current service specifications and a good service matchmaking algorithm should take the interface dependencies into consideration.

The remainder of this paper is organized as follows. First, a formal service model with interface dependencies is given in Section 2. Based on it, the novel service matchmaking algorithm is presented in Section 3. After that, its implementation in our service composition framework - DartFlow is described in Section 4. The major related work and their comparison with the proposed algorithm are discussed in Section 5. Finally, Section 6 concludes this paper.

2 A Formal Service Model

Definition 1. A service is a 9-tuple: $S = (\eta, \sigma, \upsilon, \pi, I, O, p, e, \psi)$ where:

(1) η is a service name.

(2) σ depicts some general information about the service in natural language for human reading, such as the functional description.

(3) υ is a provider description of the service, which contains information about the service provider such as the provider name and the corresponding method.

(4) π is a category name of the service based on the taxonomies such as NAICS[1] and UNSPSC[2].

(5) $I = \{i_1, i_2, \ldots, i_n\}$ is the set of inputs.

(6) $O = \{o_1, o_2, \ldots, o_n\}$ is the set of outputs. $I \cup O$ is called interface set of the service. $\forall e \in I \cup O$ is expressed using a domain-dependent ontology class with some properties.

(7) p is the precondition.

(8) e is the effect.

(9) $\psi : O \to 2^I$ is the dependency function from the output set to the input power set.

For an output $o \in O$, $\psi(o) = \omega \in 2^I$, meaning that o depends on input set ω. ψ can be regarded as an extension to OWL-S, which as the specification of SWS is an

1 The North American Industry Classification System (NAICS) published by the US Census.

2 The United Nations Standard Product and Services Classification (UNSPSC) System developed jointly by the UNDP (United Nations Development Program) and D&B (Dun & Bradstreet Corporation) in 1998.

ontology language for Web services with three main parts: the service profile that provides public information for advertisement and discovery, the process model that tells "how the service works" in detail, and the grounding that tells "how to access the service" [1]. The service model extends the service profile of OWL-S by providing a mechanism for service providers to depict and publish interface dependency information. The meaning of dependency between outputs and inputs is defined below.

Definition 2. Given an output *o* and an input *i* of a service *S*, *o* depends on *i* (denoted as $o \prec i$) if and only if *i* must be provided in order to get *o* in the service invocation.

Definition 3. Given a service $S = (\eta, \sigma, \upsilon, \pi, I, O, p, e, \psi)$ and an output $o \in O$, if $o \prec I$ i.e. $\psi(o) = I$, o is a fully-dependent output. If $\psi(o) \subset I$, o is a partially-dependent output.

As Fig. 1 shows, both outputs o_1 and o_2 depend on i_1 and i_2 while o_3 depends on only i_1. So o_1 ad o_2 are fully-dependent outputs and o_3 is a partially-dependent output. We represent a fully-dependent output as a dot-filled rectangle and a partially-dependent output as a fork-filled rectangle as shown in Fig.1.

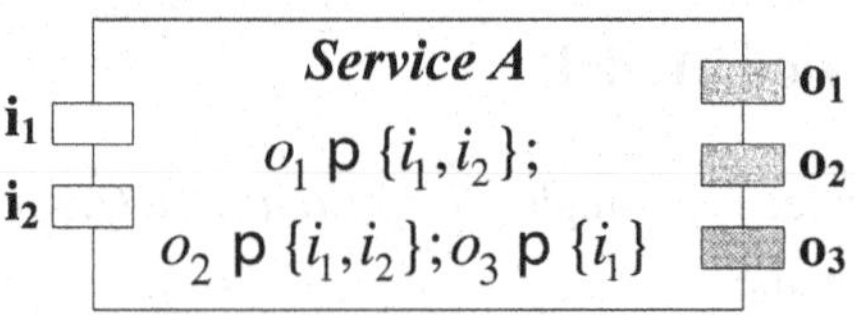

Fig. 1. An example of a service

Note that a service specification based on Definition 1 is used not only for service matchmaking algorithms but also for service providers to publish their services. It has the same purpose as the service profile of OWL-S and covers not only all the content of the service profile, but also provides additional mechanisms for service providers to depict and publish interface dependencies. The extended service profile ontology for OWL-S is illustrated in Fig. 2. Compared with the standard service profile ontology of OWL-S, the extended one has a new ontology classes named partially-dependent output. It has three properties named *output*, *dependOnInput* and *dependOnInputs*, respectively.

3 A Service Matchmaking Algorithm

This section presents a novel algorithm that is based on the extended service model, which considers the interface dependencies implied in a service. In fact, this algorithm is an improved version of our pre-published algorithm [16], in which we present some semantic similarity definitions and computations in order to do service matchmaking based on semantics. In this paper, the improved version also makes use of the semantic similarity definitions and computations shown as below.

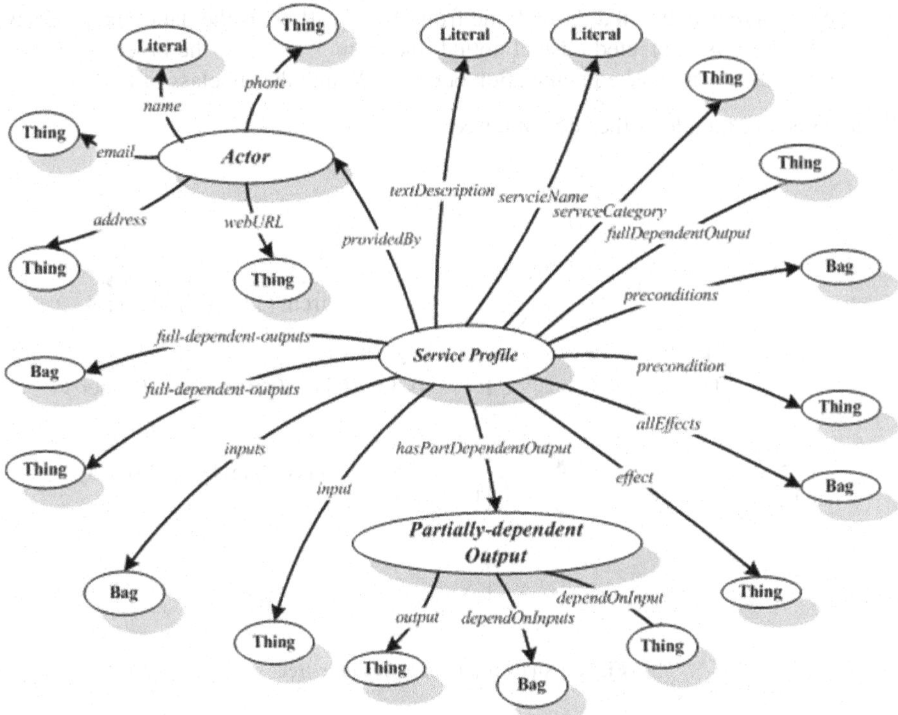

Fig. 2. An extended service profile ontology for OWL-S

3.1 Semantic Similarity Computation

Definition 4. For two ontology classes X and Y, X is semantically similar to Y (denoted as $X \square Y$) if they have one of the following four relations:

(1) X and Y are the same class (denoted as $X = Y$).
(2) Inherited relation (denoted as $X \rightarrow Y$). X is the subclass of Y, hence X inherits properties of Y. Thus they are semantically similar to some extent.
(3) Property relation (denoted as $X \prec Y$). Class X is the property of class Y, hence X can partly provide the information of Y.
(4) Mixed relation (denoted as $X \propto Y$).Class X has the property relation with some class named Z ($X \prec Z$), while class Y has the inherited relation with Z ($Y \rightarrow Z$), the relation between X and Y is called mixed relation. Since Y inherits all the properties of Z, including X, they are partly matched.

Definition 5. The relations among ontology classes construct a semantic tree $G = \{V, E\}$, where:

(1) V is the set of finite and nonempty vertexes, and each vertex represents an ontology class or a data type.
(2) $E \subseteq V \times V$ is the set of the relations between the two vertexes. If X is a subclass of Y, there is a directed real line from Y to X. If X is the object property

of Y, there is a directed dashed line from Y to X. If X is the data type property of Y, there is a directed dashed dotted line from Y to X. In the latter two situations, there is no dashed connection between X and the subclass of Y.

Figure 3 is an example of the semantic tree.

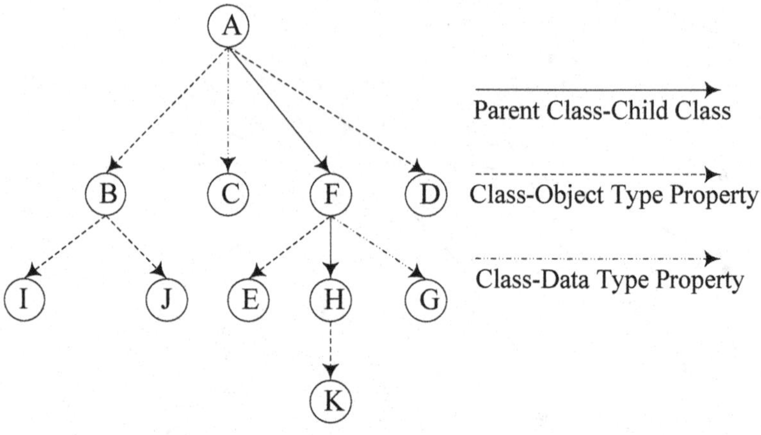

Fig. 3. An example of a semantic tree

Definition 6. Given a semantic tree $G(V,E)$, the property degree of vertex a (denoted as $PropertyNum(a)$) is the number of the directed dashed lines and directed dashed dotted edges emitted from the vertex a.

Definition 7. Inheriting vertex set $VexI(a,b)$. If there is a path connected by directed real lines from vertex a to vertex b in G, $VexI(a,b)$ contains all the vertexes in the path, including a and b.

Definition 8. Property vertex set $VexP(a,b)$. In a semantic tree $G(V,E)$, if there exists a path connected the dashed edges and dashed dotted edges from vertex a to vertex b, $VexP(a,b)$ contains all the vertexes in the path except b.

Definition 9. $Similarity(X,Y)$ is the matching degree of class X to class Y. If X can provide all the properties that Y embodies, they are totally matched. If X can only partially provide the properties that Y embodies, they are partially matched. The value of $Similarity(X,Y)$ ranges from 0 to 1. The value 0 means X is not semantically similar to Y at all, while the value 1 means X is the same as Y. Note that $Similarity(X,Y)$ and $Similarity(Y,X)$ represent different matching degrees. Different relations between X and Y result in different formulae of similarity evaluation.

(1) $X = Y$: $Similarity(X,Y) = Similarity(Y,X) = 1 = 1$.

(2) $X \rightarrow Y$: $Similarity(X,Y)$=1, since X inherits all the properties that Y embodies. For example, in Fig. 3, Similarity (H, A) =1.

$Similarity(Y,X) = \dfrac{\sum_{node \in Vex1(X,Z)} PropertyNum(node)}{\sum_{node \in Vex1(Y,Z)} PropertyNum(node)}$, where Z is the primal ancestor of X and Y. We hypothesize that the whole information of some class can be described by its properties. Child class possesses not only its own properties, but also those inherited from its ancestors. So $Similarity(Y,X)$ is the ratio of the number of properties they possess. For example, in Fig. 3, Similarity (A, H) =3/6.

(3) $X \prec Y$: $Similarity(Y,X)$=1.

For example, in Fig. 3, Similarity (A, I) =1.

$$Similarity(X,Y) = \frac{1}{\prod_{node \in Vex2(Y,X)} PropertyNum(node)}.$$

We hypothesize that all the properties of some class are of the same weight. If some class possesses n properties, then any one of the properties, namely X , contains 1/n information. If the class itself is a property of some class, namely Y , with m properties, then X contains 1/n*m information of Y . Analogically, $Similarity(X,Y)$ is defined as the above formula. For example, in Fig. 3, Similarity (I, A) =1/6.

(4) $X \propto Y$: $Similarity(Y,X)$ =1, since Y inherits the property X from its ancestor. For example, in Fig.3, Similarity (H, B) = 1.

$$Similarity(X,Y) = \frac{1}{\prod_{node \in Vex2(Z,X)} PropertyNum(node)} \bigg/ \sum_{node \in Vex1(Z,Y)} PropertyNum(node),$$

where $X \prec Z$ and $Y \rightarrow Z$. For example, in Fig.3, similarity (B, H) =1/18.

(5) Otherwise, $Similarity(X,Y) = Similarity(Y,X)$ =0

3.2 Service Matchmaking Based on Semantics and Interface Dependencies

In general, a service request specifies its input/output requirements, optional QoS criteria and additional information such as the service category name and description in its specification. In fact, the input/output requirements are the critical factors for matchmaking algorithms. For the purpose of simplicity, this paper discusses only the input/output requirements in a service request.

Definition 10. A service request is a 2-tuple: $R = (I^r, O^r)$, where

(1) $I^r = \{i^r{}_1, i^r{}_2, ..., i^r{}_m\}$ is the set of inputs, and

(2) $O^r = \{o^r{}_1, o^r{}_2, ..., o^r{}_n\}$ is the desired set of outputs.

Note that all the elements in I^r and O^r can be expressed using a domain-dependent ontology class with some properties.

Definition 11. Given a service $S=(\eta,\sigma,\upsilon,\pi,I,O,p,e,\psi)$ and a service request $R=(I^r,O^r)$, the matching degree between *S* and *R* is denoted as $\Omega(S,R)$, which is calculated according to the algorithm *SERVICE_MATCHMAKING* below.

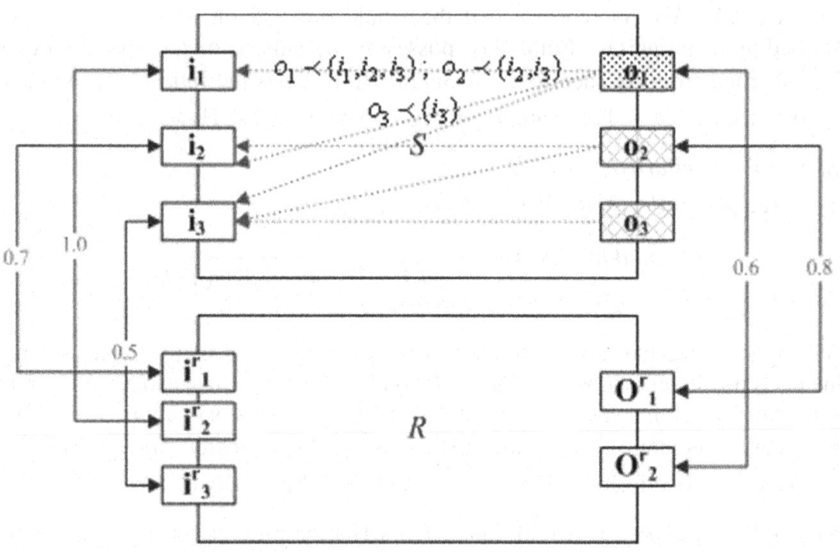

Fig. 4. An example to illustrate the principle of *SERVICE_MATCHMAKING*

This algorithm ensures the value of a matching degree ranging from 0 to 1. Due to space limitation, we just use the example in Fig. 4 to show how to calculate the matching degree. If there are the following relations in the example:

(1) $\chi(o_1^r)=o_2$, $similarity(o_1^r,o_2)=0.8$ (2) $\chi(o_2^r)=o_1$, $similarity(o_2^r,o_1)=0.6$

(3) $\gamma(i_1)=i^r_2$, $similarity(i_1,i_2^r)=1.0$ (4) $\gamma(i_2)=i_1^r$, $similarity(i_2,i_1^r)=0.7$

(5) $\gamma(i_3)=i_3^r$, $similarity(i_3,i_3^r)=0.5$

The matching degree between *S* and *R* calculates as follows according to *SERVICE_MATCHMAKING*. The relation $\chi(o_1^r)=o_2$ means that within the set *S.O* the most similar concept to o_1^r of $R.O^r$ is o_2, while $\gamma(i_2)=i_1^r$ means that within the set $R.I^r$ the most similar concept to i_2 of *S.I* is i_1^r.

$$\Omega(S,R)=\frac{(0.6\times(1.0+0.7+0.5))/3+(0.8\times(0.5+0.7))/2}{2}=0.46$$

4 DartFlow: A Framework of Service Composition

The proposed formal service model and the *SERVICE_MATCHMAKING* algorithm have been applied in DartFlow [7], which as a sub-project of DartGrid (http://ccnt.zju.edu.cn/projects/dartgrid) [8, 9] is a framework for service composition in the grid environment. It is oriented towards providing a convenient and efficient way for TCM (Traditional Chinese Medicine) researchers to collaborate with each other in research activities and experiments. It offers interfaces to allow researchers to register, query, compose and execute services at the semantic level.

So far we have teamed up with China Academy of Chinese Medical Sciences (http://www.catcm.ac.cn/) to establish the TCM domain ontology using Protégé and the OWL-plug-in, which covers about 8000 class concepts and 50,000 instance concepts [10]. Figure 5 (A) is a snapshot of our TCM ontology in Protégé. Moreover, we have implemented a novel semantic-based grid client called Semantic Browser as shown in Fig. 5 (B), which not only sketches out a semantic view of domain-ontology for end-users but also provides a friendly interface for end-users to browse and search for different resources such as TCM services and databases.

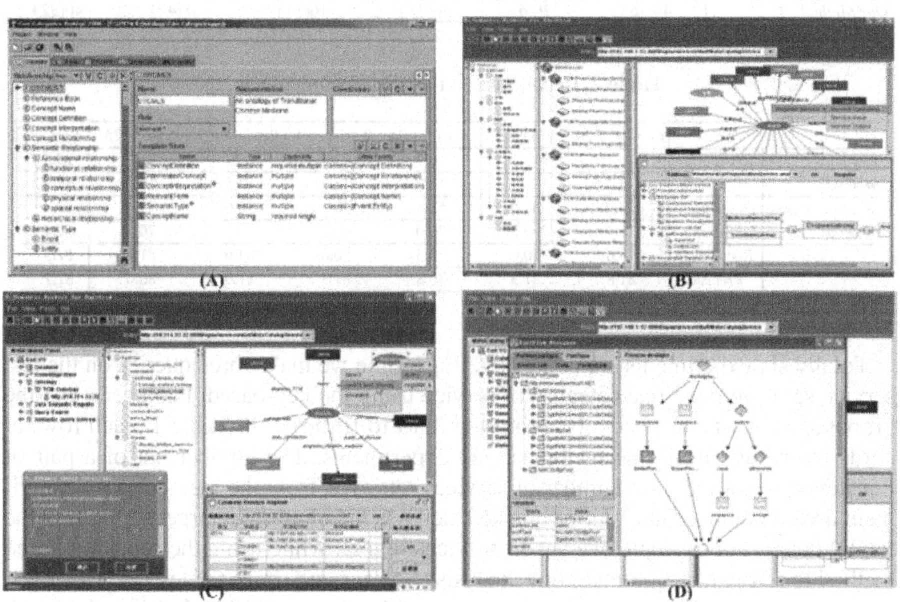

Fig. 5. Some screenshots of DartFlow

Based on the TCM domain ontology, we have developed a service registration portal as shown in Fig. 5 (C). So far DartFlow has been injected with more than 60 categories of TCM services and the total number of services reaches about 800. All services are provided by different TCM research organizations distributed in over 20 provinces of China. When users want to query services, they also provide a service profile specifying their requirements to the portal. The portal invokes the matchmaking agent to retrieve target services for users. The agent has implemented the proposed *SERVICE_MATCHMAKING* algorithm. Figure 5 (D) illustrates the workspace for service composition.

5 Evaluation and Comparison

In order to display its advantages, we have carried out a series of experiments in DartFlow. We select the standard UDDI and Paolucci's method as reference. Here we randomly select 200 services from 6 different categories registered in DartFlow as the test set. The name of category and the number of services of each category are shown in the top two rows of Table 1.

Table 1. Experiment results

Service Category Name	*Pharmacology Analysis (PhA)*	*Toxicology Analysis (TA)*	*Pathology Analysis (PA)*	*Symptomatology Analysis (SA)*	*Prescription generation (PG)*	*TCM Mining (TM)*
Service Number	42	30	24	15	52	37
Key-based Method	51(*7*)	35(*4*)	31(*4*)	14(2)	64(8)	45(*6*)
Semantic-Based Method	35(*25*)	26(*18*)	20(*14*)	13(9)	44(31)	31(22)
Our Method	44(*36*)	32(*26*)	26(*21*)	16(*13*)	58(*47*)	40(*32*)

Table 2. Recall rate and precision comparison

	(%)	*Retrieve PhA*	*Retrieve TA*	*Retrieve PA*	*Retrieve SA*	*Retrieve PG*	*Retrieve TM*	*Average*
Key-based Method	*Recall Rate*	16.7	13.3	16.7	13.3	15.3	16.2	***15.5***
	Precision	13.7	11.4	12.9	14.3	12.5	13.3	***12.9***
Semantic-Based Method	*Recall Rate*	59.5	60.0	58.3	60.0	59.6	59.4	***59.5***
	Precision	71.4	69.2	70.0	69.2	70.5	70.9	***70.4***
Our Method	*Recall Rate*	78.6	80.0	83.3	80.0	84.6	81.1	***81.5***
	Precision	81.8	81.3	80.8	81.3	81.0	80.0	***81.1***

Totally six experiments are conducted. Each time we make three queries on the test service set to retrieve one category of service using the key-based, Paolucci's and the proposed methods, respectively. From the third to fifth row in Table 1, each row records the results from one method in six experiments. The number out of a pair of brackets denotes the total number of services retrieved from the method in an experiment and the number in a pair of brackets denotes the number of target services in the total number. For example, we get 13 services in total while using the semantic-based method to retrieve symptomatology analysis (SA) services from the test set. However, only 9 from 13 services indeed belong to the SA category. Table 2 shows the recall rate and precision calculated from Table 1. The average recall rates for these methods are 15.5%, 59.5% and 81.5%, respectively. The average precisions are 12.9%, 70.4% and 81.1%, respectively. It shows that the semantic-based method can get better recall rate and precision than the key-based method and our method gets better results than the semantic-based method. Compared to the semantic-based method, our proposed method gains improvements of 22% and 10.7% in recall rate and precision, respectively. Thus we can draw a conclusion that mining functional unit relations and considering interface dependencies within services will enhance the performance of matchmaking algorithms.

6 Related Work

Service matchmaking has captured many researchers' attraction and much work has been done [2-6]. Researchers aim at pursuing high recall rate and precision while designing their service matchmaking algorithms. Precision is the proportion of retrieved documents that are relevant, and recall is the proportion of relevant documents that are retrieved [11]. Most service matchmaking algorithms can be classified into two categories: keyword and semantic-based methods. As a de-facto standard registry for Web services, UDDI provides the typical keyword-based service matchmaking function based on only names, comments and service descriptions. Because the keyword-based search fails to recognize the similarities and differences between the capabilities provided by Web services, UDDI does not yield a satisfactory recall rate and precision. To address this limitation, great efforts have been made to import service semantics and non-functional attributes into UDDI and to propose alternative ways to enhance its search functions [4, 12].

As a result, many semantic-based service query/matchmaking algorithms appear [2, 3, 6]. Klein [2] defines a fully-typed process ontology and then proposes an ontology-based approach that employs the characteristics of process taxonomy to increase recall without sacrificing precision and computational complexity of the service retrieval process. Paolucci [3] introduces a matchmaking algorithm based on the service profile of DAML-S, which considers the matching of input/output concepts defined by the same ontology. And also his group has developed a system called DAML-S Matchmaker to augment current UDDI architecture with semantic service descriptions. The matchmaker improves the discovery process by allowing location of services based on their capabilities described in DAML-S. Syeda-Mahmood [6] explores the use of domain-independent and domain-specific ontologies to find matching service descriptions. The domain-independent relationships are derived using an English thesaurus after tokenization and part-of-speech tagging.

Besides what is mentioned above, there are still many other semantic-based service matchmaking algorithms [13, 14, 15]. They will gain better recall rate and precision if they take into consideration the interface dependency information within a service.

7 Conclusion and Future Work

This paper proposes a novel service matchmaking algorithm to retrieve target services in an accurate, efficient and automatic way based on the extended service profile ontology of OWL-S. The main contributions of this work are (1) it is the first time to point out the presupposition accepted by the current service matchmaking algorithms and find out that it lower the recall rate and the precision of matchmaking algorithms; (2) it extends the service profile ontology of OWL-S with feasible and convenient mechanisms to describe and publish interface dependencies implied in services for matchmaking algorithms. Those mechanisms can be regarded as important supplements to the current service specification languages; (3) it proposes a novel service matchmaking algorithm. Compared with other algorithms, the proposed one takes into account the interface dependencies implied within a functional unit. The experiments carried out in DartFlow show that the proposed algorithm has both a better recall rate and precision than others. However, this work has not taken into account the QoS and other additional requirements in service requests. They also influence the matchmaking results to some extent. They should be taken into further consideration in the future research.

Acknowledgement

This work is supported by China 973 fundamental research and development project: The research on application of semantic grid on the sharing of knowledge and service of Traditional Chinese Medicine; Intel / University Sponsored Research Program: DartGrid: Building an Information Grid for Traditional Chinese Medicine; and China 211 core project: Network-based Intelligence and Graphics.

References

1. Paolucci M. and Sycara K., 2004. *Semantic Web Services: Current Status and Future Directions.* In: Proceeding of the IEEE International Conference on Web Services (ICWS'04), p12-31.
2. Klein M. and Bernstein A., 2001. *Searching services on the semantic Web using process ontologies.* In: Proceeding of the Int'l Semantic Web Working Symposium. (SWWS'01), p159-172.
3. Paolucci M, Kawamura T, Payne TR, Sycara K., 2002. *Semantic matching of Web services capabilities.* In: Proceeding of the International Semantic Web Conference (ISWC'02), p36-47.
4. Kawamura T., Blasio JD., Hasegawa T., Paolucci M., Sycara K., 2004. *Public Deployment of Semantic Service Matchmaker with UDDI Business Registry.* In: Proceeding of the International Semantic Web Conference (ISWC'04), p752-766.
5. Benatallah B., Hacid M., Alain L. Christophe R., Farouk T., 2005. *On automating Web services discovery.* VLDB Journal, 14(1), p84-96.
6. Syeda-Mahmood T., Shah G., Akkiraju R., Ivan A.-A, Goodwin R. 2005. *Searching Service Repositories by Combining Semantic and Ontological Matching.* In: Proceeding of the IEEE International Conference on Web Services (ICWS'05), p13-20.
7. Deng S.G., Wu Z.H., 2004. *Management of Serviceflow in a Flexible Way,* In: Proceeding of the 5th International Conference on Web Information Systems Engineering (WISE'04), p428-438
8. Wu Z.H., Chen H.J., 2004. *DartGrid: Semantic-Based Database Grid.* In: proceeding of the International Conference on Computational Science (ICCS'04), p59-66.
9. Wu Z.H., Tang S.M, Deng S.G, 2005. *DartGrid II: A Semantic Grid Platform for ITS.* IEEE Intelligent Systems 20(3), p12-15.
10. Zhou X.Z., Wu Z.H. et al, 2004. *Ontology Development for Unified Traditional Chinese Medical Language System,* Journal of Artificial Intelligence in Medicine, 32(1), p183-194.
11. Voorhees E., 1998. *Using WordNet for Text Retrieval. WordNet: An Electronic Lexical Database,* The MIT Press.
12. Zhou C., Chia L.T., Lee B.S., 2004. *QoS-Aware and Federated Enhancement for UDDI.* International Journal of Web Services Research 1(2), p58-85.

13. Verma K., Sivashanmugam K., Sheth A., Patil A., Oundhakar S., Miller J., 2004. METEOR-S WSDI: A Scalable Infrastructure of Registries for Semantic Publication and Discovery of Web Services. Journal of Information Technology and Management 6(1), p17-39.
14. Sivashanmugam K., Verma K., Sheth A., Miller J., 2003. Adding Semantics to Web Services Standards. In: Proceeding of the 1st International Conference on Web Services (ICWS'03), p23-26.
15. Hausmann, J.H., Heckel, R. and Lohmann, M., 2005. Model-Based Development of Web Services Descriptions Enabling a Precise Matching Concept. International Journal of Web Services Research 2(2), p67-84.
16. Kuang L. Wu J. Deng S.G. et al. Exploring Semantic Technologies in Service Matchmaking. In: Proceeding of the Third European Conference on Web Services (ECOWS'05), p226-234.

Crawling Web Pages with Support for Client-Side Dynamism*

Manuel Álvarez[1], Alberto Pan[1,**], Juan Raposo[1], and Justo Hidalgo[2]

[1] Department of Information and Communications Technologies,
University of A Coruña, 15071 A Coruña, Spain
{mad, apan, jrs}@udc.es
[2] Denodo Technologies Inc, 28039 Madrid, Spain
jhidalgo@denodo.com

Abstract. There is a great amount of information on the web that can not be accessed by conventional crawler engines. This portion of the web is usually known as the Hidden Web. To be able to deal with this problem, it is necessary to solve two tasks: crawling the client-side and crawling the server-side hidden web. In this paper we present an architecture and a set of related techniques for accessing the information placed in web pages with support for client-side dynamism, dealing with aspects such as JavaScript technology, non-standard session maintenance mechanisms, client redirections, pop-up menus, etc. Our approach leverages current browser APIs and implements novel crawling models and algorithms.

1 Introduction

The "Hidden Web" or "Deep Web" [1] is usually defined as the part of WWW documents that is dynamically generated. The problem of crawling the "hidden web" can be divided in two tasks: crawling the client-side and crawling the server-side hidden web. Client-side hidden web techniques are concerned about accessing content dynamically generated in the client web browser, while server-side techniques are focused in accessing to the valuable content hidden behind web search forms [3] [6]. This paper proposes novel techniques and algorithms for dealing with the first of these problems.

1.1 The Case for Client-Side Hidden Web

Today's complex web pages use scripting languages intensively (mainly JavaScript), session maintenance mechanisms, complex redirections, etc.

Developers use these client technologies to add interactivity to web pages as well as for improving site navigation. This is done through interface elements such as

* This research was partially supported by the Spanish Ministry of Education and Science under project TSI2005-07730.

** Alberto Pan's work was partially supported by the "Ramón y Cajal" programme of the Spanish Ministry of Education and Science.

J.X. Yu, M. Kitsuregawa, and H.V. Leong (Eds.): WAIM 2006, LNCS 4016, pp. 252–262, 2006.
© Springer-Verlag Berlin Heidelberg 2006

pop-up menus or by disposing content in layers that are either shown or hidden depending on the user actions.

In addition, many sources use scripting languages, such as JavaScript [10], for a variety of internal purposes, including dynamically building HTTP requests for submitting forms, managing HTML layers and/or performing complex redirections. This situation is aggravated because most of the tools used for visually building web sites generate pages which use scripting code for content generation and/or for improving navigation.

1.2 The Problem with Conventional Crawlers

There exist some problems that make it difficult for traditional web crawling engines to obtain data from client-side hidden web pages. The most important problems are described in the following sub-sections.

1.2.1 Client-Side Scripting Languages

Many HTML pages make intensive use of JavaScript and other client-side scripting languages (such as Jscript or VBScript) for a variety of purposes such as:

- Generating content at runtime (e.g. `document.write` methods in JavaScript).
- Dynamically generating navigations. Scripting code may be for instance in the `href` attribute of an anchor, or can be executed when some event of the page is fired (e.g. *'onclick'* or *'onmouseover'* for unfolding a pop-up menu when the user clicks or moves the mouse over a menu option). It is also possible for the scripting code to rewrite a URL, to open a new window or to generate several navigations (more than URL to continue the crawling process).
- Automatically filling out a form in a page and then submitting it.

Successfully dealing with scripting languages requires that HTTP clients implement all the mechanisms that make it possible to a browser to render a page and to generate new navigations. It also involves following anchors and executing all the actions associated to the events they fire. Using a specific interpreter (e.g. Mozilla Rhino for JavaScript [7]) does not solve these problems, since real world scripts assume a set of browser-provided objects to be available in their execution environment. Besides, in some situations such as multi-frame pages, it is not always easy to locate and extract the scripting code to be interpreted. That is why most crawlers built to date, including the ones used in the most popular web search engines, do not provide support for this kind of pages.

To provide a convenient execution environment for executing scripts is not the only problem associated with client-side dynamism. When conventional crawlers reach a new page, they scan it for new anchors to traverse and add them to a master list of URLs to access. Scripting code complicates this situation because they may be used to dynamically generate or remove anchors in response to some events. For instance, many web pages use anchors to represent menus of options. When an anchor representing an option is clicked, some scripting code dynamically generates a list of new anchors representing sub-options. If the anchor is clicked again, then the script code may "fold" the menu again, removing the anchors corresponding with the sub-options. A crawler dealing with the client-side deep web should be able to detect these situations and to obtain all the "hidden" URLs, adding them to the master URL list.

1.2.2 Session Maintenance Mechanisms

Many websites use session maintenance mechanisms based on client resources like cookies or scripting code to add session parameters to the URLs before sending them to the server. A number of challenges to deal with:

- While most crawlers are able of dealing with cookies, we have already stated that is not the case with scripting languages.
- Another problem arises for distributed crawling. Conventional architectures for crawling are based on a shared "master list" of URLs from which crawling processes (maybe running in different machines) pick URLs and access them independently in a parallel manner. Nevertheless, with session-based sites, we need to insure that each crawling process has all the session information it requires (such as cookies or the context for executing the scripting code). Otherwise, any attempt to access the page will fail. Conventional crawlers do not deal with these situations.
- Accessing the documents at a later time. Most web search engines work by indexing the pages retrieved by a web crawler. The crawled pages are usually not stored locally but they are indexed with their URLs. When at a later moment a user obtains the page as result of a query against the index, he can access the page through its URL. Nevertheless, in a context where session maintenance issues exist, the URLs may not work when used at a later time. For instance, the URL may include a session number that expires a few minutes after being created.

1.2.3 Redirections

Many websites use complex redirections that are not managed by conventional crawlers. For instance, some pages include JavaScript redirections executed after an on load page event (the client redirects after the page has been completely loaded);

```
<BODY onload="executeJavaScriptRedirectionMethod()">
```

In these cases, the HTTP client would have to analyze and interpret the page content to detect and correctly manage these types of redirections.

1.2.4 Applets and Flash Code

Other types of client technology are applets or flash code. They are executed on the client side, so it has to implement a container component to process them. Although accessing the content shown by programs written in these languages is difficult due to their "compiled" nature, a web crawler should at least be able to deal with the common situation where these components are used as an "introduction" that finally redirects the user to a conventional page where the crawler can proceed.

1.2.5 Other Issues

Web page elements such as frames, dynamic HTML or HTTPS, accentuate the aforementioned problems. In general terms, we can say that it is very difficult to consider all the factors, which make a Website visible and navigable through a web browser.

1.3 Our Approach

Due to all the reasons mentioned above, many designers of web sites avoid these practices in order to make sure their sites are on good terms with the crawlers. Nevertheless, this forces them to either increment the complexity of their systems by moving functionality to the server, or reducing interactivity with the user. Neither of these situations is desirable: web site designers should think in terms of "improving interactivity and friendliness of sites", not about "how the crawlers work".

This paper presents an architecture and a set of related techniques to solve the problems involved in crawling web pages with support for client-side dynamism. Our system has already been successfully used in several real applications in the fields of corporate search and technology watch.

The main features of our approach are the following:

- Our crawling processes are not based on http clients. Instead, they are based on automated "mini web browsers", built using standard browser APIs (our current implementation is based on the MSIE – Microsoft Internet Explorer [4] - WebBrowser Control). These "mini-browsers" understand NSEQL (see section 2), a language for expressing navigation sequences as "macros" of actions on the interface of a web browser. This enables our system to deal with executing scripting code, managing redirections, etc.
- To deal with pop-up menus and other dynamic elements that can generate new anchors in the actual page, it is necessary to implement special algorithms to ma-nage the process of generating new "routes to crawl" from a web page (see section 3.4).
- To solve the problem of session maintenance, our system uses the concept of *route* to a document, which can be seen as a generalization of URL. A route specifies a URL, a session object containing the needed session context for the URL, and a NSEQL program for accessing the document when the session used for crawling the document has expired.
- The system also includes some functionality to access pages hidden behind forms. More precisely, the system is able to deal with authentication forms and with *value-limited forms.* We term the ones exclusively composed of fields whose possible values are restricted to a certain finite list as *value-limited* forms (e.g. forms composed exclusively of fields 'select', 'checkbox', 'radio button',…).

2 Introduction to NSEQL

NSEQL [5] is a language to declaratively define sequences of events on the interface provided by a web browser. NSEQL allows to easily express "macros" representing a sequence of user events over a browser.

NSEQL works "at browser layer" instead of "at HTTP layer". This lets us forget about problems such as successfully executing JavaScript or dealing with client redirections and session identifiers.

Figure 1 shows an example of an NSEQL program, which is able to execute the login process at YahooMail [11] and navigate to the list of messages from the Inbox folder.

The `Navigate` command tells the browser to navigate to the given URL. Its effects are equivalent to that of a human user typing the URL on his/her browser address bar and pressing the ENTER key.

The `FindFormByName(name, position)` command looks for the position-th HTML form in the page with the given name. Then, the `SetInputValue(fieldName, position, value)` commands are used to assign values to the form fields.

The `ClickOnElement(name, type, position)` command, clicks on the position-th element of the given type and name from the current selected form. In this case, it is used to submit the form and load the result page. The `ClickOnAnchorByText (text, position, exactToken)` command looks for the position-th anchor, which encloses the given text and generates a browser click event on it. This will cause the browser to navigate to the page pointed by the anchor.

```
Navigate(http://mail.yahoo.com);
FindFormByName(login_form,0);
SetInputValue(login,0,loginValue);
SetInputValue(passwd,0,passwordValue);
ClickOnElement(_NULL_,INPUT,24);
ClickOnAnchorByText(Go to Inbox,1,true);
```

Fig. 1. NSEQL Program

Although not included here, NSEQL also includes commands to deal with frames, pop-up windows, MS Windows events, etc.

3 The Crawling Engine

As well as in conventional crawling engines, the basic idea consists of maintaining a shared list of routes (pointers to documents), which will be accessed by a certain number of concurrent crawling processes, distributed into several machines. The list is initialized with a list of routes. Then, each crawling process picks a route from the list, downloads its associated document and analyzes it in order to obtain new routes from its anchors, which are then added to the master list. The process ends when there are no routes left or when a specified depth level is reached. The value proposition in our approach is the way we obtain new routes.

The structure of this section is as follows. In section 3.1, we introduce the concept of *route* in our system, and how it enables us to deal with sessions. Section 3.2 provides some detail about the mini-browsers used as the basic crawling processes in the system, as well as the advantages they provide us with. Section 3.3 describes the architecture and basic functioning of the system. Finally, section 3.4 shows the algorithm used for generating new routes from anchors and forms controlled by scripting code (e.g. JavaScript).

3.1 Dealing with Sessions: Routes

In conventional crawlers, routes are just URLs [12]. Thus, they have the problems with session mechanisms that we have already mentioned in section 1.2.2. We propose a new concept for "route", which will be composed by three elements:

- A URL pointing to a document. In the routes from the initial list, this element may also be an NSEQL program. This is useful to start the crawling in a document, which is not directly accessible through a URL (for instance, this is usually the case with websites requiring authentication).
- A session object containing all the required information (cookies, etc.) to restore the execution environment in which the crawling process was running in the moment of adding the route to the master list.
- An NSEQL program representing the navigational sequence followed by the system to reach the document.

The second and third elements are automatically computed by the system for each route. The second element allows a crawling process to access a URL added by other crawling process (even if the original crawling process was running in another machine). The third element is used to access the document pointed by the route when the session originally used to crawl the document has expired. This is useful when session expiration times are short and, as we will see later, to allow for later access to crawled documents.

3.2 Mini-browsers as Crawling Processes

Conventional engines implement crawling processes by using http clients. Instead, the crawling processes in our system are based on automated "mini web browsers", built by using standard browser APIs (our current implementation is based on the MSIE WebBrowser Control), and which are able to execute NSEQL programs.

This allows our system to:

- Access the content dynamically generated through scripting languages (e.g. JavaScript document.write methods).
- Evaluate the scripting code associated with anchors and forms, so we can obtain the real URLs these elements are pointing to.
- Deal with client redirections: after executing next navigations, the mini-browser waits until all the navigation events of the actual page have finished.
- Provide an execution environment for technologies such as Java applets and Flash code. Although the mini-browsers cannot access the content shown by these "compiled" components, they can deal with the common situation where these components are used as a graphical introduction, which finally redirects the browser to a conventional web page.

3.3 System Architecture / Basic Functioning

The architecture of the system is shown in Figure 2.

When the crawler engine starts, it reads its configuration parameters from the Configuration Manager Component. The metainformation required to configure the system includes a list of URLs and/or NSEQL navigation sequences to access the initial sites, the desired depth for each initial route, download handlers for different kinds of documents, content filters, a list of regular expressions representing DNS domains to be included and excluded from the crawling, and other metainformation not dealt with here.

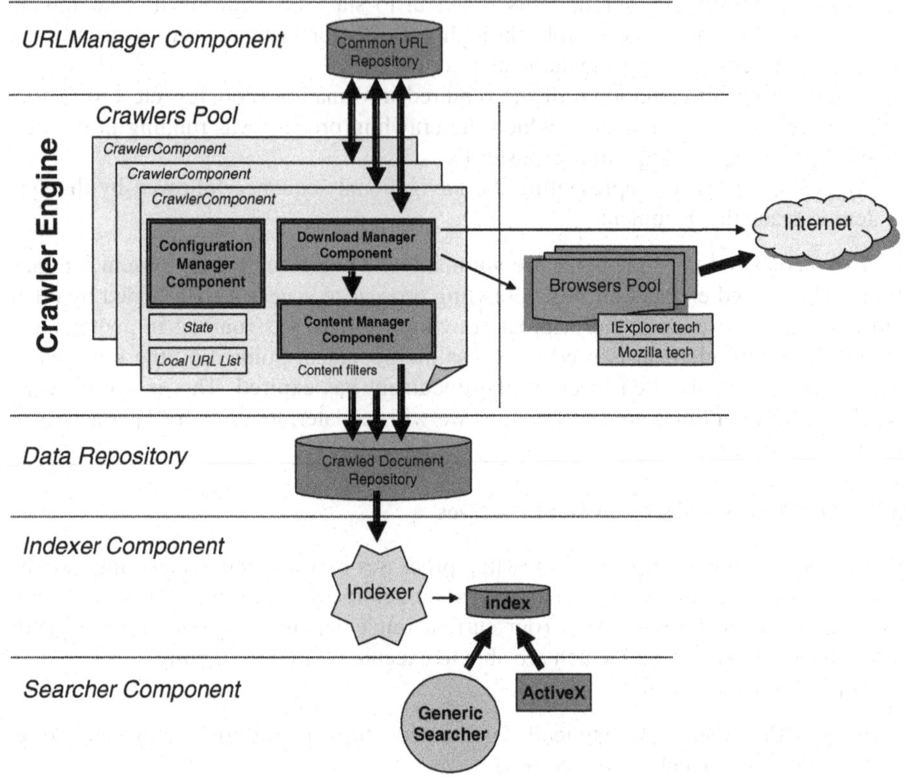

Fig. 2. Crawler Architecture

The following step consists of starting the URL Manager Component with the list of initial sites for the crawling, as well as starting the pool of crawling processes.

The URL Manager is responsible for maintaining the master list of *routes* to be accessed; all the crawlers share this list.

Once the crawling processes have been started, each one picks a route from the URL Manager. It is important to note that each crawling process can be executed either locally or remotely to the server, thus allowing for distributed crawling. As we have already remarked, each crawling process is a mini web-browser able to execute NSEQL sequences.

Then the crawling process loads the session object associated to the route and downloads the associated document (it uses the Download Manager Component to choose the right handler for the document, such as PDF, MS Word, etc). If the session has expired, the crawling process will use the NSEQL program for accessing the document again.

The content from each downloaded document is then analyzed by using the Content Manager Component. This component specifies a chain of filters to decide if the document can be considered relevant and, therefore, if it should be stored and/or indexed. For instance, the system includes filters which allow checking if the document verifies a keyword-based boolean query with a minimum relevance in order to decide whether to store/index it or not. Another chain of filters is used for post-processing the document. For instance, the system includes filters to extract relevant content from HTML pages or to generate a short document summary.

Finally, the system tries to obtain new routes from analyzed documents and adds them to the master list. In a context where scripting languages can dynamically generate and remove anchors and forms, this involves some complexities. See section 3.4 for detail.

The system also includes a chain of filters to decide whether the new routes must be added to the master list or not. In the most usual configuration, while the maximum desired depth is not reached, all the anchors of the documents will generate new routes. Value-limited forms (those having only fields with a finite list of possible values, as commented on section 1.3) will generate a new route for each possible combination of the values of its fields.

The architecture also includes components for indexing and searching the crawled contents, using state of the art algorithms. The crawler generates an XML file for each crawled document, including metainformation such as its URL and the NSEQL sequence needed to access it.

The NSEQL sequence will be used by another component of the system architecture: the ActiveX for automatic navigation Component. This component receives as a parameter a NSEQL program, downloads itself into the user browser and makes it execute the given navigation sequence. In our system this is used to solve the problem of *access to documents at a later time* (see section 1.2.2). When the user executes a search against the index and the list of answers contains some results, which cannot be directly accessed by using its URL due to session issues, the anchors associated to those results in the list will invoke the ActiveX component passing as parameter the NSEQL sequence associated to the page. Then, if the users click on the anchor, the ActiveX will make their browser automatically navigate to the desired page.

3.4 Algorithm for Generating New Routes

This section describes the algorithm used in our system to generate new routes to be crawled given a HTML page. This algorithm deals with the difficulties associated with anchors and forms controlled by scripting languages.

In general for the new routes to be crawled from a given HTML document, it is necessary to analyze the page looking for anchors and *value-limited* forms. A new route will be added for each anchor and for each combination of all possible values of the fields from each *value-limited* form. The anchors and forms which are not controlled by scripting code can be dealt with as in conventional crawlers: for anchors, a new route is built from the value of its *href* attribute, while for static forms, the new routes for each combination of values can also be routinely built by analyzing the *action* attribute of the *form* tag and the tags representing the form fields and their possible values.

Nevertheless, if the HTML page contains client-side scripting technology, the situation is more complicated. The main idea of the algorithm consists of generating click events over the anchors controlled by scripting languages in order to obtain valid URLs (NOTE: we will focus our discussion on the case of anchors. The treatment of value-limited forms is analogous), but there are several additional difficulties:

- Some anchors may appear or disappear from the page depending on the scripting code executed (e.g. pop-up menus).
- The script code associated to anchors must be evaluated in order to obtain valid URLs.
- One anchor can generate several navigations.
- In pages with several frames, it is possible for an anchor to generate new URLs in some frames and navigations in others.

Now we proceed to describe the algorithm. Remember that our crawling process is a "mini-browser" able to execute NSEQL programs. The browser can be in two states: in the *navigational* state the browser functions normally, and when it executes a click event on an anchor or submits a form, it performs the navigation and downloads the resulting page; in turn, in the *simulation* state the browser only captures the navigation events generated by the click or submit events, but it does not download the resource.

1. Let P be an HTML page that has been downloaded by the browser (navigational state).
2. The browser executes the scripting sections, which are not associated to conditional events.
3. Let A_p be all the anchors of the page with the scripting code already interpreted.
4. For each a_i Є A_p, remove ai, and:
   - If the *href* attribute from a_i does not contain any associated scripting code and it has not got an *onclick* attribute (or, if the system is configured to do so, other attributes used to assign scripting code to specific events such as *onmouseover*), the anchor a_i is added to the master list of URLs.
   - Otherwise, the browser changes to simulation state, and generates a *click* event on the anchor -and, if configured to do so, other relevant events such as *mouse-over*-:
     - There exist some anchors that, when clicked, can generate undesirable actions (e.g. a call to the "javascript:close" method closes the browser). The approach followed to avoid this is to capture these undesirable events and to ignore them.
     - The crawler captures all the new navigation events that happen as a consequence of the click. Each navigation event produces a URL. Let A_n be the set of all the new URLs.
     - $A_p = A_n$ U A_p.
     - Once the execution of the events associated to a click over an anchor has fi-nished, the crawler analyzes again the same page looking for new anchors that could have been generated by the click event (for instance, new

options corresponding to pop-up menus), A_{np}. New anchors are also added to A_p, $A_p = A_{np} \cup A_p$.
5. The browser changes to navigational state, and the crawler is ready to process a new URL.

If the processed page has several frames, then the system will process each frame in the same way.

Note that the system processes the anchors in a page following a bottom-up approach, so new anchors are added on the list before the existing ones. This way, new anchors will be processed before some other click can remove them from the page. Also notice that the added anchors will have to match the filters for adding URLs mentioned in section 3.3.

4 Related Work and Conclusions

A well-known approach for discovering and indexing relevant information is to "crawl" a given information space (e.g. the WWW, the repositories of a corporate Intranet, etc.) looking for information verifying certain requirements. Nevertheless, today's web "crawlers" or "spiders" [2] do not deal with the hidden web.

During the last few years, there have been some pioneer research efforts dealing with the complexities of accessing the hidden web [3] [6] using a variety of approaches. Nevertheless, these systems are only concerned with server-side hidden web (that is, learning how to interpret and query HTML forms).

Some crawling systems [9] have included JavaScript interpreters [7] [8] in the HTTP clients they use in order to provide some limited support for dealing with JavaScript. Nevertheless, our system offer several advantages over them:

- It is able to correctly execute any scripting code in the same manner it would be executed by a conventional web browser.
- It is able to deal with session maintenance mechanisms for both crawling and later access to documents (the latter is made through an ActiveX component able to execute NSEQL programs).
- It is able to deal with anchors and forms generated dynamically in response to events produced by the user (e.g. pop-up menus).
- It is able to deal with redirections (including those generated by Java applets and Flash programs).

Finally, we want to remark that the system presented in this paper has already been successfully used in several real-world applications in fields such as corporate search and technology watch.

We have found the need for crawling the client-side hidden web to be very frequent in these application domains. The reason is that, although most popular "mainstream" websites avoid using JavaScript and other similar techniques in order to be correctly indexed by large-scale engines such as Google, many medium-scale websites containing information of great value continue to use them intensively.

This is specially the case for websites requiring subscription or user authentication: since these sites do not have any incentive for easing the work of the large scale search engines, many of them make intensive use of client dynamism. Nevertheless, this kind of sites usually is the most valuable for many focused search applications, like technology watch or vertical search engines. Thus, our experience says the efforts for accessing the client-side deep web are valuable and should be continued.

References

1. Bergman, M. The Deep Web. Surfacing Hidden Value. http://www.brightplanet.com/technology/deepweb.asp
2. Brin, S., Page, L. The Anatomy of a Large-Scale Hypertextual Search Engine. In Proceedings of the 7th International World Wide Web Conference (1998)
3. Ipeirotis, P., Gravano, L. Distributed Search over the Hidden Web: Hierarchical Database Sampling and Selection. In Proceedings of the 28th International Conference on Very Large Databases (VLDB 2002).
4. Microsoft Internet Explorer WebBrowser Control, http://www.microsoft.com/windows/ie
5. Pan, A., Raposo, J., Álvarez, M., Hidalgo, J., Viña, A. Semi-Automatic Wrapper Generation for Commercial Web Sources. In Proceedings of IFIP WG8.1 Working Conference on Engineering Information Systems in the Internet Context (EISIC 2002).
6. Raghavan S., García-Molina, H. Crawling the Hidden Web. In Proceedings of the 27th International Conference on Very Large Databases (2001)
7. Mozilla Rhino - JavaScript Engine (Java). http://www.mozilla.org/rhino/
8. Mozilla SpiderMonkey – JavaScript engine (C) http://www.mozilla.org/js/spidermonkey/
9. WebCopier – Feel the Internet in your Hands. http://www.maximumsoft.com/
10. Scripts in HTML Documents. http://www.w3.org/TR/html4/interact/scripts.html
11. Yahoo Mail. http://mail.yahoo.com
12. Naming and Addressing: URIs, URLs, ... http://www.w3.org/Addressing/

RecipeCrawler: Collecting Recipe Data from WWW Incrementally

Yu Li[1], Xiaofeng Meng[1], Liping Wang[2], and Qing Li[2]

[1] School of Information, Renmin Univ. of China, China
{liyu17, xfmeng}@ruc.edu.cn
[2] Computer Science Dept., City Univ. of Hong Kong, HKSAR, China
50095373@student, itqli@.cityu.edu.hk

Abstract. WWW has posed itself as the largest data repository ever available in the history of humankind. Utilizing the Internet as a data source seems to be natural and many efforts have been made. In this paper we focus on establishing a robust system to collect structured recipe data from the Web incrementally, which, as we believe, is a critical step towards practical, continuous, reliable web data extraction systems and therefore utilizing WWW as data sources for various database applications. The reasons for advocating such an incremental approach are two-fold: (1) it is impractical to crawl all the recipe pages from relevant web sites as the Web is highly dynamic; (2) it is almost impossible to induce a general wrapper for future extraction from the initial batch of recipe web pages. In this paper, we describe such a system called *RecipeCrawler* which targets at incrementally collecting recipe data from WWW. General issues in establishing an incremental data extraction system are considered and techniques are applied to recipe data collection from the Web. Our *RecipeCrawler* is actually used as the backend of a fully-fledged multimedia recipe database system being developed jointly by City University of Hong Kong and Renmin University of China.

1 Introduction

WWW has posed itself as the largest data repository ever available in the history of humankind, which also is highly dynamic as there are web pages created and/or deleted on a daily basis. Utilizing WWW as a data source seems to be natural and many efforts have been made according to the literatures. However, devising generic methods for extracting Web data is a complex (if not impossible) task, because the Web is very heterogeneous as well as there are no rigid guidelines on how to build HTML pages and how to declare the implicit structure of the Web pages. Various systems, either prototypes or commercial products, try to solve the problem in two specific domains: (1) data intensive pages (such as the search results on Amazon) usually generated by online database search engines, and (2) data record pages (such as a single product page on Amazon) usually for product descriptions. The main difference between the two domains is that in the former case, there is more than one data record in each page whereas in the latter case, there is only one record in each page. Furthermore, data records of the first case share a common keyword since the web page is generated by a search engine, but for the second case the web pages usually share the same page template as they are formatted by a web page generator.

J.X. Yu, M. Kitsuregawa, and H.V. Leong (Eds.): WAIM 2006, LNCS 4016, pp. 263–274, 2006.
© Springer-Verlag Berlin Heidelberg 2006

In this paper we focus on the latter case through building a robust system to collect structural data from WWW continuously. It is a part of a collaborative project between Renmin University of China and City University of Hong Kong, the goal of which is to build a fully-fledged multimedia recipe database by collecting as many recipe web pages as possible. We extract the data records from the collected recipe pages which will be later on used in a multimedia database application–*RecipeView* (Fig.2). Generally speaking, recipe web pages are very similar to online product web pages in that (a) one web page contains only one record, (b) they follow an underlying template, and (c) there are many optional attributes. Some examples of recipe pages are shown in Fig.1. Thus by applying existing techniques, which are roughly classified into two categories– wrapper induction and automatic extraction, our goal may be achieved. However, this turns out to be a non-trivial task because of the following reasons:

- It is impractical to crawl all the recipe pages from a web site. In Fig.1(c), there is an example of a recipe category list. The webmaster will add/update some new recipe links (shown in red circle) while updating other links such as advertisements and activities. Naive crawling of all updated links will not only lead to an inefficient strategy but also impact the latter steps by introducing some noisy web pages. Thus we have to consider how to identify real recipe links while crawling pages incrementally.
- It is almost impossible to induce a general wrapper with initial batch of recipe web pages. Because of the continuous updating of recipe web sites, the changes of the underlying schema may cause the existing wrapper broken. For example, Fig.1(a) is a typical recipe web page when the web site was created. It only contains a name, a picture, a material list, a seasoning list and some cooking steps. As time elapses, the webmaster provides us with some new recipes, one of which is shown in Fig.1(b). Because some complex new optional attributes are added (e.g. two styles of sauce in Fig.1(b)) and the existing attributes are revised (e.g. seasoning turns to be repeatable), such of these variations not only cover simple representation changes, but also involve serious schema evolutions, which definitely makes conventional extraction techniques inapplicable.

Due to these observations, our approach is to build a system (called *RecipeCrawler*) that can automatically extract relevant content data, and be able to do so incrementally so that the new web pages containing new recipe records may be added dynamically. To this end it must support the following incremental features in extraction of newly crawled web pages from the recipe websites.

1. **Incrementally crawling specific web pages.** In our system, some web data sources, such as recipe web site's categories, recipe blog pages, or even recipe online forums, are monitored. Whenever the links are updated, crawler should not only grab the web page pointed by the link, but also justify whether it is the one we need. It is possible as we have some extracted recipe data records, which can give us the domain knowledge of recipes.
2. **Incrementally extracting web pages for data records.** Either wrapper based or automated method faces the problem of web site's schema evolutions. The extraction program should not only be able to adapt itself to meet the schema revision,

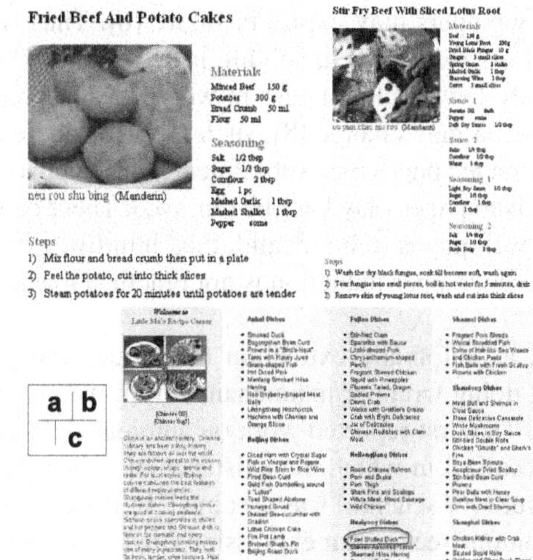

Fig. 1. Examples of Recipe and Category List Web Pages

but also be able to identify new attributes. This is important to help applications which rely on the extraction system to be of more concrete, useful, and valuable services. And it also enables the extraction system to be a reasonable and practical web data extraction system.

By putting all things together, we aim to build our system as a practical robust system which supports incremental automated data extraction. It is different from existing systems in that novel modifications are made upon the tradition architecture. In a nutshell, our contributions in this paper include: 1) a framework for building incremental web data extraction system, which is implemented in our prototype system for collecting recipe data from WWW incrementally; 2) solutions for adopting and adapting existing data extraction techniques under incremental scenarios.

In this paper we describe our *RecipeCrawler* system in detail. The rest of this paper is organized as follows. In section 2, we briefly review some existing techniques on web data extraction. Section 3 gives out an overview of *RecipeCrawler*. Section 4 and 5 discuss our main considerations in designing and implementing each component. Finally we give out a conclusion and future works in section 6.

2 Related Work

One of the reasons why the Web has achieved its current huge volume of data is that a great and increasing number of data-rich web sites automatically generate web pages according to the data records stored in their databases. Taking advantage of this fact, several approaches have been proposed and systems have been built to extract these data in literature. Generally these systems fall into two categories: wrapper induction versus automatic extraction.

With wrapper induction techniques, some positive web pages are selected as positive examples and then wrappers are trained. Though using wrappers to do continuous extraction is possible, wrappers may expire in future [6]. Thus wrapper maintenance problems arose and efforts were paid in solving it. However, to our knowledge, it assumes that there are only few small changes in web pages' representation whereas in fact the underlying schema may change [8], such as:(1) attributes that have never appeared in previously extracted pages may subsequently be added; (2) attributes appeared in previously extracted web pages may later be removed. These can cause the templates induced from existing web pages to be invalid, thus intuitive extraction strategies can not be applied. Therefore wrapper induction is not practical towards long-time, continuous data extraction.

On the other hand, as automatic extraction techniques can automatically extract structural data without doing wrapper maintenance from web pages, it becomes more popular recently years. The first reported work on automated data extraction was done by Grumbach and Mecca [5], in which the existence of collections of data-rich pages bearing a similar structure (or schema) was assumed. In RoadRunner [3], an algorithm was proposed to infer union-free regular expressions that represent page templates. Unfortunately, this algorithm has an exponential time complexity hence it is impractical for real-life data extraction systems. Then Arvind and Hector [1] proposed an improved version with a polynomial time complexity by employing several heuristics. Both of these works view web pages in HTML as a sequence of tokens (single words and tags), so when it comes to infer a template from complex web pages with many nesting structures, their solutions are still inapplicable. Other researchers have tried to solve the automated data extraction problem by viewing web pages as a long string, through employing similar generalization mechanisms (e.g., [2] and [10]). Be aware of the tree structure of web pages, [9] and [11] presented techniques based on tree edit distance for this problem. Both of them utilize a restricted tree edit distance computation process to find mapping between two web pages and then do future data extraction. In [9], wildcards are attached to tree nodes and heuristics are employed when there is a need to generalize them. In [11], a more advanced technique named partial tree alignment was proposed, which can align corresponding data fields in data records without doing wildcards generalizations. In our system, we use a similar technique and make it applicable under incremental data extraction.

While some major works have been done on clustering or classifying web pages, few of them are on automated data extraction as far as we can see from the literature. In [4], several web page features were proposed for wrapper-oriented classification. In the news extraction system [9], a hierarchical clustering technique was proposed to cluster web pages according to their HTML tree structures. A basic distance measure-edit distance is calculated by comparing two HTML DOM trees, which can tell us how similar the two web pages are. When the web page contains more than one data record, there is almost no need to do the clustering. But new problems do arise. For example, how to identify data regions containing data records in such kind of web pages is a problem. In particular, several strategies have been proposed in [7] and [12].

Combining these existing automated data extraction techniques may lead us to a generic system that is able to crawl, cluster and extract structured data from a whole web site once for all. For our recipe collection scenarios, we need to continuously collect recipe data from the web, hence modifications to such techniques or other novel techniques are needed. In the rest of this paper we show our approach to build an incremental data extraction system by adopting and adapting the existing web data extraction techniques.

3 *RecipeCrawler* - A Recipe Data Collection System

Starting from this section, we will discuss the general considerations on how to build a system to support incremental features in conventional architecture by introducing our recipe data collection system. As Fig.2 illustrates, general architecture of current existing extraction systems were applied. Besides adopting and adapting the classic components such as web crawler, web data extractor and annotator, a new component called "*Monitor*" is advocated to keep a close watch on recipe sources. Instead of digging into the details on how it is designed and implemented as well as how it supports incremental features, in this section we would like to give an overview on how recipe data are collected.

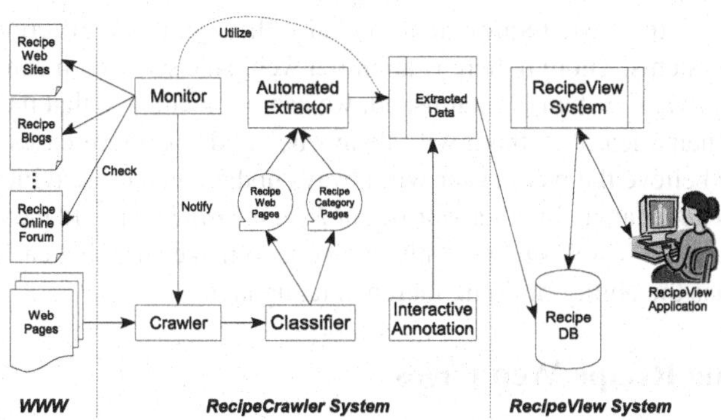

Fig. 2. Recipe Data Extraction System - An Overview

The mission of *RecipeCrawler* is to provide *RecipeView* with the recipe data records which are embedded in web pages. Here *RecipeView* is a user-centered multimedia view application built on top of the recipe database and means to provide user continuous, flexible user experience. It requires the extraction system (viz. *RecipeCrawler*) to be incremental because it needs recipe data updated every day on WWW.

Fig.2 shows an overall picture on how *RecipeCrawler* works. In particular, we incrementally grab recipe web pages by monitoring some data sources, which are as shown in the left part of Fig.2, including recipe web sites, recipe blogs and recipe online forums et. al. Considering that their indices are usually accessible (such as category lists in recipe web sites, taxonomy pages in recipe blogs and archive lists in recipe online forums), we establish a module called "*Monitor*" to find out the updated links from these sources. In order to identify whether the specific updated link is just the one we need, extracted data has been used as domain knowledge to do data clarifications. And survivors, which are definitely the ones we need, are sent to "*Crawler*" which does basic crawling as well as validation and repairing on HTML pages.

Next the crawled web pages are delivered to the "*Classifier*" which puts pages into different categories. In this procedure, an algorithm proposed in [9] has been adopted and adapted to classify web pages according to their underlying structures (or underlying template). Two categories–"*Recipe Web Pages*" and "*Recipe Category Pages*" are derived through this step, where the former one usually contains the detailed information of each recipes and the latter one usually maintains taxonomy of recipes.

In the extraction procedure, web pages in each category are processed by an "*Automated Extractor*" and thus category information and recipe data are retrieved. Annotation was done by a module named "*Interactive Annotation*" which is operated by human, who tells the system what attribute is about what. As our system means to work in incremental way, being able to handle schema changes is critical so we proposed a method by adopting algorithms in [11]. We will further discuss it in section 5 as well as the mechanism of annotation process. So finally we get the desired data with corresponding annotations and thus can import them into DBMS for future applications, which is *RecipeView* in our case.

Before we go to the sections that discuss the details of each component, we want to emphasize the incremental nature of *RecipeCrawler* again. Incremental features in *RecipeCrawler* are the basic requirements and also the significant differences comparing with other systems. Though there is an initial web page set, which can be extracted before the *RecipeView* system is established, we can not guarantee that the wrapper induced or the schema learnt in them will always be valid for future cases, because we can not naively believe the webmaster will always update recipes activities, or assume the schema will not change. In other words, our *RecipeCrawler* should face the very dynamic perspective of WWW and the only choice is to make sure that each component of our system has the ability of doing incremental update.

4 Retrieving Recipe Web Pages

Monitoring, crawling and classifying procedures in *RecipeCrawler* are implemented to retrieve recipe web pages. In this section we mainly focus on the mechanism of monitoring and classifying procedures whereas crawling procedure is omitted because its implementation is fairly simple and straightforward.

4.1 Monitoring Recipe Data Sources

Recipe data sources on WWW usually have an index facility, such as category lists in recipe web sites, taxonomy pages in recipe blogs and archive lists in recipe online forums and so on. Monitoring them for updated recipe links generally should (1) find out whatever new/updated links, and (2) identify whether they are recipe-related links or not. The former step is easy by simply comparing current web page with history version whereas the latter one is complicated. The link discovery procedure of conventional crawler usually does simple identifications based on several rules, such as URL domains, file types and so on. Few works are done on semantic link discovery because: (1) crawlers are usually of general use; (2) insufficient domain knowledge can be utilized to do it. However, in *RecipeCrawler*, we focus on recipe web pages, concerning not to introduce noisy web pages to subsequent procedures; we can even have domain knowledge by analyzing the extracted data of the initial set, which can always be selected out when first time we crawl the web site. With these characteristics in mind, we proceed to present a semantic link discovery method.

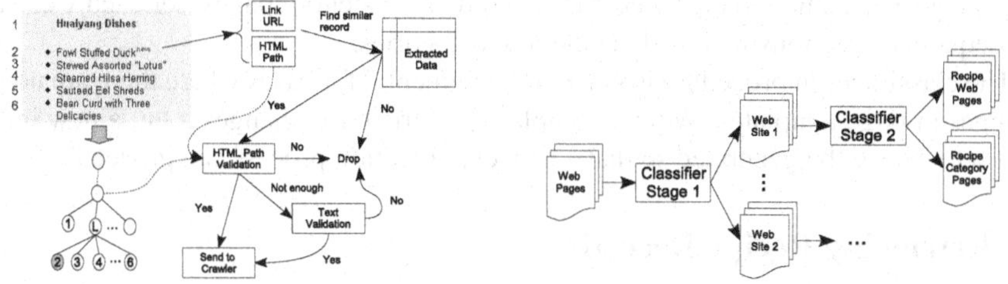

Fig. 3. Identifying Recipe Links Based on the Extracted Data - An Example

Fig. 4. Classifying Recipe Web Pages

As illustrated in Fig.3, our strategy of identifying recipe links on the basis of the extracted data works as follows. First, the current index of a web page is compared to the old one. In this way, the updated links, texts and HTML paths can be retrieved. For example, "Fowl Staffed Duck"(in short, FSD) with its link and HTML DOM path can be retrieved. Secondly we try to find records in extracted data which have similar links, as machine does not know whether it is a recipe link. Two links are similar if we can find a common pattern in them (In our system, we uses common URL prefix). Only considering URL pattern is sometimes not enough as there are still some links such as activities may survive. Therefore we utilize HTML paths and texts for further clarifications. After finding out similar records of a specified link, we first check how many records residing in the same subtree according to HTML paths. Referring back to the example, as we have FSD's DOM path, we also know similar records' DOM path (which are recorded in last time's extraction), by finding common parent nodes, such as "L" node of the DOM tree in right bottom corner of Fig.3. Note that we only give a simple DOM tree here due to the space reason, in which number denotes the content. If we can not find any, this link is probably not a recipe link so we discard it. If we can only find few (in our system, we use 0.5 as the threshold, which means half out of total records), the text is used as the third judgment, which is simple keyword matching in our system, in the hope of finding common recipe keywords(such as "Beef", "Pork" and so on). If most records reside in the same subtree, we let the link survive. Figure 3 illustrates the whole process we have just described, which, based on our practice, has been quite effective and efficient.

4.2 Classifying Recipe Web Pages

In the next step, we build a module "*Classifier*" to handle the web page classification. The classifier program in our system has two stages, as shown in Fig.4. In the first stage we organize the web pages according to URLs, thus obtaining categories of web sites. This stage is relatively easy. Next we further classify crawled web pages according to the tree structures. A clustering algorithm based on tree edit distance [9] has been adopted and adapted. As mentioned before, recipe web pages in our scenario may contain repeatable attributes, so we have modified the matching process to cover repeatable cases. It is called sibling matching which is also used in automated extraction procedure and the details will be given in section 5.1. After classification we will get two categories, namely recipe web pages and recipe category pages, for each web site. Subsequent extractions will be done in these categories.

The classification procedure is in nature incremental for cases where there are no big changes in page templates. When a template (or structure) changes a lot, a new initial data set needs to be generated so that a new classification process can proceed.

5 Retrieving Recipe Records

We now describe how *RecipeCrawler* retrieves recipe data from the crawled recipe web pages. There are two modules involved, namely "*Automated Extrator*" and "*Interactive Annotation*". Though they do different functions in retrieving recipe data, there is no rigid execution order. In *RecipeCrawler*, they are actually invoked asynchronously. Fig.5 gives an illustration on how these two modules cooperate with each other. The *Automated Extractor* continuously does extraction on web pages while the *Interactive Annotation* is notified each time new attributes are identified. *Automated Extrator* will generate two data tables, namely "*Recipe Data*" and "*Category Data*", from recipe web pages and recipe category pages, respectively. Each table may contain some new attributes during the incremental extraction. Thus an execution of annotation procedure is needed. Then we select data fields that have been annotated from these two tables, and join them according to URLs. Finally data is extracted and ready to be imported into DBMS.

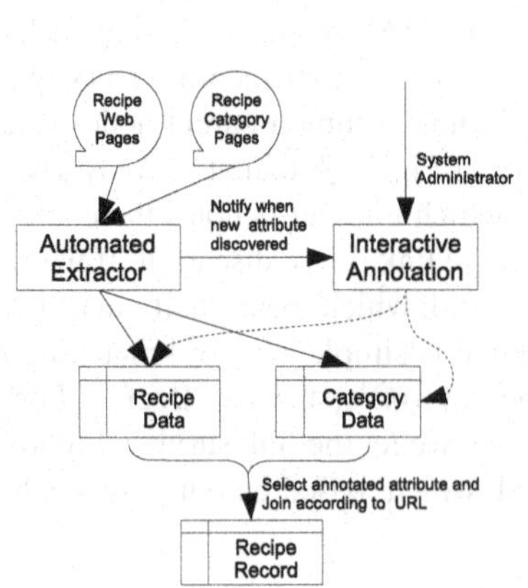

Fig. 5. Retrieving Recipe Data from Web Pages

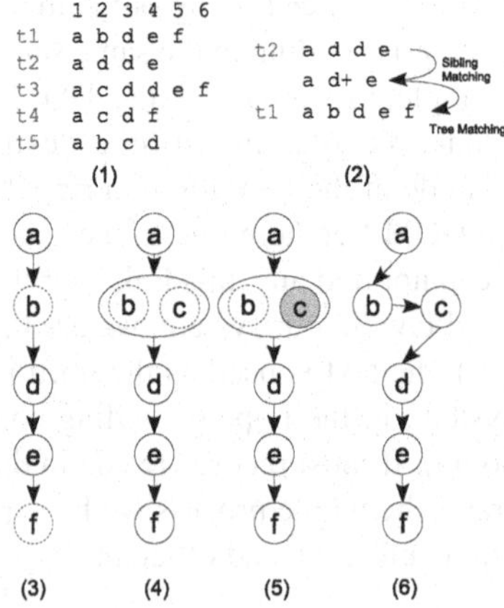

Fig. 6. Illustration of How Automated Recipe Data Extraction Works

5.1 Automated Extraction

In this module, we adopt techniques proposed in [11] for automated extraction. As reported in [11], an algorithm named *partial tree alignment* based on the simple tree matching was used to extract data records in data intensive web pages, such as result pages returned by online retailer web sites. The recipe category web pages in our system are also data intensive web pages, so data records can be directly extracted by applying this algorithm. But we need to modify it in order to extract new/updated records in it for supporting incremental features. This can be done by comparing currently extracted results to the former ones, so the details are omitted here.

On the other hand, extracting data from recipe web pages is not so easy. It is a non-trivial problem because: (1) attributes that have never appeared in previously extracted pages may subsequently be added; (2) attributes that appeared in previously extracted web pages may later be removed; (3) attributes that appeared as singleton in previously extracted web pages may be modified to be repeatable. For example, referring back to Fig.1, the "sauce" attribute appearing in Fig.1(b) is an example of added attributes, and the "seasoning" attribute appearing both in Fig.1(a) and Fig.1(b) is an example of revised attributes, which later can be repeatable. There is no example of removed attributes in Fig.1, but it is easy to give out: any optional attribute can be it when we start from web pages containing it to web pages without it. Though the technique proposed in [11] can roughly handle these situations by selecting and starting from the maximal web page in the hope of that it contains as many optional nodes as possible, it is unfortunately inapplicable in our incremental crawling scenario. So we have adapted it to fulfill the incremental requirements.

Instead of explaining the detailed algorithm used by *RecipeCrawler*, we give an illustrative example in Fig.6 to show how it works. We suppose there are 5 recipe web pages, and to be simple, we present them in simple characters sequence, in which each character denoting a subtree directly contains text values, such as "<LI>Materials:
Beef 150g</LI>" . We can get the sequence by specific traversal of HTML tree [11], and we use pre-order traversal here. According to [11], partial tree alignment first selects the biggest web page as the seed and then do multiple tree alignment. In our example, the biggest one is t3. But in an incremental situation, t3 may not be in the initial set because it is not created by any webmaster at all. In our example, we assume that the initial set has t1 t2, whereas t3, t4 and t5 are added subsequently.

For the initial set we apply the partial tree alignment technique. First we do a sibling matching (as shown in Fig.6(2)), which is used to handle repeatable attributes ("d" in t2). The sibling matching scans each tree and tries to match siblings in it. If two sibling nodes match, they will be replaced by a single example node (we simply take the first one). We do not consider non-sibling nodes because usually a list of repeatable attributes will not be interrupted by other attributes. (For example, the webmaster will not insert some cooking steps in the middle of listing materials.) And the sibling matching performs whenever we match a web page to another (as well as the template, see below). After doing that we make the tree matching based on the edit distance computation to find mappings. By taking the biggest one t2 as the template, we can align t1 to it and by applying partial tree alignment techniques [11] we can also align optional nodes. The basic idea of partial template alignment is trying to find the unique insertion location for each unmatched nodes. In our example, "b" of t1 is unmatched, but we can find a unique insertion location in t2 for it, because "a" and "d" are matched and there is nothing between them in t2. So "b" should be inserted between "a" and "d" in t2 to form a template. After inserting all optional nodes as proven in [11], recipe data is extracted and a template (shown in Figure 6(3)) is induced. Then an annotation process may be invoked, but at this time we are not sure that the nodes "b" and "f" are the data attributes we need (they can be useless values such as "copyright by" et. al.). Another reason is that they may be disjunctions as we have only few instances. So, in our example, we simply suppose no annotation in it, so actually we only extract "a", "d" and "e".

Now we come to the part of incremental extraction. Supposing that t3, t4 and t5 will be updated and crawled one by one, Fig.6(4,5,6) shows how the extraction is done. The basic idea is to match new crawled web pages with the existing template and insert the unmatched nodes into the template. When there is no unique insertion location for the specific node, we insert it by merging it as a possible value into a possible node. In our example, when t3 comes, we find that "c" does not have a unique insertion location as there is already an unannotated "b" between "a" and "d", so we merge "c" as a possible value into "d", thus the template can cover t3 (as shown in Fig.6(4)). At this time t3 can be partially extracted with some part left in the induced template, which may be further matched or annotated (extraction process will give annotation process a notification at this time). Another node, say "f", matches with the one in the template, thus we have enough instances to identify "f" as an attribute and both "f" nodes in t2 and t3 will be extracted.

After processing t3, t4 comes in subsequently. This time we match it with the template too. The difference is that when matching with node "b c", we need to match two times to find the best one. We can see that "c" will be matched thus attribute "c" will be identified. But we can not take it out from the "b c" node for there is still no unique insertion location. The template after matching and extracting t4 is as be seen in Fig.6(5). After t5 comes, matching with t5 will identify the attribute "b" too. And the order of attributes "b" and "c" can be identified since we have t5 as the instance (there is a "b" "c" sequence in t5). Thus all attributes are identified and can be extracted. The induced template is shown in Fig.6(6). Next time when new web pages come in, the same processing techniques can be used.

Note that currently we do not consider disjunctions in our strategy due to two reasons. Firstly, disjunctions are actually not that serious when we are doing incremental extraction. By using following web pages as examples (Fig.6(6)), identifying whether there are disjunctions is easy. Secondly, the chances of disjunctions making our strategy broken are fairly few. For example, considering a web page t6("a c b d e"), our strategy would break while handling it. But this is rare because t6 means that web master changes the order of attributes (such as giving "cooking steps" before "materials"). It is almost unlikely and we did not find any cases in our practice, so we leave this problem to be a possible future work.

5.2 Interactive Annotation

Currently in *RecipeCrawler* the annotation procedure is designed as an interactive program. It can be asynchronously invoked by a system operator while the system does automated extraction. The template induced by automated extraction will be presented to the operator for annotation instead of requiring him to do annotation on each record. When a new attribute is identified, a notification will be given. Then the system operator can check the revised template and examples to decide what kind of attribute it is. Having annotations made to the extracted recipes and category data, they will be selected out and joinned based on URLs to generate the final extraction results. Unannotated data will be reserved in the extracted data storage for future annotation. This mechanism ensures us to be able to incrementally extract meaningful recipe data for *RecipeView* as soon as newly crawled web pages come in. In our practice, we perform the interactive annotation when the initial set was extracted and when enough (e.g., 10) new web pages are extracted. The current practice of *RecipeCrawler* shows that such an approach is quite reasonable and effective.

5.3 Importing Recipe Data Records

As shown in Fig.2, the extracted recipe data records by *RecipeCrawler* are to be utilized by a front-end application system called *RecipeView*. Since the retrieved recipe data records come from various sources, they should go through an importation procedure before they can be fully utilized. This procedure is called "Preprocess" in *RecipeView*, which involves *Filtering* and *Standardization*. The *Filtering* module makes sure that all the recipe records are qualified for the system requirements (e.g. by checking whether the data fields of each record are correctly identified). In the *Standardization* module, all the recipe records have to conform to a standard presentation by fusing different data formats together. For instance, the display sequence of the data fields in each record must be the same. Thus they become uniform and consistent. After the "Preprocess" procedure, the recipe data records are imported into an underlying DBMS for possible user manipulations within the *RecipeView* system.

6 Conclusion and Future Work

As we believe, building incremental data extraction is a critical step towards practical, continuous, reliable web data extraction systems that utilize WWW as the data source for various database applications. In this paper, we have described such a system (viz., *RecipeCrawler*) which targets at incrementally collecting recipe data from WWW. General issues in establishing an incremental data extraction system are considered and techniques applied to recipe data collection from the Web. Our *RecipeCrawler* has served as the backend of a multimedia database application system (called *RecipeView*) and offers good experimental results. Various techniques proposed in literature for data extraction from WWW are adopted and adapted to do the automated recipe data extraction as well as to support incremental features. As for future research, besides evaluating and improving our system, we also plan to address other important issues, including better crawling strategies and automated annotation algorithms.

Acknowledgments

This research was partially supported by the grants from the Natural Science Foundation of China under grant number 60573091, 60273018; the National 973 Basic Research Program of China under Grant No.2003CB317000 and No.2003CB317006; the Key Project of Ministry of Education of China under Grant No.03044 ; Program for New Century Excellent Talents in University(NCET).

References

1. A. Arasu and H. Garcia-Molina. Extracting structured data from web pages. In *Proceedings of the* 22th *ACM SIGMOD International Conference on Management of Data*, pages 337–348, 2003.
2. C.H. Chang and S.C. Lui. Iepad: information extraction based on pattern discovery. In *Proceedings of the* $10th$ *International World Wide Web Conference*, pages 681–688, 2001.
3. V. Crescenzi, G. Mecca, and P. Merialdo. Roadrunner: Towards automatic data extraction from large web sites. In *Proceedings of* 27th *International Conference on Very Large Data Bases*, pages 109–118, 2001.
4. V. Crescenzi, G. Mecca, and P. Merialdo. Wrapping-oriented classification of web pages. In *Proceedings of the* 17th *ACM Symposium on Applied Computing (SAC)*, pages 1108–1112, 2002.
5. S. Grumbach and G. Mecca. In search of the lost schema. In *ICDT '99*, pages 314–331, 1999.
6. N. Kushmerick. Wrapper verification. *World Wide Web*, 3(2):79–94, 2000.
7. B. Liu, R. L. Grossman, and Yanhong Zhai. Mining data records in web pages. In *Proceedings of the* 9th *ACM SIGKDD International Conference on Knowledge Discovery and Data Mining*, pages 601–606, 2003.
8. X. Meng, D. Hu, and C. Li. Schema-guided wrapper maintenance for web-data extraction. In *the* 5th *ACM CIKM International Workshop on Web Information and Data Management*, pages 1–8, 2003.
9. D.C. Reis, P.B. Golgher, A.S. Silva, and A.H.F. Laender. Automatic web news extraction using tree edit distance. In *Proceedings of the* 13th *international conference on World Wide Web*, pages 502–511, 2004.
10. J. Wang and F. H. Lochovsky. Data extraction and label assignment for web databases. In *Proceedings of the* 12th *International World Wide Web Conference*, pages 187–196, 2003.
11. Y. Zhai and B. Liu. Web data extraction based on partial tree alignment. In *Proceedings of the* 14th *international conference on World Wide Web*, pages 76–85, 2005.
12. H. Zhao, W. Meng, Z. Wu, V. Raghavan, and C. T. Yu. Fully automatic wrapper generation for search engines. In *Proceedings of the* 14th *international conference on World Wide Web*, pages 66–75, 2005.

CCWrapper: Adaptive Predefined Schema Guided Web Extraction*

Jun Gao, Dongqing Yang, and Tengjiao Wang

Department of Computer Science and Technology, Peking University, Beijing, China
{gaojun, dqyang, tjwang}@pku.edu.cn

Abstract. In this paper, we propose a method called CCWrapper (Classification-Cluster) to extract target data items from web pages under the guide of the predefined schema. CCWrapper extracts and combines the different HTML nodes features, including the style, structure, thesaurus and data type attributes into one unified model, and generates the extraction rules with Bayes classification in the training step. When the new HTML page is handled, CCWrapper generates the probability of the target element for each HTML node and clusters the HTML nodes for extraction based on the intra-document relationship in the HTML document tree. The preliminary experimental results on real-life web sites demonstrate CCWrapper is a promising extraction method.

1 Introduction

With the web becoming the abundant information resource, web data extraction, which can map loosely-structured data from web pages into a formal structure, has received much attention in the past few years [1-11]. The extracted web data can be used to provide users with better service. The module of web extraction is also called the wrapper.

How to extract data from web pages of different web sites while at the same time to reduce the human involvement is a big challenge. Since the initial purpose of HTML is for human browsing rather than computer processing, the structure, style, or the layout of web pages are different from each other. In addition, some web sites take the anti-extraction strategy to prevent their data from being extracted. The structures for HTML document trees may be changed dynamically with time. Although the users may not be aware of those changes, some HTML page structure based wrapper cannot work.

There are several types of data extractions from web pages: (1) region extraction (extracting the interesting region in the form of HTML from the original HTML page); (2) target data extraction (extracting individual data items scattered on web pages, such as name of a product and its price); (3) schema guide data extraction (extracting individual data items scattered and annotating individual data according to

* Project 60503037 supported by NSFC, Project 4062018 supported by Beijing Natural Science Foundation.

J.X. Yu, M. Kitsuregawa, and H.V. Leong (Eds.): WAIM 2006, LNCS 4016, pp. 275–286, 2006.
© Springer-Verlag Berlin Heidelberg 2006

the predefined schema). Our method falls into the third category, but also borrows some ideas from the methods in the first two categories.

Although the current methods have made great achievement in the web extraction, they can be improved in the following aspects: improving the quality of the extracted data; improving the adaptability of the wrapper; reducing the human burden in the web extraction.

In order to overcome the limitation of the existing methods and handle the problems in extraction, we attempt to propose a method called CCWrapper. Specifically, the contributions of this paper can be summarized as follows:

- Rather than treating a HTML document as a sequence of tokens, we exploit more semantic features, including the style, structure, thesaurus and data type attributes, from the HTML nodes. We extract the features of HTML node which is mapped to the target element in the training phase. The Bayes network classification method is used to generate the extraction rules based on the HTML nodes features set.
- Based on the probability produced from the Bayes network classifier over the HTML nodes in a new HTML tree, we cluster these nodes and establish the mapping from the nodes in HTML tree to the target elements based on a benefit model. In addition, we discuss how to exploit the intra-document relationship for HTML nodes to improve the quality of the web extraction.
- The experiments on the real data set demonstrate the effectiveness of CCWrapper.

The rest of the paper is organized as follows. Section 2 introduces some preliminary knowledge. Section 3 proposes the extraction rules generation and application in CCWrapper. Section 4 shows experimental results, and Section 5 reviews the related work. Section 6 concludes the whole work and discusses the further work.

2 Preliminary Background

This section reviews the preliminary knowledge including HTML and target schema for the extracted information, and discusses the criteria to evaluate the web extraction methods.

2.1 HTML

HTML can be modeled as a node labeled tree. Each node is annotated with one node name and may have different sub nodes and attributes. There are different kinds of nodes according to the role of the nodes in the HTML tree. The structure node can describe the structure of the HTML web page, for example, <body>, <td>, <tr>…etc. The text nodes are always the leaf nodes in the HTML document tree, which contains the target data for extraction. If the text node is not a hyperlink node, it is called a *normal text node*, or else, it is a *hyperlink text node*. The style node controls the appearance of the HTML text nodes. The code nodes include the scripts codes which can run in the HTML page.

2.2 The Target Predefined Schema

Due to the heterogeneous nature of web pages, we use the flexible DTD to represent the schema of extracted data. DTD can support the element definition with the regular expression of the sub elements. Given a regular expression definition *R* of element *e*, the "*" annotated on sub element e_1 of *e* indicates zero-many occurrence of sub element e_1, denoted as $Card(e_1)$=*; the "?" annotated on the sub element e_1 indicates zero-one occurrence of sub element e_1, denoted as $Card(e_1)$=?. The one time occurrence of sub element e_1 in the expression is represented by $Card(e_1)=1$. If the element definition is not recursive, DTD can be represented by a schema tree.

2.3 The Evaluation of Web Extraction Methods

Given a set of the web pages *W* from the web sites set *S*, the data set D_1 behind the web pages set *W*, the data set D_2 extracted from the web pages *W* with method *M*, the **recall** of *M* can be defined as $|D_1 \cap D_2|/|D_1|$, the **precision** of *M* can be defined as $|D_1 \cap D_2|/|D_2|$.

A web wrapper can be represented as a set of extraction rules. Suppose the rules of a web wrapper *E* are not specific to some given web sites, we call *E* the **adaptive** wrapper. Suppose the rules of web wrapper *E* can be generated on the training set automatically rather than hand crafting, we call *E* the **semi-automatically generated** web wrapper.

3 CCWrapper: Adaptive Predefined Schema Web Extraction

The problem handled in the paper can be described as follows: Given a training set *W* of web pages from a web sites set *S*, the target schema *T* with the regular expression element definition including "*" or "?", how to build a web wrapper *W* to extract data from web page under the guide of target schema *T*, while to improve the recall and precision of the extracted data, to improve the adaptability of *W* and to reduce the human burden in the process.

3.1 The Framework of CCWrapper

The framework of CCWrapper can be illustrated in the following figure. First, a user establishes mappings from the nodes in training HTML document to the target elements with a user friendly interface. Second, CCWrapper extracts the features including the structure features, style features, data type feature and layout features of the HTML nodes which have been mapped to the target elements. Third, CCWrapper generates a Bayes network classifier *C* to represent the extraction rules over the features set. Fourth, CCWrapper uses classifier *C* to get the probability of target element for each node in a new HTML page. In the final step, CCWrapper exploits the intra-document relationship in HTML page to cluster the nodes and annotate the HTML nodes with the target elements in the schema.

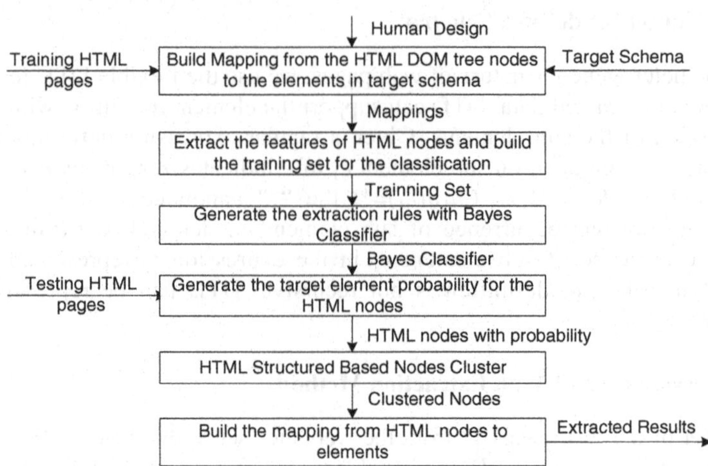

Fig. 1. The framework of the Web extraction

3.2 Extraction Rules Generation Based on Classification

With the mappings from the HTML tree to the target schema tree, the next step is to extract the features of the corresponding HTML nodes for each target schema node, which can be used as the basis for the extraction rules. CCWrapper combines different features of HTML nodes into one unified model. The attributes of HTML node used as the nodes features in CCWrapper can be divided into four categories: style attributes, structure attributes, thesaurus attributes and the data type attributes.

Style Attributes: The style attributes control the appearance of the web page. Different HTML nodes may have different style features. In addition, it is observed that the web pages in the same domain are often displayed in a similar way. For example, the font size of the news title is always largest in the whole web page. The product name in the E-commerce domain is always emphasized, etc. As a result, the extraction rules based on the site independent features can be used in the web sites not in the training set. Some selected style attributes on the HTML node used in CCWarpper are described in the following table:

Table 1. The Style Attributes of the HTML Node

AF/RF	The Absolute (Relative) Font size
BD	Whether the node is emphasized
LN/CLN	The length (context length) of the node text
PS/RPS	The Position (Relative Position) of the node

Structure Attributes: The structure attribute in the HTML page represents the path from the root node to the leaf node in the HTML page. Since many data intensive web sites are generated from the backend database, the paths for the HTML node corresponding to the same element in the target schema are similar for HTML pages in the one web site. In order to exploit structure attribute as one of the important features of the HTML node, we give the following definition:

Definition 1. (the similarity between the paths). Given two HTML paths p_1 and p_2, we create a mapping M from p_1 to p_2, where the mapped element node n_2 in p_2 denoted as $M(n_1)$ is annotated with the same node name as that of element node n_1. In addition, if node n_{11} is a preceding node of n_{12} in path p_1, $M(n_{11})$ is a preceding node of $M(n_{12})$ in path p_2. The similarity between two paths can be defined as $|A|/|B|$, where A is the mapped element nodes set in path p_1 and p_2, B is all element nodes set in path p_1 and p_2.

In the extraction rules training, we can construct the HTML paths set $P(e)$ for target element e from different training HTML pages. In the extraction rules application, given a path p from the root node to the leaf node n in a new HTML tree, the similarity between p and the path set $P(e)$ for element e can be obtained as the maximum similarity between p and every path in $P(e)$.

Thesaurus Attributes: The thesaurus attribute *TA* of node n_1 is the content of node n_2, where n_2 is the preceding node of n_1 in the HTML layout and the content of n_2 describes the content of node n_1.

Different web pages may have different thesaurus attributes for the same element node in the target schema. For example, in the E-commerce domain, the preceding node of the *Price* node for product may be labeled by "the price" or "the discounted price" or "our price". In order to handle this problem, we extract the thesaurus attributes from the HTML nodes in different pages which are mapped to the target element e, organize the thesaurus into ontology $O(e)$ and annotate $O(e)$ on the target element e in the training phase. In the rule application phase, given a node n_1 in a HTML web page, we can locate its thesaurus attribute *ta*. If *ta* is one of the concepts in the ontology $O(e)$ for target element e, we know that it is highly likely that node n_1 can be mapped to element e.

The Data Type Attribute: The data types of the contents on different nodes can also reveal some differences among nodes. For example, the data type of "publication time" of news is date time, and the price values of "product price" in E-commerce web sites are numerical data. The currently supported data types in CCWrapper include money, date time, and user defined date types, for example, address, telephone, e-mail, postal code, etc.

The given predefined schema is only validated for one specific domain. As for the web extraction in one domain, we need to select the features used in the extraction rules. For example, we need not combine the thesaurus features into the training set in new domain since there are little useful thesaurus features of the HTML nodes in news domain. However, the thesaurus attributes play very important roles in the extraction rules in E-Commerce domain.

3.3 Basic Extraction Rules Application

With the generated Bayes network classifier based on the HTML nodes features set, we can determine the probability of the target element e for each HTML node n, denoted as *Prob*(n, e). In the following, the probability can be used as the basis to build a valid mapping from the HTML tree to target schema tree.

Definition 2. (Mapping M from HTML DOM tree T_1 to Target Schema Tree T_2). A mapping M can be defined in the form of nodes pair (n_1, n_2), where n_1 is a leaf node in T_1, $n_2=M(n_1)$ is a leaf node of schema tree T_2. There is one mapping node in T_1 in the case of $Card(n_2)=1$. There are zero or more mapping nodes in T_1 in the case of $Card(n_2)=*$. There is at most one mapping node in T_1 in the case of $Card(n_2)=?$.

Since there are many valid mappings from a HTML DOM tree to a target schema tree, we need a benefit model to evaluate which mapping is better than others.

Definition 3. (The weight of mapping M from a HTML DOM tree T_1 to a Target Schema Tree T_2). The weight of the mapping M denoted as *Weight(M)* can be defined as the production of the *Weight*(e) for each element e in the target schema. As for each target element, *Weight*(e) can be defined as *Prob*(n, e) in the case of $Card(e)=1$, where $M(n)=e$; *Weight*(e) can be defined as $Prob(n_1,e)*\ldots Prob(n_k,e)(1-Prob(n_{k+1},e))*(1-Prob(n_m,e))$ in the case of $Card(e)=*$, where $M(n_1)=e,\ldots M(n_k)=e$ and $M(n_{k+1})\neq e\ldots M(n_m)\neq e$; *Weight*($e$) can be defined as $Prob(n_1,e)*(1-Prob(n_2,e))..(1-Prob(n_m, e))$ in the case of $Card(e)=?$, where $M(n_1)=e$ and the rest of nodes do not map to element e.

In the case of $Card(e)=1$, we select a HTML node n with the maximum *Prob*(n, e) among all HTML nodes. In the case of $Card(e)=?$, we select a HTML node n with maximum *Prob*(n, e) among all HTML nodes if *Prob*(n, e) is greater 50%, or else, we do not create the mapping for element e. In the case of $Card(e)=*$, we select all HTML nodes $\{n_0,..n_k\}$with $Prob(n_i, e)$ $(0\leq i\leq k)$ greater than 50%.

The above rules can be used to establish the mapping from the HTML tree nodes to the node in the target schema tree. In addition, the rules works well for the element with $Card(e)=1$ if the necessary features are used. However, the simple strategy may lead to the problem in the mapping to the element with $Card(e)=*$. Taking the news content extraction as example, the hyper link node n may have low *Prob*(n, e) due to the limited length of the text even though n belong to the news content; The advisement node n may has high *Prob*(n, e) if the feature of n is similar to those of news content nodes. In order to handle this problem, we not only consider the HTML node n itself, but also consider the context of node n. We make the following assumption:

Assumption 1. The leaf nodes $\{n_1,..n_k\}$ which map to a target element e with $Card(e)=*$ are adjacent in the preorder traversal of leaf nodes in tree T. In addition, the HTML node mapping to element e with $Card(e)=1$ can not be in the middle of adjacent nodes set $\{n_1,..n_k\}$.

Assumption 1 can be accepted in many domains. For example, the nodes for the content of the news web page are always adjacent. In addition, it is less likely that the nodes for the news title are located in the middle of the news content nodes.

Definition 4. (Stub Node) Given one target element e with $Card(e)=1$, if there exists one HTML node n with *Prob*(n, e) much greater (10 times or higher) than $Prob(n_1, e)$, where n_1 is any HTML leaf node and $n_1\neq n$, we call HTML node n the Stub node.

Since it is likely to map the stub node n to the correct target element node e with $Card(e)=1$, we know that node n is less likely in the middle of the adjacent nodes sub sequence for the element with $Card(e)=*$. Therefore, the stub node can be used to divide the whole HTML leaf nodes sequence into a set of the node units:

Definition 5. (HTML Nodes Unit) Given a HTML leaf nodes sequence $S=\{n_0,\ldots,n_k\}$ in a preorder traversal and a stub node n_i ($0\leq i\leq k$) in the sequence S, the stub node divides the sequence S into two sub sequence with $S_1=\{n_0,\ldots n_{i-1}\}$ and $S_2=\{n_{i+1},\ldots n_k\}$. S_1 or S_2 is called nodes unit.

With the HTML node units, we avoid the case that we map the nodes from different nodes unit to element *e* with *Card*(*e*)=*. The basic extraction process with the HTML node units can be described in the following algorithm.

Algorithm 1. The basic extraction rule application

Input: the HTML web page *P*, the Classifier *C*, the target schema *S*
Output: the mapping *M* for the extraction on the web page *P*
For each leaf node *n* in the web page *P*
    Calculate *Prob*(*n*, *e*) with Classifier *C* for each target element *e*
For each element *e* with *Card*(*e*)=1
    Select node *n* with the maximum *Prob*(*n*, *e*)// *n* maps to *e*;
    If node *n* meets the requirement of stub node
        Divide the whole nodes sequence into HTML node units with node n.
For each element *e* with *Card*(*e*)=* or *Card*(*e*)=?
    For each HTML node unit *U*
        Generate the weight of the mapping *M* from the node in *U* to element *e*;
    Select the mapping *M* with the maximum weight.
Return the mapping from HTML nodes to all target elements.

3.4 Extraction Rules Application Based on Cluster over the HTML Tree

Although the basic method can implement the web extraction, the precision of the basic method can be further improved. For example, even if we can select the mapping with the maximum weight from the nodes in HTML nodes unit *U* to the element node *e* in the case *Card*(*e*)=*, it is likely that some nodes in *U* should not map to element *e*.

We make a deep analysis on the basic method in section 3.3. The reason that the basic method cannot remove the unrelated nodes from the HTML node units correctly lies in that the features used to generate the extraction rules only include the features of the single HTML node itself, which ignores the HTML tree structure as a whole totally. Next, we make another assumption on the HTML tree structure in the News or E-commerce domain.

Assumption 2. The web page p_1 contains a region with adjacent hyperlinks, for example, the related news links in the news web page or the lists of products in E-commerce web page. Since the content of one hyperlink p_2 can be retrieved fully from another web page which is pointed by p_2, we assume that users are not interested in the extraction of hyperlink p_2 in the process of the extraction of p_1.

In order to remove these adjacent hyperlink nodes more reasonable, we also need to consider the internal structure in one HTML nodes unit. We introduce the notation of the weight of the internal node to decide which nodes in one HTML nodes unit can be removed.

Definition 6. (the weight of the Internal Node for HTML nodes Unit). Given a HTML nodes unit *U*, for each node *n* in *U*, we locate an ancestor node *a* for *n*, nodes set $S=Des(a)\cap Unodes(U)$, where *Des*(*a*) is a descendant nodes set of *a*, *Unodes*(*U*) is a nodes set in nodes unit *U*, the weight of node *a* for target element *e*, denoted as *weight*(*a*, *e*), can be defined as *(TotalLen-LinkLen)/Totallen*(TotalNodes-LinkNodes)/TotalNodes*P*, where *TotalLen* is the total length of the node content for all nodes in *S*, *LinkLen* is the total length of the node content for all hyperlink text nodes in *S*, *TotalNodes* is the number of the all nodes in *S*, *LinkNodes* is the number of the hyperlink text nodes in nodes *S*. *P* is the sum of *Prob*(*s*, *e*), where $s\in S$.

The above definition conforms to the assumption 2. We notice that the more the hyperlink nodes under internal node *a* are, the less the weight of node *a* is. In other words, the weight of the internal node for the normal text nodes (extraction target nodes) is much higher than that of the internal node for the leaf hyperlink nodes. Such a characteristic can be used to locate one internal node "cover" *all* and *only* extraction target nodes for one HTML node unit.

Definition 7. (the lowest common ancestor *LA* for a nodes unit *U* with the threshold *T*). Given an internal node *n*, and the direct child set $C=\{c_1,..c_k\}$, if there does *NOT* exist a child node *c*, where $weight(c)\geq weight(c_1)*T$, c_1 is any node in *C*, $c_1\neq c$, node *LA* is called the lowest common ancestor of a nodes unit *U* with threshold *T*.

The location of lowest common ancestor *LA* from HTML nodes unit *U* with threshold 30 can be illustrated in Fig.2. We start to locate the lowest common ancestor *LA* from the root *HTML* node. Since the weight of one direct child node *Body* of *HTML* node is much higher (more than 30 times) than that of other child nodes, we know that it is more likely that the nodes interesting to the users are under node *Body*. We handle the internal nodes similarly until we find the last *TD* node. Notice that the lowest common ancestor can be used to improve the recall of web extraction, especially when there is a hyperlink node *h* in the middle of the text nodes sequence. That is, although the weight of node *h* itself is 0, such as the third *P* node under the last *TD* node in Fig.2, it will be extracted since it is under the lowest common ancestor node *TD*.

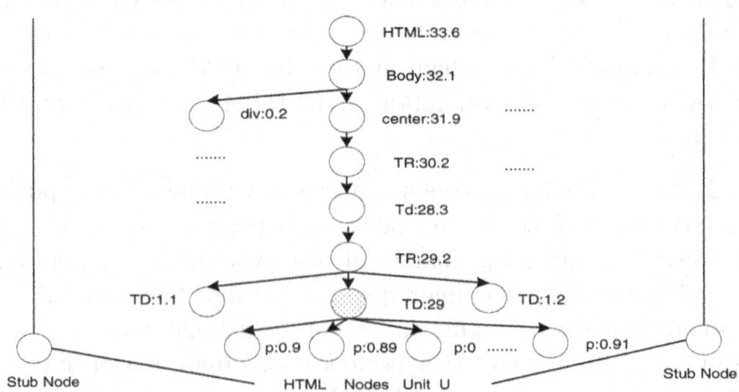

Fig. 2. An example of the lowest common ancestor for a HTML nodes unit

Compared with the basic method, we improve the precision of CCWrapper by exploiting the HTML internal structure to remove the unrelated nodes, mainly the adjacent hyperlink text nodes, from the HTML nodes unit when mapping HTML nodes to the target element *e* with *Card(e)*=*. Such a process can be described as Algorithm 2.

Algorithm 2. The HTML structure based node cluster for the nodes mapping

Input: the HTML nodes units set in web page *P*, the element *e* with *Card(e)*=*, the threshold *T*

Output: the nodes mapping *M* from the nodes in web page *P* to *e*

For each HTML nodes unit *U*

Calculate the weight for each internal node *a* for nodes unit *U*;

Determine the lowest common ancestor *LA* with the maximum probability given the threshold *T* in a top down fashion;

Build mapping *M* from all nodes $n_1 ..... n_k$ under node *LA* to element *e*;

Calculate the weight of mapping *M*;

Select a nodes unit *Umax* with the maximum *Weigtht*(*M*);

Output the mapping *M* from the nodes under the lowest common ancestor node in nodes unit *Umax* to element *e*;

4 The Performance Study

We implemented CCWrapper with the JDK 1.4 on Windows 2000 running on a Dell Optiplex GX260 with P4 2GHz CPU and 512MB RAM. The Bayes Classifier package used in CCWrapper is JBNC[13]. We evaluate CCWrapper against the news web pages from the influential web sites in China. The target schemas in the experiments contain the element *e* with *Card(e)*=*.

4.1 The Analyze of CCWrapper

The precision of CCWrapper is related to the features used in the extraction rules. In the news or the E-commerce domain, it is relatively easy to find the features that distinguish the node from others, especially for the target element *e* with *Card(e)*=1. The recall of CCWraper can be improved by the notation of the lowest common ancestor. All leaf descendant nodes under the lowest common ancestor node will be extracted, regardless what the mapping probabilities of these nodes are.

The threshold used in locating the lowest common ancestor affects the recall and recall of the web extraction. The increase of threshold denotes that it is less likely to find a child node whose weight meets the requirement. Therefore, we cannot lower the common ancestor for the HTML nodes unit, which leads to the increase of recall and decrease of precision. On the other hand, the decrease of threshold indicates the decrease of the recall and increase of the precision.

The adaptability of CCWrapper is addressed by the extracted rules based on the site independent features of HTML nodes for the different web sites. These features include the style attributes or the thesaurus attributes or date type attributes, etc. The extraction rules based on these features can also be applied on the web pages from web site not in the training set. In addition, assumptions 1 and 2 are always true on the web pages from different web sites, which also improve the adaptability of CCWrapper.

As for the human involvement in CCWrapper, human needs to select features used in extraction for target elements in a given predefined schema. In addition, user needs to establish the mapping from HTML nodes to target element nodes. The remaining steps in extraction rules generation from the training web pages and the application of these rules over the testing web pages can be performed automatically.

4.2 The Real Data Set Test

We evaluate CCWrapper over the web pages in the news domain. The training set includes three HTML pages from www.sina.com.cn, www.sohu.com.cn, www.tom.com.cn. The target schema includes the *news title*, *news source*, *news publish date*, *news content*, *news link* with *Card*(*news content*)=*. We build the mapping from the HTML pages to the target schema. The evaluation data set also includes the web pages from other web sites. The precision and recall can be obtained from the nodes mapping generated from the CCWrapper.

From the results in table 2, the average of the precision and recall is 92.5% and 94.7% for the web pages in 9 different web sites. The main reason behind the error mapping is the irregularity of the real web page. For example, there may be only one picture as the main content of the HTML news, or the features of the news content are similar to those of other parts of the HTML pages. In addition, we also notice that the average precision and recall of the extracted result for the web sites not in the training set is not as high as that in the training set. This is because the features on the HTML nodes are a little different for the web pages from different web sites. On the other hand, the results in table 2 also demonstrate the adaptability of CCWrapper.

Table 2. the web extraction over the real test set

Web site	Total web pages	Total Target Data Items	precision	Recall
www.sina.com.cn	115	2875	94.3	96.8
www.sohu.com.cn	114	2736	95.2	97.2
www.tom.com.cn	128	3072	95.1	98.2
www.qq.com.cn	35	910	92.1	93.2
www.gmv.com	45	990	89.3	92.1
www.chinadaily.com.cn	49	1029	88.9	93.2
www.xinhua.com	75	1725	94.2	97.3
www.cnradio.com.cn	67	1474	91.1	90.2
www.hf365.com	58	1334	92.3	94.2
Total	686	16145	92.5	94.7

The CCWrapper can be implemented efficiently. Given n HTML leaf nodes and m target schema elements, we generate $n*m$ probability with the trained classifier. The calculation of the weight for each internal node n takes the linear time in the size of the total descendant leaf nodes of node n. The lowest common ancestor can be detected in the linear time in the size of internal node in the HTML tree. Fig.3 also demonstrates the efficiency of CCWrapper. The extraction time cost in CCWrapper is even less than that of parser time cost for some web pages.

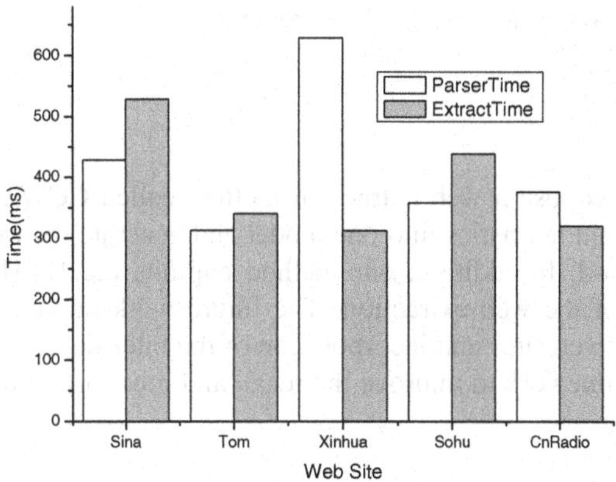

Fig. 3. The time cost of CCWrapper over Real set

5 The Related Work

As for the target data extraction, RoadRunner[2], EXALG[3],Omini[5],MDR[6], Meng[4] do not need manual labeling, but need a set of positive pages of the same template. Our method also shares some ideas from their work. For example, the generalized node [6] plays the similar role as low common ancestor node in our method. However, the location of low common ancestor in our method is guided not only by the HTML tree structure, but also by the probability generated on the features of the HTML nodes. The method [4] also utilizes the visual information to extract the data. Our method supports an open framework which can incorporate different kinds of the heuristic features, including the visual features. Most important, the difference between CCWrapper and this kind of methods lies in that CCWrapper not only extracts the data items, but also annotates the extracted item with the target element.

The schema guide data extraction can be divided into the automatic wrapper induction and handed crafted wrapper. Traditional Information extraction approach [7] treats web documents as tokens streams and use delimiter-based patterns to extract the web pages. If the query interface on the web is available, the fully automatic extraction and annotation method is studied in [8]. Compared with this kind of methods, CCWrapper can exploit more semantic features rather than frequent tokens sequence. In addition, CCWrapper does not need the support from the query interface.

The hand crafted wrapper receives high attention [9,10,11]. Although this kind of method can extract the web pages precisely, the construction and maintenance of the wrapper is costly. In addition, there is little chance that the path based wrapper designed for one specific site is still valid on other web sites.

The problem of schema mapping is studied recently in the data integration system [12]. The web data extraction can be regarded as a special case of the schema mapping. Different rules can be generated based on the structure, thesaurus, and date type attributes or the similarity between instances. We also share the similar idea in the features selection and extraction rules generation with Bayes classification. However, the HTML tree structure and the semantic meaning of the HTML node can also provide the heuristic knowledge in the rules application, which is ignored totally in the schema mapping in the relational database context.

6 Conclusion

In this paper, we propose a web extraction method called CCWrapper. Our method can combine different heuristics into one model and generate the extraction rules with classification method. In addition, our method exploits the HTML structure to improve the quality of the web extraction. The future work includes the extensive experiments on more web sites and incorporation of the inter-document relationship into our CCWrapper framework to improve the recall and precision of the web extraction.

Reference

[1] A.H. F. Laender, B.A. Ribeiro-Neto, A.S.Silva, J.S.Teixeira. A Brief Survey of Web Data Extraction Tools. In SIGMOD Record, Volume 31(2002), No.2.

[2] V.Crescenzi, G.Mecca, P.Merialdo. RoadRunner: Towards Automatic Data Extraction from Large Web Sites. In Proc. of VLDB, 2001,pp:109-118.

[3] A.Arasu, H.G.Molina: Extracting Structured Data from Web Pages. In Proc. of SIGMOD 2003, pp:337-348

[4] H. Zhao, W. Meng, Z. Wu, V. Raghavan, C. Yu. Fully Automatic Wrapper Generation for Search Engines. In Proc. of WWW, 2005.

[5] D. Buttler, L. Liu, C. Pu. A Fully Automated Object Extraction System for the World Wide Web. In Proc. of ICDCS, 2001.

[6] B. Liu, R. Grossman and Y. Zhai. Mining Data Records in Web Pages. In Proc. of SIGKDD, 2003.

[7] D Freitag, N. Kushmerick, Boosted wrapper generation. In Proc of AAAI, 2000.

[8] J.J.Wang, J.R.Wen, F.H. Lochovsky, W.Y.Ma: Instance-based Schema Matching for Web Databases by Domain-specific Query Probing. In Proc of VLDB, 2004, pp:408-419

[9] L.Liu, C.Pu, W.Han. XWRAP: An XML-enabled Wrapper Construction System for Web Information Sources. In Proc. of ICDE, 2000, pp: 611-621.

[10] T.J.Wang, S.W.Tang, D.Q.Yang, J.Gao, et al. COMMIX: Towards Effective Web Information Extraction, Integration and Query Answering. In Proc. of SIGMOD, 2002, pp:620.

[11] L.Y.Li, S.W.Tang, D.Q.Yang, T.J.Wang, Z.H.Su, EGA: An algorithm for automatic semi-structured web documents extraction. In Proc. of DASFAA, 2004, 787-789

[12] R.B.Dhamankar, Y.Lee, A.H.Doan, A.Y.Halevy, P.Domingos: iMAP: Discovering Complex Mappings between Database Schemas. In Proc. of SIGMOD, 2004, pp: 383-394

[13] Java Bayes Package http:// jbnc.sourceforge.net

MiniTasking: Improving Cache Performance for Multiple Query Workloads

Yan Zhang[1], Zhifeng Chen[2], and Yuanyuan Zhou[3]

[1] National laboratory on machine perception, Peking Univ., Beijing, 100871, China
zhy@cis.pku.edu.cn
[2] Google, USA
zhifeng.chen@gmail.com
[3] Department of Computer Science, University of Illinois at Urbana-Champaign, USA
yyzhou@cs.uiuc.edu

Abstract. This paper proposes a novel idea, called MiniTasking to reduce the number of cache misses by improving the data *temporal locality* for *multiple* concurrent queries. Our idea is based on the observation that, in many workloads such as decision support systems (DSS), there is usually significant amount of data sharing among different concurrent queries. MiniTasking exploits such data sharing characteristics to improve data temporal locality by scheduling query execution at three levels: (1) It batches queries based on their data sharing characteristics and the cache configuration. (2) It groups operators that share certain data. (3) It schedules mini-tasks which are small pieces of computation in operator groups according to their data locality without violating their execution dependencies.

Our experimental results show that, MiniTasking can significantly reduce the execution time up to 12% for joins. For the TPC-H throughput test workload, MiniTasking improves the end performance up to 20%. Even with the Partition Attributes Across (PAX) layout, MiniTasking further reduces the cache misses by 65% and the execution time by 9%.

1 Introduction

1.1 Motivation

With the increasing size of main memory, most of query processing working set can fit into main memory for many database workloads. As a result, the main memory latency is becoming a major performance bottleneck for many database applications, such as DSS (Decision Support System) applications [2, 20, 31]. This problem will get worse as the processor-memory speed gap increases. Previous work demonstrates that the L2 data stall time is one of the most significant components of the query execution time [2]. We conducted similar measurements using IBM DB2 with DSS workloads. Our results demonstrate that on Pentium 4, the L2 cache misses contribute 18%-56% of CPIs (cycle per instructions) for most TPC-H queries. Therefore, improving the L2 cache hit ratio is critical to reduce the number of expensive memory accesses and improve the end performance for database applications.

An effective method for improving the L2 data cache hit ratio is to increase data locality, which includes *spatial locality* and *temporal locality*. Many previous studies

J.X. Yu, M. Kitsuregawa, and H.V. Leong (Eds.): WAIM 2006, LNCS 4016, pp. 287–299, 2006.
© Springer-Verlag Berlin Heidelberg 2006

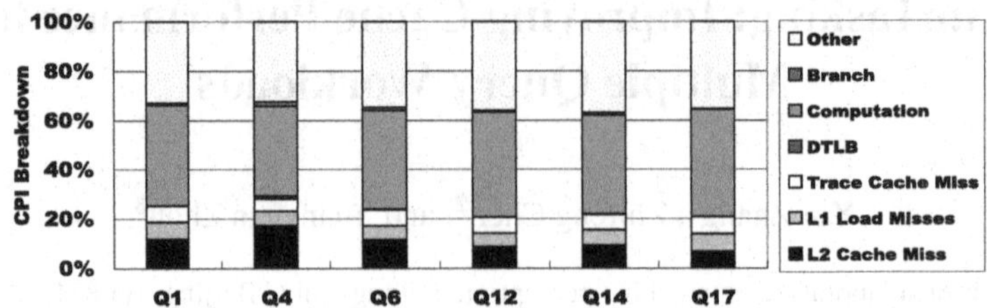

Fig. 1. CPI breakdown of some TPC-H queries on Shore using PAX

have proposed clever ideas to improve the data spatial locality of a *single* query by using cache-conscious data layout. Examples include PAX (Partition Attributes Across) by Ailamaki et al. [1], data morphing by Hankins and Patel [14] and wider B^+-tree nodes by Chen et al. [8]. These layout schemes place data that are likely to be accessed together consecutively so that servicing one cache miss can "prefetch" other data into the cache to avoid subsequent cache misses.

While the above techniques are very effective in reducing the number of cache misses, the memory latency still remains significant contributor for the query execution time even though the amount of contribution is not as high as before. For example, as shown in Figure 1, with the PAX layout, the L1 and L2 cache misses still contribute around 20% of CPIs for TPC-H queries. Therefore, it is still necessary to seek other complementary techniques to further reduce the number of cache misses.

Improving temporal locality is a potential complementary technique to reduce cache miss ratio by improving data temporal reuse. This approach has been widely studied for scientific applications. Most previous work in this category maximizes data temporal locality by reordering computation, e.g., compiler-directed tiling or loop transformations [32, 18, 11, 3], fine-grained thread scheduling [23, 34]. While these techniques are very useful for regular, array-based applications, it is difficult to apply them to database applications that usually have complex pointer-based data structures, and whose structure information is known only at run-time after the database schema is loaded into the main memory. So far few studies have been conducted to improve the temporal cache reuse for database applications.

1.2 Our Contributions

In this paper, we propose a technique called MiniTasking to improve data temporal locality for concurrent query execution. Our idea is based on the observation that, in a large scale decision support system, it is very common for multiple users with complex queries to hit the same data set concurrently [16], even though these queries may not be identical. MiniTasking exploits such data sharing characteristics to improve temporal locality by scheduling query execution at three levels:(1) It batches queries based on their data sharing characteristics and the cache configuration. (2) It groups operators that share certain data. (3) It schedules mini-tasks which are small fractions of operator groups according to their data locality without violating their execution dependencies.

MiniTasking is complementary to previously proposed solutions such as PAX [1] and data morphing [14], because MiniTasking improves temporal locality while cache conscious layouts improve spatial locality. MiniTasking is also complementary to multiple query optimization (MQO) techniques that produce a global query plan for them [13,28,27].

We implemented MiniTasking in the Shore storage manager [6]. Our experimental results with various DSS workloads using the TPC-H benchmark suite show that, MiniTasking improves the end performance up to 20% on a real compound workload running TPC-H throughput testing streams. Even with the Partition Attributes Across (PAX) layout, MiniTasking reduces the L2 cache misses by 65% and the execution time of concurrent queries by 9%.

The remainder of this paper is organized as follows. Section 2 presents the related work. Section 3 introduces data temporal locality. Section 4 describes MiniTasking in detail. Section 5 demonstrates the experimental evaluation. Finally, we show our conclusions in Section 6.

2 Related Work

Multiple Query Optimization. endeavors to reduce the execution time of multiple queries by reducing duplicated computation and reusing the computation results. Previous work proposes to extract common sub-expressions from plans of multiple queries and reuse their intermediate results in all queries [10,13,27,28]. Early work shows that the multiple query optimization is an NP-hard problem and proposes heuristics for query ordering and common sub-expressions detection and selection [13,27]. Roy et al. propose to materialize certain common sub-expressions into transient tables so that later queries can reuse the results [26]. Instead of materializing the results of common sub-expressions, Davli et al. focus on pipelining the intermediate tuples simultaneously to several queries so as to avoid the prohibitive cost of materializing and reading the intermediate results [10]. Harizopoulos et al. propose a operator-centric engine Qpipe to support on-demand simultaneous pipelining [15]. O'Gorman et al. propose to reduce disk I/O by scheduling queries with the same table scans at the same time and therefore achieve significant speedups [22]. However, reusing intermediate results requires exactly same common sub-expressions. For example, a little change in the selection predicate of one query will render previous results not usable.

Improving Data Locality. is another important technique to improve performance of multiple queries, especially when the memory latency becomes a new bottleneck for DSS workload on modern processors. Ailamaki et al. show that the primary memory-related bottleneck is mainly contributed by L1 instruction and L2 data cache misses [2].

Many recent studies have focused on improving data spatial locality to reduce cache misses in database systems [1,9,19,33,25]. Cache-conscious algorithms change data access pattern of table scan [4] and index scan [33] so that consecutive data accesses will hit in the same cache lines. Shatdal et al. demonstrate that several basic database operator algorithms can be redesigned to make better use of the cache [29]. Cache-conscious index structures pack more keys in one cache lines to reduce cache misses during lookup in an index tree [9,19,25]. Cache-conscious data storage models partition tables vertically so that one cache line can store the same fields from several records [1,24]. Although these techniques effectively reduce cache misses within a single query, data fetched into processor caches are not reused across multiple queries.

Much previous work studies improving data temporal locality for general programs [7, 5, 12]. For example, based on the temporal relationship graph between objects generated via profiling, Calder et al. present a compiler directed approach for cache-conscious data placement [5]. Carr and Tseng propose a model that computes temporal reuse of cache lines to find desirable loop organizations for better data locality [7, 21]. Although these methods are effective in increasing cache reuse, it is difficult to apply them directly to DSS workload because it is hard to profile *ad hoc* DSS queries.

3 Feasibility Analysis: Improving Temporal Locality

Processor caches are used in modern architectures to reduce the average latency of memory accesses. Every memory load or store instruction is first checked inside the processor cache (L1 and L2). If the data is in the cache, a.k.a. a cache hit, the access is satisfied by the cache directly. Otherwise, it is a cache miss. Upon a cache miss, the accessed data is fetched into the cache from the main memory. Because accessing the main memory is 10–30 times slower than accessing the processor cache, it is performance critical to have high cache hit ratios to avoid paying the large penalty of accessing main memory.

There are two kinds of locality: spatial locality and temporal locality. Our work focuses on improving temporal locality via locality-based scheduling. Temporal locality is the tendency that individual locations, once referenced, are likely to be referenced again in the near future. Good temporal locality allows data in processor caches to be reused (called as *temporal reuse*) multiple times before being replaced and thereby improving the cache effectiveness.

In most real world workloads, database servers usually serve multiple concurrent queries simultaneously. Usually, there is significant amount of data sharing among many of such concurrent queries. For example, Query 1 (Q1) and Query 6 (Q6) from the TPC-H benchmark [30] share the same table *Lineitem*, the largest one in the TPC-H database.

However, due to the locality-oblivious multi-query scheduling that is commonly used in modern database servers, such significant data sharing is not fully exploited in databases to improve the level of temporal reuse in processor caches and reduce the number of processor cache misses. As a result, before a piece of data can be reused by another query, it has already been replaced and needs to be fetched again from main memory when it is needed by another query.

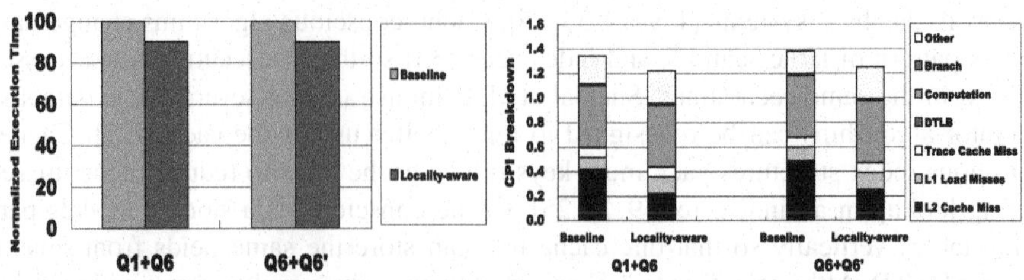

Fig. 2. Comparison between locality-oblivious and locality-aware multi-query scheduling

Let us looking at an example using Q1 and Q6 from the TPC-H benchmark. Suppose *Lineitem* has 1M tuples, with each tuple occupying one cache line of 64 bytes (for the simplicity of description), and the L2 cache holds only 64K cache lines (total of 4 MBytes). Suppose that the scheduler decides to execute Q1 first in concurrent to some other queries that do not share any data with Q1 and Q6. After Q1 accesses the 128K-th tuple, Q6 is scheduled to start from the 1st tuple. Since the L2 cache can only hold 64K tuples, the first tuple of *Lineitem* is already evicted from L2. Therefore, the database needs to fetch this tuple again from main memory to execute Q6.

In contrast, if we use a locality-aware multi-query scheduling and execution, we can schedule Q1 and Q6 together in an interleaved fashion so that, after a query fetches a tuple from main memory into L2, this tuple can be accessed for both queries before being replaced from L2.

Figure 2 shows that, for multiple queries of different types (Q1+Q6), the locality-aware scheduling is able to reduce the number of cache misses by 41.7% and result in 9.7% reduction in execution time. For multiple queries of the same type but with different arguments (Q6+Q6'), the locality-aware scheduling reduces the number of cache misses by 42.4% and the execution time by 9.9%. These results indicate that locality-awareness in multi-query scheduling is very helpful to reduce the number of cache misses and improve database performance, which is the major focus of our work.

4 MiniTasking

4.1 Overview

To exploit data sharing among concurrent queries for improving temporal locality, MiniTasking schedules and executes concurrent queries based on data sharing characteristics at three levels: query level batching, operator level grouping and mini-task level scheduling. While each level is different, all levels share the same goal: improving

```
Algorithm Greedy-Selecting:
;; Given n queries Q_1,...,Q_n, return a batch of
;; queries that will be processed as a whole.
S={Q_a, Q_b | max_{i,j} AmountDataSharing(Q_i, Q_j)}
while |S| < MaxBatchSize
do
  Find Q ∉ S s.t. ∃Q' ∈ S
    AmountDataSharing(Q, Q') is maximized
  if AmountDataSharing(Q, Q') ≠ 0
    S=S ∪ {Q}
  else
    exit the loop ;; No more queries sharing with S
return S
```

Fig. 3. Greedy batch selecting algorithm

temporal data locality. Therefore, at each level, all decisions are made based on data sharing characteristics with consideration of other factors that are specific to each level.

At the query level, due to the processor cache capacity limit, it is not beneficial to execute together all concurrent queries (queries that have already arrived at the database management server and are waiting to be processed). Therefore, MiniTasking carefully selects a *batch* of queries based on their data sharing characteristics and the processor cache configuration to maximize the level of temporal locality in the processor cache. Queries in the same batch are then processed together in the next two levels.

At the second level, MiniTasking produces a locality-aware query plan tree for each batch of queries. MiniTasking does this by starting from the query plan tree produced by the optimizer and group together those operators that share significant amount of data. Operators that do not share data with others remain untouched.

At the third level, MiniTasking further breaks each operator into mini-tasks, with each mini-task operating on a fine-grained data block. Then all mini-tasks from the same of query plan tree are executed one after another following an order to maximize temporal data reuse in the processor cache.

4.2 Query Level Batching

Obviously, the first criteria for query batching should be data sharing. If two queries access totally different data, there is no chance of reusing each other's data from the processor cache. Such case can happen even when two queries access the same table but access different fields that do not share the same cache line. In this case, we call that these two queries do not have overlapping *working sets*, which is defined as the set of data (cache lines) accessed by a query.

Therefore, to batch queries based on data sharing characteristics, MiniTasking needs to estimate the amount of sharing between any two concurrent queries. A metric, called as $AmountDataSharing$ is introduced to measure the estimated amount of data sharing, i.e. the amount of overlapping in working set, between two given concurrent queries. Since only coarse-grain data access characteristics are known at the query level, we estimate a query's working set based on the tables and the fields accessed by this query.

MiniTasking schedules queries in batches and processes these batches one by one. Given a large number of concurrent queries that share data with each other, intuitively, it sounds beneficial to execute concurrently as many queries as possible so that the amount of data reuse can be maximized.

However, in reality, due to the limited L2 cache capacity, scheduling too many concurrent queries can result in even poor temporal locality because data from different queries can replace each other in the cache before being reused. Therefore, we should carefully decide how many and which concurrent queries should be batched together. To address this problem, we use a threshold parameter, $MaxBatchSize$, to limit the number of concurrent queries in a batch.

Based on the above analysis, we use a heuristic greedy algorithm to select batches of queries, as shown in Figure 3. It works similar to a clustering algorithm: divide all concurrent queries into clusters smaller than $MaxBatchSize$ to maximize the total amount of data sharing.

4.3 Operator Level Grouping

Since queries consist of operators, MiniTasking goes one step further to group together operators from the same batch of queries according to their data sharing characteristics. MiniTasking scans every physical operator tree produced by the query optimizer for each query in a batch and groups operators that share some certain data. The evaluation process is similar to the one used at the query level. If the results of an operator is pipelined to other operators, MiniTasking also puts these related operators into the same group. Each group of operators is then passed to the mini-task level. Operators that do not share data with others are all put into the last group and is executed last using the original scheduling algorithm.

MiniTasking supports operator dependency by maintaining a pool of ready operators. An operator is ready and joins the ready pool when it does not dependent on other unexecuted operators. MiniTasking selects a group of operators from the ready pool using a similar algorithm to the one used in query batching described in Figure 3. After this group of operators finishes execution via mini-tasking (described in the next subsection), some operators that depend on the ones just executed will be "released" and join the ready pool if they do not have other dependencies. MiniTasking will select the next group of operators and so on so forth until all operators are executed.

Figure 4 uses an example to demonstrate how MiniTasking works at the operator level. Suppose there are two queries, namely Q and Q'. Op_1 to Op_5 are operators of query Q, and Op'_1 to Op'_4 are operators of query Q'. As both Op_1 and Op'_1 access table T_1, they are grouped together. Suppose Op'_3 and Op_4 are implemented using pipelining. MiniTasking also puts them into the same group as Op_1, Op'_1, Op_2 and Op'_2. This group does not contain Op'_4 or Op_5, because the results of Op'_3 and Op_4 are materialized.

4.4 Mini-task Level Scheduling

At the mini-task level, the challenge is how MiniTasking breaks various query operators into mini-tasks and achieves benefit from rescheduling them. We show our method by

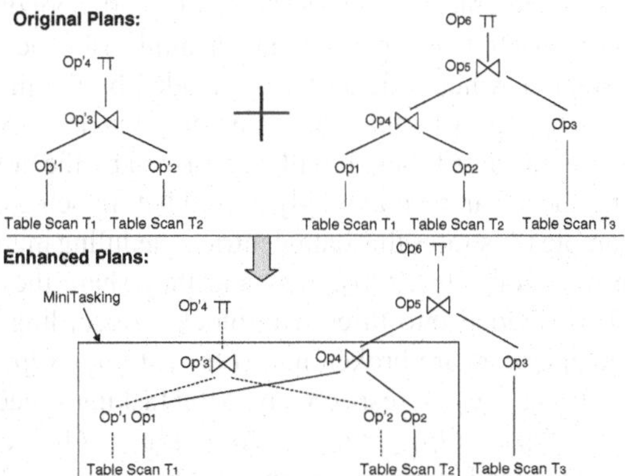

Fig. 4. An example of the operator grouping process. The output of Op'_3 to Op'_4 and the output of Op_4 to Op_5 are materialized.

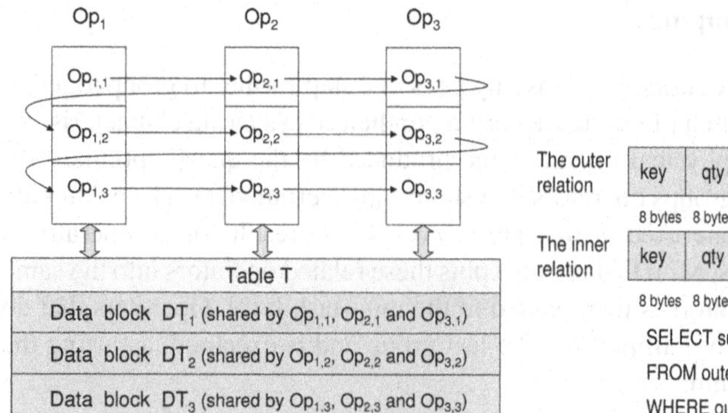

Fig. 5. MiniTasking breaks the operators into mini-tasks and schedules them

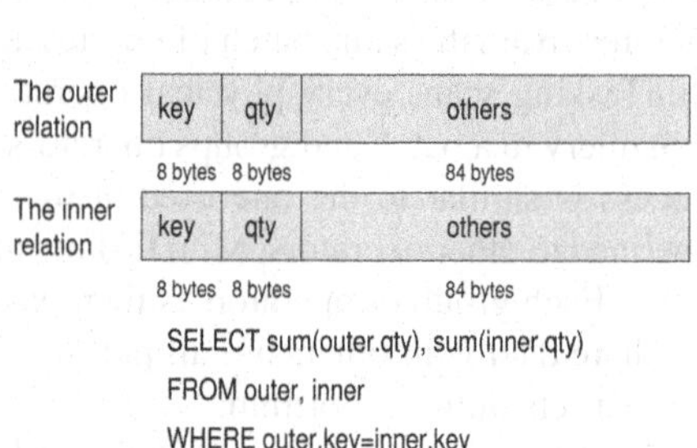

Fig. 6. The layouts for the two join relations and the join query

illustrating a data-centric method applied to a table scan. The idea can be extended to handle other query operators.

The goal of MiniTasking is to make the data loaded into the cache reused by queries as much as possible before it is evicted from the cache. Therefore, MiniTasking carefully chooses an appropriate value for the whole working set size, which means the total size for all the data blocks that can reside in the cache. It has a big impact on the query performance. If it is too large, some data may be evicted from the cache before being reused. However, decreasing it will result in more mini-tasks and thereby heavier switching overhead.

Generally, this parameter is related to the target architecture, the data layouts and the queries, especially the L2 cache size, the L2 cache line size and the associativity. According to our experiments, it is not very sensitive to the type of queries. Once the target architecture and the data layouts are specified, it is feasible to run some calibration experiments in advance to determine the best value for this parameter.

Therefore, for a table scan, MiniTasking divides the table into n fine-grained data blocks, with each block suitable for the working set. Correspondingly, MiniTasking breaks the execution of each scan operator into n mini-tasks, according to the data blocks they use. Thereafter, when a data block is loaded by the first mini-task, MiniTasking schedules other mini-tasks that share this data block to execute one by one. When no mini-tasks use this data block, it will be replaced by the next data block. Thus the data resided in the cache can be maximally reused before being evicted.

The following example illustrates this data-centric scheduling method. Suppose there are three table scan operators Op_1, Op_2, Op_3 and they share the table T, as shown in Figure 5. Table T is divided into three data blocks. According to the data blocks they access, the three operators are broken into ($Op_{1,1}$, $Op_{1,2}$, $Op_{1,3}$), ($Op_{2,1}$, $Op_{2,2}$, $Op_{2,3}$), and ($Op_{3,1}$, $Op_{3,2}$, $Op_{3,3}$), respectively. MiniTasking schedules them in such an order: $Op_{1,1}$, $Op_{2,1}$, $Op_{3,1}$, $Op_{1,2}$, $Op_{2,2}$, $Op_{3,2}$, $Op_{1,3}$, $Op_{2,3}$, and $Op_{3,3}$. In this way, the data block (DT_j) loaded into the cache by $Op_{1,j}$ (j=1, 2, 3) can be reused by the subsequent mini-tasks $Op_{2,j}$ and $Op_{3,j}$.

5 Experimental Evaluation

5.1 Evaluation Methodology

We implement MiniTasking in the Shore database storage manager [6], which provides most of the popular storage features used in a modern commercial DBMS. Previous work show that Shore exhibits memory access behaviors similar to several commercial DBMSes [1]. Since Shore's original query scheduler is fairly serialized (executing one query after another), we have extended Shore to use a slightly more sophisticated scheduler which switches from one query to another after a certain time quantum or when this query yields voluntarily due to other reasons (e.g. I/Os). This scheduler emulates what would really happen with a multi-threaded or multi-processed commercial database server. Our results also show that this scheduler performs slightly better than the original scheduler in Shore. Therefore, we use this time quantum-based scheduler as our baseline to compare with MiniTasking.

Experimental Workloads. For DSS workloads, we use a TPC-H-like benchmark, which represents the activities of a complex business that manages, sells and distributes a large number of products [30]. The following are the table sizes in our TPC-H-like database: 600572 tuples in *Lineitem*, 150000 tuples in *Orders*, and 20000 tuples in *Part*.

Experimental Platform. Our evaluation is conducted on a machine with a 2.4GHz Intel Pentium 4 processor and 2.5GB of main memory. The processor includes two levels of caches: L1 and L2, whose characteristics are shown on Table 2. The operating system is Linux kernel 2.4.20. For measurements, we use a commercial tool, the Intel VTune performance tool [17], which collect performance statistics with negligible overhead.

5.2 Results for *Micro-Join*

We use a two-relation join query to examine MiniTasking, as shown in Figure 6. We vary the number of tuples in the two relations and examine four representative combinations for them, as shown in Table 1.

Our experiments show that MiniTasking improves the performance of join operations by 4%–12%. When a hash join is used, if the hash table on the inner relation is small enough to be put into the cache, MiniTasking can be effectively applied to the outer relation. For example, when two instances of the join query are running, MiniTasking improves the query performance by 9% in the case of Hash-1 and 12% in the case of Hash-2, as shown in Figure 7. MiniTasking has similar speedup for the index-based join

Table 1. The sizes of the outer and inner relations used by *Micro-join*

	Hash Joins		Index Joins	
Tuples	Hash-1	Hash-2	Index-1	Index-2
Outer	10^6	10^6	10^6	5,000
Inner	5,000	100	500,000	10^6

Table 2. Processor cache parameters of the evaluation platform

Parameters	L1 D cache	L2 cache
Size	8KB	512KB
Associativity	4-way	8-way
Cache line	64B	64B
Cache miss latency	7 cycles	350 cycles

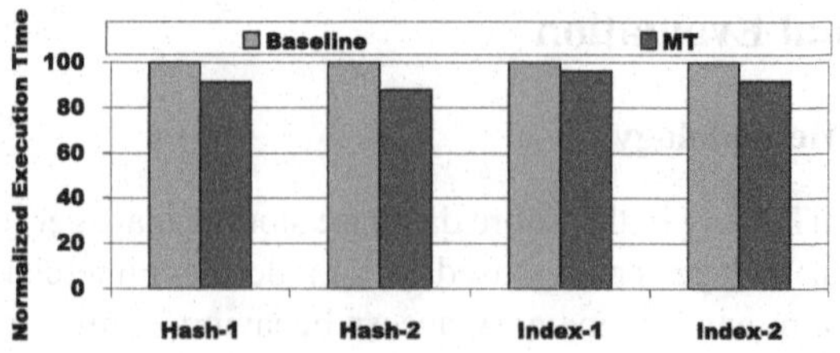

Fig. 7. Performance of join operations. MiniTasking reduces execution time up to 12.1% for hash joins and 8.2% for index nested-loops joins. MT stands for MiniTasking.

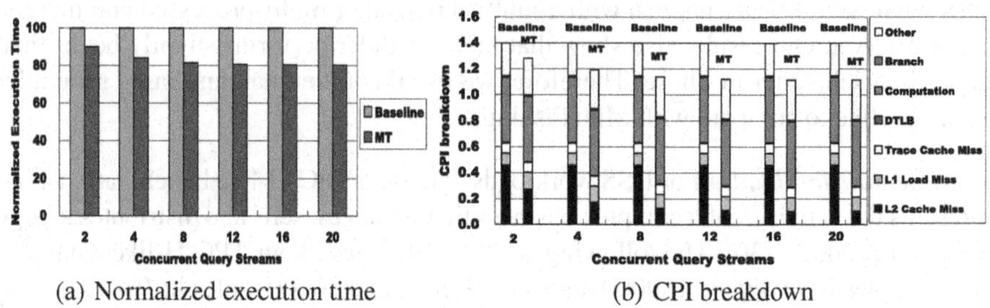

(a) Normalized execution time (b) CPI breakdown

Fig. 8. Performance of *throughput-real* tests. Each test runs several concurrent streams. The execution time of each test is normalized to the baseline without MiniTasking.

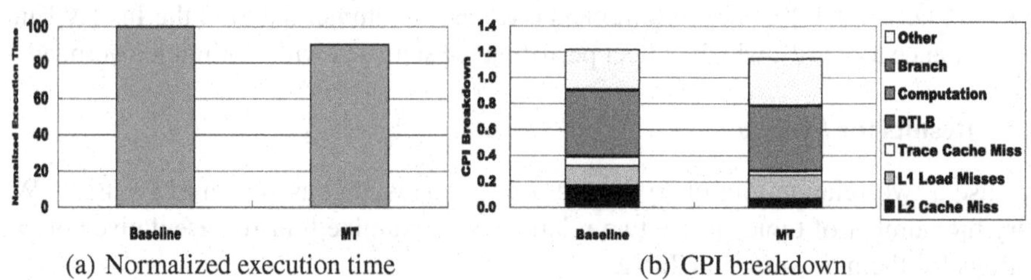

(a) Normalized execution time (b) CPI breakdown

Fig. 9. The execution time and the CPI breakdown of four concurrent queries (TPCH-Q1). The PAX data layout is used in Shore and MT.

since it can break the index probing into mini-tasks. As a result, MiniTasking reduces the query execution time by up to 8.2% for two concurrently running instances of the join query.

5.3 Results for *Throughput-Real*

We validate our MiniTasking strategy using a real workload, modeling after the throughput test of TPC-H benchmark. The standard TPC-H throughput test is composed of multiple concurrent streams. Each stream contains a sequence of TPC-H queries in an order which TPC-H benchmark specifies. Accordingly, our experiment follows these sequences and let each stream execute the six TPC-H queries we implemented.

Our experimental results show that MiniTasking is very effective for this workload. Figure 8(a) shows that the execution time of each test is reduced by 11%-20% for various number of concurrent query streams. As shown on Figure 8(b), the performance gain comes from the reduction in L2 cache misses: MiniTasking significantly reduces the number of L2 cache misses by 41%-79%. This is all because MiniTasking's locality-aware query scheduling and execution effectively improves the access temporal locality. Meanwhile, MiniTasking do not affect other processor events very much since it adds little overhead. Therefore, the improved L2 cache hit ratios is proportionally reflected into the end performance.

5.4 Improvement upon PAX Layout

Figure 9 shows the effects of MiniTasking on cache-conscious data layout such as PAX [1]. MiniTasking can still effectively reduce the number of L2 cache misses by 65% and the execution time by 9%. The performance speedup is less pronounced with PAX than with the default NSF layout because, with PAX that has significantly improved spatial locality in accesses, the L2 cache miss time contributes less to the execution time than with NSM.

6 Conclusion

In this paper, we propose a technique called MiniTasking to improve database performance for concurrent query execution by reducing the number of processor cache misses via three levels of locality-based scheduling. Through query level batching, operator level grouping and mini-task level scheduling, MiniTasking can significantly reduce L2 cache misses and execution time. Our experimental results show that, MiniTasking can significantly reduce the execution time up to 12% for joins. For the TPC-H throughput test workload, MiniTasking reduces the number of L2 cache misses up to 79% and improves the end performance up to 20%. With the Partition Attributes Across (PAX) layout, MiniTasking further reduces the cache misses by 65% and the execution time by 9%, which indicates that our technique well compliments previous cache-conscious layouts.

References

1. A. Ailamaki, D. J. DeWitt, and M. D. Hill. Data page layouts for relational databases on deep memory hierarchies. *The VLDB Journal*, 11(3):198–215, 2002.
2. A. Ailamaki, D. J. DeWitt, M. D. Hill, and D. A. Wood. DBMSs on a modern processor: Where does time go? In *VLDB '99*, pages 266–277, 1999.
3. A.-H. A. Badawy, A. Aggarwal, D. Yeung, and C.-W. Tseng. Evaluating the impact of memory system performance on software prefetching and locality optimizations. In *International Conference on Supercomputing*, pages 486–500, 2001.
4. P. A. Boncz, S. Manegold, and M. L. Kersten. Database architecture optimized for the new bottleneck: Memory access. In *VLDB '99*, pages 54–65, 1999.
5. B. Calder, C. Krintz, S. John, and T. Austin. Cache-conscious data placement. In *ASPLOS '98*, pages 139–149, 1998.

6. M. J. Carey, D. J. DeWitt, M. J. Franklin, N. E. Hall, M. L. McAuliffe, J. F. Naughton, D. T. Schuh, M. H. Solomon, C. K. Tan, O. G. Tsatalos, S. J. White, and M. J. Zwilling. Shoring up persistent applications. In *SIGMOD '94*, pages 383–394, 1994.
7. S. Carr, K. S. McKinley, and C.-W. Tseng. Compiler optimizations for improving data locality. In *ASPLOS '94*, pages 252–262, 1994.
8. S. Chen, P. B. Gibbons, and T. C. Mowry. Improving index performance through prefetching. In *SIGMOD '01*, pages 235–246, 2001.
9. S. Chen, P. B. Gibbons, T. C. Mowry, and G. Valentin. Fractal prefetching b+-trees: optimizing both cache and disk performance. In *SIGMOD '02*, pages 157–168, 2002.
10. N. N. Dalvi, S. K. Sanghai, P. Roy, and S. Sudarshan. Pipelining in multi-query optimization. In *PODS '01*, pages 59–70, 2001.
11. C. Ding and K. Kennedy. Inter-array data regrouping. In *Languages and Compilers for Parallel Computing*, pages 149–163, 1999.
12. C. Ding and M. Orlovich. The potential of computation regrouping for improving locality. In *ACM/IEEE SC2004*, Nov. 6-12, 2004.
13. S. Finkelstein. Common expression analysis in database applications. In *SIGMOD '82*, pages 235–245, 1982.
14. R. A. Hankins and J. M. Patel. Data morphing: An adaptive,cache-conscious storage technique. In *VLDB '03*. Morgan Kaufmann, 2003.
15. S. Harizopoulos, V. Shkapenyuk, and A. Ailamaki. Qpipe: A simultaneously pipelined relational query engine. In *SIGMOD '05*, pages 383–394, 2005.
16. IBM. Personal communication with IBM, Jan. 2005.
17. Intel Corporation. Intel vtune performance analyzer. http://www.intel.com/software/products/vtune/, 2004.
18. K. Kennedy and K. S. McKinley. Maximizing loop parallelism and improving data locality via loop fusion and distribution. In *Proceedings of the 6th International Workshop on Languages and Compilers for Parallel Computing*, pages 301–320. Springer-Verlag, 1994.
19. K. Kim, S. K. Cha, and K. Kwon. Optimizing multidimensional index trees for main memory access. In *SIGMOD '01*, pages 139–150. ACM Press, 2001.
20. J. L. Lo, L. A. Barroso, S. J. Eggers, K. Gharachorloo, H. M. Levy, and S. S. Parekh. An analysis of database workload performance on simultaneous multithreaded processors. In *ISCA '98*, pages 39–50. IEEE Computer Society, 1998.
21. K. S. McKinley, S. Carr, and C.-W. Tseng. Improving data locality with loop transformations. *ACM Transactions on Programming Languages and Systems*, 18(4):424–453, July 1996.
22. K. O'Gorman, D. Agrawal, and A. E. Abbadi. Multiple query optimization by cache-aware middleware using query teamwork. In *ICDE '02*, page 274. IEEE Computer Society, 2002.
23. J. Philbin, J. Edler, O. J. Anshus, C. C. Douglas, and K. Li. Thread scheduling for cache locality. In *ASPLOS '96*, pages 60–71. ACM Press, 1996.
24. R. Ramamurthy, D. J. DeWitt, and Q. Su. A case for fractured mirrors. In *VLDB '02*, pages 430–441, 2002.
25. J. Rao and K. A. Ross. Making b+- trees cache conscious in main memory. In *SIGMOD '00*, pages 475–486, New York, NY, USA, 2000. ACM Press.
26. P. Roy, S. Seshadri, S. Sudarshan, and S. Bhobe. Efficient and extensible algorithms for multi query optimization. In *SIGMOD '00*, pages 249–260. ACM Press, 2000.
27. T. Sellis and S. Ghosh. On the multiple-query optimization problem. *IEEE Transactions on Knowledge and Data Engineering*, 2(2):262–266, 1990.
28. T. K. Sellis. Multiple-query optimization. *ACM Trans. Database Syst.*, 13(1):23–52, 1988.
29. A. Shatdal, C. Kant, and J. F. Naughton. Cache conscious algorithms for relational query processing. In *VLDB '94*, pages 510–521, 1994.
30. Transaction processing performance council. http://www.tpc.org.

31. P. Trancoso, J.-L. Larriba-Pey, Z. Zhang, and J. Torrellas. The memory performance of DSS commercial workloads in shared-memory multiprocessors. In *HPCA '97*, 1997.
32. M. E. Wolf and M. S. Lam. A data locality optimizing algorithm. In *PLDI '91*, 1991.
33. J. Zhou and K. A. Ross. Buffering accesses to memory-resident index structures. In *VLDB '03*, pages 405–416, 2003.
34. Y. Zhou, L. Wang, D. W. Clark, and K. Li. Thread scheduling for out-of-core applications with memory server on multicomputers. In *IOPADS '99*, pages 57–67. ACM Press, 1999.

Cache Consistency in Mobile XML Databases

Stefan Böttcher

University of Paderborn, Computer Science, Fürstenallee 11, 33102 Paderborn, Germany
stb@uni-paderborn.de
http://wwwcs.upb.de/cs/boettcher/

Abstract. Whenever an XML database is used to provide transactional access to mobile clients in multi-hop networks, standard database technologies like query processing and concurrency control have to be adapted to fundamentally different requirements, including limited bandwidth and unforeseeable lost connections. We present a query processing approach that reduces XML data exchange to the exchange of difference XML fragments wherever possible. Additionally, within our approach transactions can even use cached results of outdated queries and of neighbor clients, wherever they result in a reduction of data exchange. Furthermore, our approach supports a pipelined exchange of queries and partial answers. Finally, we present a timestamp-based approach to concurrency control that guarantees cache consistency and minimizes data exchange between the mobile clients and the XML database server.

1 Introduction

XML has become a widely accepted standard for data exchange in the Web, and XPath [16] is most widely used in query languages accessing Web data and XML databases. Whenever an XML database is used by multiple clients in mobile ad-hoc networks, database technologies face new challenges. For example, transaction management has to consider unpredictable disconnections of clients for applications that require transactional guarantees like serializability of histories of concurrent transactions. Similarly, limited bandwidth and limited energy supply require new approaches to query processing which includes data exchange, replication, and caching of query results. Within a multi-hop mobile network, it appears to be promising to interchange data between mobile participants that cache different XML data fragments. However, the identification of outdated data and an integration of caching with transaction synchronization become even more challenging than in traditional client-server systems.

In this paper, we present an integrated approach to XML query processing, transaction synchronization and caching in multi-hop mobile networks that guarantees transaction serializability and that is optimized towards minimal data exchange. By minimizing the data exchange required for correct transaction processing, our approach saves the consumption of limited resources like bandwidth and also of energy supply, whenever the energy required for sending and receiving data significantly exceeds the energy required for internal computations. In order to achieve this goal, our paper addresses and solves the following four problems. First, how we can reuse cached XML fragments of multiple mobile clients for query processing in multi-hop networks instead of retrieving all the data from the XML database. Second, how can

J.X. Yu, M. Kitsuregawa, and H.V. Leong (Eds.): WAIM 2006, LNCS 4016, pp. 300–312, 2006.
© Springer-Verlag Berlin Heidelberg 2006

we efficiently identify which XML fragments are missing in the cache of a network node. Third, how can we identify outdated data without additional communication overhead. Forth, how can we guarantee transaction serializability with a minimum of data exchange.

In order to solve the problems mentioned, our paper presents the following new contributions. First, we show how cached query results can be reused. Second, we provide a fast detection technique for missing XML data fragments. Third, we reuse the serializability check results of validation for cache consistency checking and maintenance. Finally, we provide a variety of techniques to minimize XML data exchange. Therefore, we consider our approach to be useful to almost all applications which need transactional guarantees during their work on XML fragments and for which access to an XML database from single-hop and multi-hop mobile networks is a major bottleneck, i.e. is most energy or time consuming.

The related works to our research involve approaches based on data replication [8,9,11], works that discuss caching but do not take advantage of transaction synchronization for cache consistency checking (e.g. [6,7]) as well as protocols for the synchronization of mobile transactions (e.g. [15]). A previous approach to the combination of caching and synchronization ([4]) considers only transactions that involve at most one client, i.e. it does neither synchronize transactions that involve multiple clients, nor does it optimize cache access in multi-hop environments. As a consequence, it does neither propagate nor re-compute forwarded queries or partial answers. In addition to propagation and computation of forwarded queries and partial answers, our approach includes a bit-vector based test for reusing cached results. Therefore, to the best of the author's knowledge, our integration of XML data caching and transaction synchronization in multi-hop ad-hoc networks has not been proposed anywhere before.

2 Reusing Cached XML Data

We apply a variety of techniques to reduce the bandwidth consumed for the transport of XML fragments from one node of the network to another node. These techniques include XPath query translation, XML fragment caching, pipelined reuse of cached XML fragments, and computation of forwarded queries. In order to preserve correctness of transactions, transactions are separated into the following phases: a *read phase* where they are allowed to read cached and possibly outdated data, followed by a *validation phase* where cache consistency is checked and repaired, and an optional *write phase* for successfully validated writing transactions.

2.1 XPath Query Translation

In order to answer an application's XPath database query AQ, it is sometimes necessary to access more data than we get as the query result of AQ. This occurs especially in the cases, where we have to access data in order to evaluate the filter expressions of AQ that would reduce the selected answer fragment. In order to retrieve the relevant data, we use the technique of projecting XPath expressions as described in [13]. We use this technique to translate AQ into a set of queries S={Q1,...,Qn} such that the results to the queries of S are sufficient to answer AQ. For the following discussion, we assume that the translation of AQ into S has been performed and we discuss how to treat the queries Qi∈ S within our approach.

2.2 Fragment Caching and Reuse

During the read phase, we reuse the cached query results regardless of whether they are outdated or incomplete. Note that errors are detected and repaired within the following validation phase. The whole process of transferring an XML fragment to the client can be considered as a pipelined process where sub-fragments of the queried fragment are retrieved from the next node on the shortest path to the server (c.f. Figure 1). Whenever these sub-fragments are sufficient to answer the query, we do not need to retrieve the queried fragment from the server. In other words, our goal is that the server transfers only those sub-fragments which are not cached in a node on the shortest path from the requesting client to the server.

Of course, a query only has to be forwarded, if there is still data missing to answer the query. That is the reason why the set of queries forwarded to the next node on the path to the server may change, say from Qs to Qs1 to Qs2. As long as the complete answer to a given query set Qs on the requesting client is not yet computed, each cache on the way from the requesting client to the server submits a pair (Qsi/PAi) consisting of a forwarded XPath query set Qsi and the XPath string PAi that describes the partial answer to Qs(i-1) collected so far. In the opposite direction XML fragments are sent to the clients, however we only send XML difference fragments, i.e. data that are not contained in any cache on the path to the client.

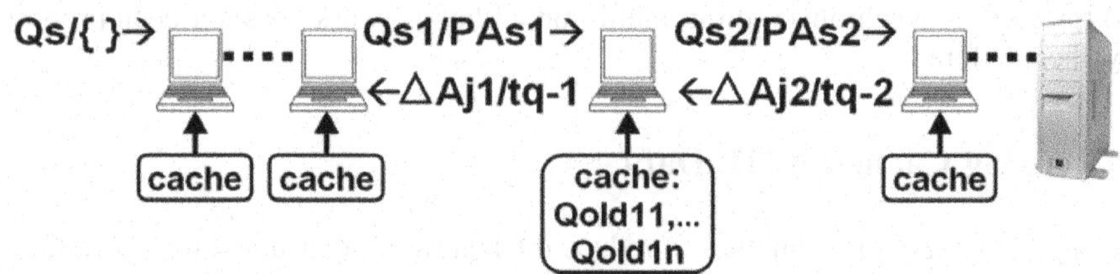

Fig. 1. Answering a set Qs of generated queries in the read phase

2.3 Reusing Old Data During the Read Phase

During the read phase, cached data is reused regardless of the time-stamps associated with the data. This may result in the use of outdated data. The motivation behind this is that usually XML databases contain a lot of data that very rarely changes. For example, let us look at changes in a commercial XML database that contains customer and product descriptions: the name or the address of a given customer or the name or the description of an ordered product will change very rarely. Even if that data changes from time to time, no error occurs because each transaction is validated. Only if the data has been changed since the last time when it was validated, it is outdated, i.e. only in this case outdated data has been used by a query. But even then, it is quite common that only a small portion of the data has changed, e.g. a phone number in the customer's contact data. Because we can compute outdated data from the global write set (defined in Section 3.1), within our approach, only this changed XML difference fragment is transferred from one node to the next on the way from the server to the clients. This offers the clients on that path the chance to actualize their cached data using the transferred fragment, i.e. they are again up to date without re-submitting their query to the XML database server.

2.4 Using Incomplete Data and Data Integration During the Read Phase

When a query can be partially answered by a fragment that is cached on a client, it is not necessary to retrieve the whole fragment from the server. Instead, the query result can be combined from both, the cached fragment and the remaining part that is not found in the cache but has to be retrieved from the server. We use a unique document numbering scheme outlined in [2] for the server-side XML document and all partial copies on a client. This numbering scheme allows each node to integrate XML fragments received over the network into its locally stored XML fragments at the correct position.

Within the next subsections, we outline how we identify which data is contained in a cache and which is missing and whether the query set Qsi must be forwarded.

2.5 Forwarding Queries and Returning Partial Answer Fragments

The computation of partial answers is based on asynchronous messages that are sent back and forth on the shortest path from the requesting client to the server. There are two kinds of incoming messages to a client and two kinds of outgoing message calls from a client. The first incoming message, `Query`, is querying for an XML fragment which is required to answer a query on the requesting client. The first outgoing message calls `Query` again on the next client on the path to the server and asks for the same or for a smaller XML fragment.

A second outgoing message `Answer` contains a partial answer fragment to a query set `Qs1` received as part of a previous `Query` message. Finally, the second kind of incoming message receives such a partial answer fragment that is contained in an `Answer` message that has been sent by the next client on the path to the server. While the `Query` messages are forwarded from each client to the next node on the shortest path to the server, the `Answer` messages are forwarded in the opposite direction, i.e. towards the requesting client.

When `Query` messages are forwarded from one client to the next on the shortest path to the server, they contain not only a set of queries, but also a set of XPath expressions describing partial answers found in the caches of previous clients on the path to the server. To achieve this goal, the implementation of the `Query` message computes two sets for a given set `Qs1` of queries and a given set `PAs1` of partial answer XPath expressions: the set `Qs2` of queries to be forwarded and the set `PAs2` of partial answer XPath expressions. The implementation of the `Query` message is outlined in Algorithm 1 below.

Algorithm 1. Implementation of the asynchronous method used for querying

```
Query(in:Qs1,PAs1)
// used in asynchr. output messages: Qs2, PAs2
{ Qs2 = ∅ ;  PAs2 = empty ;
  for each Qi in Qs1
  { computeXPathExpr( Qi, XPA, QF ) ;
```

```
(6)      if ( QF!=empty )    Qs2 = Qs2 ∪ {QF} ;
(7)      if ( XPA!=empty)    PAs2 = PAs2 | XPA ;
(8)    }
(9)    send( NextClientOnPathToRequestingClient,
(10)         Answer( computeLocalAnswer(PAs2-PAs1) ) ) ;
(11)   if ( Qs2 != Ø )
(12)     send( NextClientOnPathToServer,
(13)       Query(Qs2, (PAs1|PAs2) );
(14) }
```

The input parameters of the `Query` message (line (1)) are a set `Qs1` of given queries and a set `PAs1` of XPath expressions describing partial answers to `Qs1` that have already been found. In (line(3)), two local variables, i.e. `Qs2` and `PAs2` are initialized to the empty set and to the empty XPath query string respectively. `Qs2` describes the set of queries to be forwarded, and `PAs2` describes the cached query results of the actual client node that are relevant to the queries in `Qs2`.

Then (within lines (4)-(8)), the set Qs2 of queries and the XPath expression `PAs2` are computed. Qs2 simply collects the queries QF to be forwarded (line (6)) and `PAs2` collects the XPath expressions `XPA` describing reusable cached query results (line (7)) from each call of the procedure `computeXPathExpr`. The procedure `computeXPathExpr` (given in Section 2.6) computes a query `QF` to be forwarded and a partial answer XPath expression `XPA` for a single query `Qi` contained in `Qs`.

Within line (10), the partial answer fragment Ans1 is computed from the difference XPath expression `(PAs2-PAs1)`, and it is sent back to the next client on the path to the requesting client. We use the difference `(PAs2-PAs1)` here, because it is not necessary to include a fragment described by `PAs1` in the answer as this fragment of the answer has already been found.

Finally, if the XPath query string `Qs2` to be forwarded is non-empty (line (11)), a `Query` message is sent to the next client on the shortest path to the server (lines (12)-(13)). The parameters are the computed set Qs2 of queries to be forwarded and the XPath expression `(PAs1|PAs2)`, which is the union of the XPath expression `PAs1` of previously found partial answer fragments and the XPath expression `PAs2` describing the partial answer fragment found on the actual client.

To answer a query, that partial answer `PAs2` of the locally cached fragment `F` that is not covered by the partial answers `PAs1` of previous clients, i.e. `PAs2-PAs1` is transferred to the requesting client (line (10)). A straight-forward implementation of the message `Answer` simply forwards each partial answer XML fragment to the requesting client by sending the message `Answer` again. The server simply answers an incoming query by accessing the XML database and returns the answer fragment within a separate `Answer` message. The `Answer` message contains also the actual time-stamp generated for the purpose of transaction synchronization and cache consistency checking.

2.6 Conditions for Query Forwarding and Using a Containment Test

As we can see from lines (11)-(13) of Algorithm1, queries are forwarded only if the set `Qs2` contains at least one non-empty query `QF`. Given Query `Qi`, the computation of a query `QF` to be forwarded is done by a procedure `computeXPathExpr` (outlined in Figure 2 below), which additionally computes an XPath expression `XPA` describing the partial answer found in a local cache. A call to computeXPathExpr returns that QF is empty (line (10) of Figure 2), i.e. an XPath query Qi∈Qs is not forwarded, if the answer to Qi is contained in the cached query result of a previous query Qold. This could be tested by checking query containment (c.f. line (9) of Figure 2). The containment tester tries to prove that Qi *is subsumed by* Qold, i.e. every answer to Qi is also an answer to Qold - independently of the database state. When the test yields that Qi is subsumed by Qold, this is sufficient to guarantee that every node selected by Qi is also selected by Qold. Therefore, Qold is sufficient to search for the fragment F that answers Qi.

However, the execution time needed for a complete XPath containment test would exhaust the mobile devices' power and time resources (e.g. [12]). Therefore, we have added a number of optimizations that avoid the containment test in most cases, i.e. compute XPA and QF from Qi without performing an XPath containment test at all. Instead, wherever possible, we substitute an XPath containment test with a more efficient test based on *DTD node bit-vectors* which are described in the next section. Furthermore, we simplify the remaining XPath containment tests by using a fast but incomplete tester [5].

```
(1)  computeXPathExpr( in: Qi ; out: XPA, QF )
(2)  { XPA = empty ;
(3)    for each query Qold, the result of which is cached do
(4)    { if ( (Qi.bitvector and Qold.bitvector) == 0 )    skip;
         //Qold is not relevant,as they have no bit in common
(5)      else
(6)      if ((Qi.bitvector and complement(Qold.bitvector))==0)
(7)       //test  containment  only  if  every  bit  set  in  the
            bit-vector of Qi is set in the bit-vector of Qold
(8)      and (     Qi.querystring == Qold.querystring
(9)            or Qi is subsumed by Qold )
(10)      { QF = empty ;   XPA = Qi ; return ; }
(11)     else
(12)      { XPA = XPA | Qold ; }
(13)   }
(14)   QF=Qi ;                         // forward Qi unchanged
(15) }
```

Fig. 2. Computing partial answer and forwarded XPath expression for a query Qi

2.7 Mapping of Queries to DTD Node Bit-Vectors

The requesting client, that submits a query Qi, generates a DTD node bit-vector for Qi as an approximation to decide whether or not a cached result of a query Qold can be reused for answering Qi. The idea behind DTD node bit-vectors is that Qold can be reused, only if Qold and Qi select at least one common attribute or element. In such a case, we call Qold *relevant to* Qi.

A *DTD node bit-vector* contains one bit for each element or attribute defined in a DTD. Basically a query Qi is translated into its bit-vector by setting a bit for each *leaf element* and for each attribute selected by Qi or accessed by a filter of Qi. Within a query Qi = /E1[./E2[E3]/E4]/E5/E6, the elements E3, E4 and E6 are the *leaf elements of* Qi whereas E1, E2 and E5 are not. Note that an element can be a leaf element of a query, although all elements in an XML database with the same name represent inner XML element nodes.

Note however that the DTD node bit-vector is changed for a query `Qold`, the result of which is cached. `Qold` is translated into its bit-vector by setting a bit only for each leaf element and for each attribute selected by `Qold`, i.e. the elements or attribute occurring only in a filter are ignored. For example, the bit for E6 is the only bit set in the bit-vector of a query `Qold`=/E1[./E2[E3]/E4]/E5/E6.

Whenever a query result of an old query `Qold` is cached, the query string and the bit-vector of `Qold` are cached too. The bit-vectors are used to restrict the number of XPath containment tests as follows. Only if each bit set in the bit-vector of `Qi` is also set in the bit-vector of `Qold` (line (6) of Figure 2), we perform the fast containment test for XPath queries described in [5]. Otherwise, `Qi` can not be answered completely by `Qold`, i.e. we do not need an XPath containment test.

Now, we can explain the remaining parts of the procedure `computeXPathExpr`. This procedure processes one cached query `Qold` after the other (line (3)) and stops immediately if a containment test was successful (line (10)). It distinguishes the following cases for reducing the number of containment tests.

First, if the bit-vectors of `Qi` and `Qold` have no bit set in common (line (4)), we are then sure that there is no leaf element or attribute node in any valid XML document that is both selected by `Qold` and required to answer `Qi`. In other words, we are sure that the cached query result for `Qold` cannot contribute to answer `Qi`. If this condition holds for all old query results `Qold` in a client, then the query `QF` forwarded to answer `Qi` is simply the same as `Qi` (line (14)), i.e. `Qi` is forwarded to the next client on the path to the server.

Second, if `Qi` selects or a filter of `Qi` depends on at least one leaf element or attribute that is not selected by `Qold`, there is at least one bit in set in the bit-vector of `Qi` that is not set in the bit-vector of `Qold` (i.e. the test in line (6) fails). As the query result `Qold` may partially contribute to the answer of Qi, the XPath query expression of `Qold` is added to `XPA`, the XPath query expression of partial answers to `Qi`. Note that the containment test (line (9)) is skipped, and the only tests required so far are two fast tests on bit-vectors.

Third, if the bit-vectors of `Qi` sets a subset of the bits of the bit-vector of `Qold` (line(6)), it is first checked whether the query strings of `Qi` and `Qold` are identical (line (8)). If the query strings are identical, the fragment that is cached for `Qold` is exactly what we need to answer `Qi`. Therefore, forwarding of `Qi` is stopped.

Finally, only if none the above three conditions applies, the fast but incomplete containment test described in [5] is performed. If the containment test yields the result that `Qi` is subsumed by `Qold`, `Qold` can be searched for the fragment `F` that answers `Qi`. Therefore again, the forwarding of `Qi` is stopped.

To summarize the contributions of Section 2: After translating an application query AQ into a set Qs of queries Qi, we have suggested to reduce data transfer by using cached results and outdated data, and to ask only for missing data fragments. Furthermore, we have shown how to compute XPath queries for missing data fragments and how to check whether or a cached result can be reused and whether or not a query has to be forwarded. The advantages of these techniques are that queries are sent only when necessary and only to as few nodes on the path to the server as necessary and that the size of transferred answer fragments is reduced to a minimum.

3 Cache Consistency and Synchronization of Mobile Transactions

3.1 Overview of Our Validation Based Approach to Synchronization

As mobile clients have a higher chance to loose their connection to the database server than traditional static clients, we do not grant locks to resources accessed by mobile clients. Instead, we use a server-side scheduler that combines time-stamps and an optimistic approach. While this idea has been applied to relational databases, we use XML databases and want to minimize data exchange within multi-hop environment, both of which lead to new requirements - to be discussed later.

As within the traditional validation protocols ([10]), our transactions are divided into phases. A read phase is followed by a validation phase, which in case of successful validation is eventually followed by a write phase. Transactions are ordered according to the end of their read phase, i.e. transaction `Told` is defined to be older than a transaction `T`, if `Told` ends its read phase (and thereby starts its validation phase) before `T` ends its read phase. Younger transactions `T` are validated against older transactions `Told`. As the scheduler's decision on commit or abort during the validation phase of a `T` depends on timestamps and data read or written by `T`, each transaction `T` uses a *read set* and a so called *private write set* to inform the scheduler about XML data fragments that have been read or shall be written by `T`. The scheduler combines the private write sets received by all (non-aborted) transactions into the so called *global write set*, which is used to check whether an actually validating transaction `T` conflicts with the write operations of previous transactions `Told`.

Inspired by the idea of [14] that uses queries in predicative validation, we use XPath expressions instead of XML fragments within the read set and, wherever possible, within the private write set too. This significantly reduces the amount of data exchanged for the purpose of validation as the XPath expressions are usually much smaller than the XML fragments read by a transaction.

Within the *read phase*, transactions query the XML database itself or the cached copies of XML fragments in the network which may contain outdated data. Furthermore, write operations during the read phase of a transaction are performed on the client's local copy of an XML database fragment, and both the operations and the new values of altered fragments are stored in the *private write set* of the transaction. Finally, at the end of the read phase, a writing transaction transfers its *private write set* to the server. Note however that the private write set is not applied to the server-side XML database as long as the transaction has not been validated successfully.

During the *validation phase*, the transactions' queries together with the time-stamps computed for the query results are compared with the write operations performed by concurrent transactions as described below. As a result of the validation phase, an XML difference fragment is returned from the database server to all the mobile clients participating in the transaction. This *XML difference fragment* contains all the information needed to bring the client up to date, i.e., the new values of outdated data and the information which data has been inserted or deleted on the server by concurrent transactions since the data used by the client has been read from the server. If this XML difference fragment is empty, the transaction has only used actual data; therefore the clients know that the transaction has been completed successfully. Otherwise, the clients use the XML difference fragment to refresh their cached data and assign a new time-stamp to the refreshed data before they restart the transaction. By using XML difference fragments to refresh cached data, we avoid the conflicts that previously lead to the abortion of the transaction, and we bring the client up to date without reading all the data used by the client again.

Within the *write phase*, the server-side transaction scheduler applies all the write operations contained in the private write set of a successfully validated transaction to the XML database. Then the scheduler generates a time-stamp for the write operations and copies the transaction's private write set together with the generated time-stamp into the server-side global write set, which is now actualized for the validation of further concurrent transactions.

3.2 Time Stamp Generation

As mentioned earlier, the scheduler generates a new timestamp during the write phase of each transaction *after* the transaction's changes have been made permanent to the database. Timestamp generation is the only mutual exclusive step, i.e. the only step that has to be done in a critical section. Furthermore, the actual time-stamp is assigned to each query submitted to the server, *before* the query is applied to the server-side XML database. The resulting answer XML fragment is associated with this timestamp and reflects the time at which data collection for this fragment started. This time-stamp will be used in the validation phase. Finally, a new time-stamp is generated *before* the data collection for an XML difference fragment is started.

Time-stamps are assigned to the query results and XML difference fragments *before* the data collection for the query and the XML difference fragment starts, whereas time-stamps for write operations are generated *after* the data has been written to the XML database. This is required for the following reason. When a query (or an XML difference fragment computation) of transaction `T` with a time-stamp `t` conflicts with write operations of a transaction `Told` with an older time-stamp `told`, we are then sure that the write operations performed by `Told` on the XML database are completed before the read operations of the query or the XML difference computation for `T` start. This allows us to conclude that no transaction dependency "T reads dirty data that has been changed by `Told`" can result from this particular query and this particular write phase.

Whenever a cached XML fragment is transferred to another client, the original time-stamp set by the database server for this fragment is associated with the copy too.

3.3 Details of the Validation Phase

Within the validation phase, each transaction `T` is validated against older writing transactions `Told`. As we allow for parallel validation of transactions, we have to check for read-write conflicts and for write-write conflicts. Note however that it is not necessary to validate a transaction `T` against older reading transactions, as they did not chance the XML database and therefore did not change the data read by `T`.

In comparison to node-based locking or validation approaches, we use the XPath expressions that have been used in the data collection phase of a query also in the validation phase. These XPath expressions are applied to the XML difference fragments F that are stored in the global write set, i.e. to the old values of updated and deleted fragments and to the new values of updated and inserted fragments. A read operation *read(Q)* that uses an XPath expression Q and a write operation *write(F)* that modifies a fragment F are defined to be in conflict if Q(F), i.e. Q applied to F, is non-empty. Whenever *read(Q)* and *write(F)* are in conflict, the time-stamps associated to

Q and to F are used to check whether or not *read(Q)* was a dirty read. Whenever, the time-stamp of F is at least as old as the time-stamp of Q, we are then sure that the values read by *read(Q)* could not have been invalidated by the operation *write(F)*. Therefore, Q(F) is added to the XML difference fragment only if the time-stamp of Q is older than the time-stamp of F.

Some write-write conflicts have to be checked because at validation time, we can not be sure whether the older transaction writes conflicting data first. Similarly as for queries, we use the XPath expressions X that occur in write operations and that are stored as operations in the validating transaction's private write set. A write operation using an XPath expression X is *in conflict* with a write operation modifying a fragment F, if and only if X(F) is non-empty. Similarly as with read-write conflicts, a write-write conflict of an older transaction `Told` and a validating transaction `T` can not yield a lost update if we are sure that `Told` writes before `T` writes. This is the case, if the time-stamp generated in the write phase of `Told` is older than the time-stamp for `T`'s validation phase begins.

If however, we have a write-write conflict and the time-stamp of the write phase of `Told` either is not older than the time-stamp for `T`'s validation begins or has not yet been created, we can not be sure whether write-write conflicts between `Told` and `T` yield lost updates. In this case, we have to prevent that `T` writes before `Told` writes. This can either be done by restarting `T` or by suspending the write phase of `T` until `Told`'s write phase is completed. Which option is the best choice, depends on the server's stability considerations, i.e. we decided for a stable server to suspend the start of `T`'s write phase until `Told`'s write phase is completed instead of aborting and restarting `T` as in the standard parallel validation protocol. The advantage of fewer restarts than in the standard parallel validation protocol is that we reduce the amount of data that has to be exchanged between server and client, which is essential in mobile environments.

4 Reducing Data Exchange for Validation

4.1 Reduced Data Exchange at the End of the Read Phase

Data exchange at the end of the read phase is minimized because the data needed for validation is restricted to a minimum as follows. The largest reduction is to exchange XPath expressions or IDs for XPath expressions instead of exchanging read XML fragments. A second reduction applies to delete operations, for which the client sends only paths to the deleted fragments instead of sending the deleted fragment to the server. Each insert operation is sent as a pair consisting of an inserted fragment and the path to it. A third reduction applies to update operations. We use the path to each updated fragment for both, deleting the old fragment and inserting the new fragment, i.e. we avoid sending the old fragment back to the server. Finally, whenever the XPath expressions are stored on the server-side and associated with IDs, the system can exchange IDs instead of strings for XPath expressions except for the first time when an XPath expression is transmitted.

4.2 XML Difference Fragment Computation in the Validation Phase

In the validation phase, the scheduler computes which data is missing or outdated but required on the clients to correctly answer all its computed queries Qi. The scheduler compiles an XML difference fragment containing this required data. The XML difference fragment contains the answer fragment X to the union of all queries Qi of the transaction minus those fragments that have been transferred or validated before and have not been changed since the last transfer or validation. In order to check whether or not a fragment has been changed since the last transfer or validation, the time-stamps are used as described in Section 3.2. After all the fragments have been subtracted from X which, according to the time-stamps, may contain outdated data, the remaining XML difference fragment is transferred to the client.

4.3 XML Difference Fragment Propagation to the Client

Once computed, the XML difference fragment is transferred hop by hop on the shortest path from the server to the requesting client. This fragment can be used to actualize the cache content of the inner network nodes. Whenever the cache of a requesting client or of an inner network node caches an XML fragment that is actualized by applying the updates of an XML difference fragment, the actualized fragment inherits the time-stamp of the XML difference fragment.

Note that this cache actualization of intermediate network clients results in a more actual state of is their cached data without extra bandwidth consumption. The advantage of this more actualized intermediate caches is that transactions started on other clients may eventually reuse this cached data, i.e., we can reduce the number of required data exchange steps of further queries or it may lead to fewer failing validation steps of other transactions. Furthermore, note that this advantage holds even if the difference fragment is empty. Then, all the clients on the shortest path from the server to the requesting client know the following. All the data that is needed for the queries of the actual transaction and that these clients have in their cache is up to date. Therefore, all the clients on the path to server including the requesting client can modify their time-stamps without exchanging additional data.

5 Time-Stamp Computation for Mixed Fragments

When queries are partially answered by cached query results, there are in principle two options for computing the time-stamp of the query. First, the query result can combine the data and take the oldest time-stamp as the time-stamp of the combined result. Second, the query can be split, i.e. it can be replaced with two or more queries, each representing one cached fragment. Both approaches have their pros and the cons. The first approach is easy to implement and does not require to communicate and to manage extra query strings. In comparison, the second approach, in general, attaches newer time-stamps which may lead to fewer failing validations.

6 Summary and Conclusions

As mobile clients may lose their connection to a database server, we do not grant locks to resources accessed by mobile clients. Instead, we use an optimistic approach that allows unprepared disconnections of clients at any time without blocking the server. Additionally, our approach allows repairing lost connections, i.e. continuing interrupted transactions after link failures have been repaired without restarting a running transaction. Furthermore, it allows for cross-transaction optimization, i.e. to use cached and outdated data of previous transactions, and it allows using cached data of other clients.

Data exchange during the read phase is further reduced by a pipelined data exchange technique that considers partial answers that have already been found and transports only missing XML difference fragments. Furthermore, missing XML difference fragments are taken from the first client found in order to keep the transportation distance as short as possible.

Data exchange in the validation phase is reduced to an absolute minimum as the XML difference fragments contain only the required information about outdated fragments and fragments not yet cached at the client. Furthermore, the difference fragments can be used by the inner mobile network nodes to update their caches.

Cache consistency is checked and guaranteed within our approach as a result of the validation step during the transactions' commit-request and does not require any additional data exchange. We regard this as a significant contribution as validation-based synchronization appears to be appropriate for mobile transactions, and our approach reduces the major bottle-neck and most energy consuming process in mobile networks, i.e. the size of exchanged data fragments.

Although, we have used a validation based approach on the server, our approach of validating clients, that perform a cache consistency check without extra XML fragment exchange, is not restricted to client-server architectures that use validation as a server-side synchronization protocol. [3] shows that that client-side cache-consistency checking integrates well with centralized or distributed servers in wired networks that use a lock-based protocol. Finally, although we have described our approach for a single stable XML database server, we consider the approach to be applicable also to transactions running on multiple databases located on different MANET nodes, if it is appropriately combined with an atomic commit protocol for MANETs as e.g. [1].

References

[1] Joos-Hendrik Böse, Stefan Böttcher, Le Gruenwald, Sebastian Obermeier, Heinz Schweppe, Thorsten Steenweg. An Integrated Commit Protocol for Mobile Network Databases. The 9th International Database Engineering and Applications Symposium (IDEAS 2005). Montreal, Canada, July 2005.

[2] Stefan Böttcher, Adelhard Türling. Caching XML Data for Mobile Web Clients. International Conference on Internet Computing IC'04, Las Vegas, June 2004.

[3] Stefan Böttcher, Adelhard Türling. Transaction Synchronisation for XML Data in Client Server Web Applications. In: Informatik 2001 , Tagungsband der GI-Jahrestagung 25.-28. September 2001, Vienna, Austria , Volume 1, pages 388-395.

[4] Stefan Böttcher. Repairing lost connections of mobile transactions with minimal XML data exchange. IFIP TC8 Working Conference on Mobile Information Systems (MOBIS). Oslo, Norway, September 2004.

[5] Stefan Böttcher, Rita Steinmetz. Testing Containment of XPath Expressions in order to Reduce the Data Transfer to Mobile Clients. 7th East-European Conference on Advances in Databases and Information Systems, Dresden, Germany, September 2003.

[6] Çetintemel, Ugur, Peter J. Keleher, Bobby Bhattacharjee and Michael J. Franklin: Deno: A Decentralized, Peer-to-Peer Object-Replication System for Weakly Connected Environments. IEEE Trans. Computers 52(7): 943-959 (2003)

[7] Chung, I.-Y., Hwang, C.-S.: Transactional Cache Management with Aperiodic Invalidation Scheme in Mobile Environments. ASIAN 1999: 50-61

[8] Hara, T., and Madria, S.: Consistency management among replicas in peer-to-peer mobile ad hoc networks, Proc. of Int'l Symposium on Reliable Distributed Systems (SRDS 2005), pp.1-8, 2005.

[9] Karumanchi, G., Muralidharan, S., and Prakash, R.: Information dissemination in partitionable mobile ad hoc networks, Proc. Int'l Symposium on Reliable Distributed Systems (SRDS'99), pp.4-13, 1999.

[10] Kung, H.T., Robinson, J.T.: On Optimistic Methods for Concurrency Control. ACM TODS, 6, 2, 1981.

[11] Luo, J., Hubaux, J.P., and Eugster, P.: PAN: Providing reliable storage in mobile ad hoc networks with probabilistic quorum systems, Proc. ACM MobiHoc'03, pp.1-12, 2003.

[12] Frank Neven, Thomas Schwentick: XPath Containment in the Presence of Disjunction, DTDs, and Variables. ICDT 2003: 315-329.

[13] Amelie Marian, Jerome Simeon: Projecting XML Documents, VLDB 2003.

[14] Manuel Reimer: Solving the Phantom Problem by Predicative Optimistic Concurrency Control, 9th VLDB, Florenz, 1983.

[15] Türker, Can, Klaus Haller, Christoph Schuler and Hans-Jörg Schek. "How can we support Grid Transactions? Towards Peer-to-Peer Transaction Processing". In: Proceedings of the Second Conference on Innovative Data Systems Research, CIDR 2005, January 4-7, 2005, Asilomar, CA, USA, pp. 174-185, 2005.

[16] World Wide Web Consortium (W3C), XML Path Language (XPath) Version 1.0, *W3C Recommendation*, http://www.w3.org/TR/xpath/, 1999.

Bulkloading Updates for Moving Objects*

Xiaoyuan Wang, Weiwei Sun, and Wei Wang

Department of Computing and Information Technology
Fudan University, Shanghai, China
{xy_wang, wwsun, weiwang1}@fudan.edu.cn

Abstract. Supporting frequent updates is a key challenge in moving object indexing. Most of the existing work regards the update as an individual process for each object, and a large number of separate updates are issued respectively in update-intensive environments. In this paper, we propose the bulkloading updates for moving objects (BLU). Based on a common framework, we propose three bulkloading schemes of different spatial biases. By grouping the objects with near positions, BLU prefetches the nodes accessed on the shared update path and combines multiple disk accesses to the same node into one, which avoids I/O overhead for objects within the same group. We also propose a novel MBR-driven flushing algorithm, which utilizes the dynamic spatial correlation and improves the buffer hit ratio. The theoretical analysis and experimental evaluation demonstrate that BLU achieves the good update performance and does not affect the query performance.

1 Introduction

The rapid advances in wireless communications and electronic technologies enable a wide range of emerging location-aware applications in mobile environments, such as traffic monitoring and intelligent transportation systems. Moving objects with positioning devices move continuously and their location information is reported to the server for further processing. Efficiently tracking the changing positions of moving objects can substantially improve the quality of these applications.

Spatial indexes like R-tree provide a basis for indexing moving objects. The key challenge is to handle the frequent updates because the sampled location values are dynamically changing and need to be updated frequently. The high demand for updates is motivated by most location-aware applications. Several indexing technologies have been proposed for moving objects [12, 6, 9, 16, 4, 2, 17]. One way is to accelerate the location steps of the old and new entries in leaf nodes, and reduces the number of disk accesses to internal nodes in traverse of the index structure [6, 9, 16, 17]. Another way is to model the objects' movement as a function of time to support the future trajectory queries [12, 4]. Only when the function parameters change, is an update issued, which reduces the number

* This work was supported in part by Natural Science Foundation of China under grant number No. 60503035.

J.X. Yu, M. Kitsuregawa, and H.V. Leong (Eds.): WAIM 2006, LNCS 4016, pp. 313–324, 2006.
© Springer-Verlag Berlin Heidelberg 2006

of location updates. Most of the existing work regards the update as an individual process for each object, and separate updates are issued respectively in update-intensive environments. With a large number of moving objects, this one-by-one manner causes a high volume of update path traverses and duplicate disk accesses to same nodes by different objects.

In this paper, we propose the bulkloading updates (BLU) for moving objects, which efficiently utilize the spatial correlation between different updates and achieve significantly lower update cost. We first present a framework of BLU, in which there is no need to modify any existing disk-based update or query algorithm. Thus BLU can be applied to the existing moving object indexes as a flexible component. Based on it, we propose three bulkloading schemes with different spatial biases. Each of them utilizes its spatial bias to group objects with near positions. Within the same group, shared update paths are prefetched into the buffer and multiple disk accesses to the same node can be combined into one. In this way, BLU avoids I/O overhead for objects with the same group. We also propose a novel MBR-driven flushing algorithm. It organizes the flushing order in an MBR-driven manner and improves the buffer hit ratio. We conduct the theoretical analysis and experimental evaluation. As shown in the analysis, one distinguishing feature of BLU is that its query performance is lossless, that is, it does not affect the query I/O cost of the index it is applied to. Both the analysis and experimental results demonstrate that BLU has the good update performance.

The rest of the paper is organized as follows. Section 2 reviews the related work. Section 3 presents the bulkloading updates (BLU) in detail. Section 4 conducts the experimental evaluation and we conclude the paper in Section 5.

2 Related Work

The bulkloading technique [5, 7, 15] is usually used for the construction phase of an index structure and can improve the overall performance with fairly static data. However, for dynamic data, especially frequently updated data like moving objects, the effect of bulkloading for the initial index construction is trivial. Several group updates for spatial indexes [1, 10] have been proposed and little work is favorable to moving object applications. Recently [8] proposes a lazy group update method for moving objects. With a disk-based insertion buffer for each internal node in R-tree, it improves the update throughput and also incurs additional I/O overhead in query evaluation.

Moving object indexing problems are generally categorized into three kinds: (1) Indexing the historical trajectories of objects [11, 13]. (2) Indexing the current positions of objects [6, 9, 16, 2, 17]. (3) Indexing the near future positions of objects [12, 4]. Among category (2) and (3), how to support frequent updates as well as efficient query processing is the key challenge to the existing index technologies.

To support frequent updates, several indexing methods have been proposed recently. Different from the traditional deletion-insertion way, Lazy R-tree [6] updates the index only when an object moves out of the corresponding MBR. Q+Rtree [16] differentiates fast-moving objects and quasi-static objects, and constructs a hybrid tree structure consisting both an R*-tree and a Quadtree. The Frequently Updated R-tree (FUR-tree) [9] incorporates the localized bottom-up strategies into R-tree. It locates the leaf node via a secondary object-ID index, and a bottom-up search is issued from the leaf node to find the new entry to be inserted. [4] proposes a B^+-tree based structure B^x-tree for indexing current and near future positions of moving objects. [2] proposes the change tolerant indexing for high update environments. The MBR is defined based on the changes to data values and thus can reduce the number of updates that cross MBR boundaries. [17] presents an R-tree variant that avoids disk accesses for purging old entries during an update process. Most of the existing work regards the update as an individual process, and a large number of separate updates are issued respectively in update-intensive environments. In this paper, we propose the bulkloading update (BLU) and apply it to FUR-tree [9], a typical moving object index that has been widely used. Meanwhile, the proposed technique is also applicable to other moving object index structures.

3 Bulkloading Updates

3.1 Motivation

The basic idea behind BLU is to group the objects with close positions and combine their individual updates into a common process. An example is illustrated in Figure 1. The location updates for object $o1$ and $o2$ are issued in FUR-tree. Both of them are deleted in leaf node A and respectively inserted into leaf node B and C in a bottom-up way. We assume an LRU buffer of four disk pages. In the traditional way where a separate update for each object is issued one by one, there is no correlation between the update for $o1$ and the one for $o2$. Figure 1(b) shows the buffer states and disk page swapping occurs frequently between two individual update phases. It incurs 8 disk accesses totally (here we do not account the I/O cost for accessing the secondary object-ID index). Now we consider the bulkloading way. $o1$ and $o2$ are clustered together and then a common update process is issued. Two objects almost share the same update path in FUR-tree. As shown in Figure 1(c), it incurs only 5 disk accesses. In fact the update path ADE has been prefetched into the buffer before the update for $o2$.

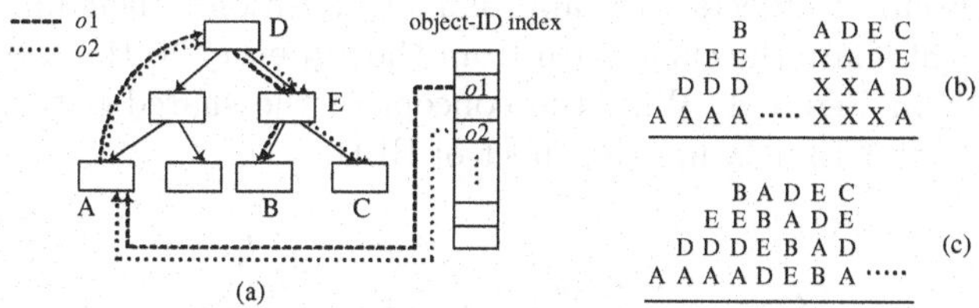

Fig. 1. An example to show the update path and buffer state

3.2 A Framework of Bulkloading Updates

We first present a framework of bulkloading updates for moving objects, as shown in Figure 2. It consists of two phases *loading* and *flushing*. An in-memory loading pool is maintained for buffering the incoming location information. When a new tuple (oid, pos) comes at each time step, it is first put into the loading pool according to a certain criteria. When the loading pool has not enough memory to accommodate the new incoming tuples, the flushing phase is issued. The location values in the loading pool are group by group flushed into the disk-based index. Then an ordinary update operation is performed for each object in a group. Two points should pointed out here.

1. In this framework, there is no need to modify any disk-based update (insertion/deletion) algorithm in the existing moving object indexes. Therefore BLU can be applied to the current moving objet databases as a flexible component.

2. When a new ad hoc query comes, BLU first checks whether the loading pool is empty. If not, it flushes the remaining values in the loading pool and then performs the query evaluation, as shown in Figure 2. In this way, only one active copy of each object's location information is kept at the same time, and no additional overhead is incurred to keep the data values consistent between the loading pool and the disk index. Similarly, there is no need to modify any disk-based query algorithm and BLU remains adaptive in dynamic environments.

Within the above framework, two problems become critical to the performance of BLU: *the grouping criteria* and *the flushing algorithm*. According to the grouping criteria, we propose three bulkloading schemes in Section 3.3, and the flushing algorithm will be investigated in Section 3.4.

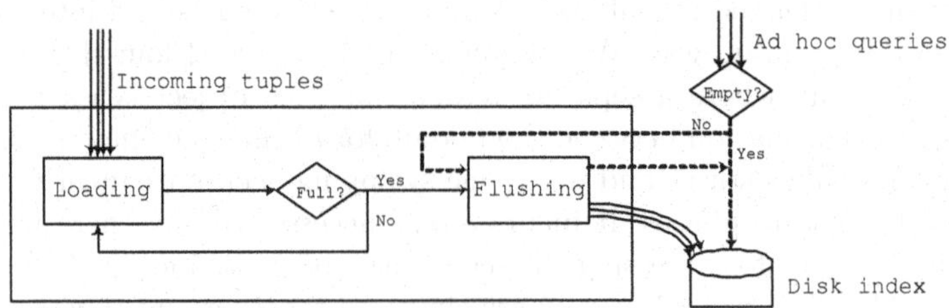

Fig. 2. A framework of bulkloading updates

3.3 Bulkloading Scheme

For a given group of objects with approximate positions, their updates in the disk index might share the same path from the old entry to the new entry, like the path ADE in Figure 1. With the concept of the shared path, we use the relative cost ratio ξ to measure the effect of BLU,

$$\xi = \frac{Cost_{BLU}}{Cost_{non-BLU}} = \frac{l_s + \sum_{i=1}^{n} l_i}{l_s \cdot n_s + \sum_{i=1}^{n} l_i} \tag{1}$$

where l_s is the shared path length, n_s is the number of objects whose update path contains the shared path, n is the total number of objects in this group, and l_i is the length of object i's update path excluding the shared path. The path length is referred to the number of nodes accessed on it. For example, in Figure 1 $l_s = 3$, $n_s = 2$ and $\xi = \frac{3+2}{6+2} = \frac{5}{8}$. In the BLU schemes, we expect both l_s and n_s to be large so that the nodes on the shared path repeatedly accessed by multiple objects can be prefetched into the buffer and efficiently combined into one disk access. We first introduce the concept of bulkloading bias, which forms the basis of bulkloading schemes.

Definition 1. (Bulkloading Bias) *The bulkloading bias is defined as the spatial unit based on which the moving objects are grouped. The objects are called neighbors if their positions are within the same spatial unit.*

According to the bulkloading bias, the loading pool is partitioned into a set of buckets, each of which forms a group and accommodates the continuously incoming tuples. A hash-based bucket function h is used to determine which bucket a new tuple (*oid*, *pos*) should be put into. The processing logic of BLU is described in Algorithm 1. We present three bulkloading schemes of different spatial biases, each of which has its own bucket function.

Algorithm 1. BLU(new tuple (oid, pos), scheme S)

```
if the loading pool is full
    collect the buckets and flush the data to the disk-based index.
    for each bucket bk
        for each tuple (oid, pos) in bk
            issue a bottom-up update in FUR-tree.
    return.
obtain the new tuple's key of the bucket function according to scheme S.
put the new tuple (oid, pos) into the bucket h(key) in the loading pool.
```

MBR Biased Scheme(MBS)

In this scheme, the bulkloading bias is the MBR (Minimum Bounding Rectangle) in R-tree based indexes. Note that we distinguish two kinds of positions, the old position and the new position. The former is reported at last time step and currently stored in the index structure. The latter comes from the new tuple (*oid*, *pos*) and will be processed. For each object, its old and new positions respectively correspond to the old and new MBRs the position lies in. We employ the old MBR in MBS since the new MBR of an object is unknown before traverse of the index structure. In this way, objects whose old positions are located in the same MBR are grouped in the same bucket. In R-trees, the leaf node and the leaf MBR have a one-to-one relationship. Two objects reside in the same MBR if and only if their corresponding entries are within the same leaf node. Thus the leaf node serves as a tag of the MBR and becomes the key of the bucket function. Especially in FUR-tree, the leaf node N can be directly located via the secondary object-ID index before a bottom-up search is issued. The new tuple (oid, pos) is then put into the bucket $h(N)$ in the loading pool.

Grid Biased Scheme(GBS)

Different from MBS that objects with near old positions are grouped together, we take into consideration the grouping effect of new positions in GBS. Although the new MBR of each object is not known in the loading phase, we use the grid partition as approximation. The space is uniformly divided into $k * k$ grids of same size. For a new position $pos(x, y)$, it is easily to obtain the grid cell that pos lies in. With row-major ordering, the grid cell id gid is $(y/yunit) * k + x/xunit$, where $yunit$ and $xunit$ are the grid cell side length of y-axis and x-axis respectively. The new tuple (oid, pos) is put into the bucket $h(gid)$ in the loading pool.

It should be noted that GBS is approximate grouping while MBS is precise grouping. In MBS, it is concerned with the old positions and objects keep consistent between the buckets and the old MBRs. In GBS, it considers the new positions and the grid is just the spatial approximation to the new MBR. Objects in the same grid might be in the same new MBR and there are also chances that they reside in different MBRs. In other words, MBS is a *look-back* scheme and GBS is a *look-ahead* scheme.

Hybrid Biased Scheme(HBS)

Based on MBS and GBS, we propose the hybrid biased scheme (HBS). We combine the grouping effect of both MBS and GBS in a unified way. The key of the bucket function is (N, gid), where N is the leaf node located in MBS and gid is the grid cell id calculated in GBS. Thus objects are clustered in a more compact way. Only those whose old positions are located in the same MBR and new positions are approximately neighboring can be grouped in the same bucket and then a common disk-based update is issued. In fact, the concern in HBS is a trajectory between two time steps rather than a single position. The shared update path is expected to be longer in HBS while the number of objects in each bucket might be less.

Figure 3 illustrates three bulkloading schemes. The objects $o1$, $o2$, $o3$ move from the old positions to the new positions respectively. In MBS, two groups are formed $h(MBR1) = \{o1, o2\}$ and $h(MBR2) = \{o3\}$. In GBS, $h(g1) = \{o1\}$ and $h(g2) = \{o2, o3\}$. In HBS, three groups are formed because of the finer granularity, $h(t1) = \{o1\}$, $h(t2) = \{o2\}$, and $h(t3) = \{o3\}$.

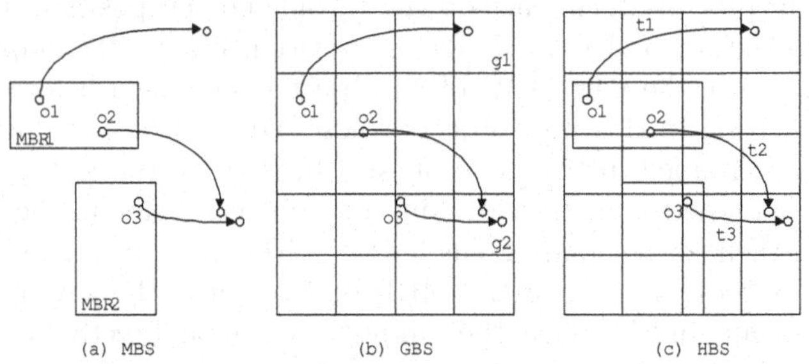

Fig. 3. An example of bulkloading schemes

3.4 MBR-Driven Flushing Algorithm

When the loading pool can not accommodate new tuples, the data values in the buckets are flushed into the disk index. The flushing algorithm considers *in what order the buckets are collected.* The buckets reflect the spatial location of the objects in it, and different flushing orders lead to different buffering effects as well as disk I/O cost. Intuitively, the spatial units preserving proximity should be close in the flushing order. We propose an MBR-driven flushing algorithm. A stack-like MBR Table (MT) with LRU replacement is used to maintain the leaf nodes recently accessed. The size of MT is a parameter that can be dynamically adjusted.

Algorithm 2. MBR-driven Flushing for MBS

```
While there are non-empty buckets
    choose a non-empty bucket and set N to the bucket key.
    push N into MT.
    while MT is not empty
        N = MT.pop().
        if the bucket h(N) is not empty
            for each tuple (oid, pos) in the bucket h(N)
                issue a bottom-up update.
                if leaf node N' is pinned into the buffer
                    push N' into MT.
            clear the bucket h(N) to empty.
```

The flushing algorithm for the MBR biased scheme is described in Algorithm 2. Note that N and N' are referred to the leaf node ID rather than the actual page. When a leaf node is pinnned into the buffer by previous updates, its ID is pushed into MT. In this way, MT records the leaf nodes that have been accessed and still reside in the buffer. The subsequent buckets driven by the leaf node (MBR) popped from MT can directly access the in-buffer nodes without I/O overhead. Even some of consecutive buckets share a common update path, which has been prefetched into the buffer. It should be noted that the shared path here is subtly different from that in Section 3.3. We distinguish them as *in-bucket shared path* and *between-bucket shared path* respectively. The former means that the update path is prefetched into the buffer and shared by objects within the same bucket, as described in Section 3.3. The between-bucket shared path here means that it is commonly accessed by objects belonging to different buckets, which is the immediate effect of the flushing algorithm.

The flushing algorithm for the grid biased scheme is different from that for MBS in two points: (1) The key of the bucket function h is the grid id *gid* instead of the leaf node id N. (2) To find which grid to be driven by the MBR popped from MT, we map the MBR to the grid space and select the grids whose region overlap with the MBR as the next one in the flushing order. Since the grid partition is uniform, the mapping calculation is simple. For example, in Figure 3, when MBR1 is popped from MT, the grids that MBR1 intersects are selected and their corresponding buckets will be next collected for flushing. The MBR-driven order is distinguished from other space-filling curves like row-major order or Hilbert curve, since it utilizes the dynamic spatial correlation based on buffer hit, instead of a predefined visiting order. As for the hybrid biased scheme, the above MBR-driven flushing algorithm either for MBS or for GBS can be employed.

3.5 Cost Analysis

We first introduce a theorem to show the query performance of BLU. Let T be the original index structure and $BLU\text{-}T$ be the corresponding index with the proposed bulkloading updates.

Lemma 1. *Let o_1 and o_2 be two objects to be updated. For an R-tree based index, two updates of different orders, o_1-$first$-o_2-second and o_2-$first$-o_1-second, have the same average query I/O cost.*

Theorem 1. *The query performance of BLU is lossless, that is, the query I/O cost of $BLU\text{-}T$ is not more than that of T.*

Proof. Let T_0 be the index before the update, n be the total number of objects, $C_q(T, n)$ and $C_q(BLU\text{-}T,\ n)$ be the query I/O cost of T and $BLU\text{-}T$. An update is an index structure change denoted as a binary tuple, that is, (T_0, T) and (T_0, $BLU\text{-}T$) respectively. For all the objects, there is an update sequence $(o_1, o_2, ..., o_n)$ in (T_0, T), and the sequence is $(o_{i_1}, o_{i_2}, ..., o_{i_n})$ in (T_0, $BLU\text{-}T$). We prove that $C_q(BLU\text{-}T,\ n)$ is not larger than $C_q(T, n)$ by induction of n. (1) When $n = 1$, there is only one object and the conclusion exists. (2) When $n > 1$, there exist the update sequence $(o_1, ...S_1..., o_{i_n}, ...S_2..., o_n)$ for (T_0, T) and $(o_{i_1}, ...S'_1..., o_n, ...S'_2..., o_{i_n})$ for (T_0, $BLU\text{-}T$). We make a series of bubble swapping for the first sequence so that o_n swaps with its left neighbor and o_{i_n} swaps with its right neighbor repeatedly until it turns a new sequence $(o_1, ...S_1..., o_n, ...S_2..., o_{i_n})$. According to Lemma 1, $C_q(T, n)$ is not affected by the bubble swapping. Now for the sequence $(o_1, ...S_1..., o_n, ...S_2..., o_{i_n})$ for T and $(o_{i_1}, ...S'_1..., o_n, ...S'_2..., o_{i_n})$ for $BLU\text{-}T$, we consider their $(n-1)$-length form $(o_1, ...S_1..., o_n, ...S_2..., o_{n-1})$ and $(o_{i_1}, ...S'_1..., o_n, ...S'_2..., o_{i_{n-1}})$. By induction, $C_q(BLU\text{-}T,\ n-1)$ is not larger than $C_q(T, n-1)$. Therefore the same for the n-length sequence and we have the conclusion when $n > 1$. □

From Theorem 1, we see that BLU keeps the good query performance of the existing R-tree variants. Different from some of the previous approaches, which sacrifice the query performance for the update performance, BLU does not need to make a compromise between them. In fact, since objects with close positions are updated together, $BLU\text{-}T$ keeps a more compact index structure than T and even might slightly improve the query performance.

Update Cost. We first analyze the update I/O cost of the bottom-up approach. For simplicity, we use the form *cost(read or write, the accessed object)* in the following analysis. If the new entry remains in the old leaf node, the cost = 1(R, secondary index) + 2(R/W, leaf node) = 3. If the new entry is inserted into some sibling of the old leaf node, the cost = 2(R/W, secondary index) + 2(R/W, leaf node) + 2(R/W, sibling node) = 6. Otherwise, a bottom-up search is issued and the nodes on the top-down path are accessed to locate the new entry. The cost = 2(R/W, secondary index) + 2(R/W, old leaf node) + $(h-1)$(R, internal nodes on the top-down path) + 2(R/W, new leaf node) = $5+h$, where h is the height of the top-down path in the search. Let p_1, p_2 and p_3 be the probability that a new entry is located in the old leaf node, in the sibling node, and in the new leaf node respectively. The cost of a bottom-up update is $3p_1+6p_2+(5+h)p_3$. For a group of m objects in a bucket, the total cost is $3mp_1+6mp_2+(\sum_{i=1}^{m}(5+h_i))p_3$.

For the bulkloading update of MBR biased scheme, the objects in a bucket reside in the same old MBR and multiple node accesses can be combined into one. Let l_s be the length of the shared update path as described in Section 3.3. For m objects in a bucket, we analyze the I/O cost in the above three cases. In case 1, the cost = $m\cdot 1$(R, secondary index) + 2(R/W, leaf node) = $m+2$. In case 2, the cost = $m\cdot$(2(R/W, secondary index) + 2(R/W, sibling node)) + 2(R/W, leaf node) = $4m+2$. In case 3, the cost = $m\cdot$(2(R/W, secondary index) + 2(R/W, new leaf node)) + 2(R/W, old leaf node) + $\sum_{i=1}^{m}(h_i-1-l_s)$ $= 4m+2+\sum_{i=1}^{m}(h_i-1-l_s)$. Therefore the total cost is

$$Cost_{BLU} = (m+2)p_1 + (4m+2)p_2 + (4m+2+\sum_{i=1}^{m}(h_i-1-l_s))p_3 \qquad (2)$$

From the above equation we see that the longer shared update path, the more cost reduced. Note that here we only consider the in-bucket shared path and do not take into account the effect of the between-bucket shared update path as described in Section 3.4.

Memory Requirement. The additional memory requirement in BLU is the size of the loading pool S_{lp}, which is the maximum number of accommodated tuples. Given a fixed available memory of size S_{total}, how to allocate S_{total} to S_{lp} and the buffer size S_{buf} is an interesting problem, and we will investigate it in the experiments.

4 Experimental Evaluation

4.1 Experimental Setup

We compare the following four approaches: FUR-tree [9], BLU-based FUR-tree with MBR biased scheme (BLU-MBS), BLU-based FUR-tree with grid biased scheme (BLU-GBS), and BLU-based FUR-tree with hybrid biased scheme (BLU-HBS). All the experiments are conducted on Pentium IV 2.0GHz with 512 MB RAM running Windows Server 2003. The size of disk page is set to 4KB. We use synthetic datasets generated by GSTD [14]. All the objects are uniformly distributed in a unit-square space and can move arbitrarily with a maximum moving distance of 0.2. The default number of objects is 100K. The performance metric is the number of disk accesses. Since BLU does not affect the query I/O cost according to Theorem 1, in the following experiments we focus on the update performance and do not report the results of query performance.

For a fair comparison, we allocate the same memory size (10% of dataset size) to all the approaches. For FUR-tree, the buffer size is set to the whole available memory size. For BLU, the same memory size is allocated to the buffer and the loading pool respectively, and the allocation ratio $\lambda = \frac{S_{lp}}{S_{buf}}$ is 0.25. We employ an LRU buffer with the write-through strategy. The setting of k in BLU-GBS (grid cell number per dimension) depends on the size of loading pool S_{lp}. Let N_{lp} be the number of tuples the loading pool can accommodate, we set k to $\sqrt{\frac{N_{lp}}{\eta}}$, where η is a tuning parameter and set to 2 in the experiments.

4.2 Results and Discussion

We conduct a set of experiments to investigate the effect of maximum moving distance, memory size, number of objects and allocation ratio respectively.

We first vary the maximum moving distance of objects from 0.01 to 0.15 and investigate its effect on the update performance. Figure 4(a) gives the update I/O cost for all the approaches. With the increase in objects' moving distance, the update cost rises up slightly. This is due to the fact that in FUR-tree more objects move far from old leaf nodes to new leaf nodes. The larger moving distance indicates the longer bottom-up and top-down update path, which further results in more accesses to index nodes. BLU-based FUR-trees outperform that without BLU. The bulkloading manner enables objects with similar positions to issue updates together, and reduces the additional disk access to common update paths. Figure 4(a) also shows that MBR biased scheme has the lower cost than grid biased scheme. This reveals a look-back bulkloading scheme performs better than a look-ahead one. An interesting result is that BLU-MBS and BLU-HBS almost have the same I/O cost. This is because the MBR bias puts more effects on the performance and the hybrid scheme prefers to it. Meanwhile HBS employs the same MBR-driven flushing algorithm with MBS, and the flushing unit of both of them is MBR instead of Grid. In this way, BLU-HBS can be regarded as a finer-granularity version of BLU-MBS.

We then study the effect of memory size by varying it from 0% to 15% of dataset size. For BLU, the allocated memory serves as the loading pool besides buffer space. As shown in Figure 4(b), when no memory is allocated, all the approaches have the same I/O cost because of each direct disk access to index nodes without buffering. When memory size is increased to 5% of dataset size, there is a great drop in the update cost. Update performance continues to improve with the increasing memory size, as can be expected. From Figure 4(b) we see that the enlargement of memory size has a strong impact on the performance of BLU due to variety of the loading pool size.

Figure 4(c) gives the update performance with different number of objects from 100K to 1M. BLU keeps the update cost steady with the increasing number of objects. Still BLU-MBS and BLU-HBS have the lowest I/O cost. It should be noted that although the dataset size is increasing, it does not affect the tuple load of the loading pool in each flushing phase due to a fixed loading volume.

In Figure 4(d) we investigate the effect of the allocation ratio. We set the allocation ratio λ, that is, the percentage of loading pool size to buffer size, to 1/4, 2/3, 3/2, and 4/1 respectively. The variety indicates more memory size allocated to the loading pool. BLU improves its update performance when λ changes from 1/4 to 3/2. This is because the larger loading pool can accommodate more tuples, and thus the shared update path can be longer and accessed by more objects, as discussed in Section 3.5. When λ varies from 3/2 to 4/1, the update cost does not change too much, which means the performance turns stable and does not fluctuate in this interval. Figure 4(d) also shows that under different allocation ratios BLU-MBS and BLU-HBS still have the similar performance and performs better than BLU-GBS. In actual applications, MBS or HBS is a good choice.

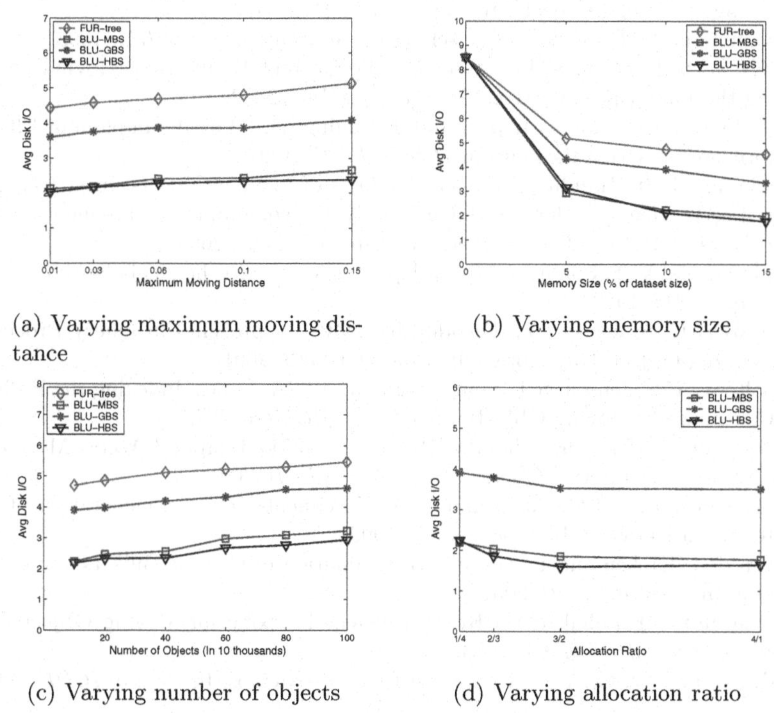

(a) Varying maximum moving distance

(b) Varying memory size

(c) Varying number of objects

(d) Varying allocation ratio

Fig. 4. Update Performance Results

5 Conclusion

We propose an efficient method, the bulkloading updates (BLU), for moving object databases. It is adaptive to the existing moving object indexes and can be applied to commercial systems as a flexible component. Both the theoretical analysis and experimental results demonstrate that BLU significantly improves the update performance while keeping the good query performance all the same. In future work, we would like to extend BLU to other types of index structures, and accelerate the update process in various update-intensive environments.

References

1. L. Arge, K. Hinrichs, J. Vahrenhold and J. Vitter. Efficient Bulk Operations on Dynamic R-trees. In *Proc of Workshop on Algorithm Engineering and Experimentation*, 1999.
2. R. Cheng, Y. Xia, S. Prabhakar, and R. Shah. Change Tolerant Indexing for Constantly Evolving Data. In *Proc of ICDE*, 2005.
3. A. Guttman. R-trees: A Dynamic Index Structure for Spatial Searching. In *Proc of SIGMOD*, 1984.
4. C. S. Jensen, D. Lin, and B. C. Ooi. Query and Update Efficient B^+-Tree Based Indexing of Moving Objects. In *Proc of VLDB*, 2004.
5. I. Kamel and C. Faloutsos. On Packing R-trees. In *Proc of CIKM*, 1993.
6. D. Kwon, S. Lee, and S. Lee. Indexing the Current Positions of Moving Objects Using the Lazy Update R-Tree. In *Proc of MDM*, 2002.
7. S. T. Leutenegger, M. A. Lopez, and J. Edgington. STR: A Simple and Efficient Algorithm for R-tree Packing. In *Proc of ICDE*, 1997.
8. B. Lin and J. Su. Handling Frequent Updates of Moving Objects. In *CIKM*, 2005.
9. M.L. Lee,W. Hsu, C.S. Jensen, B. Cui, and K. L. Teo. Supporting Frequent Updates in R-trees: A Bottom-Up Approach. In *Proc of VLDB*, 2003.
10. L. Malmi and E. S. Soininen. Group Updates for relaxed height-balanced trees. In *Proc of PODS*, 1999.
11. D. Pfoser, C. S. Jensen, Y. Theodoridis. Novel Approaches in Query Processing for Moving Object Trajectories. In *Proc of VLDB*, 2001.
12. S. Saltenis, C.S. Jensen, S.T. Leutenegger, and M.A. Lopez. Indexing the Positions of Continuously Moving Objects. In *Proc of SIGMOD*, 2000.
13. Y. Tao and D. Papadias. The MV3R-Tree: A Spatio-Temporal Access Method for Timestamp and Interval Queries. In *Proc of VLDB*, 2001.
14. Y. Theodoridis, J.R.O. Silva, and M.A. Nascimento. On the Generation of Spatiotemporal Datasets. In *Proc of SSD*, 1999.
15. J. van den Bercken and B. Seeger. An Evaluation of Generic Bulk Loading Techniques. In *Proc of VLDB*, 2001.
16. Y. Xia and S. Prabhakar. Q+Rtree: Efficient Indexing for Moving Object Databases. In *Proc of DASFAA*, 2003.
17. X. Xiong and W. G. Aref. R-trees with Update Memos. In *Proc of ICDE*, 2006.

Finding the Plateau in an Aggregated Time Series

Min Wang[1] and X. Sean Wang[2]

[1] IBM T. J. Watson Research Center
Hawthorne, NY 10532, USA
min@us.ibm.com

[2] Department of Computer Science, The University of Vermont
Burlington, VT 05405, USA
xywang@cs.uvm.edu

Abstract. Given d input time series, an aggregated series can be formed by aggregating the d values at each time position. It is often useful to find the time positions whose aggregated values are the greatest. Instead of looking for individual top-k time positions, this paper gives two algorithms for finding the time interval (called the plateau) in which the aggregated values are close to each other (within a given threshold) and are all no smaller than the aggregated values outside of the interval. The first algorithm is a centralized one assuming that all data are available at a central location, and the other is a distributed search algorithm that does not require such a central location. The centralized algorithm has a linear time complexity with respect to the length of the time series, and the distributed algorithm employs the Threshold Algorithm by Fagin et al. and is quite efficient in reducing the communication cost as shown by the experiments reported in the paper.

1 Introduction

Given a set of d input time series, by aggregating the d values at each time position, we obtain an aggregated time series A. A top-k query is to determine the top k time positions on A, namely, the time positions with the k greatest aggregated values. The well-known threshold algorithm (TA) [2] may be used to answer this type of query.

Recently, there has been active research on data aggregation in sensor networks [5, 6, 7, 1] and the top-k query can be very useful. For example, in an environmental monitoring system, multiple sensors may be used in an interested area to measure the temperature, humility, etc., at every minute. The measured data are stored in these sensors, and the system may need to find, within a specific time period, the time positions with the k highest average temperatures [3].

Assume the aggregated time series contains the average temperature for each minute during the past week and $k = 3$. If Friday is the warmest day during the week and the highest temperature during the week is at 1:30pm on Friday, we may very likely get the following three time positions as the answer to our top-3 query: 1:29pm on Friday, 1:30pm on Friday, and 1:31pm on Friday.

J.X. Yu, M. Kitsuregawa, and H.V. Leong (Eds.): WAIM 2006, LNCS 4016, pp. 325–336, 2006.
© Springer-Verlag Berlin Heidelberg 2006

We believe that a more interesting query is to find the *plateau* over the aggregated time series. The plateau is defined as the maximum interval such that all the values on the time positions in the interval are no less than all the values at the time positions outside of the interval. Compared to the top-k time positions, the plateau may give us more information. The plateau definition becomes more interesting and useful when we add another constraint: all the values in the plateau should be "close enough" to the top-1 value of the whole sequence. How close is "close enough" can be a value specified by the user.

In the example above, assume that the user considers two degrees as close enough, and asks for the plateau. The answer will be the interval [1:10pm on Friday, 1:45pm on Friday] if the temperature at each time position in this interval is at most two degrees lower than the highest temperature observed at 1:30pm on Friday, and all the time positions outside of this interval have temperature values no higher than the value of each time position in the interval. Obviously, the plateau carries more information about high-temperature time positions than that of the k time positions we get from a traditional top-k query.

In this paper, we formally define the plateau over time series and present efficient algorithms to find the plateau in both centralized and distributed settings. We show that the plateau can be found in linear time with respect to the length of time series in the centralized setting. For the distributed setting, we develop a distributed search algorithm and through experiments we show that it significantly outperforms a direct extension of the TA algorithm in terms of number of accesses to the distributed sources.

The rest of the paper is organized as follows. In the next section, we introduce some basic notions and formally define the key concept of *plateau*. Sections 3 and 4 describe our algorithms for finding the plateau in an aggregated time series in a centralized setting and a distributed setting, respectively. We present our experimental results in Section 5 and draw conclusions in Section 6.

2 Preliminary and Basic Assumptions

We first define time series. A *time series* is a finite sequence of real numbers and the number of values in the sequence is its *length*. We assume all time series are sampled at the fixed (discrete) time positions $t_1, \ldots, t_n$. A time series is denoted as s, possibly with subscripts, and its value at time t is denoted $s(t)$.

An *aggregated time series* is a time series whose value at time position t is from aggregating the values from multiple *input time series*. Specifically, given $s_1, \ldots, s_d$ and an aggregation function f, the aggregated time series is s_f with $s_f(t) = f(s_1(t), \ldots, s_d(t))$ for each t. We shall use A to denote aggregated time series, and omit the mentioning of function f when it is understood. A "normal" time series can be considered as a degenerated aggregated time series, and hence we shall use A to denote both "normal" time series and aggregated ones.

Definition 1. *Given a time series A and a real value ε, a time interval $[t_l, t_r]$ is said to be an* ε-plateau *of A if for each time position $t \in [t_l, t_r]$, we have (1) $|A(t) - A(t')| \le \varepsilon$ for all $t' \in [t_l, t_r]$, and (2) $A(t) \ge A(t'')$ for all $t'' \notin [t_l, t_r]$.*

Intuitively, an ε-plateau in a time series is the largest time interval that has values no less than the value of any time position outside of the interval, and the difference between the values within the time interval is at most ε. An ε-plateau must contain a time position with the greatest value in the time series.

We abbreviate ε-plateau to simply plateau when ε is implicit or irrelevant. A *maximum ε-plateau* is an ε-plateau that is not a proper subinterval of another ε-plateau. In the sequel, when not explicitly stated and clear from the context, we will use the term plateau to mean the maximum plateau.

When there are more than one top-1 time position in the aggregated time series, two cases arise: all the top-1 time positions are either contiguous or not. In the former case, we will have only one maximum plateau. For the latter, the only (maximum) plateaux we will find are formed by top-1 time positions, regardless of the ε value. This is rather trivial algorithmically since it is equivalent to finding all top-1 time positions (and possibly combine these positions that are contiguous with each other). We do not pursue this case any further. Since the former case is equivalent to having a unique top-1 position, we will in the sequel assume that the top-1 position is unique in each aggregated time series, and hence we will have a unique maximum plateau for each ε value.

Example. Consider the maximum plateau in the (aggregated) time series shown in Fig. 1. The top-1 time position is $t_d = t_{10}$ with value 12. If $\varepsilon = 2$, then the plateau is $[t_9, t_{10}]$. If $\varepsilon = 10$, then the plateau is $[t_8, t_{11}]$. □

An equivalent way of defining a plateau is by a minimum value threshold τ. That is, instead of condition (1) in the definition, we would insist that $A(t) \geq \tau$ for all $t \in [t_l, t_r]$. Obviously, this is equivalent to the original definition if we take $\tau = A(t_m) - \varepsilon$, where t_m is a time position with the greatest value. In the sequel, we may use plateau to mean an ε-plateau or equivalently a plateau with a minimum value threshold.

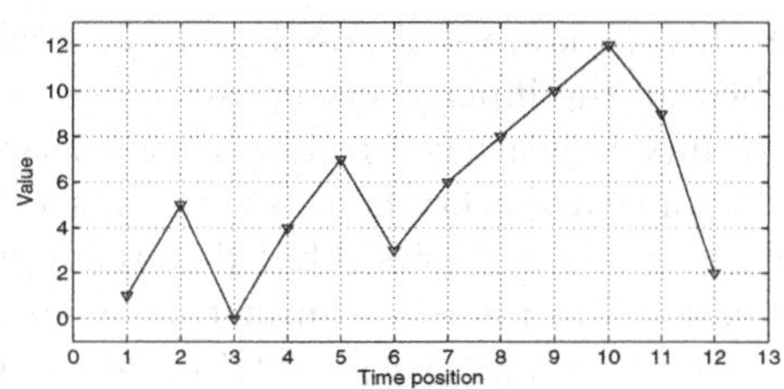

Fig. 1. Example time series

We may also define the ε-plateau via the notion of rank as follows.

Definition 2. *Given a time series, the* top-rank, *or simply* rank, *of a time position t, denoted $R(t)$, is defined as* 1 *plus the number of time positions that have greater values, that is, $R(t) = 1 + |\{t' | A(t') > A(t)\}|$.*

If $R(t) \leq k$, we will also say that t is a *top-k time position*. Hence, a top-1 time position has a value that is no less than that of any other time positions.

Given a time series and real value ε, if $[t_l, t_r]$ is an *ε-plateau*, then for each time position $t \in [t_l, t_r]$, all the time positions with ranks higher (or $R()$ values smaller) than $R(t)$ must be in $[t_l, t_r]$. For example, if the plateau includes a rank 3 time position then all the rank 1 and rank 2 time positions must also be in the plateau.

Much has appeared in the literature for algorithms that look for top-k items from multiple data sources (e.g., [4]). Many algorithms use a variant of Fagin et al.'s threshold algorithm (TA), which has been shown to be optimal [2]. In TA, the aggregation function f is assumed to be *monotonic*, i.e., $x_1 \leq y_1, \ldots, x_d \leq y_d$ implies $f(x_1, \ldots, x_d) \leq f(y_1, \ldots, y_d)$. Many practical aggregation functions, like sum, average, maximum, are monotonic.

We now briefly review TA, as applied to look for top-k time positions in the aggregated time series. Assume we have d input time series $s_1, \ldots, s_d$. We sort each time series based on the values (from large to small), and keep the time position information with the values. Thus, we have d such sorted lists: $L_1, \ldots, L_d$. In TA, we proceed as follows.

1. Do sorted access in parallel (or using a round-robin schedule) to each of the d sorted lists. As a value v is retrieved under the sorted access from one list (assuming the associated time position is t), do random access to the other time series to find the values $s_i(t)$ for all i, and compute $A(t) = f(s_1(t), \ldots, s_d(t))$. We say time position t has been "seen" and $A(t)$ is kept for each "seen" time position t.
2. For each list L_i, let v_i be the last value returned under the sorted access. Define the *threshold value* θ to be $f(v_1, \ldots, v_d)$. Stop as soon as there are at least k distinct $A(t)$ values on the "seen" time positions that are greater than θ, and then output the top-k time positions among all the "seen" time positions.

3 Centralized Algorithm

In this section, we discuss how to find the plateau for an aggregated time series when all the input time series are available at a central point. For example, we can imagine each sensor in a sensor network sends its measurement data to the control center every hour. In such a setting, the central point can calculate the aggregated time series A based on the input time series and the given aggregation function. We present a linear time algorithm for finding the plateau on A.

We first define a *left ε-plateau* of the time series A to be an ε-plateau when we only consider the time series on the left of (and including) the top-1 time position. That is, it is an ε-plateau we find in $A(t_1), \ldots, A(t_m)$, where t_m is the top-1 time position. Right ε-plateaux are defined analogously. We define the maximum left and right ε-plateaux in a similar way as we defined the maximum ε-plateau, and use the term *left* and *right plateau* to mean the maximum left and right plateau, respectively, when the context is clear. Note, however, the union of a left and a right ε-plateaux does not necessarily form an ε-plateau as will be shown in the example at the end of this section.

The following result directly follows the definitions.

Theorem 1. *Denote* $min\_right(i) = min\{A(t_j) \mid i \leq j \leq m\}$, *and* $max\_left(i) = max\{A(t_j) \mid 1 \leq j < i\}$. *Interval* $[t_l, t_m]$ *(*$l \leq m$*) is a left ε-plateau if and only if* $min\_right(l) \geq A(t_m) - \varepsilon$ *and* $min\_right(l) \geq max\_left(l)$ *where* t_m *is the top-1 time position.*

In the above theorem, we assume *max_left(1)*=$-\infty$. We have an analogous theorem for the right ε-plateaux. These theorems give the basis for our linear time algorithm in finding the maximum left and right ε-plateaux. It is obvious that *min_right* and *max_left* for the time positions before t_m (and *min_left* and *max_right* for the positions after t_m) can be computed in an incremental fashion with two sequential scans, using for example the recurrence relation $min\_right(i) = min\{min\_right(i+1), A(i)\}$. Assume these values are available and assume $\tau = A(t_m) - \varepsilon$. Then we can easily design the procedure:

$$find\_left\_plateau\left([t_L, t_m], \tau\right) : [t_l, t_m], \tau_l$$

The input parameters are $[t_L, t_m]$ and τ, where t_L is the left boundary of the time series to be considered, t_m is the right boundary of the time series to be considered (t_m is also the top-1 position in $[t_L, t_m]$), and τ is the required minimum value threshold. The output parameters are $[t_l, t_m]$ and τ_l, where $[t_l, t_m]$ is the maximum left plateau and $\tau_l = max\{\tau, A(t_i) \mid i = l, \ldots, l-1\}$. The procedure simply scans from t_L towards t_m and finds the first time position t_l such that $min\_right(l) \geq max\_left(l)$ and $min\_right(l) \geq \tau$.

The correctness of this procedure follows Theorem 1 directly. It is also clear that the time complexity of the procedure is $O(l - L + 1)$.

The question now is how to get the global ε-plateau. Assume *find_left_plateau* and *find_right_plateau* return $[t_l, t_m]$ and τ_l, and $[t_m, t_r]$ and τ_r, respectively. By Theorem 1, all the positions in $[t_l, t_m]$ have values no smaller than τ_l while all the positions in $[t_1, t_l)$ have values no greater than τ_l. We have similar conclusions for $[t_m, t_r]$ and τ_r. If $\tau_l = \tau_r$, we can merge the left and right ε-plateaux to obtain the maximum ε-plateau. Otherwise, we should shrink the side with the smaller τ using the greater τ. This shrinking process is repeated until $\tau_l = \tau_r$ and we then merge the left and right ε-plateaux into the ε-plateau. The whole process is summarized in Fig. 2. The algorithm finds the maximum ε-plateau $[t_l, t_r]$ of time series A. It also returns a real value τ such that all the values in $[t_l, t_r]$ are no smaller than τ while all the values not in $[t_l, t_r]$ are no greater than τ.

Algorithm *Find_Plateau*
Input: Time series A of length n, and ε.
Output: $[t_l, t_r]$: maximum ε- plateau
$\tau = max\{A(t_m) - \varepsilon, A(t_j) | t_j \notin [t_l, t_r]\}$, where t_m is the top-1 time position
(1) Find the top-1 time position t_m.Set $\tau = A(t_m) - \varepsilon$, and compute *min_right*, *max_left*, *min_left* and *max_right* as described earlier.
(2) Call *find_left_plateau*($[t_1, t_m], \tau$). Return $[t_l, t_m]$, τ_l.
(3) Call *find_right_plateau*($[t_m, t_n], \tau$). Return $[t_m, t_r]$, τ_r.
(4) Let $t_L = t_l$ and $t_R = t_r$. If $\tau_l = \tau_r$ then $\tau = \tau_l$. Return $[t_L, t_R], \tau$. Done.
(5) If $\tau_l > \tau_r$ then call *find_right_plateau*($[t_m, t_R], \tau_l$). Return $[t_m, t_r]$, τ_r. Goto Step 4.
(6) If $\tau_l < \tau_r$ then call *find_left_plateau*($[t_L, t_m], \tau_r$). Return $[t_l, t_m]$, τ_l. Goto Step 4.

Fig. 2. The *Find_Plateau* algorithm

Theorem 2. *Algorithm Find_Plateau correctly finds the ε-plateau of time series A in linear time and space.*

Proof. The space complexity of the algorithm is obvious since we only need to store two numbers for each time position. Now we analyze its time complexity. Steps 1-3 take linear time as mentioned earlier. The nontrivial part of the proof is that *find_left_plateau* and *find_right_plateau* may be called multiple times due to Steps 5 and 6. However, each repeated call to *find_left_plateau* will start the scan from the stopping position of the previous call. That is, even in the worst case, the multiple calls to *find_left_plateau* will scan up to m positions and thus the complexity of all calls is $O(m)$. Similarly, the complexity of all possible multiple calls to *find_right_plateau* is $O(n-m+1)$. Hence, the time complexity of Algorithm *Find_Plateau* is $O(n)$.

The correctness follows the correctness of the procedures *find_left_plateau* and *find_right_plateau*. Indeed, with Steps 2 and 3, we find the respective maximum plateaux with $A(t_m) - \varepsilon$ as the minimum value threshold for the plateaux. It is clear that Steps 5 and 6 will both still return ε-plateaux. The question is whether the final result is the maximum ε-plateau. The answer is positive since each time we used smallest τ_l and τ_r value that is necessarily to maintain the combined interval to be a plateau. □

Example. We want to find the 10-plateau in the time series shown in Fig. 1. The top-1 time position is $t_m = t_{10}$ with value 12. Given $\varepsilon = 10$, we have threshold $\tau = 12 - 10 = 2$ initially. The call to *find_left_plateau*$([t_1, t_{10}], 2)$ returns with the maximum left plateau $[t_8, t_{10}]$ and $\tau_l = 7$, and *find_right_plateau*$([t_{10}, t_{12}], 2)$ returns with the maximum right plateau $[t_{10}, t_{12}]$ and $\tau_r = 2$. Note that we cannot combine the left and right plateaux into one yet since $\tau_l \neq \tau_r$ (actually, $[t_9, t_{12}]$ is not a plateau). Since $\tau_l > \tau_r$, so we call *find_right_plateau*$([t_{10}, t_{12}], 7)$. This time, it returns a new right plateau $[t_{10}, t_{11}]$ and a new $\tau_r = 7$. Now we can combine the left and right plateaux into $P = [t_8, t_{11}]$. We also output $\tau = 7$. □

4 Distributed Algorithm

In this section, we discuss how to find the plateau for an aggregated time series without bringing all the data into a centralized server. The reason for this may include the large size of the time series from the data sources, and the high communication costs. In this setting, we would like to calculate the ε-plateau with a minimum amount of communication. To do this, we assume that data sources have some computation power to support the local processing as required by the Threshold Algorithm (TA) of [2].

In the distributed setting, as required by the TA, we assume the aggregation functions are *monotonic*.

4.1 A Naive Algorithm

A straightforward way of finding the plateau in a distributed setting is to find the top-1 time position t_m in the aggregated time series, and then to find all the time positions whose aggregated values are no smaller than $A(t_m) - \varepsilon$.

The top-1 time position t_m and its aggregated value $A(t_m)$ can be found by a direct use of TA. We may trivially extend the TA algorithm to proceed, after finding top-1 time position, to repeatedly find the next top time positions and their associated aggregated values until the threshold θ is smaller than $A(t_m)-\varepsilon$. In this way, we find all the time positions with values no smaller than $A(t_m)-\varepsilon$. With these time positions, we can use our linear algorithm to find the maximum ε-plateau. Indeed, a little deeper analysis of the linear algorithm indicates that if we change all the values smaller than $A(t_m)-\varepsilon$ to a very small number (smaller than all possible values), then the plateau found by the linear algorithm is the same as the one found with all the data available.

4.2 A Distributed Search Algorithm

In some situations, the above naive algorithm performs very poorly. Indeed, consider the following aggregated time series of length n:

$$2, 2, \ldots, 2, 1, 3$$

and consider 1-plateau (i.e., $\varepsilon = 1$). Clearly, the top-1 time position is t_n, and the 1-plateau is $[t_n, t_n]$. However, the above naive algorithm will need to retrieve all the time positions t_1 through t_{n-2}, in addition to t_n. The run time and the communication cost will be proportional to n. A simple observation will yield that if we find out that the time position t_{n-1} has a value 1 that is lower than $A(t_n) - \varepsilon = 3 - 1 = 2$ and the greatest value between t_1 and t_{n-1} is 2, then we can safely conclude that $[t_n, t_n]$ is the plateau we are seeking.

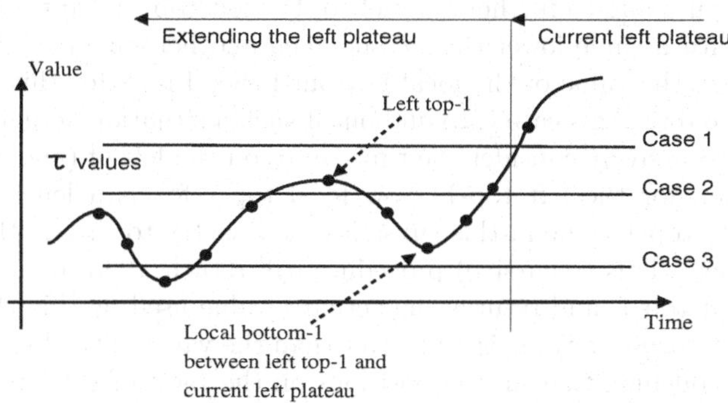

Fig. 3. Three cases for the distributed algorithm

Similar to the linear centralized algorithm in Section 3, we first concentrate on finding the left and right plateaux, separately, and then combine them into a single plateau. The above example is for the left plateau. Let us examine it a little closer with the help of the diagram in Fig. 3. In this diagram, the current (not necessarily maximum) left plateau is the one we have already found (e.g., $[t_m, t_m]$ where t_m is the top-1 point in the whole series), and we would like to see if we can extend the current left plateau towards the left in order to find the maximum left plateau. For this purpose, we find the top-1 time position (called "left top-1" in the digram) on the left of the current left plateau, and then we find the bottom-1 time position (called "local bottom-1" in the diagram) between the left top-1 and the current left plateau.

Three cases arise based on the τ value as depicted in Fig. 3. (Recall that τ gives the restriction that all the values in the plateau must be no less than τ). Consider Case 2 first as this is the case for the above example. In this case, the τ value is between the left top-1 value and the local bottom-1 value. The following are two useful observations for this case:

(1) Any value in the maximum plateau must be no less than the value of this left top-1. This gives us a new τ value for the left plateau.
(2) The left plateau cannot be extended to the time position of the local bottom-1. This gives us a new boundary when extending the left plateau.

By using these observations, we can extend the left plateau by using the new τ value and the boundary. This can be done with a recursive call to the extending procedure itself. One condition for the recursion to stop is if the new boundary is actually the current plateau. Going back to the above example, the procedure stops after we find the local bottom-1 is at position t_{n-1}, which is at the immediate left of the current left plateau (i.e., $[t_n, t_n]$).

Now consider Case 1. Since the left top-1 value is below τ, we know no time positions on the left of the current left plateau can be in the maximum left plateau. In this case, the current left plateau is the maximum left plateau.

Finally consider Case 3. In this case, we may be tempted to conclude that the left plateau can be extended to the time position of left top-1. However, this would be wrong if going to further left (left of the left top-1), we would meet a time position with a value lower than τ and then another time position with a value higher than the value of the local bottom-1. See Fig. 3 for this situation. What we need to do in this case is to find out if such a situation actually occurs. To do this, we recursively consider the time series on the left of (and including) the time position for the left top-1. Now local top-1 forms a left plateau by itself since it is a top-1 value in this subseries, and we try to extend the "local" plateau to the left. This (recursive) procedure will return a "local" left plateau starting from left top-1, and returns the actual τ value used by this "local" left plateau. If this returned τ value is still lower than the value of the local bottom-1, then we can conclude that all the positions on the right of the left top-1 are indeed in the left plateau (together with all the time positions in the "local" left plateau). Otherwise (i.e., the returned τ value is greater than the value of the local bottom-1), then we can conclude that the left plateau cannot be extended to the time position of left top-1, and the new τ value to use is the returned τ value from the "local" left plateau procedure.

We can now summarize our search algorithm in Fig. 4. In this algorithm, we refine the TA algorithm to look for top-1 and bottom-1 time positions (in terms of aggregated values) in an interval of [*left*, *right*] of the time series. We assume TA will return the aggregated values associated with the top-1 and bottom-1 time positions. This extension can be obtained straightforwardly without requiring the data sources maintain separate sorted lists for each different time interval.

Procedure: *find_left_plateau*
Input: $[t_l, t_m]$ where t_l is the left boundary of the time interval to be considered and t_m is the top-1 position in $[t_l, t_m]$ and the right boundary of the time series to be considered, τ: the minimum value threshold for the left plateau
Output: $[t_{l'}, t_m]$: maximum left plateau $\tau' = max\{\tau, A(t_i) | i = l, \ldots, l' - 1\}$.

(0) If $l = m$, then return $[t_m, t_m]$ and τ.
(1) Let $t_t = top[t_l, t_{m-1}]$, and $t_b = bot[t_t, t_{m-1}]$.
(2) Three cases.
  (2.1) if $A(t_t) < \tau$, then return $[t_m, t_m]$ and τ.
  (2.2) if $A(t_t) \geq \tau$ and $A(t_b) < \tau$, then
    if $b = m - 1$, then return $[t_m, t_m]$ and $A(t_t)$;
    else recursively call *find_left_plateau* with $[t_{b+1}, t_m]$ and $\tau = A(t_t)$, and return what's returned from recursive call
  (2.3) if $A(t_b) \geq \tau$, then
    if $t_t = t_l$, then return $[t_l, t_m]$ and τ;
    else recursively call *find_left_plateau* with $[t_l, t_t]$ and τ
      assume the returned values are $[t_{l'}, t_t]$ and τ'
      (2.3.1) if $\tau' \leq A(t_b)$, then return $[t_{l'}, t_m]$ and τ
      (2.3.2) if $\tau' > A(t_b)$, then set $\tau = \tau'$ and goto Step (2).

Fig. 4. The *find_left_plateau* procedure for the distributed setting

We will use the notation top[*left*, *right*] and bot[*left*, *right*], where *left* and *right* are time positions, to denote the top-1 and bottom-1 time positions found by TA within the interval [*left*, *right*], respectively.

Theorem 3. *The algorithm in Fig. 4 correctly finds the maximum left plateau.*

The procedure to find the right plateau is similar. The complete algorithm that finds the plateau is the same as for the centralized algorithm, but will use TA to find the top-1 time position (Step 1, without computing the four arrays) and the search algorithms to find the left/right plateaux (Steps 2-6). It is easily seen that this complete procedure will find the correct plateau.

Example. Consider the time series in Fig. 5. We will only show how to find the left 8-plateau with $t_m = t_6$ and $\tau = 2$. During the initial call (*C-1*) with $[t_1, t_6]$, we find left top-1 is at $t_t = t_4$, and local bottom-1 is at $t_b = t_5$. Since $A(t_b) = A(t_5) = 3 > \tau = 2$, we are in Case 3 (Step 2.3), and we make a recursive call (*C-2*) with interval $[t_1, t_4]$ and $\tau = 2$. In *C-2*, we have $t_t = t_2$ and $t_b = t_3$, and we are looking at Case 2. Since $b = 3 = m - 1 = 4 - 1$ in this case, we return

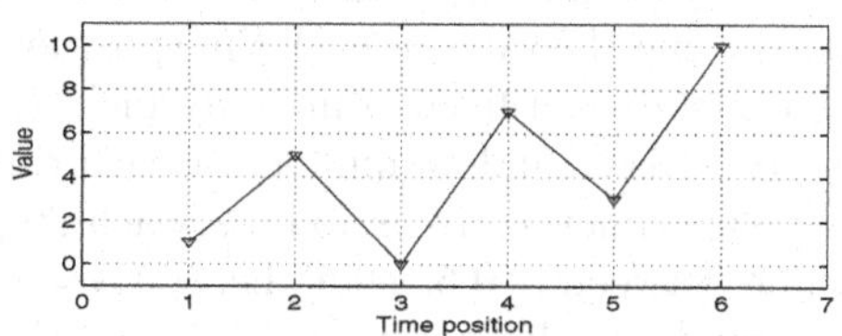

Fig. 5. Another example time series

to *C-1* with $[t_4, t_4]$ and a new $\tau = A(t_2) = 5$. In *C-1*, we were in Case 3 with returned $\tau' = 5$, and since $\tau' = 5 > A(t_b) = A(t_5) = 3$, we set $\tau = 5$ and go back to Step 2. Now we are looking at Case 2 since $A(t_t) = A(t_4) = 7 > \tau = 5 > A(t_b) = A(t_5) = 3$. Since $5 = b = m - 1 = 6 - 1$, we return $[t_6, t_6]$. Hence, we have found the maximum left 8-plateau to be $[t_6, t_6]$ and the return $\tau = A(t_t) = A(t_4) = 7$. □

4.3 Optimizing the Distributed Search Algorithm

There are many optimization techniques to add to the search algorithm. Here we only mention three of them that are used in our implementation. Other opportunities are abundant but are not pursued in this paper.

To start with, for Step 1, we may want to find the leftmost $top[t_l, t_{r-1}]$ and rightmost $bot[t_t, t_{r-1}]$ if there are multiple left top-1 and local bottom-1 time positions. While the algorithm is still correct if we use an arbitrary $top[t_l, t_{r-1}]$ and $bot[t_t, t_{r-1}]$ time positions among the multiple possibilities, the use of the leftmost and rightmost time positions, respectively, generally gives us the advantage in obtaining the plateau faster.

For Step 2.3, if $t_t = t_b$, then we know that all the time positions between $[t_b, t_m]$ have values no less than $A(t_t)$ (also no less than τ), then we may immediately extend the left plateau to $[t_b, t_m]$ without any recursion (although recursion will eventually find this extension as well).

Since we repeatedly use TA to find $top[t_l, t_r]$ and $bot[t_l, t_r]$, it is possible to reuse of the results across the different runs. For example, we may need to find $top[t_l, t_r]$ and later $top[t_l, t_{r-k}]$. During the search for $top[t_l, t_r]$, the final threshold value θ for TA used may be on a time position within $[t_l, t_{r-k}]$. In this case, we have already obtained the $top[t_l, t_{r-k}]$.

5 Experimental Results

In this section, we report the experimental evaluation of our distributed search algorithm. For the purpose of comparison, we also implemented the naive algorithm as mentioned in Section 4.1.

In order to control the experiments, we used synthetically generated data sets. We are interested in the situation that all the distributed data sources are monitoring the same phenomenon and hence the data should be somewhat correlated. In order to simulate this, to generate one data set, we first use a random walk to generate a *core time series* s_c, and then generate each input time series by (1) adding to the core with a fixed "shift" value, and then (2) randomly perturbing the value at each time position. That is, $s(t) = s_c(t) + shift + randpert$, where *shift* is a fixed (randomly picked) value for the entire time series s, and *randpert* is a random number at each time position. The parameters we used in our experiments are as follows: each step of the random walk takes a random value between $[-0.5, +0.5]$, i.e., $s_c(i) = s_c(i-1) + rand[-0.5, 0.5]$, and the shift is a random value between $[-5, 5]$ and the *randpert* is a random number between $[-2.5, 2.5]$. We used the sum as our aggregation function.

To give a "trend" to the random walk data, we modified the above generation of s_c with a slight bias. For the first half of the core time series, we add a small value (0.01 is used in the experiments) to each step, i.e., add 0.01 to $s_c(i)$, and in the second half of the core time series, we subtract the same small bias. This way, it's more likely that the time series will peak when reaching the middle of the time series. Since the bias is rather small, the trend is not prominent in our data sets.

Basically, three parameters affect the performance: the length of time series, the number of time series, and the ε value used for the plateau. Therefore, we tested our distributed search algorithm in three different ways, each varying one parameter while keeping the other two constant. The performance of our algorithm is measured on the number of accesses needed to the data sources (i.e., the number of sorted and random accesses required by the TA). For each fixed set of parameters, we generated 10 different data sets as described above and report the average number of accesses.

The result of the first experiment is reported in Fig. 6. In this experiment, we fixed number of series to 30, and ε to 90. As can be seen, the length of the series do not affect the performance too much on both algorithms, although our distributed algorithm performs better with one scale of magnitude. Intuitively, the naive algorithm would be affected by the series length because there may be more time positions with aggregated value above $A(t_m) - \varepsilon$. However, in our particular setting, due to the one "peak" nature of our time series, the performance of the naive algorithm does not degenerate as series length increases. As we observed (but not reported here), if we use a larger ε value, the performance of the naive algorithm generally goes poorer as the series length increases. In general, however, the performance of our distributed algorithm scales well with series length even in *multiple-peak* situations.

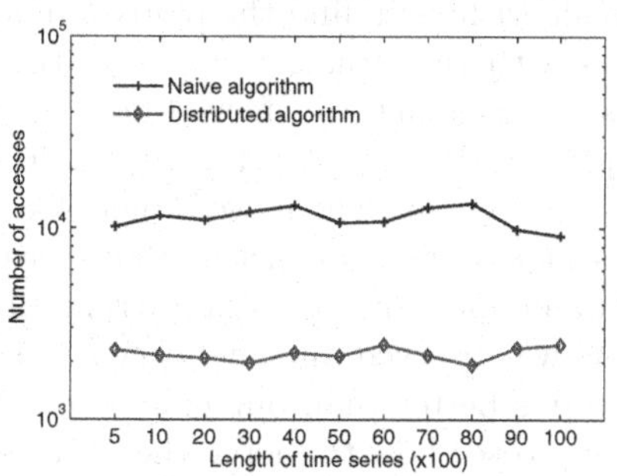

Fig. 6. Varying series length

The result of the second experiment is reported in Fig. 7. In this experiment, we fixed the time series length to 3,000, but varied the number of input time series from 1 to 100. Since we used sum as our aggregation, we varied the ε value in proportion to the number of time series. Specifically, ε is three times the number of time series (thus, if we have 30 time series, $\varepsilon = 90$). As can be seen that our distributed algorithm performs much better than the naive algorithm, with one scale of magnitude, consistently.

The result of the third experiment is reported in Fig. 8. In this experiment, we fixed the time series length to 3,000 and the number of time series to 30. Interestingly, when ε value is very small, the naive algorithm performs better than our distributed algorithm. In such cases, the naive algorithm retrieves almost

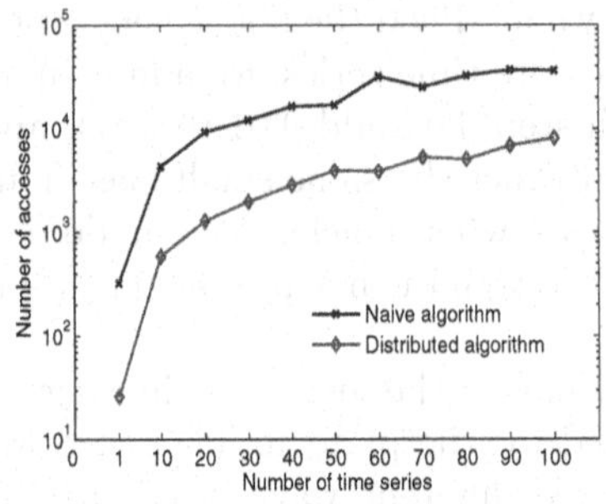

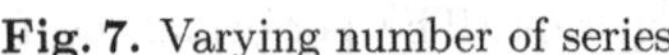

Fig. 7. Varying number of series

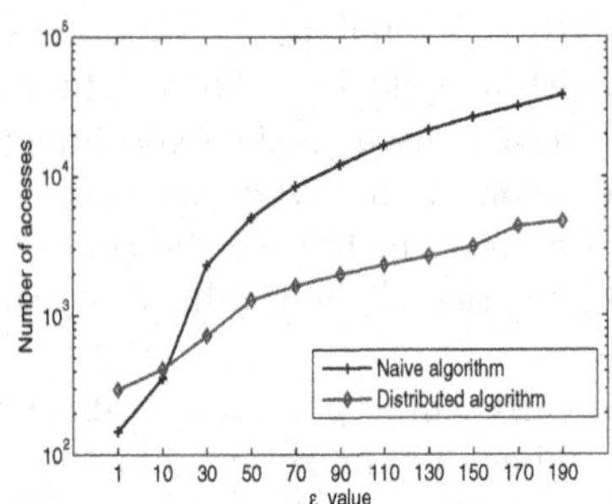

Fig. 8. Varying ε value

exactly all the time positions in the plateau. In general, if the plateau consists of all (or most of) the points that is above $A(t_m) - \varepsilon$, then the naive algorithm works very well. However, such cases should be rare in practice.

6 Conclusion

In this paper, we introduced the notion of the plateau in time series and presented two algorithms to find the plateau in aggregated time series. The first algorithm deals with the situation when all the data are available at a central location. In such a setting, we showed how the plateau can be found in linear time with respect to the length of the time series. The second algorithm is for distributed data sources in which we would like to reduce the communication cost. We presented a search algorithm that gives one scale of magnitude reduction in terms of communication cost over a straightforward use of the Threshold Algorithm [2].

As we observed, in some very special situations, the naive algorithm actually performs better than our more sophisticated search algorithm. It will be interesting to see how to merge the naive strategy into the search algorithm to take advantage of the special situations.

References

1. A. Deligiannakis, Y. Kotidis, and N. Roussopoulos. Hierarchical in-network data aggregation with quality guarantees. In *Proceedings of EDBT*, 2004.
2. R. Fagin, A. Lotem, and M. Naor. Optimal aggregation algorithms for middleware. *Journal of Computer and System Sciences*, 66:614–656, 2003.
3. D. Gunopulos. Data storage and analysis in sensor networks with large memories, presentation at IBM Watson Research Center, 2005.
4. C. A. Lang, Y.-C. Chang, and J. R. Smith. Making the threshold algorithm access cost aware. *IEEE Trans. Knowl. Data Eng*, 16(10):1297–1301, 2004.
5. S. Madden, M. J. Franklin, and J. M. Hellerstein. TAG: A tiny aggregation service for ad-hoc sensor networks. In *Proceedings of OSDI*, 2002.
6. A. Manjhi, S. Nath, and P. B. Gibbons. Tributaries and deltas: Efficient and robust aggregation in sensor network streams. In *Proceedings of ACM SIGMOD*, 2005.
7. M. Sharifzadeh and C. Shahabi. Supporting spatial aggregation in sensor network databases. In *Proceedings of ACM-GIS*, 2004.

Compressing Spatial and Temporal Correlated Data in Wireless Sensor Networks Based on Ring Topology

Siwang Zhou[1], Yaping Lin[1,2], Jiliang Wang[1], Jianming Zhang[1], and Jingcheng Ouyang[1]

[1] College of Computer and Communication, Hunan University, Changsha, China
[2] College of Software, Hunan University, Changsha, China
myswzhou@hotmail.com, yplin@hnu.cn, {jilwang, eway_chang, oyjchen}@hotmail.com

Abstract. In this paper, we propose an algorithm for wavelet based spatio-temporal data compression in wireless sensor networks. By employing a ring topology, the algorithm is capable of supporting a broad scope of wavelets that can simultaneously explore the spatial and temporal correlations among the sensory data. Furthermore, the ring based topology is in particular effective in eliminating the "border effect" generally encountered by wavelet based schemes. We propose a "Hybrid" decomposition based wavelet transform instead of wavelet transform based on the common dyadic decomposition, since temporal compression is local and far cheaper than spatial compression in sensor networks. We show that the optimal level of wavelet transform is different due to diverse sensor network circumstances. Theoretically and experimentally, we conclude the proposed algorithm can effectively explore the spatial and temporal correlation in the sensory data and provide significant reduction in energy consumption and delay compared to other schemes.

1 Introduction

Wireless sensor networks are widely used in military and civil fields, such as battle monitoring, environmental exploration, and traffic control [1, 2]. Sensor networks usually have limited energy and link bandwidth and hence sending the original data directly is not feasible. Wavelet data compression has been attracting extensive research efforts in wireless sensor networks targeting at reducing network load and hence energy consumption and delay. Wavelets are a mathematics technique that can simultaneously represent the data's time and frequency behavior. This representation inherently provides the multi-resolution analysis view needed by applications while still preserving the data's statistical interpretation regardless of the scale or compression ratio. It's fairly promising for wavelets in both theory and application in sensor networks. WISDEN

J.X. Yu, M. Kitsuregawa, and H.V. Leong (Eds.): WAIM 2006, LNCS 4016, pp. 337–348, 2006.
© Springer-Verlag Berlin Heidelberg 2006

system [3] is designed for structural monitoring; it performs the wavelet compression in single sensor node firstly and then wavelet coefficients are sent for further processing centrally. Aiming at time-series sampled by a single sensor node, RACE [4] proposes a rate adaptive Haar wavelet compression algorithm. The support of Haar wavelet is 1 and its structure is simple, so the algorithm can come true easily. However, those wavelet algorithms do not exploit the fact that data originated from spatially close sensors are likely to be correlated. Energy would be wasted with the transmission of redundant data. DIMENSIONS [5] proposes a hierarchical routing with its wavRoute protocol, which exploits temporal data redundancy of sensor nodes in the bottom firstly, and then spatial data reduction in the middle hierarchy. Obviously, there exists the transmission of spatial redundancy from the bottom to middle hierarchy. Noticeably, a series of papers have pioneered in wavelet based distributed compression [6, 7, 8] recently. While these papers have provided certain insights in employing distributed wavelet transform(WT) to exploit spatial correlation among data, they are often limited to the cursory application of wavelet function. Although these algorithms are shown to be simple, they lack the consideration of property of WT, such as "border effect" [9], the level of WT, and so on. Furthermore, existing schemes have often focused on either exploiting the temporal correlation or spatial correlation of the sensory data, but not both simultaneously. This, in turn has limited their performance and application scope.

Motivated thereby, in this paper, we propose a ring topology based distributed wavelet compression algorithm. Our scheme simultaneously exploits the spatial and temporal correlation residing in the sensor data within a cluster. Furthermore, our scheme is capable of accommodating a broad range of wavelets which can be designated by different applications. Moreover, the ring model will naturally eliminate the "border effects" encountered by WT and hence further strengthen its support to general wavelets. The common dyadic decomposition based WT is not feasible in sensor networks, since temporal compression is local and far cheaper than spatial compression. We propose a "Hybrid" decomposition based WT and show that the optimal level of WT is different due to diverse natures of data and the distance between sensor nodes and cluster head. Theoretically and experimentally, we analyze the performance of the ring based WT and perform comparison with non-distributed approach.

The remainder of this paper is organized as follows. In Section 2, we detail the ring model and describe the WT thereon. In Section 3, we analyze the performance of the proposed framework and study the optimal level WT theoretically. Experimental study is presented in Section 4 and we conclude in Section 5.

2 Spatio-temporal Wavelet Compression Algorithm

In this section, we first present the network model and the construction of the virtual ring topology. The wavelet based algorithm for compressing spatial and temporal correlated data is then detailed.

2.1 Virtual Grid and Ring Topology

We assume that the sensor network is divided into different clusters, each of which is controlled by a cluster head [10]. Our focus is given to energy-efficient gathering of the sensory data from various cluster members to the cluster head. Routing the data from the cluster head to the sink is out of the scope of this paper although it may benefit from the compression algorithm presented in this paper. We assume that in each cluster, nodes are distributed in a virtual grid as illustrated in Fig. 1. Due to redundancy, one node in each grid cell is required to report its data to the cluster head. Without confusion, we will simply use node to refer to this reporting sensor. We remark that this model is neither restrictive nor unrealistic. In the worst case, a single node can be logically reside in one grid cell and can be required to report its data corresponding to every query or during every specified interval.

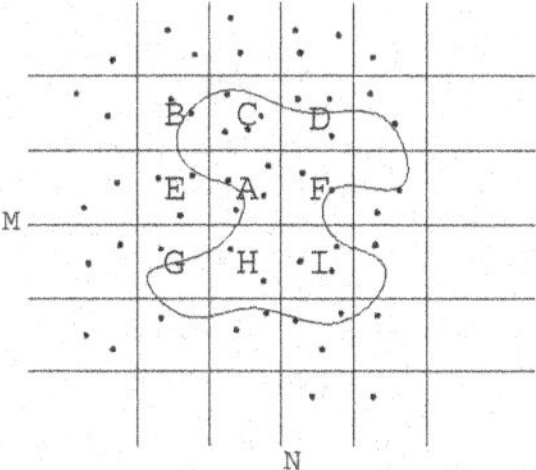

Fig. 1. Ring topology based on virtual grid

The key for our construction is that we form a ring topology among the reporting sensor nodes, as illustrated in Fig. 1. In this ring topology, neighboring nodes belong to spatial adjacent grid cells. A node on the ring receives data from one of its neighbors, fuses the data with its own, and further forward the results to the other neighbor. As the nodes are relaying the sensory data, WT will be executed and certain wavelet coefficients will be actually stored locally and some others will be actually forwarded. Indeed, nodes in a particular grid cell can alternatively participate in the ring and hence the data gathering procedure. This way, energy consumption can be more evenly distributed among the nodes and thus extend the network lifetime. Readers are referred to [11] for approaches of scheduling nodes within one grid, for example, power on and off, for this purpose.

Given the ring topology, in each data gathering round, a node will be chosen as the "head" of the ring and the nodes will be indexed accordingly as $s_0, s_1, \cdots, s_i, \cdots, s_{N-1}$, where N is the number of nodes on the ring. In addition, we assume that sensor i stores data $c_{ji}, j = 0, 1, \cdots, M-1$, where j is the temporal index and c_{ji} represents the sensory data of sensor i at time index j. Evidently, dependent on M, each sensor will window out history data. Accordingly, we can arrange the sensory data on the ring according to their spatial and temporal relationship to a matrix $C^0 = \{c_{ji}\}, 0 \le i < N, 0 \le j < M$, where column i represent the data of sensor node i. For ease of notation, we will use $\boldsymbol{C}_i$

to denote column i. Notice that $\boldsymbol{C}_0$ and $\boldsymbol{C}_{N-1}$ are adjacent on the ring topology and hence will possess relatively higher correlation. As we will detail later, this unique feature of ring topology can effectively help us eliminate the "border effects" of WT.

2.2 "Hybrid" Decomposition Based Distributed Spatio-temporal Wavelet Transform

Our goal is to employ the WT for compression sensory data on the ring so that it can be energy efficiently transmitted to the cluster head. The approach is to simultaneously exploit the temporal and spatial correlation among the nodes' data and reduce the redundancy thereby. As the data is represented by matrix C^0, the temporal (within a node) and spatial (among multiple nodes) correlation is then captured by the columns and rows respectively.

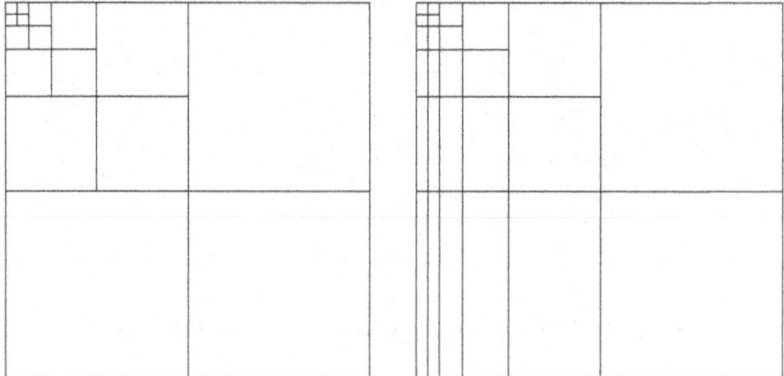

(a) Dyadic tree decomposition (b) "Hybrid" decomposition

Fig. 2. The structure of five-level decomposition

Intuitively, we can perform two-dimensional WT on the matrix C^0 to exploit the spatio-temporal correlation. For two-dimensional tensor product WT, the common structure of decomposition is dyadic tree decomposition as illustrated in Fig. 2(a). Using the structure of dyadic tree decomposition, we will first perform WT on each row, and then perform WT on the column. These row WT and column WT will be performed recursively to achieve a K-level WT. Communication constraints in sensor networks drive a time first, space next approach to compressing the sensory data, since temporal compression is local and far cheaper than spatial compression. Correspondingly, the common dyadic tree decomposition will not adapt to sensor networks.

In this section, we propose a "hybrid" decomposition based distributed WT, as illustrated in Fig. 2(b). We will first perform K-level WT on all columns to exploit temporal correlation, followed by a dyadic WT on the row to exploit spatial correlation. Notice that column WT is within a single node hence no communication is required although data shall be buffered. On the contrary, the row WT is among the sensor nodes and hence require additional communications.

This way, by reducing the temporal data firstly, the communication overhead of column WT is reduced. Without loss of generality, we consider $K = 2$ levels distributed spatio-temporal WT.

Our first step is to perform K-level transform on the columns of C^0 to exploit temporal correlation. Let L_n and H_n be lowpass analysis filter and highpass analysis filter respectively, we have

$$c_{m,i}^{L_c^1} = \sum_n L_{(n-2m)} \boldsymbol{C_i}(n) \tag{1}$$

$$c_{m,i}^{H_c^1} = \sum_n H_{(n-2m)} \boldsymbol{C_i}(n), \quad 0 \leq m \leq M/2 - 1 \tag{2}$$

$$c_{m,i}^{L_c^2} = \sum_n L_{(n-2m)} c_{n,i}^{L_c^1} \tag{3}$$

$$c_{m,i}^{H_c^2} = \sum_n H_{(n-2m)} c_{n,i}^{L_c^1}, \quad 0 \leq m \leq M/4 - 1 \tag{4}$$

where $C_{m,i}^{L_c^k}$ represents the mth approximation wavelet coefficient in i^{th} column in the kth level of the column WT, $C_{m,i}^{H_c^k}$ is the corresponding detail wavelet coefficient, where $1 \leq k \leq K$ and $\boldsymbol{C}_i(n)$ denotes the nth element of $\boldsymbol{C}_i$. Notice that this transform is performed within each node on its own sensory data and thus does not require any communication among the nodes on the ring. Subsequently, we can realign the resultant wavelet coefficients and obtain matrix

$$C_1 = \left\{ \begin{matrix} c_{0,0}^{L_c^2} & c_{0,1}^{L_c^2} & \cdots & c_{0,N-1}^{L_c^2} \\ \vdots & \vdots & \ddots & \vdots \\ c_{\frac{M}{4}-1,0}^{L_c^2} & c_{\frac{M}{4}-1,1}^{L_c^2} & \cdots & c_{\frac{M}{4}-1,N-1}^{L_c^2} \\ c_{0,0}^{H_c^2} & c_{0,1}^{H_c^2} & \cdots & c_{0,N-1}^{H_c^2} \\ \vdots & \vdots & \ddots & \vdots \\ c_{\frac{M}{4}-1,0}^{H_c^2} & c_{\frac{M}{4}-1,1}^{H_c^2} & \cdots & c_{\frac{M}{4}-1,N-1}^{H_c^2} \\ c_{0,0}^{H_c^1} & c_{0,1}^{H_c^1} & \cdots & c_{0,N-1}^{H_c^1} \\ \vdots & \vdots & \ddots & \vdots \\ c_{\frac{M}{2}-1,0}^{H_c^1} & c_{\frac{M}{2}-1,1}^{H_c^1} & \cdots & c_{\frac{M}{2}-1,N-1}^{H_c^1} \end{matrix} \right\}$$

Given matric C_1, our second step is to perform K-level transform on its rows to explore the spatial correlation among the nodes. Note that the first and the last column are adjacent on the ring topology, and this resembles "the periodic extension to signal". Towards this end, for general wavelets with arbitrary supports whose lowpass analysis filter is L_n, $-i_1 \leq n < j_1$ and highpass analysis filter is H_n, $-i_2 \leq n < j_2$, where $i_1, i_2, j_1, j_2 \geq 0$, we analyze the different cases of the row transform based on whether j_1 and j_2 are even or odd.

Case I: If j_1 is even and j_2 is odd, by performing the first WT on the rows in a similar way to the column WT, we obtain

$$C_2 = \left\{ \begin{array}{ccccc}
c_{0,l_0}^{L_r^1 L_c^2} & c_{0,h_0}^{H_r^1 L_c^2} & \cdots & c_{0,l_{\frac{N}{2}-1}}^{L_r^1 L_c^2} & c_{0,h_{\frac{N}{2}-1}}^{H_r^1 L_c^2} \\
\vdots & \vdots & \ddots & \vdots & \vdots \\
c_{\frac{M}{4}-1,l_0}^{L_r^1 L_c^2} & c_{\frac{M}{4}-1,h_0}^{H_r^1 L_c^2} & \cdots & c_{\frac{M}{4}-1,l_{\frac{N}{2}-1}}^{L_r^1 L_c^2} & c_{\frac{M}{4}-1,h_{\frac{N}{2}-1}}^{H_r^1 L_c^2} \\
c_{0,l_0}^{L_r^1 H_c^2} & c_{0,h_0}^{H_r^1 H_c^2} & \cdots & c_{0,l_{\frac{N}{2}-1}}^{L_r^1 H_c^2} & c_{0,h_{\frac{N}{2}-1}}^{H_r^1 H_c^2} \\
\vdots & \vdots & \ddots & \vdots & \vdots \\
c_{\frac{M}{4}-1,l_0}^{L_r^1 H_c^2} & c_{\frac{M}{4}-1,h_0}^{H_r^1 H_c^2} & \cdots & c_{\frac{M}{4}-1,l_{\frac{N}{2}-1}}^{L_r^1 H_c^2} & c_{\frac{M}{4}-1,h_{\frac{N}{2}-1}}^{H_r^1 H_c^2} \\
c_{0,l_0}^{L_r^1 H_c^1} & c_{0,h_0}^{H_r^1 H_c^1} & \cdots & c_{0,l_{\frac{N}{2}-1}}^{L_r^1 H_c^1} & c_{0,h_{\frac{N}{2}-1}}^{H_r^1 H_c^1} \\
\vdots & \vdots & \ddots & \vdots & \vdots \\
c_{\frac{M}{2}-1,l_0}^{L_r^1 H_c^1} & c_{\frac{M}{2}-1,h_0}^{H_r^1 H_c^1} & \cdots & c_{\frac{M}{2}-1,l_{\frac{N}{2}-1}}^{L_r^1 H_c^1} & c_{\frac{M}{2}-1,h_{\frac{N}{2}-1}}^{H_r^1 H_c^1}
\end{array} \right\}$$

where $l_i = (\frac{N-j_1+2i}{2} mod \frac{N}{2})$, $h_i = (\frac{N-j_2+2i+1}{2} mod \frac{N}{2})$, $c_{m,l_i}^{L_r^{k_1} L_c^{k_2}}$ or $c_{m,l_i}^{L_r^{k_1} H_c^{k_2}}$ represents the ${l_i}^{th}$ approximation wavelet coefficient of mth row in the k_1^{th} level of the row WT to the approximation or detail coefficients generated by the k_2^{th} level column WT, and $c_{m,l_i}^{H_r^{k_1} L_c^{k_2}}$ or $c_{m,l_i}^{H_r^{k_1} H_c^{k_2}}$ represents the corresponding detail coefficients. We remark that for a node with index i, if i is even, the node stores coefficients $c_{m,\frac{N-j_1+i}{2} mod \frac{N}{2}}^{L_r^{k_1} L_c^{k_2}}$ and $c_{m,\frac{N-j_1+i}{2} mod \frac{N}{2}}^{L_r^{k_1} H_c^{k_2}}$; if i is odd, the node stores coefficients $c_{m,\frac{N-j_2+i}{2} mod \frac{N}{2}}^{H_r^{k_1} L_c^{k_2}}$ and $c_{m,\frac{N-j_2+i}{2} mod \frac{N}{2}}^{H_r^{k_1} H_c^{k_2}}$, where $1 \leq k_1, k_2 \leq K$, $0 \leq m \leq M/2-1$.

Notice that this transform is performed among the sensor nodes on the ring to harvest the spatial correlation and hence resultant wavelet coefficients cannot be realigned as in the column WT.

Based on the the approximation coefficients in C_2, we can obtain matrix C_3 as follow:

$$C_3 = \left\{ \begin{array}{cccc}
c_{0,l_0}^{L_r^1 L_c^2} & c_{0,l_1}^{L_r^1 L_c^2} & \cdots & c_{0,l_{\frac{N}{2}-1}}^{L_r^1 L_c^2} \\
\vdots & \vdots & \ddots & \vdots \\
c_{\frac{M}{4}-1,l_0}^{L_r^1 L_c^2} & c_{\frac{M}{4}-1,l_1}^{L_r^1 L_c^2} & \cdots & c_{\frac{M}{4}-1,l_{\frac{N}{2}-1}}^{L_r^1 L_c^2} \\
c_{0,l_0}^{L_r^1 H_c^2} & c_{0,l_1}^{L_r^1 H_c^2} & \cdots & c_{0,l_{\frac{N}{2}-1}}^{L_r^1 H_c^2} \\
\vdots & \vdots & \ddots & \vdots \\
c_{\frac{M}{4}-1,l_0}^{L_r^1 H_c^2} & c_{\frac{M}{4}-1,l_1}^{L_r^1 H_c^2} & \cdots & c_{\frac{M}{4}-1,l_{\frac{N}{2}-1}}^{L_r^1 H_c^2}
\end{array} \right\}$$

We perform the second level row WT on matrix C_3 as those to matrix C_2 and extend to the Kth level row WT.

After K-level distributed spatial-temporal WT are performed, the original data gathered by the nodes on the ring are transformed to wavelet domain. Since the spatial and temporal correlations are exploited, we can represent the original data using fewer bits. In lossless compression, all the wavelet coefficients are encoded and sent to the cluster head. In lossy compression, according to different application-specific requirements, such as error bound, energy cost, etc., we can accordingly select the wavelet coefficients, and then they are encoded and sent to the cluster head.

Case II: If j_1 and j_2 are both odd, while we can perform the transform following similar procedure, the matrices C_2 will be significantly different. Due space limitation, we omit them here but remarks that those nodes whose indexes are even will not store wavelet coefficients and become pure delays.

When j_1 is odd and j_2 is even, it will be similar to the first case, and when j_1 and j_2 are all even, it will be similar to the second case discussed above. i_1 and i_2 will not affect the distribution of wavelet coefficients. The reason is that when we perform row WT, the first group of approximation coefficients are calculated using the data stored in the $((N - i_1)modN)^{th}$ node to the $(j_1 modN)^{th}$ node and are stored in the $(j_1 modN)^{th}$ node. The corresponding detail coefficients are calculated using the data stored in the $((N-i_2)modN)^{th}$ node to the $(j_2 modN)^{th}$ node and are stored in the $(j_2 modN)^{th}$ node.

2.3 Discussion

In the above WT, the ring head can be alternated among different nodes when performing the data gathering procedure. Consequently, the wavelet coefficients will be distributed to different nodes accordingly which in turn will balance the energy consumption within the cluster. Furthermore, neighboring nodes on the ring belong to spatial adjacent virtual grids, so the data gathered by the neighboring nodes are more likely spatially correlated. Because the calculation of approximation and detail wavelet coefficients are for neighboring nodes within a support length, performing WT based on the ring can make full use of spatial correlation to remove the data redundancy and hence reduce transmission cost.

More importantly, performing WT based on ring topology naturally eliminates the "border effect" problem inherent in WT. It is well known that general wavelet functions are defined on the real axis R while the signal is always limited in a finite region K. Therefore, the approximate space $L^2(\mathrm{R})$ will not match the signal space $L^2(\mathrm{K})$ which will result in the "border effect" and thus introduce errors during signal reconstruction. One of the general methods to deal with "border effect" is extending border. The ring topology resembles a periodic extension to the signal that naturally dissolves the "border effect".

3 Analysis

We now briefly analysis the total energy consumption and delay of the proposed scheme and study the optimal level spatio-temporal WT. For this purpose, we adopt the first order radio model described in [10]. In this model, a radio dissipates E_{elec} amount of energy at the transmitter or receiver circuitry and ϵ_{amp} amount of energy for transmit amplifier. Signal attenuation is modelled to proportional to d^2 on the channel, where d denotes distance. For k bits data and a distance d, the transmission E_{Tx} and reception energy consumption E_{Rx} can be calculated respectively as follows:

$$E_{Tx}(k,d) = E_{Tx-elec}(k) + E_{Tx-amp}(k,d) \quad (5)$$

$$E_{Tx}(k,d) = E_{elec} * k + \epsilon_{amp} * k * d^2 \quad (6)$$

$$E_{Rx}(k) = E_{Rx-elec}(k) = E_{elec} * k \quad (7)$$

We further assume that the sensor nodes can transmit simultaneously and neglect the processing and propagation delay. Let the transmission time of one data unit be one unit time. For performance comparison, we employ a *non-distributed approach* for data gathering. In this approach, sensor nodes in the cluster will send their data to the cluster head directly, and thus no inter-nodes communications are required.

3.1 Energy Consumption and Delay Analysis

In this subsection, We analysis the total energy consumption and delay of the proposed scheme. Let E_{IN} and D_{IN} represents the energy consumption and delay resulting from communication among the nodes within this cluster for performing the proposed WT, We can derive the following theorem.

Theorem 1. *For general wavelets with arbitrary supports, let the lowpass analysis be $L_n, -i_1 \leq n < j_1$, and the highpass analysis be $H_n, -i_2 \leq n < j_2$, where $i_1, i_2, j_1, j_2 \geq 0$. For a K-level distributed spatial-temporal WT based on the ring topology proposed above, to gather the sensory data in a cluster of N nodes, we have*

$$E_{IN} = \sum_{k=1}^{K} \sum_{l=0}^{N/2^k-1} (E_{k,l}^P + 2E_{elec}(\sum_{i=0}^{i_1+j_1+1} q_{ikl}^L + \sum_{i=0}^{i_2+j_2+1} q_{ikl}^H) + \epsilon_{amp}(\sum_{i=0}^{i_1+j_1+1} (q_{ikl}^L \cdot d_{ikl}^L) + \sum_{i=0}^{i_2+j_2+1} (q_{ikl}^H \cdot d_{ikl}^H))) \quad (8)$$

$$D_{IN} = \sum_{k=1}^{K} (\max_{0 \leq l \leq \frac{N}{2^k}-1} (\sum_{l=0}^{i_1+j_1-1} q_{ikl}^L) + \max_{0 \leq l \leq \frac{N}{2^k}-1} (\sum_{l=0}^{i_2+j_2-1} q_{ikl}^H)) \quad (9)$$

where

$$q_{ikl}^L = q_{k,(-i_1+N+2^k l+(2^{k-1}-1)(i_1+j_1)+2^{k-1}i) mod N},$$

$$q_{ikl}^H = q_{k,(-i_2+N+2^k l+(2^{k-1}-1)(i_2+j_2)+2^{k-1}i) mod N},$$

$$d_{ikl}^L = (\sum_{j=-i_1+N+2^k l+(2^{k-1}-1)(i_1+j_1)}^{-i_1+N+2^k l+(2^{k-1}-1)(i_1+j_1)+2^{k-1}-1} d_{j mod N})^2,$$

$$d_{ikl}^H = (\sum_{j=-i_2+N+2^k l+(2^{k-1}-1)(i_2+j_2)}^{-i_2+N+2^k l+(2^{k-1}-1)(i_2+j_2)+2^{k-1}-1} d_{j mod N})^2,$$

$q^L_{k,i}$ and $q^H_{k,i}$ are the data amount transmitted by the ith node when the lth approximation coefficient and the corresponding detail coefficient in the kth level row WT are calculated respectively, d_{jmodN} is the distance between the $(jmodN)^{th}$ node and the $((j+1)modN)^{th}$ node, $E^P_{k,l}$ is the processing energy of when the lth wavelet coefficients is calculated in the kth level WT.

Proof. When the lth approximation wavelet coefficient in the kth level row WT is calculated, the transmitting cost $E^L_{k,l}$ is: $E^L_{k,l} = E_{Tx} + E_{Rx} = 2E_{elec}\sum_{i=0}^{i_1+j_1} q^L_{ikl} + \epsilon_{amp}\sum_{i=0}^{i_1+j_1}(q^L_{ikl}\cdot d^L_{ikl})$ (10). When the lth detail wavelet coefficient in the kth level row WT is calculated, the transmitting cost $E^H_{k,l}$ is: $E^H_{k,l} = 2E_{elec}\sum_{i=0}^{i_2+j_2} q^H_{ikl} + \epsilon_{amp}\sum_{i=0}^{i_2+j_2}(q^H_{ikl}\cdot d^H_{ikl})$ (11). When the kth level WT is performed, the processing cost E_p is: $E_P = \sum_{l=0}^{\frac{N}{2^k}-1} E^P_{k,l}$ (12). Then, the energy consumption in the kth WT is $E_{k,IN}$: $E_{k,IN} = E_P + \sum_{l=0}^{N/2^k-1}(E^L_{k,l} + E^H_{k,l})$ (13). if K-level WT are performed, the energy cost E_{IN} is: $E_{IN} = \sum_{k=1}^{K}(E_p + \sum_{l=0}^{\frac{N}{2^k}-1}(E^L_{k,l} + E^H_{k,l}))$ (14). Taking (10), (11) and (12) into (14), we can obtain (8). The network delay of the kth WT is $D_{k,IN}$: $D_{k,IN} = \max_{0\le l\le \frac{N}{2^k}-1}(\sum_{l=0}^{i_1+j_1-1} q^L_{ikl}) + \max_{0\le l\le \frac{N}{2^k}-1}(\sum_{l=0}^{i_2+j_2-1} q^H_{ikl})$ (15). Hereby, it is easy to get (9).

Notice that $E^P_{k,l}$ includes two parts: one is the processing cost when nodes perform column WT in single node, the other is the processing cost when nodes fuse data obtained from the proceeding nodes. We can conclude from the theorem that, along with increasing levels of the WT, the energy cost also increases. However, the detail wavelet coefficients stored by the nodes also increase. As a result, the data can be coded using fewer bits.

3.2 The Optimal Level Spatio-temporal Wavelet Transform

In this subsection, we will study how many levels WT needed to be performed to obtain optimal network performance. From the viewpoint of information theory, only by decreasing entropy of wavelet coefficients is WT worthy. As we known, entropy corresponds to the average encoding bits. If the entropy of wavelet coefficients is smaller than those in above level WT, the average encoding bits would be decreased. Generally speaking, the entropy of wavelet coefficients lies on the magnitude of signal (set), the specific measured signal (data) and the wavelet function (wavelet). Let B_{k-1} and B_k are the average encoding bits of wavelet coefficients in the $(k-1)^{th}$ and k^{th} level respectively, then we have:

$$B_{k-1} - B_k = f(set, data, wavelet)$$

Compared to non-distributed approach, our scheme reduces the data by eliminating the spatio-temporal correlation among the sensory data. However, performing WT requires inter-nodes communication and computation within nodes, and thus need additional energy consumption and delay. Apparently, there are a trade-off point between WT and non-distributed approach. Studying the optimal level spatio-temporal WT, we have the following theorem:

Theorem 2. *Let the average distance between nodes and the cluster head be D meters,* $K_1 = \max(k : E_{k,IN} - E_{elec}(B_{k-1} - B_k) - \epsilon_{amp}(B_{k-1} - B_k)D^2 \leq 0)$, $K_2 = \max(k : D_{k,IN} - B_k + B_{k-1} \leq 0)$, $E_{k,IN}$ *and* $D_{k,IN}$ *are illustrated in (13) and (15) in the above subsection respectively, then, the optimal level of spatio-temporal WT is K:* $K = \max(K_1, K_2)$.

Proof. The energy consumptions of sending $(B_{k-1} - B_k)$ bits are $(E_{elec}(B_{k-1} - B_k) + \epsilon_{amp}(B_{k-1} - B_k)D^2)$ and delays are $(B_{k-1} - B_k)$. If the energy consumptions and delays generated by the kth level WT are less than or equal to them respectively, the kth level WT would be performed. So, according to the theorem 1, we can easily obtain the theorem 2.

4 Simulation and Results

In this section, using Haar wavelet we evaluate the performance of our algorithm and in particular compare it with the non-distributed approach.

We consider a ring composed of 96 nodes, assuming that the nodes are uniformly distributed and the average distance among the neighboring nodes is 5 meters.We use real life data obtained from the Tropical Atmosphere Ocean Project (http://www.pmel.noaa.gov/tao/), which are the ocean temperatures sampled by 96 sensor nodes from different mornings at different depths at 12:00pm from 1/20/2004 to 5/26/2004. In the experiment, we employ uniform quantization and no entropy coding. Two cases are compared: optimal level Haar WT and non-distributed approach. The results are shown in Fig. 3 and 4. The relations among optimal level of WT(Opt-level), distance between nodes and cluster head(Distance), peak signal to noise ratio($PSNR$), energy consumption(E_D) and delay(D_D) are shown in Table 1.

As we can see, when the proportion of the discarding detail coefficients to total wavelet coefficients in the WT reachs 73 percent, the $PSNR$ is still reach 49dB. We believe that the reasons are the data used in the simulation have strong spatio-temporal correlations and our algorithm can move them efficiently. In our simulation, the optimal level of WT is 0 when the distance between nodes and cluster head is less than 20 meters. This indicates that WT is not

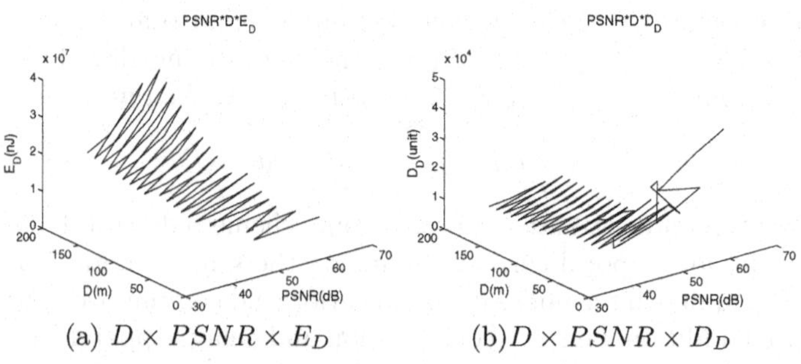

(a) $D \times PSNR \times E_D$ (b)$D \times PSNR \times D_D$

Fig. 3. For optimal level WT

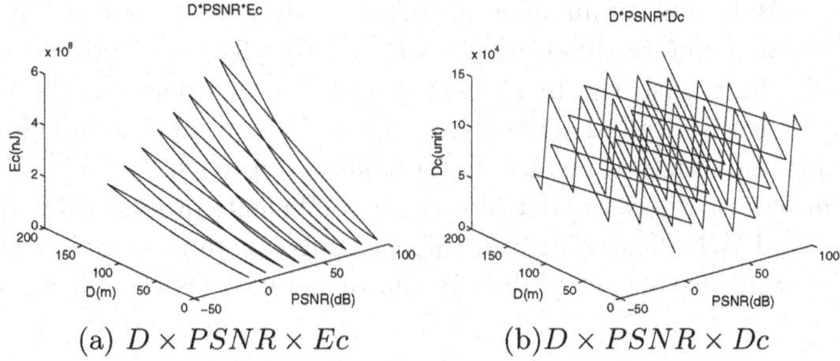

(a) $D \times PSNR \times Ec$ (b)$D \times PSNR \times Dc$

Fig. 4. Non-distributed Approach

Table 1. The optimal level WT

Opt-level	Distance(m)	PSNR(dB)	$E_D(10^7 nJ)$	$D_D(10^4 unit)$
1	20	47.6	0.7	2.6
1	30	47.6	0.9	2.6
2	40	48.9	1.0	1.3
3	50	47.0	1.1	0.7
3	60	47.0	1.2	0.7
3	70	47.0	1.2	0.7
3	80	47.0	1.3	0.7
3	90	47.0	1.4	0.7
3	100	47.0	1.5	0.7
4	110	46.2	1.5	0.5
4	120	46.2	1.5	0.5
4	130	46.2	1.6	0.5
4	140	46.2	1.7	0.5
4	150	46.2	1.8	0.5
4	160	46.2	1.9	0.5
4	170	46.2	2.0	0.5
4	180	46.2	2.1	0.5
4	190	46.2	2.2	0.5
4	200	46.2	2.3	0.5

necessary under this case, for the non-distributed approach has no additional energy consumption. However, with increasing distance between the nodes and the cluster head, the benefit of compression outweigh the energy due to inter-node communication for performing the WT, and then the proposed algorithm will save more energy.

5 Conclusion

In this paper, we have proposed a distributed spatio-temporal compression algorithm based on the ring model. Our algorithm accommodates to a broad range of wavelet function, and can remove the temporal and spatial correlation of original data simultaneously, the ring mode can cope with "border effect" and thus benefit WT. We have analyzed the energy cost and network delay and studied the optimal level WT. The Simulation experiment suggests that the optimal level of WT is different due to different $PSNR$ and the distance between nodes and cluster head, along with the increasing of the distance between the nodes and cluster head, the distributed spatio-temporal wavelet compression algorithm has better performance than that of non-distributed approach.

How to accept or reject the detail wavelet coefficients produced by distributed spatio-temporal WT effectively, and thus gaining constant or limited bit rate to improve the transmitting scheduling in sensor networks is our future work.

References

1. D. Estrin, R. Govindan, J. Heideman and S. Kumar, Next century challenges: scalable coordination in sensor networks, in Proc. MOBICOM, Seattle, USA, Aug., 1999.
2. S. Lindsey, C. Raghavendra and K. Sivalingam, Data gathering algorithms in sensor networks using energy metrics, IEEE transactions on parallel and distributed systems, vol.13, pp.924-935, 2002.
3. N. Xu, S. Rangwala, K. Chintalapudi, D. Ganesan, A. Broad,R. Govindan, and D. Estrin, A wireless sensor network for structuralmonitoring, in Proc. ACM SenSys, Maryland, USA, Nov., 2004.
4. H. Chen, J. Li and P. Mohapatra, RACE: Time Series Compression with Rate Adaptive and Error Bound for Sensor Networks, in Proc. MASS, Fort Lauderdale, USA, Oct., 2004.
5. D. Ganesan, D. Estrin, and J. Heidemann, DIMENSIONS: Why do we need a new data handling architecture for sensor networks?, SIGCOMM Comput. Commun. Rev., vol. 33, no. 1, pp. 143-148, 2003.
6. S. Servetto, Distributed signal processing algorithms for the sensor broadcast problem, in Proc. CISS, Philadelphia, USA, Mar., 2003.
7. A. Ciancio and A. Ortega, A distributed wavelet compression algorithm for wireless multihop sensor networks using lifting, in Proc. ICASSP, Philadelphia, USA, Mar., 2005.
8. J. Acimovic, R. Cristescu and B. Lozano, Efficient distributed multiresolution processing for data gathering in sensor networks, in Proc. ICASSP, Philadelphia, USA, Mar., 2005.
9. G. Karlsson and M. Vetterli, Extension of finite length signals for subband coding, Signal processing, vol.17, pp.161-168, 1989.
10. W. Heinzelman, A. Chandrakasan, and H. Balakrishnan, Energy- Efficient Communication Protocol for Wireless Microsensor Networks, in Proc. HICSS, Hawaii, USA, Jan., 2000.
11. Y. Xu, J. Heidemann, and D. Estrin, Geography-informed energy conservation for ad hoc routing, in Proc. MobiCom, Rome, Italy, Jul., 2001.

Discovery of Temporal Frequent Patterns Using TFP-Tree

Long Jin, Yongmi Lee, Sungbo Seo, and Keun Ho Ryu

Database/Bioinformatics Laboratory, Chungbuk National University, Korea
{kimlyong, ymlee, sbseo, khryu}@dblab.chungbuk.ac.kr
http://dblab.chungbuk.ac.kr/index.html

Abstract. Mining temporal frequent patterns in transaction databases, time-series databases, and many other kinds of databases have been widely studied in data mining research. Most of the previous studies adopt an Apriori-like candidate set generation-and-test approach. However, candidate set generation is still costly, especially when there exist prolific patterns and long patterns. In this paper, we propose an efficient temporal frequent pattern mining method using the TFP-tree (Temporal Frequent Pattern tree). This approach has three advantages: (i) one can scan the transaction only once for reducing significantly the I/O cost; (ii) one can store all transactions in leaf nodes but only save the star calendar patterns in the internal nodes. So we can save a large amount of memory. Moreover, we divide the transactions into many partitions by maximum size domain which significantly saves the memory; (iii) we efficiently discover each star calendar pattern in internal node using the frequent calendar patterns of leaf node. Thus we can reduce significantly the computational time. Our performance study shows that the TFP-tree is efficient and scalable for mining, and is about an order of magnitude faster than the classical frequent pattern mining algorithms.

1 Introduction

Frequent pattern mining plays an essential role in mining association, correlations, causality, sequential patterns, episodes, multidimensional patterns, max-patterns, partial periodicity, emerging patterns, and many other important data mining tasks [1,2,3]. For example *egg* → *coffee* (support: 3%, confidence: 80%) means that 3% of all transactions contain both *egg* and *coffee*, and 80% of the transactions that have *egg* also have *coffee* in them. In real dataset, time is one of the important factors. For example, *eggs* and *coffee* may be ordered together primarily between 7AM and 11AM. Therefore, we may find that the above association rule has a support as high as 40% among the transactions that happen between 7AM and 11AM and has a support as low as 0.005% in other transactions. So we can discover more useful knowledge if we consider the time interval.

Informally, we refer to the association rules along with their temporal intervals as temporal association rules. The discovery of temporal association rules has been discussed in the literature. For example, in [4], the discovery of cyclic association rules

J.X. Yu, M. Kitsuregawa, and H.V. Leong (Eds.): WAIM 2006, LNCS 4016, pp. 349 – 361, 2006.
© Springer-Verlag Berlin Heidelberg 2006

(i.e., the association rules that occur periodically over time) was studied. However, periodicity has limited expressiveness in describing real-life concepts such as the first business day of every month since the distances between two consecutive such business days are not constant. In general, the model does not deal with calendric concepts like year, month, day, and so on. In [5], the work of [4] was extended to treat user-defined temporal patterns. Although the work of [5] is more flexible than that of [4], it only considers the association rules that hold during the user-given time intervals described in term of a calendar algebraic expression. In other words, a single set of time intervals is given by the user and only the association rules on these intervals are considered. This method hence requires user's prior knowledge about the temporal patterns. In calendar based temporal association rules [6], this work was about temporal association rules during time intervals that follow some user-given calendar schemas. Generally, the use of calendar schemas makes the discovered temporal association rules easier to understand. An example of calendar schema is (year, month, day), which yields a set of calendar-based patterns of the form $<d_3, d_2, d_1>$, where each d_i is either an integer or the symbol "*". Such calendar-based patterns represent all daily, monthly, and yearly patterns. For example, <2005, *, 10> is such a pattern, which corresponds to the time intervals consisting of all the 10th day of all months in year 2005. But [6] adopts an Apriori-like candidate set generation-and-test approach. So it is costly to handle a huge number of candidate sets and tedious to repeatedly scan the database and check a large set of candidates by pattern matching, which is especially true for mining long patterns.

In this paper, we propose an efficient temporal frequent pattern mining method using TFP-tree (Temporal Frequent Pattern tree). We propose a completed TFP-tree for efficient mining. This approach has three advantages: (i) this method only scans database once and maintains all transactions using FP-tree. So we can reduce significantly the I/O cost; (ii) this method stores all transactions in leaf nodes but only saves the star calendar patterns in the internal nodes. So we can save a large amount of memory. Moreover, we separate the transactions into many partitions by maximum size domain for saving the memory; (iii) we efficiently discover each star calendar patterns of internal node using the frequent calendar patterns of leaf node. So we can reduce significantly the run time.

The remaining of this paper is organized as follows. Section 2 designs the TFP-tree structure and its construction method is shown in Section 3. Section 4 develops a TFP-tree based frequent pattern mining algorithm, TFP-tree Mining. Section 5 presents our performance study. Section 6 summarizes this paper.

2 Design Frequent Pattern Tree and Other Definitions

Table 1 show the first running example of a transaction database. For convenience of later discussions, we continue to use this example and describe each part.

Let $I=\{a_1,a_2, \ldots,a_m\}$ be a set of items, and a transaction database $DB=<T_1,T_2,\ldots,T_t>$, where $T_i(i\in [1..t])$ is a transaction which contains a set of items in I. The support (or occurrence frequency) of a pattern A, which is a set of items, is the number of transactions containing A in DB. A is a frequent pattern if A's support is no less than a predefined minimum support threshold, ε.

Table 1. A transaction database as a running example

TID	Items	Time Stamp
01	**c,d,e,f,g,i**	**<1,1,1,1>**
02	**a,c,d,e,m,b**	**<1,1,1,1>**
03	**a,c,d,e,b**	**<1,1,1,1>**
04	**a,c,d,h**	**<1,1,1,3>**
05	**a,b,d,h,i**	**<1,1,1,3>**
06	**a,b,d,e,g,k**	**<1,1,1,3>**
07	**c,d,f,g,b**	**<1,1,3,1>**
08	**b,c,d,e**	**<1,1,3,1>**
09	**a,c,e,k,m**	**<1,1,3,3>**
10	**b,d,e,m**	**<1,1,3,3>**

We present a class of calendar related to temporal patterns called calendar patterns. Calendar pattern represents the sets of time intervals in terms of calendar schema specified by user. Calendar schema is a relational schema $R=(f_n:D_n, f_{n-1}:D_{n-1}, ..., f_1:D_1)$, where each attribute f_i is a time granularity name such as year, month, day, and so on. Each D_i is a domain value corresponding to f_i. In the example of Table 1, there is given a calendar schema (year:{1,2}, month:{1,2}, week:{1,2,3}, day:{1,2,3,4}). And a calendar pattern on the calendar schema R is a tuple on R of the form $<d_n, d_{n-1},...,d_1>$. Each d_i is a positive integer in D_i or the symbol "*". "*" denotes all the values corresponding to domain and means "every." Exactly, it represents periodic cycles on the calendar pattern such as every week, every month, and so on. According to the above example 1, the calendar pattern <1,1,*,3> represents time intervals which means the third day of every week of January in the first year.

To design a compact data structure for efficient temporal frequent pattern mining, we define TFP-tree as follows.

Definition 1. (TFP-tree) If a calendar schema R has n attributes, then a temporal frequent pattern tree (or TFP-tree in short) is a tree structure defined below:

1. It consists of one node of all the star patterns *all_star*, a two dimensional array of internal nodes *internal_array[n-2][n]*, and one dimensional array of leaf nodes *leaf_array[n]*.
2. The structure of the internal nodes of a TFP-tree that is called *internal_node* is as follows. It consists of one label of star calendar pattern label and a large k itemset *large_itemset* which is constructed by a star calendar pattern and an *internal_pattern* point, where the structure of *internal_pattern* is constructed by one label of star calendar pattern *calendar_pattern* and a frequent pattern list *freqnt_list*. If there is an internal node that is ith subtree of m level, the label of internal node is as follows.

$$node\ label = \begin{cases} <\overbrace{0,......}^{i-1},\overbrace{1,......}^{m},\overbrace{0,......}^{n-(i-1)-m}>, (i-1)+m \le n \\ <\overbrace{1,......}^{(i-1)+m-n},\overbrace{0,......}^{n-m},\overbrace{1,......}^{n-(i-1)}>, (i-1)+m > n \end{cases} \quad \text{(Formula 1)}$$

where $0 < i \le n$ and $0 < m \le n-2$.

3. The structure of the leaf node of a TFP-tree that is called *leaf_node* is as follows. It consists of one label of star calendar pattern label and a large 1-itemset *large_itemset* which is constructed by a star calendar pattern and a

leaf_pattern point, where the structure of *leaf_pattern* is constructed by one label of star calendar pattern *calendar_pattern*, a transaction list *tran_list*, a FP-tree point *FP_T*, and a frequent pattern list *freqnt_list*. The label of the *i*th leaf node is as follows.

$$node\ label = \begin{cases} <\overbrace{0,\ldots\ldots}^{i-1},\overbrace{1,\ldots\ldots}^{n-1},\overbrace{0,\ldots\ldots}^{2-i}>, i \le 2 \\ <\overbrace{1,\ldots\ldots}^{i-2},0,\overbrace{1,\ldots\ldots}^{n-(i-1)}>, i > 2 \end{cases} \quad \text{(Formula 2)}$$

$where\ 0 < i \le n.$

From the above definition, we can generally construct a TFP-tree shown in the example of Table 1 and Fig. 1.

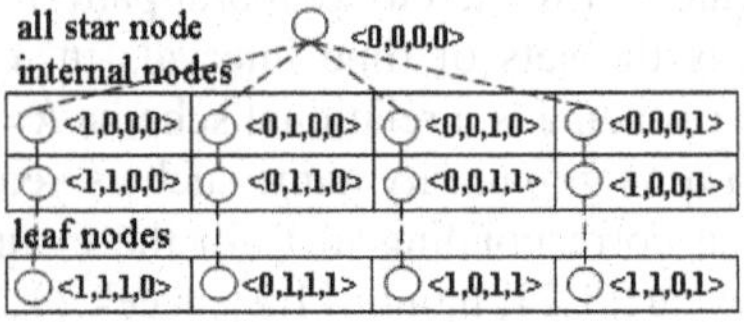

Fig. 1. The TFP-tree in example 1

Why do we use the arrays and are there not any missing or overlapping transactions? We prove this problem in Problem A of Appendix.

3 Construction of Temporal Frequent Pattern Tree

This section shows how to construct a TFP-tree based on Definition 1. The construction process consists of two important procedures: (i) *insert_tree()* procedure inserts

Algorithm 1 (TFP-tree construction)

Input: A transaction database *DB* and calendar schema *R*.
Output: Its frequent pattern tree, *TFP-tree*
Method: The *TFP-tree* is constructed in the following steps.

```
1. Select maximum size domain d from the calendar schema R.
2. Sort and scan the transaction database DB according to d.
3. Create the root of a TFP tree T.
   And label the internal node and leaf node according to formula 1 and 2, respectively.
4. Create a parameter max_domain and initialize 1;
5. For each transaction Trans in DB do {
     Filter the maximum domain schema tem_max from the basic time e0 of Trans.
     If max_domain is equal to tem_max then {//inset the Trans into TFP-tree
        insert_tree(Trans,T);
     } Else {//refresh the TFP-tree
        refresh_tree(max_domain,T);
        max_domain = tem_max;
        insert_tree(Trans,T);
   } }
   refresh_tree(max_domain,T);//fresh all of remaining 1-star calendar pattern
```

transactions into TFP-tree and (ii) *refresh_tree()* procedure constructs FP-tree. Based on Definition 1, we have the following TFP-tree construction algorithm in detail.

Scanning the transactions, we sort the transactions according to maximum size domain. There are several reasons. (i) For saving the memory, TFP-tree only saves transactions into the array of leaf nodes and the array of internal nodes does not store the transactions but saves only the corresponding to star calendar patterns. But there is still a need of n times memory space of the total number of all transactions. Consider example 1 above, there needs 4 times memory space. So a solution to save the memory efficiently is necessary. Solving this problem, we use maximum size domain to separate many partitions of transactions. Why do we select maximum size domain? This reason is that the leaf node is 1-star calendar pattern and only one domain is "*". Therefore we must select maximum size domain and can separate many partitions of transactions by it. (ii) Scanning each part of transactions and inserting these into leaf_array of TFP-tree, we construct all of FP-trees that the 1-star calendar pattern contains this domain value of maximum size domain before scanning next part of transactions. Completing the process of constructing FP-Tree, we delete transactions in each 1-star calendar pattern for saving the memory space. From these reasons, we can guarantee to not only save the memory but also discover frequent patterns efficiently. In example 1, the maximum size domain is D_1 and we sort the transactions. It is shown in the left table of Fig. 2.

The procedure of *insert_tree()* is a function that inserts each transaction into the transaction list of the covering the basic time in leaf node.

```
Procedure 1 (Inserting transactions into leaf node)
insert_tree(Trans, T) {
 1. Filter basic time e0 from Trans.
 2. Insert Trans into T.leaf_array[n] as follows.
    For each i in n do
      k ← (i+n)%(n+1);
      e is 1-star calendar pattern that kth of e0 is the star calendar.
      If T.leaf_array[i].large_itemset(e) is null then
        Create a leaf_pattern temp_leaf,
        temp_leaf.calendar_pattern ← e; temp_leaf.tran_list ← Trans;
        Insert temp_leaf into T.leaf_array[i].large_itemset(e);
      Else
        Insert Trans into T.leaf_array[i].large_itemset(e).trans_list;
 3. Insert star calendar pattern into T.internal_array as follows.
    For each m in (n-2) do //m level
      For each i in n do {//ith subtree
        e is star calendar pattern that is derivable from formula 1.
        If T.internal_array[m][i].large_itemset(e) is null then
          Create a internal_pattern temp_internal;
          temp_internal.calendar_pattern ← e;
          Insert temp_internal into T.internal_array[m][i].large_itemset(e);
} }
```

This *insert_tree()* procedure consists of two parts: inserting transactions into leaf node and star calendar patterns into internal node. In the process of inserting into leaf node, each transaction is inserted into each leaf node in TFP-tree. In the process of inserting into internal node, all of star calendar patterns that cover the basic time are inserted into the corresponding to internal node. In this case, we insert the star calendar pattern into internal node only if the internal node does not contain it. The example is shown in Fig. 2.

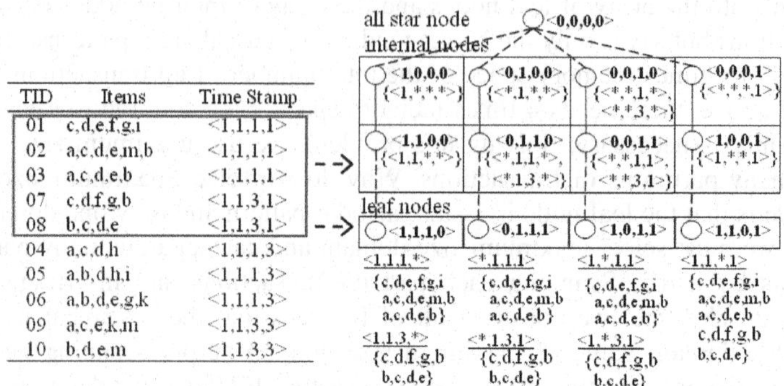

TID	Items	Time Stamp
01	c,d,e,f,g,i	<1,1,1,1>
02	a,c,d,e,m,b	<1,1,1,1>
03	a,c,d,e,b	<1,1,1,1>
07	c,d,f,g,b	<1,1,3,1>
08	b,c,d,e	<1,1,3,1>
04	a,c,d,h	<1,1,1,3>
05	a,b,d,h,i	<1,1,1,3>
06	a,b,d,e,g,k	<1,1,1,3>
09	a,c,e,k,m	<1,1,3,3>
10	b,d,e,m	<1,1,3,3>

Fig. 2. TFP-tree of inserting first partition of transactions in example 1

The procedure of *refresh_tree()* is a function of creating FP-tree that the 1-star calendar pattern contains *max_domain* at leaf nodes.

```
Procedure 2 (Creating the FP-tree)
refresh_tree(max_domain,T) {
 For each i in n do {
  For each calendar pattern e in T.leaf_array[i].large_itemset do {
   If max_domain ∈ e then
    Create a parameter temp of leaf_pattern;
    Create the root of an FP-tree, FP_T, and label it as "null".
    Scan the transaction T.leaf_array[i].large_itemset(e).tran_list once.
    Collect the set of frequent items F and their supports.
    Sort F in support descending order as L, the list of frequent items.
    For each transaction Trans in T.leaf_array[i].large_itemset(e).tran_list do
      Select and sort the frequent items in Trans according to the order of L.
      Let the sorted frequent item list in Trans be [p|P],
      where p is the first element and P is the remaining list.
      Call FP_insert tree([p|P]; FP_T);
    T.leaf_array[i].large_itemset(e).FPT_link ← FP_T;
    Delete T.leaf_array[i].large_itemset(e).tran_list.
}}}
```

Completing the process of inserting a part of transactions, we construct all of FP-trees that the 1-star calendar pattern contains this part of domain value of maximum size domain and delete the corresponding to transactions for saving the memory. So we only maintain this FP-tree and do not need the transactions. If there are a large amount of databases, we can save so much memory and do not affect the mining frequent patterns. Where the procedure of FP-insert_tree([*p*|P]; T) is the creating FP-tree function in [7]. The example is shown in Fig. 3.

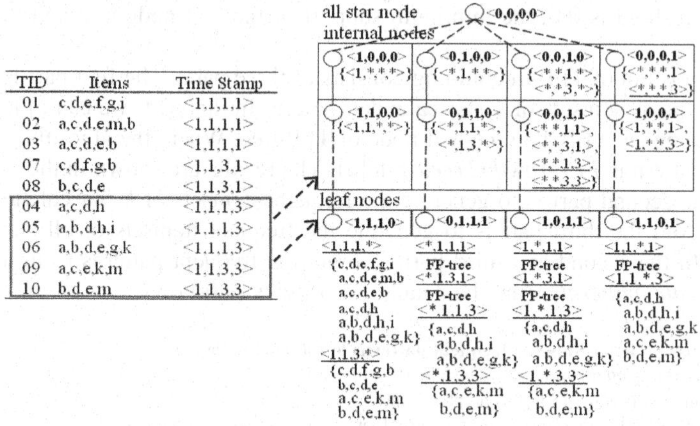

Fig. 3. TFP-tree of inserting second partition of transactions in example 1

4 Mining Frequent Patterns Using TFP-Tree

Construction of a compact TFP-tree can be performed with a rather compact data structure. However, this does not generate the frequent patterns. In this section, we will study how to explore the compact information stored in a TFP-tree and to develop an efficient method for mining the complete set of frequent patterns.

Given a transaction database *DB* and a minimum support threshold, ε, the problem of finding the complete set of frequent patterns is called the frequent pattern mining problem. Based on the above section, we have the following algorithm for mining frequent patterns using TFP-tree.

Algorithm 2 (TFP-tree Mining)

Input: TFP-tree *T*, a minimum support threshold *ε*.
Output: The complete set of frequent patterns.
Method: Generate the frequent star calendar pattern as follows.

1. Generate the frequent itemsets of 1-star calendar pattern.
   For each *i* in *n* **do**
      For each calendar pattern *e* in *T.leaf_array[i].large_itemset* **do**
         Create a parameter *temp* of leaf_pattern;
         temp ← *T.leaf_array[i].large_itemset(e)*;
         temp.freqnt_list ← FP-growth(*temp.FP_T,null*);
         Delete *temp.FP_T* of FP-tree.
2. Generate the frequent itemsets of k-star calendar pattern (k>1).
   For each *i* in *n* **do**
      For each *m* in (*n*-2) **do**
         generate_star_pattern(*T.internal_array[m][i].large_itemset*, *T.leaf_array[i].large_itemset, ε*);
3. Generate the frequent itemsets of all star calendar pattern.
   generate_star_pattern(*T.all_star,T.leaf_array[1].large_itemset, ε*);

To help the understanding of TFP-tree mining algorithm, we illustrate frequent patterns mining in Fig. 4 using 3-subtree of TFP-tree in Fig. 3. Where the minimum support threshold is 0.6, the minimum support of the leaf node is 2 and the internal node is 5.

The algorithm of TFP-tree mining consists of three parts. The first part is to generate the frequent itemsets of 1-star calendar pattern. In this part, we can mine frequent patterns using each FP-T in the leaf node of TFP-tree. Where the algorithm of mining frequent pattern is *FP-growth(Tree,α)* in [7]. The results are shown in the top right of Fig. 4. The second part is to generate the frequent itemsets of *k*-star calendar pattern ($1<k<n$). And the third part is to generate the frequent itemsets of all star calendar patterns. In the second and third parts, we get the frequent patterns using the procedure *generate_pattern()*. And the detail of process is as follows.

```
Procedure 3 (Generating the frequent patterns in internal node)
generate_star_pattern(internal_itemset,leaf_itemset,ε) {
   //freqnt_list is consist of {freqnt_ptn,count}
   For all calendar pattern e' in leaf_itemset that cover e in internal_itemset do {
      For each l∈leaf_itemset(e').freqnt_list do {
         If l ∩ internal_itemset(e).freqnt_list ≠ Ø then
            internal_itemset(e).freqnt_list(l.freqnt_ptn).count += l.count;
         Else
            Insert l into internal_itemset(e).freqnt_list;
   } }
   For each calendar pattern e in internal_itemset do {
      For each temp in internal_itemset(e).freqnt_list do {
         If temp.count < ε then
            Delete temp from internal_itemset(e).freqnt_list;
} } }
```

The procedure *generate_pattern()* is the function that generates the frequent calendar pattern. For each sub-tree, each internal node scans the leaf node of this sub-tree and generates frequent pattern itemsets. In other words, we scan each itemset of 1-star

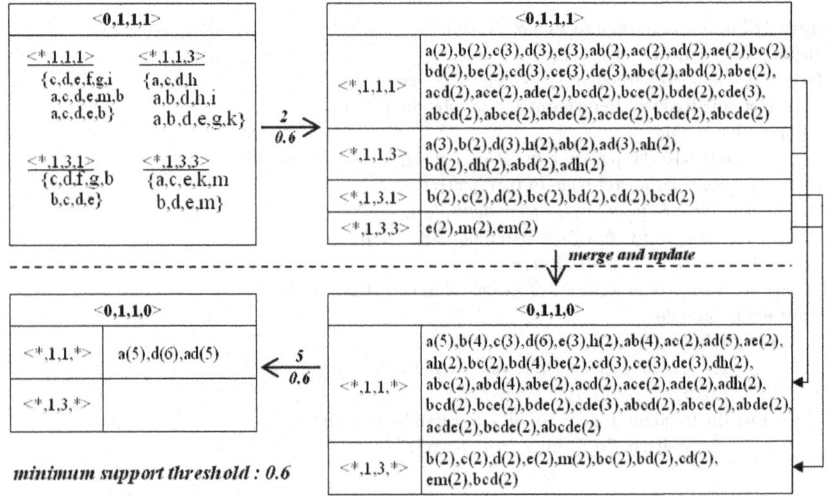

Fig. 4. The illustration of mining the frequent patterns using TFP-tree in example 1

calendar pattern in a leaf node and merge these frequent itemsets into the star calendar pattern that covers this 1-star calendar pattern. If there already exists an itemset, we only add the count. Otherwise, we insert the itemset into there. An example of these results is shown in the bottom right of Fig. 4. And we eliminate the itemsets that do not satisfy the minimum support 5 and select the frequent itemsets. The results are shown in the bottom left of Fig. 4.

Does this TFP-tree mining guarantee the frequent patterns in internal node without missing any frequent itemsets? We prove this problem in Problem B of Appendix.

5 Experiment and Evaluation

In this section, we perform a series of experiments for evaluating the performance of TFP-tree with the classical frequent pattern mining algorithms on synthetic data. All the experiments are performed on a Windows 2000 Server desktop with Pentium PC 2.8GHz and 512 Mbytes of main memory. Also we use JDK 1.4, MS-SQL 2000 database and JDBC driver for connecting MS-SQL 2000.

Our data generation procedure takes the calendar schema (D_4:{1,…,4}, D_3:{1,…,6}, D_2:{1,…,12}, D_1{1,…,30}). The number of items is 100 and the pattern-ratio is 0.5. The average number of per-internal itemsets and transactions per basic time interval are 100 and 1000, respectively. The average size of the transactions and per-interval itemsets are 10 and 4, respectively. For examining the performance, we generate a series of data sets, most of which are generated by varying one parameter while keeping others at their default values. The size of the data sets ranges from 500MB to 5GB.

In our experiments, we compare three algorithms: nontemporal association match (NTA match), calendar temporal association match (CTA match), and temporal frequent pattern match (TFP match).

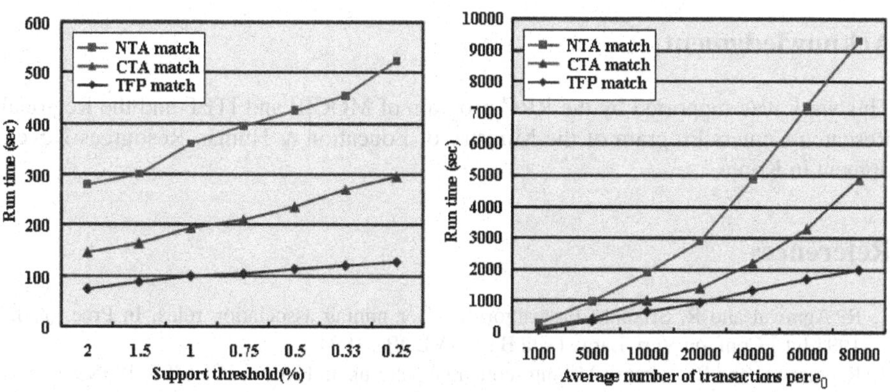

Fig. 5. Comparison of the run time of TFP-tree with other algorithms

The first experiment studies the run time versus support threshold by decreasing support threshold from 2 to 0.25 on the left of Fig. 5. It also shows that TFP match method has good scalability with the reduction of support threshold. The second experiment is about the run time versus average number of transactions per e_0, increasing from 1000 to 80000 on the right of Fig. 5. Both NTA match and CTA match have linear scalability with the number of transactions, but TFP match is more scalable. In both experiments, the run time of TFP match method is increasing more smoothly than others. This reason is that only the run time of mining the frequent pattern using TFP-tree is increased according to decreasing the support threshold while all constructions of TFP-tree have same time. Therefore, discovery temporal frequent patterns using TFP-tree has a better performance than the classical frequent pattern mining algorithms.

6 Conclusion

We have proposed a novel data structure, that is temporal frequent pattern tree (TFP-tree), for storing compressed, crucial information about temporal frequent patterns, and developed a pattern growth method, TFP-tree mining, for efficient mining of frequent patterns in large databases. TFP-tree has several advantages compared to other approaches: (i) one scans the transaction only once for reducing significantly the I/O cost; (ii) one stores all transactions in leaf nodes but saves only the star calendar patterns in the internal nodes, then we can save a large amount of memory. For saving the memory efficiently, we divide the transactions into many partitions by maximum size domain. We prove that there are no transactions missed in Section 2 and Appendix; (iii) we efficiently discover each star calendar pattern of internal node using the frequent calendar patterns of leaf node. We prove that there are not any missing frequent itemsets in Section 4 and Appendix.

Our performance study showed that the TFP-tree is efficient and scalable for mining, and is about an order of magnitude faster than the classical frequent pattern mining algorithms.

Acknowledgment

This work was supported by the RRC program of MOCIE and ITEP and the Regional Research Centers Program of the Ministry of Education & Human Resources Development in Korea.

References

1. R. Agrawal and R. Srikant.: Fast algorithms for mining association rules, In Proc. of the 1994 Int'l Conf. on Very Large Data Bases (VLDB), 1994.
2. R. Agrawal and R. Srikant.: Mining sequential patterns, In Proc. of ICDE'95, 1995.
3. S. Brin, R. Motwani, and C. Silverstein.: Beyond market basket: Generalizing association rules to correlations, In Proc. of SIGMOD'98, 1998.
4. B. Ozden, S. Ramaswamy, and A. silberschatz.: Cyclic association rules, In Proc. of the 14th Int'l Conf. on Data Engineering , 1998.

5. S. Ramaswamy, S. Mahajan and A. Silberschatz.: On the discovery of interesting patterns in association rules, In Proc. of the 1998 Int'l Conf. on Very Large Data Bases (VLDB), 1998.
6. Y. Li and P. Ning.: Discovering Calendar-based Temporal Association Rules, In Proc. of the 8th Int'l Symposium on Temporal Representation and Reasoning, 2001.
7. J. Han, J. Pei, and Y. Yin.: Mining frequent patterns without candidate generation, In Proc. of 2000 ACM-SIGTMOD Int. Conf. Management of Data (SIGMOD'00), 2000.
8. Y. J. Lee, Y. J. Lee, H. K. Kim, B. H. Hwang, and K. H. Ryu.: Discovering Temporal Relation Rules from Temporal Interval Data, EurAsia-ICT2002, 2002.
9. Sungbo Seo, Long Jin, Jun Wook Lee, Keun Ho Ryu, Similarity Pattern Discovery using Calendar Concept Hierarchy in Time Series Data, Asia Pacific Web Conference (APWeb), 2004.

Appendix

Proof of Problem A. Why do we use the arrays and are there not any missing or overlapping transactions? We can use two parts to answer this question.

1. The leaf nodes of each sub-tree has all transactions.
   If there give transaction T_i(i□[1...t]) in *DB* and a sub-tree of 1-star calendar pattern that D_j(j□[1...n]) in the calendar schema *R* is star calendar, there is maximum size of D_n *x* ··· *x* D_1(D_j is except from there) of 1-star calendar patterns in the leaf node of this sub-tree. And all of these 1-star calendar patterns cover the basic time e_0 in T_i. So the leaf node of this sub-tree contains all transactions.
2. Each internal node covers all transactions not any missing or overlapping transactions.

   Case 1:

$$<\overbrace{0,\ldots\ldots}^{i-1},\overbrace{1,\ldots\ldots}^{m},\overbrace{0,\ldots\ldots}^{n-(i-1)-m}> \quad from\ formula1 \quad (1)$$

$$<\overbrace{0,\ldots\ldots}^{i-1},\overbrace{1,\ldots\ldots}^{n-1},\overbrace{0,\ldots\ldots}^{2-i}> \quad from\ formula2 \quad (2)$$

First part of star calendar is same.

From second part,

$$m \le n-2 \Rightarrow m+1 \le n-1$$

$$\therefore m < n-1$$

$\therefore$ *The numer of basic time in* (2) *is large than* (1).

From third part,

$$m \le n-2 \Rightarrow m+2 \le n$$

$$\therefore n-(i-1)-m \ge m+2-(i-1)-m$$

$$= 2-i+1 = (2-i)+1 > (2-i)$$

$\therefore$ *The number of star calendar in* (1) *is large than* (2).

$\therefore$ *The star calendar of* (1) *covers* (2).

Case 2:

$$< \overbrace{1,\ldots\ldots}^{(i-1)+m-n},\overbrace{0,\ldots\ldots}^{n-m},\overbrace{1,\ldots\ldots}^{n-(i-1)} > \quad \textit{from formula} 1 \qquad (3)$$

$$< \overbrace{1,\ldots\ldots}^{i-2},0,\overbrace{1,\ldots\ldots}^{n-(i-1)} > \qquad \textit{from formula} 2 \qquad (4)$$

From first part,

$$m \le n-2$$

$$\therefore (i-1)+m-n \le (i-1)+n-2-n$$

$$= (i-2)-1 < (i-2)$$

$\therefore$ *The number of basic time in* (4) *is large than* (3).

From second part,

$$m \le n-2 \Rightarrow n-m \ge 2$$

$$\therefore n-m > 1$$

$\therefore$ *The number of star calendar in* (3) *is large than* (4).

Third part of basic time is same.

$\therefore$ *The star calendar of* (3) *covers* (4).

So each internal node covers all the transactions, without any missing or overlapping transactions.

Proof of Problem B. We prove the correctness of the frequent patterns in internal node without missing any frequent itemsets.

If there is a *m*-star calendar pattern *P* in the internal node of a sub-tree and *k* of 1-star calendar patterns, $p_1,\ldots,p_k$, respectively that are covered with *P*, we express $P = \{p_1,\ldots,p_k\}$ in short and the domain is $\{D_1,\ldots,D_m\}$. So we can consider that the transactions are partitioned into k parts. Hence this problem is converted into the problem of partition algorithm for mining the frequent itemsets.

Let *L* be the set of actual frequent itemsets in *P*. Since the global frequent itemsets are generated by counting the support for every itemset in C^G, it is sufficient to show that $C^G \supseteq L$. Assume there exists an itemet *l* that is actually frequent but does not appear in C^G, i.e., $l \in L$ but $l \notin C^G$. But $C^G = U_{i=1,\ldots,k} L^i_j$. Hence $l \notin L^i$ for i=1,2,…,*k*. Let $|p_i|$ be the size of 1-star calendar pattern p_i. And $|P|$ is the size of *m*-star calendar pattern *P*. Let $|p_i(l)|$ be the number of transaction containing the itemset *l* in p_i. Since $l \notin L^i$, it must be true that

$$\frac{|p_1(l)|}{|P_1|} < minSup \wedge \frac{|p_2(l)|}{|P_2|} < minSup \wedge \ldots \wedge \frac{|p_k(l)|}{|P_k|} < minSup$$

or

$$|p_1(l)| < minSup \times |p_1| \wedge |p_2(l)| < minSup \times |p_2| \wedge \ldots \wedge |p_k(l)| < minSup \times |p_k|$$

This is equivalent to

$$|p_1(l)| + |p_2(l)| + \ldots + |p_k(l)| < minSup \times (|p_1| + |p_2| + \ldots + |p_k|)$$

But $|p_1|+|p_2|+\ldots+|p_k|$ is the total size of 1-star calendar pattern in leaf node and $|p_1(l)|+|p_2(l)|+\ldots+|p_k(l)|$ is the total number of transactions containing *l* in *DB*.

$$|D_1|+|D_2|+...+|D_m|=|p_1|+|p_2|+...+|p_k|$$
$$\because |P|=|D_1|\times|D_2|\times...\times|D_m|$$
$$\therefore |p_1|+|p_2|+...+|p_k|<|P|$$
$$\therefore |p_1(l)|+|p_2(l)|+...+|p_k(l)|< minSup\times(|p_1|+|p_2|+...+|p_k|)$$
$$< minSup\times|P|$$

Therefore *support*(l) < *minSup* and so $l \notin L$. But this is a contradiction.

Hence the internal node contains all of the frequent patterns without missing any frequent itemsets.

DGCL: An Efficient Density and Grid Based Clustering Algorithm for Large Spatial Database*

Ho Seok Kim[1], Song Gao[2], Ying Xia[2], Gyoung Bae Kim[3], and Hae Young Bae[1]

[1] Department of Computer Science and Information Engineering, Inha University
Yonghyun-dong, Nam-gu, Incheon, 402-751, Korea
hskim@dblab.inha.ac.kr, hybae@inha.ac.kr
[2] College of Computer Science and Technology,
Chongqing University of Posts and Telecommunications,
Nan'an Distinct ChongQing City, 400065, P.R. China
gao_fly@hotmail.com, xiaying@cqupt.edu.cn
[3] Department of Computer Education, Seowon University, 231
Mochung-dong Heungduk-gu Cheongju-si Chungbuk, 361-742, Korea
gbkim@seowon.ac.kr

Abstract. Spatial clustering, which groups similar objects based on their distance, connectivity, or their relative density in space, is an important component of spatial data mining. Clustering large data sets has always been a serious challenge for clustering algorithms, because huge data set makes the clustering process extremely costly. In this paper, we propose DGCL, an enhanced Density-Grid based Clustering algorithm for Large spatial database. The characteristics of dense area can be enhanced by considering the affection of the surrounding area. Dense areas are analytically identified as clusters by removing sparse area or outliers with the help of a density threshold. Synthetic datasets are used for testing and the result shows the superiority of our approach.

1 Introduction

Spatial data mining is the discovery of interesting characteristics and patterns that may exist in large spatial databases. Usually the spatial relationships are implicit in nature. Because of the huge amounts of spatial data that may be obtained from satellite images, medical equipments, Geographic Information System (GIS) etc, it's expensive and unrealistic for the users to examine spatial data in detail. Spatial data mining aims to automate the process of understanding spatial data by representing the data in a concise manner and reorganizing spatial databases to accommodate data semantics.

The aim of data clustering algorithms is to group the objects in spatial databases into meaningful subclasses. A good clustering algorithm should have the following characteristics. First, due to the huge amount of spatial data, an important challenge

* This research was supported by the MIC (Ministry of Information and Communication),Korea, under the ITRC (Information Technology Research Center) support program supervised by the IITA (Institute of Information Technology Assessment).

J.X. Yu, M. Kitsuregawa, and H.V. Leong (Eds.): WAIM 2006, LNCS 4016, pp. 362–371, 2006.
© Springer-Verlag Berlin Heidelberg 2006

for clustering algorithm is to achieve good time efficiency. Second, a good clustering algorithm should be able to identify clusters irrespective of their shapes or relative position. Third, it should have better ability to handle noise or outliers. Fourth, it should be order insensitive with respect to input data. Last, the parameter count should be minimized for users.

This paper presents an enhanced density-grid based clustering algorithm, DGCL, which can handle huge amount of spatial data with noise efficiently and find natural clusters correctly. In this algorithm, we set a default number of intervals according to the number of input data. The time complexity mostly depends on the grid number N, and it can be O(N). It's also order insensitive.

The rest of this paper is organized as follows. Section 2 reviews related work. The detail algorithm is described in Section 3. Section 4 we analyze the time complexity. Section 5 shows the results of experiments. A conclusion is presented in the last section.

2 Related Work

Density-based and grid-based clustering are two main clustering approaches. The former is famous for its capability of discovering clusters of various shapes and eliminating noises, while the latter is well known for its high speed. Shifting grid and GDILC are two kinds of clustering methods which are based on density and grid. Both of them have advantages and disadvantages.

Density–based [1] clustering algorithms regard clusters as dense regions of objects in the data space that are separated by regions of low density. A density-based cluster is a set of density-connected objects that is maximal with respect to density-reachability. Every object not contained in any cluster is considered to be *noise*. Typical example is DBSCAN. It grows regions with sufficiently high density into clusters and discovers clusters of arbitrary shape in spatial databases with noise. It has two parameters (ε, MinPts). But the users usually don't know clearly about the suitable values of these two parameters for some data sets. Other drawback of this technique is the high computational complexity because of examining all the neighborhoods in checking the core condition for each object. Specially when the algorithm runs on very large datasets, this step is very expensive. Its time complexity is O(n log n), where n is the number of data objects [2].

Grid-based [1] clustering algorithms use a multi-resolution grid data structure. It quantizes the space into a finite number of cells that form a grid structure on which all of the operations for clustering are performed. The main advantage is its fast processing time, which is typically independent of the number of data objects, yet dependent on only the number of cells in each dimension in the quantized space.

A shifting grid [3] clustering algorithm uses the concept of shifting grid. This algorithm does not require users inputting parameters. It divides each dimension of the data space into certain interval to form a grid structure in the data space. Based on the concept of sliding window, shifting of the whole grid structure is introduced to obtain a more descriptive density profile. It clusters data in a way of cell rather than in points [4]. Because of its recursive execution, the performance is not better even though it can enhance the accuracy of the results.

GDILC [5] is a grid-based density-isoline clustering algorithm. The idea of clustering using density-isoline comes from contour figures, density-based and grid-based clustering algorithms. When clustering, density-isoline figure obtained from the distribution densities of data sample can be used to discover clusters. Because this algorithm needs to calculate the distance between each data sample and every data sample in its neighbor cells, the cost is also too high, especially for huge data set.

3 The Density and Grid Based Algorithm

In this part, the structure of this algorithm and the detail of the sub-procedure will be described.

3.1 Procedure of DGCL

In DGCL, we regard each spatial data as a point in the space. There are 7 steps in DGCL. In step 1, get the total number of the data points. According to the total number, construct the grid cell. In step 2, read the data set from the disk. If there is not sufficient memory to contain the whole data set, this algorithm divides them to several parts and read one part at a time to calculate the density of each cells until all parts have been read for one time. In step 3, calculate the density threshold DT by using the equation in GDILC. The aim is to remove the outliers and empty cells as much as possible in step 4. And the fourth step can be regarded as a pre-clustering. The remainder cells will be regarded as *useful cells*. In the following steps, only the useful cells will be considered. So the number of useful cells is small compared to the number of data. In step 5, from the remainder cells, assign the adjacent cells to the same group which should be regarded as a cluster. But that's not the final result, because the fifth step can only find groups in the sub-region, and some groups are adjacent with each other. So, it's necessary to merge the adjacent groups together to become one group in step 6. There are still some outliers exiting in the groups, so in the last step, DGCL removes the outliers again to optimize the result. In the end, each group is a cluster. The sketch of DGCL is shown in Fig.1.

1: Construct grid cell according to the number of data points.
2: Load data set.
3: Distribute the data points into cells and calculate the density threshold DT.
4: Remove outliers and empty cells.
5: Group assignment.
6: Group mergence procedure.
7: Optimization.

Fig. 1. The sketch of DGCL

3.2 Number of Intervals

In this step, setting the number of intervals is a very critical procedure. If the size of the cells is too large, the algorithm will merge two or more clusters into one. Another drawback is that even though it can find the cluster at the right place, it still has so many blank spaces in the large size of the cell. So the result is not exact and satisfying. If the size of cell is too small, the algorithm may make the number of cells equal or close to the number of points. For large dataset, the cost of calculation is too expensive even though we regard the cell as the minimum unit for clustering. So it's necessary to find a method to set a suitable interval value to get both a better clustering result and a good efficiency. Here we adopt the method of GDILC [5]. The following formula is used to calculate the number of intervals *m*.

$$m = \sqrt{\frac{n}{coefM}} \tag{1}$$

In equation 1, *n* is the number of data points. *coefM* is a coefficient to adjust the value of *m*. we propose it as an positive integer. In fact, it stands for the average number of data samples in a cell. But we don't want to regard it as a fixed value. Because in the experiments, we find the relationship between the number of cells and that of data points is not linear. So *coefM* also need to be adjusted to get a better result. In our experiments, *coefM* changes according to the following curve in Fig. 2. And it can get a better result as we expect.

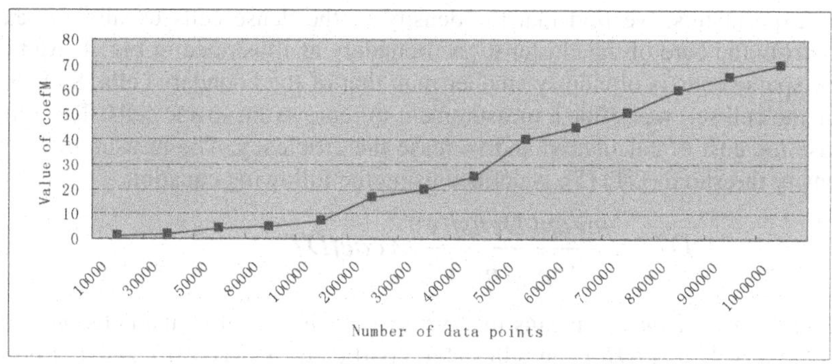

Fig. 2. *coefM* depends on the number of data

3.3 Density of the Cell

In general, we term the density as the number of data points in the cell. The original grid-based clustering algorithm just considers about the density of the current cell itself [6]. The disadvantage is that it may decrease the relationship of neighbor cells which have similar data points. The attributes of a spatial object stored in a database may be affected by the attributes of the spatial neighbors of that object [4]. To improve this situation, we calculate the density of the considered cell with considering the data points in its neighbor cells such as what the shifting grid clustering algorithm does [3] as illustrated in Fig. 3. L means the width of each cell. And we never consider about the empty cells.

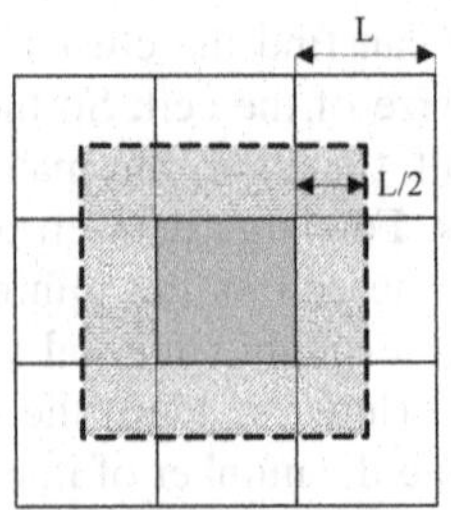

Fig. 3. The cell with gray color is the considered cell. The density of the considered cell is the sum of the density of the grey area and the line-shadowed part.

The definition of neighbor cells satisfies the following inequation. Assume that cell $C_{i_1 i_2}$ and $C_{j_1 j_2}$ are neighbor cells. *m* is the number of intervals.

$$\left| i_p - j_p \right| \leq 1, (p = 1,2;\ 1 \leq i, j \leq m) \tag{2}$$

3.4 Selection of the Density Threshold DT

The dense cells are surrounded by the sparse cells which are regarded as outliers. From the experiments, we find that the density of the dense cells usually decrease gradually from the core of the cluster to the boundary as illustrated in Fig. 4. And the density of sparse cells is obviously smaller than that of the boundary cells. So before clustering the cell set, we define a measurement to remove the sparse cells. The aim is to decrease the cost of calculation and increase the efficiency. The measurement, we call it density threshold (DT) [5], is defined using the following equation.

$$DT = \frac{mean(Density)}{\log_{10}(m^2)} \times coefDT \tag{3}$$

In equation 3, *mean(Density)* means the average density of all of the cells. *m* is the number of intervals. *coefDT* is an adjustable coefficient between 0.7 and 1. Lots of experiments show that when setting it to 0.95, good clustering result can be achieved in most conditions. All the cells of which the density is smaller than DT will be

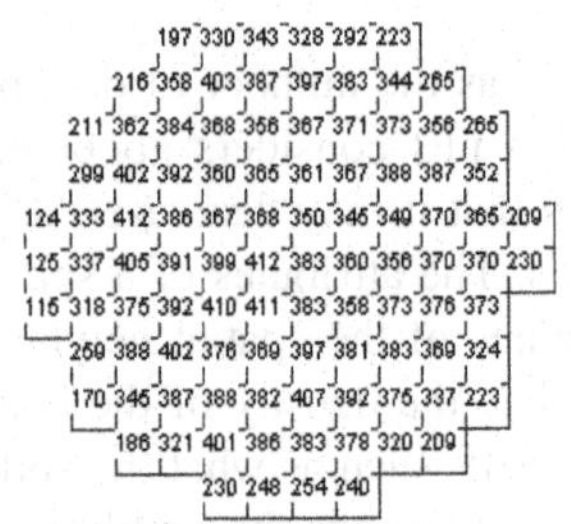

Fig. 4. Varying grid density within a circle cluster

removed from the cell set. The remainder cells will be regarded as *useful cells*. In the following steps, the algorithm only considers about the useful cells, so compared with the number of data points, they're really few enough. The remainder cells also contain some unexpected cells. They will be further removed in step 7 (optimization).

3.5 Group Assignment

This procedure starts from the first useful cell. If the considered cell C_i and all its *useful neighbors*, all belonging to set S_i, haven't been assigned a group ID, the algorithm assigns a new group ID for all the cells in the set S_i. If some cells in S_i have had group IDs, the algorithm finds the ID of the cell with the maximum density in S_i and assigns it to the other cells in S_i. This procedure will not stop until all *useful cells* have been checked. Fig. 5 shows the sketch of group assignment.

```
DO {
select a useful cell Ci.
IF ( there is no group assigned to the cell Ci and its neighbors )
   assign a new group to the cell and all its neighbors.
ELSE
   find proper group ID and assign it to the other cells.
} WHILE ( there are still useful cells which haven't been checked )
```

Fig. 5. The sketch of group assignment

3.6 Group Mergence

The procedure of group assignment only considers the current cell and its neighbors, so it clusters the similar cells into the same group in a sub-area. In the whole data space, the adjacent groups need to be merged together to form one group as we expected. The sketch of group mergence is shown in Fig. 6.

```
DO {
   select one group gi.
   IF ( there are some groups adjacent with gi ){
        merge them into one group gi'.
        select the smaller group ID among them.
        assign this ID to the new group gi'. }
} WHILE ( there are still groups which haven't been checked )
```

Fig. 6. The sketch of group mergence

3.7 Optimization

As we mentioned in the previous part, after step 4, the remainder cells also contain some cells which we are not expect.

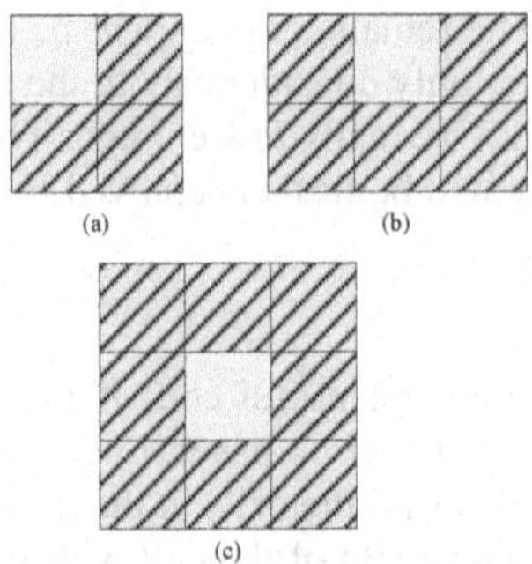

Fig. 7. Situations of neighbors: (a) 3 neighbors in the corner and (b) 5 neighbors at the edge and (c) 8 neighbors inside

In DGCL, we calculate the cell density with considering about its neighbors. There are three kinds of situations of neighbors in 2-D space as illustrated in fig. 7. The problem is that if the considered cell only contains a few data points, its useful neighbors contribute so much to calculate its density. It also includes into a group. But in fact, this cell should be regarded as a cell which contains outlier. And lots of experiments show that these situations often happen at the boundary of the group. Fig. 8 shows one situation of the problem. The fuscous cell is the considered cell. It only contains a relatively few data points compared with its neighbors when calculating the density. So this cell should be removed. The removed cells are regarded as *unuseful cells*. And the final result only contains the useful cells. We remove the cells which satisfy the following inequation.

$$RD < \frac{TD}{Num+1} \tag{4}$$

In equation 4, *RD* means the real number of data points which are contained in the considered cell. *TD* means the total density of the considered cell. *Num* is the number of its useful neighbors and 1 means the considered cell itself.

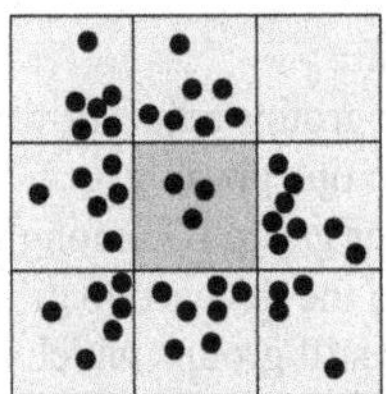

Fig. 8. The fuscous cell should be removed

4 Time Complexity

In DGCL, we use the following equation which we have mentioned previously to calculate the number of intervals.

$$m = \sqrt{\frac{n}{coefM}} \tag{1}$$

The total number of cells is m^2, namely n/coefM, in which n is the number of data points. After we get the data set, both the data distribution and removing outlier procedure need check or calculate all the cells. After that, only few cells need to be checked for group assignment, merge procedure and optimization. So in most of the situations, the time complexity is smaller than $O(n)$. It much more depends on the number of the *useful cells*.

5 Experimental Results

We performed experiments using a personal computer with 768MB of RAM and Pentium(R) 4 CPU 1.8GHz and running Windows XP Professional. The data sets are generated ourselves. In the data set, the data points are generated randomly according to certain kinds of distributions. Noises are randomly distributed. And the clustering results are tagged by different colors. Fig. 9 (a) shows a data set with 100000 data points, including 30000 for circle, 40000 for rectangle, 25000 for sine curve and 5000 noises.

The result shows that DGCL can find the clusters correctly and eliminate outliers efficiently. Furthermore it also fast enough. If users want to get more exact result, they can adjust the coefficient *coefM*. The smaller the *coefM* is, the more exact result DGCL gets. But it need more time for calculation. Because GDILC has higher performance than shifting grid algorithm, we only show the comparison of DGCL and GDILC in Fig. 10. From that graph, we know that this algorithm has higher performance than GDILC. Other data sets are also used to test this algorithm, the result is shown in Fig. 11.

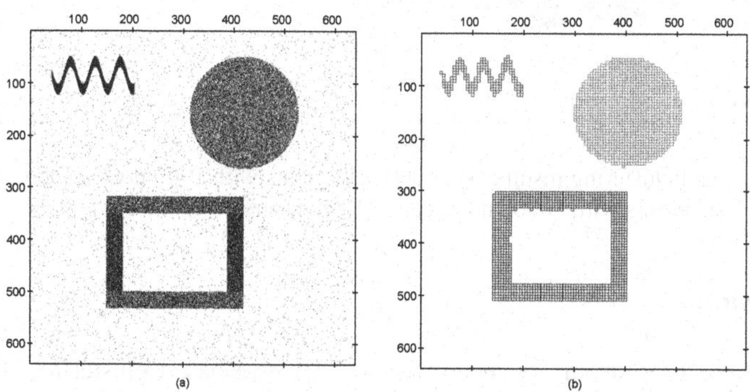

Fig. 9. (a) test data set includes 100000 data points with 5000 noises and (b) clustering result (3 clusters)

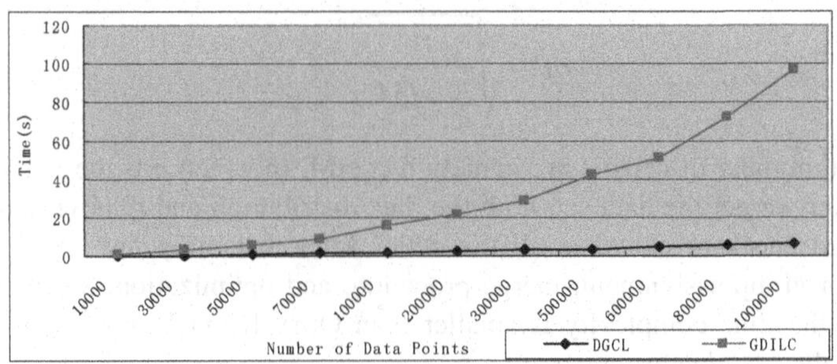

Fig. 10. Comparison between DGCL and GDILC

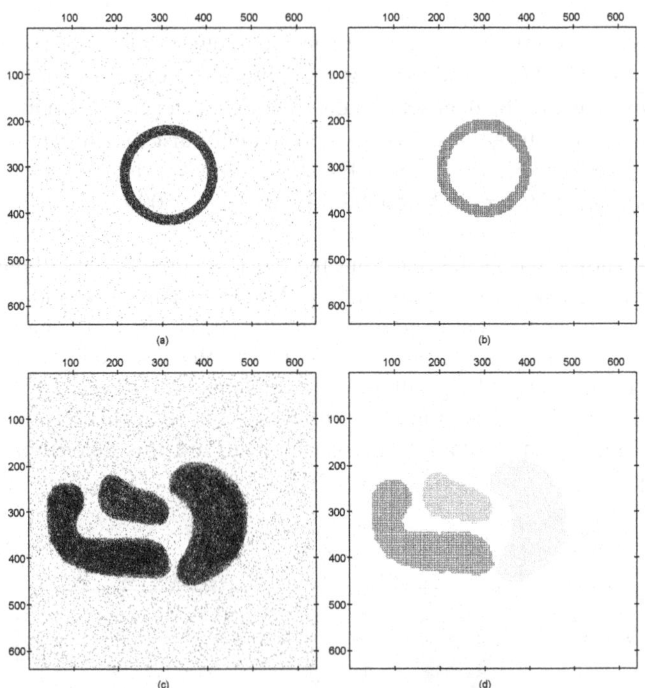

Fig. 11. Datasets and clustering results (a) 20000 data points with 1000 noises and (b) 1 cluster and (c) 250000 data points with 10000 noises and (d) 3 clusters

6 Conclusion

In this paper, we present an enhanced density and grid based clustering algorithm, DGCL. By considering the neighbor cells when calculating the density of current cell and removing the outliers efficiently with the help of a proper measurement, a better clustering result can be provided by this algorithm. Compared with the shifting grid clustering algorithm and GDILC, it's much faster because it doesn't need to cluster recursively or calculate the distance between data points. The time complexity depends on the number of cells. Drawback of this algorithm is that all the cluster boundaries are either horizontal or vertical. Moreover, it is not affected by the outliers and can handle them properly. And DGCL is order insensitive. A faster method to do I/O, such as an efficient indexing method or parallel control, will make the algorithm a whole lot faster. In conclusion, the experiments show that DGCL is a stable and efficient clustering method for large spatial data set.

References

1. Jiawei Han, Micheline Kamber: <<Data Mining: Concepts and Techniques>>. 2001 by Academic Press
2. Yasser El-Sonbaty, M.A. Ismail, Mohamed Farouk: An Efficient Density Based Clustering Algorithm for Large Databases. ICTAI (2004)
3. Ma, W.M., Eden, Chow, Tommy, W.S.: A new shifting grid clustering algorithm. Pattern Recognition 37(3), 503-514 (2004)
4. A.H. Pilevar, M. Sukumar: GCHL: A grid-clustering algorithm for high-dimensional very large spatial data bases. Elsevier B.V. (2004)
5. ZHAO Yanchang, SONG Junde: GDILC: A Grid-based Density-Isoline Clustering algorithm. IEEE (2001)
6. Xiaowei Xu, Martin Ester, Hans-peter Kriegel, Jorg Sander: Clustering and Knowledge Discovery in Spatial Databases (1997)
7. Yanchang Zhao, Chenqi Zhang, Yi-Dong Shen: Clustering High-Dimensional Data with Low-Order Neighbors. Proceedings of the IEEE/WIC/ACM International Conference on Web Intelligence (WI' 04)
8. Yu Qian, Kang Zhang: GraphZip: A Fast and Automatic Compression Method for Spatial Data Clustering. SAC '04, March 14-17, 2004, Nicosia, Cyprus
9. Yu Qian, Gang Zhang, Kang Zhang: FACADE: A Fast and Effective Approach to the Discovery of Dense Clusters in Noise Spatial Data. SIGMOD 2004

Scalable Clustering Using Graphics Processors

Feng Cao[1], Anthony K.H. Tung[2], and Aoying Zhou[1]

[1] Dept. of Computer Science and Engineering, Fudan University, China
{caofeng, ayzhou}@fudan.edu.cn
[2] School of Computing, National University of Singapore, Singapore
atung@comp.nus.edu.sg

Abstract. We present new algorithms for scalable clustering using graphics processors. Our basic approach is based on k-means. By changing the order of determining object labels, and exploiting the high computational power and pipeline of graphics processing units (GPUs) for distance computing and comparison, we speed up the k-means algorithm substantially. We introduce two strategies for retrieving data from the GPU, taking into account the low bandwidth from the GPU back to the main memory. We also extend our GPU-based approach to data stream clustering. We implement our algorithms in a PC with a Pentium IV 3.4G CPU and a NVIDIA GeForce 6800 GT graphics card. Our comprehensive performance study shows that the common GPU in desktop computers could be an efficient co-processor of CPU in traditional and data stream clustering.

1 Introduction

The rapid growth of data volume in real-life databases has intensified the need for scalable data mining methods. Data warehouse and data stream applications are very data and computation intensive, and therefore demand high processing power. As a building block of data mining, clustering derives clusters which can be visualized more efficiently and effectively than the original data. Researchers have actively sought to design algorithms to perform efficient clustering.

Assuming that the data sets are in the secondary memory, effort to enhance the scalability of clustering algorithms often focus on reducing the number of disk I/O. Work in this direction have effectively reduce the scan on data sets into one or two rounds. As such, it is difficult to further enhance scalability by reducing I/O cost.

Meanwhile, CPU cost is no longer a minor factor for scalability improvement in clustering algorithms (see Figure 1). In data stream applications, CPU cost becomes more important because each data object needs to be processed in real time. Therefore, new techniques for reducing CPU cost will greatly improve the scalability of online and offline clustering algorithms.

Recently, the Graphics Processing Unit (GPU) has provided a programmable pipeline, allowing users to write fragment programs that are executed on pixel processing engines. At the same time, the computing capability of common GPU

J.X. Yu, M. Kitsuregawa, and H.V. Leong (Eds.): WAIM 2006, LNCS 4016, pp. 372–384, 2006.
© Springer-Verlag Berlin Heidelberg 2006

is becoming increasingly powerful. For example, a NVIDIA GeForce6800 chip contains more transistors than an Intel Pentium IV 3.73GHz Extreme Edition processor. In addition, the peak performance of GPUs has been increasing at the rate of 2.5 – 3.0 times a year, much faster than the rate that Moore's law predicted for CPUs. Furthermore, due to economic factors, it is unlikely that dedicated general vector and stream processors will be widely available on desktop computers [14].

Driven by the programmability and computational capabilities of GPUs, many GPU-based algorithms have been designed for scientific and geometric computations [10][12], database operations [5], stream frequency and quantiles approximation [6], etc. However, as far as we know, the computational power of GPUs has not been well exploited for scalable clustering yet. In this paper, we will make the following contribution:

1. Having identify distance computation and comparison as the most expensive operations for clustering algorithms, we propose a new, highly parallelized distance computation technique which utilizes the fragment vector processing and *multi-pass rendering* capabilities of GPUs. We further apply multi-texturing technology to deal with high-dimensional distance computing.
2. Our basic approach is based on k-means. By changing the order of determining object labels, and exploiting the high computational power and pipeline of graphics processing units (GPUs) for distance computing and comparison, we speed up the k-means algorithm substantially. We then further extend the algorithm to perform clustering on data stream.
3. A comprehensive performance study proves the efficiency of our algorithms. The GPU-based algorithm for stream clustering reduces clustering cost by about 20 times as compared to prior CPU-based algorithms. The basic k-means-based algorithm obtains 3 – 8 times speedup over CPU-based implementations. We thus bring forward the conclusion that the GPU can be used as an effective co-processor for traditional and stream clustering.

The rest of the paper is organized as follows. Section 2 analyzes existing clustering algorithms. Section 3 gives an overview of GPU. Section 4 presents our GPU-based clustering algorithms. Section 5 presents the performance study. Section 6 briefly surveys related work. Section 7 concludes the paper.

2 Analysis of Existing Clustering Algorithms

Existing clustering algorithms can be classified into partitioning [11], hierarchical [8, 16], density-based [4], streaming methods [1, 2, 7], etc. Since multiple scan of out of core data sets often create a bottleneck due to the I/Os, many methods have been proposed to reduce the number of scans on data sets into one pass or two. These include: random sampling technology in CURE [8], R*-Tree indexing approach adopted in DBSCAN [4], the divide and conquer strategy in STREAM [7] to process large data sets chunk by chunk, and the CF-tree in BIRCH [16] for performing preclustering. These methods have reduced I/O cost back to a level in which the CPU cost become significant again. Specifically, distance computation and comparison often become the most expensive operations in existing clustering algorithms.

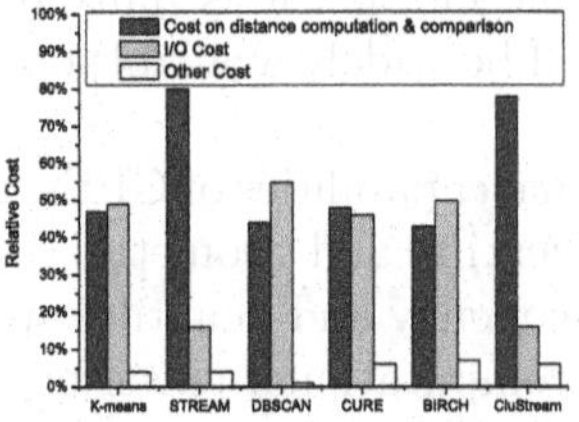

Fig. 1. Relative costs in clustering methods

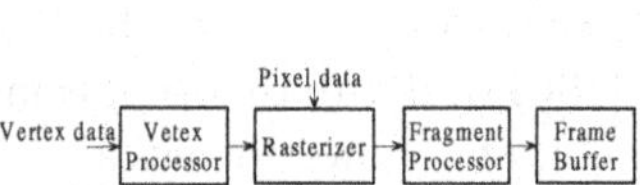

Fig. 2. Graphics pipeline overview

The popular partitioning-based method – k-means [11] contains three steps: (1)Initialization: Choosing k points representing the initial group of centroids. (2)Assignment: Assigning each point to its closest centroid. When all points have been assigned, recalculate the positions of the k centroids. (3)Termination condition: Repeating Steps 2 and 3 until the centroids no longer move. Having load the data into memory, the most time consuming computation is assignment, i.e., distance computation and comparison (see Figure 1). The number of distance computation and comparison in k-means is $O(kmn)$, where m denotes the number of iteration and n is the number of point in memory.

An effective hierarchical clustering algorithm, CURE [8], starts with the individual points as individual clusters. At each step, the closest pair of clusters is merged to form a new cluster. The process is repeated until there are only k remaining clusters. Figure 1 shows that distance computation and comparison are about 45% of the total cost. Because these operations widely exist in methods of finding the nearest cluster and merging two clusters. The number of distance operations is $O(n^2 \log n)$, where n denotes the number of points in a sampling. To find the nearest cluster, we can load the clusters to the GPU and apply our GPU-based distance computation technique to these clusters.

In order to determine the density of a given point p, density-based methods (such as DBSCAN [4]) need to compute the distance from point p to its nearby points and compare the distance with a pre-defined threshold ϵ. Therefore, the cost on distance computation and comparison becomes an important factor (see Figure 1). To determine the density for each point, we could load nearby data points into the GPU, apply our GPU-based distance computation, and compare the distance results with ϵ by GPU.

In the data stream environment, I/O cost no longer exists or could be ignored. Figure 1 shows the relative costs in STREAM [7] and CluStream [1] when accessing data from the hard disk. Ideally, we should adopt new GPU-based methods to improve the scalability of stream clustering.

3 Preliminaries of GPU

3.1 Graphics Pipeline

Figure 2 shows a simplified structure of the rendering pipeline. A vertex processor receives vertex data and assembled them into geometries. The rasterizer constructs fragments at each pixel location covered by the primitive. Finally, the fragments pass through the fragment processor. A series of tests (such as depth test) can be applied to each fragment to determine if the fragment should be written to the frame buffer. Frame buffers may be conceptually divided into three buffers: *color buffer*, storing the color components of each pixel; *depth buffer*, storing a depth value associated with each pixel; and *stencil buffer* which stores a stencil value for each pixel and can be regarded as a mask on the screen.

3.2 Data Representation and Terminology

We store the data points to be clustered on the GPU as *textures*. A *texture* is an image, usually a 2D array of values, which often contains multiple channels. For example, an RGBA texture four channels: red, blue, green and alpha. To perform clustering using the GPU, the attribute of each tuple is stored in multiple channels of a single texel (i.e., individual elements of the texture), or the same texel location in multiple textures. Several data formats are supported in textures, e.g., 8-bit bytes. In particular, the textures in *Pbuffer* (an off-screen frame buffer) support the 32-bit IEEE single precision floating-point.

The term *multi-texturing* refers to the applications of more than one texture on the same surface. *Multi-pass rendering* is a technique for generating complex scene. That is, the GPU renders several passes and combines the resulting images to create a final frame. *Stencil test* is used to restrict computation on a portion of the frame buffer. When a new fragment arrives, stencil test compares the value at the corresponding location in the stencil buffer and a reference value. The new fragment is discarded if it fails the comparison.

A group of stencil operations are provided to modify the stencil value, e.g., keeping the stencil value in the stencil buffer or replacing the stencil value to the reference value. Typically, if stencil test is passed, depending on the result of depth test, the user could define different stencil operations.

4 Clustering Using GPUs

K-means is a basic method for clustering which has wide applications. When the algorithm is implemented on the CPU, distances to the k centroids are evaluated for a single output object label at a time, as illustrated in Figure 3(a).

Instead of focusing on computation of the label for a single object one at a time, we calculate the distances from a single input centroid to all objects at one go, as shown in Figure 3(b). The distances to a single input centroid can be computed in the GPU for all objects simultaneously. In this case, the final label of a single object is only available when all input centroids have been processed.

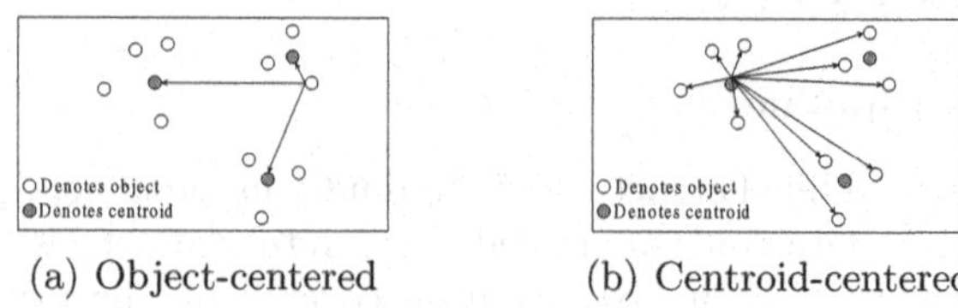

(a) Object-centered (b) Centroid-centered

Fig. 3. Object-centered vs. centroid-centered distance computation

The rationale for the approach is as follow: GPU essentially operates by applying simple, identical operations to many pixels simultaneously. Naturally, these operations have access to a very limited number of inputs. However, in the k-means algorithms, k inputs are needed in order to calculate the label of a single data point. Furthermore, centroid-oriented distance computation allows comparison operations to be done outside each fragment, thus greatly reducing the number of operations in the fragment program.

4.1 Distance Computing

Typically, Euclidean distance is a used as a similarity measure for clustering. The Euclidean distance between 2 d-dimensional points X and Y is defined as follows: $dist(\overrightarrow{X} - \overrightarrow{Y}) = \sqrt{\Sigma_{i=1}^{d}(x_i - y_i)^2}$.

Assuming that there are a set of d-dimensional points $X_i (1 \leq i \leq N)$ and k centroids Y_j, where $1 \leq j \leq k$. We arrange X_i into an array A (named point array) as follow, where R denotes the number of rows , L denotes the number of columns, $R * L$ equals the number of points N. In the actual implementation, a point array is a texture (see Section 3.2). If the number of points is above the maximal size of one texture, the point array can be partitioned into multiple textures. In order to better utilize the parallelism of GPU, R and L are set at $\lceil\sqrt{N}\rceil$. The unused portion of the array could be simply masked by stencil.

$$A = \begin{vmatrix} X_1 & \cdots & X_L \\ \multicolumn{3}{c}{\cdots\cdots\cdots\cdots} \\ X_{(R-1)*L+1} & \cdots & X_{R*L} \end{vmatrix} \qquad D_j = \begin{vmatrix} dot2(X_1 - Y_j) & \cdots & dot2(X_L - Y_j) \\ \multicolumn{3}{c}{\cdots\cdots\cdots\cdots} \\ dot2(X_{(R-1)*L+1} - Y_j) & \cdots & dot2(X_{R*L} - Y_j) \end{vmatrix}$$

Each element $a[m][n]$ in array A corresponds to point $X_{(m-1)*L+n}$. We calculate the result array D_j (named distance array) for each centroid Y_j as above, where $dot2(X)$ is the dot product of vector X with itself. Each element $e[m][n]$ in D_j corresponds to the distance from point $X_{(m-1)*L+n}$ to centroid Y_j. Without loss of generality, we adopt squared Euclidean distance as the goodness measurement here. GPUs are capable of computing dot product on vectors in parallel giving high efficiency. Here, we propose a GPU-based method for distance computation.

ComDistance (Algorithm 1) computes the distance array for the point array in tex to centroid v_{cen}. To allow a more precise fragment, Line 1 actives Pbuffer. Line 2 enables the fragment program. Line 3 renders a textured quadrilateral using FComDist. SUB and DOT are hardware optimized vector subtract and dot product instructions, respectively. Finally, the distance array is stored in the depth component of each fragment. In case of very large databases, we can swap textures in and out of video memory using out-of-core techniques.

Algorithm 1. ComDistance (tex, v_{cen})

```
ActivePBuffer();
Enable fragment program FComDist;
RenderTexturedQuad(tex);
Disable fragment program FComDist;
```

FComDist(v_{cen})

```
v_tex = value from tex
tmpR = SUB(v_tex,v_cen)
result.depth = DOT(tmpR,tmpR);
```

The ARB_fragment_program OpenGL extension allows depth values to be assigned in the fragment program. We exploit this feature to accelerate the comparison step described in Section 4.2 by avoiding the storage of the distance array in a texture which mean reloading the texture into the depth buffer.

High-dimensional Distance Computing. In case of $d > 4$, we divide every four dimensions of points into a point array, calculate each of these $\lceil \frac{d}{4} \rceil$ arrays with the corresponding section of Y_j, and sum up them to get the final Y_j.

Our algorithm uses multi-texturing technology to handle high-dimensional data. Although current GPUs only support eight simultaneous texture units resulting in at most 32 dimensions in one pass, we believe that future generation of GPU will provide more simultaneous texture units. At the current stage, we adopt *multi-pass rendering* in case of $d > 32$. Assuming a given GPU support m simultaneous texture units, the number of passes will be equal to $\lceil \frac{d}{4m} \rceil$.

4.2 Labeling

In k-means clustering, labeling is achieved by comparing the distances between the point and each centroid. We utilize *multi-pass rendering* to realize this operation. Depth test is enabled to compare the depth value of the arriving fragment to the corresponding pixel in the depth buffer. The stencil buffer is configured to maintain the label of the nearest centroid. Finally, the distance array D_j is rendered for each j ($1 \leq j \leq k$). Algorithm 2 describes this procedure in detail.

We compute and store distance array D_1 directly in the depth buffer, and initialize the stencil buffer with 1. That is, all the points are labelled to centroid 1 at first. Then, depth test is enabled and set to pass if the depth value of arriving fragment is less than the corresponding pixel. Stencil test is set to always being passed. If the arriving fragment passes depth test, the corresponding pixel is updated with the new depth value, and Line 9 replace the stencil value in

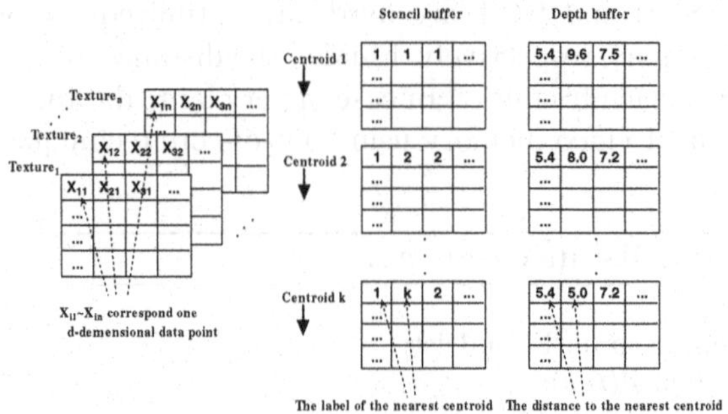

Fig. 4. Labeling

corresponding position with the new label $i+1$. Otherwise, we keep the depth and stencil values. Therefore, after each distance array D_i is generated, the stencil buffers contains the label of the nearest centroid for each point (named label array). The depth buffer contains the corresponding minimal distance value. Figure 4 illustrates this process. In the pipeline of the labeling algorithm, various operations can be processed simultaneously: the fragment program computes distance arrays; depth test compares depth value in the depth buffer; and stencil test updates the labels in the stencil buffer.

4.3 Generating New Centroids

It is a bottleneck of current hardware to retrieve data from GPU to the main memory (sending data from the main memory to GPU is much faster by say ten times). According to the data retrieved, we design the following two strategies to generate new centroids, corresponding to GPU-C (GPU-based clustering by retrieving centroids) and GPU-L (GPU-based clustering by retrieving label array) algorithms, respectively:

1. **Retrieve Centroids.** One way is to compute the centroids in GPU and retrieving them from GPU. Stencil test is utilized to filter out points in the same cluster and summarize them by mipmaps. Mipmaps are multi-resolution textures consisting of multiple levels. The highest level contains the average of all the values in the lowest level. A group of *occlusion query*s must be called in order to obtain the number of points in each cluster. An occlusion query returns the number of fragments that pass the variance tests. In our case, the test is a stencil test. The procedure is shown in Algorithm 3. In case of $d > 4$, we need to render $\lceil \frac{d}{4} \rceil$ times for each centroid. Finally, we retrieve the highest level of the mipmaps $tex_{out}[i]$ and the result of the occlusion query q_i from GPU in order to calculate the final centroid results. Although this strategy has the advantage of reducing communication cost, its computation cost overwhelms the saving on communication cost, as our experiments in Section 5.4 will show.

2. **Retrieve the Label Array.** In this strategy, we retrieve the label array from the stencil buffer directly. To reduce communication cost, the label array is retrieved from the stencil buffer by an impact mode GL_BYTE. Although 8-bit value constraint exists in this mode (that is the upper bound of k is 256), it can meet the requirements of most real applications. After retrieving the label array, we generate the new centroids in CPU by adding up the points with the same label.

Algorithm 2. Labeling $(tex_{in}, v_{centroid}[k])$

```
glClearStencil(1);
ComDistance(tex_in, v_centroid[0]);{ generate distance array D_1 and store it in depth
  buffer}
glEnable(GL_DEPTH_TEST);
Set depth test to pass if incoming fragment is less than the corresponding value in
  depth buffer.
for i = 1; i < k; i++ do
  Set stencil test to always pass;
  ComDistance(tex_in, v_centroid[i]);{ generate a frame of fragments corresponding
    to distance array D_{i+1}}
  if depth test passed then
    replace stencil value with the reference value i + 1;
  else
    keep the stencil value;
  end if
end for
glDisable(GL_DEPTH_TEST);
```

Algorithm 3. GetControids $(tex_{in}, tex_{out}[i])$

```
for i = 1; i ≤ k; i++ do
  Set stencil reference value as i;
  Set stencil test to pass if stencil value is equal to the reference value.
  Enable Occlusion query i;
  RenderTexturedQuad(tex_in);{ generate a frame of fragments which correspond
    to all the points belonging to centroid i}
  Disable Occlusion query i;
  MipMap the fragments in framebuffer into tex_out[i]
end for
```

4.4 Clustering Data Stream

We extend our GPU-based method to data stream clustering, specifically, landmark window [7] and sliding window clustering [2]. The pipe-line architecture and parallel processing of the GPU are well suited for stream processing [14].

1. **Landmark Window Clustering.** We adopt the divide-and-conquer methodology [7] and our GPU-L method (abbr. STREAM-GPU) to cluster

a data stream. We compare STREAM-GPU with three CPU-based algorithms: BIRCH-KM, STREAM-KM and STREAM-LS [7]. Figures 5(a)(b) show that STREAM-GPU achieves the highest processing rate with competitive SSQ (the sum of square distance). Although STREAM-LS achieves the lowest SSQ, its processing rate is 15 times slower than STREAM-GPU. STREAM-GPU is more efficient than BIRCH-KM with 200% effectiveness gain. Considering only clustering cost, STREAM-GPU is nearly 20 times faster than an optimized CPU-based implementation.

2. **Sliding Window Clustering.** In sliding window clustering, only the N most recent points contribute to the results at any time. We adopt the algorithm in [2], and the basic operation in combination procedure is implemented by our GPU-L method. Figure 5(c) shows the comparison result with window size $N = 100,000$. GPU-based clustering is always better than an optimized CPU-based implementation by about 19 – 20 times.

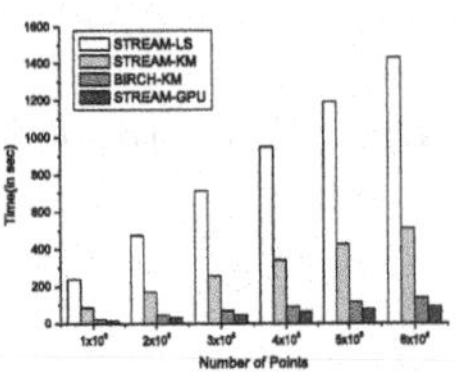

(a) Efficiency comparison in landmark window

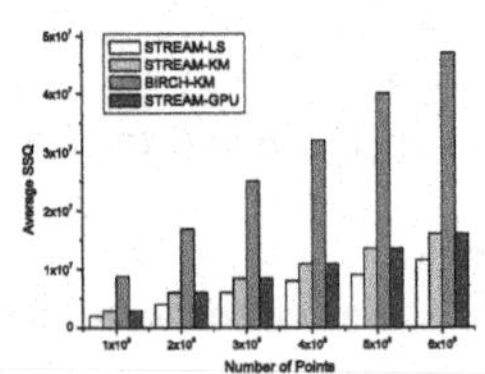

(b) Effectiveness comparison in landmark window

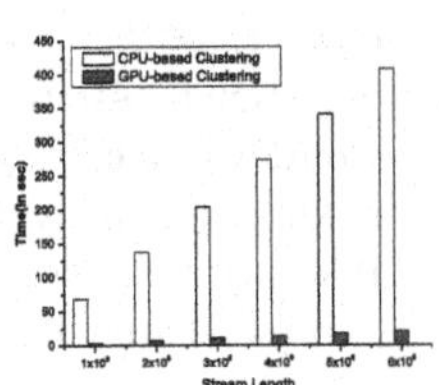

(c) Efficiency comparison in sliding window

Fig. 5. GPU-based vs. CPU-based stream clustering

5 Experiments and Results

5.1 Experimental Setting

We tested our algorithms on a Dell workstation with a 3.4 GHz Pentrium IV CPU and a NVIDIA GeForce 6800GT graphics card. To generate the fragment programs, we used NVIDIA's CG compiler. The CPU algorithms were compiled using an Intel compiler with hyper-threading technology and SIMD execution option. Data exchange between GPU and CPU was implemented with an AGP 8X interface. The points in synthetic data sets followed Gaussian distributions. The data sets had between 10K and 10,000K points each, varied in the number of clusters from 8 to 256, and ranged in dimensionality from 4 to 28.

Execution time was adopted to evaluate various costs. The costs of the CPU-based k-means algorithm (abbr. CPU-K) are: (1)$tc = cc + I/O\ cost$, where tc is total cost; cc is clustering cost. (2)$cc = pt * m$, where pt is the cost of one iteration; m is the number of iterations. (3)$pt = dc + gc$, where dc is the cost of distance computation and comparison; gc is the cost of generating new centroids. The costs of the GPU-based algorithm are: (1)$cc_{gpu} = pt_{gpu} * m + m2g$, where $m2g$ is the cost of sending data from CPU to GPU. (2)$pt_{gpu} = dc + gc + g2m$, where $g2m$ is the cost of retrieving data from GPU to CPU. Unless otherwise mentioned, the experiments adopted $d = 8$, $k = 8$ normal distributed data set.

5.2 Total Cost

Figure 6(a) shows that the total costs of GPU-L, GPU-C and CPU-K increase linearly to the size of data sets. The total cost of GPU-L is about 60% of CPU-K's. However, the total cost of GPU-C almost equals to CPU-K's. We will discuss this phenomenon in Section 5.4. Because total cost includes I/O cost and the number of iteration is about 20, the influence of I/O cost on the total cost is very big. The impact of I/O cost reduces as the number of iterations increases. And the performance improvement of GPU-L and GPU-C will be greater.

5.3 Clustering Cost and Cost of One Iteration

Figure 6(b) illustrates that the clustering cost of GPU-L is about 1/4 that of CPU-K. First, the performance improvement benefits from the parallel computation of pixel processing engines. For example, a NVIDIA GeForce 6800 GT graphic processor can process 16 pixels in parallel. Second, the vector instructions in the GPU are well optimized, which greatly improves the process rate of distance computation. Third, as the distance is compared via depth test, no branch mispredictions exist in the GPU implementation, which leads to further performance gain. Branch mispredictions can be extremely expensive on modern CPUs. For example, a branch misprediction on a Pentium IV CPU costs 17 clock cycles. Figure 6(c) compares the costs of one iteration. It shows the same tendency of Figure 6(b). GPU-L constantly outperforms CPU-K by four times.

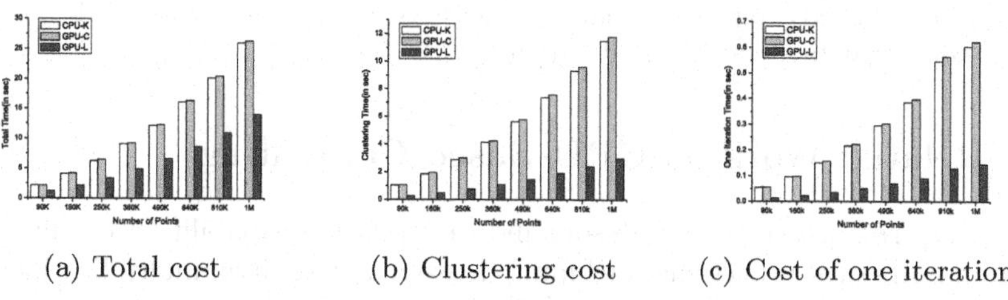

(a) Total cost (b) Clustering cost (c) Cost of one iteration

Fig. 6. GPU-based vs. CPU-based clustering

5.4 Costs of Generating Centroids and Retrieving Data

We compare the cost of generating centroids gc in GPU-C and GPU-L. Figure 7 shows the gc in GPU-C is about 10 times larger than the gc in GPU-L. This is because in order to generate centroids, GPU-C needs to perform several times of slow texture writing, which is often a relatively slow operation.

Figure 7 shows GPU-C has the advantage of retrieving data from GPU at low cost. The cost of retrieving data from GPU $g2m$ is a constant in GPU-C because it only needs to retrieve k centroids and the number of points in each cluster. However, this advantage is overwhelmed by its great cost on generating centroids in GPU-C. Therefore, the overall clustering cost of GPU-L is much smaller than that of GPU-C.

Figure 8 illustrates the cost of retrieving data from GPU $g2m$ in GPU-L. As the number of points grow, $g2m$ increases linearly. However, as we adopt a compact mode of data retrieval, the cost of retrieving data in GPU-L is not significant compared to the cost of one iteration.

5.5 Clustering Cost vs. k and d

Because the number of centroids k and dimensions d may significantly effect the clustering cost, we test several data sets with 16,000 data points for various k and d. Figure 9 shows as k increases, the costs of GPU-L, GPU-C and CPU-K increase linearly. GPU-C has almost the same cost as CPU-K, while the cost of GPU-L is much lower than that of CPU-K. As k grows, the advantage of GPU-L becomes more obvious. This is because the larger k is, the advantage of parallelism is better utilized. Figure 10 shows that the clustering cost in CPU-K, GPU-L and GPU-C increase linearly as d increases.

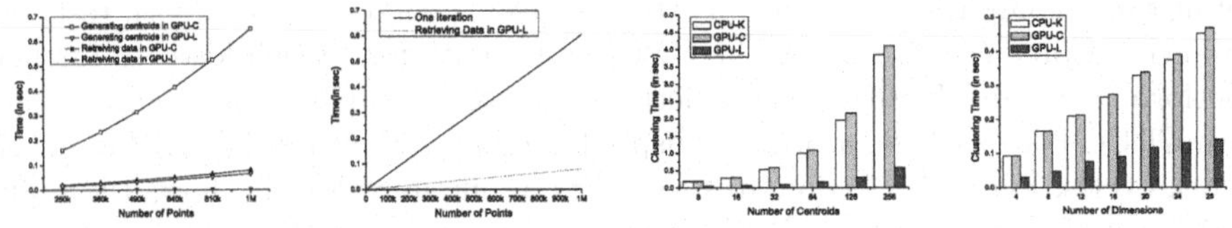

Fig. 7. Costs of generating centroids and retrieving data

Fig. 8. Cost of retrieving data vs. cost of one iteration

Fig. 9. Clustering cost vs. k

Fig. 10. Clustering cost vs. d

6 Related Work on GPU-Based Computing

High performance vertex processors and rasterization capability are utilized for certain numerical processing, including dense matrix-matrix multiplication [12], general purpose vector processing [15], etc. Different from these vertex-based methods, our algorithm achieves vector processing ability at the fragment level, which possesses higher parallel ability. Hall et al provided a GPU-based iterative clustering method [9]. As being designed for geometry processing, it doesn't fully utilize the pipeline of GPUs for mining large databases, let alone data streams. New techniques have been developed to take advantage of the highly optimized GPU hardware functions, e.g, 2D discrete Voronoi Diagrams [10] and 3D object collision detection [3]. Different from these 2D or 3D approximate algorithms, our clustering methods yield exact results for high-dimensional data points.

There has been interest in using GPUs to speed up database computations. Sun et al [13] used GPUs for spatial selection and join operations. Govindaraju et al [5] presented algorithms for predicates and aggregates on GPUs. Another work [6] presents algorithms for quantile and frequency estimation in data streams.

7 Conclusion

In this paper, we have presented a novel algorithm for fast clustering via GPUs. Our algorithm exploits the inherent parallelism and pipeline mechanism of GPUs. Distance computing and comparison are implemented by utilizing the fragment vector processing and multi-pass rendering capabilities of GPUs. Multi-texturing technology is applied to handle high-dimensional distance computing. We have also extended our method to stream clustering. Our implementation of the algorithms on a PC with a Pentium IV 3.4G CPU and a NVIDIA 6800GT graphics card highlights their performance. Our future work includes developing algorithms for other data mining tasks such as outlier detection and classification.

References

1. C. C. Aggarwal, J. Han, J. Wang, and P. S. Yu. A framework for clustering evolving data streams. In *Proc. of VLDB*, 2003.
2. B. Babcock, M. Datar, R. Motwani, and L. O'Callaghan. Maintaining variance and k-medians over data stream windows. In *Proc. of PODS*, 2003.
3. G. Baciu, S. Wong, and H. Sun. Recode: An image-based collision detection algorithm. *Visualization and Computer Animation*, 10(4):181–192, 1999.
4. M. Ester, H.-P. Kriegel, J. Sander, and X. Xu. A density-based algorithm for discovering clusters in large spatial databases with noise. In *Proc. of KDD*, 1996.
5. N. K. Govindaraju, B. Lloyd, W. Wang, M. Lin, and et al. Fast computation of database operations using graphics processors. In *Proc. of SIGMOD*, 2004.
6. N. K. Govindaraju, N. Raghuvanshi, and D. Manocha. Fast and approximate stream mining of quantiles and frequencies using graphics processors. In *Proc. of SIGMOD*, 2005.
7. S. Guha, A. Meyerson, N. Mishra, R. Motwani, and L. O'Callaghan. Clustering data streams:theory and practice. In *IEEE TKDE*, pages 515–528, 2003.
8. S. Guha, R. Rastogi, and K. Shim. Cure: An efficient clustering algorithm for large databases. In *Proc. of SIGMOD*, pages 73–84, 1998.
9. J. D. Hall and J. C. Hart. Gpu acceleration of iterative clustering. In *Proc. of SIGGRAPH poster*, 2004.
10. K. E. Hoff III, J. Keyser, M. Lin, D. Manocha, and T. Culver. Fast computation of generalized voronoi diagrams using graphics hardware. In *Proc. of SIGGRAPH*, pages 277–286, 1999.
11. A. Jain and R. Dubes. Algorithms for clustering data. *New Jersey*, 1998.
12. E. S. Larsen and D. K. McAllister. Fast matrix multiplies using graphics hardware. In *Proc. of IEEE Supercomputing*, 2001.
13. C. Sun, D. Agrawal, and A. E. Abbadi. Hardware acceleration for spatial selections and joins. In *Proc. of SIGMOD*, pages 455–466, 2003.
14. S.Venkatasubramanian. The graphics card as a stream computer. In *SIGMOD Workshop on Management and Processing of Data Streams*, 2003.

15. C. J. Thompson, S. Hahn, and M. Oskin. Using modern graphics architectures for general-purpose computing: A framework and analysis. In *Proc. of IEEE/ACM International Symposium on Microarchitectures*, pages 306–317, 2002.
16. T. Zhang, R. Ramakrishnan, and M. Livny. Birch: An efficient data clustering method for very large databases. In *Proc. of SIGMOD*, pages 103–114, 1996.

TreeCluster: Clustering Results of Keyword Search over Databases

Zhaohui Peng[1], Jun Zhang[1,2], Shan Wang[1], and Lu Qin[1]

[1] School of Information, Renmin University of China, Beijing 100872, P.R. China
{pengch, zhangjun11, swang, qinlu}@ruc.edu.cn
[2] Computer Science and Technology College, Dalian Maritime University, Dalian 116026, P.R. China

Abstract. A critical challenge in keyword search over relational databases (KSORD) is to improve its result presentation to facilitate users' quick browsing through search results. An effective method is to organize the results into clusters. However, traditional clustering method is not applicable to KSORD search results. In this paper, we propose a novel clustering method named TreeCluster. In the first step, we use labels to represent schema information of each result tree and reformulate the clustering problem as a problem of judging whether labeled trees are isomorphic. In the second step, we rank user keywords according to their frequencies in databases, and further partition the large clusters based on keyword nodes. Furthermore, we give each cluster a readable description, and present the description and each result graphically to help users understand the results more easily. Experimental results verify our method's effectiveness and efficiency.

1 Introduction

Based on the full text indexing provided by RDBMS, keyword search over relational databases (KSORD) enables casual users to use keyword queries (a set of keywords) to search relational databases just like searching the Web, without any knowledge of the database schema or any need of writing SQL queries[1, 2]. The recent studies on KSORD can be categorized into two types according to the search mechanism, *schema-graph-based* and *data-graph-based*. The former includes DBXplore[5], DISCOVER[6], IR-Style[7]. The latter can be further classified into two types based on the search results. One is those that return a single tuple as result, e.g. ObjectRank[8]. The other, e.g. BANKS[3, 4], called *tree-like data-graph-based* KSORD (TD-KSORD), return a tuple connection tree. In this paper, we focus on TD-KSORD systems.

One of the most critical challenges in KSORD research is how to present the query results[1, 16]. This is not easy for the following reasons. Firstly, the results need to be semantically meaningful to users. However, a result which is a tuple or a tuple connection tree is not easy to be quickly understood by end users. Secondly, it is important to avoid overwhelming users with a huge number of

J.X. Yu, M. Kitsuregawa, and H.V. Leong (Eds.): WAIM 2006, LNCS 4016, pp. 385–396, 2006.
© Springer-Verlag Berlin Heidelberg 2006

trivial results. However, lots of similar results are often produced, which makes users tired or confused. As we will see in section 5, previous works in KSORD do not solve these problems very well.

Organizing search results into clusters facilitates users' quick browsing through search results. Users can determine whether a group is relevant or not by examining simply its description: they can then explore just the relevant clusters and ignore the remaining ones, so that their browsing efficiency can be improved. This method has been widely used in presenting Web search results, while to the best of our knowledge, it has not been employed in KSORD research.

In this paper, we propose clustering to improve the presentation of search results, so as to improve the efficiency of users' browsing. Although many works about clustering have been done in related domains, traditional clustering methods are not applicable to KSORD results as is explained in section 5. In this paper, we focus on TD-KSORD systems, and propose a novel results clustering method named TreeCluster. It combines the structure and content information together and includes two steps of pattern clustering and keyword clustering. In the first step, we use labels to represent schema information of each result tree and cluster the trees into groups. The trees in each group are isomorphic. In the second step, we rank user keywords according to their frequencies in the database, and further partition the large groups based on the content of keyword nodes. Furthermore, we give each cluster a readable description, and present the description and each result tree graphically to help users understand the results more easily. Experimental results verify our methods' effectiveness and efficiency.

Organization: Section 2 introduces the basic concepts needed. Section 3 provides the detail of our solution and algorithms. The experimental results are shown in section 4. Section 5 reviews the related work. Finally, Section 6 concludes this paper.

2 Basic Concepts

We define some terms we will use in the following sections. They are based on [3] and have been adjusted slightly for simplification.

Definition 1 (Data Graph). Database can be represented as an undirected Data Graph G(V,E) which is composed of weighted nodes and weighted edges.

Nodes: For each tuple t in the database, the graph has a corresponding node $u_t \in V$. We will speak interchangeably of a tuple and the corresponding node in the graph.

Edges: For each pair of tuples t_1 and t_2 such that there is a foreign key from t_1 to t_2, the graph contains an undirected edge $< u_{t_1}, u_{t_2} >$.

Weights: Each node and edge is assigned a weight.

Definition 2 (Keyword Query). User's input is defined as a keyword query, which generally consists of n ($n \geq 1$) search terms $k_1, k_2, ..., k_n$.

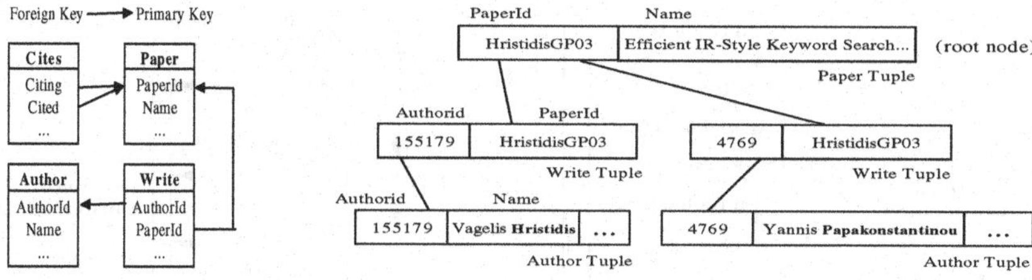

Fig. 1. DBLP Schema

Fig. 2. An Example of result tree

A node is relevant to a search term if it contains the search term as part of an attribute value. It is called a **keyword node**. Generally, the first step of search algorithms is to locate the set of keyword nodes S_i that are relevant to k_i for each k_i in the query.

Definition 3 (Result Tree). An answer to a query is a rooted weighted tree containing at least one node from each S_i.

The relevance score of a result tree is computed from the weights of its nodes and edges. Result trees should be ranked in descending order of relevance score to meet the requirement of top-k query.

We call the root node of a result tree a **information node**, which connects all the keyword nodes, and strongly reflects the relationship among them.

For example, Figure 1 shows the schema of DBLP[14] dataset. Given a keyword query (*Hristidis, Papakonstantinou*), TD-KSORD systems find top-k result trees from the datagraph of DBLP. Figure 2 shows an example of one of the result trees, which is a subgraph of DBLP's data graph and means *Hristidis* and *Papakonstantinou* coauthor a paper.

3 TreeCluster

The problem we will solve is to find a clustering method to organize result trees into significant groups. First, we introduce the intuition of our method, and then describe the implementation, finally introduce the graphical user interface.

3.1 Intuition

We did much observation on different datasets, and found that many of the result trees were of the same pattern. For example, in DBLP, keyword query (*Jim Gray, Transaction*) may lead to many results. Some of them belong to the pattern that *Jim Gray* writes papers about *transaction*, while some of them belong to the one that *Jim Gray's* papers are cited by papers about *transaction*, and others may belong to the one that *Jim Gray's* papers cites papers about *transaction*. Thus, we can cluster all these results into various groups according to different patterns, and give a readable description for each group.

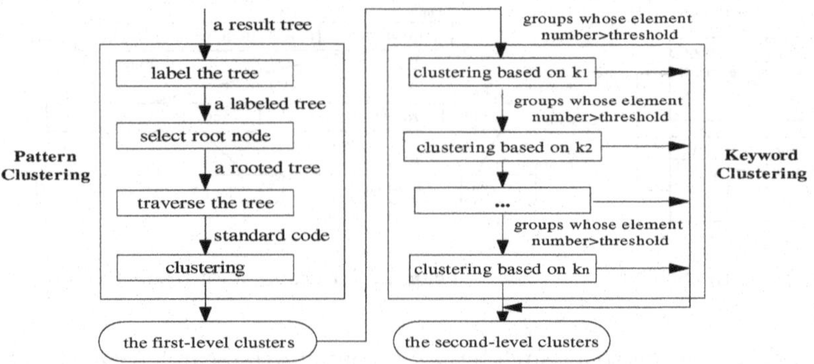

Fig. 3. Architecture of TreeCluster

Furthermore, we find that the resulting clusters in some patterns are quite large. So we decide to partition the large clusters further based on the content. From users' viewpoints, the most meaningful things are the keywords they input, so we can do partitioning based on the content of keyword nodes. The keywords should not be treated equally however. In fact, different keywords have different "frequencies" in the database. For instance, in DBLP, for keyword query (*Gray, Transaction*), *Gray* only appears in a few tuples, while *Transaction* appears in lots of tuples. We can partition large clusters based on the content of nodes relevant to low frequency keywords first. In this example, we partition a large group according to nodes relevant to *Gray* first. Thus result trees relevant to different "Gray"s, e.g. *Jim Gray* and *W.A.Gray*, are separated. Users need only examine the label (*Jim Gray*) or (*W.A.Gray*) for each subgroup to determine which one they are interested in instead of browsing through each result in the large group.

Figure 3 shows the framework of TreeCluster. It includes two steps, and produces two levels of clusters. After pattern clustering, we get the first-level groups, each of which corresponds to a kind of tree pattern. The large groups, whose numbers of elements exceed the threshold, will be processed by keyword clustering, after which, we get the second-level groups.

3.2 Pattern Clustering

Firstly, we cite definitions and conclusions about labeled trees from [9, 10], without detailed explanations due to space limitations.

Theorem 1. Two rooted ordered labeled trees are isomorphic if and only if their preorder traversal codes are equal.

Definition 4 (Standard Code). Let T be a rooted unordered labeled tree. All rooted ordered trees derived from T are named $T_1, T_2, ..., T_n$, whose preorder traversal codes are $S_1, S_2, ..., S_n$ respectively. We call the minimum code S_{min} of $S_1, S_2, ..., S_n$ the standard code of T.

Algorithm 1: GetStandardCode(t)

```
Global: special symbols '#' and '$' ('#' >' $' >all the label symbols)
Input: t: the root of a rooted unordered labeled tree T
Output: the standard code of T
St ← label(t)+"$"; // "+" means connecting
for each edge e that comes from t to its sons do
    St2 ← label(e); get another node n of e;
    insert St2+GetStandardCode(n)+"$" into set S;
end
sort strings in S in ascending order;
for each string s in S do
    append s to St;
end
return St+"#";
```

Theorem 2. Algorithm 1 computes the standard code of a rooted unordered tree correctly.

Theorem 3. Two rooted unordered labeled trees are isomorphic if and only if their standard codes are equal.

Now, we label the nodes and edges with schema information, so that we can express the pattern using traversal code of the tree. For an ordinary node (not keyword nodes), we may easily use the relation name it belongs to as its label. For a keyword node, things are more complex, because a keyword node may contain several keywords, and a keyword may appear in several attributes of a node. For an edge, what we concern is the primary-foreign key relationship. Thus we get the following rules.

Rule 1. Assume a node t, $t \in$ relation R. If t is an ordinary node, the label of t is [R]. If t is a keyword node, which contains keywords $k_1, k_2, ..., k_n$, and k_i is contained in attributes $A_{i_1}, A_{i_2}, ..., A_{i_{m_i}}$ $(1 \le i \le n)$, then the label of t is $[Rk_1(A_{1_1}A_{1_2}...A_{1_{m_1}})...k_i(A_{i_1}A_{i_2}...A_{i_{m_i}})...k_n(A_{n_1}A_{n_2}...A_{n_{m_n}})]$.

Rule 2. Assume an edge $< t_1, t_2 >, t_1 \in$ relation $R_1, t_2 \in$ relation R_2, and assume the corresponding foreign key is $(A_1, ..., A_r)(A_i \in R_1, 1 \le i \le r)$, the corresponding primary key is $(B_1, ..., B_r)(B_i \in R_2, 1 \le i \le r)$, then the label of $< t_1, t_2 >$ is $\{(A_1, ..., A_r), (B_1, ..., B_r)\}$.

Because of the search mechanism in TD-KSORD systems, the roots of result trees in the same pattern may not be correspondent. For example, different result trees (the two authors coauthor different papers) in Figure 4 and Figure 2 have the same pattern, but their root nodes are not in correspondence. Therefore, we need to select a new root for each result tree to ensure the roots of trees in the same pattern are correspondent. In addition, such root nodes should contain as much information as possible. In this example, the root node of the tree in Figure 4 should be the "Paper Tuple".

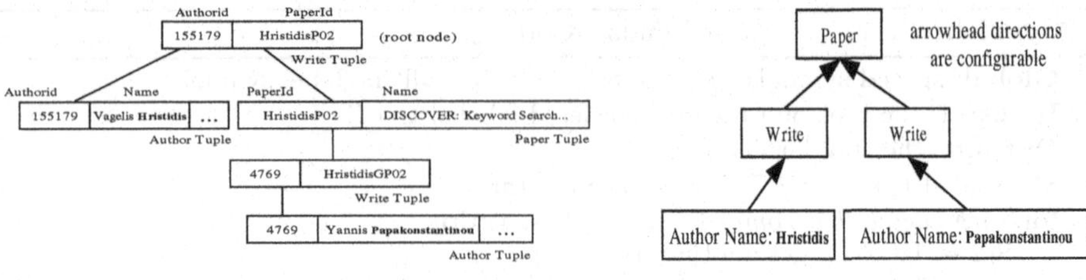

Fig. 4. A result tree in the same pattern with the tree in Figure 2

Fig. 5. An Example of the first-level cluster description

We consider firstly the nodes having the maximum degree, if there are many such nodes, we select those closest to the center of the tree. Usually, there is only one candidate node meeting the above two conditions. If there are more than one however, we use each of the candidate nodes in turn as the root and employ Algorithm 1 to compute the standard codes of the tree respectively. The one with the minimum standard code is selected as the information node. If there are more than one root node resulting in the minimum standard code, we can use any of them as the root node, because they produce the same standard code and do not affect the judging of isomorphism.

Now we get a rooted unordered labeled tree, we could use algorithm 1 to compute its standard code. According to Theorem 3, trees having the same standard codes are isomorphic and are clustered into a group. Thus we get the first-level clusters.

3.3 Keyword Clustering

We firstly rank the keywords according to their frequencies in the database, i.e. the number of keyword nodes which contain the specified keyword. Assume the new order is k_1, k_2,...,k_n. Then, we examine each group. If the number of elements in the group exceeds the threshold, we partition it firstly based on k_1, that is, if the contents of nodes in two trees relevant to k_1 are the same, the two trees are put into one group, otherwise separated into different groups. If the new groups still contain more than the threshold number of elements, we will continue to partition them based on k_2, and etc, until the number of elements in each cluster is less than the threshold or all the keywords are used up. Algorithm 2 shows the details.

3.4 GUI and Cluster Description

We build a graphic user interface for result representation, as demonstrated in Figure 6, in windows explorer style. For the results in each cluster, we rank them according to the relevant score in descending order. Furthermore, we get the maximum relevant score of each cluster, and rank clusters based on their maximum scores in descending order too.

In order to make the results semantically meaningful to users, we give a readable description for each cluster and present the description and each result graphically. Each tuple connection tree is presented in graph, as shown in Figure 2. The first-level cluster description mainly has the following characteristics. Firstly, it uses alias for database relations and attributes, so that database schema information is shielded to end users and improve the readability. Secondly, in order to focus on the pattern information, an ordinary node is only annotated with its relation alias, while a keyword node annotated with its relation alias, attribute alias and keyword itself. Thirdly, the direction of the edges between nodes can be configured in advance to provide more semantical meaning. Figure 5 is the cluster description of Figure 2 and Figure 4. Apparently, it can be understood quickly by users. For the second-level clusters, we label them with the keywords based on which the group is produced.

Algorithm 2: Group(S, k)

```
Global: THRESHOLD; KeyWord[ ]: an array of ranked keywords according to
their frequencies in ascending order
Input: S: a group (set of trees) to be clustered; k: the index of current keyword
Output: set of the subgroups of S
if k > KeywordNum then {insert S into V; return V;}
for each tree t in S do
    search set S2 in V, requiring the content of nodes relevant to KeyWord[k] of
    trees in S2 is the same as that of t;
    if S2 exists then {add t into S2;}
    else {NEW(S2), add t into S2, and insert S2 into V;}
end
for each set S2 in V do
    if |S2| < THRESHOLD then { add S2 into V2;}
    else
        V3 ← group(S2, k + 1);
        for each set S3 in V3 do
            add S3 into V2;
        end
    end
end
return V2;
```

---

4 Experiments

A search result clustering system is designed using Java, as shown in Figure 6. The system accepts query inputs from users and passes them to KSORD systems. Users can select one of the two result presentation manners: list or cluster. The former is the traditional method that simply presents ranked results in order, while the latter is this paper's work of presenting ranked results in clusters. As experiments demonstrates below, the latter is almost as fast as the former.

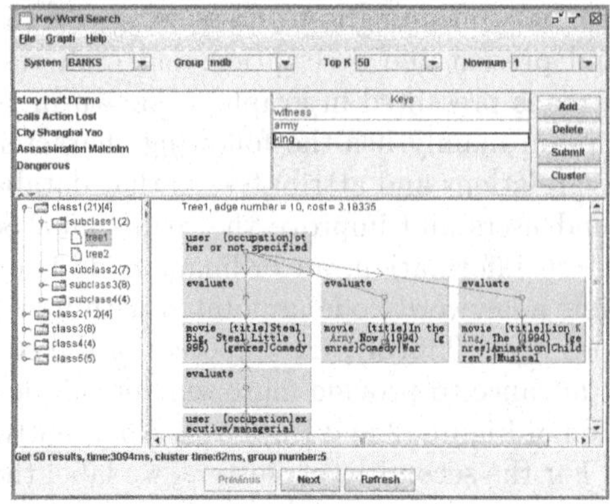

Fig. 6. The GUI of Search Result Clustering

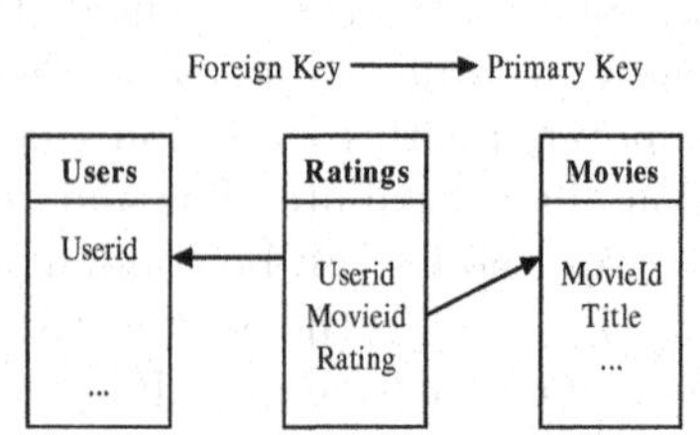

Fig. 7. MDB Schema

We conduct tests using Oracle9i on a AMD844*4 CPU and 4G memory Dawning server running Windows 2000 Advanced Server, using BANKS as KSORD system and it connects to Oracle9i through JDBC. In our figures, C-BANKS means BANKS using cluster as presentation manner, while L-BANKS means BANKS using list manner. For each test, we experiment on two real datasets, a subset of DBLP and a subset of MDB[15]. Our DBLP consists of about 497,000 nodes and 567,000 edges. Our MDB consists of about 506,000 nodes and 997,000 edges. The schema of MDB is shown in Figure 7.

For each experiment, we randomly generate 100 queries, and test the average effectiveness and efficiency. We partition the keywords extracted from the two datasets into three category according to their frequencies: high(H), medium(M), and low(L). We will show the experimental results of various patterns of keyword queries, although we only use keywords in medium and high frequency to do tests in order to meet the real-life case.

Due to space limitations, we always set the threshold of keyword clustering to 10 and do not report experimental results of other threshold. Apparently, as the threshold arise, the group number of the second-level will decrease.

4.1 Effectiveness

We call the average group number of the first-level **F-Num**, and use it to evaluate the effectiveness of pattern clustering. We use the number of overall groups including groups of the first-level that do not have subgroups and groups of the second-level to evaluate the overall effectiveness, and call it **O-Num**. Apparently, neither too many nor too few groups is good, and only medium F-Num and O-Num helps to improve users' browsing efficiency.

Number of Keywords. In Figure 8 and 9, we fix result number to 100 and vary the number of keywords from 2 to 6, to test F-Num and O-Num. We can see that in most cases, F-Num and O-Num are medium, which verifies our methods' effectiveness.

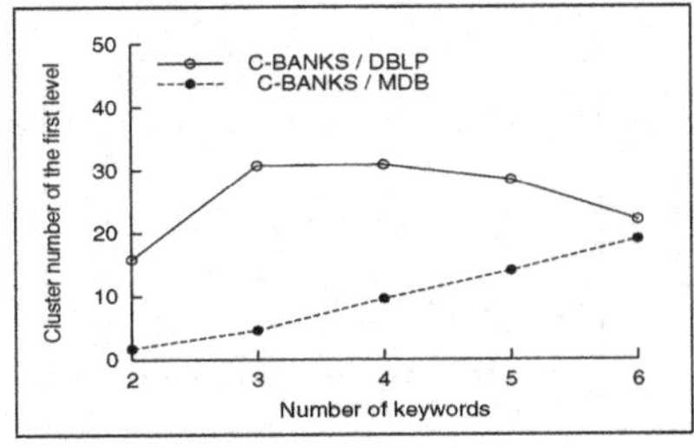

Fig. 8. Effectiveness(a): F_Num. Fix *Top-k* = 100, and vary KeywordNum.

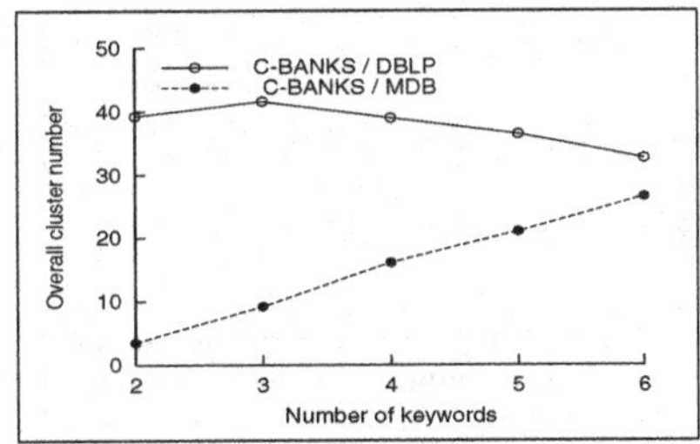

Fig. 9. Effectiveness(b): O_Num. Fix *Top-k* = 100, and vary KeywordNum.

In Figure 8, F-Num in DBLP is always larger than that in MDB, because the schema of MDB (primary-foreign key relationship) is simpler than that of DBLP, so that top-k results are likely in the same pattern. As keyword number increases, F-Num in MDB increases while that in DBLP decreases with over 3 keywords. The reason is that keyword frequencies in MDB are significantly lower than those in DBLP, so results that contain more keywords in MDB are not likely in the same pattern, while in DBLP, results containing more keywords are more likely produced by one Cartesian product[3] and thus in the same pattern.

It's easy to understand that if F-Num is small, the element number of each group is more likely to exceed the threshold and will be partitioned further by keyword clustering. Thus in Figure 9, although the varying trend of O-Num is similar to that of F-Num, it varies more gently.

Number of Results. In Figure 10 and 11, we fix keyword number to 3 and vary the number of returned results from 20 to 120. We can see F-Num and O-Num basically linearly increase as the top-k increases, which demonstrates our methods' good scalability.

Keyword Patterns. In Figure 12 and 13, we fix the number of keywords to 3, and the number of returned results to 100, and report 10 representative keyword patterns. For instance, pattern MML represents two medium frequency and one low frequency keywords.

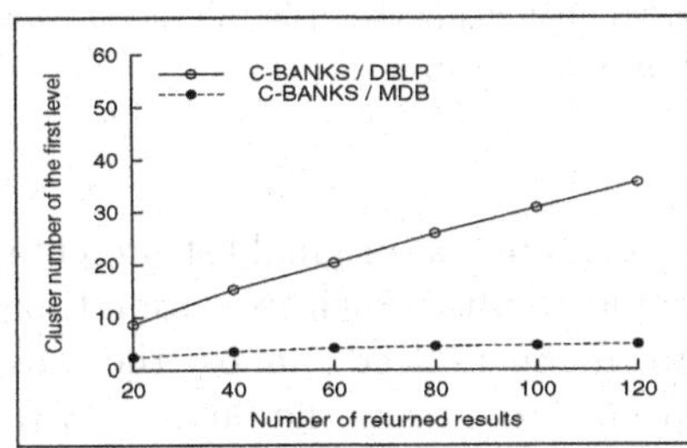

Fig. 10. Effectiveness(c): F_Num. Fix *KeywordNum* = 3, and vary Top-k.

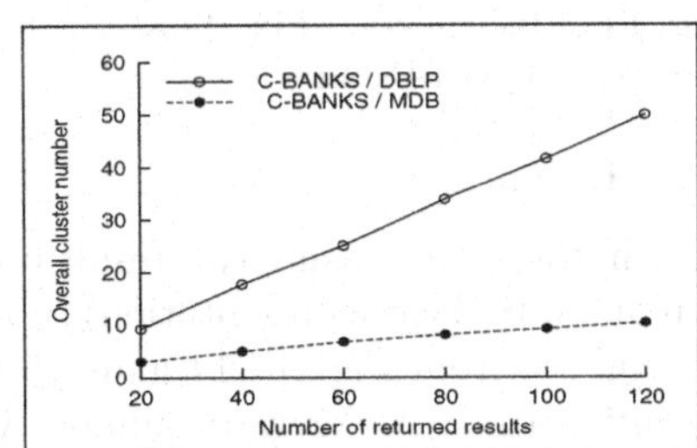

Fig. 11. Effectiveness(d): O_Num. Fix *KeywordNum* = 3, and vary Top-k.

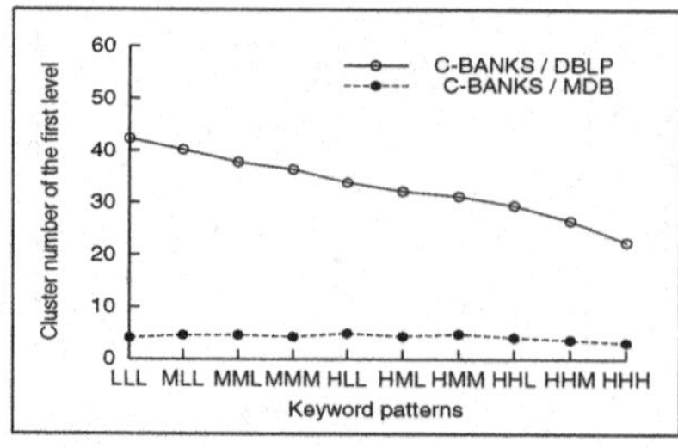

Fig. 12. Effectiveness(e): F_Num. Fix *KeywordNum* = 3, *Top-k* = 100, and vary Keyword Pattern.

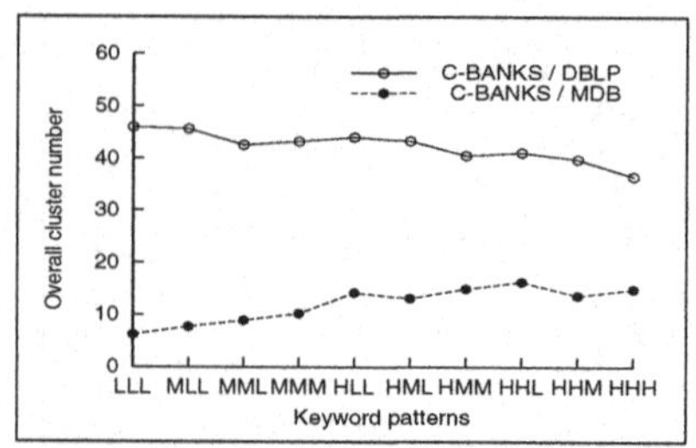

Fig. 13. Effectiveness(f): O_Num. Fix *KeywordNum* = 3, *Top-k* = 100, and vary Keyword Pattern.

In Figure 12, as keyword pattern contains higher frequency keywords, F-Num decreases in DBLP, which shows that keywords in higher frequency is more likely to produce results in the same pattern. F-Num varies a little in MDB because most of the keywords in MDB appear only a few times.

Figure 13 shows that higher frequency words play an import role in keyword clustering, because they appear in many tuples and the contents of these tuples are usually not equal.

Discussion. In general, simpler database schema and higher frequency keywords incline to decrease F-Num, while lower frequency keywords incline to increase F-Num. Higher frequency keywords incline to increase the group number of the second-level resulting in the increment of O-Num.

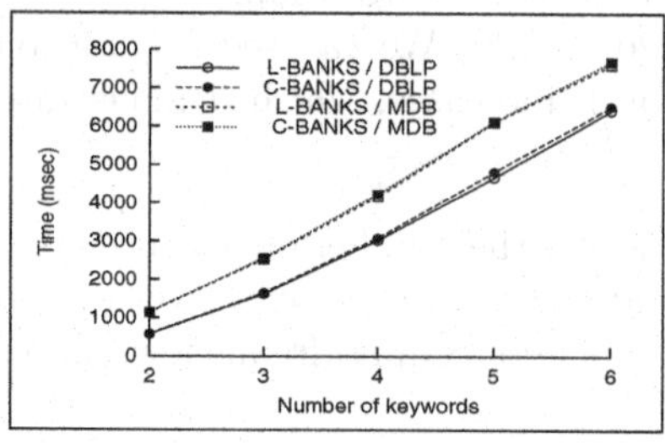

Fig. 14. Efficiency(a). Fix *Top-k* = 100 and vary KeywordNum.

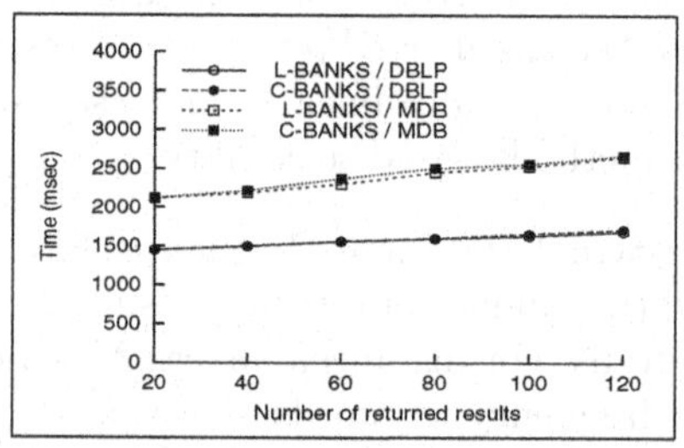

Fig. 15. Efficiency(b). Fix *KeywordNum* = 3 and vary Top-k.

4.2 Efficiency

We run the system using two result presentation manners (original list presentation and our cluster presentation) separately and compare their execution time. We can see from Figure 14 and 15 that two manners needs almost the same execution time. As keyword number varies from 2 to 6 or as the number of returned results varies from 20 to 120, clustering time increases only a little (the difference between C-BANKS/dataset and L-BANKS/dataset means the value of clustering time). The efficiency of BANKS on MDB is lower than that on

DBLP, which is also because keyword frequencies in MDB are lower than those in DBLP.

Usually, clustering search results always hurts the efficiency of systems, as previous works in Web search do. However, our method has slightly effect on original system efficiency.

5 Related Work

In KSORD research, many ways are used to present query results. BANKS[3] shows the query results in a nested table, based on which [13] improves the answer format by addressing readability. DbSurfer[12] uses tree-like structures to display all trails, while DataSpot[11] uses a distinguished answer node to represent a result. However, these works do not solve the problem of lots of similar results. In this paper, we organize the results into clusters and present them graphically to improve users' browsing efficiency.

[9] proposes a result classification method. In preprocessing, the system produces various patterns, and in processing a query, users select a particular pattern and the system searches the results matching the selected pattern. [13] mentions the similar idea, however with no implementation details. This method has to be implemented inside the search engine of a KSORD system, and closely bundled with the system. Our method can be implemented outside the system and applicable to various TD-KSORD systems.

Clustering results has been investigated in many works in the context of Web search. These works (e.g. [17, 18, 19]) are based on the content similarity and cluster documents into topically-coherent groups. Vivisimo[20] is a real demonstration of clustering Web search results. However, clustering methods used in Web are not applicable to KSORD. On the one hand, results of KSORD belong to a community (a professional database, such as DBLP or MDB), clustering based on content similarity usually can not get distinguished groups. On the other hand, information of RDBMS schema which is not available in Web search should be employed to instruct clustering.

[21] proposes to categorize the results of SQL queries, and generates multi-level category structure. However, according to the characteristics of our method, we only produce two levels of categorization, including the results of pattern clustering and keyword clustering respectively.

Traditional clustering research includes partitioning method, hierarchical method, density-based method, and etc[22]. Our method is different from them, aiming at the character of KSORD results. There are many works about judging isomorphism of rooted labeled trees. We directly cite the conclusions from [9, 10] without detailed explanations due to space limitations.

6 Conclusion and Future Work

In this paper, we proposed a novel clustering method named TreeCluster to organize search results of TD-KSORD system to improve users' browsing efficiency.

Furthermore, we generated readable cluster description, and presented the description and each result graphically to help users understand the results more easily. Experimental results verify effectiveness and efficiency of our method. This is the first proposal for clustering search results of KSORD.

In future work, we will detect more database schema information in the search process of KSORD and utilize it to improve the clustering results.

Acknowledgement

This work was supported by the National Natural Science Foundation of China (No.60473069 and No.60496325).

References

1. Shan Wang and Kun-Long Zhang. Searching Databases with Keywords. Journal of Computer Science and Technology, Volume 20, No.1, January 2005.
2. A. Hulgeri, G. Bhalotia, C. Nakhe et al. Keyword Search in Databases. IEEE Data Engineering Bulletin, vol. 24, pages 22-32, 2001.
3. G. Bhalotia, A. Hulgeri, C. Nakhe et al. Keyword Searching and Browsing in Databases using BANKS. ICDE'02.
4. Varun Kacholia, Shashank Pandit, Soumen Chakrabarti et al. Bidirectional Expansion For Keyword Search on Graph Databases. VLDB'05, pages 505-516.
5. S. Agrawal et al. DBXplorer: A System For Keyword-Based Search Over Relational Databases. ICDE'02.
6. V. Hristidis et al. DISCOVER: Keyword Search in Relational Databases. VLDB'02.
7. V. Hristidis et al. Efficient IR-Style Keyword Search over Relational Databases. VLDB'03.
8. A. Balmin et al. ObjectRank: Authority-Based Keyword Search in Databases. VLDB'04.
9. Kun-Long Zhang. Research on New Preprocessing Technology for Keyword Search in Databases. PH.D thesis of Renmin University of China, 2005.
10. A.V. Aho, J.E. Hopcroft, and J.D. Ullman. The Design and Analysis of Computer Algorithms, Addison-Wesley, 1974.
11. S. Dar et al. DTL's DataSpot:Database Exploration Using Plain Language. VLDB'98.
12. R. Wheeldon et al. DbSurfer: A Search and Navigation Took for Relational Databases. The 21st Annual British National Conference on Databases, 2004.
13. B. Aditya et al. User Interaction in the BANKS System: A Demostration. ICDE'03, Demo.
14. DBLP Bibliography. http://www.informatik.uni-trier.de/ ley/db/index.html.
15. J. Riedl and J. Konstan. MoveLens. http://www.grouplens.org/.
16. V. Hristidis et al. Keyword Proximity Search on XML Graphs. ICDE'03.
17. Cutting D. R. et al. Constant Interaction-Time Scatter/Gather Browsing of Very Large Document Collections. SIGIR'93.
18. Zamir O. et al. Web Document Clustering: A Feasibility Demonstration. SIGIR'98.
19. Hua-Jun Zeng et al. Learning to Cluster Web Search Results. SIGIR'04.
20. Vivisimo clustering engine,(2004) http://vivisimo.com.
21. K.Chakrabarti et al. Automatic Categorization of Query Results. SIGMOD'04.
22. A.K. Jain et al. Data Clustering: A Review. ACM Computing Surveys, Vol 31, No.3, 1999: 264-323.

A New Method for Finding Approximate Repetitions in DNA Sequences

Di Wang[1], Guoren Wang[1], Qingquan Wu[1,2], Baichen Chen[1], and Yi Zhao[1]

[1] College of Information Science & Engineering
Northeastern University, Shenyang 110004, China
wangdeedee@vip.sina.com
http://mitt.neu.edu.cn

[2] Shanghai Baosight Ltd., Shanghai 201900, China

Abstract. Searching for approximate repetitions in a DNA sequence has been an important topic in gene analysis. One of the problems in the study is that because of the varying lengths of patterns, the similarity between patterns cannot be judged accurately if we use only the concept of ED (Edit Distance). In this paper we shall make effort to define a new function to compute similarity, which considers both the difference and sameness between patterns at the same time. Seeing the computational complexity, we shall also propose two new filter methods based on frequency distance and Pearson correlation, with which we can sort out candidate set of approximate repetitions efficiently. We use SUA instead of sliding window to get the fragments in a DNA sequence, so that the patterns of an approximate repetition have no limitation on length. The results show that with our technique we are able to find a bigger number of approximate repetitions than that of those found with tandem repeat finder.

1 Introduction

In the human, coding sequences comprise less than 5% of the genome, whereas repeat sequences account for at least 50% or much more [1] [2].They embody a large amount of information concerning key clue of human evolution and abundant information of antiquated life [2]. Nowadays the repeat sequence as a heretical mark is widely applied in the fields of tumor biochemistry, forensic medicine individual recognition, parent-child appraisal, population genetics and so on [3] [4]. For example, the recent research shows that CCG trinucleotide repetitions have important effect on pre-mutation of X chromosome [5].

Finding repetitions is a difficult task and the first obstacle in the way is how to give a formal definition of repetitions as was once pointed out by G. Benson [6]. The search of the repetitions can be classified into two kinds, perfect repetitions and approximate repetitions, the patterns of one perfect repetition being all the same. We have proposed a new definition LPR for prefect repetitions and designed an index SUA for finding LPRs [14]. However, events such as mutations, translocations and reversal events will often render the copies imperfect over

J.X. Yu, M. Kitsuregawa, and H.V. Leong (Eds.): WAIM 2006, LNCS 4016, pp. 397–409, 2006.
© Springer-Verlag Berlin Heidelberg 2006

time, so the approximate repetitions are present, whose patterns are not all the same. Finding approximate repetitions is harder work than finding perfect repeats and has been studied by many researchers during recent years. In this paper, we will focus on the search for approximate repetitions, whose copies of a repetition are tandemly.

The approximate repetitions search methods can be classified into two kinds according to the search result: the exact method by which all the repetitions can be found according to the given definition and the heuristic method with which we cannot be sure to find all the repetitions. In the exact methods, Landau and Schmidt [7] proposed the algorithm for finding the tandem repeats where the hamming or edit distance of the two patterns of the repeat has some given value. Kurtz proposed the algorithm for finding all the maximal repeat pairs under the given hamming distance. Sagot and Myers designed the algorithm for finding approximate tandem array [8], but the algorithm requires the length of a pattern be less than 40 and the continuous occurrence of the pattern be given in advance. Compared with exact methods, heuristic methods are not so good in that we cannot with those methods find all the approximate repetitions according to the definitions of the repetitions that we are able to find with exact methods, but the definitions are more acceptable to the biologist. Most of the methods are based on statistic, with which we find possible approximate repetitions according to the statistics information, and then discover the approximate repetitions from them [9] [10]. One of the most popular algorithms is Tandem Repeat Finder [10].

In this paper we'll present a new approach to detect approximate repetitions in DNA sequence. Similar to [10] and [11], we use a two-phased algorithm, which consist of candidate phase and verification phase. Our main contributions are i) we use a new criterion to express the percentage differences between patterns even though the lengths of the copies may not be equal; ii)in candidate phase we employ frequency distance and Pearson correlation as filter to find the candidates; iii) our method requires no priori knowledge such as the pattern, pattern size or the number of copies; iv) we use SUA index instead of sliding window to find patterns which has no limitation on the size of copies in a repetition.

The remainder of this paper is organized as follows. In section 2, we import a new criterion for approximate repetitions. We design the filters for detection of candidates of approximate repetitions in section 3. In section 4, we first use SUA to attain copies of repetitions and then use the two-phased method to find the approximate repetitions. In section 5 the algorithm is tested thoroughly. Finally, in Section 6 we draw our conclusion.

2 New Criterion for Approximate Sequences

To process approximate matching, one common and simple approximation metric is called edit distance.

Definition 1. Edit distance *The edit distance between two sequences is defined as the minimum number of edit operations (i.e. insertions, deletions and* *substitutions) of single characters needed to transform the first string into the second. Ed(S, P) is used to denote the edit distance between sequence S and P.*

Given the two sequences S1 and S2, the similarity between them is the fixed number of differences in traditional methods, i.e. Edit distance. But Edit distance suitable for short patterns would be unreasonably restrictive for long patterns in the repetitions comparison. Conversely, Edit distance suitable for long patterns would be not strict enough for short patterns. Another criterion of similarity is percentage difference proposed in [10], which takes the Edit distance and the lengths of patterns into account. But the lengths of copies in an approximate repetition are different so that we cannot use this percentage difference directly. Take S1=ACCT ACG ACGTA for instance, the Edit distances between every two copies are the same but the lengths of copies are different. In this case we cannot evaluate the similarity of copies by percentage difference. But it is obvious that in the process of the comparison between two copies of chars, in which we change one copy into the other copy with the minimum number of deletions, insertion or replacements, the number of chars which remain unchanged in their original positions is fixed.

Definition 2. ReservedChar *Let S1, S2 be two sequences from the alphabet $\sum = \{a_1, a_2, \cdots, a_n\}$; Let S' be the alignment result sequence of S1, S2 by dynamic programming. If c_j is a char of S1 with index j ($0 \leq j < |S1|$), and c_j still occurred (not been deleted or replaced) in S' with index j',we call c_j is a ReservedChar of S1 to S2. In the same way, if c_k is a char of S2 with index k ($0 \leq k < |S2|$), and c_k still occurred in S' with index k', we define c_k is a ReservedChar of S2 to S1.*

Definition 3. ReservedChar Pair *Let S' be an alignment result sequence of S1, S2 by dynamic programming, c_j is a ReservedChar of S1 to S2 occurring in S' with index j' , and c_k is a ReservedChar of S2 to S1 occurring in S' with index k', if j' == k', then we define (c_j, c_k) a ReservedChar Pair of S1, S2.*

For example, given S1 = ACATTA and S2 = AATG, we denote X^i as char X occurred at index j in a given sequence, if S' = AATG, then A^1, A^3, T^4 are reserved chars of S1 to S2 (T^5 is deleted); all chars of S2 are reserved chars of S2 to S1; (A^1, A^1), (A^3, A^2), (T^4, T^3) are reserved char pairs of S1, S2. However, if S'= ACATTA, then all chars of S1 are reserved chars of S1 to S2; A^1, A^2, T^3 are reserved chars of S2 to S1; (A^1, A^1), (A^3, A^2), (T^4, T^3) are reserved char pairs of S1, S2.

Evidently, we have Property 1 as follows:

Property 1. If c_j is a ReservedChar of S1(to S2) or S2(to S1), then c_j belongs to at most one ReservedChar Pair of S1 and S2.

Definition 4. Reserved Number *Let S1, S2 be two sequences from the alphabet $\sum = \{a_1, a_2, \cdots, a_n\}$; We define the Reserved Number of S1,S2 as the total number of ReservedChar Pairs of S1 and S2, abbreviate as ResNum (S1, S2).*

As is known, Edit Distance (ED) expresses the difference between two sequences S1, S2, and here we describe the meaning of ResNum (S1, S2). According to the definition of ReservedChar pair , c_j and c_k in ReservedChar Pair (c_j , c_k) can be looked upon as a char pair which are matched with no need of insertion, replacement or deletion operation. So the Reserved Number of S1, S2 expresses the sameness between S1 and S2.

Property 2. Let S1, S2 be two sequences from the alphabet $\sum=\{a_1, a_2, \cdots, a_n\}$; then ResNum (S1, S2) is a definite value, which is determined by ED(S1, S2).

We define a new function based on ED and ResNum to find similarity of two sequences.

Definition 5. Similar(S1, S2). *Let S1, S2 be two sequences from the alphabet $\sum = \{a_1, a_2, \cdots, a_n\}$. We define Similar(S1, S2) as: Similar(S1, S2) = ResNum(S1, S2)/ED(S1, S2).*

For example, if S1 = ACATTA and S2 = AATG, then ResNum(S1,S2)=3, ED(S1,S2)=3, so Similar(S1,S2)=3/3=1.

In fact, Similar(S1, S2) expresses the ratio of the sameness to the difference between S1 and S2. So, it is reasonable to take Similar(S1, S2) as the criterion to the similarity between sequences. Obviously, Similar(S1, S2) has the following properties.

Property 3. The more similar S1 and S2 are, the bigger the value of Similar(S1, S2) is.

According to the property 3, given a lower bound of similarity value γ, all the sequence pairs (Si, Sj) that meet Similar(Si, Sj) $\geq \gamma$ are the results of the similarity search. If we improve γ, the more similar pairs could be found.

Note that, given two sequences S1 and S2, ED(S1, S2) and the ResNum(S1, S2) is got by DP, then Similar(S1, S2) can be computed. Because of the time and space complexity of ED computation, we will propose two appropriate filters in order to produce the smaller candidate set to compute edit distance.

3 Filters Design

Let m and n be the lengths of sequences S1 and S2, then the edit distance, ED(S1, S2), and the corresponding edit operations can be determined in O(mn) time and space [12]. In the search of approximate repetitions in DNA sequences, firstly, the sequences are usually large, even as long as tens of giga bps; secondly, given a sequence of length n, the number of its substring is as large as $O(n^2)$. If we directly compute edit distance to abtain the value of the function Similar between sequences, the time and space complexity is unacceptable. So we design two kinds of filters, and we compute only the function Similar of the sequences chosen by the filters. We will introduce some background about the filters.

3.1 Proposed Techniques

Frequency Distance

Definition 6. Frequency Vector. *Let S be a string over the alphabet* $\sum = \{a_1, a_2, \cdots, a_n\}$, *then the frequency vector of S, called f(S) is defined as: f(S) =* $[f_1, \cdots, f_n]$*,where each* f_i (≥ 0) *corresponds to the occurrences of* a_i *in S.*

For example, if S=ACTAT is a genomic sequence (i.e. from alphabet $\sum = \{A, C, G, T\}$), then f(S) = [2, 1, 0, 2].

Definition 7. Frequency Distance. *Let u and v be integer points in dimensional space. The frequency distance, FD(u, v), between u and v is defined as the minimum number of steps in order to go from u to v (or equivalently from v to u) by moving to a neighbor point at each step.*

Let u and v be vectors in the same dimension, let $Pos = \sum_{u_i > v_i} u_i - v_i$ and $Neg = \sum_{u_i < v_i} v_i - u_i$, then FD(u, v) = max($Pos$, Neg). It is obvious that the computation of FD is linear, so the time and space complexity of FD is much lower than that of ED. The detail about FD is in [13]. An important property of frequency distance is that, given two sequences S1 and S2, FD(f (S1), f(S2))≤ ED(S1, S2) [13].

Pearson Correlation

Pearson Correlation, i.e. linear correlation, measures the strength of a linear relationship between two variables. It ranges from -1 to 1. A correlation of +1 means that there is a perfect positive linear relationship between variables and a correlation of -1 means the perfect negative linear relationship between variables. And 0 means there isn't a clear linear relationship between variables.

For two vector X=$[x_1, x_2, \cdots, x_n]$ and Y=$[y_1, y_2, \cdots, y_n]$, their Pearson correlation is expressed as follows:

$$Pearson(X, Y) = \frac{\sum(X - \overline{X})(Y - \overline{Y})}{\sum(X - \overline{X})^2 \sum(Y - \overline{Y})^2}$$

$$\overline{X} = \sum_{i=1}^{n} x_i \Big/ n, \overline{Y} = \sum_{i=1}^{n} y_i \Big/ n$$

In the section of filter design, we will describe how to construct the vectors X and Y according to the sequences, and take Pearson correlation as the criterion for sequences similarity.

3.2 Filters Design

FD Based Filter

Frequency distance is widely used as a simple and efficient filter in search of similar sequences. We propose a FD based filter Similar_FD for the function Similar. As mentioned above, given the sequences S1 and S2, FD(S1, S2) can be seen as a filter for ED(S1, S2), so the key problem is to define the filter for ResNum(S1, S2).

Definition 8. ResNum_FV. *Let S1, S2 be two sequences from the alphabet* $\sum = \{a_1, a_2, \cdots, a_n\}$. *The frequency vectors of S1 and S2 are f(S1)=*$[f1_{S1}, f2_{S1}, \cdots, fn_{S1}]$ *and f(S2)=* $[f1_{S2}, f2_{S2}, \cdots, fn_{S2}]$ *respectively. ResNum_ FV is defined as:*

$$ResNum\_FV(S1, S2) = \sum_{i=1}^{n} \min(fi_{S1}, fi_{S2}).$$

Definition 9. Similar_FD. *Let S1, S2 be two sequences from the alphabet* $\sum = \{a_1, a_2, \cdots, a_n\}$. *Similar_FD is defined as: Similar_FD(S1, S2) = ResNum_FV (S1, S2) / FD(S1, S2).*

Lemma 1. *Let S1, S2 be two sequences from the alphabet* $\sum = \{a_1, a_2, \cdots, a_n\}$, $ResNum\_FV(S1, S2) \geq ResNum(S1, S2)$.

Theorem 1. *Let S1, S2 be two sequences from the alphabet* $\sum=\{a_1, a_2, \cdots, a_n\}$, $Similar\_FD(S1, S2) \geq Similar(S1, S2)$.

In the interest of space, we omit the proofs of the properties, lemma and theorem in this paper.

Given the two sequences S1 and S2 and the valve value of Similar() γ, we can prune S1 and S2 without computing Similar(S1, S2) if $Similar\_FD(S1, S2) < \gamma$. So we take Similar_FD() as the filter for Similar().

We give the performance of the FD based filter in the experiments. Similar to other methods based on FD, the performance of Similar_FD() is quite satisfactory when the sequences are short, however, it descends rapidly when the sequences are long. So, regarding the longer sequences, we give the following PC based filter.

PC Based Filter

Experiments show that the performance of the filter based on frequency function descended with the increasing of the lengths of sequences. We can come to the same conclusion by theoretical analysis. Let's take the frequency distance function FD for example. It uses the occurrence frequency of a char in the compared sequences as the similarity filter feature. If the sequences are short, it is really done. However, with the sequence length increasing, the occurrence frequency of a char will approach some statistical values, which is independent of the sequences. For example, in a genetic sequence of length more than 1M, there will be about 1/4M 'A' char. That means, when the sequences are long enough, they will have almost the same frequency vectors. So the FD filter will not function.

So, when the compared sequences are long, the statistical feature of a char frequency will cover up their every local difference. To solve the problem we propose a new filter method based on Pearson correlation coefficient.

The new method is sourced from the following idea directly:

1. According to the analysis above, when the compared sequences are short, the frequency feature can judge the similarity between two sequences well, so we will split a long sequence into many short subsequences, and then compute the frequency vector of these subsequences.

2. If two long sequences S1 and S2 have high similarity, their subsequences in corresponding region will have high similarity. Reflected to char frequency feature of the sequences, it means the same char's frequency value in every corresponding subsequences of S1 and S2 will be equal almost, that is, the same char's distributions in the subsequences are similar. If we take the char's frequency value serial in subsequences as two vector respectively, then the two vector will be high correlated. We measure the correlation by Pearson's correlation.

So, given two long sequences S1, S2 to be compared, we propose the filter method as the following, which includes two step-operation:

Step1: Divide two genomic sequences S1, S2 both into n subsequences and we get $S1_1$, $S1_2$,..., $S1_n$ of S1 and $S2_1$, $S2_2$,..., $S2_n$ of S2. Then compute t frequency vectors of the 2n subsequences and we get f (A_{11}, C_{11}, G_{11}, T_{11}), $\cdots$, f (A_{1n}, C_{1n}, G_{1n}, T_{1n}) and f (A_{21}, C_{21}, G_{21}, T_{21}), $\cdots$, f(A_{2n}, C_{2n}, G_{2n}, T_{2n}). For A, C, G and T, we can get vectors $((A_{11}, \cdots, A_{1n}), (A_{21}, \cdots, A_{2n}))$, (($C_{11}$, $\cdots$, C_{1n}), (C_{21}, $\cdots$, C_{2n})), ((G_{11}, $\cdots$, G_{1n}), (G_{21}, $\cdots$, G_{2n})) and ((T_{11}, $\cdots$, T_{1n}), (T_{21}, $\cdots$, T_{2n})) respectively. Here, we get two vectors for each char to compute Pearson's correlation. Take 'A' as example, we get vector $X_A = [A_{11}, \cdots, A_{1n}]$ from S1 and vector $Y_A = [A_{21}, \cdots, A_{2n}]$ from S2.

Step2: Compute Pearson(X_A, Y_A), Pearson(X_C, Y_C), Pearson(X_G, Y_G), and Pearson(X_T, Y_T). And set a valve r, if the four coefficient value above are all higher than $r * \frac{Similar()}{Similar()+1}$, we think the two sequences to be compared are similar probably and add them into the candidate set.

Here are some explanations. The method presumes if the two sequences to be compared are similar; the frequency vector got from their subsequences will have high correlation. In most cases, it is the fact. However, there also are some exceptional cases. So the filter method will probably filter out some sequence pairs which are really similar. Fortunately, the lost pairs are very few, but the filter method can filter long sequences efficiently. In the last part of the paper, we will show the efficiency of the filter method through thorough experiments.

Hybrid of the Two Filters

In the previous section, we proposed two filters to construct candidate set. The Similar_FD filter will function well if the compared sequences are short while the PC based filter is efficient for long sequences. So, we integrated the two methods in practice according to the lengths of sequences and we perform experiments to determine the borderline value of the two methods. In the experiment section we will give a detailed discussion about it.

4 Two-Phased Algorithm

4.1 Sequence Partition

Here we design efficient filters for the similar sequences search in database based on Similar. A key phase for the search of approximate repetitions is to partition the query sequence into fragments and filter the adjacent fragments by the functions discussed above. A general method of partitioning the sequence is sliding window method and its fatal shortcoming is that only the tandem fragments with the same length can be found. To avoid this shortcoming we use SUA [15].

SUA is an index structure that we design for finding perfect repetitions [14]. In repetitions finding, the copy of a repetition is generally called pattern. For example, in repetition ACGACGACG, ACG is the pattern. Through further analysis of the patterns in the repetitions, we find that a pattern comprises some units with the same characteristics.

Definition 10. pattern unit. *Let S be a sequence and substr be a substring starting with symbol X (it is A, C, G, T or $ in DNA sequence) of S. If the successor of substr is X or $ and there is no X in substr except for the first symbol, we call substr a pattern unit of X in S.*

For example, in the sequence ACGAGATC$, the substring ACG, AG and ATC are pattern units of A but ACGAC and AT are not. For the purpose of convenience, '$' is seen as a pattern unit although it cannot be a part of any pattern.

Definition 11. Succeeding Unit Array (SUA). *Let S be a DNA sequence of length* n. *We sort all the pattern units in ascending order (the regulation of the sorting is the same as the regulation of string sorting. If two pattern units are equal, we sort them according to their succeeding string) and get* n *pattern units. Every pattern unit and the position of its succeeding pattern unit (succeeding pattern unit of a pattern unit* pu *is the pattern unit of the succeeding symbol of* pu*) after sorting (the position of $ ' s succeeding pattern unit is marked as -1) compose a new array – Succeeding Unit Array.*

For example, in the sequence ACACACTAT$, there are four pattern units of A (one is ACT , one is AT, and the other two are AC), three pattern units of C (one is CTAT and the other two are CA) and two pattern units of T (one is T and the other is TA). The SUA is illuminated in figure 1.

pos	pattern unit	successor pos
0	$	-1
1	AC	2
2	AC	3
3	ACT	4
4	AT	0
5	CA	6
6	CA	7
7	CTAT	0
8	T	0
9	TA	8

Fig. 1. SUA on sequence ACACACTAT$

The construction and the performance of SUA has been discussed in [15]. For the purpose of convenience, given a sequence S, we call the substring of S a *compound pattern unit* which comprises some pattern units of the same symbol.

4.2 Candidate Phase

In candidate phase, we first take all the pattern units as the copies of repetitions and then add every pattern unit and its successor pattern unit which is gained according to the succeeding information in SUA as a pair to candidate set if they meet the filter function. Secondly, similar to perfect repetitions search in [14], compound pattern units are produced according to the succeeding information of pattern units. And then we push the compound pattern units and its successor into candidate set if they meet the filter function. The details are shown in [14].

Algorithm 1. candidate set

```
/*Tmin=the minimal length of pattern in repetition which requestor need.*/
/*Tmax=the maximal length of pattern in repetition which requestor need.*/
/*allDone=1 means there might still be candidates.*/
allDone=1;
while allDone==1 do
   allDone=0;
   for each position of sequence do
      pattern1 = the (compound) pattern unit which starts at the position;
      pattern2 = the pattern unit which is the successor of pattern1;
      if the length of pattern1 and pattern2 in [Tmin ··· Tmax] then
         allDone=0;
      end if
      if pattern1 and pattern2 are satisfied with the filter function then
         Add them as a pair in to candidates;
      end if
   end for
   for each position do
      pattern1=pattern unit which start at the position;
      if pattern1 can connect its successor then
         Connect the pattern1 and successor, procedure a compound pattern unit;
      end if
   end for
end while
```

4.3 Verification Phase

Given a list of candidates, the verification phase will work out the real the approximate repetitions.

The researchers have defined the types of repetitions, the simple, neighboring and pairwise approximate repetitions [14]. Clearly, different types of approximate repetitions lead to different verification procedures. Here, for neighboring approximate repetitions a two-phased verification procedure is performed.

Firstly, the Similar() of every pair in the candidate set is computed by DP to determine whether the pair meets the query.

Secondly, these two-copy approximate repetitions are connected into repetitions which contain more repeats if the last copy LC of the former repetition is the first copy FC of the latter repetition. The information of connection can be got by the succeeding information provided by SUA (the details can be found in [16]). We also found the pairwise approximate repetitions in [16].

In the search for approximate repetitions, we avoid two kinds of redundant results:(1) For a repetitions $P_1P_2 \cdots P_k$,which have k copies and P_i is one copy $(1 \leq i \leq k)$, we only produce the repetitions $P_i \cdots P_j$ $(1 \leq j \leq k)$with i = 1 and j = k. (2) For the repetitions which have the same start position and end position but different expressions, we only output the expression which has the most copies.

5 Experiments

In this section, we'll evaluate performance of filters and compare the repetitions we found with the result of Tandem Repeat Finder. The test data is DNA fragments from Human chr18 and chr22.

We implement the algorithms in C++ under Windows XP. All the experiments are run on a Dell PC with 2.6GHZ Intel Pentium processor with 512M memory. And we set the valve value of Similar=3.

We have mentioned the performance of FD based filter will drop rapidly with the increment of lengths of copies. Let frag_short be the shorter one of every two adjacent fragments, let candidate_Num[l] be the number of the candidates with frag_short = l and result_Num [l] be the number of correct results with frag_short = l. We use Performance_FD(l) = candidate_Num [l]/result_Num [l] to evaluate the performance of FD based filter, and in the experiment we set 12 $\leq l \leq$ 34. When the length of frag_short is larger than 18, the curve tendency of Performance_FD increases rapidly. For the efficiency of the method, we use PC based filter when the copies are longer and our method becomes a heuristic method because some results will be lost. According to Fig.2, we decide to use the PC based filter when lengths of the two adjacent fragments are both bigger than 18. Otherwise, we use FD based filter.

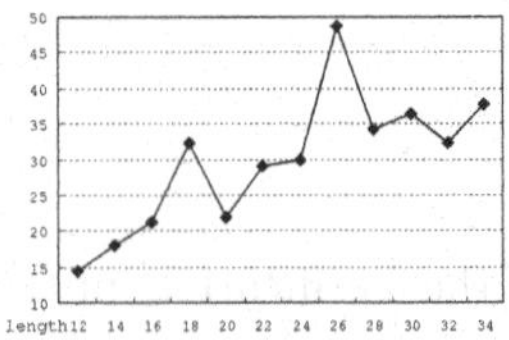

Fig. 2. Illustration for choosing length

Before using PC based filter to produce candidate set, we need to decide two parameters, the valve value of the correlation and the value of partitions that we divide the copies into. We choose these two values according to the proportion of results and candidates found with PC based filter to those found with FD based filter in experiments. We use 2 to 5 as the number of partitions and 0.3 to

0.6 as the valve value of the correlation. We take two fragments with the size of 60K from human chr18 and chr22 as test data. The (A) and (C) of Fig.3 shows that there is quite a rapid decrease of the proportion of right results found with PC based filter when valve value of correlation is bigger than 0.4 on different partitions. But the proportion of candidates decreases smoothly from 0.3 to 0.6 in (B) and (D) of Fig.3. So we choose 0.4 as the valve value of correlation. We choose partition=3 through the experiments for similar reason for choosing valve value of correlation. And we use partition=3 and valve value=0.4 to accomplish following experiments.

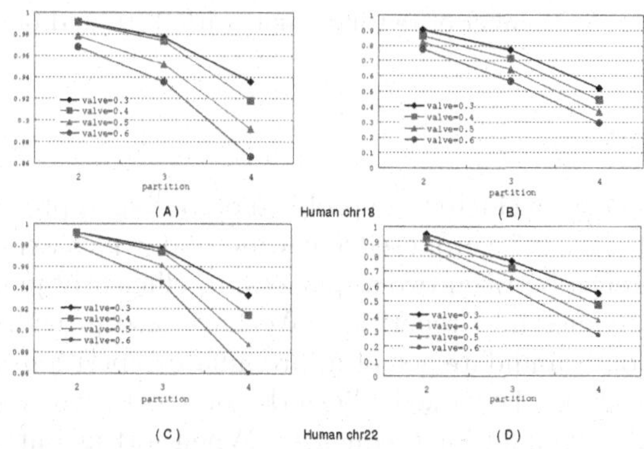

Fig. 3. Illustration to determine valve value and partitions of PC based filter

We compare the efficiency of FD based filter and the hybrid method by execution time and the number of right results and candidates. Fig.4 shows that the right results we lost is smaller than 3% but we cut down more than 35% on candidates and the saving of execution time is satisfactory.

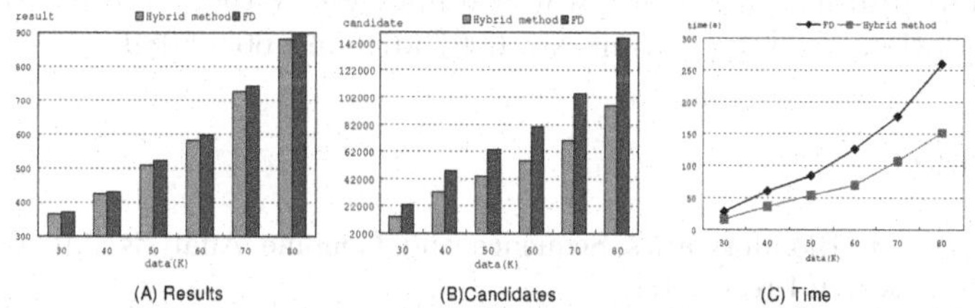

Fig. 4. Hybrid of the filters

In order to prove the validity of our method, we compare approximate repetitions found with our methods with the results found with Tandem Repeat Finder under the same condition in Fig.5. Our results always cover almost 95% of the results found with Tandem Repeat Finder and our results are much more than that of TRF using TRF's definition as shown in Fig.5, which proves the efficiency of our methods. The detailed analysis of the results can be found in http://mitt.neu.edu.cn.

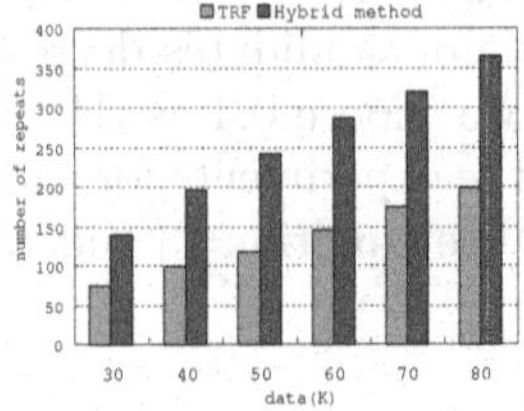

Fig. 5. Number of repeats found with TRF and ours

6 Conclusion

In this paper, we have considered the problem of finding approximate repetitions in a DNA sequence. We have proposed a new method, which expresses the ratio of sameness to difference between two sequences, to efficiently judge the similarity between any two copies in a repetition. We have also provided two new filter methods to sort out candidate set of approximate repetitions: the Similar_FD filter function based on FD worked efficiently for short sequences; the PC based filter method worked well for long sequences. When sorting out candidate set, by using SUA instead of sliding window, we can get patterns of different lengths. And in this paper, we have given some theoretical analysis and experimental results to validate the efficiency of our method.

However, the PC based filter method has its limitation in not being able to work out the complete candidate set. So, the next step for us to take is to search for some more efficient filter methods for long sequences and to try to apply our method to looking for dispersed repetitions in DNA sequences to see if it is efficient enough.

Acknowledgment. This research was supported by the National Natural Science Foundation of China (Grant No. 60273079 and 60573089).

References

1. David W. M. Bioinformatics Sequence and Genome Analysis [M], Cold Spring Harbor Laborary Press. 2001.
2. International Human Genome Sequencing Consortium. Initial sequencing and analysis of the human genome. Nature 409(15): 860-921, Feb, 2001.
3. IBeleza, S., Alves, C., Gonzalez-Neira, A., Lareu, M., Amorim, A., Carracedo, A., and Gusmao, L. Extending STR markers in Y chromosome haplotypes. Int.J.Legal Med. 117(1): 27-33, 2003.
4. Young, D. R., Tun, Z., Honda, K., and Matoba, R. Identifying sex chromosome abnormalities in forensic DNA testing using amelogenin and sex chromosome short tandem repeats. J.Forensic Sci. 46(2): 346-348, 2001.

5. Moore CJ, Daly EM, Tassone F and *et al.*The effect of pre-mutation of X chromosome CGG trinucleotide repeats on brain anatomy.Brain. Oct, 2004.
6. G. Benson. An algorithm for finding tandem repeats of unspecified pattern size. RECOMB98, pp. 20-29, ACM Press, 1998.
7. G. M. Landau and J. P. Schmidt. An algorithm for approximate tandem repeats. Proc. Of the 4th Annual Symposium on Combinatorial Pattern Matching. Vol. 684: 120-133, Italy, 1993.
8. S. Kurtz, J.V. Choudhuri, E. Ohlebusch, C. Schleiermacher, J, Stoye, R. Giegerich. REPuter: the manifold applications of repeat analysis on a genomic scale. Nucl. Acids Res. 29(22): 4633-4642. 2001.
9. G. Benson and M. Waterman. A method for fast database search for all k-nucleotide repeats. Nucl. Acids Res. 22:4828-4836, 1994.
10. G. Benson. Tandem repeats finder: a program t analyze dna. Nucl. Acids Res. 27(2):573-580, 1998.
11. Y. Wexler, Z. Yakhini, Y. Kashi and D. Geiger. Finding approximate tandem repeats in genomic sequences. RECOMB04, pp. 223-232, ACM Press, 2004.
12. D. Gusfield. Algorithms on string, trees and sequences: Computer science and computational biology. Cambridge University Press, 1997.
13. T. Kahveci and A. K. Singh. An efficient index strction of string databases. VLDB01, pp. 351-360, 2001.
14. D. Wang, G. Wang, Q. Wu and B. Chen. Finding LPRs in DNA sequence based on a new index SUA. BIBE05, pp. 281-284, IEEE Computer Science, 2005.
15. D. Wang, G. Wang, B. Chen, Q. Wu, B. Wang and D. Han. A new lightweight index SUA for biological sequence anlysis. J. Huazhong Univ. of Sci. & Tech. 33(12):207-210, 2005.
16. D. Wang, G. Wang. Q. Wu and B. Chen. Finding approximate repetitions in DNA sequence based on SUA. Technology Report. http://mitt.neu.edu.cn. 2005.

Dynamic Incremental Data Summarization for Hierarchical Clustering

Bing Liu, Yuliang Shi, Zhihui Wang, Wei Wang, and Baile Shi

Department of Computing and Information Technology,
Fudan University, Shanghai, China
{031021057, 031021056, 041021056, weiwang1, bshi}@fudan.edu.cn

Abstract. In many real world applications, with the databases frequent insertions and deletions, the ability of a data mining technique to detect and react quickly to dynamic changes in the data distribution and clustering over time is highly desired. Data summarizations (e.g., data bubbles) have been proposed to compress large databases into representative points suitable for subsequent hierarchical cluster analysis. In this paper, we thoroughly investigate the quality measure (data summarization index) of incremental data bubbles. When updating databases, we show which factors could affect the mean and standard deviation of data summarization index or not. Based on these statements, a fully dynamic scheme to maintain data bubbles incrementally is proposed. An extensive experimental evaluation confirms our statements and shows that the fully dynamic incremental data bubbles are effective in preserving the quality of the data summarization for hierarchical clustering.

1 Introduction

Knowledge discovery in databases (KDD) is the non-trivial process of identifying valid, novel, potentially useful, and understandable patterns. Detecting patterns effectively and efficiently is a challenging task since these patterns usually reside in large amounts of high dimensional and noisy data. As time goes by, the data distribution and the underlying clustering structure may change whereby previously uncovered patterns may become obsolete. The ability of a data mining technique to detect and react quickly to dynamic changes in the data patterns is highly desirable.

One of the primary data analysis tasks in KDD is cluster analysis. The main goal of a clustering algorithm is to partition a set of data points into groups such that similar points belong to the same group and dissimilar points belong to different groups. There are two main kinds of clustering algorithms: partitioning and hierarchical. Partitioning algorithms like *k*-means [1] create *k* partitions of the points. Hierarchical clustering algorithms like the OPTICS [2] or Single-Link method [3] compute a representation of the possible hierarchical clustering structure of the database in the form of a dendrogram or a reachability plot from which clusters at various resolutions can be extracted, as has been shown in [4].

In general, clustering algorithms do not scale well with the size of the data set. However, many real-world databases contain thousands or even millions of objects.

J.X. Yu, M. Kitsuregawa, and H.V. Leong (Eds.): WAIM 2006, LNCS 4016, pp. 410–421, 2006.
© Springer-Verlag Berlin Heidelberg 2006

To be able to perform a cluster analysis of such databases, a very fast method is required. Therefore, the development of scalable clustering algorithms has received a lot of attention in recent years. One approach for scaling up a clustering algorithm is to apply the clustering algorithm to only a summary of the database instead of the whole database. In data summarization methods such as Data Bubbles [5] and BIRCH [6], the database is partitioned into a small number of subsets, where each subset represents its elements by a number of sufficient statistics. A modified version of the preferred clustering algorithm can be applied to those data summarizations to detect the interesting patterns. For example, OPTICS [2] was shown to uncover the clustering structure effectively and very efficiently from data bubbles [5].

Various dynamic updates of deletions and insertions to very large databases add new challenges to the clustering task by possibly changing the underlying data distribution and the associated clustering structure over time. The naive approach is to reapply the data mining algorithms and extract the hidden patterns every time following a certain fraction of updates to the database. However, this approach is prohibitively slow for fast changing and large databases, especially if an up-to-date clustering structure is required frequently, e.g., in order to detect the changes in the data distribution after a small fraction of updates occur and important decisions are based on the current data distribution. Therefore in this paper we focus on achieving incremental summaries of dynamic databases.

There are two main strategies to address the problem of incremental clustering in a database environment. In the first strategy, a specialized incremental clustering algorithm is designed to directly handle dynamic changes in the database. In the second strategy, a data summarization technique is developed and used to compress the database incrementally, and then a slightly modified, standard clustering algorithm is subsequently applied to the generated data summarizations.

We first discuss some of the proposed algorithms for the first strategy. There are several incremental clustering algorithms that do not use the data summarization technique but attempt to directly restructure the clusters to reflect the dynamic changes of the dataset.

Chen et al. [7] propose the incremental hierarchical clustering algorithm GRIN for numerical datasets, which is based on gravity theory in physics. Ester et al. [8] present a new incremental clustering algorithm called Incremental DBSCAN suitable for mining in a data-warehousing environment. Incremental DBSCAN is based on the DBSCAN algorithm [9] which is a density based clustering algorithm. However, the proposed method does not address the problem of changing point densities over time, which would require adapting the input parameters for Incremental DBSCAN over time. Widyantoro et al. [10] present the agglomerative incremental hierarchical clustering (IHC) algorithm that utilizes a restructuring process while preserving homogeneity of the clusters and monotonicity of the cluster hierarchy. Charikar et al. [11] introduce new deterministic and randomized incremental clustering algorithms while trying to minimize the maximum diameters of the clusters.

Unlike the above algorithms that typically invent yet another "new" incremental algorithm for a particular application, the second strategy is more flexible and generic as it allows the application of a broad range of existing standard clustering algorithms (hierarchical and partitioning) to the data summaries. The adaptation of a standard clustering algorithm to data summarization typically requires only minor modifications, as has been shown in [5]. It also has the advantage that the data summaries can be used for other data mining tasks such as computing approximate statistics of data sets or quickly approximating the number of objects in a database within certain attribute ranges of interest.

Samer et al. [12] use the second approach and propose a scheme to incrementally maintain data summaries of a dynamic database, i.e., they enhance data summarizations to become incremental and capable to adapt to insertions and deletions into a database. Furthermore, by using a measure of the compression quality called data summarization index (the fraction of points in the database compressed by the data bubble), they can identify the data bubbles that still compress their points well following the insertions and the deletions.

For the scheme proposed by Samer et al. [12], there are some remaining works needed to solve. First, they use data summarization index as the measure of the compression quality and Chebyshev's Inequality to judge the quality of data bubbles. Using Chebyshev's Inequality needs to know the mean and standard deviation of the data summarization index. But they do not give an analysis about how to get the mean and standard deviation, and do not illustrate which factors will affect them. Second, they can not deal with the situations where the number of data points or data bubbles is changed. And they only consider where there is an equal number of insertions and deletions for each update and the number of data bubbles are unchanged. This is because they can not judge which data bubbles are not good if the number of points or data bubbles is changed. In this paper, we will give a thorough analysis about the incremental update of data bubbles.

The rest of the paper is organized as follows. In section 2, we first present the background related to the problems of incremental data summarization. Then we show how to get the theoretic mean and give some statements about the standard deviation of the data summarization index. Also we propose an algorithm about fully dynamical incremental data bubble maintenance. In section 3, we perform an extensive experimental evaluation to our methods, confirming the statements presented in section 2, and showing that incremental data bubbles can preserve the quality of the data summarization for hierarchical clustering. The conclusions and some future directions are presented in section 4.

2 Dynamic Incremental Data Summarization

In this section, we present a detail discussion about the data summarization index. Previously it has been shown that for hierarchical clustering algorithms, the data bubbles [5] are much more effective than basic clustering features $CF=(n, LS, SS)$, where LS is the linear sum of the points and SS is their square sum, as proposed, e.g., for BIRCH. Data bubbles summarize a set of n points by "compressing" the points into special sufficient statistics that are required for effective hierarchical clustering based on data summarizations. Data bubbles have been evaluated in [5], using OPTICS [2], and were shown to reduce the runtime of OPTICS dramatically while still producing high-quality hierarchical clustering structures.

A data bubble has been defined as follows:

Definition 1. A data bubble B for a set of points $X = \{X_i\}$, $1 \leq i \leq n$ is a tuple $B = (rep, n, extent, nnDist)$ where

- *rep* is a representative, defined as the mean of the points in X
- n is the number of points in X
- *extent* is the radius of B around *rep* that encloses the majority of the points in X
- $nnDist(k,B)$ is a function that estimates the average k nearest neighbor distances in B.

Although the information in a data bubble is more specialized than the basic sufficient statistics (n, LS, SS), it has been shown in [5] that the representative *rep*, the *extent*, and assuming a uniform distribution of points within a data bubble, the average nearest neighbor distances $nnDist(k,B)$ can be easily derived from n, LS, SS.

The method that has been proposed to construct data bubbles consists of the following two steps:

1. Retrieve randomly s points from the database as "seeds".
2. Scan the database, and assign each point in the database to the closest seed in the set obtained in step 1.

We assume that we have initially constructed a set of data bubbles that summarize a large database of d-dimensional points following the above description. If the database is dynamic, new points are inserted and old points are deleted over time, possibly changing the underlying data distribution. We are interested in the updated clustering structure and hence the underlying data summarization after a set of updates.

For incrementally updating a set of data bubbles following a batch of updates to the underlying database, the sufficient statistics of affected data bubbles are decremented when deleting the old points and incremented when inserting the new points. When deleting a point p, the sufficient statistic (n, LS, SS) of the data bubble B where p was previously assigned are updated to (n-1, LS-p, SS-p^2), whereas when inserting a point p, the sufficient statistics (n, LS, SS) of the data bubble B that is closest to p are updated to (n+1, LS+p, SS+p^2).

After these updates, it is possible that some data bubbles do not represent their points well or lost all of their points such that the overall compression quality is poor, possibly resulting in a distorted clustering structure based on these data bubbles. In order to recover from structural distortions due to changes in the data distribution, we have to identify those data bubbles that significantly degrade the quality of the data summarization and re-build them quickly, while at the same time maintaining a given compression rate.

The measure for determining the quality of a data bubble is the number of points it summarizes relative to the total database size. Roughly speaking, "good" data bubbles summarize not too many and not too few points. Samer et al. [12] introduce the data summarization index β to capture the quality of a data bubble.

Definition 2. Given a database D *of* N points and a set Ω of data bubbles that compress the points in D, the data summarization index β_i of a data bubble i that compresses n points is defined as $\beta_i = n/N$.

Based on Chebyshev's Inequality theorem: $P(|X-\mu_X|<k\sigma_X)\geq 1-1/k^2$, paper [12] distinguishes three classes of data bubbles according to their compression quality.

Definition 3. Given a database D of N points and a set Ω of data bubbles that compress the points in D, let μ_β and σ_β be the mean and standard deviation of the distribution of the β values for all data bubbles in Ω. Given a probability p (where the corresponding k value is computed according to Chebyshev's Inequality), a data bubble B with the data summarization index β is called:

1. "good" iff $\beta \in [\mu_\beta - k\sigma_\beta, \mu_\beta + k\sigma_\beta]$
2. "under-filled" iff $\beta < \mu_\beta - k\sigma_\beta$
3. "over-filled" iff $\beta > \mu_\beta + k\sigma_\beta$

Figure 1 shows the pseudo code for improving the quality of an over-filled data bubble [12] while keeping the number of data bubbles unchanged. The quality of $B_{over\text{-}filled}$ is improved by first merging $B_{under\text{-}filled}$ and then splitting $B_{over\text{-}filled}$.

```
DevideOverFilledBubble()
{
  Select a random under-filled data bubble Bunder-filled (if
none exists, select the "good" data bubble with lowest
quality in the "good" data bubbles set);
  Free Bunder-filled by assigning its points to their next
closest data bubble(s);
  Migrate Bunder-filled to the region compressed by Bover-filled
by selecting a new seed s1 for it from the points of Bover-
filled;
  Select a new seed s2 for Bover-filled from the points of
Bover-filled ;
  Split Bover-filled by reassigning its points between s1
and s2;
}
```

Fig. 1. Improving the quality of an over-filled data bubble

Although Samer et al. [12] use the data summarization index to judge the quality of data bubbles, they do not give a further analysis about how to get the mean and standard deviation of it when the number of points or data bubbles are changed. In their paper's last conclusion, they also indicate that the problem of how to dynamically increase or decrease the number of data bubbles is needed to solve to further improve the compression of a database. They assume that when building data bubbles from scratch, the majority of the data bubbles have good compression. So they use the initial data bubble distribution to compute the mean and standard deviation of the data summarization index. In their experiments, in order to use these two estimation values, they keep the number of points and the number of data bubbles unchanged, i.e.

they delete and insert the same number of points for each update. But in real world applications, with the dynamic update of deletions and insertions to database, the total number of points may change dramatically. And sometimes, in order to adapt to the change of database, we also need to change the number of data bubbles. At this time, the mean and standard deviation estimated from initial data bubble distribution are useless. So we will give further explore about the mean and standard deviations of the data summarization index. We will show which factors can affect the mean and standard deviation and which can not.

We illustrate how to compute the mean of data summarization index in theory, and also give some statements about the relationships between standard deviation and some database factors. In the next section, we present the detail experiments supporting for these statements. Also, based on these observations, we propose a fully dynamic incremental data summarization maintenance algorithm in this section.

Samer et al. [12] use experiment to evaluate the mean of data summarization index. In this paper, we give a theorem to show how to compute the mean of data summarization index in theory.

Theorem 1. Given a database D of N points and a set Ω of s data bubbles that compress the points in D, μ_β is the mean of the data summarization index β for all data bubbles in Ω.. There is $\mu_\beta=1/s$.

Proof: Assume β_i is the ith data bubble that compresses n_i points. According to the definition of mean, there is $\mu_\beta = \frac{1}{s}\sum_{i=1}^{s}\beta_i = \frac{1}{s}\sum_{i=1}^{s}\frac{n_i}{N} = \frac{1}{sN}\sum_{i=1}^{s}n_i = \frac{1}{sN}\times N = \frac{1}{s}$. Thus $\mu_\beta=1/s$. □

Theorem 1 shows that μ_β is only decided by the number of data bubbles and inverse proportional to it. If we know the number of data bubbles in advance, we can compute the mean of the data summarization index even in the situations where the database dramatically changes.

Next we give analysis and statements about the standard deviation of data summarization index (σ_β). According to the definition of standard deviation, there is: $\sigma_\beta^2 = \frac{1}{s}\sum_{i=1}^{s}(\beta_i-\mu_\beta)^2 = \frac{1}{s}\sum_{i=1}^{s}(\frac{n_i}{N}-\frac{1}{s})^2 = \frac{1}{s}(\sum_{i=1}^{s}\frac{n_i^2}{N^2}+\sum_{i=1}^{s}\frac{1}{s^2}-\sum_{i=1}^{s}\frac{2n_i}{Ns}) = \frac{1}{s}(\frac{1}{N^2}\sum_{i=1}^{s}n_i^2-\frac{1}{s})$ where $1\le n_i\le N\text{-}s+1$ and $n_1+n_2+\ldots+n_s=N$. This formula shows that σ_β is related to the actual number of points in each data bubble, so it is difficult to give a theoretical value independent to each sampling process. But we can give some statements about which factors will affect σ_β or not. Also we give the intuitional explanations about these statements. In the next section, we will use experiments to confirm our statements.

First, we show the relationships between σ_β and the number of points, the distribution of points, and the dimensions of points.

Statement 1: Given a database D, σ_β is the standard deviation of the data summarization index β for all data bubbles in Ω. σ_β is independent to the number of points, the distribution of points, and the dimensions of points in the database.

We give some explanations about statement 1. In statement 1, we argue that σ_β is not related to the number of points in database. We know that β represents the fraction of points in the database compressed by the data bubble, and the mean of it is independent to the number of points proven by theorem 1. So we speculate that the standard deviation of β is also not affected by the number of points in database. Statement 1 also says that σ_β is independent to the distribution of points, which means that the clustering structure can not affect σ_β. In paper [12], although they do not say explicitly, they just use this fact. In their experiments, they do not change the number of points in database, but they change the underlying data distribution and the associated clustering structure when updating database. We can think that where data distributions are dense, the sample points are also dense, so it is possible that σ_β is not related to the data distribution. In statement 1, we also argue that σ_β is independent to

```
IncrementalDataBubble ( )
Input: A batch of data update, original data bubble number m, new data bubble number n
{
  Delete old points and decrease the sufficient statistics of the corresponding data bubbles;
  Insert new points and assign them to their closest data bubbles;
  k=|n-m|;
  if (n>m)    //increase the number of data bubbles
  {
     for (i=0;i<k;i++)
     {
        Find the data bubble B that has the maximum number of points;
        Random select two new seed s1 and s2 from B;
        Split B by reassigning its points to s1 and s2;
     }
  }
  if (n<m)    //decrease the number of data bubbles
  {
     For (i=0;i<k;i++)
     {
        Find the data bubble B that have the minimum number of points;
        Free B by assigning its points to their next closest data bubble(s);
     }
  }
  Use n to compute the new μβ and σβ;
  Use the new μβ and σβ to determine the upper and lower boundary for the data bubble quality;
  while (exist data bubble B over-filled)
     Invoke the DevideOverFilledBubble() for B in figure 1;
}
```

Fig. 2. Incremental data bubble maintenance

the data dimensions. This statement is easy to understand. Because we use distance between points to build data bubbles, the dimensions are not related to σ_β. In real world applications, it is common to change the number of data points and data distribution. But it is rare that the data structure (dimensions) will change, so dimensions do not have too much effect to σ_β. In the next section, we will use experiments to confirm the arguments in statement 1.

Although it is hard to give a precise value about σ_β, we can use experiments to estimate it. In this section, we first give the statement about how to compute σ_β, and in the next section, we use experiments to confirm this statement.

Statement 2: Given a database *D*, there are *s* data bubbles, and σ_β is the standard deviation of the data summarization index β for all data bubbles in Ω. There is $\sigma_\beta = 0.546/s$.

Statement 2 claims that σ_β is also only decided by the number of data bubbles and it is inverse proportional to *s*. And the correlation coefficient is 0.546. Using theorem 1, the above formula in statement 2 can also be written as $\sigma_\beta = 0.546\mu_\beta$.

Using these statements and theorem, we can give a fully dynamic incremental data bubble maintenance algorithm. This algorithm can deal with the change to the number of points or data bubbles, which can not be dealt with in paper [12]. We can dynamically increase or decrease the number of data bubbles or keep it unchanged when the original database is updated.

Figure 2 shows the pseudo code for this algorithm. We first update the existing data bubbles according to data deleting and inserting. If need to change the number of data bubbles, we increase or decrease the number of data bubbles to meet the condition of new data bubble number. Next, according to the new data bubble number we compute the new μ_β and σ_β based on theorem 1 and statement 2. And we use the new μ_β and σ_β to decide which data bubbles are good or over-filled. The sequence of synchronized merging and splitting of data bubbles is repeated after updating the database with each batch of insertions and deletions.

3 Experiments

In this section, we perform an extensive evaluation to confirm our statements presented in section 2, and show the efficiency of our new method for incremental data bubble maintenance in hierarchical clustering. All results in this section are average values of 10 repetition tests.

First we give an experiment to illustrate that the standard deviation of data summarization index is independent to the number of points. Figure 3 shows the relationship between the number of points and standard deviation. We use a 2-dimensional database, and choose 100 data bubbles, the points are randomly generated. According to theorem 1, the mean of data summarization index is 0.01. In figure 3, the trend of the standard deviation with the increase of the number of points is nearly a straight line.

Furthermore, we use the following formula to define the difference between the maximum and minimum standard deviation. And the difference can also give us some indication about the relationship between standard deviation and other factors. The difference in figure 3 is about 4.6%. Thus, we can say that the standard deviation of data summarization index is independent to the number of points, which confirms our statement 1.

$$\text{difference} = \frac{(\text{maximum} - \text{minimum}) * 2}{(\text{maximum} + \text{minimum})}$$

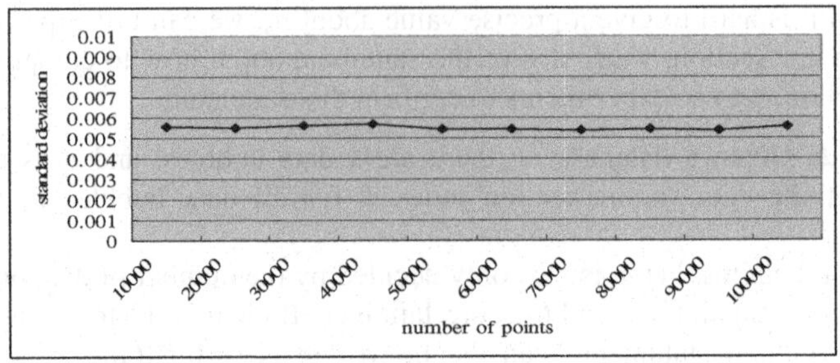

Fig. 3. The standard deviation for different number of points in database

Figure 4 gives the relationship between the dimensions of points and standard deviation of data summarization index. We use 10000 points and 100 data bubbles for different dimensions, and the points are randomly generated. The mean of the data summarization index is 0.01. In figure 4, the trend of the standard deviation with the increase of the dimensions is also nearly a straight line. The maximum and minimum standard deviation's difference is about 7.1%. Thus, we can say that the standard deviation of data summarization index is independent to the dimensions of points, which confirms our statement 1. Because for most real world applications, the dimensions of point rarely change, so we can ignore the effect of this factor when incrementally building data bubbles.

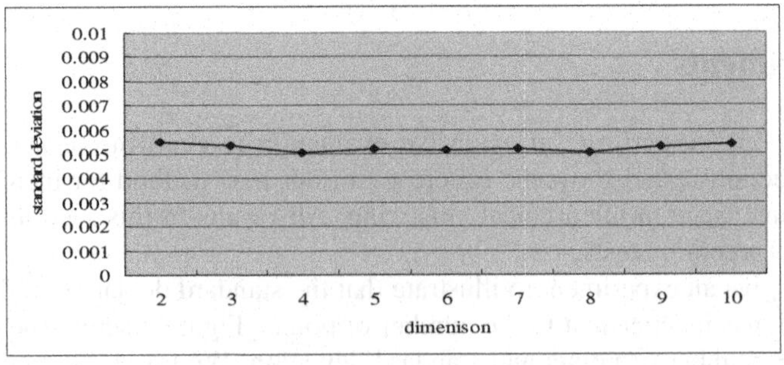

Fig. 4. The standard deviation for different dimensions of points

Figure 5 gives the relationship between the distribution of points and standard deviation of data summarization index. We use 10000 points and 100 data bubbles for 2-dimensional database. In this experiment, we generate seven types of data distribution: Random, two clusters (2clus), four clusters (4clus), two clusters where each cluster contains two sub clusters (2clus2sub), four clusters where each cluster contains two sub clusters (4clus2sub), two clusters where each cluster contains four sub clusters (2clus4sub), and four clusters where each cluster contains four sub clusters (4clus4sub). In figure 5, the standard deviation is also nearly a straight line. The maximum and minimum standard deviation's difference is about 1.7%. Thus, we can say that the standard deviation of data summarization index is independent to the distribution of points, which confirms our statement 1. Also, we confirm paper [12]'s assumption, where they use this conclusion but not state explicitly.

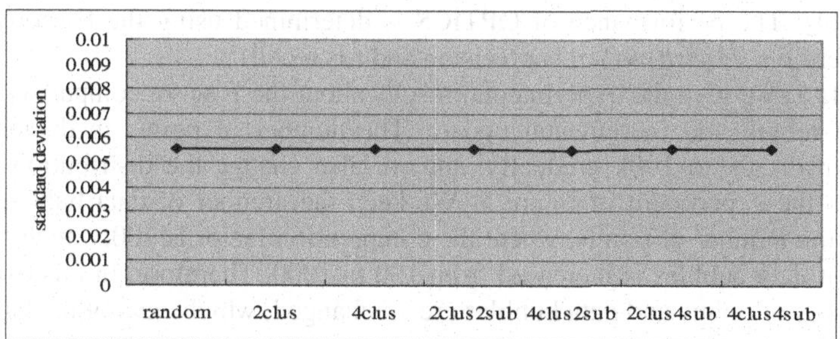

Fig. 5. The standard deviation for different distribution of database

Now we discuss the relationship between the number of data bubbles and standard deviation. Figure 6 gives the line representing the multiplication of standard deviation (σ_β) and the number of data bubbles (s). In this experiment, we use 50000 2-dimensioal points which are randomly generated. Figure 6 shows that (bubble num)*(standard deviation) is nearly a straight line. Then we can speculate that the standard deviation is inverse proportional to the number of data bubbles. So there is $\sigma_\beta=k/s$. Using linear regression analysis, we can give an estimation that k=0.546. Therefore the statement 2 in section 2 is acquired.

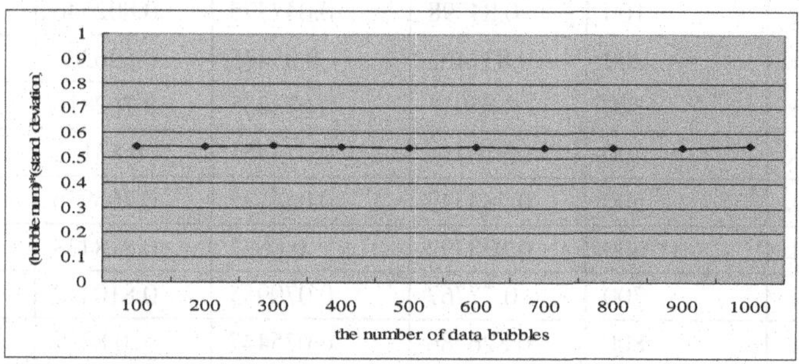

Fig. 6. The relationship between the standard deviation and the number of data bubbles

Above experiments confirm the statement 1 and 2 in section 2. Thus, when we maintain data bubbles incrementally, we know which factors will affect the quality of data bubbles. And using these conclusions we can dynamically build data bubbles.

To further analyze how our scheme of incremental data bubbles given in figure 2 affects the quality of the data summarization technique, we measure the quality and effectiveness of the incremental data bubbles by studying their effect on the performance of a clustering algorithm relative to its performance when using completely rebuilt data bubbles. After each batch of update, we summarize each database of the current points by building separate incremental and completely rebuilt data bubbles. Next OPTICS is applied to these data bubbles separately to generate the reachability plots of the completely rebuilt and incremental clustering structures. The clusters are extracted from these plots using a modified version of an automatic method developed in [4]. The performance of OPTICS is determined using the F score measure [13] (where F = 2*p*r/(p+r), p is precision and r is recall).

In table 1, we give the experimental results about the F score comparison between complete rebuilt and incremental update. The number of points in database is increased from 10k to 100k gradually, and we also change the distribution of points similar to the experiment of figure 5. We keep the number of data bubbles proportional to the number of points, where the compression factor is 100, which means the number of data bubbles is increased from 100 to 1000. Therefore, in this experiment, the numbers of points and data bubbles are all changed, which can not be dealt with in paper [12].

We notice from Table 1 that the F score of the clustering algorithm (OPTICS) using our dynamic incremental scheme is always very similar to (and sometimes higher than) the F score when using completely rebuilt data bubbles. Thus, our scheme for dynamically maintaining the incremental data bubbles is effective in preserving the quality of the clustering algorithm as measured by the F score.

Table 1. Comparison of performance using complete and incremental construction

		complete		incremental	
Number of points	number of data bubbles	mean	standard deviation	mean	standard deviation
10k	100	0.84798	0.047775	0.802546	0.066559
20k	200	0.831402	0.05445	0.826384	0.068536
30k	300	0.85953	0.078435	0.762816	0.063264
40k	400	0.810414	0.073953	0.83152	0.068132
50k	500	0.783372	0.044135	0.766926	0.04517
60k	600	0.873392	0.0572	0.818438	0.067877
70k	700	0.77767	0.070965	0.810492	0.067218
80k	800	0.826786	0.075447	0.8377	0.0582
90k	900	0.839904	0.04732	0.875772	0.067626
100k	1000	0.831828	0.046865	0.795815	0.05529

4 Conclusions

In this paper, we have discussed the data summarization index and presented a fully dynamic scheme for incrementally maintaining data summarization. We show that the data summarization index is independent to the number of points, the distribution of points, and the dimensions of points in the database. It is only related to the number of data bubbles and inverse proportional to it. An extensive experimental evaluation for various cases confirm our statements, and show that the incremental data bubbles provide an efficient data summarization technique for dynamically changing large databases, and is effective in preserving the quality of the clustering algorithm.

References

[1] MacQueen, J. Some Methods for Classification and Analysis of Multivariate Observations. In 5th Berkeley Symp. Math. Statist. Prob., 281-297, 1967.
[2] Ankerst, M., Breuing, M., Kriegel, H-P., Sander, J. OPTICS: Ordering Points to Identify the Clustering Structure. In SIGMOD'99, 49-60, 1999
[3] Sibson, R. SLINK: An Optimally Efficient Algorithm for the Single-link Cluster Method. The Computer Journal, 16(1): 30-34, 1973.
[4] Sander, J., Qin, X., Lu, Z., Niu, N, Kovarsky, A. Automated Extraction of Clusters from Hierarchical Clustering Representations. PAKDD'03.
[5] Breuing, M., Kriegel, H-P, Kroger, P., Sander, J. Data Bubbles: Quality Preserving Performance Boosting for Hierarchical Clustering. In SIGMOD'01, 79-90, 2001.
[6] Zhang, T., Ramakrishnan, R., Linvy, M. BIRCH: An Efficient Data Clustering Method for Very Large Databases. SIGMOD'96, 103-114, 1996
[7] Chen, C., Hwang, S., Oyang, Y. An Incremental Hierarchical Data Clustering Algorithm Based on Gravity Theory. In 6th Pacific Asia Conference on Knowledge Discovery and Data Mining, 2002.
[8] Ester, M., Kriegel, H-P., Sander, J. Wimmer, M., Xu, X. Incremental Clustering for Mining in a Data Warehousing Enviornment. VLDB'98, 323-333, 1998.
[9] Ester, M., Kriegel, H-P., Sander, J., Xu, X. A Density Based Algorithm for Discovering Clusters in Large Spatial Databases with Noise. KDD'96, 226-231, 1996.
[10] Widyantoro, D. H., Ioerger, T. R., Yen, J. An Incremental Approach to Building a Cluster Hierarchy. ICDM'02, 705-708, 2002.
[11] Charikar, M., Chekuri, C., Feder, T., Motwani, R. Incremental Clustering and Dynamic Information Retrieval. In 29th Symposium on Theory of Computing, 626-635, 1997.
[12] Samer Nassar, Jorg Sander, Corrine Cheng. Incremental and Effective Data Summarization for Dynamic Hierarchical Clustering. SIGMOD'04, 467-478, 2004
[13] Larsen, B., Aone, C. Fast and Effective Text Mining Using Linear-time Document Clustering. In KDD'99, 16-22, 1999.

Classifying E-Mails Via Support Vector Machine

Lidan Shou[1], Bin Cui[2], Gang Chen[1], and Jinxiang Dong[1]

[1] College of Computer Science, Zhejiang University, Hangzhou, 310027, P.R. China
{should, cg, djx}@cs.zju.edu.cn

[2] School of Computing, National University of Singapore, Singapore 117543
cuibin@comp.nus.edu.sg

Abstract. For addressing the growing problem of junk E-mail on the Internet, this paper proposes an effective E-mail classifying technique. Our work handles E-mail messages as semi-structured documents consisting of a set of fields with predefined semantics and a number of variable length free-text contents. The main contributions of this paper include the following: First, we present a Support Vector Machine (SVM) based model that incorporates the Principal Component Analysis (PCA) technique to reduce the data in terms of size and dimensionality of the input feature space. As a result, the input data become classifiable with fewer features, and the training process has faster convergence speed. Second, we build the classification model using both the $\mathcal{C}$-support vector machine and υ-support vector machine algorithms. Various control parameters for performance tuning are studied in an extensive set of experiments. The results of our performance evaluation indicate that the proposed technique is effective in E-mail classification.

1 Introduction

As the Internet grows at a tremendous speed, E-mail has become a widely used form of communication. E-mail has gained enormous popularity not only as a means for letting friends and colleagues exchange messages, but also as a medium for conducting electronic commerce. Unfortunately, the convenience and inexpensiveness of E-mail also make it overused by companies, organizations or people to promote products and spread information, which serves their own purposes. The unsuspecting mailboxes of users may often be crammed with E-mail messages a large portion of which are not of interest to them. Searching for interesting messages out of a thousand unread ones is tedious and annoying. As a consequence, the need for a personal E-mail filter is pressing.

For the problem of classifying E-mail documents, the objects to be classified are semi-structured textual documents consisting of two portions. One portion is a set of structured fields with well-defined semantics and the other portion is a number of variable length sections of free text. We would like to emphasize this feature in our study because information from both portions is important. In the case of E-mail messages, the fields in the mail header such as the sender and the recipient are very informative when we determine how interesting the

J.X. Yu, M. Kitsuregawa, and H.V. Leong (Eds.): WAIM 2006, LNCS 4016, pp. 422–434, 2006.
© Springer-Verlag Berlin Heidelberg 2006

message part is. On the other hand, the interestingness of an E-mail message from the same sender also depends on the content of the body message.

There have been a number of approaches developed for E-mail classification [8, 4, 10, 2]. In this paper, we propose a novel approach to classifying E-mails using the Support Vector Machine (SVM). In particular, we treat E-mail messages as a specific kind of plain text files with structured features, the implication being that our feature set is relatively large (since there are thousands of different terms in different E-mail files). To speed up the process and reduce the space/computational cost, we enhance SVM with Principal Component Analysis (PCA) [7] which is used as a preprocessor to reduce the data in terms of dimensionality so that the input data becomes more classifiable. Note that, PCA only pre-processes the input features to SVM classification model. We also evaluate the performance of E-mail classification with two SVM mechanisms, i.e. $\mathcal{C}$-support vector machine and v-support vector machine algorithms. We conduct a series of experiments on a relatively large dataset composed of real personal E-mails, and discuss the behaviors of the classification approach in detail. The experimental results show that this approach provides superior performance in terms of recall and precision.

The rest of this paper is organized as following: The next section introduces some related work. In section 3, we present our method for E-mail classification. In sections 4, we present the experimental results and the analysis. Finally, we give the conclusions in section 5.

2 Related Work

This section reviews related work in the area of junk E-mail filtering and Principal Component Analysis. There are a lot of research works on junk E-mail filtering in the literature [2, 10, 4, 3]. Sahami et al. proposed a Bayesian approach to filtering junk E-mail in [10]. The proposal considers domain specific features in addition to raw text of E-mail messages. It enhances the performance of a Bayesian classifier by handcrafting and incorporating many features indicative of junk E-mail. The authors proposed two classifications as the Probabilistic Classification and the Domain Specific Properties. Representing each individual message as a binary vector, the proposed method detects junk mail in a straightforward manner using a given pre-classified set of training messages. In [2], the authors compared methods for learning text classifiers focusing on the kinds of classification problems that might arise in filtering personal E-mail messages. In [4], the E-mail documents to be classified are regarded as semi-structured textual documents comprising two parts. One part is a set of structured fields with well-defined semantics, while the other is a number of variable-length sections of free text. However, not many text classifiers take both portions into consideration. Moreover, conventional classification techniques may not be effective when handling variable-length free text. In [3], a model based on the Neural Network was proposed, which handles fields which having pre-defined semantics as well as the variable length free-text fields for obtaining higher accuracy. In [5], the authors propose an E-mail classifying system using Support Vector Machine. The results outperform other three conventional methods in that it provides acceptable test performance in terms of accuracy and speed, without compromising with long training time.

In this paper, we propose a new model based on a hybrid technique to improve the efficiency of the system, which integrates Support Vector Machine and Principal Component Analysis together. PCA [7] is a widely used method for applications in signal/image filtering and pattern classification. It can transform data in the original space into another feature space, reduce the dimensionality of the input data, while keeping the most significant information. It examines the variance structure in the dataset and determines the directions along which the data exhibits high variance. The first principal component accounts for as much of the variability in the data as possible, and each succeeding component accounts for as much of the remaining variability as possible. Working as a preprocessor of SVM E-mail classifier, it can make the input data more classifiable and reduce the dimensionality of the training and validation dataset by using only the first several features, thereby speeding up the convergence of the training process, e.g. 10% number of features after PCA transformation can capture more than 95% information of the data.

3 The E-Mail Classification Technique

In this section, we discuss the main phases of proposed method for E-mail classification in detail. We first introduce the background information for our technique. Second, a model for E-mail classification based on SVM is presented. Third, we describe how to integrate the PCA technique in the SVM-based model.

3.1 Support Vector Machine

The Support Vector Machine (SVM) [1] can be simply regarded as a task that is to find an optimal hyperplane which linearly separates the sample set in their feature space. More precisely, suppose we have a sample set, say $\mathbf{X}_i$, (i = 1, 2, , N), where $\mathbf{X}_i$ is a k-dimensional vector which means that $\mathbf{X}$ can be expressed as a vector of k features. Then, we can map the sample space into their k-dimension feature space. For each sample $\mathbf{X}_i$, we assign a target value or class label d_i with value -1 or 1. After that, we try to find a hyperplane which linearly separates the samples according to their target values. There might be many hyperplanes satisfying the requirement if there exists one such hyperplane. For these hyperplanes, we define the *margin of separation*, denoted as R, as the separation between the hyperplane and the closest data points. The goal of SVM is to find the optimal hyperplane with the maximum margin of separation.

Here, we give some more details of SVM-based classification algorithms. SVM is a relatively new learning approach to solve two class pattern recognition problems based on structural risk minimization principles. Figure 1 shows a very simple example of SVM classifier. Each circle in the figure represents a document in the feature space.

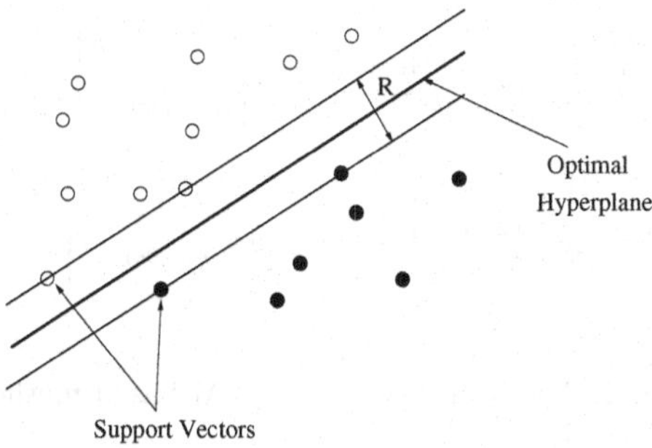

Fig. 1. Example of SVM classifier

The algorithms to obtain the optimal hyperplane have been well studied, such as using quadratic programming technique, e.g. method of Lagrangian multipliers. We show one method as follows:

Given: training sample (d_i, y_i) i = 1 ... N, where d_i, is a training document and y_i is the desired output, either 1 or -1.

- The problem is to solve for w and b:
  $w^T.d_i + b \geq 0, \text{for } y_i = 1$
  $w^T.d_i + b < 0, \text{for } y_i = -1$
  where w is the weight vector and b is the bias.
- The decision formula is $g(d) = w^T.d + b$ and the hyperplane for decision is described by equation $g(d) = w^T.d + b = 0$

3.2 Model of SVM for E-Mail Classification

The work on E-mail filtering can be mapped onto the framework of text classification. An E-mail message is regarded as a document. A judgment of whether it is *interesting* or not is viewed as a class label given to the E-mail document. The processing via the SVM involves three steps, namely *pre-processing*, *training* and *testing*, as shown in figure 2. The *Feature Extraction* box refers to pre-processing, which we will discuss shortly. For the training data, once we obtain the selected features, we feed them into the SVM and generate a classifier. The testing data are used to validate the efficiency of the SVM model. We adopt two classes of SVM algorithms, namely the $\mathcal{C}$-support vector machine algorithm and the v-support vector machine algorithm, to handle the training problem. Details about these algorithms would be discussed shortly.

The reasons that we use SVM are described as following: (1) Firstly, when training E-mail classifiers, one has to deal with very many features. As SVM uses over-fitting protection, which does not necessarily depend on the number of features. It has the potential of handling these large features. (2) Secondly, there are few irrelevant features in E-mail classification. One way to avoid these high dimensional input spaces is to assume that most of the features are irrelevant. The feature selection process tries to determine these irrelevant features.

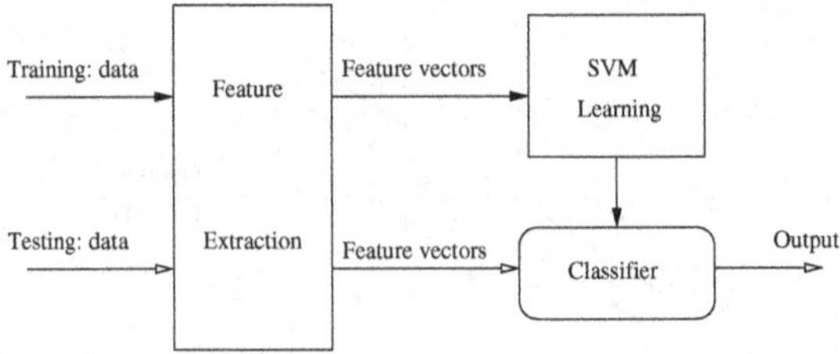

Fig. 2. The overview of the SVM based method

Unfortunately, in E-mail categorization, there are only very few irrelevant features. A good classifier should combine many features (learn a "dense" concept), while that an aggressive feature selection process may cause loss of information. (3) Thirdly, document vectors are usually sparse. For each E-mail document, the corresponding document vector contains only few entries that are non-zero. SVM is well suited for problems with dense concepts and sparse instances. (4) Finally, most text categorization problems are linearly separable, and the motivation of SVM is to find the optimal linear separators.

The dataset is divided into the following disjoint sets:

1. Training set: This dataset is used to train the SVM. In the pre-processing stage, we employ cross-validation and early stopping before presenting the data to the SVM for training or testing.
2. Validation set: The error of the SVM output averaged over this dataset is used to decide when the training algorithm has found the optimal approximation to the data.
3. Testing set: After the validation process, the SVM classifier is applied to the testing set, and the performance over the testing set is collected.

Pre-processing of the Dataset. E-mail messages are semi-structured documents that possess a set of structured fields with predefined semantics as well as a number of variable-length free text fields. The headers of a message are structured fields and usually contain information pertaining to the document, such as the sender, the date, the domain etc. The main contents of the message are variable length free text fields, such as the subject and the body. Both the structured fields and the free-text portion may contain important information for determining the class which a message belongs to. Therefore, an effective E-mail classifier should be able to collect features from both the structured fields and the free text. In our work, we generate two kinds of input features for each E-mail in the dataset. The features are as follows:

1. *Structured features* are features represented by structured fields in the header part of an E-mail message. These include:
   - Attachment: If the attachment occurs in the E-mail, *true*; else, *false*.
   - Content Type: If the content type of E-mail is "plain text", *true*; else *false*.

- Sender Domain: The sender domain from E-mail header, if it contains "edu", *1*; contains "com", *2*; else *3*.
- FW: "Subject" of E-mail header starts with word "FW", *true*, else *false*.
- Re: "Subject" of E-mail header starts with word "Re", *true*, else *false*.
- To group: The E-mail is sent to a group, *true*; else, to a single person, *false*.
- CC: The content of "CC" in the header of E-mails is not empty, *true*; else, *false*.

2. *Textual features.* We use general text processing method to handle the textual features. The terms occur in the body of E-mails and the "Subject" of E-mail are extracted and preprocessed. These data are regarded as the features of the body of E-mails. We use *Document Frequency Threshold* to remove some features that have little influence on classification work. In this work, we extract 2160 text features most frequently used. We represent the feature values of the term in two methods: (1) the simple *TF-IDF* (Term Frequency-Inverse Document Frequency) method; and (2) the *binary* method, where a value +1 or -1 indicates if the word occurs in the document or not.

Training of SVM. With the results of pre-processing, we perform the training of SVM and generate a classifier for E-mail filtering. A two-dimensional array of feature vector is obtained for *interesting* and *uninteresting* E-mail messages. The vector contains features extracted from both the message header and the body. In this work, we use the $\mathcal{C}$-support vector machine and the v-support vector machine algorithms to learn the SVMs. These two methods are briefly described in the following.

There are two class labels $\{-1, 1\}$ as the result space for the classification. Given L training vectors $\mathbf{x}_i \in R^n$, where n is the dimensionality of the vector, $i = 1, \ldots, L$, there are L labeled training examples: $(\mathbf{x}_1, y_1), \ldots, (\mathbf{x}_L, y_L)$, where $y_i \in \{-1, 1\}$. The primal problem of $\mathcal{C}$-support vector algorithm is defined as:

$$min(\frac{1}{2}W^T W + \mathcal{C}\sum_{i=1}^{L} \xi_i)$$

subject to following constraints:

$$y_i(W^T \Phi(\mathbf{x}_i) + b) \geq 1 - \xi_i \ , \quad where \quad \xi_i \geq 0, (i = 1, \ldots, L)$$

Parameter $\mathcal{C}$ is used to penalize variable ξ_i. However, it is often hard to select an appropriate $\mathcal{C}$ value. Schölkopf et al. proposed the v-support vector classification in [11]. They introduce a new parameter v which allows one to control the number of support vectors and errors. The primal problem of v-SVM is defined as:

$$min(\frac{1}{2}W^T W - v\rho + \frac{1}{L}\sum_{i=1}^{L} \xi_i)$$

subject to following constraints:

$$y_i(W^T \Phi(\mathbf{x}_i) + b) \geq \rho - \xi_i \ , \quad where \quad \rho \geq 0 \ \text{ and } \ \xi_i \geq 0, (i = 1, \ldots, L)$$

More specifically, it has been proved that parameter v is an upper bound of the fraction of the margin errors and a lower bound of the fraction of support vectors.

Testing of SVM. In the testing stage, we will test the efficiency of the classifier.

1. Like the process in the training part, we generate a feature vector from the header and the body of the message being tested.
2. We apply the classifier, which has been trained in the training stage, to the feature vector for each E-mail to compute the output class label.

3.3 Principal Component Analysis of Datasets

We use the PCA method to accelerate the training process of the SVM. The purpose of using PCA is to reduce the dimensionality of the feature space while retaining the most feature information. Finding the principal components is basically a mathematical problem of finding the principal singular vectors of the input dataset using the singular value decomposition method.

In our approach, we use the PCA method as following: Firstly, in the training phase, we apply the principal component analysis on the training and validation dataset. We transform the training and validation dataset into the singular vector space and calculate the eigenvectors and eigenvalues for the covariance matrix of the dataset. The dataset for the new data space can then be produced by multiplying the eigenvector matrix with the original data. In the experiments, we select a number of the most principal components in the new data space as the dataset with reduced dimensionality. Secondly, in the testing phase, we transform the testing dataset into the same space as the training and validation data. This is done by simply multiplying it with the eigenvector matrix produced in the first step.

4 Experimental Results

In the experiments, we use the mySVM software tool for computation of the $\mathcal{C}$-support vector machine and the v-support vector machine algorithms [9]. MySVM uses a novel decomposition algorithm that attains optimality by solving a sequence of much smaller sub-problems. It proved to be better to iteratively decompose the problem into a small working set S and minimize the target function on the working set only, keeping the other variables fixed [6].

All the experiments have been conducted on a SUN E450 machine with SUN OS 5.7. We have used a total of 2000 personal E-mails as the dataset for our experiments. We manually label each E-mail as *interesting* or *uninteresting* for the experiments. The number of messages that are *interesting* is 1500, while that of those *uninteresting* is 500. The whole dataset was split into three portions randomly for different purposes, i.e. training set, validation set, and testing set. The meanings of these datasets are self-explanatory.

We use *recall* and *precision* as the performance metrics of the classifier. Although the training stage is relatively more time-consuming, the testing stage is very efficient. The recall and precision for interesting E-mails are defined as: $recall = \frac{N_{ii}}{N}$, $precision = \frac{N_{ii}}{N_i}$, where N is the total number of *interesting* E-mails, N_i is the total number of E-mails classified as *interesting*, and N_{ii} is the number of *correctly-classified* interesting E-mails.

4.1 Effect of Feature Selection

As we described before, the E-mails have structural features and free-text content features. The subject of E-mail message usually contains much more information about whether the E-mail is interesting or not. Therefore, if subjects are given double weights, the result may be more accurate. The primary content features which appear at least in four messages have 2160 dimensions. In other words, there are totally 2160 word features. We can then obtain the following schemes (The following strings in the parentheses are the respective notations for them):

1. The scheme with only body and subject features (sub+con);
2. The scheme with structure features and E-mail body features (str+con);
3. The scheme with structure features, subject features and body features (str+sub+con);
4. The scheme with structure features, double weighted subject features and the body features (str+dousub+con);
5. The scheme with structure features, triple weighted subject features and the body features (str+3sub+con).

In each scheme, the dataset has two representations, i.e. TF-IDF and binary form. The results are shown in table 1 and plotted in figure 3.

Table 1. The performance of various feature selection schemes

	TF-IDF		Binary	
	precision(%)	recall(%)	precision(%)	recall(%)
sub+con	95.83	95.60	96.5	94.82
str+con	91.33	90.76	91.24	90.96
str+sub+con	96.17	95.60	96.83	95.60
str+dousub+con	96.33	95.60	96.83	95.60
str+3sub+con	96.17	95.60	96.83	95.60

From the results, we can see that the binary feature of the structure, subject and body of E-mail has the best performance. From the results of scheme "sub+con" and "str+con", we can see that the structured features contain less classification information than the subject features. However, comparing the results of "sub+con", "str+sub+con", and "str+dousub+con", we can assert that the structured features do contribute to improving the classification problem. It is important to note that the structured features and the subject features contain a lot of classification information, despite the fact that, when more weight is put on the subject features, the overall performance improves only marginally.

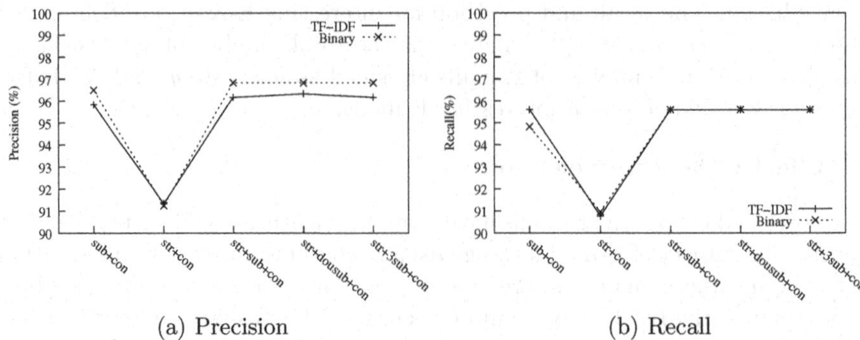

(a) Precision (b) Recall

Fig. 3. The precision and recall of various feature selection schemes

4.2 Effect of PCA

We use the 2160 features of the dataset, and do the principal component analysis and generate the new feature space with different dimensions (PCs). The performance of the SVM after PCA is depicted in figure 4.

The PCA method allows us to select the most important features for the classification effectively and efficiently. From the results, we can see that the average precision and recall of E-mail classification are above 92% even for the first 28 features, compared with about 95% when the PCA method is not used, where 2160 features are used (as shown in table 1). Moreover, when the number of dimensions is small(< 200), the performance after PCA processing is very stable. When the number of dimensions is 100, the result is near optimal, i.e. as good as full features used. Furthermore, the training time and space cost is only around 5% of the original method when PCA is not used. From these results, we can see that PCA could select a small set of features which can describe the whole features of the dataset. Therefore, the time and space costs could be reduced without compromising the performance. We also observe that adding many "unimportant" features to the SVM does not necessarily improve

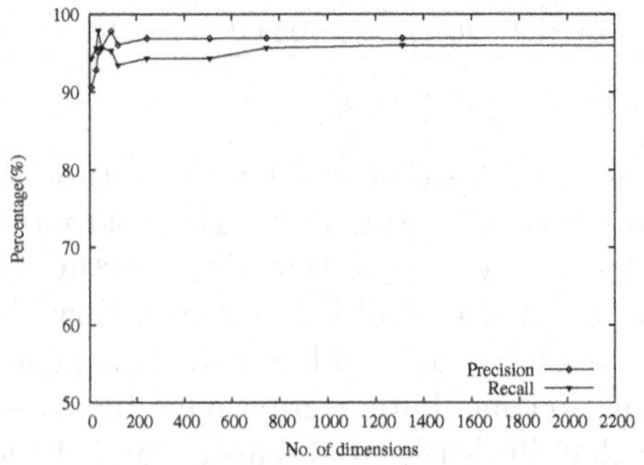

Fig. 4. The effect of PCA

the performance of the classification, as the performance does not improve as the number of dimensions increases.

4.3 Results of the $\mathcal{C}$-SVM

In the $\mathcal{C}$-support vector algorithm, parameter $\mathcal{C}$ affects the performance for the case when the training data is not linear separable by a linear SVM. In general, there should be an optimal value for this parameter. However, the optimal value of $\mathcal{C}$ cannot be obtained by examining the training data and it is unfair to do so by examining the test data. Only by using a validation set, would it be possible to optimize $\mathcal{C}$. The experiment is conducted as follows: (1) First, use the default $\mathcal{C}$, conduct the experiment to solve the optimal problem, and then find the performance on the validation set; (2) Pick another $\mathcal{C}$ and repeat step (1) until the performance on the validation set is optimal.

We use the dot and the radial kernel in this experiment. We also use binary feature vectors composed with structure features, subject features and body features. The result of the dot kernel algorithm is shown in table 2.

Table 2. Dot kernel training

$\mathcal{C}$	precision (%)	recall(%)	#support vectors	#Bounded SVs
600	96.83	95.60	149	2
60	96.83	95.60	148	2
6	96.83	95.60	148	2
0.6	96.83	95.60	148	2
0.06	96.54	95.60	152	2
0.006	96.33	95.60	179	9
0.0006	93.5	95.60	209	25
6e-5	89.5	96	249	105

When parameter $\mathcal{C}$ is decreased, the number of support vectors increases. MySVM provides the mechanism to search for the optimal $\mathcal{C}$ by adding or multiplying some delta increase to the current $\mathcal{C}$ value. From the table we can see that when $\mathcal{C}$ is set bigger than 0.6, there is no improvement of the precision performance. Therefore, we can search for the optimal $\mathcal{C}$-value between 6e-5 and 0.6 with pace 5 (by multiplication). The optimal $\mathcal{C}$ is 0.1875, with the respective performance results as follows: $precision_{op} = 96.83\%$, $recall_{op} = 95.60\%$.

Table 3. Radial Kernel Training

	$\gamma = 0.6$			$\gamma = 0.8$			$\gamma = 1$			$\gamma = 1.2$		
$\mathcal{C}$	precision	recall	#SV	precision	recall	#SV	precision	recall	#SV	precision	recall	#SV
600	81	80	445	81	90	444	81	90	444	81	90	444
6	81	80	444	81	90	444	81	90	444	81	90	442
0.06	80	90	443	80	90	443	80	90	443	80	90	442
6e-5	80	90	186	80	90	186	80	90	186	80	90	186

Table 3 shows the results of the radial kernel algorithm. Same as the dot kernel algorithm, the number of bounded SVs increases as C decreases (the result is not presented here). However, when parameter C is increased, the precision and the number of support vectors both increases. This is different from the dot kernel support vector machine. When C is greater than 6, the performance improves little as C increases. From the three criteria listed in the table, namely the *precision*, the *recall*, and the *number of support vectors*, we can see when γ is in [0.8, 1.0], the performance is optimal. We also note that the dot kernel algorithm is more suitable for E-mail classification compared to the radial kernel algorithm, and we only show the results of dot kernel algorithm in the following part of the paper.

4.4 Results of the v-SVM

Parameter v controls the upper bounds of the fraction of errors and the lower bounds of the fraction of support vectors. An increase in v allows for more errors and wider margin. The larger the v value is selected, the more points are allowed to lie inside the margin. As for the kernel, we use the popular radial kernel function $k(x, y) = exp(-\gamma\|x - y\|^2)$, where $\gamma = 1.0$. The result is shown in table 4. Although the v-SVM was proposed to better control the number of support vectors and errors, it does not show better performance than C-SVM, i.e. the C-SVM algorithm is more suitable in E-mail classification scenario.

Table 4. v-support training results

v	0.1	0.2	0.3	0.4	0.5
Precision	0.95	0.95	0.94	0.93	0.92
Recall	0.94	0.94	0.94	0.93	0.91
margin ($\rho/\|W\|$)	0.0002	0.0005	0.0007	0.0009	0.0023
fraction of SVs	0.23	0.28	0.41	0.47	0.58

Table 5. Comparison with other schemes

	precision	recall	space	time
PSVM	96.8%	96%	0.4K	0.02S
NN	93%	95%	1K	0.03S
SVM	95%	95.6%	8.6K	0.1S
Decision Tree	90%	91%	8.6K	0.1S
Bayesian Classifier	91%	91%	8.6K	0.1S

4.5 Comparison with Other Schemes

We also compare our model with the Decision Tree [4], the Naive Bayesian Classifier method [10], the Neural Network method [3] and the original SVM method [5]. Because of different feature selections, we only compare the optimal performance for the five methods. To clarify the presentation, we name our method as

PSVM which adopts $\mathcal{C}$-support vector algorithm, features selected from "structured fields+subject+body", binary feature representation and enhanced with PCA.

Table 5 shows the performance comparison with other schemes, where the space is the feature size used for classification. We can see that PSVM method yields comparable precision and recall rate with NN and original SVM methods, but is more effective in terms of space and CPU cost. The reason is that our proposed PSVM method captures all the features including structure information, subject and body text. Additionally, the PCA transformation makes the input data more classifiable with fewer features.

5 Conclusion

This paper models E-mail messages as a combination of structured features and textual features, which motivates the work of classifying such documents based on these features. We presented a SVM model which embeds PCA as a preprocessor to E-mail classification. Different ways of feature selection for the model were also evaluated. Our study indicated that the classification process could be enhanced by selecting features from both the structured part and the content part of the E-mails. The experiments showed that our SVM model provided good performance in filtering junk E-mails.

For future work, we plan to incorporate other techniques (e.g. E-mail address analysis, filthy word identification) into our method for better performance in classification. We can also expand the work from 2-class classification to multiple-class method, and further to a hierarchy of classes as well.

References

1. C. J. C. Burges: A Tutorial on Support Vector Machine for Pattern Recognition Data Mining and Knowledge Discovery, 2(2), (1998) 121–167
2. W. W. Cohen: Learning rules that classify e-mail. Proc. AAAI Spring Symposium on Machine Learning in Information Access, (1996) 124–143
3. B. Cui, A. Mondal, J. Shen, G. Cong and K.-L. Tan: On Effective E-mail Classification via Neural Networks. Proc. Database and Expert Systems Applications (DEXA), Copenhagen, Denmark, (2005) 85–94
4. Y. Diao, H. Lu and D. Wu: A Comparative Study of Classification Based Personal E-mail Filtering. Proc. of PAKDD, Kyoto, Japan, (2000) 408–419
5. H. Drucker, D. Wu and V. N. Vapnik: Support Vector Machine for Spam Categorization. IEEE Trans. on Neural Networks, 10(5), (1999) 1048–1054
6. T. Joachims: Making large-Scale SVM Learning Practical. *Advances in Kernel Methods - Support Vector Learning*, Chapter 11, MIT Press (1999)
7. I. T. Jolliffe: Principal Component Analysis. Springer-Verlag, (1986)
8. S. Kiritchenko and S. Matwin: E-mail Classification with Co-Training. Proc. of CASCON, Toronto, Canada, (2001) 192–201

9. S. Rüping: mySVM-Manual. University of Dortmund, Lehrstuhl Informatik 8, (2000) http://www-ai.cs.uni-dortmund.de/SOFTWARE/MYSVM/
10. M. Sahami, S. Dumais, D. Heckerman and E. Horvitz: A bayesian approach to filtering junk e-mail. Proc. AAAI Workshop Learning for Text Categorization, Madison, Wisconsin, (1998)
11. B. Schölkopf, A. J. Smola, R. C. Williamson and P. L. Bartlett: New support vector algorithms. Neural Computation, 12, (2000) 1207–1245

A Novel Web Page Categorization Algorithm Based on Block Propagation Using Query-Log Information

Wenyuan Dai, Yong Yu, Cong-Le Zhang, Jie Han, and Gui-Rong Xue

Apex Data & Knowledge Management Lab
Department of Computer Science and Engineering
Shanghai Jiao Tong University, 200240, Shanghai, China
{dwyak, yyu, zhangcongle, hanjie, grxue}@apex.sjtu.edu.cn

Abstract. Most existing web page classification algorithms, including content-based, link-based, or query-log analysis methods, treat the pages as smallest units. However, web pages usually contain some noisy or biased information which could affect the performance of classification. In this paper, we propose a Block Propagation Categorization (BPC) algorithm which deep mines web structure and views blocks as basic semantic units. Moreover, with query log information, BPC propagates only suitable information (*block*) among web pages to emphasize their topics. We also optimize the BPC algorithm to significantly speed up the block propagation process, without losing any precision. Our experiments on ODP and MSN search engine log show that BPC achieves a great improvement over traditional approaches.

1 Introduction

Classifying web pages into meaningful semantic categories plays an important role in the domain of web mining. The content-based classification algorithms only concern word occurrence statistics of document samples; the link-based categorization methods utilize the relationships between different web pages; and the traditional query log analysis methods improve the performance of categorization using the associations between queries and web pages. However, all these categorization techniques have some shortcomings. First, they failed to consider that most web pages contain noisy information. Second, not like pure text, huge amount of web pages are composed by different semantic parts. These biased parts will blur the topic of the web pages. Moreover, through page-like transmission or iterative reinforcement steps, they will further weaken the categorization performance.

Our motivation is to deeply use the structure of the web to propagate suitable information among web pages to emphasize each page' topic, and hence improve the categorization result. We noticed that web pages are usually composed by multiple units, including paragraphs, tables, lists, headings and so on. We denote these units as *blocks*. In most cases, blocks have purer topics than web pages. Thus, it is nature to believe, the reason for user to click one page associated with one query is that he was interested in certain blocks (usually the blocks share some information with search results' snippets) of that page rather than the whole. Therefore, query-page

J.X. Yu, M. Kitsuregawa, and H.V. Leong (Eds.): WAIM 2006, LNCS 4016, pp. 435–446, 2006.
© Springer-Verlag Berlin Heidelberg 2006

association should be looked upon as query-block association essentially. Our opinion is that if we could find users' really interested blocks in web pages according to their queries, and explore the association between queries and blocks, we would deeper utilize the query log information to further improve the performance of categorization. Our experiment results well prove this opinion.

Based on query-block association, we proposed a novel model to make one page mine blocks close related to itself. Then, through propagating these blocks to the page, its topic becomes more centralized, and hence the precision of classification increases. We denote the pages after propagation process as *virtual pages*. Those virtual pages, whose topics are purer than before, will be classified instead of the original pages.

The contributions of our work are:

1. We explored a query-block relationship and thus deeper mining web information could be realized;
2. We proposed Block Propagation Categorization (BPC) algorithm to propagate only useful and related blocks, while traditional link-based methods always propagate biased information;
3. We optimized the BPC algorithm to reduce the time usage of Block Propagation, without loss of any accuracy.

To evaluate our algorithm, the experiments are performed on the Open Directory Project (ODP) data set together with the click-through log from MSN search engine. The experiments show that, BPC achieves a significant improvement over traditional approaches, with an excellent performance in time. More details of the experiments will be reported later.

The rest of the paper is organized as follows. In section 2, we review some related work on traditional classification techniques. In section 3, we propose our BPC algorithm and explain it in detail. The experimental results are reported in section 4. Finally, we conclude the whole paper in section 5.

2 Related Work

Among all the related works, the content-based classification methods should be the most popular ones. *k*NN [7] is one of the most well-known classifiers, which is based on the categories assigned to the *k* nearest training documents to the input. Lewis [10], Lang [9] and Joachims [11] designed a document classifier by Naïve Bayes Classifier, and Joachims proposed the methods of using Support Vector Machines (SVM) [6, 12] to classify documents. However, all these approaches only consider the content information, while neglecting the ubiquitous relationships among interrelated objects. Thus, the content-based categorization algorithms are less powerful in web domain.

In the link-based techniques, learning algorithms are applied to handle both text information of web pages and hyperlink relationships among them. Slattery et al. [17] explored the hyperlink topology using an extended HITS algorithm. Similarly, Cohn et al. [5] and Glover et al. [8] improved the classification performance by combining link-based and content-based techniques. Chakrabati et al. [2] showed that directly incorporating words from neighboring page might not improve the categorization results. Panteleeva [14] filters the neighboring pages in order to take only useful pages to enrich the pages' representation and ignore noisy pages that drift the topic of source page. As pages usually contain noisy information and the relevance of hyperlinks is not high enough, link-based techniques have limited abilities for classifying web pages.

Analyzing query log information, Beeferman et al. [1] proposed an innovative query clustering method based on click-through data. They treat click-though data sets as a bipartite graph and identify the mapping between queries and the associated URLs. Queries with similarly clicked URLs can be clustered together. Chuang et al. [4] propose a technique for categorizing web query terms from the click-through logs into a predefined subject taxonomy based on their popular search interests. Wang et al. [19] proposed a method of using query click-through log to iteratively reinforce query and web page clusters, while Xue et al. [18] categorize the query and web page by iterative reinforcement technique. However, all these approaches treat web page as basic unit, and bring the noisy or biased information into other web pages, and hence reducing the categorization performance.

3 Block Propagation Categorization

According to the discussion in Section 2, most traditional methods are dealing with noisy or biased information in classification, which affects the results of categorization. In order to tackle these problem, we propose a Block Propagation Categorization (BPC) Algorithm which deeply uses the relationship between the heterogeneous web objects (queries, web pages and blocks), and propagates only useful information (block) to emphasize the topics of web pages. In our paper, *block* denotes the unit composing web pages, such as paragraphs, tables, lists and headings. Compared with web pages, blocks usually have more centralized topic. We will take advantage of this property to improve categorization performance.

We first define an interrelated objects model for this problem. Then we explain the algorithm in detail. Finally, optimization is designed to improve the efficiency.

3.1 Problem Definition

We consider the web as a model contains three types of objects: queries, web pages and blocks composing these pages. Besides, there also exist query-page, query-block and page-block relationships.

However, in order to describe the problem clearly, let's first consider the model without blocks (only consist of queries and web pages).

The Web Model Without Blocks. Let's see Figure 1. $P = \{p_1, p_2, \ldots, p_N\}$ is used to denote the set of web pages, while each page p_i contains n_i blocks. $Q = \{q_1, q_2, \ldots, q_M\}$ denotes the set of queries. $W_{N\times M}$ represents the adjacent matrix whose (i, j)-element w_{ij} represents the *weight* from web page p_i to query q_j (higher weight means more relevance).

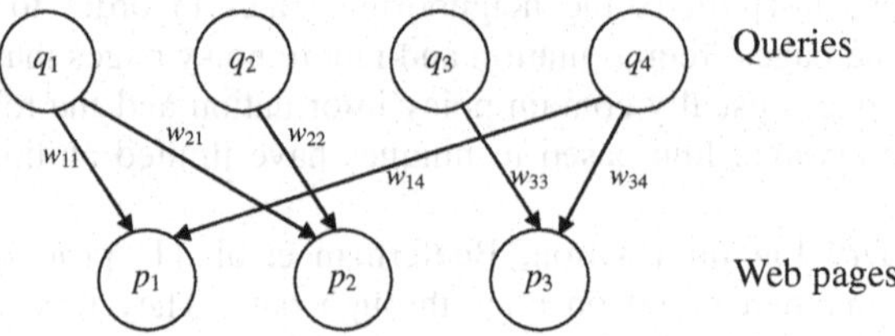

Fig. 1. Interrelation between Queries and Web pages

The Web Model with Blocks. Now, the feature of blocks will be added into the model. We use the sets $B_i = \{b_{ij} \mid 1 \le j \le n_i\}$ (b_{ij} denotes the jth block of page p_i) and $S_i = \{s_{ij} \mid 1 \le j \le n_i\}$ (s_{ij} denotes the *degree of similarity* (See Equation 1) between b_{ij} and p_i) to represent the blocks composing p_i and their contribution to p_i.

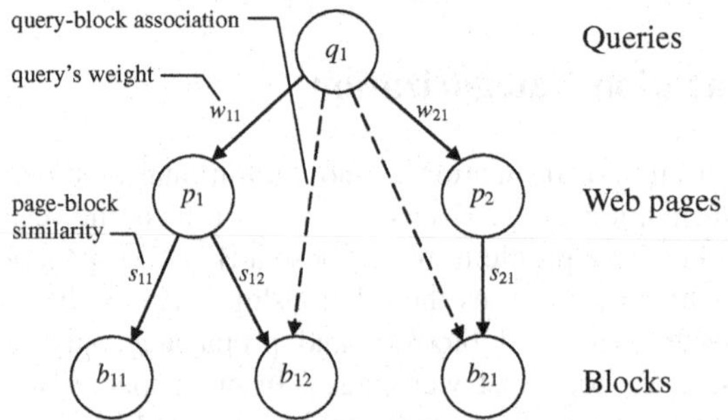

Fig. 2. Interrelation between Queries, Web pages and Blocks

Figure 2 shows the interrelation between queries, web pages and blocks. But, there is a relation we haven't defined in the figure – that is the query-block association.

Query-Block Association. A many-to-many mapping $\{<q_i, b_{jk}>\}$ is defined to represents the query-block association between q_i and b_{jk}. Here, the query-block association exists when b_{jk} contains some keywords of q_i.

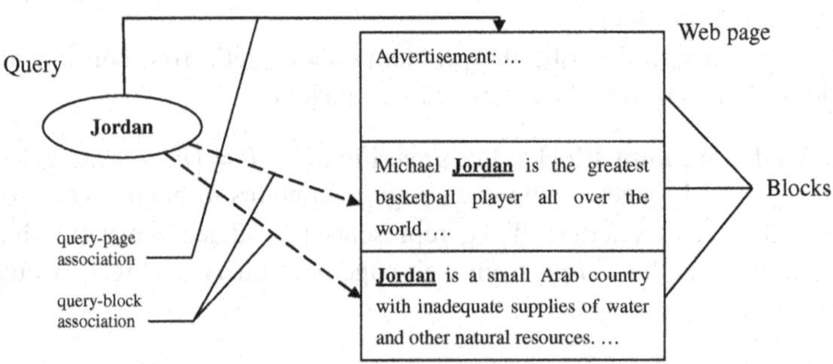

Fig. 3. Query-Block Association

Figure 3 illustrates the query-block association. The web page on the right contains three blocks: first is an advertisement; second and third introduce something about Michael Jordan and the country Jordan. Since there is a query-page association between the query and the page and the last two blocks contains the keyword "Jordan", there are two query-block associations between the query and the last two blocks.

Based on the web model we defined above, our problem is how to deeply utilize the relationships between queries, web pages and blocks to enhance the performance of categorization. Formally, given the graph $G = \{V = \{Q, P, B\}, E = \{W, R, f\}\}$, we aim to classify the web pages P into a set of predefined categories.

3.2 Block Propagation Categorization Algorithm

First, we segment each web page into several blocks from the html DOM tree [3]. After removing stop words and feature selection, we establish the interrelated model between queries, web pages and blocks, as depicted in Section 3.1 and Figure 3.

We propose a novel block propagation method to enhance the topic of each page, and thus improving the performance of categorization. Our basic idea is that when a block and a page are simultaneously associated with an identical query (the block contains some keywords of the query where query-page association already exists), the block has high possibility to share the same topic with the page. Hence, propagating the block to the page will reinforce the topic of the page in most cases.

Thus, in the case of blocks and pages associated with one same query, we set a threshold to propagate the most similar blocks, together with their contributions (See Equation 1), to the pages during the block propagation process. After this process, each page may obtain some new blocks. We use *virtual pages* to denote the pages after propagation process.

At last, we classify the virtual pages, instead of the original ones, based on their contents and contribution of blocks.

The block propagation categorization algorithm is described as follow:

Block Propagation Categorization (BPC) Algorithm

1. Segment each web page p_i into a set of blocks $B_i = \{b_{ij} \mid 1 \leq j \leq n_i\}$ from html DOM tree and then establish query-page and query-block association;
2. For each block b,
   - 2.1 For each the query q_i that is associated with b,
     - 2.1.1 Propagate the block b to all the q_i-associated web pages which are similar with the block (i.e. block's contribution to the page is above a predefined threshold, Equation 1 shows its calculation);
3. After the step 2, we obtain a set of virtual pages VP instead of the original web page set P.
4. Classify the virtual pages based on their contents and contribution of blocks.

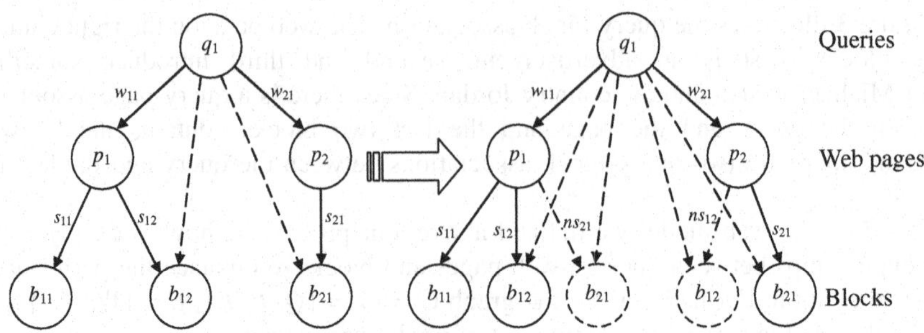

Fig. 4. An illustration of Block Propagation Process

Suppose the b_{12} and b_{21} are both the related blocks which should be propagated. Figure 4 illustrates the changes of graph after block propagation process. The result after the process is, p_1 obtains a new block b_{21} with the contribution ns_{21} (See Equation 1), and p_2 obtains a new block b_{12} with the contribution ns_{12}.

In the following, we will describe the process in detail.

Degree of Similarity (Contribution) Between Blocks and Web Pages. The degree of similarity (contribution) between blocks and web pages is an important measurement in our algorithm. A popular technique to quantify this measurement is based on the *Vector Space Model* (VSM) [15, 16] for documents. Here, we convert the blocks' and web pages' content into vectors in VSM. Let p_i be the vector of p_i, and b_{ik} be the vector of p_i's block b_{ik}. Then, the degree of similarity between p_i and b_{ik} is defined as the *cosine of the angle* between p_i and b_{ik},

$$\mathrm{sim}(\boldsymbol{p}_i, \boldsymbol{b}_{ik}) = \frac{\boldsymbol{p}_i \cdot \boldsymbol{b}_{ik}}{|\boldsymbol{p}_i| \times |\boldsymbol{b}_{ik}|} = \frac{\sum_j \boldsymbol{p}_i(j) \cdot \boldsymbol{b}_{ik}(j)}{\sqrt{\sum_j \boldsymbol{p}_i^2(j)} \sqrt{\sum_j \boldsymbol{b}_{ik}^2(j)}} \tag{1}$$

Content-Based Classification. The last step of the algorithm is to classify the web pages based on their content together with their contribution. We use a weighted Naïve Bayes Classifier (NBC) which treats the contribution (or degree of similarity) of blocks as the weight of content. For example, if a word in a block that has a contribution of 0.5, we would say that the word appears 0.5 time in the block. Thus, NBC is converted to weighted NBC as

$$c_{NB} = \arg\max_{c_j \in C} P(c_j) \prod_i P^{w_i}(a_i \mid c_j), \quad w_i = \alpha \cdot s_i \tag{2}$$

Here, c_{NB} represents the categorization result of weighted NBC, a_i represents a word in some block of a page, s_i represents the contribution of the block, and α is a parameter.

3.3 Optimization

In the experiments, propagating block content could be rather inefficiency. Based on mathematic knowledge, we convert the problem to propagate some other information, such as vector space or probability distribution, instead of block content.

According to Naïve Bayes Classifier, for blocks b_i, the classifier works as following

$$P(c_j \mid b_i) = P(c_j) \prod_{a_k \in b_i} P^{w_i}(a_k \mid c_j)$$

Thus, it is not difficult to find the probability distribution of $b_1 \oplus b_2 \oplus \ldots \oplus b_n$ (the combination of two blocks)

$$\begin{aligned} P(c_j \mid \oplus_{1 \le i \le n} b_i) &= P(c_j) \prod_{1 \le i \le n} \prod_{a_k \in b_i} P^{\tilde{w}_i}(a_k \mid c_j) \\ &= P^{1-n}(c_j) \prod_{1 \le i \le n} [P(c_j) \prod_{a_k \in b_i} P^{\tilde{w}_i}(a_k \mid c_j)] \\ &= P^{1-n}(c_j) \prod_{1 \le i \le n} [P(c_j) \prod_{a_k \in b_i} P^{w_i}(a_k \mid c_j)]^{\frac{\tilde{w}_i}{w_i}} P^{1-\frac{\tilde{w}_i}{w_i}}(c_j) \\ &= P^{1-\sum_{1 \le i \le n} \frac{\tilde{w}_i}{w_i}}(c_j) \prod_{1 \le i \le n} P^{\frac{\tilde{w}_i}{w_i}}(c_j \mid b_i) \end{aligned} \tag{3}$$

Here, $\tilde{w}_i$ represents the contribution of block b_i to the new page.

From Equation 3, we observe that we could only propagate the blocks' probability distribution and lead to the same accuracy result. Thus, there is no need for propagating contents. Hence, the time and space complexity got much reduced.

4 Experiment

4.1 Data Set

To evaluate the performance of our algorithm, we performed the experiments on a set of classified web pages from the Open Directory Project (ODP) (http://dmoz.org). ODP contains about 1.2 million web pages, in which each web page is classified by human experts into 17 top level categories (*Arts, Business and Economy, Computer and Internet, Games, Health, Home, Kids and Teens, News, Recreation, Reference, Regional, Science, Shopping, Society, Sports, Adult and World*). We removed the Regional and World categories, because the web pages in Regional category are also in other categories and the pages in World category are not in English. Thus, there remain 15 categories in our experiments.

We collected a real MSN query click-through log as our experiment data set. The log collection contains about 1.2 million query requests recorded over 12 hours in August 2003.

Some preprocesses have been applied to the raw queries and web pages. First, we converted the queries into lower case, and stemmed them using the Porter algorithm, while the stop words were removed too. The query sessions sharing the same query and URL are merged into a single one, with the frequencies summed up. Then, we removed, from the data set, the web pages which are not associated with some query session, and the blocks are extracted from the web pages. Finally, we got 131,788 web pages in 15 top-level categories, 199,564 associated queries and 468,696 query sessions. Figure 5 shows the distribution of the web pages in 15 categories.

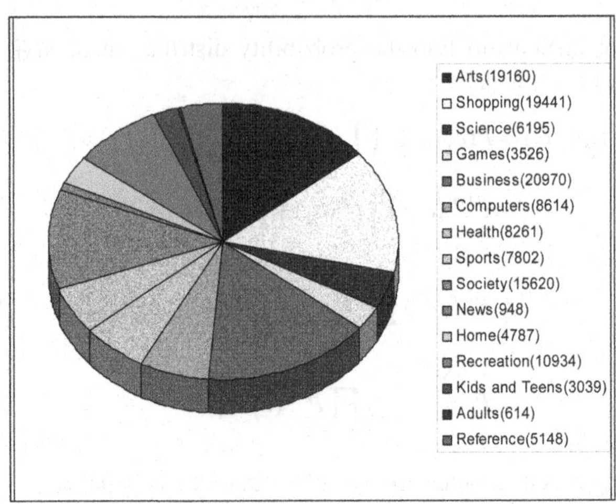

Fig. 5. Distribution of web pages in the 15 categories

4.2 Feature Selection

We used a popular feature selection method, Document Frequency (DF) Thresholding [20], to cut down the number of features, and speed up the classification. Based on Y. Yang et al. [20], DF thresholding is suggested, as the method, which has comparable performance with IG or CHI, is simplest with lowest cost in computation. In our experiments, we set the DF threshold as 3.

4.3 Evaluation Criteria

The performance of the algorithms was evaluated by precision, recall and F_1 measures [21], while micro-average and macro-average [21] were applied to get single performance value over all classification tasks.

4.4 Performance

We use the *pure content-based Naïve Bayes Classifier* (NBC) as the baseline. Besides, the traditional "Query + Content" (QC) method [18], which use the query metadata as additional features of web pages, is introduced for compare use. In order to evaluate the effect of block propagation, we also compare our Block Propagation Categorization (BPC) algorithm with the Link-based Page Propagation (LBPP) method [14] which we have mentioned in the section 2.

We fixed several parameters in our experiments. First, when selecting features, we set the DF threshold as 3. Second, when propagating blocks, the threshold of similarity is set as 0.5. Third, the parameter α in Equation 2 is set as 0.2. Using these values, our experiment gave a good performance. Table 1 shows the performance of each classification algorithms.

Table 1. Performance of the four algorithms

MICRO-AVERAGE			
	Precision	Recall	F_1 measure
NBC	0.597	0.597	0.597
QC	0.631	0.631	0.631
LBPP	0.633	0.633	0.633
BPC	**0.669**	**0.669**	**0.669**
MACRO-AVERAGE			
	Precision	Recall	F_1 measure
NBC	0.594	0.512	0.537
QC	0.631	0.557	0.580
LBPP	0.610	0.559	0.575
BPC	0.650	0.586	0.602

The result in Table 1 shows that the content-based classification method (NBC) gives poor result, which indicates it is not sufficient to only concern text contents for classifying web pages. The performance of "Query + Content" (QC) method is much better, since it utilizes the information of queries. Link-based Page Propagation (LBPP) has a comparable performance with QC, as it collects the neighborhood pages' contents to enrich each page's topic. However, our BPC algorithm archives the best categorization result, compared with other three approaches. We believe that is because BPC deeper uses the information of contents and relationships in the web. It filters much more noise than most traditional methods during the reinforcement process (Block Propagation Process).

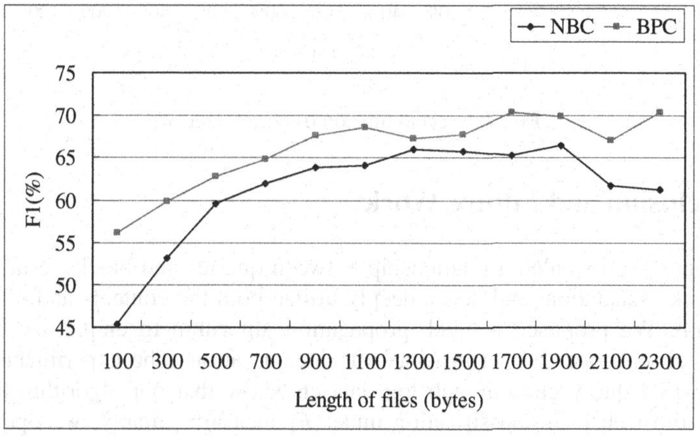

Fig. 6. Performance on different file length

We conduct the further experiment to show the other performance of our algorithm. Figure 6 shows that NBC has a poor performance when the lengths of files are too short or too long. The reason is simple. When the length is too short, there is no sufficient text information for NBC to give confident predictions; when the length is too long, there is usually amount of noisy information in the web page, which could affect the categorization results. These web pages may have unclear or confused topics. BPC propagates useful blocks to emphasize the topic of the each page, and hence emphasizes the topics of these pages. We see that, in Figure 6, BPC achieves bigger improvement when the lengths of files are quite short or quite long. Comparatively, the less improvement is given for the files with normal lengths.

Different sizes of data (in number of web pages) were tested in the experiments. We run our BPC algorithm on the Pentium IV 2.4G PC with 1GB memory. Figure 7 shows the executed CPU time by BPC before and after optimization (Section 3.3). We see that before optimization, BPC (Naïve BPC) consumes huge amount of time, while after optimization, BPC (Optimized BPC) has a time complexity which is approximately linear with the data size. That indicates our algorithm has a good scalable ability for large data.

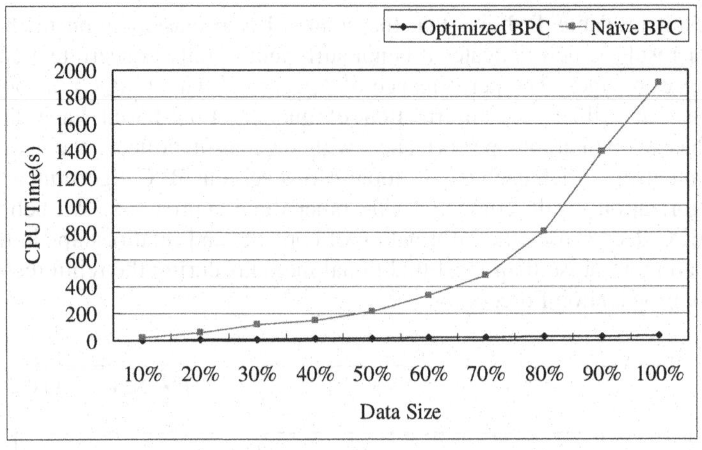

Fig. 7. Execute time on different data size

5 Conclusion and Future Work

In this paper, we revealed a relationship between queries and blocks, established the query-block association, and hence deeply utilize both the contents and relationships in the web. We proposed a block propagation algorithm to emphasize the pages' topic, which enhance the performance of categorization. The experiments on ODP and real MSN query click-though log datasets show that our algorithm thoroughly improves the web page classification under F_1 measure. Finally, we optimized the classification algorithm to speed up it. And the experiment shows that our algorithm is scalable well for large web data.

In this paper, we only propagate the blocks for one step. Maybe propagating for more steps will further improves the performance of classification. But, the difficulty is how to update the query-block association after block propagation, which could take huge amount of time and space. Thus, in order to propagate the blocks for more than one step, we have to design an efficient algorithm to real-time update the query-block association.

We have already shown that block propagation could improve the traditional web page classification algorithm. How about the web page clustering?

References

1. D. Beeferman and A. Berger. "*Agglomerative clustering of a search engine query log.*" In Proceedings of the sixth ACM SIGKDD International Conference on Knowledge Discovery and Data Mining, pages 407-415, 2000.
2. S. Chakrabati, B. Dom and P. Indyk. "*Enhanced hypertext categorization using hyperlinks.*" In Proceedings of the ACM SIGMOD International Conference of Management of Data, pages 307-318, Seattle, Washington, June 1998.
3. S. Chakrabarti. "*Mining the Web: Discovering Knowledge from Hypertext Data.*" Morgan Kaufmann Publishers, 2002.
4. S. L. Chuang and L. F. Chien. "*Enriching Web taxonomies through subject categorization of query terms from search engine logs.*" Decision Support System, Volume 35, Issue 1, April 2003.
5. D. Cohn and T. Hofmann. "*The missing link – a probabilistic model of document content and hypertext connectivity.*" In Advances in Neural Information Processing Systems 13, pages 430-436. MIT Press, 2001.
6. C. Cortes and V. Vapnik. "*Support Vector Networks.*" Machine Learning, 20:1-25, 1995.
7. T. Cover and P. Hart, "*Nearest neighbor pattern classification.*" IEEE Transactions on Information Theory, 13, 21-27, 1967.
8. E. J. Glover, K. Tsioutsiouliklis, S. Lawrence, D. M. Pennock and G. W. Flake. "*Using Web structure for classifying and describing Web pages.*" In Proceedings of WWW-02, International Conference on the World Wide Web, 2002.
9. K. Lang. "*Newsweeder: Learning to filter netnews.*" Proceedings of the 12th International Conference on Machine Learning, pages 331-339. San Francisco, 1995.
10. D. Lewis. "*Representation and learning in information retrieval.*" (COINS Technical Report 91-93). Dept. of Computer and Information Science, University of Massachusetts, 1991.
11. T. Joachims. "*A probabilistic analysis of the Rocchio algorithm with IFIDF for text categorization.*" Computer Science Technical Report CMU-CS-96-118. Carnegie Mellon University.
12. T. Joachims. "*Text categorization with support vector machines: learning with many relevant features.*" In Proceeding of ECML-98, 10the European Conference on Machine Learning, pages 137-142, Chemnitz, Germany, April 1998.
13. T. M. Mitchell, "*Machine Learning.*" McGraw-Hill, 1997.
14. N. Panteleeva, "*Using neighborhood information for automated categorization of Web*", http://meta.math.spbu.ru/~nadejda/papers/ista2003/ista2003.html.
15. G. Salton. "*The SMART Retrieval System – Experiments in Automatic Document Processing.*" Prentice Hall Inc., Englewood Cliffs, NJ, 1971.

16. G. Salton and M. E. Lesk. "*Computer evaluation of indexing and text processing.*" Journal of the ACM, 15(1):8-36, January 1968.
17. S. Slattery and M. Craven. "*Discovery test set regularities in relational domains.*" In Proceedings of ICML-00, 17th International Conference on Machine Learning, pages 895-902, Stanford, US, 2000.
18. G. R. Xue, D. Shen, Q. Yang, H. J. Zeng, Z. Chen, Y. Yu and W. Y. Ma. "*IRC: An Iterative Reinforcement Categorization Algorithm for Interrelated Web Objects.*" Proceedings of the 2004 IEEE International Conference on Data Mining (ICDM-2004). Brighton, United Kingdom, November 2004.
19. J. D. Wang, H. J. Zeng, Z. Chen, H. J. Lu, L. Tao, and W. Y. Ma. "*ReCoM: reinforcement clustering of multi-type interrelated data objects.*" In Proceedings of the ACM SIGIR Conference on Research and Development in Information Retrieval, pages 274-281, Toronto, CA, July 2003.
20. Y. Yang and J. O. Pedersen. "*A comparative study on feature selection in text categorization.*" In Proceeding of the Fourteenth International Conference of Machine Learning, 1997.
21. Y. Yang, "*An evaluation of statistical approaches to text categorization.*" Journal of Information Retrieval, Vol 1, No. 1/2, pages 67-88 , 1999.

Counting Graph Matches with Adaptive Statistics Collection*

Jianhua Feng, Qian Qian, Yuguo Liao, and Lizhu Zhou

Department of Computer Science and Technology
Tsinghua University, Beijing 100084, China
{fengjh, dcszlz}@tsinghua.edu.cn,
{qqpeter99, liaoyg03}@mails.tsinghua.edu.cn

Abstract. High performance of query processing in large scale graph-structured data poses a pressing demand for high-quality statistics collection and selectivity estimation. Precise and succinct statistics collection about graph-structured data plays a crucial role for graph query selectivity estimation. In this paper, we propose the approach SMT, Succinct Markov Table, which achieves high precision in selectivity estimation with low memory space consumed. Four core notions of SMT are constructing, refining, compressing and estimating. The efficient algorithm SMTBuilder provides facility to build adaptive statistics model in the form of SMT. Versatile optimization rules, which investigate local bi-directional reachability, are introduced in SMT refining. During compressing, affective SMT grouping techniques are introduced. Statistical methods are used for selectivity estimations of various graph queries basing on SMT, especially for twig queries. By a thorough experimental study, we demonstrate SMT's advantages in accuracy and space by comparing with previously known alternative, as well as the preferred optimization rules and compressing technique that would favor different real-life data.

1 Introduction

Graph is widely used to model complex and schemaless data, ranging from XML, proteins, to chemical compounds. The key problem for many graph-related applications is how to efficiently process graph query and retrieve corresponding sub-graphs. For achieving the best query performance in graph-structured data, effective and accurate estimations for selectivities of both simple and complex path queries are crucially needed by determining the optimal query-execution plan. Accurate selectivity estimation becomes challenging as it relies on exact graph statistics information which always can't be afforded in real-life system for time and space constraints..

As the standard for data exchange and integration nowadays, XML is a kind of directed labeled graph, which is self-describing and cycle-enabled in nature. The underlying labeled graph model of XML consists of element nodes, which can be

* The work was supported by the National Natural Science Foundation of China under Grant No.60573094, Tsinghua Basic Research Foundation under Grant No.JCqn2005022 and Zhejiang Natural Science Foundation under Grant No.Y105230.

J.X. Yu, M. Kitsuregawa, and H.V. Leong (Eds.): WAIM 2006, LNCS 4016, pp. 447–459, 2006.
© Springer-Verlag Berlin Heidelberg 2006

simple/complex type value node or composite reference node (i.e. id/idref node[2]). For all the query languages on graph, pattern-based query description is a common and essential feature. This kind of query is more complex than SQL in RDBMS because of its capability in graph navigational query, especially for complex twig and cyclic query pattern. However, similar to RDBMS, accurate selectivity estimation for graph query is critical for optimal query execution plan choosing as it provides cost evaluations for different search and traversing plans. The following example illustrates the importance of selectivity estimation for XML graph query. The query is expressed in XQuery[3]. Figure 1 is a query expression and its corresponding structure.

FOR $g in document ("")//Prof*
WHERE $g/Class = "Database"
AND $g/Year = "2000"
RETURN $g/Name

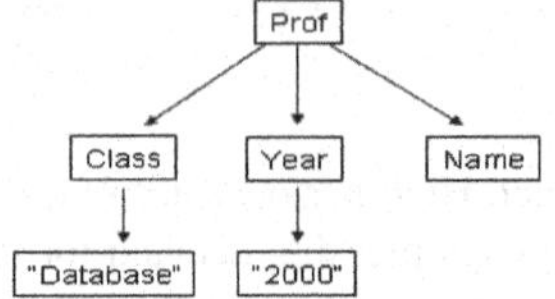

Fig. 1. A sample query and its structure

The purpose of this complex graph query is to find the names of all professors who gave "Database" class in 2000. For efficient execution of this query, we need to know the selectivities of paths //Prof/Class="Database", //Prof/Year="2000" and //Prof/name. As an assumption, selectivities of path //Prof/Class="Database" and //Prof/Year ="2000" are 20 and 400 respectively, which means totally 20 "Database" classes existed and 400 classes were given in 2000. According to the selectivities above, the optimal query plan should follow the execution order by fetching the results from path //Prof/Class="Database" firstly and matching the condition of //Prof/Year="2000" secondly. On the other hand, with selectivity estimations, optimizer in RDBMS also becomes powerful to determine the best Join execution order. In both scenarios, query optimization highly depends upon efficient and accurate selectivity estimation.

As a summary, our contributions are listed as follows:

- **SMT:** A novel graph statistics collection model. It is the core of efficient and accurate selectivity estimations for graph queries. It outperforms previous approaches by less memory cost and more precise selectivity. SMTBuilder is an efficient algorithm to generate SMT from the start point of 0-bisimilarity graph statistics collection.
- **Methods of SMT compressing:** We propose compressing techniques: *Naive method, Forward Grouping method* and *Backward Grouping method* to yield compact SMT which is fit for available memory.
- **Methods of SMT refining:** The optimization rules and the adaptive parameter m for statistical path length are incorporated in refining process. Optimization rules help to capture the correlations and distributions of different paths exactly by investigating the local bi-directional reachability. With parameter m, we can adjust the granularity of our statistical model dynamically.
- **Methods of counting matches:**. We demonstrate the effectiveness of SMT-based statistical methods for selectivity estimation on complex graph query.

The rest of this paper is organized as follows. Section 2 gives an overview about related work. Section 3 describes constructing graph statistics collection. Section 4 presents SMT refining approach for selectivity estimation. Section 5 gives three useful compressing techniques. Section 6 contains selectivity estimation methods on SMT. Section 7 is performance evaluation. Section 8 presents our conclusion.

2 Related Work

Various selectivity estimation approaches have been proposed for path query on semi-structured data, such as Path Tree and Markov Table presented in [1], which illustrate selectivity estimation methods for single path query in large-scale web data. Markov Table [1] adopts a set of pruning and aggregation techniques on the statistics information. The approach for twig query estimations is discussed in [5], which presents CST (Correlated Subpath Tree), a suffix tree representation about statistical information with value constraints on leaf nodes. It is a general selectivity estimation method for twig query so far.

Besides, A(k)[7] and D(k)[4] give new index techniques on XML data, which also can be treated as graph-structured data statistics collection methods. The concept of k-bisimilarity is introduced in A(k) index, which use a parameter k to adjust index structure granularity.By extending A(k), D(k) considers the index local features for real data. Here, k becomes a tunable parameter optimized with the length of path query. For long path, a big k is suitable; oppositely, a small k is fit for short path. Each element in D(k) index always contains two attributes: one is the supported k, the other is the data nodes contained by this element. However, index is the presentation for data pointers or offset references. In the problem of selectivity estimation, frequencies of element and path are key characteristics people concern. Another aspect different from index technique is the more strict memory constraint, which is affected by real-life system's resource restriction.

XPathLearner [8] is an on-line method for refining statistics information by gathering results from user queries as a forward feedback. It updates both of the tag and value distribution information with a self-tuning mechanism. However, when the system is running under heavy workload, the on-line tuning method poses extra burden which sometimes can't be compensated by the benefits it gives. Besides, once false feedback is taken effect, it lacks the ability of withdrawing and recovering.

3 Constructing Graph Statistics Collection

In general, a common graph statistics collection model can be described as follow: An original graph data G = (V, E) depicts a directed graph structure. In graph statistics collection S = (V', E'), each $v' \in V'$ with $extent(v') \subseteq V$ is a representation of the nodes in G classified by certain aggregation principle (i.e. 0-bisimilarity), which records the number of nodes in it. Each edge $(u', v') \in E'$ contains all the edges from extent(u') to extent(v'). Here, extent(v') indicates the set of nodes in G which are corresponding to v' in S.

Figure 2 gives the sample graph-structured data which is expressed in XML by involving ID/IDREF elements [2]. The concepts of "bisimilarity" and "k-bisimilarity" were proposed by 1-index [10] and A(K)-index[7] respectively. For the concern of different statistics collection granularity, "k-bisimilarity" can be used as the aggregation principle in statistics collection graph (S) generation. As the base for selectivity estimation, we choose "0-bisimilarity" principle for our first-step statistics collection generation. "0-bisimilarity" principle maps the nodes with identical tag in G to the same and unique node in S, which we call S(0) , the base statistics collection status in our approach. Figure 3(a) shows the S(0) of the graph data in Figure 2. Because of S(0)'s coarseness, some false and cyclic paths may be introduced during its generation. As well, exact path distribution information is always lost in S(0). That's the reason why it can't achieve satisfied selectivity estimation results..

In *Markov Table* [1], the selectivity estimations of paths with length m depend only on the selectivity estimations of sub paths with length m-1 preceding it. In fact, the process is modeled as a Markov process of order m-1, so this approach is called *Markov Table*. It represents an accurate approximation of the structure of the XML data, but it is only used for simple path query in tree-structured data [1]. In our approach, we extend it to complex twig query in graph-structured data with new features added. In order to strengthen *Markov Table*'s ability for summarizing graph-structured data, we propose *Theorem 1*.

Theorem 1. *In statistics collection S, the frequency of edge (* u_i *, v), which is one of all the edges leads to v, can be denoted as follows:*

$$\mathrm{Freq}(u_i, v) = \frac{\mathrm{Freq}(u_i)}{\sum_{u_i} \mathrm{Freq}(u_i)} \times \mathrm{Freq}(v) \tag{1}$$

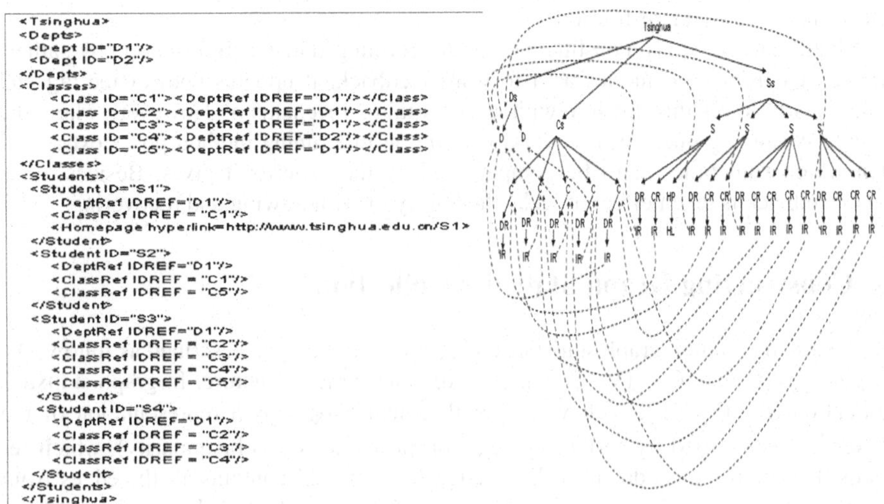

Fig. 2. XML data and its graph structure

The computation for the frequency of edge (u_i, v) mainly considers two factors. $\frac{Freq(u_i)}{\sum_{u_i} Freq(u_i)}$ presents the fraction of edges with start node u_i in all the edges leading to v. Freq(v) is the frequency of the node v in S. Thus, the product of these two factors is the approximation for frequency of edge (u_i, v). This idea is also addressed in [1] and [11], which is considered as a statistical computation based on uniformity assumption.

Applying *Theorem 1* on the S(0) in Figure 3(a), we can obtain the *Markov Table* with path length m=2 in Figure 3(b), which is the initial statistics collection for graph-structured data in Figure 2.

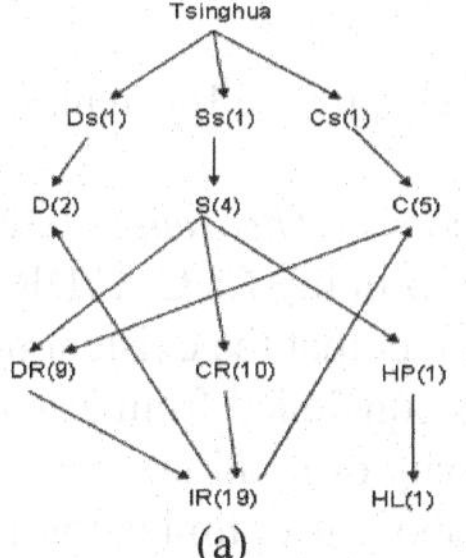

(a)

Path	Freq	Path	Freq	Path	Freq
Ts	1	HP	1	S/DR	4
Ds	1	HL	1	S/CR	10
Ss	1	IR	19	S/HP	1
Cs	1	Ts/Ds	1	C/DR	5
D	2	Ts/Ss	1	DR/IR	9
S	4	Ts/Cs	1	CR/IR	10
C	5	Ds/D	2*(1/20)	HP/HL	1
DR	9	Ss/S	4	IR/D	2*(19/20)
CR	10	Cs/C	5*(1/20)	IR/C	5*(19/20)

(b)

Fig. 3. S(0) of sample graph data in Figure 2 and Markov Table for S(0)

4 SMT Refining

Actually, in Figure 3(b), we can see the frequencies of path "IR/D", "IR/C" are 2*(19/20) and 5*(19/20) respectively which are computed by *Theorem 1.* Since the computation is based on uniformity assumption [11], it is only a coarse estimation that can't supply more exact information about correlations and distributions for them. Because of the accuracy limitation of S(0), we need to investigate optimization methods for refining graph summarization. As a base for optimization rules, we first exploit the local bi-directional reachability about edges in graph statistics collection S. Two definitions are proposed to describe the types of edges in S, which consider the forward and backward inclusions on the edges.

Definition 1. *Forward-Inclusion (FI): For each edge (u, v) in graph statistics collection S, if u can reach no nodes except v, then the type of (u, v) is FI.*

Definition 2. *Backward-Inclusion (BI): For each edge (u, v) in graph statistics collection S, if v can only be reached by u, then the type of (u, v) is BI.*

Therefore, all the edges in S can be classified into 4 types: FI, BI, FI $\wedge$ BI and NI. NI denotes the type of $\neg(FI \vee BI)$. With the definition 1 and 2, we draw two important theorems as evidences supporting accurate selectivity estimations.

Theorem 2. *Given a path P = ($/t_1/t_2/.../t_n$) in graph statistics collection S, if types of all edges (t_i/t_{i+1}) in P are BI, then Freq(t_n) is an accurate estimation for path P.*

Theorem 3. *Given a path $P = (/t_1/t_2/.../t_n)$ in graph statistics collection S, if types of all edges (t_i/t_{i+1}) in P are FI, then each node in extent(t_i) ($1 \leq i<n$) has connected path reaching some node in extent(t_n).*

As an example for twig query in sample graph data, the query P = /Tsinghua[Cs/C /DR/IR]/Ds/D has the purpose to find all the D nodes having the pattern matched with the structure Figure 4(a) describes.

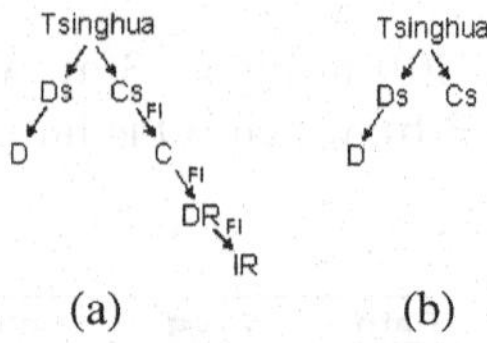

Fig. 4. Original query pattern and Optimized query pattern after applying Theorem 3

Because Cs/C, C/DR and DR/IR have types of FI in common, as *Theorem 3* defined, Freq (P) = Freq (/Tsinghua[Cs]/Ds/D) which is simplified by pruning Cs/C, C/DR and DR/IR. The intrinsic sense of this simplification is based on a fact that the existent probability of sub path Cs/C/DR/IR is a hundred percent which is concluded from *Theorem 3*. So the Figure 4(b) shows the simplified structure for selectivity estimation.

In order to leverage *Theorem 2* and *3* sufficiently, we propose 4 optimization rules with goals to depict the graph statistics collection containing more BI and FI type edges.

Optimization Rule 1: *Given an edge (u, v) with $\neg FI$ type in graph statistics collection S, let the type of (u, v) be T. The node u in S can be split into two nodes u_1 and u_2, where $set(u) = set(u_1) \cup set(u_2)$ and $set(u_1) \cap set(u_2)= \phi$, then the new types of (u_1, v) and (u_2, v) are $FI \cup T$ and T respectively.*

Optimization Rule 2: *Given an edge (u, v) with $\neg BI$ type in graph statistics collection S, let the type of (u, v) be T. The node v in S can be split into two nodes v_1 and v_2, where $set(u) = set(u_1) \cup set(u_2)$ and $set(u_1) \cap set(u_2)= \phi$, then the new types of (u, v_1) and (u, v_2) are $BI \cup T$ and T respectively.*

Optimization Rule 3: *Given n edges with $\neg FI$ types which start from node u in graph statistics collection S, let them be denoted as (u, v_1), (u, v_2), ..., (u, v_n). As an assumption, the average frequency of these n edges is **a**, which is computed by the formula of $Avg(u, v_i)=\frac{\sum_{vi} Freq(u, vi)}{n}$. The node u can be split into two nodes u_1 and u_2, where $set(u) = set(u_1) \cup set(u_2)$ and $set(u_1) \cap set(u_2)= \phi$, such that $Freq(u_1, v_i)>$**a** with v_i connected by u_1 and $Freq(u_2, v_j) \leq$ **a** with v_j connected by u_2.*

Optimization Rule 4: *Given n edges with $\neg BI$ types which start from node u in graph statistics collection S, let them be denoted as (u_1, v), (u_2, v), ...,(u_n, v). As an assumption, the average frequency of these n edges is **a**, which is also computed by the formula of $Avg(u_i, v)=\frac{\sum_{ui} Freq(ui, v)}{n}$. The node v can be split into two nodes v_1 and v_2, where $set(u) = set(u_1) \cup set(u_2)$ and $set(u_1) \cap set(u_2)= \phi$, such that $Freq(u_i, v_1)>$**a** with ui leads to v_1 and $Freq(u_j, v_2) \leq$ **a** with u_j leads to v_2.*

Clearly, dynamic combination of optimization rules offers a flexible and satisfied solution to produce more precise graph statistics collections and selectivity estimations. Versatile advantages of different optimization rules for complicated and style-varied data is an important advantage of our approach which also will be illustrated in following part. Basing on the optimization rules, we give a concrete demonstration on the SMT construction algorithm: SMTBuilder.

```
Algorithm:    SMTBuilder
Input:        G: Original data graph
              m: Maximum path length supported in SMT
              RuleSet: Optimization Rules Set
Output:       SMT that is optimized by RuleSet
        S(0):=GenS(G);//S(0) contains type of each edge;
        SMT:=GenMT(m, S(0));
        For each R in RuleSet do
           SMT:=ApplyRule(SMT, R);
        Return SMT;
```

Figure 5(a)(b)(c) present the local structure changes when IR is split. (d) and (e) show the statistics collection and SMT by applying RuleSet {1} on IR/D of S(0).

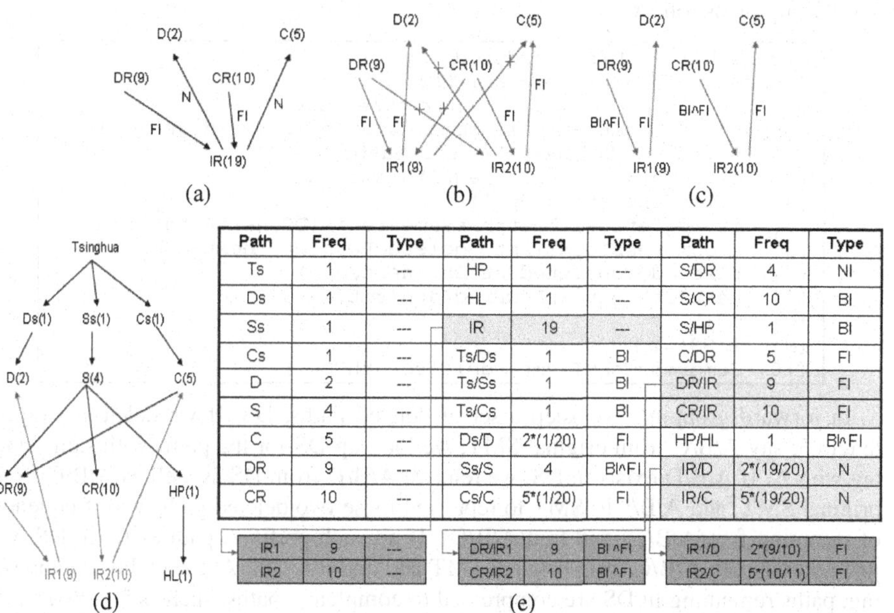

Path	Freq	Type	Path	Freq	Type	Path	Freq	Type
Ts	1	---	HP	1	---	S/DR	4	NI
Ds	1	---	HL	1	---	S/CR	10	BI
Ss	1	---	IR	19	---	S/HP	1	BI
Cs	1	---	Ts/Ds	1	BI	C/DR	5	FI
D	2	---	Ts/Ss	1	BI	DR/IR	9	FI
S	4	---	Ts/Cs	1	BI	CR/IR	10	FI
C	5	---	Ds/D	2*(1/20)	FI	HP/HL	1	BI∧FI
DR	9	---	Ss/S	4	BI∧FI	IR/D	2*(19/20)	N
CR	10	---	Cs/C	5*(1/20)	FI	IR/C	5*(19/20)	N

Path	Freq	Type	Path	Freq	Type	Path	Freq	Type
IR1	9	---	DR/IR1	9	BI∧FI	IR1/D	2*(9/10)	FI
IR2	10	---	CR/IR2	10	BI∧FI	IR2/C	5*(10/11)	FI

Fig. 5. Process of applying Optimization Rule 1 on IR/D, optimized graph statistics collection and optimized SMT

5 SMT Compressing

Note that SMT represents an accurate approximation of graph-structured data, which may not be fit in the available memory for its large size. This problem is also bewared in our former work [6]. An efficient and natural idea to compress SMT is discarding and grouping the paths with the lowest frequencies in SMT. With respect to compensating the loss of accurate structural information, we try to preserve the information represented in the deleted paths by adding them into groups of deleted paths. Though with coarser granularity, high scalability can be achieved by appropriate size of statistical information. The precision under compressed SMT turns out to be somehow the same or quite close to accurate approximation, which will be demonstrated by our experiments in real life data.

***Naïve Method*:** The first method for compressing SMT, which we call it Naïve method, uses the strategy of "simply discarding". Low-frequency paths in SMT are simply discarded without further grouping. When using SMT to estimate selectivity by Naïve compressing, if any of the required paths is not found, we estimate a selectivity of zero. In Naïve compressing, it is appropriately assumed that paths, which do not exist in the compressed SMT, neither exist in the original SMT.

***Forward Grouping Method*:** The second method for compressing SMT, which we call forward grouping, uses a special path *-paths [1] to represent all deleted paths with different length, such as * presents all the deleted paths with length 1, while */*/* for all the deleted paths with length 3. We develop the algorithm SMTForwardGrouping as follow:.

```
Algorithm:     SMTForwardGrouping
Input:         smt: Original SMT
               n: low frequency threshold
Output:        smt that is compressed by forward grouping
DS :=φ; //Deleted Set for paths in SMT
nextPath := nextLowFreqPath(smt, n);
while(nextPath!= null)
  if((deletedPathSet=hasSamePrefix(DS,nextPath))!= φ)
    compressToSMT(smt, deletedPathSet, nextPath);
  else addToDeletedSet(DS, nextPath)
  nextPath = nextLowFreqPath(smt, n);
End;
If(DS!=φ)
CompressToSMT(smt, deleledPathSet);
```

In forward grouping, we keep a set of deleted paths, DS. If we delete a path of length 3, say A/B/C from original SMT, we look up DS for the paths with same start tag with A. If A/B/D exists in DS, we remove A/B/D from DS as well as A/B/C from original SMT, add A/B/* to SMT to represent these two deleted paths with frequency of summing freq(A/B/C) and freq(A/B/D). If no such prefix-A path exists in DS, we just remove path A/B/C from original SMT and add it to DS. At the end of compressing, paths remaining in DS are compressed to complete * paths, such as */*, */*/* etc. The average frequency of these remained paths is the frequency for their corresponding *-paths. During the process of selectivity estimation, say for path A/B/C, if A/B/C is not found in SMT, we search A/B/*, A/*/*, and */*/* for its frequency sequentially.

***Backward Grouping Method*:** The third method for compressing SMT, which we call backward grouping, adopts an opposite direction to group low frequency paths contrasted to forward grouping method. In our example, if path A/B and C/B individually qualify for deletion, then they are combined into */B. With SMT compressed by backward grouping method, selectivity also needs estimating reversely. It is inevitable that backward grouping may delete fewer paths to compress SMT, but it has advantages in estimating complex queries with wildcard "//" and "*".

6 SMT-Based Selectivity Estimation for Complex Graph Query

In this section, we give formal identification of our approach and demonstrate accuracy enhancement in selectivity estimation by real case.

Theorem 1 in section 3 defines a universal method to calculate the frequency of edge (u, v). For a given simple path query P = ($//t_1/t_2/\ldots/t_n$), the selectivity of it can be computed by the following formula based on SMT with path length up to m:

$$\mathbf{Freq}(/t_1/t_2/\ldots/t_n) = \mathbf{Freq}(/t_1/t_2/\ldots/t_m) \times \prod_{i=1}^{n-m} \frac{\mathrm{Freq}(/t_{1+i}/t_{2+i}/\ldots/t_{m+i})}{\mathrm{Freq}(/t_{1+i}/t_{2+i}/\ldots/t_{m+i-1})} \quad (2)$$

Equation (2) can be inferred from *Theorem 1* extending from length 1 to m. Essentially, only with exact correlation information supplied, accurate estimations can be performed. SMT is a step-by-step optimized graph statistics collection for selectivity estimation, which has the ability in nature to offer the precision on the statistical information needed in estimations. Given a complex twig path query having two sub paths, $P=/t_1/t_2/\ldots/t_n[t_{n+1}/t_{n+2}/\ldots/t_{n+m}]/t_{n+m+1}/t_{n+m+2}/\ldots/t_{n+m+k}$, here we assume $P1=/t_1/t_2/\ldots/t_n$ with length n, $P2=/t_{n+1}/t_{n+2}/\ldots/t_{n+m}$ with length m and $P3=/t_{n+m+1}/t_{n+m+2}/\ldots/t_{n+m+k}$ with length k. According to the statistical model for twig query selectivity estimation in [11], we can use following equation to compute the selectivity of P:

$$\mathbf{Freq\ (P1[P2]/P3) = [r(P1) \times r(P2|P1) \times r(P3|P1)] \times Freq(t_{n+m+k})} \quad (3)$$

in which r(P1) denotes occurrence probability of P1, also posterior beliefs with r(P2|P1) and r(P3|P1). Because of the path independence assumption in [11], we have r(P2|P1) $\approx$ r(P2), r(P3|P1) $\approx$ r(P3).

As a detail example, the complex path query is P=/Tsinghua/Ss/S[DR/IR/D]/CR/IR/C. From original graph data in Figure 2, we find that 5 is the accurate count for the node C which corresponds to the query pattern described above. The selectivity for P can be decomposed into following parts according to equation (3).

$$\mathrm{r(Tsinghua/Ss/S)} = \frac{\mathrm{Freq(Tsinghua/Ss)}}{\mathrm{Freq(Tsinghua)}} \times \frac{\mathrm{Freq(Ss/S)}}{\mathrm{Freq(Ss)}}$$

$$\mathrm{r(S/CR/IR/C)} = \frac{\mathrm{Freq(S/CR)}}{\mathrm{Freq(S)}} \times \frac{\mathrm{Freq(CR/IR)}}{\mathrm{Freq(CR)}} \times \frac{\mathrm{Freq(IR/C)}}{\mathrm{Freq(IR)}}$$

$$\mathrm{r(S/DR/IR/D)} = \frac{\mathrm{Freq(S/DR)}}{\mathrm{Freq(S)}} \times \frac{\mathrm{Freq(DR/IR)}}{\mathrm{Freq(DR)}} \times \frac{\mathrm{Freq(IR/D)}}{\mathrm{Freq(IR)}}$$

which derivate from the formulas in [11].

If without SMT approach, we look up original Markov Table in Figure 4 to estimate the selectivity of P.

r(Tsinghua/Ss/S)=$\frac{1}{1}\times\frac{4}{1}$=4; r(S/CR/IR/C)=$\frac{10}{4}\times\frac{10}{10}\times\frac{5\times(19/20)}{19}$=0.625; r(S/DR/IR/D)=$\frac{4}{4}\times\frac{9}{9}\times\frac{2\times(19/20)}{19}$=0.10. Freq(C) = 5. Thus, Freq(P1[P2]/P3) = [4×0.625×0.10)]×5=1.25 with relative error rate $\mu_1=\frac{5-1.25}{5}=0.75$. With the help of SMT, we look up SMT in Figure 9(e). As the split of IR, the sub path CR/IR, DR/IR, IR/C, IR/D are converted to CR/IR2, DR/IR1, IR2/C, IR1/D respectively. Therefore,

r(Tsinghua/Ss/S)=$\frac{1}{1}\times\frac{4}{1}$=4; r(S/CR/IR/C)=$\frac{10}{4}\times\frac{10}{10}\times\frac{5\times(10/11)}{10}$=1.136

r(S/DR/IR/D)=$\frac{4}{4}\times\frac{9}{9}\times\frac{2\times(9/10)}{9}$=0.20.

So, Freq(P1[P2]/P3) = [4 × 1.136 × 0.20)] × 5=4.55 with relative error rate $\mu_2=\frac{5-4.55}{5}=0.09$. Satisfyingly, the relative error rate is reduced from 0.75 to 0.09, totally 88 percentages decrease.

7 Performance Evaluation

In this section, we report our experiments that validate the efficiency and flexibility of SMT. The experiments mainly focus on three parts: efficiency of SMT by comparing with CST[5], the benefits of flexible combination about Optimization Rules, and different compressing methods on SMT .

Experiment Data and Query Set. We use three kinds of standard XML testing datasets in our experiments: Shakespeare[12], XMark[13] and DBLP[9]. Table.1 records the major features of these three datasets with the terms of element number, document size, S(0) Size and SMT Size. The SMT Size here is generated with 4 Optimization Rules applied once for each S(0).

We choose 1000 complex path queries for each dataset. These queries are obtained by off-line scanning of the graph statistics collection generated by our GenS() function in SMTBuilder.

Evaluation Criterion AER and Experiment Results. We use AER, Average Error Rate, as our evaluation criterion which has strong ability to apperceive the effects brought by different methods, queries, memory sizes, and graph data. CST[5] both do well in trading off the accuracy and memory space, in which Correlated Suffix Trees are used to depict graph summarization. The range for memory size is from 0 to 50 KB in our experiments.

Table 1. Features of three datasets

	Shakespeare	XMark	DBLP
Element number	65,006	67,514	89,170
Document Size (MB)	19.3	36.0	42.0
S(0) Size (KB)	6.5	5.4	15.2
SMT Size (KB)	18.2	48.5	32.6

Experiment 1: Comparison between SMT and CST.

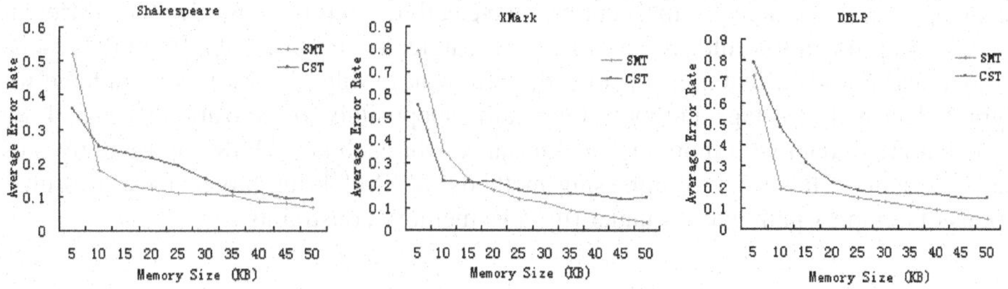

Fig. 6. AER on three datasets

In Figure 6, with the change in memory space constraints, the results of comparisons between SMT and CST show the advantages of SMT in AER. Optimization Rules 1 to 4 are repeatedly applied until reaching the memory size constraint.

Experiment 2: AER with different Rule Sets.

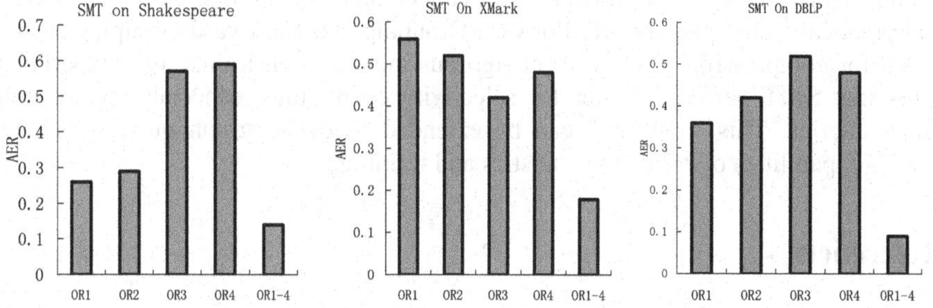

Fig. 7. AER with different ORs

Figure 7 shows results by different choosing and combination strategies of optimization rules named ORs.

Experiment 3: Experiments on different compressing methods.

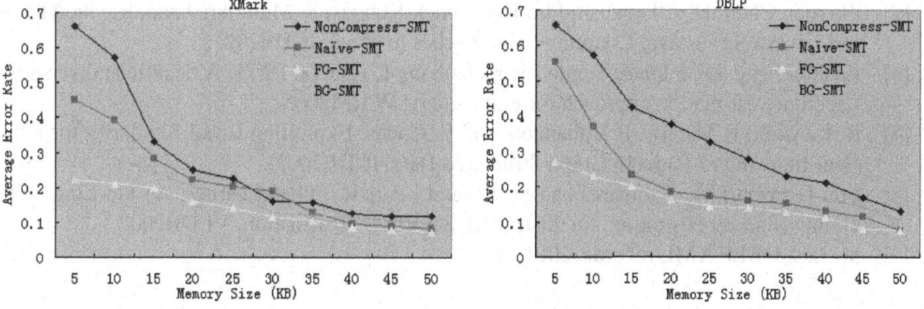

Fig. 8. AER of different compressing methods on SMT

There are three sub conclusions we can draw from three-step experiments. First, with the comparisons between SMT and CST on three standard datasets, we believe that SMT has advantages in accuracy of selectivity estimations. Second, different usage of optimization rules fits for different features of real-life data. From the results above and real data features considered, optimization rules 1, 2 are more suitable for graph data with less tags and more long paths. Oppositely, optimization rules 3, 4 are good at graph data with more tags and instances for each tag. Third, Figure 8 gives us evidences to believe our compressing methods on SMT bring advantages in estimations of complex path queries under rigorous memory constraints.

8 Conclusion

In this paper we presented SMT, a precise and adaptive approach for selectivity estimation of complex graph query. Our approach has been validated to be precise and scalable for estimating the selectivities of complex graph queries. With the trading off between memory space constraints and accuracy, we exploit the important features of local forward/backward inclusions and propose 4 Optimization Rules for SMT construction. SMTBuilder, as a core algorithm for SMT generation, is fulfilled with dynamic characteristics on optimization rules choosing and combination. Three affective and practical techniques: Naïve, Forward Grouping and Backward Grouping are proposed for compressing SMT to meet rigorous memory constraints. Our experiments show that SMT performs better for selectivity estimations, especially for complex graph queries. This work also can be extended to cyclic graph queries based on SMT's capabilities of collecting statistics and refining.

References

[1] A. Aboulnaga, A. R. Alameldeen, and J. F. Naughton. Estimating the selectivity of XML path expressions for internet scale applications. VLDB2001.

[2] T. Bray, J. Paoli, C.M. Sperberg-McQueen, and E. Maler. Extensible Markup Language (XML) 1.0 (Second Edition). W3C Recommendation , October 2000.

[3] D. Chamberlin, J. Clark, D. Florescu, J. Robie, J. Simeon, and M. Stefanescu. XQuery 1.0: An XML query language. W3C Working Draft, June 7, 2001.

[4] Q. Chen, A. Lim, and K. W. Ong. D(k)-index: An adaptive structural summary for graph-structured data. SIGMOD2003.

[5] Zhiyuan Chen, H.V. Jagadish, Flip Korn, Nick Koudas, S. Muthukrishnan, Raymond Ng, and Divesh Srivastava. Counting twig matches in a tree. ICDE2001.

[6] Jianhua Feng, Qian Qian, Yuguo Liao, Guoliang Li, Na Ta. DMT: A flexible and versatile selectivity estimation approach for graph query. WAIM2005.

[7] R. Kaushik, P. Shenoy, P. Bohannon, and E. Gudes. Exploiting Local Similarity for Efficient Indexing of Paths in Graph Structured Data. ICDE2002.

[8] Lim L., Wang M., Padmanabhan S., Vitter J., Parr R.: XPathLearner: An On-Ling Self-Tuning Markov Histogram for XML Path Selectivity Estimation. VLDB2002.

[9] M. Ley. DBLP XML records, 2001.

[10] T. Milo and D. Suciu. Index structures for Path Expressions. ICDT1999.
[11] N. Polyzotis, M. Garofalakis, Statistical Synopses for Graph-Structured XML Databases, SIGMOD2002.
[12] Shakespeare dataset. http://www.cs.kuleuven.ac.be/~ml/ie/
[13] XMARK: The XML-benchmark project. http://monetdb.cwi.nl/ xml, 2002

Tight Bounds on the Estimation Distance Using Wavelet

Bing Liu, Zhihui Wang, Jingtao Li, Wei Wang, and Baile Shi

Department of Computing and Information Technology,
Fudan University, Shanghai, China
{031021057, 041021056, lijt, weiwang1, bshi}@fudan.edu.cn

Abstract. Time series similarity search is of growing importance in many applications. Wavelet transforms are used as a dimensionality reduction technique to permit efficient similarity search over high-dimensional time series data. This paper proposes the tight upper and lower bounds on the estimation distance using wavelet transform, and we show that the traditional distance estimation is only part of our lower bound. According to the lower bound, we can exclude more dissimilar time series than traditional method. And according to the upper bound, we can directly judge whether two time series are similar, and further reduce the number of time series to process in original time domain. The experiments have shown that using the upper and lower tight bounds can significantly improve filter efficiency and reduce running time than traditional method.

1 Introduction

The quantity of data stored in computers is growing rapidly. Many of these data, particularly collected automatically by sensing or monitoring applications, are time series data. Thus time series data are of growing importance in many new database applications, such as data warehouse and data mining etc. A time series is a real-valued sequence, which represents the status of a single variable over time. Typical examples include stock prices and currency exchange rates, biomedical measurements, weather data, etc … collected over time. Therefore, it is hardly surprising that much of research has recently been devoted to the efficient management of time series data. Analysis of time series data is rooted in the ability to find similar time series [1, 2]. Similarity is defined in terms of a distance metric, most often Euclidean distance. For different applications, there are also other distance metrics to define the similarity of time series, such that Lp-norms and DTW may also be used. Because of the high dimensionality of most time series, the direct indexing and searching of time series is prohibitive. As a result, dimensionality reduction appears to be the most promising method for overcoming this problem.

Wavelet Transform (WT) or Discrete Wavelet Transform (DWT) [3] has been found to be effective in many applications in signal processing, speech, computer graphics and image processing [4, 5]. Recent Studies have also demonstrated the applicability of wavelets in database fields, such as similarity search in time series

J.X. Yu, M. Kitsuregawa, and H.V. Leong (Eds.): WAIM 2006, LNCS 4016, pp. 460–471, 2006.
© Springer-Verlag Berlin Heidelberg 2006

[6~10], approximate query processing over massive relational tables [11~13], and clustering in very large databases [14], etc.

For wavelet transform applied to time series, paper [6] first proposes to use Haar wavelet transform for time series similarity search and show that DWT outperforms Discrete Fourier Transform (DFT) in query performance. Paper [7] gives another type of wavelet transform to show the superiority of wavelet in time series similarity search. In paper [8], they present a detail performance study using different wavelets on the similarity search for time series data. In this paper, based on previous researches as shown in papers [6~8] and other related works [9~10], we give the tight upper and lower bounds on the estimation distance using wavelet transform. The experiments have shown that we can further reduce the number of original time series to process and improve filter efficiency.

The rest of the paper is organized as follows. Section 2 gives distance function definitions and wavelet transform related to this paper. In section 3, we discuss the upper and lower tight bounds on the estimation distance using wavelet transform and give a new range query algorithm based on the tight bounds. Our experimental results are reported and discussed to show its superiority to traditional methods in section 4. Finally, section 5 contains conclusions and the direction of future work.

2 Related Concepts

Before into the details of our proposed method, we first give the similarity models usually used in time series similarity search. The first definition is the Euclidean distance between two time series X and Y.

Definition 1. Given a threshold ε, two time series $X(x_0 \ldots x_{n-1})$ and $Y(y_0 \ldots y_{n-1})$ are said to be Euclidean distance similar if

$$D(X,Y) = (\sum_{i=0}^{n-1} (y_i - x_i)^2)^{1/2} \le \varepsilon$$

A shortcoming of definition 1 demonstrated in figure 1 is that it does not consider the effect of vertical offset to similarity. From human interpretation, X and Y may be quite similar if Y can be shifted down vertically to obtain X or vice versa. However, they will be considered not similar by definition 1 because errors are accumulated at each pair of x_i and y_i. Therefore, another similarity model is given by definition 2.

Definition 2. Given a threshold ε, two time series $X(x_0 \ldots x_{n-1})$ and $Y(y_0 \ldots y_{n-1})$ are said to be v-shift similar if

$$D(X,Y) = (\sum_{i=0}^{n-1} ((y_i - x_i) - (y_A - x_A))^2)^{1/2} \le \varepsilon$$

where $x_A = \frac{1}{n}\sum_{i=0}^{n-1} x_i \quad y_A = \frac{1}{n}\sum_{i=0}^{n-1} y_i$

According to definition 2, any two time series are said to be v-shift similar if the Euclidean distance is less than or equal to a threshold ε neglecting their vertical offsets. This definition can give a better estimation of the similarity between two time series with similar trends running at two completely different levels.

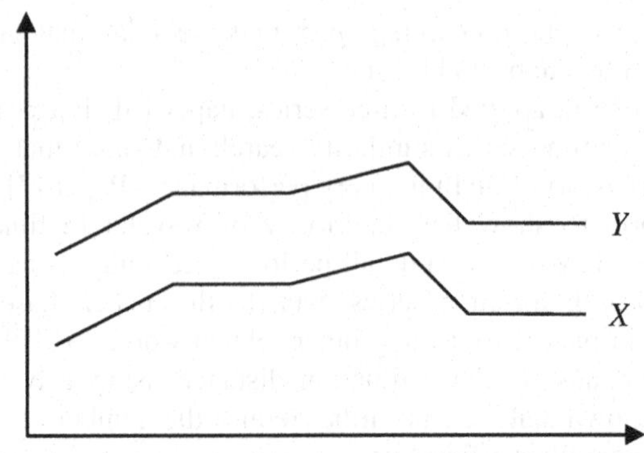

Fig. 1. Example of vertical shifts of time series

Because Haar wavelet transform allows good approximation with a subset of coefficients and it can be computed quickly and easily, it has been used as a research tool in many database fields, including time series similarity search.

Haar wavelet transform can be seen as a series of averaging and differencing operations on a discrete time function. We first give the normalized Haar wavelet definition as following and the detail description can be found in [4].

$$\Psi_i^j(x) = 2^{j/2}\Psi(2^j x - i),\ i = 0,\ldots,2^j\text{-}1$$

where

$$\Psi(x) = \begin{cases} 1 & \text{for } 0 \le x < 1/2 \\ -1 & \text{for } 1/2 \le x < 1 \\ 0 & \text{otherwise} \end{cases}$$

An example to find the normalized Haar wavelet transform of a time series $f(x)$ = (5, 3, 8, 6) is shown in table 1. The wavelet transform discussed in this paper all refers to normalized Haar wavelet transform.

Table 1. The wavelet transform of time series (5, 3, 8, 6)

Resolution	Averages	Coefficients
4	(5,3,8,6)	
2	$((5+3)/\sqrt{2}, (8+6)/\sqrt{2})$	$((5-3)/\sqrt{2}, (8-6)/\sqrt{2})$
1	$((5+3+8+6)/(\sqrt{2}\times\sqrt{2}))$	$((5+3-8-6)/(\sqrt{2}\times\sqrt{2}))$

Resolution 4 in table 1 is the full resolution of the time series $f(x)$ representing the time series itself. In resolution 2, $((5+3)/\sqrt{2}$, $(8+6)/\sqrt{2})$ is the sums of (5, 3) and (8, 6) divided by $\sqrt{2}$ respectively. $((5-3)/\sqrt{2}$, $(8-6)/\sqrt{2})$ is the differences of (5, 3) and (8, 6) divided by $\sqrt{2}$ respectively. This process is recursively continued until resolution 1 is reached. The wavelet transform $H(f(x))$ = ((5+3+8+6)/($\sqrt{2}\times\sqrt{2}$), (5+3-8-6)/($\sqrt{2}\times\sqrt{2}$), (5-3)/ $\sqrt{2}$, (8-6) / $\sqrt{2}$) = (11,-3, $\sqrt{2}$, $\sqrt{2}$) is obtained.

3 Tight Bound Estimation Using Wavelet

Generally speaking, the superiority of using wavelet transform is that it allows good approximation with a subset of coefficients. We can use these coefficients as synopses to the original time series. Because the basis function of normalized Haar wavelet transform is orthonormal, there is the following lemma [4]:

Lemma 1. $R(r_0 \ldots r_{n-1})$ is the wavelet transform of time series $X(x_0 \ldots x_{n-1})$, there is $\|X\|^2=\|R\|^2$, which means:

$$\sum_{i=0}^{n-1} x_i^2 = \sum_{i=0}^{n-1} r_i^2$$

According to lemma 1, we can deduce lemma 2:

Lemma 2. R and S are the wavelet transform of time series X and Y, there is:

$$\|X-Y\|^2=\|R-S\|^2$$

Proof: Because R and S are the wavelet transform of X and Y, there are $R=AX$, $S=AY$ (A is the wavelet transform basis function satisfying orthonormality). We have $R-S=AX-AY=A(X-Y)$, which means $R-S$ is the corresponding wavelet transform of $X-Y$. According to lemma 1, there is $\|X-Y\|^2=\|R-S\|^2$. □

Above two lemmas show that Haar wavelet transform can keep the original time series' energy unchanged, which means that the Euclidean distance between two time series data is also preserved after wavelet transform.

For the general similarity search methods based on wavelet transform for time series database, they first transform the time series using wavelet, and then keep the first k wavelet coefficients as synopses, and search in wavelet domain. If the two wavelet synopses' distance is less than a predefined threshold ε, the methods use original time series to remove all false alarms. Otherwise, it is known that they are not similar. The algorithms use wavelet as a filter and no false dismissal will occur, which is guaranteed by lemma 1 and lemma 2. Therefore the aim of using wavelet is to reduce the number of time series to process in original time domain.

In order to present this paper's main contribution, we first give another lemma.

Lemma 3. There are two time series $P(p_0,\ldots,p_{n-1})$, $Q(q_0,\ldots,q_{n-1})$, the distance between them satisfying the following inequality:

$$(P_T - Q_T)^2 \le \|P-Q\|^2 \le (P_T+Q_T)^2$$

$$\text{where } P_T^{\,2} = \sum_{i=0}^{n-1} p_i^2 \,,\; Q_T^{\,2} = \sum_{i=0}^{n-1} q_i^2 \quad (P_T \ge 0 \quad Q_T \ge 0)$$

This lemma is easy to understand. P, Q and P-Q can be seen as three edges of a triangle. Therefore lemma 3 is the statement of triangle inequality and reverse triangle inequality.

Depending on analysis to the wavelets transform and above lemmas, we present the following theorem:

Theorem 1. $R(r_0 \ldots r_{n-1})$ and $S(s_0 \ldots s_{n-1})$ are the wavelet transform of time series X and Y, there is:

$$\sum_{i=0}^{k-1}(r_i - s_i)^2 + (R_T - S_T)^2 \le \|X-Y\|^2 \le \sum_{i=0}^{k-1}(r_i - s_i)^2 + (R_T + S_T)^2$$

$$\text{where } R_T^2 = \sum_{i=k}^{n-1} r_i^2 \quad S_T^2 = \sum_{i=k}^{n-1} s_i^2 \quad (R_T \ge 0 \quad S_T \ge 0)$$

Proof: According to lemma 2, because $\|X-Y\|^2 = \|R-S\|^2$, the inequality can be written as $\sum_{i=0}^{k-1}(r_i - s_i)^2 + (R_T - S_T)^2 \le \|R-S\|^2 \le \sum_{i=0}^{k-1}(r_i - s_i)^2 + (R_T + S_T)^2$. Since $\|R-S\|^2 = \sum_{i=0}^{n-1}(r_i - s_i)^2$, we only need to prove $(R_T - S_T)^2 \le \sum_{i=k}^{n-1}(r_i - s_i)^2 \le (R_T + S_T)^2$, and according to lemma 3, this holds true. Therefore we complete the proof of theorem 1. □

```
RangeQuery()
Input: query time series Y(y0...yn-1), query radius ε
{
   Compute wavelet sequence S(s0...sn-1) from Y, and compute
 the corresponding ST;
   for(p=1 to m) /*m is the number of time series in da-
tabase*/
   {
    /*If the query radius is less than the lower bound in
theorem 1, Xp and Y are not similar; finish this loop and
continue next loop */
   (1)  if (ε ≤ Σ_{i=0}^{k-1}(r_{p,i} − s_i)^2 + (R_Tp - ST )^2 )
            { print("Xp is not similar to Y"); continue; }
   /*If the query radius is greater than the upper bound
in theorem 1, Xp and Y are similar; finish this loop and
continue next loop */
   (2)  if (Σ_{i=0}^{k-1}(r_{p,i} − s_i)^2 + (R_Tp+ST) ^2≤ε)
            { print( "Xp is similar to Y"); continue; }
   (3)  Compute the actual distance between Xp and Y to
judge whether their distance is less than ε;
   }
}
```

Fig. 2. The range query algorithm for time series database

Theorem 1 gives lower and upper bounds on the distance between two time series using wavelet. Based on theorem 1, we can give a range query algorithm using it. Suppose there is a database including time series $X_1(x_{1,0}\ldots x_{1,n-1})\ldots X_m(x_{m,0}\ldots x_{m,n-1})$, and the number of time series in database is m. The corresponding wavelet sequences are $R_1(r_{1,0}\ldots r_{1,n-1})\ldots R_m(r_{m,0}\ldots r_{m,n-1})$. For the given preserved number of wavelet coefficients k, we can compute $R_{T1}\ldots R_{Tm}$, where $R_{Tp}{}^2 = \sum_{i=k}^{n-1} r_{p,i}^2$ ($1 \le p \le m$, $R_{Tp} \ge 0$). Figure 2 shows the pseudo code for range query based on upper and lower bounds in theorem 1.

In order to compare the difference between our new algorithm and traditional algorithm, we give a description about traditional method using wavelet in figure 3.

```
TraditionalRangeQuery()
Input: query time series Y(y0...yn-1), query radius ε
{
    Compute wavelet sequence S(s0...sn-1) from Y;
    for(p=1 to m)
    {
        if (ε ≤ Σ_{i=0}^{k-1} (r_{p,i} - s_i)^2 )
        { print("Xp is not similar to Y"); continue; }
        Compute the actual distance between Xp and Y to
judge whether their distance is less than ε;
    }
}
```

Fig. 3. The traditional range query algorithm

Now we give further explanations about above algorithms. Because the original time series is usually very long, and sometimes the length is greater than a few hundreds, it is not efficient to compute the distance directly in time domain. Wavelet transform is used as a dimensionality reduction method, and only a few dimensions are remained as data synopses. The algorithms first compute in the wavelet domain using synopses. Compared to original time domain, the cost of computing in wavelet domain is relative low. The aim of using wavelet is to reduce the computation amount in original time domain to improve query efficiency, namely avoiding the execution of step (3) in figure 2. And this is usually used as the criterion to judge algorithm's efficiency. As shown in figure 3, the traditional method only uses $\varepsilon \le \sum_{i=0}^{k-1}(r_{p,i}-s_i)^2$ as the filter criterion in wavelet domain. Our algorithm's step (1) $\varepsilon \le \sum_{i=0}^{k-1}(r_{p,i}-s_i)^2 + (R_{Tp} - S_T)^2$ can filter out more dissimilar time series compared to traditional methods for the given ε. And the traditional method does not have the filter criterion of step (2) in figure 2, which can directly judge whether two time series are similar. We can see that $\varepsilon \leq \sum_{i=0}^{k-1}(r_{p,i}-s_i)^2$ for traditional method is contained in the lower bound of our algorithm. Our algorithm proposes stricter upper and lower distance bounds between two time series in wavelet domain. According to the lower bound, we can exclude more unmatched time series than traditional method. And according to the upper bound, we can directly judge whether two time series are similar, then further reduce the number of original time series to compare in time domain. Therefore compared to traditional methods, our method can significantly reduce the number of original time series to process in time domain and improve query efficiency.

We give an example to illustrate our new algorithm's superiority to traditional method. There are 3 time series in database: $X_1(1+1/\sqrt{2}, 1-1/\sqrt{2}, 0, 0)$, $X_2(1, 1, \sqrt{2}, -\sqrt{2})$, $X_3(1+1/\sqrt{2}, 1-1/\sqrt{2}, 1/\sqrt{2}, -1/\sqrt{2})$. The corresponding wavelet sequences are R_1 (1,1,1,0), R_2 (1,1,0,2), R_3 (1,1,1,1). If k=2, there are R_{T1}= 1□R_{T2}=2□$R_{T3}=\sqrt{2}$. For a query time series Y(1,1,0,0) and query radius 3, the corresponding wavelet sequence is S (1,1,0,0) and there is S_T =0. According to our range query algorithm in figure 2, step (1) can directly judge that X_2 is not similar to Y, and step (2) can directly judge that X_1 and X_3 are similar to Y. Now we need not to compute the actual distance in the original time domain, which means that step (3) needs not to execute one time. But for traditional method in figure 3, it can not judge which time series is similar or dissimilar to the query time series in wavelet domain. Now it has to compute the actual distances in the original time domain three times.

4 Experiments

In this section, we perform an extensive evaluation using the method given in this paper. The experiments use two types of data. The first type is computer generated random walk time series: $p_i = p_{i-1} + x_i$. And another type is real-world data: stock data from Dow Jones Industrials [15]. We use sliding windows to cut the long sequences and every time series' length is 128. The number of time series generated for each type is 100K. We use the same method to create query time series. All experimental results given in this section are the average of 10 trials.

After transforming time series from time domain to wavelet domain, we keep the first three wavelet coefficients as synopses. We will compare the filter efficiency and running time of our new algorithm and traditional algorithm. From section 3, we know that the aim of using wavelet is to reduce the number of original time series to process, namely try to avoid the execution of step (3) of the range query algorithm in figure 2. In order to compare our new method and traditional method, we define filter efficiency as:

$$\text{filter efficiency} = \frac{\text{the number of time series filtered in wavelet domain}}{\text{the number of time series in database}}$$

For the above formula, the number of time series filtered in wavelet domain also refers to those that can be determined whether they are similar or dissimilar to query time series directly in wavelet domain. The example in section 3 shows that traditional method can not judge which time series in database is similar or dissimilar to query time series only using wavelet synopses, so its filter efficiency is 0. But our new algorithm can directly determine the similarity between time series in database and query time series only using wavelet synopses, so the filter efficiency is 100%. Also, the running time is related to the filter efficiency for similarity search. If the filter efficiency is relative high, the number of time series needed to process in original time domain is less, therefore the query time is reduced.

Figure 4 and 5 give the filter efficiency and running time comparison between traditional algorithm and our new algorithm given in section 3. They use computer generated random walk data and Euclidean distance. Figure 4 shows the filter efficiency comparison as the query radius increases. This figure illustrate that our new algorithm is always better than traditional algorithm in filter efficiency for any query radius. And with the query radius increasing, the filter efficiency of new algorithm is further better than that of traditional algorithm. Figure 5 shows the running time comparison. Although the running time of new algorithm is a little longer than that of traditional method when query radius is relative short, as query radius increases new algorithm's running time is better than that of traditional method at most situations.

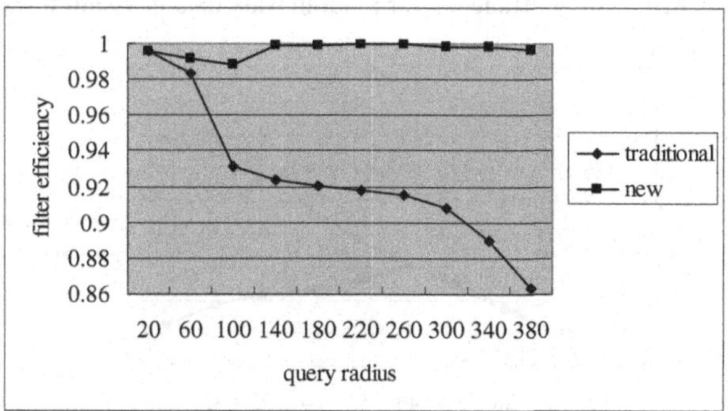

Fig. 4. The filter efficiency for random walk data in Euclidean distance

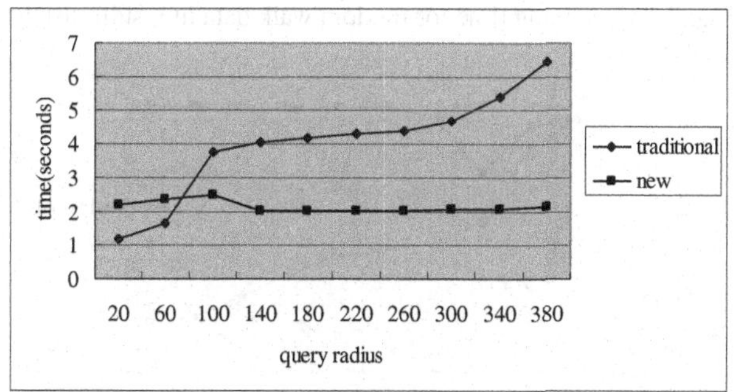

Fig. 5. The running time for random walk data in Euclidean distance

Figure 6 and 7 give the comparisons of filter efficiency and running time using computer generated random walk data and v-shift distance defined in section 2.

Figure 6 gives the filter efficiency comparison for traditional algorithm and new algorithm as the query radius increases. It also shows that new algorithm is better than traditional algorithm. The running time comparison in figure 7 further confirms this conclusion.

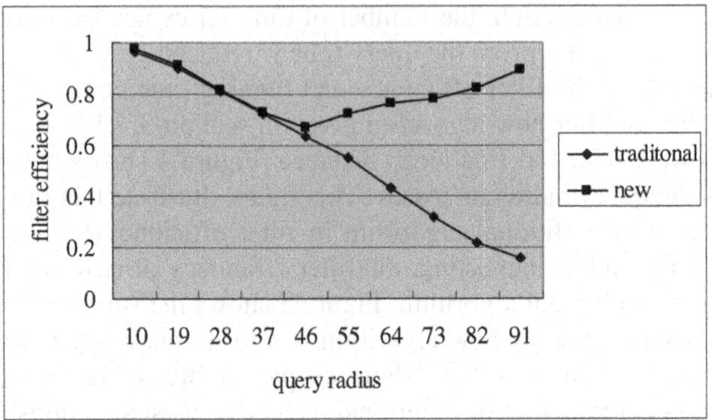

Fig. 6. The filter efficiency for random walk data in v-shift distance

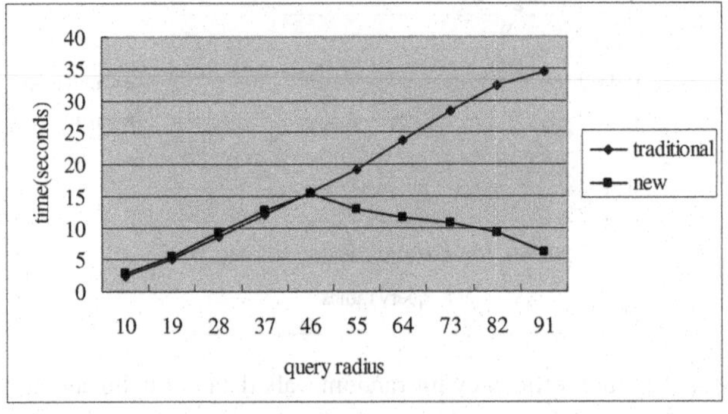

Fig. 7. The running time for random walk data in v-shift distance

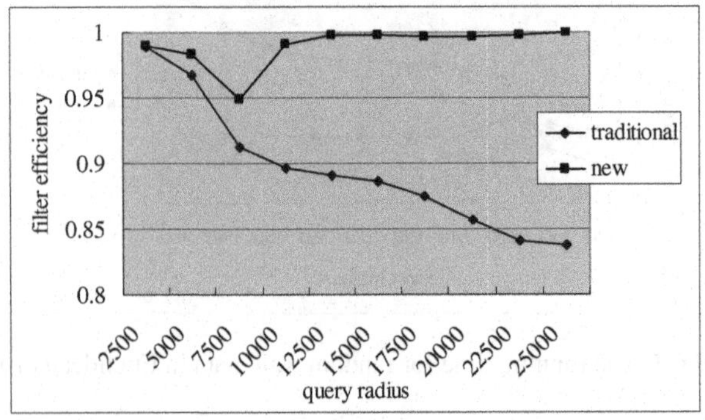

Fig. 8. The filter efficiency for Dow Jones Industrials data in Euclidean distance

Figure 8 and 9 give the comparisons of filter efficiency and running time using Dow Jones Industrials data and Euclidean distance. Also they show that the filter efficiency and running time of new algorithm are gradually better than that of traditional algorithm.

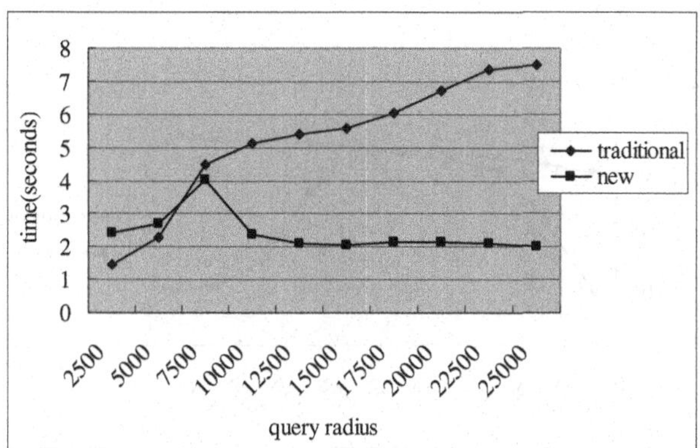

Fig. 9. The running time for Dow Jones Industrials data in Euclidean distance

Figure 10 and 11 give the comparisons of filter efficiency and running time using Dow Jones Industrials data and v-shift distance. Similar to above observations, the filter efficiency and running time of new algorithm are better than that of traditional algorithm.

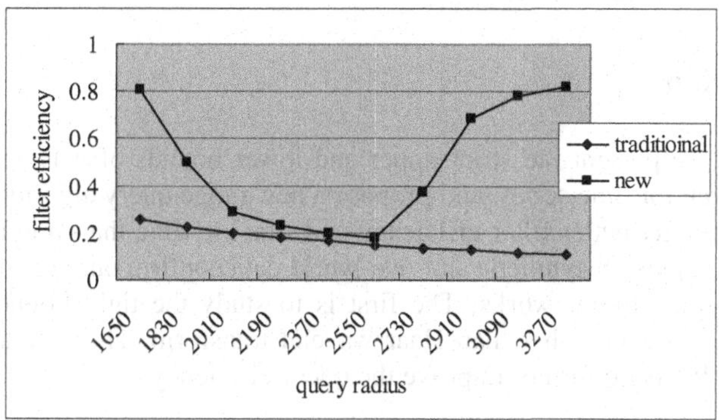

Fig. 10. The filter efficiency for Dow Jones Industrials data in v-shift distance

Observed from above figures, the filter efficiency of traditional algorithm gradually reduces when the query radius increases. This is because that the traditional algorithm only uses lower bound as filter criterion. When the query radius ε increases, the filter effect of $\varepsilon \leq \sum_{i=0}^{k-1}(r_i - s_i)^2$ reduces. For the new algorithm given in this paper, when the query radius increases, the filter efficiency first reduces, and then increases, which is especially obvious in figure 10. This is because that the new algorithm uses upper and lower bounds as filter criterion. When the query radius increases, the filter effect of lower bound reduces similar to traditional algorithm, but the power of upper bound is gradually strengthened. Since the running time is approximately proportional to the filter efficiency, the comparisons for running time have the similar trend as the filter efficiency.

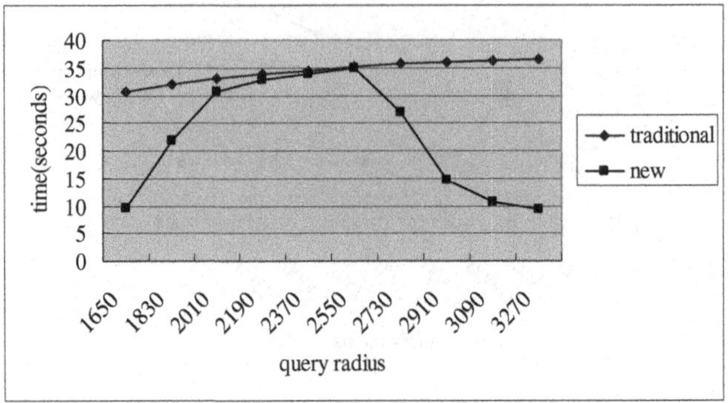

Fig. 11. The running time for Dow Jones Industrials data in v-shift distance

In a summary, for different data sets, distance functions and query radiuses, the filter efficiency and running time of new algorithm is better than that of traditional algorithm at most situations. And sometimes the filter efficiency and running time of new algorithm significantly outperform traditional method.

5 Conclusion

In this paper, we present the strict upper and lower bounds of wavelet transform in similarity search for time series, and propose a new range query algorithm based on it. Using it we can get better filter efficiency and running time than traditional method. Experimental results on synthetic and real-world data confirm our conclusion.

There are some future works. The first is to study the tight bound for different wavelet basis functions other than Haar wavelet transform. The second is to use indexes such as R-tree to further improve the query efficiency.

Acknowledgement. We thank Prof. Jian Pei (Simon Fraser University, Canada) and Haixun Wang (IBM T. J. Watson Research Center) for discussing some issues about this paper.

References

[1] C. Faloutsos, M. Ranganathan, Y. Manolopoulos. Fast subsequence matching in time-series databases. In Proc. of SIGMOD 1994

[2] R. Agrawal, C.Faloutsos, A.Swami. Efficient similarity search in sequence databases. In Proc. Of the 4th FODO, 1993

[3] C. Siney Burrus, R. A. Gopinath, H. Guo. Introduction to Wavelets and Wavelet Transforms, A Primer. Prentice Hall, 1997

[4] Eric J. Stollnitz, Tony D. Derose, David H. Salesin. Wavelets for Computer Graphics. Morgan Kaufmann, 1996

[5] Han Hua, Wang Xueling, Peng Silong. Image Restoration Based on Wavelet-Domain Local Gaussian Model. Journal of Software, 2004,15 (3):443-450

[6] Kinpong Chan, Ada Waichee Fu. Efficient time series matching by wavelets In Proc of ICDE 1999

[7] Zhang Haiqin, Cai Qingsheng. Time Series Similar Pattern Matching Based on Wavelet Transform. Chinese Journal of Computers, 2003,26(3) :372-377

[8] Ivan Popivanov, Renee J. Miller. Similarity search over time series data using wavelets. In Proc of ICDE 2002

[9] Zhao Hui, Hou Jianrong, Shi Baile. Research on Similarity of Stochastic Non-Stationary Time Series Based on Wavelet-Fractal. Journal of Software, 2004,15 (5):633-640

[10] Zheng Cheng, Ouyang Weiming, Cai Qingsheng, An Efficient dimensionality reduction technique for times series data sets. Mini-Macro System, 2002,23(11):1380-1383

[11] J.S Vitter, M. Wang. Approximate computation of multidimensional aggregates of sparse data using wavelets. In Proc of SIGMOD 1999

[12] Kaushik Chakrabarti, Minos Garofalakis, Rajeev Rastogi, Kyuseok Shim. Approximate Query Processing Using Wavelets. The VLDB Journal, 2001,10(3):199-223

[13] A. Deligiannakis, N. Roussopoulos. Extended wavelets for multiple measures. In Proc of SIGMOD 2003

[14] G. Sheikholeslami. S., Chatterjee., A, Zhang. Wavecluster: a wavelet based clustering approach for spatial data in very large databases. VLDB Journal, 2000: 289-304

[15] http://finance.yahoo.com/

Load Shedding for Window Joins over Streams

Donghong Han, Chuan Xiao, Rui Zhou, Guoren Wang,
Huan Huo, and Xiaoyun Hui

Northeastern University, Shenyang 110004, China
wanggr@mail.neu.edu.cn

Abstract. We present a novel load shedding technique over sliding window joins. We first construct a dual window architectural model including join-windows and aux-windows. With the statistics built on aux-windows, an effective load shedding strategy is developed to produce maximum subset join outputs. For the streams with high arrival rates, we propose an approach incorporating front-shedding and rear-shedding, and then address the problem of how to cooperate these two shedding processes through a series of calculations. Based on extensive experimentation with synthetic data and real life data, we show that our load shedding strategy delivers superb join output performance, and dominates the existing strategies.

1 Introduction

Data stream applications such as network monitoring, on-line transaction flow analysis, intrusion detection and sensor networks pose tremendous challenges to traditional database systems. Unbounded continuous input streams require specific processing techniques different from fixed-size stored data sets.

As for "join", a traditional important operator, it is not practical to compare every tuple in one infinite stream with every tuple in another, thus, *sliding window join* is put forward [1]. It restricts the set of the most recent tuples that participate in the join within a bounded-size window, and produces acceptable approximate join outputs. There are mainly two types of windows: time-based window and tuple-based window [3]. As for time-based window, the number of tuples in window is not fixed. The higher the stream arrival rate is, the more tuples the window memory holds. For tuple-based window, the number of tuples in window is fixed. The higher the arrival rate is, the newer the window tuples are. In our paper, we primarily focus on tuple-based window, and time-based window is reserved for future work.

Note that even with a window predication, join operator may lack of CPU or memory resources when streams have high arrival rates. Therefore, we need load shedding (drop some tuples to reduce system load) to facilitate the join processing, so as to keep pace with the incoming streams. There are two types of join approximation [5]: max-subset results and sampled results. We take max-subset approximation as the evaluation criterion for shedding strategies.

For time-based window joins, we have two kinds of resource limitations, CPU deficiency and memory shortage [4]. For tuple-based joins, the two limitations

J.X. Yu, M. Kitsuregawa, and H.V. Leong (Eds.): WAIM 2006, LNCS 4016, pp. 472–483, 2006.
© Springer-Verlag Berlin Heidelberg 2006

can attribute to CPU deficiency exclusively, because the buffer memory that holds tuples will not overflow if CPU is fast enough. Considering the evaluating process of joins, since probes(checking the opposite window for matching tuples) take up most of the CPU resources, we develop a novel shedding strategy by letting part of the tuples enter window without performing probes. We "drop" the tuples in this way rather than discard them directly, for the sake that future tuples from the other stream may produce join results with these ones. Furthermore, we implement a semantic selection of the shedding tuples based on statistics of aux-windows(Section 2), which shows good performance on producing max-subset outputs and is denoted as rear-shedding stategy(Section 3). If stream arrival rates are high, a large percent of tuples will be dropped. CPU resources are primarily spent on the operation of entering/leaving windows. Considering an extreme case, stream speeds are so high that no probes can be performed, then no join outputs will be obtained. Paradoxically, if we discard part of tuples beforehand, some CPU resource will be saved to perform probes, with a subset of join outputs gained. We name the shedding strategy here front-shedding, and address the problem of how to cooperate these two shedding processes through a series of calculations(Section 4). Experiment results are shown in Section 5. Related literatures are fully summarized in Section 6.

2 Dual Window Model

Our goal is to process a sliding window equi-join between two streams A and B producing maximum subset of join outputs with load shedding if necessary.

We adopt the join process similar to those presented in [1,5]. Assume the two streams are Stream A and Stream B. On each arrival of a new tuple from Stream A, three tasks must be performed:

1. Scan Stream B's window, looking for matching tuples, and propagate them to the result. This task is called probing.
2. Insert the new tuple into Stream A's window.
3. Invalidate the oldest tuple in Stream A's window.

From the above, we conclude that there are two kinds of tasks for CPU to perform: **probe** (1) and **updates** (2,3). As for tuple-based window, for one tuple, updates (replacing the oldest tuple in the join window with a new coming one) can be performed more efficiently than probe. In cases of high stream speeds, CPU is unable to perform the whole join process (both probe and updates) for every arriving tuple, therefore we need to shed load by letting part of the tuples enter window without performing probes, yet the other tuples perform probes as normal. Notice that we do not discard the tuples that do not perform probes, for future tuples from the other stream may produce join results with these tuples. Consequently, CPU can keep pace with the streams whose speeds are faster than CPU's processing ability. Figure 1 shows our model on window joins. We divide the memory into three parts. For each stream, we have :

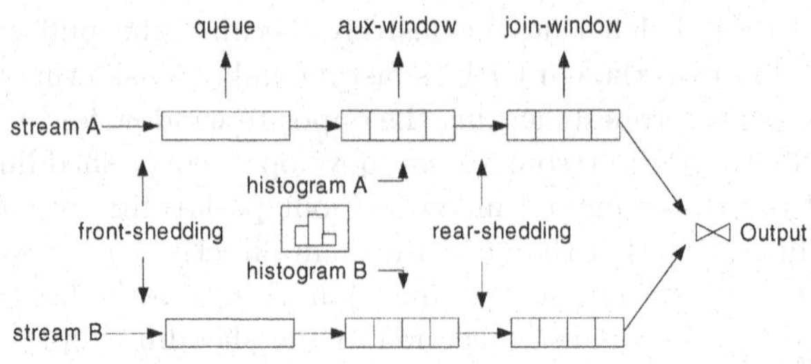

Fig. 1. Dual Window Model

1. **join-window**, the join window holding the tuples with which a new arriving tuple from the opposite stream will perform join.
2. **aux-window**, auxiliary window, which is the same size as the join-window. We also construct a window-histogram based on the aux-window, and with the help of its statistics we can implement effective load shedding by dropping those tuples producing fewer join results.
3. **queue**, serves as a buffer. We can detect stream speeds by monitoring the queue size of each stream.

When the queue length reaches the threshold when buffer is about to overflow, and the stream speeds are still faster than CPU processing rate, we start load shedding by keeping part of the tuples from performing probes. Hence CPU can process more tuples per time interval, though some join results are left out. We denote this load shedding process as rear-shedding, whose evaluation is executed when a tuple leaves aux-window, and preparing to enter join-window. If the incoming stream speeds further increase, exceeding another threshold (interpreted in sections below), we start front-shedding to cooperate with rear-shedding to produce max-subset join results.

3 Rear-Shedding

For convenience, in Table 1, we introduce notations for the constants and variables used in this paper. These notations are also used in the following sections. W, D are set up according to specific application, while V_j and V_w are determined by CPU processing ability and can be tested from experiments.

3.1 Determining k_r

We do not need load shedding if CPU can perform the joins of every tuple. In order to keep the queue from overflow, we need to maintain an approximately constant queue length. Based on this prerequisite, we have the following deduction:

The time for one tuple to enter queue is $\frac{1}{V_q}$, and the time for one tuple to leave aux-window and to join is $\frac{1}{V_w} + \frac{1}{V_j}$. Since the window size is fixed, the time for one tuple to leave aux-window is equal to that for one tuple to enter aux-window, which is equal to the time for one tuple to leave queue. For a constant

Table 1. Constants and Variables

Name	Description
V_s	speed of stream
V_q	speed of tuples entering queue
V_j	maximum number of tuple probes per time interval without considering the cost of entering and leaving windows
V_w	maximum number of tuples entering/leaving window per time interval without considering the cost of probes
k_r	rear-shedding rate
k_f	front-shedding rate
W	window size
D	domain of the join attribute

queue length, the time for one tuple to enter queue and the time for one tuple to leave queue are equal, thus we have:

$$\frac{1}{V_q} = \frac{1}{V_w} + \frac{1}{V_j}$$

Likewise, we can get the following equation when performing load shedding:

$$\frac{1}{V_q} = \frac{1}{V_w} + \frac{1 - k_r}{V_j}$$

Then k_r is determined as:

$$k_r = 1 - V_j\left(\frac{1}{V_q} - \frac{1}{V_w}\right) \tag{1}$$

Furthermore, for a constant queue length, we obtain $V_q = V_s$. V_s can be detected by the system, thus we can find a shedding rate k_r to let CPU coordinate with the incoming streams. The faster the streams are, the higher k_r is adopted.

3.2 Determining Which Tuple to Shed

Suppose we perform joins on tuple's attribute *Attr*, and take integer as data type for simplicity. For each stream, we build a **window-histogram** based on its aux-window by mapping the values of *Attr* into an array of counters. The array size is D. Figure 2 gives an example. There are two 1s, four 2s, one 3, zero 4, and one 5 in aux-windowB. Window-histogram is maintained dynamically, and when a new tuple enters aux-window or when an old one leaves, updates will be carried out by means of increasing or decreasing the corresponding counter of the tuple's attribute value.

Assume the two streams have the same speed(Processing of different speed ratio is omitted due to space limitation. Readers can refer to our technical report [14].), for such speed ratio 1:1, we let the aux-windows and join-windows of the two streams have the same size. CPU alternatively takes out a tuple from one of the aux-windows and performs joins with the opposite join-window.

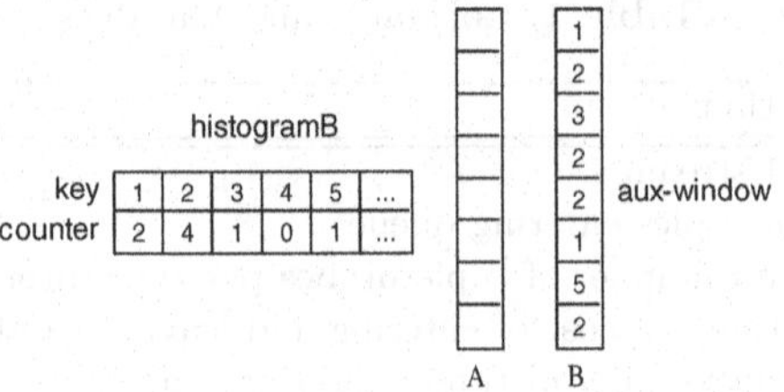

Fig. 2. Window-histogram

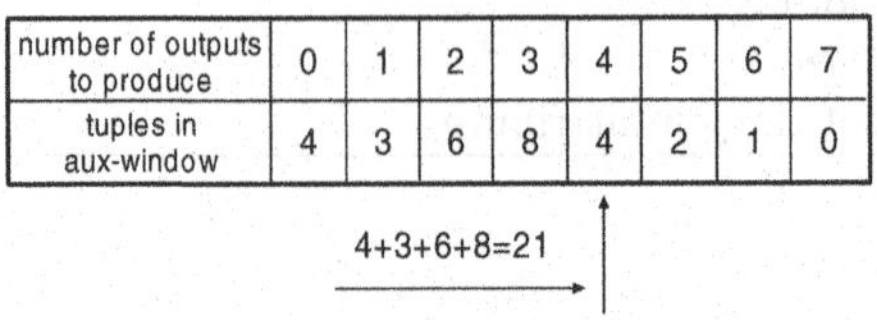

number of outputs to produce	0	1	2	3	4	5	6	7
tuples in aux-window	4	3	6	8	4	2	1	0

Fig. 3. Calculating n with Frequency Array

Now we introduce the strategy to determine which tuple should be shed. Take Stream A for example. When a tuple g is about to enter aux-windowA, we check its join attribute value in the window-histogram of the opposite window (window-histogramB), find how many join outputs it will produce, and save this number N. Accordingly, we construct an array C for all the tuples in aux-windowA, recording the number of join outputs that each tuple will produce. Moreover, a frequency array is built on the array C, counting how many tuples in aux-windowA will produce a specific number($C[i]$) of join outputs. Therefore, when g leaves aux-windowA, it is able to count how many tuples in aux-windowA will produce less join outputs than N, denoted as n. Figure 3 provides an example: the tuple being judged will produce 4 join outputs, we need to count how many tuples in its aux-window will produce less than 4 join outputs. There are 4 tuples will produce 0 join outputs, 3 will produce 1, 6 will produce 2, and 8 will produce 3, there are 4+3+6+8=21 (n=21) tuples in all to produce less than 4 outputs. From Algorithm 1, we know that for a tuple g leaving aux-windowA, if the aux-windowA has $k_r W$ or more tuples that will produce join outputs fewer than N, g will not be shed.

Algorithm 1. SheddingAlgorithm()

Function: Judge whether a tuple should be shed or not

```
if n/W < k_r then
    update(enter its own join-window without probing the opposite join-window);
else
    probe; update;
end if
```

Considering a case that many tuples in aux-windowA have the same number of join outputs. For example, suppose window size is 100, and of the 100 tuples in aux-windowA, 20 tuples will produce 0 join result, 50 tuples will produce 1 join result, and 30 tuples will produce 2 join results. Now we have the shedding rate k_r=0.6, thus we should shed all 20 resultless tuples and also 40 tuples from 50 which will produce 1 join result. The 40 tuples will be chosen randomly. The algorithm is easy and omitted here.

4 Front-Shedding

Suppose stream speeds are extremely high, e.g. $V_s > V_w$. We have to shed all the tuples (k_r=1), and CPU resources are all spent on performing updates, with no join results produced. Nevertheless, the speed of tuples entering queue is still higher than the speed of tuples leaving queue. The queue length will increase with no limit, and the system will become unstable. However, if we discard part of the incoming tuples before pushing them into the queue, letting $V_q < V_w$, some CPU resources will be saved to perform probes, and some join results will be obtained. We introduce front-shedding, controlling $V_q < V_w$. Figure 4 shows an approximate join outputs curve without front-shedding. When $V_s <= V_j * V_w/(V_j + V_w)$ (we can get it from equation 1), system needs no load shedding (k_r=0), and output results will increase in proportion to the stream speeds. As the stream speeds become higher, shedding rate increases correspondingly. When the stream speeds reach V_w, the shedding rate k_r is 1, and the output results are 0. Since the stream speeds and the shedding rate k_r are continuous, there exists a maximum number of join outputs at a certain speed, V_{opt}. (opt means optimal.) Next, we will calculate V_{opt}.

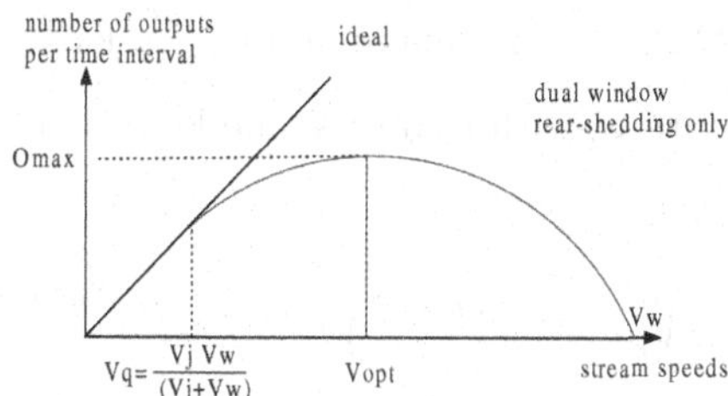

Fig. 4. Rear-shedding Outputs

Suppose the two incoming stream have the same distribution. Take uniform distribution as an example. Other types of distribution, such as Zipfian can be deduced similarly. For a tuple g with attribute value a, the probability it appears is $1/D$, where D is the value domain of the attribute. The probability that in the opposite window, there are exactly i tuples with the same attribute value a as tuple g is:

$$P_i = \binom{W}{i} (\frac{1}{D})^i (1 - \frac{1}{D})^{W-i}$$

Suppose we will shed all the tuples producing outputs fewer than $M(M \in [0, W])$, and part of the tuples producing M outputs, denote the ratio as r, i.e. among the tuples that will produce M outputs, the number of tuples to be shed divided by all such tuples. Thus the shedding rate k_r is determined as:

$$k_r = \sum_{i=0}^{M-1} P_i + r \cdot P_M (0 \leq r \leq 1)$$

And tuples joined per time interval is: $V_q(1 - k_r)$. The average number of join outputs each tuple can produce is:

$$O_{tuple} = (1 - r) \cdot M \frac{P_M}{1 - k_r} + \sum_{i=M+1}^{W} i \cdot \frac{P_i}{1 - k_r}$$

Thus the total number of outputs per time interval is:

$$O = V_q(1 - k_r) \cdot O_{tuple} = V_q[M(\sum_{i=0}^{M} P_i - k_r) + \sum_{i=M+1}^{W} i \cdot P_i]$$

Our goal is to achieve the max-subset of join output results, letting O reach the maximum O_{max}. As is known in equation (1), k_r is a function of V_q. Substitute k_r with V_q, we obtain:

$$\begin{cases} O = V_q[M(\sum_{i=0}^{M} P_i + \frac{V_j}{V_q} - \frac{V_j}{V_w} - 1) + \sum_{i=M+1}^{W} i \cdot P_i] \\ \sum_{i=0}^{M-1} P_i \leq k_r = 1 - V_j(\frac{1}{V_q} - \frac{1}{V_w}) \leq \sum_{i=0}^{M} P_i \end{cases} \quad (2)$$

Let $V_q = V_{opt}$, when O reaches its maximum O_{max}. let $\lambda = V_j/V_w$, then $V_q = V_j/(\lambda+1-k_r)$. Substitute V_q with k_r and λ; and let $\alpha = M \sum_{i=0}^{M} P_i + \sum_{i=M+1}^{W} i \cdot P_i$, $\beta = \lambda + 1$, we can get:

$$O = V_j \cdot \frac{\alpha - M k_r}{\beta - k_r} = V_j \cdot (M + \frac{\alpha - \beta M}{\beta - k_r}) \quad (3)$$

In equation (3), for a definite M, α, β, V_j are all constant. Hence O changes monotonically with k_r. As a result, there is no such k_r:

$$\sum_{i=0}^{M-1} P_i < k_r < \sum_{i=0}^{M} P_i$$

that produces O_{max}. O_{max} is obtained only at endpoints, i.e. the ratio $r = 0$. The following equation can be deduced:

$$k_r = \sum_{i=0}^{M-1} P_i \ \ or \ \ k_r = \sum_{i=0}^{M} P_i$$

Equation (2) can be reduced to:

$$\begin{cases} O = V_q \sum_{i=M+1}^{W} i \cdot P_i \\ \sum_{i=0}^{M} P_i = k_r = 1 - V_j(\frac{1}{V_q} - \frac{1}{V_w}) \end{cases}$$

M is in $[0,W]$. For a given window size and distribution, W and P_i are fixed; only M is variable. Therefore O_{max} can be easily found through a search of M among W+1 values. V_{opt} and k_r can be then determined by M. Furthermore we can use a binary search to reduce the searching cost remarkably, for the function O has the shape like "Λ", which means it first increases, and then decreases. The proof is omitted due to page limitation.

Based on the discussions above, we summarize the applying of front-shedding and rear-shedding strategies as follows:

- If $V_s <= V_{opt}$, only rear-shedding will be adopted.
- If $V_s > V_{opt}$, rear-shedding and front-shedding will cooperate. Control V_q by front-shedding, letting $V_q = V_{opt}$.

Front-shedding rate k_f is determined as $k_f = 1 - \frac{V_{opt}}{V_s}$. Semantic information is ignored in front-shedding, because the long queue may impair its efficacy in prediction over joins. Therefore, we choose a subset of the streams in a random way, namely a simple but efficient way.

5 Experiments

To assess the practical performance of our model, we perform several sets of experiments on both synthetic and real life datasets. We compare the performance of our strategies (referred to as DUAL) with another two load shedding strategies. One is dropping tuples randomly from the join input buffers (referred to as RAND); the other is a heuristic strategy [4] (referred to as PROB). Additionally, we use an optimal offline strategy [4] (referred to as OPT) to better evaluate the results. All the experiments are performed on P4 3.2G, 512M, Windows XP. The experiments indicate that our dual-window model histogram-based load shedding strategy works surprisingly well in practice.

5.1 Experiments on Front-Shedding

Our first set of experiments is focused on studying the function of front-shedding. We compare two strategies, both front-shedding and rear shedding (referred to as DUAL), and rear-shedding only (referred to as REAR). We use window size 400, domain size 50, and input data generated from Zipfian distribution with skew parameter 1. From the tested speed of join probes and that of the tuples entering/leaving window, we obtain that $V_{opt} = 117.396$ by calculation, which accords with our experiment results. V_{opt} is determined similarly in subsections

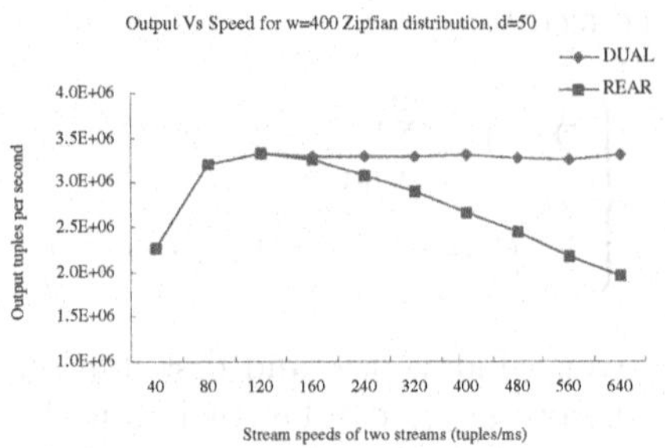

Fig. 5. Front-shedding and Rear-shedding

5.2 and 5.3, with respect to fixed data distributions and predefined window sizes. Figure 5 shows the comparison between the two strategies.

When stream speeds are lower than V_{opt}, front-shedding has not been started, thus two strategies have the same results. As the stream speeds increase, we can easily see the difference: the result from DUAL keeps approximately a constant number, because front-shedding controls the tuples entering queue at a constant speed, and rear-shedding drops tuples at a constant shedding rate.

5.2 Effect of Window Size

Figures 6 and 7 show the number of join outputs for window sizes of 400 and 800 respectively. In this set of experiments, we use input data generated from Zipfian distribution with skew parameter 1, domain size 50. Four load shedding strategies are to be compared: OPT, RAND, PROB, and DUAL.

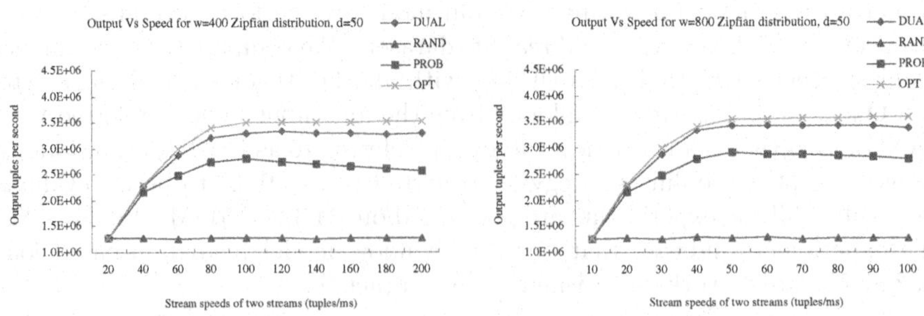

Fig. 6. Window Size (W=400)

Fig. 7. Window Size (W=800)

As shown in the figures, DUAL works much better than PROB and RAND, especially when stream speeds are high. The performance of the different strategies do not change much as the window size is varied. Increased window size only produces more join outputs at one stream speed, for a tuple needs to probe more tuples in the opposite window; but not impacts the performance of the load shedding strategies.

5.3 Effect of Distribution

Figure 8 shows the performance of the different load shedding strategies for a window size of 400 when both the incoming streams have a uniform data distribution in a domain size of 50. The experiment results indicate that for less regular input data, shedding by heuristic information is not a good option, while our strategy has a significant advantage over shedding by heuristic information or random selection.

The input data streams consist of tuples with uniformly distributed attribute values have different affects on the performance of different load shedding strategies. Since all the tuples have the same probability of finding a tuple with equal attribute value in the opposite window, heuristic information is trivial in judging which tuple will produce more join results. Therefore PROB will be as poor as RAND, however, DUAL is able to perform as well as on Zipfian distributed input data. Aux-windows are introduced to predict the number of join outputs that each tuple can produce, therefore enable the selection among tuples within a range of window size. Such preferences are accumulated through large streams, and finally lead to the advantage over the other two strategies.

5.4 Real Life Dataset Experiments

We use CO_2 data available at [10] as our real life datasets for experiments. We perform a streaming sliding window join using the air temperature at 38.2 meters in two years - 1995 and 1998 - as two datasets, and we set window size as 1000. After deleting invalid data items and considering the warmup phase [4], 15471 tuples are left for join queries. Such join query results can be potentially used to research the change of ambient CO_2 concentration at the same temperature in the three years. For the calculation of V_{opt}, we perform a sampling of the datasets, and then obtain an approximate distribution of the input data, thus V_{opt} can be determined as described in Section 4. Figure 9 shows the results from different strategies as a percentage of ideal case, namely the results produced by fast enough CPU.

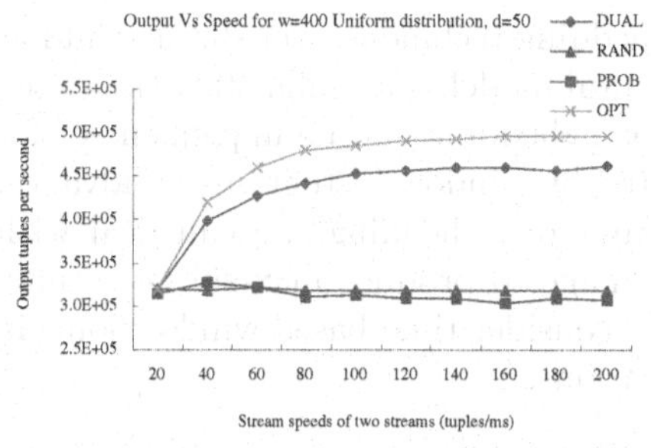

Fig. 8. Uniform Distribution

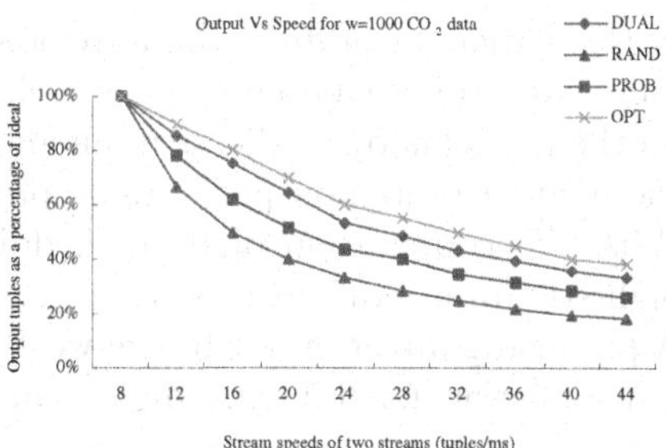

Fig. 9. Real Life Datasets

From the figure, it is observed that our strategy DUAL performs much better than PROB and RAND. The real life datasets are neither as random as uniform distribution data, nor as regular as Zipfian distribution data. Therefore, heuristic information may be used to judge which tuple will produce more join outputs, but the judgment might not be accurate, in other words, the tuples with attribute value that produced more join outputs in the past might not produce more join outputs in the future. At the same time, DUAL performs well because the judgment is within one window instead of among all the tuples, and therefore more accurate than selection by heuristic information.

6 Related Work

There has been considerable work on data stream processing. The survey in [11] gives an overview of stream work, and has summarized the issues of building a data stream management system. Specialized systems have been built to process streaming data, such as Aurora [6], STREAM [2], NiagaraCQ [7] and TelegraphCQ [9].

The papers [1, 4, 5, 12, 13] focus on performing joins over streaming data. [1] introduces an implementation of join process, and addresses the cost models of nested loop joins and hash joins, which adopts the simplest random shedding strategy. [4] provides an architectural model, primarily discusses the offline load-shedding strategies, and introduces some heuristic online strategies. [5] puts forward the concepts of sampled results and age-based model, apart from max-subset results and frequency-based model in [1,4]. Our work consider max-subset results and frequency-based model. We also construct an architectural model, and develop an online shedding strategy according to window statistics. In the literature of multi-joins, [12] analyzes the cost of nested loop joins and hash joins, and proposes join ordering heuristics to minimize the processing cost per unit time. [13] provides a symmetric multi-join operator for multiple joined streams to minimize memory usage as opposed to using multiple binary join operators.

7 Conclusions and Future Work

In this paper, we addressed a novel load shedding technique over sliding window joins. We propose a dual window architectural model, and build statistics based on the aux-windows. Effective semantic load shedding can be implemented, for the number of join outputs can be predicted by window-histograms in advance. With the cooperation of front-shedding and rear-shedding, we can deal with high stream arrival rate scenarios, and manage to produce max-subset results. A promising direction for future work is to consider time-based window joins in order to serve for different kinds of applications.

Acknowledgments. This research was partially supported by the National Natural Science Foundation of China (Grant No. 60273079 and 60573089) and Specialized Research Fund for the Doctoral Program of Higher Education (SRFDP).

References

1. J. Kang, J. F. Naughton, and S. D.Viglas. Evaluating Window Joins over Unbounded Streams. In *Proc. 2003 Intl. Conf. on Data Engineering*, Mar. 2003.
2. The STREAM Group. STREAM: The Stanford Stream Data Manager. *IEEE Data Engineering Bulletin* ,26(1):19-26,March 2003.
3. A. M. Ayad, J. F. Naughton. Static Optimization of Conjunctive Queries with Sliding Windows Over Infinite Streams. In *Proc. ACM SIGMOD Conf.*, June 2004.
4. A. Das, J. Gehrke, and M. Riedewald. Approximate Join Processing Over Data Streams. In *Proc. 2003 ACM SIGMOD Conf.*, June 2003.
5. U. Srivastava, J. Widom. Memory-Limited Execution of Windowed Stream Joins. In *Proc. 30th Int. Conf. on Very Large Data Bases*, 2004.
6. D. Abadi, D. Carney, et al. Aurora: a new model and architecture for data stream management. *VLDB Journal*, Vol.12(2),pp.120-139,2003.
7. J. Chen, D. J. DeWitt, F. Tian, and Y. Wang. NiagaraCQ: A scalable continous query system for internet databasses. In *Proc. ACM SIGMOD Int. Conf. on Management of Data*, pages 379-390, 2000.
8. P. M. Fenwich. A New Data Structure for Cumulative Frequency Tables. *Software - Practice and Experience*, Vol 24, No 3, pp 327-336, Mar 1994.
9. J. M. Hellerstein, M. J. Franklin, S. Chandrasekaran, et al. Adaptive query processing: Technology in evolution. *IEEE data Engineering Bulletin*, 23(2):7-18,2000.
10. D. Baldocchi, K. Wilson, et al. Half-Hourly Measurements of CO2, Water Vapor, and Energy Exchange Using the Eddy Covariance Technique from Walker Branch Watershed, Tennessee, 1995-1998. http://cdiac.esd.ornl.gov/ftp/ameriflux/data/us-sites/walker-branch/
11. B. Babcock, S. Babu, M. Datar, R. Motwani, and J. Widom. Models and issues in data stream systems. In *Proc. Principles of Database Systems (PODS)*, June 2002.
12. L. Golab, M. T. Ozmu. Processing Sliding Window Multi-joins in Continuous Queries over Data Streams. In *Proc. Conf. on Very Large Databases*, Sept. 2003.
13. S. D. Viglas, J. F. Naughton, J. Burger. Maximizing the Output Rate of Multi-Way Join Queries over Streaming Information Sources. In *Proc. Int. Conf. on Very Large Databases (VLDB)*, Sept. 2003.
14. D. Han, R. Zhou, C. Xiao. Load shedding for Window Joins over Data Streams, June 2004, Technical report, Northeastern University. http://mitt.neu.edu.cn/publications/HZX05-Joins.pdf

Error-Adaptive and Time-Aware Maintenance of Frequency Counts over Data Streams*

Hongyan Liu[1], Ying Lu[2], Jiawei Han[2], and Jun He[3]

[1] Tsinghua University, China 100084
hyliu@tsinghua.edu.cn
[2] University of Illinois, Urbana-Champaign, USA 61801
{yinglu, hanj}@uiuc.edu
[3] Renmin University of China, China 100872
hejun@ruc.edu.cn

Abstract. Maintaining frequency counts for items over data stream has a wide range of applications such as web advertisement fraud detection. Study of this problem has attracted great attention from both researchers and practitioners. Many algorithms have been proposed. In this paper, we propose a new method, *error-adaptive* pruning method, to maintain frequency more accurately. We also propose a method called *fractionization* to record time information together with the frequency information. Using these two methods, we design three algorithms for finding frequent items and top-*k* frequent items. Experimental results show these methods are effective in terms of improving the maintenance accuracy.

1 Introduction

With the emergence of data stream applications, data mining for data streams has attracted great attention from both researchers and practitioners. Among the mining tasks for stream data, maintaining frequency counts over data streams is a basic mining problem with a wide range of applications, such as web advertisement fraud detection and network flow identification[1][2]. A number of algorithms have been proposed to tackle this problem [1] [2] [3] [4] [5] [6] [7] [8]. A comprehensive introduction to these algorithms is given in reference [2]. Most of these algorithms are designed to maintain a set of approximate frequency counts satisfying an error requirement within a theoretical memory bound, and they are mostly false-positive oriented. Usually the error bound is given by an end user. To satisfy this error bound, different algorithms use different methods to consume as less memory as possible. Among these algorithms, an algorithm called *space-saving* [2] uses an integrated approach for finding both frequent items and top-*k* frequent items. Both theoretical analysis and experimental results show that this method achieves a better performance in terms of accuracy and memory usage compared to other algorithms, such as

* This work was supported in part by the National Natural Science Foundation of China under Grant No. 70471006 and 70321001, and by the U.S. National Science Foundation NSF IIS-02-09199 and IIS-03-08215.

J.X. Yu, M. Kitsuregawa, and H.V. Leong (Eds.): WAIM 2006, LNCS 4016, pp. 484 – 495, 2006.
© Springer-Verlag Berlin Heidelberg 2006

GroupTest [3], *FREQUENT* [4], *CountSketch* [7] and *Probabilistic-InPlace* [4]. However, after studying these existing algorithms, we have following observations:

- Timestamp information is ignored at processing each data arrival. Stream data are temporally ordered, fast changing, massive, and potentially infinite sequences of data. So time dimension is an important point of view to look at the data. Also, people are usually interested in recent changes of the data streams. However, as far as we know, all of these existing algorithms for approximating the frequency counts do not take this kind of information into account.
- Precision and recall may not be enough to measure the performance of an algorithm. Many algorithms use precision and recall as important measures to judge if an algorithm is good. However, precision and recall depend on minimum support parameter (*minsup* in short) and top-*k* parameter (*k* in short). For high *minsup* or low *k* value in a skewed data stream, they are usually 1. From these two measurements, it is hard for us to know how well an algorithm does for maintaining the frequency counts as a whole. For example, if we use 10000 counters to monitor frequency counts of items over a data stream with length of 100,000 and 10000 distinct items. More than 50% of the frequency counts maintained by *space-saving* are 1, and in the meantime they also have the highest estimation error among all the counts maintained, while the exact answer tells us that only 4% of these counts are 1. But this aspect is not easy to be seen from precision and recall.

In this paper we focus on addressing these two issues described above. We propose three algorithms: *SSTime*, *Adaptive,* and *AdaTime*. Following are some contributions made in this paper:

- We propose to make use of time dimension information when designing the pruning strategy. In order to do that, we propose a method, called *fractionization* , to compress timestamp of each arrival for an item into existing count and error data. We also propose several methods to utilize this information to achieve better pruning result.
- We propose to use the sum of *maintained error* and the error of *estimation error* as well as the sum of *all errors* to measure the quality of mining algorithm. In order to improve the quality of mining results in terms of these measurements, we develop a pruning strategy, called *error-adaptive pruning*, to prune items adaptively so that the error bound can be achieved and in the meantime a low maintained error can also be achieved.
- We develop and implement an algorithm named *Adaptive* to use *error-adaptive pruning* technique to maintain frequency counts over data streams. Comprehensive experimental studies indicate that this algorithm can achieve better performance.
- We design and implement two algorithms, *SSTime and AdaTime,* to extend the existing *space-saving* algorithm and the new algorithm *Adaptive* by taking the time dimension into consideration. Experimental results show that time information is effective in terms of improving the mining quality.

The remainder of the paper is organized as follows. Section 2 describes how to keep and use time dimension, and give the description of algorithm *SSTime*. Section 3 describes the error-adaptive pruning technique, and presents two new algorithms

Adaptive and *AdaTime*. Section 4 gives three measures as a complement to existing measures for performance study and presents experimental results, and section 5 concludes the paper.

2 Keeping and Using Time Information

In this section, we describe our method to consider time information while summarizing the dynamic data stream.

2.1 Problem Definition

Let I be a set of single items, $I = \{e_1, e_2, \ldots, e_n\}$. Given a single item stream D of size N, an item e_i is called *frequent* if its frequency count, f_i, in this stream exceeds a user-specified support $\lceil \varphi N \rceil$, where φ is a user-specified threshold, called minimum support (*minsup*). An item e_j is called a *top-k frequent item* if its frequency count is among the k highest frequencies, where k is specified by user.

For a data stream application, the exact solution of finding all of the frequent items or finding all of the top-k frequent items is usually impractical due to time and space limitation. Therefore, the problem becomes finding an approximate set of frequent items and top-k items. To solve this problem, except for the parameter *minsup* and k, an error rate, ε, is also given by a user. With the relaxation of the original problem, the task of mining frequent items becomes finding all of frequent items whose estimated frequency counts exceeds $\lceil \varphi N \rceil$, where the difference between the estimated counts and their true counts is at most εN. Similarly, the task of finding top-k frequent items becomes finding k items with highest estimated frequency counts, where the difference between the estimated counts and their true counts is also at most εN.

2.2 *Fractionization:* A Method to Keep Time Information

Existing algorithms for mining frequent items in data streams can be categorized into two kinds of techniques: *counter-based* and *sketch-based.* Counter-based method use an individual counter for each item monitored. In this paper we only discuss this method.

Due to the space limitation and the big size of the stream, usually only a subset of all of items can be monitored in the main memory. Suppose we use m counters in memory to keep frequency counts, then at any point of time, only m distinct items are monitoring.

Almost all of the counter-based algorithms use the following method to maintain item's frequency. If the newcome item is currently monitored, its frequency is increased. Otherwise, an item currently monitored is pruned to make room for the new item. Although these existing algorithms are different from each other in terms of pruning method, they all neglect the time information of each item arrival. In real applications, items in data stream are changing as time changes. For example, old frequent items may become infrequent as time goes on. Therefore, a straightforward way to use time information is that whenever pruning is required, among candidates, we choose old one instead of recent one to prune. But how can we judge which one is older than others?

The answer to this question depends on how time information for every arrival of items is recorded. If we have enough space, it is easy to record time information. But in order to achieve high accuracy, we need to use as less memory as possible for each counter. Therefore, how to put time information into existing information that a counter keeps is important.

Suppose for each counter we maintain three pieces of information for an item: *key, guaranteed count,* and *maximum error*, which can be represented as a triple (*item, count, error*), where each element of this triple is usually saved as an integer. Our method to save time information of each item arrival is called *Fractionization* , which means that we first transform the information of each item into a decimal fraction, and then save it as a decimal part of existing triple element such as error. In this case, we use *float* rather than *integer* to represent it. However, even by this way, we still cannot record every occurrence of an item. In order to save space, we sum all of time information of its occurrence, and then save it as a subpart of the error element.

Now the problem becomes how to express the time information of an occurrence of an item. There are many ways to do that. A simple one is that we use the occurrence order to represent the timestamp of each item arrival. For example, the timestamp of the first item in the stream is 1, and second is 2, and so on. In this way, since the length of stream increases continually, the sum of timestamp may become very big. After *fractionization* , it may become very small. To prevent this problem, before *fractionization* , we can do logarithm computation such as natural logarithm. Taking natural logarithm as an example, in order to transform the sum of timestamp into a decimal, we can get the inverse of this number. So the sum of time stamp should be greater than one. As a result, if we use natural logarithm computation, the time stamp of the first item in the stream could be 3.

In sum, we could use the following formula (1) to record the time information of a monitored item (e_i, $count_i$, $error_i$):

$$error_i = error_i + \frac{1}{\ln(\sum_{j=1}^{count_i} timestamp_j)} \tag{1}$$

Besides the linear sum of the timestamp information of an item's each monitored arrival, we can also record the square sum of the timestamp information by a similar way as shown in formula (2). Here, we put the time information in the *item* element, and the timestamp of an item's arrival can use the natural logarithmic value of its occurrence order. For example, the timestamp of the first item in a stream is *ln*(3).

$$e_i = e_i + \frac{1}{\ln(\sum_{j=1}^{count_i} timestamp_j^2)} \tag{2}$$

2.3 Algorithm: *SSTime*

To show the effectiveness of using item's time information, we integrate the time keeping and using method with the *space-saving* algorithm [2]. The algorithm called *SSTime* is outlined in Fig.1.

This algorithm is similar to *space-saving*. There are two differences between them. The first is that *SSTime* records not only the *count* and *error* information of an item, but also its time information. In Fig. 1, we use formula (1) to record the time information (line 6-8 and line 14). We can also use both formulae (1) and (2) to record more information about time. When an item is pruned from the memory, i.e., it is not monitored currently, its time information is lost at the same time (line 13-15). We can also record this information in the item that replaces it. The second difference is that when choosing the pruning item, *SSTime* takes time into consideration. Among all of items with the same (*count* + *error*), where *error* means the integer part of the counter's error element, the "oldest" item is chosen to prune first. To judge which item is old is not an easy job. In this algorithm, we use a straightforward method. The smaller the sum of timestamps of an item is, the older the item is. This method is shown in formula (3). We can also use some complex method, which will be discussed in the next section.

$$e_p = \arg\max_{e_i \in candidate}(error_i - (\text{int})error_i) \quad (3)$$

```
Algorithm: SSTime( m counters, stream D)
1    timestamp=2;
2    For each item, e_i, in D {
3    timestamp++;
4    If e_i is monitored by counter (e_i, count_i, error_i) {
5            count_i= count_i+1;
6    temp=exp(1/(error_i-(int)error_i));
7    temp=temp+timestamp;
8    error_i=(int)error_i+1/ln(temp);
9    }
10   else {
11           candidate={e_j | e_j has the least value of min=(count+(int)error)}
12           Let e_p be the "oldest" item among items in candidate
13           Replace e_p with e_i.
14           error_i= min+1/ln(timestamp);
15           The counter for e_i becomes (e_i, 1, error_i)
16   }
17   }
```

Fig. 1. Algorithm *SSTime*. This algorithm is an extending of the algorithm *space-saving* by incorporating time information of items to it.

With the information maintained by this algorithm, at any point of time, a query could be submitted to output all of the frequent items according to a user-specified *minsup*, or to output k most frequent items when the user gives the value of k. The method to fulfill these two kinds of queries is the same as given in *space-saving*, and we do not give them here due to the space limitation. This is the same for the other two algorithms which will be described in the following sections.

3 Error-Adaptive Pruning Method and Algorithm

3.1 *Error-Adaptive* Pruning Method

As discussed in section 1, using the pruning method proposed in *space-saving*, most of the frequency counts maintained in memory have only one guaranteed frequency count, whereas they have the highest estimated error. In other words, most of them are very untrustworthy, and the estimation error as a whole is high. In order to improve this, we propose a new pruning method, called *error-adaptive*.

The pruning method used in *space-saving* is that whenever an existing monitored item needs to be pruned, one of the items (we call them *candidate items*) with the minimum estimated count, i.e. (*count* + *error*), is selected. The problem of this method is that among these candidate items, some have very high guaranteed counts, and others have only one guaranteed count. Treating them equally during pruning will lead to high estimation error. Therefore, in our new pruning method, we try to treat them differently, and in the meantime, we need to guarantee the error rate and high recall and precision. This method is shown in Definition 2.

Definition 1. *(pruning point N) A time point is called a pruning point if at this time point, a new coming item in data stream cannot find a counter to monitor its frequency count. Let the current length of the stream is N, then this pruning point is called pruning point N.*

Definition 2. *(error-adaptive pruning method) Suppose user-specified error rate is* ε, *at pruning point N. Let* $ecount_i$ *be the estimated count,* $(count_i + error_i)$ *for each monitored item* e_i. *The error-adaptive pruning method selects all of items* e_j *satisfying both of the following conditions as candidate items:*

1) $\text{ecount}_j \leq N/m$ where $m=\lceil 1/\varepsilon \rceil$
2) $count_j = \min(count_i)$ i=1, 2, …, m

At pruning point N, the N*th* item, e_n, of the stream comes, and one of the candidate items is selected. Suppose the counter for the selected item is (e_p, count_p, error_p). Then after pruning, this counter becomes (e_n, 1, $count_p + error_p$) and is used to monitor e_n.

Using error-adaptive pruning method, we have the following lemmas.

Lemma 1. Let N be the current length of a data stream, then at any time point the following equation (4) holds.

$$N = \sum_{\forall i | e_i \text{ is monitored}} (count_i + error_i) \tag{4}$$

Proof. Each item arrival in data stream D only increases one counter's count by 1. This is obviously true when this item is currently monitored. Even when it is not monitored, it will replace one existing item. The counter for the existing item will be used to monitor the new arrival item. This counter's original *count* and *error* will be saved to *error* and its *count* will be set to 1. So the count of old arrival is kept, and the new arrival is also recorded. Hence, at any time point, the summation of any counter's *count* and *error* equals the number of item arrivals currently in data stream.

Lemma 2. At any pruning point N, there is always at least one candidate item that can be found to prune.

Proof. Lemma 1 means at any pruning point there is at least one monitored item satisfying $(count + error) \leq N/m$. The proof is by contradiction. Assume every item monitored has an estimated count $> N/m$, then the sum of the estimated counts of m counters must satisfy: $\text{sum}(count_i + error_i) > N/m*m = N$, which is contradictory to Lemma 1.

Lemma 3. Using error-adaptive pruning method, the frequency count estimation error rate for any item is not greater than ε.

Proof. Items can be classified into two categories: items that are monitored currently, and items that are not monitored currently. For those monitored, if it is monitored before all of the counters are used up and have not been pruned yet, its estimation error is zero, which is obviously less than ε. If it is monitored at the pruning point N by replacing a monitored item, then its error should be less than or equal to $N\varepsilon$ according to definition 2. That is to say, its error rate $(error/N)$ is not greater than ε. For those not monitored, we regard its frequency count zero. Suppose it is last pruned at the pruning point N, then according to definition 2, before its pruning, the sum of its count and error (i.e., $count + error$) must be less than or equal to $N\varepsilon$. Since its estimated count is zero, the maximum error is $(count + error)$, which is not greater than $N\varepsilon$. Therefore, the lemma also holds for this case.

Using this error-adaptive pruning method for mining task given in section 2.1, the output will only include false positive, no false negative. This is already proven in algorithm *space-saving*. In *space-saving*, at every pruning point, the error for the new coming item is overestimated as the minimum estimated count, which is $\min(count + error)$. By our method, the error estimated is no less than $\min(count + error)$, so it is also an overestimation. Therefore, there is only false positive among output frequency count. This is also demonstrated by comprehensive experimental study results.

Based on this error-adaptive pruning method, we propose two algorithms, *Adaptive* and *AdaTime*, for finding frequent items and top-*k* frequent items.

3.2 Algorithm: *Adaptive*

Adative is the algorithm we design for finding frequent items and top-*k* frequent items based on *error-adaptive* pruning method. It is depicted in Fig.2.

In this algorithm we do not consider time information. Based on user-specified error rate ε, we use m (=1/ε) counters to monitor items in stream D. When a new item arrives in the stream, if it is currently monitored, its count is increased by one (lines 5-6). If it is a pruning candidate, we delete it from the candidate set (line 7). If it is not monitored and there is no candidate item in candidate set for pruning, a function, *Getcandidate*(), is called to select candidate items from all of counters based on error-adaptive pruning method described in Definition 2 (lines 13-14). Then, one candidate item is randomly picked to prune and make its counter available to the new item (line 15). If it is not monitored, but the candidate set is not empty, we choose one item from the candidates to prune instead of selecting pruning item from all of the counters again (line 15). By doing this, we could save time without affecting error rate. The items in candidate are selected during a former pruning point, say N. At that point, each of them satisfies $(count + error) \leq N\varepsilon$. Suppose the current pruning point is M, (M > N), then items in candidate satisfy $(count + error) \leq N\varepsilon \leq M\varepsilon$ too. After pruning an existing item, its counter is incremented and used to monitor the new item (lines 16-18).

```
Algorithm: Adaptive(m counters, stream D)
1  n = 0;
2  candidate={};
3  for each item, e_i, in stream D {
4       n = n+1;
5       if e_i is monitored by counter (e_i , count_i, error_i) {
6            count_i = count_i +1;
7            If e_i is in candidate, erase it from candidate
8       }
9       else {
10          if there is a free counter to use
11               New counter (e_i , 1, 0) for e_i;
12          else {
13               if candidate is empty
14                    candidate=GetCandidate(m, n);
15               Let e_p be one of the items in candidate
16                    Replace e_p with e_i
17               error_i=count_p+error_p;
18               The counter for e_i becomes (e_i, 1, error_i)
19          }
20     }
21  }
```

```
Function GetCandidate(m counters,
n current length of stream D)
min=n;
for each item, e_i, monitored currently {
     if (count_i+(int)error_i <= n/m) {
          if (count_i = =min) then
               put e_i in candidate;
          else if count_i <min {
               min = count_i;
               empty candidate;
               put e_i in candidate;
          }
     }
}
return candidate;
```

Fig. 2. This is the main procedure of algorithm *Adaptive*

The function *GetCandidate*(*m*, *n*) is called to find all of the candidate items from *m* counters at pruning point *n*. This is done by traversing from counters with the minimum estimated count, $(count_i + error_i)$. We use the same data structure used in *Space-saving*. All of the counters with the same estimated count are attached to a bucket, and all of the buckets are linked together according to the estimated count value. Therefore, when traversing buckets from the one with the lowest estimated count, once this value is greater than $n\varepsilon$, we could stop further traverse.

3.3 Algorithm: *AdaTime*

To show the effect of the time information to the error-adaptive pruning method, we propose another algorithm, *AdaTime*, which is outlined in Fig. 3.

The major difference between algorithms *Adaptive* and *AdaTime* is shown in lines 7, 15 and 18. In line 7, we record time information together with count and error information in the counter. We can use the same method used in algorithm *SSTime*. Here we introduce another way. Suppose the timestamp for the nth arrival is $ln(n+2)$, then we could put linear sum of each timestamp of this item to *error,* and put the square sum of each timestamp in the *key* of the item. We use the *fractionization* method introduced in section 2 to do that. In line 15, instead of randomly picking one item from the candidate set, we choose the relatively old item to prune. To decide which item is older, we can use the linear sum of the timestamps and square sum of the timestamps to compute a distance between the occurrences of this item and the new coming item. Due to the space limitation, we do not give the further detail of this method. The larger the distance is, the older the item is. Similar to line 7, in line 18, at the pruning point, time information is also recorded.

```
Algorithm: AdaTime(m counters, stream D)
1  n = 0;
2  candidate={};
3      for each item, e_i, in stream D {
4          n = n+1;
5          if e_i is monitored by counter(e_i , count_i, error_i) {
6              count_i = count_i +1;
7              Record timestamp information;
8              If e_i is in candidate, erase it from candidate
9          }
10         else {
11             if counters# < m, create a new counter  for e_i;
13             else {
14                 if candidate is empty, candidate=GetCandidate(m, n);
15                 Let e_p be "oldest" items in candidate
16                 Replace e_p with e_i by counter (e_i, 1, error_i)
17             error_i=count_p+(int) error_p;
18                 Record timestamp information;
19             }
20         }
21     }
```

Fig. 3. Algorithm *AdaTime* is an algorithm using *error-adaptive* pruning method, and it also considers time information when do pruning

4 A Performance Study

4.1 Measures

In order to evaluate performance of an algorithm completely, besides the measures such as recall, precision, space, and time, we propose three other measures to evaluate the effectiveness of various pruning method.

Let $|I|$ be the number of distinct items in a data stream, and m be the number of counters used to maintain frequency counts for these items. The first measure is the *average absolute error of all items*, or *aError* in short. It is defined in formula (5). The second is the *average absolute error of maintained counts*, or *mError* in short, as shown in formula (5).

$$aError = \frac{\sum_{i=1}^{|I|} truecount_i - count_i}{|I|} \qquad mError = \frac{\sum_{ei\ monitored} truecount_i - count_i}{m} \tag{5}$$

The third is *the average absolute error of maintained error*, or *eError* in short, as shown in formula (6).

$$eError = \frac{\sum_{ei\ monitored} error_i - (truecount_i - count_i)}{m} \tag{6}$$

We have implemented the three algorithms proposed in this paper in C language and run them on a Pentium IV 2GHz *IBM Thinkpad* laptop with 1.5G memory running Window 2003 Server system. For algorithm *SSTime* and *AdaTime*, when we implement them, we have tried several different methods to record and use time information. But due to space limitation, we only report the result of the simple method as shown in Fig. 1.

We use synthetic data generated by following a *Zipf*-like distribution [8].

4.2 Varying the Data Skew

In this set of experiments, we change the skew factor of the data stream, and measure the recall, precision, *aError*, *mError*, *eError*, and time. We fix the number of distinct items to be 100,000, the length of stream to be 10,000,000, and the error rate to be 0.0001. We compare the performance of our algorithms with *space-saving* which proves to have better performance than other algorithms in [2], and is implemented to our best knowledge. Since we use the data structure as used in *space-saving*, the space used by our algorithms is similar to *space-saving*. We vary the skew factor from 0.5 to 2, and the results are shown in Fig. 4 and 5.

From Fig. 4 (a) and (b) and Fig. 5 (a) we can see that algorithms *Adaptive* and *AdaTime* produce better error results than *space-saving* and *SSTime*. Furthermore, although it is hard to see from these figures, algorithm *AdaTime* is slightly better than Adaptive, and *SSTime* is slightly better than *AdaTime*.

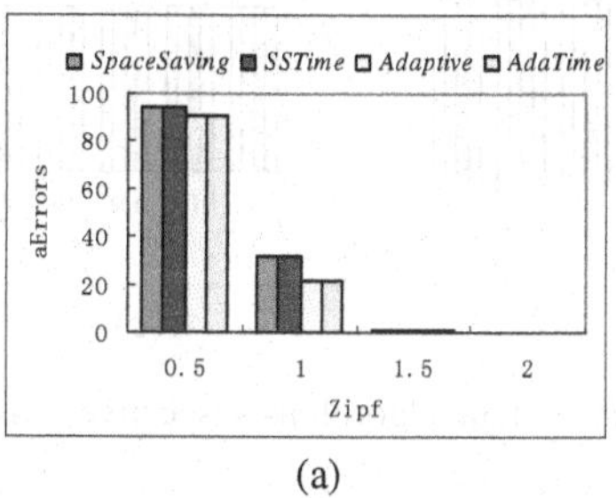

(a)

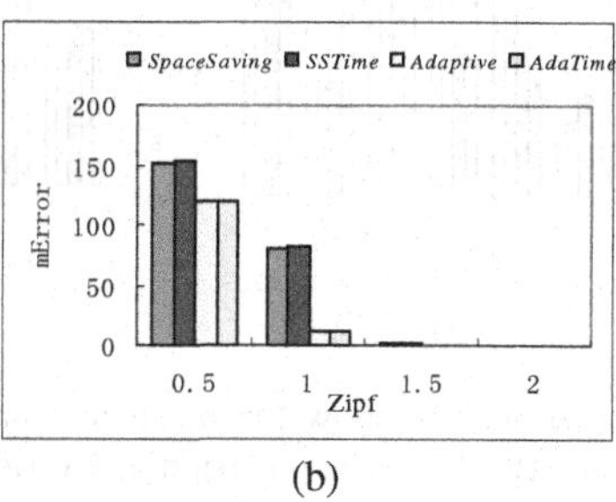

(b)

Fig. 4. These two figures show *aError* and *mError* for several data streams with length 10000000 and 100000 distinct items. Their skew factors are changed from 0.5 to 2.

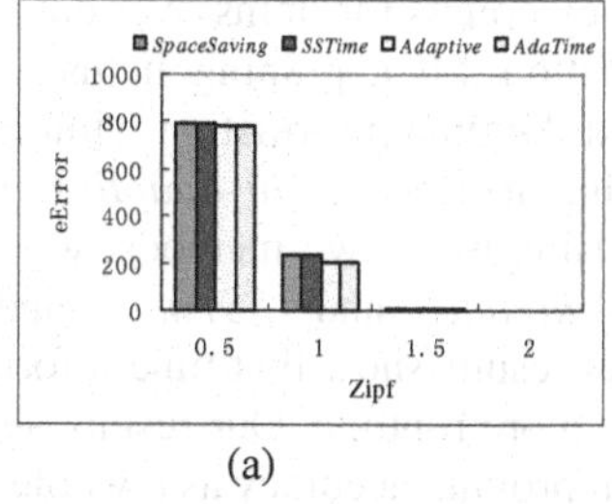

(a)

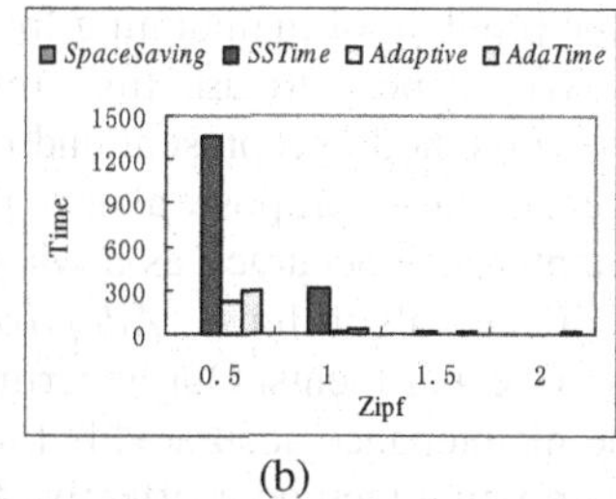

(b)

Fig. 5. These two figures show *eError* and *runtime* when running four algorithms for four data streams with length 10000000 and 100000 distinct items. Their skew factors are different.

Fig. 5 (b) indicates that among these four algorithms, *space-saving* is the fastest, and *SSTime* is slowest, while Adaptive is better than *AdaTime*. Since both recording time information and selecting candidate based on time information take more time, it is not difficult to understand this result. The reason why *SSTime* is much slower than others is that at each pruning point, every item with the min(*count* + *error*) is needed to scan and compare.

4.3 Varying the Query Parameters

In this set of experiments, we fix the number of distinct items to be 100,000, the length of stream to be 10,000,000, the error rate to be 0.0001, and skew factor to be 1. We change two parameters, *minsup* and *k*, to see the recall, precision. Since this data set is one of those used in section 4.2, the other measures for this data set remain the same as given above. The results are depicted in Fig. 6.

One can see from Fig. 6 (a) and (b), for low *minsup*, Adaptive and *AdaTime* have better recall and precision than *space-saving* and *SSTime*, whereas *AdapTime* is better than Adaptive and *SSTime* is a little better than *space-saving*. As the top-*k* query, the results for recall are the same as precision, so we do not put the figure here. Fig. 6(c) shows us that for high *k*, these algorithms have the same behavior shown in (a) and (b).

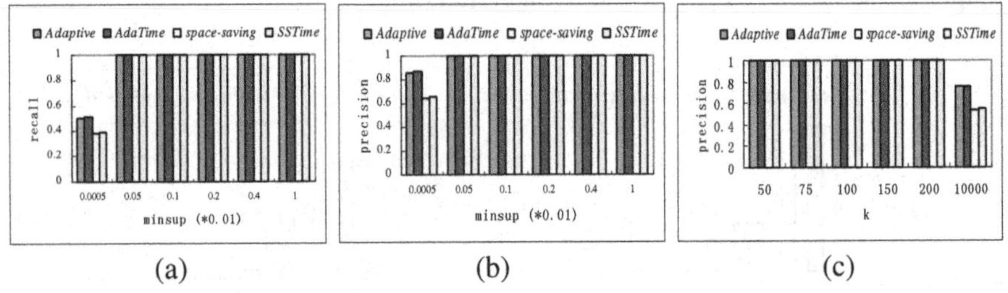

Fig. 6. (a) and (b) show the recall and precision of four algorithms respectively as *minsup* varies, and (c) shows the precision as *k* varies

5 Conclusions

We study the problem of maintaining frequency counts for items over data streams in this paper. We propose to use time information when pruning items, and give a *fractionization* method to represent and record the time information without spending much space. We also propose a new pruning method, *error-adaptive pruning*, to improve maintenance accuracy as a whole. Using these two methods, we design and implement three algorithms, *Adaptive*, *AdaTime,* and *SSTime*, and conduct comprehensive experiments. Our experimental results show that time information can improve the maintenance accuracy, but needs more runtime. Our results also indicate that the new pruning method is effective for improving accuracy as a whole.

References

1. G. S. Manku and R. Motwani. Approximate Frequency Counts over Data Streams. In *Proc. of 28th Intl. Conf. on Very Large Data Bases*, pages 346 – 357, 2002.
2. A. Metwally, D. Agrawal, and A. El Abbadi. Efficient. Computation of Frequent and Top-k Elements in Data Streams. *In Proceedings of the 10th ICDT. International Conference on Database Theory,* pages. 398–412, 2005.
3. G. Cormode and S.Muthukrishnan. What's Hot and What's Not: Tracking Most Frequent Items Dynamically. In *Proc. Of 22nd ACM Symposium on Principles of Database Systems (PODS)*, pages 296 – 306, 2003.
4. E. Demaine, A. Lopez-Ortiz, and J. Munro. Frequency Estimation of Internet Packet Streams with Limited Space. In *Proc. of 10th Annual European Symposium on Algorithms*, 2002.
5. C. Jin, W. Qian, C. Sha, J. Yu, and A. Zhou. Dynamically Maintaining Frequent Items Over a Data Stream. In *Proc. Of CIKM*, 2003.
6. J. Yu, Z. Chong, H. Lu, and A. Zhou. False Positive or False Negative: Mining Frequent Item Sets from High Speed Transactional Data Streams. In *Proc. of 30th VLDB*, pages 204–215, 2004.
7. M. Charikar, K. Chen, and M. Farach-Colton. Finding Frequent Items in Data Streams. In *Proc. of the Int. Colloquium on Automata, Languages and Programming (ICALP)*, pages 693 – 703, 2002.
8. D. E. Knuth. *The Art of Programming*. Addison-Wesley, 1973.

Supporting Efficient Distributed Top-k Monitoring*

Bo Deng, Yan Jia, and Shuqiang Yang

School of Computer Science
National University of Defense Technology
Changsha 410073, China
dengbomail@gmail.com, jiayanjy@vip.sina.com, sqyang9999@126.com

Abstract. This paper addresses the efficient processing of distributed top-*k* monitoring, which is continuously reporting the *k* largest values according to a user-specified ranking function over distributed data streams. To minimize communication requirements, the necessary data transmitting must be selected carefully. We study the optimization problem of which objects are necessary to be transmitted and present a new distributed top-*k* monitoring algorithm to reduce communication cost. In our approach, few objects are transmitted for maintaining the top-k set and communication cost is independent of *k*. We verify the effectiveness of our approach empirically using both real-world and synthetic data sets. We show that our approach reduces overall communication cost by a factor ranging from 2 to over an order of magnitude compared with the previous approach when *k* is no lees than 10.

1 Introduction

The objective of the top-*k* query is to find the "top *k*" results, according to a user-specified ranking function. In many database applications, top-*k* query processing is natural behavior, and the database research communities have studied the issue of efficient processing of top-*k* queries for a long time [9, 11, 12, 13, 17].

Recently, much attention has been focused on online monitoring of aggregate functions over data streams such as call records, sensor readings, web usage logs, network packet traces, etc. [6, 7, 15, 19]. Often, data streams originate from multiple remote sources and many online monitoring tasks, e.g. detecting distributed denial-of-service (DDoS) attacks, only require that attention be focused on atypical behavior in the environment being monitored, while habitual behavior is to be ignored.

Babcock and Olston presented an original algorithm for distributed top-*k* monitoring, which is continually identifying the top *k* data values over distributed data streams [4, 5]. In Babcock&Olston's algorithm, arithmetic constraints are maintained at remote stream sources to ensure that the most recently provided top-*k* answer remains valid to within a user-specified error tolerance. Distributed communication is only necessary on occasion, when constraints are violated. However, Babcock&Olston's algorithm needs transmitting entire top-*k* set and its current partial

* This research is partly supported by the National High Technology Research and Development Plan (863 plan) of China under Grants No.2004AA112020 and No.2003AA111020.

J.X. Yu, M. Kitsuregawa, and H.V. Leong (Eds.): WAIM 2006, LNCS 4016, pp. 496–507, 2006.
© Springer-Verlag Berlin Heidelberg 2006

data values, and a border value to the central processing system when constraints are violated. In this paper, we show that transmitting entire top-*k* set is unnecessary.The first contribution of this paper is studying the optimization problem of which objects are necessary to be transmitted to reduce communication cost of distributed top-*k* monitoring. We show that when constraints are violated, only the objects which break the constraints and two border values need to be transmitted. Our second contribution is a careful implementation of a new distributed top-*k* monitoring algorithm and the communication cost of our new algorithm is independent of *k*. Extensive experiments with real and synthetic data show that, compared to previous technique (Babcock&Olston's algorithm), our approach reduces overall communication cost by a factor ranging from 2 to over an order of magnitude when *k* is no lees than 10. The rest of the paper is organized as follows. Section 2 defines the problem of distributed top-*k* monitoring formally. Section 3 discusses the background and related work. Section 4 introduces our new *Minimal Refresh* algorithm (MR). Section 5 studies of the performance of MR. Finally, Section 6 concludes the paper.

2 Problem Statement

We address the same problem described in [4, 5]. We consider a distributed online monitoring environment with m+1 nodes: a central *coordinator node* N_0, and m remote monitor nodes $N_1, N_2, \ldots, N_m$. Collectively, the monitor nodes monitor a set U of n logical data objects $U = \{O_1, O_2, \ldots, O_n\}$, which have associated numeric (real) values $V_1, V_2, \ldots, V_n$. The values of the logical data objects are not seen by any individual node. Instead, updates to the values arrive incrementally over time as a sequence S of $\langle O_i, N_j, \Delta\rangle$ tuples, which may arrive in arbitrary order. The meaning of the tuple $\langle O_i, N_j, \Delta\rangle$ is that monitor node N_j detects a change of Δ, which may be positive or negative, in the value of object O_i. A tuple $\langle O_i, N_j, \Delta\rangle$ is seen by monitor node N_j but not by any other node N_l, $l \neq j$. For each monitor node N_j, we define *partial data values* $V_{1,j}, V_{2,j}, \ldots, V_{n,j}$ representing N_j 's view of the data stream, where $V_{i,j} = \sum_{\langle O_i, N_j, \Delta\rangle \in S} \Delta$. The overall logical data value of each object O_i, which is not materialized on any node, is defined to be $V_i = \sum_{1 \le j \le m} V_{i,j}$.

The coordinator is responsible for tracking the top k logical data objects within a bounded error tolerance. More precisely, the coordinator node N_0 must maintain and continuously report a set $T \subseteq U$ of logical data objects of size $|T| = k$. T is called the approximate top-k set, and is considered valid if and only if:

$$\forall O_t \in T, \forall O_s \in U - T : V_t + \varepsilon \ge V_s . \quad (1)$$

where $\varepsilon \ge 0$ is a user-specified approximation parameter. If $\varepsilon = 0$, the coordinator must continuously report the exact top-*k* set. For non-zero values of ε, a corresponding degree of error is permitted in the reported top-*k* set.

The goal for *distributed top-k monitoring* is to provide, at the coordinator, an approximate top-*k* set that is valid within ε at all times, while minimizing the overall cost to the monitoring infrastructure. For our purposes, cost is measured as the message size exchanged among nodes.

3 Background and Related Work

Among the ample work on top-*k* query processing, the TA family of algorithms for monotonic score aggregation [12, 13, 17] stands out as an extremely efficient and highly versatile method for centralized data management. Based on TA, many efficiency approaches have been developed for distributed top-*k* query processing [2, 3, 8, 10, 16]. However, these one-time query algorithms are not suitable for online monitoring because they do not include mechanisms for detecting changes to the top-*k* set.

Top-*k* monitoring of a single data stream was studied in [14]. This work only considers single data streams rather than distributed data streams and concentrates on reducing memory requirements rather than communication costs.

Babcock and Olston presented an original algorithm for distributed top-*k* monitoring in [4, 5]. In Babcock&Olston's algorithm, the coordinator node N_0 maintains an approximate top-*k* set T that is valid within ε. In addition to maintaining the top-*k* set, the coordinator also maintains $n(m + 1)$ numeric adjustment factors, labeled $\delta_{i,j}$, one corresponding to each pair of object O_i and node N_j, which must at all times satisfy the following two adjustment factor invariants:

Invariant 1: For each object O_i, the corresponding adjustment factors sum to zero: $\sum_{0\le j\le m}\delta_{i,j}=0$.

Invariant 2: For all pairs $\langle O_t\in T, O_s\in U-T\rangle$, $\delta_{t,0}+\varepsilon\ge\delta_{s,0}$.

At the outset, the coordinator initializes the approximate top-*k* set T by running an efficient algorithm for one-time top-*k* queries, e.g. TA. Then, a reallocation subroutine (described later) is used to set the adjustment factors that satisfy the two invariants and for each monitoring node N_j:

$$\forall O_t\in T, \forall O_s\in U-T: V_{t,j}+\delta_{t,j}\ge V_{s,j}+\delta_{s,j}\,. \tag{2}$$

If Invariant 1, 2 and formula 2 are satisfied, then formula 1 is satisfied. Whenever the constraints are violated at some monitor node N_c, a three-phase distributed process called *resolution* is initiated to maintain the current approximate top-*k* set:

Phase 1: N_c sends a message to the coordinator N_0 containing the *resolution set* $R=C\cup T$ and its current partial data values, and a special "border value" B_c, where C is the set of objects whose partial values at N_c are involved in violated constraints. (C contains one or more objects from T plus one or more objects not in T, and called C as the *conflict set*), and $B_c=\min\{\min_{O_t\in T}(V_{t,f}+\delta_{t,f}), \max_{O_s\in U-T-C}(V_{s,f}+\delta_{s,f})\}$.

Phase 2: The coordinator considers each pair $\langle O_t\in T, O_s\in U-T\rangle$ whose constraint has been violated and performs the following *validation test*: $V_{t,j}+\delta_{t,0}+\delta_{t,j}\ge V_{s,j}+\delta_{s,0}+\delta_{s,j}$. If this test succeeds, let $T' = T$, the coordinator performs reallocation to update the adjustment factors pertaining to those two nodes to reestablish all arithmetic constraints, and notifies N_c of its new adjustment factors. If the test fails, the phase 3 is required.

Phase 3: The coordinator contacts all monitor nodes other than N_c, and for each node N_j, $1 \leq j \leq m$, $j \neq c$, the coordinator requests the current partial data values $V_{i,j}$ of objects O_i in the resolution set R as well as the border value B_j (as defined above for node N_c), calculates new approximate top-*k* set *T'* , then, performs reallocation across all nodes to establish new adjustment factors to serve as parameters for those constraints, and notifies all monitor nodes of the new approximate top-*k* set *T'* and the new adjustment factors.

To reallocate the adjustment factors, let the set *participating nodes N* is: If reallocation is performed during Phase 2, then $N = \{N_0, N_c\}$, If reallocation is performed during Phase 3, then $N = \{N_0, N_1, N_2, \ldots, N_m\}$. Each node N_j, $0 \leq j \leq m$, is allocated an *allocation parameter* F_j. $0 \leq F_j \leq 1$ for all j, $\sum_{0 \leq j \leq m} F_j = 1$ and $F_j = 0$ if $F_j \notin N$. Let $V_{i,0} = 0$ for all i and $B_0 = \max_{1 \leq i \leq n, O_i \in U-R} \delta_{i,0}$. For each object O_i, O_i's *participating sum* $V_{iN} = \sum_{0 \leq j \leq m, N_j \in N} (V_{i,j} + \delta_{i,j})$. Similarly, $B_N = \sum_{0 \leq j \leq m, N_j \in N} B_j$. The detail of the subroutine *reallocation* as follows.

INPUTS: $T', R, \{B_j\}, \{V_{i,j}\}, \{\delta_{i,j}\}, \{F_j\}$

OUTPUT: $\{\delta'_{i,j}\}$

1. *For each object in the resolution set* $O_i \in R$, *compute the leeway* λ_i *:*

$$\lambda_i = \begin{cases} V_{iN} - B_N + \varepsilon & \text{if } O_i \in T \\ V_{iN} - B_N & \text{otherwise} \end{cases}$$

2. *For each object in the resolution set* $O_i \in R$ *and each monitor node* $N_j \in N$ *participating in resolution, assign:*

$$\delta'_{i,j} = \begin{cases} B_j - V_{i,j} + F_j \lambda_i - \varepsilon & \text{if } O_i \in T, j = 0 \\ B_j - V_{i,j} + F_j \lambda_i & \text{otherwise} \end{cases}$$

In Babcock&Olston's algorithm, distributed communication is only necessary on occasion, when constraints are violated. Communication cost is dominated by the size of the resolution set $R = C \cup T$. However, in Section 4, we show that transmitting the conflict set C is enough and the communication cost can be reduced significantly.

4 Minimal Refresh Algorithm

As described in Section 3, the communication cost is dominated by the size of the resolution set *R*. The basic idea behind MR is reducing the size of resolution set by transmitting the necessary objects. We show that, the monitor nodes only need transmitting the conflict set *C* and its current partial data values, and two border values in the resolution process. Note that the conflict set *C* is the minimal resolution set.

We first bring to light some key observations towards defining an efficient distributed top-*k* monitoring algorithm in Section 4.1. In Section 4.2 we introduce our new algorithm for distributed top-k monitoring termed *Minimal Refresh* (MR) algorithm and prove the correctness. In Section 4.3 we discuss the efficiency of our approach.

4.1 Key Observations

Let the *down conflict set* $C_T = T \cap C$ and the *up conflict set* $C_{U-T} = (U-T) \cap C$.

Claim 1. $\forall O_t \in T, \forall O_s \in U-T-C_{U-T} : V_t + \varepsilon \geq V_s$.[1]

Proof. $\forall O \in U$, O satisfies the invariant 1, which described in Section 3. $\forall O_t \in T$, $\forall O_s \in U-T-C_{U-T}$, $\langle O_t, O_s \rangle$ still satisfies the invariant 2 and formula (2). Therefore, $\forall O_t \in T, \forall O_s \in U-T-C_{U-T} : V_t + \varepsilon \geq V_s$. □

Claim 2. $\forall O_t \in T - C_T, \forall O_s \in C_{U-T} : V_t + \varepsilon \geq V_s$.

Proof. $\forall O \in U$, O satisfies the invariant 1. $\forall O_t \in T - C_T, \forall O_s \in C_{U-T}$, $\langle O_t, O_s \rangle$ still satisfies the invariant 2 and formula (2), Therefore, $\forall O_t \in T - C_T, \forall O_s \in C_{U-T} : V_t + \varepsilon \geq V_s$. □

Theorem 1. Let $p = |T - C_T|$. Let I is a subset of C, $|I| = k - p$ and $\forall O_t \in I, \forall O_s \in C - I : V_t \geq V_s$. Let $T' = (T - C_T) \cup I$, then T' can be a new approximate top-k set after resolution process, i.e. $|T'| = k$ and $\forall O_t \in T', \forall O_s \in U - T' : V_t + \varepsilon \geq V_s$.

Proof. There are two cases for the new approximate top-k set $T' = (T - C_T) \cup I$:

Case 1: $T' = T$, that means $\forall O_t \in C_T, \forall O_s \in C_{U-T} : V_t \geq V_s$. By Claim 2, we know that $\forall O_t \in T - C_T, \forall O_s \in C_{U-T} : V_t + \varepsilon \geq V_s$. Thereby, $\forall O_t \in T, \forall O_s \in C_{U-T} : V_t + \varepsilon \geq V_s$. By Claim 1, we know that $\forall O_t \in T, \forall O_s \in U - T - C_{U-T} : V_t + \varepsilon \geq V_s$. Therefore, $\forall O_t \in T, \forall O_s \in U - T : V_t + \varepsilon \geq V_s$, i.e. $\forall O_t \in T', \forall O_s \in U - T' : V_t + \varepsilon \geq V_s$.

Case 2: $T' \neq T$, that means $\exists O_i \in (I \cap C_{U-T}), \forall O_s \in C - I : V_i \geq V_s$. By Claim 2, we know that $\forall O_t \in T - C_T, \forall O_s \in C_{U-T} : V_t + \varepsilon \geq V_s$. Thereby, $\forall O_t \in T - C_T, \forall O_s \in C - I : V_t + \varepsilon \geq V_i \geq V_s$. From the definition of I, we know that $\forall O_t \in I, \forall O_s \in C - I : V_t \geq V_s$. Thereby, $\forall O_t \in (T - C_T) \cup I, \forall O_s \in C - I : V_t + \varepsilon \geq V_s$ On the other hand, if $T' \neq T$, $\exists O_d \in C_T \cap (C - I)$. Note that $\forall O_s \in U - T - C_{U-T} : V_d + \varepsilon \geq V_s$, and $\forall O_t \in I, \forall O_s \in C - I : V_t \geq V_s$. Therefore, $\forall O_t \in I, \forall O_s \in U - T - C_{U-T} : V_t + \varepsilon \geq V_s$. By Claim 1, we know that $\forall O_t \in T - C_T, \forall O_s \in U - T - C_{U-T} : V_t + \varepsilon \geq V_s$. Therefore, $\forall O_t \in (T - C_T) \cup I, \forall O_s \in U - T - C_{U-T} : V_t + \varepsilon \geq V_s$. Note that $T' = (T - C_T) \cup I$, and $U - T' = (C - I) \cup (U - T - C_{U-T})$, therefore, $\forall O_t \in T', \forall O_s \in U - T' : V_t + \varepsilon \geq V_s$.

---

[1] We assume that no partial values are updated during resolution. The definition of correctness ensures the convergence property described in [5].

As discussed above, $\forall O_t \in T', \forall O_s \in U - T': V_t + \varepsilon \geq V_s$ and $|T'| = p + (k - p) = k$. Therefore, T' can be a new approximate top-*k* set after resolution process. □

The implication of Theorem 1 is that, in the resolution process, we can keep the objects in the set $T - C_T$ and choose the $k - p$ objects with largest aggregation values from the conflict set C to rebuild the new approximate top-*k* set *T'*.

4.2 Algorithm

In our new algorithm MR, at the outset, the coordinator uses the same approach of Babcock&Olston's algorithm to initialize the approximate top-*k* set *T* and set the adjustment factors that satisfy the invariant 1, 2 and formula (2).

Whenever the local arithmetic constraints are violated at some monitor node N_c, a three-phase distributed process called *MR-Resolution* is initiated to maintain the current approximate top-*k* set. MR-Resolution uses the method in Theorem 1 to rebuild the new approximate top-*k* set *T'*. To make sure *T'* and $U - T'$ still satisfy the invariant 1, 2 and formula (2), we define two border values: B_c and H_c.

$$B_c = \min\{\min_{O_t \in T}(V_{t,c} + \delta_{t,c}), \max_{O_s \in U-T-C}(V_{s,c} + \delta_{s,c})\}$$

$$H_c = \max\{\min_{O_t \in T-C}(V_{t,c} + \delta_{t,c}), \max_{O_s \in U-T}(V_{s,c} + \delta_{s,c})\}$$

The detail of the subroutine MR-Resolution as follows.

Algorithm MR-Resolution

Phase 1: N_c sends a message to the coordinator N_0 containing the *conflict set C* and its current partial data values, and the two border values B_c and H_c of N_c.

Phase 2: The coordinator considers each pair $\langle O_t \in T, O_s \in U - T\rangle$ whose constraint has been violated and performs the following *validation test*: $V_{t,j} + \delta_{t,0} + \delta_{t,j} \geq V_{s,j} + \delta_{s,0} + \delta_{s,j}$. If this test succeeds, let $I = C_T$, the coordinator performs MR-Reallocation to update the adjustment factors pertaining to those two nodes to reestablish all arithmetic constraints, and notifies N_c of its new adjustment factors. If the test fails, the phase 3 is required.

Phase 3: The coordinator contacts all monitor nodes other than N_c, and for each node N_j, $1 \leq j \leq m$, $j \neq c$, the coordinator requests the current partial data values $V_{i,j}$ of objects O_i in the conflict set *C* as well as the border value B_j and H_j (as defined above for node N_c), calculates the set *I* by the method in Theorem 1, then, performs MR-Reallocation across all nodes to establish new adjustment factors to serve as parameters for those constraints, and notifies all monitor nodes of the new adjustment factors. Every node rebuilds the new approximate top-*k* set *T'*, where $T' = (T - C_T) \cup I$.

To reallocate the adjustment factors, we use the same definition of *participating nodes N*, *allocation parameter* and *participating sum* of Babcock&Olston's algorithm. In *MR-Reallocation,* let $B_0 = \min\{\min_{O_t \in T}(\delta_{t,0} + \varepsilon), \max_{O_s \in U-T-F}(\delta_{s,0})\}$, $H_0 = \max\{\min_{O_t \in T-D}(\delta_{t,0} +$

$\varepsilon), \max_{O_s \in U-T}(\delta_{s,0})\}$, $B_N = \sum_{0\le j\le m, N_j \in N} B_j$ and $H_N = \sum_{0\le j\le m, N_j\in N} H_j$. The detail of the subroutine *MR-Reallocation* as follows.

Algorithm MR-Reallocation

INPUTS: $I, C, \{B_j\}, \{H_j\}, \{V_{i,j}\}, \{\delta_{i,j}\}, \{F_j\}$

OUTPUT: $\{\delta'_{i,j}\}$

1. *Compute the threshold* τ *and the interpolation factor* α *:*

$$\tau = (\min(H_N, \min_{t' \in I}(V_{t',N} + \varepsilon)) + \max(B_N, \max_{s' \in C-I}(V_{s',N})))/2$$

$$\alpha = \begin{cases} (\tau - B_N)/H_N - B_N & \text{if } H_N > B_N \\ 0 & \text{otherwise} \end{cases}$$

2. *For each monitor node* $N_j \in N$ *, compute the threshold* τ_j *:*

$$\tau_j = \alpha(H_j - B_j) + B_j$$

3. *For each object in the conflict set* $O_i \in C$*, compute the leeway* λ_i *:*

$$\lambda_i = \begin{cases} V_{iN} - \tau + \varepsilon & \text{if } O_i \in I \\ V_{iN} - \tau & \text{otherwise} \end{cases}$$

4. *For each object in the conflict set* $O_i \in C$ *and each monitor node* $N_j \in N$ *participating in resolution, assign:*

$$\delta'_{i,j} = \begin{cases} \tau_j - V_{i,j} + F_j\lambda_i - \varepsilon & \text{if } O_i \in I, j = 0 \\ \tau_j - V_{i,j} + F_j\lambda_i & \text{otherwise} \end{cases}$$

From Theorem 1, we know that *T'* is a correct new approximate top-*k* set. Now, we prove the new adjustment factors $\delta'_{i,j}$ satisfy the invariant 1, 2 and formula (2).

Note that $\sum_{0\le j\le m, N_j\in N} \tau_j = \tau$ and $0 \le F_j \le 1$ for all *j*, $\sum_{0\le j\le m} F_j = 1$ and $F_j = 0$ if $F_j \notin N$, thereby $\sum_{N_j\in N} \delta'_{i,j} = \sum_{N_j\in N} \delta_{i,j}$, the new adjustment factors $\delta'_{i,j}$ satisfy the invariant 1.

Lemma 1. $\min(H_N, \min_{t'\in I}(V_{t',N} + \varepsilon)) \ge \max(B_N, \max_{s'\in C-I}(V_{s',N}))$.

Proof. For each node N_j ($0 \le j \le m$), $H_j \ge B_j$, therefore, $H_N \ge B_N$. Note that $\min_{t'\in I}(V_{t',N} + \varepsilon) \ge \max_{s'\in C-I}(V_{s',N})$, $\min_{t'\in I}(V_{t',N} + \varepsilon) \ge \min_{t\in T}(V_{t,N} + \varepsilon) \ge \min_{t\in T}(V_{t,N} + \varepsilon) \ge B_N$ and $H_N \ge \max_{s'\in C_{U-T}}(V_{s',N})$. If $T' = T$, then $C - I = C_{U-T}$, $H_N \ge \max_{s'\in C-I}(V_{s',N})$. If $T' \ne T$, then $\exists O_i \in (I \cap C_{U-T})$, $H_N \ge V_{i,N} \ge \max_{s'\in C-I}(V_{s',N})$. Thereby, $\min(H_N, \min_{t'\in I}(V_{t',N} + \varepsilon)) \ge \max(B_N, \max_{s'\in C-I}(V_{s',N}))$. □

By Lemma 1, we know that, in MR-Reallocation $\forall O_{t'} \in T', \forall O_{s'} \in U - T'$:

$$V_{t',N} + \varepsilon \ge \min(H_N, \min_{t'\in I}(V_{t',N} + \varepsilon)) \ge \tau \ge \max(B_N, \max_{s'\in C-I}(V_{s',N})) \ge V_{s',N} . \quad (3)$$

Furthermore, by Lemma 1, we know that, in the MR-Reallocation process, the leeway $\lambda_i \geq 0$ and $\lambda_s \leq 0$ for all $O_i \in I$ and $O_s \in C - I$. Note that the interpolation factor $\alpha \in [0,1]$, $V_{i,0} = 0$ for all i, thereby, for all pairs $\langle O_{t'} \in T', O_{s'} \in U - T' \rangle, \delta_{t',0} + \varepsilon \geq \delta_{s',0}$, i.e. the new adjustment factors $\delta'_{i,j}$ satisfy the invariant 2.

Theorem 2. Let $\delta'_{i,j}$ be the new adjustment factor output by MR-Reallocation if $O_i \in C$ and $N_j \in N$, and let $\delta'_{i,j} = \delta_{i,j}$ otherwise. It is the case that $V_{t,j} + \delta'_{t,j} \geq V_{s,j} + \delta'_{s,j}$ for all monitor nodes N_j, for all $O_t \in T'$, $O_s \in U - T'$.

Proof. Note that $\alpha \in [0,1]$, for each monitoring node N_j, $\forall O_t \in T - C_T, \forall O_s \in U - T - C_{U-T} : V_{t',j} + \delta_{t',j} \geq H_j \geq \tau_j \geq B_j \geq V_{s',j} + \delta_{s',j}$. Note that $0 \leq F_j \leq 1$, and, in the MR-Reallocation process, $\lambda_i \geq 0$ and $\lambda_s \leq 0$ for all $O_i \in I$ and $O_s \in C - I$. Thereby, for each monitoring node N_j, $\forall O_{t'} \in T'$, $\forall O_{s'} \in U - T'$: $V_{t',j} + \delta_{t',j} \geq \tau_j \geq V_{s',j} + \delta_{s',j}$. □

4.3 Efficiency

We use the message size exchanged between the monitor nodes and the coordinator during resolution as the metric of communication cost. The message size is governed by the size of the conflict set C for our algorithm MR and the size of the resolution set $R = C \cup T$ for Babcock&Olston's algorithm.

There are two types of events that can cause local arithmetic constraints to become violated, triggering resolution: either a partial value of an object that is not in the current approximate top-*k* set can increase, or a partial value of an object that is in the current approximate top-*k* set can decrease. In the first case, $|C| = |C_T| + 1$ and the size of R is always $k+1$. In the second case, $|C| = |C_{U-T}| + 1$, $|R| = k + |C_{U-T}|$. Based on our simulations, we found that, more than 98%, $|C_T| = 1$ for the first case, and $|C_{U-T}| \leq 4$ for the second case. In our simulations, the average number of $|C|$ is ranging from 2 to 4, depending on the parameters used when running the algorithm.

As discussed above, $|C|$ is independent of k and $|C| << k$ in most situations, while $R = C \cup T$ and $|T| = k$, therefore $|R|$ is always greater than k and $|C|$.

Based on our simulations (Section 5) we found that, the total number of messages exchanged of MR is higher ($< 40\%$) than Babcock&Olston's algorithm. Taking into account the size of the border values, the ratio of communication cost of our approach to Babcock&Olston's algorithm is approximate $2 \times |C| / |R|$.

To keep the size of the messages exchanged as low as possible, we modified our algorithm by an alternative resolution procedure described in [5]: whenever a change in a partial data value would result in the violation of more than Φ local arithmetic constraints. For our purposes, we set $\Phi = 20$ (these situations are less than 1%). The alternative procedure, generates $2m$ extra messages (m is the number of monitor nodes) in addition to the ones generated by the ordinary MR-Resolution procedure.

5 Experimentation

In this Section, we first give the experimental setting in Section 5.1. In Section 5.2 we discuss the leeway allocation policies. In Section 5.3 we experimentally compared the performance of our proposed algorithm MR against Babcock&Olston's algorithm.

5.1 Experimental Setting

We used both real-world and synthetic data sets to evaluate our new algorithm:

- *WorldCup*: we used a 24-hour HTTP server log from the web site for the FIFA World Cup Soccer on June 15, 1998, which consisting of 58 million page requests distributed across 29 servers that were active during that period and serving some 17,000 distinct files [1].
- *Zipf-WorldCup*: we replaced the real page requests number of each page in WorldCup by the score initialized by the Zipf's distribution [18] with a Zipf factor θ, and distributed the synthetic score in the server log by the uniform distribution.

We present two continuous monitoring queries for every data set that the administrators of the World Cub web site might have liked to have posed:

Monitoring Query 1. Which web documents are the most popular from the begging of monitoring, across all servers?

Monitoring Query 2. Which web documents are the most popular in the last one hour, across all servers?

Monitoring Query 1 represents the first case that causes local arithmetic constraints to become violated, triggering resolution, and Monitoring Query 2 represents a hybrid example of the first case and the second case.

Our implementation of the test-bed and the related algorithms was written in GNU C++. All the experiments are conducted on Intel Pentium IV CPU 2.4GHz with 512MB RAM running Red Hat Linux 9.

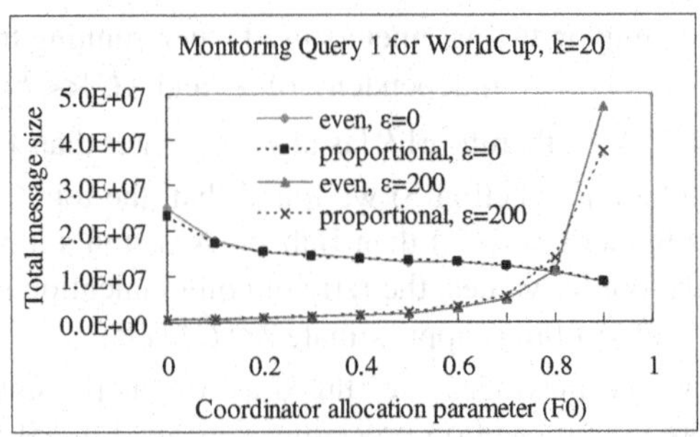

Fig. 1. Performance of difference leeway allocation policies

5.2 Leeway Allocation Policies

Recall from Section 4.2 that our MR-Reallocation algorithm is parameterized by m+1 allocation parameters F_0, F_1, …, F_m that specify the fraction of leeway allocated to the adjustment factors at each node N_j participating in resolution. We compared the two basic leeway allocation policies described in [4, 5]:

Figure 1 Shows the results of our experiments on Monitoring Query 1 for World-Cup, $k = 20$ and two different error tolerance values: $\varepsilon = 0$, and a larger value ($\varepsilon = 200$) that permits a moderate amount of error with respect to the data queried (similar results occur with all other monitoring queries, and are omitted for the space reasons).

In all cases, the value assigned to F_0 turns out to be the largest factor in determining cost. Our results suggest that an efficient allocation policy is:

Hybrid: set $F_0 = 0.5$ and using the proportional allocation when ε is small, and set $F_0 = 0$ and using the even allocation when ε is large. The cutoff point between "small" and "large" values of ε comes roughly when ε is 1/500 of the threshold τ. This conclusion is supported by the results presented in this section and also by additional experimental results not presented here due to space considerations ([4, 5] used the same hybrid policy while the cutoff point is 1/1000 of the largest data value in the data set).

5.3 Comparison Against Alternative

We compared our algorithm against Babcock&Olston's algorithm using a simulator that for both algorithms assumes that communication and computation latencies are small compared with the rate at which data values change. We used the hybrid policy for our algorithm and Babcock&Olston's algorithm.

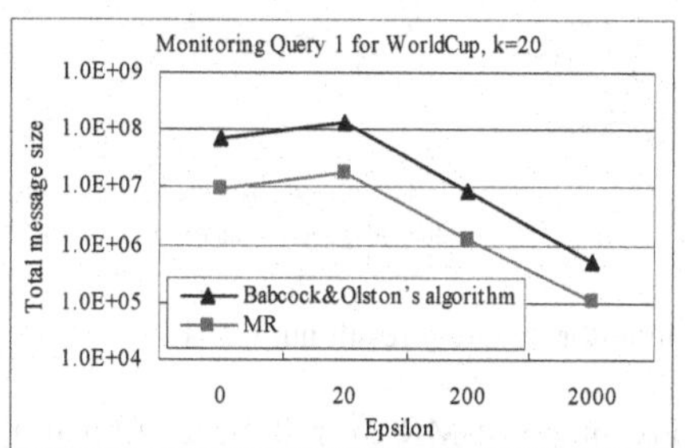

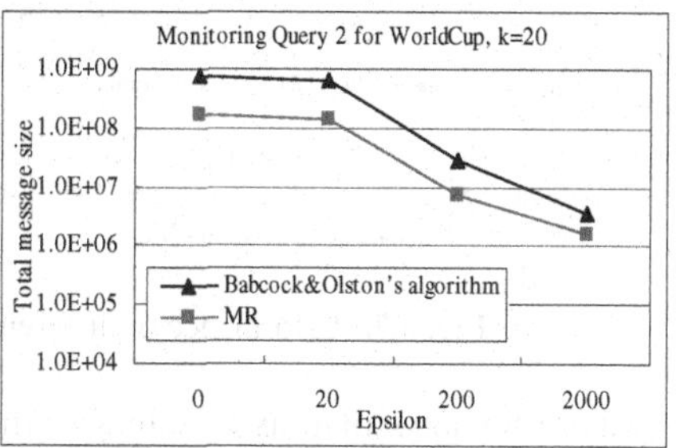

Fig. 2,3. Comparison against alternative for real-world data sets

Figure 2, 3, 4 and 5 show the results for Monitoring Queries 1 and 2 of both data sets for $k = 20$. For simplicity, we set the Zipf factor $\theta = 0.8$ (similar results occur with all other tested values of θ, and are omitted for the space reasons). In each graph, the approximation parameter ε is plotted on the x-axis. The y-axis shows total message size, on a logarithmic scale.

In all cases our algorithm achieves a significant reduction in cost compared with Babcock&Olston's algorithm. The overall performance of MR outperforms Babcock&Olston's algorithm by a factor ranging from 2 to 8. The main reason of MR outperforming Babcock&Olston's algorithm is that, when constraints are violated, MR only need take into account the conflict set C while Babcock&Olston's algorithm need take into account the resolution set $R = C \cup T$, and $|C| << |R|$ in most situations described in Section 4.3.

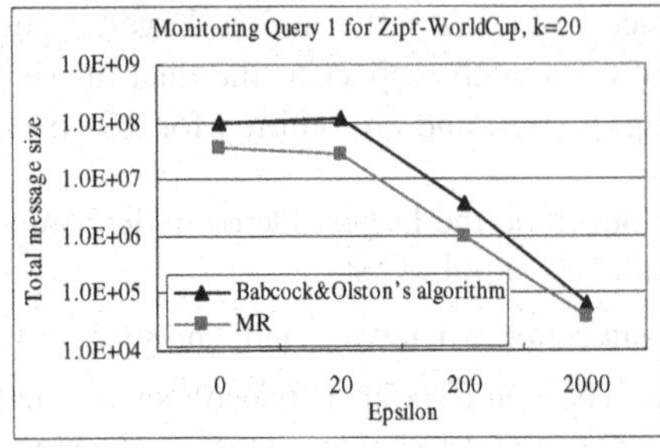

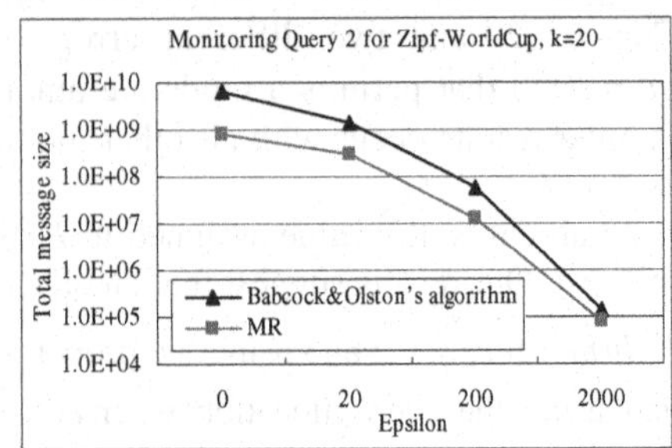

Fig. 4,5. Comparison against alternative for synthetic data sets

We measured the message size and message number of our experiments on Monitoring Query 1 of WorldCup for different monitoring query result number k from 10 to 100 with $\varepsilon = 200$ (similar results occur with all other experimental results, and are omitted for the space reasons). Figures 6, 7 show the results respectively.

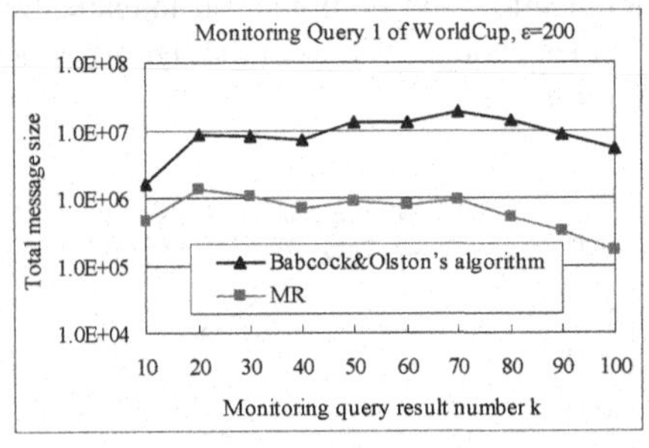

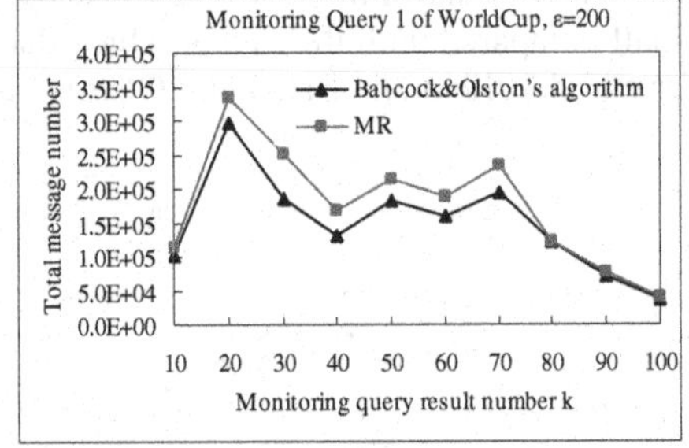

Fig. 6,7. Performance of difference monitoring query result number k

Figure 6 shows that, as k increases, the advantage of MR over Babcock&Olston's algorithm is magnified, often by over an order of magnitude (note that the y-axis is on a logarithmic scale). The main reason is that, $|C|$ is independent of k and $|C| << k$ in most situations, while $R = C \cup T$ and $|T| = k$, therefore $|R|$ is always greater than k.

Figure 7 shows that message number of MR is higher ($< 40\%$) than Babcock&Olston's algorithm. The main reason is that, in the resolution process, comparing with our algorithm, Babcock&Olston's algorithm reallocates additional adjustment factors of the set $|T - C|$, which decreases some potential constraint conflicts.

6 Conclusions

In this paper, we have studied the optimization problem of which objects are necessary to be transmitted in distributed top-k monitoring, and presented the MR algorithm, an efficient distributed top-k monitoring algorithm. In our approach, only few objects are transmitted for maintaining the top-k set and the communication cost is independent of k. We have verified the effectiveness of our approach empirically using both real-world and synthetic data sets. The experiments results have shown that our approach reduces overall communication cost by a factor ranging from 2 to over an order of magnitude compared with the previous approach (Babcock&Olston's algorithm) when k is no lees than 10.

References

1. M. Arlitt and T. Jin. 1998 world cup web site access logs, August 1998. Available at http://www.acm.org/sigcomm/ITA/.
2. N. Bruno, L. Gravano, and A. Marian. Evaluating top-k queries over web-accessible databases. In ICDE, 2002.
3. W.-T. Balke, W. Nejdl, W. Siberski, et al. Progressive Distributed Top-k Retrieval in Peer-to-Peer Networks. In ICDE 2005.
4. B. Babcock, C. Olston. Distributed Top-K Monitoring. In SIGMOD, 2003.
5. B. Babcock and C. Olston. Distributed top-k monitoring. Technical report, Stanford University Computer Science Department, 2002. http://dbpubs.stanford.edu/pub/2002-61.
6. D. Carney, U. Cetintemel, M. Cherniack, et al. Monitoring streams - a new class of data management applications. In VLDB, 2002.
7. J. Chen, D. J. DeWitt, F. Tian, et al. NiagaraCQ: A scalable continuous query system for internet databases. In SIGMOD, 2000.
8. K.C.-C. Chang, S.-W. Hwang: Minimal probing: supporting expensive predicates for top-k queries. In SIGMOD 2002.
9. M. J. Carey and D. Kossmann. On saying "Enough already!" in SQL. In SIGMOD, 1997.
10. P. Cao, Z. Wang. Efficient top-k query calculation in distributed networks. In PODC, 2004.
11. R. Fagin. Combining fuzzy information from multiple systems. In J. Comput. System Sci., pages 58:83–99, 1999.
12. R. Fagin, Amnon Lotem, and Moni Naor. Optimal aggregation algorithms for middleware. In PODS, 2001.
13. U. Güntzer, W.-T. Balke, and W. Kieβling. Optimizing multi-feature queries for image databases. In VLDB, 2000.
14. P. B. Gibbons and Y. Matias. New sampling-based summary statistics for improving approximate query answers. In SIGMOD, 1998.
15. S. Madden, J. M. Hellerstein, M. Shah, et al. Continuously adaptive continuous queries over streams. In SIGMOD, 2002.
16. S. Michel, P. Triantafillou, and G. Weikum. KLEE: A Framework for Distributed Top-k Query Algorithms. In VLDB, 2005.
17. S. Nepal and M. V. Ramakrishna. Query processing issues in image (multimedia) databases. In ICDE, 1999.
18. G. K. Zipf: Human Behavior and the Principle of Least Effort. Addison-Wesley Press, 1949.
19. R. Zhang, N. Koudas, B.C. Ooi, et al. Multiple Aggregations Over Data Streams. In SIGMOD, 2005.

Designing Quality XML Schemas from E-R Diagrams

Chengfei Liu and Jianxin Li

Faculty of Information and Communication Technologies
Swinburne University of Technology
Melbourne, VIC 3122, Australia
{cliu, jili}@ict.swin.edu.au

Abstract. XML has emerged as the standard for representing, exchanging and integrating data on the Web. To guarantee the quality of XML documents, the design of quality XML Schemas becomes essentially important. In this paper, we look into this problem by designing quality XML Schemas from given E-R diagrams. We first discuss several criteria in designing a good XML Schema. Following these criteria, transformation rules are then devised that take all constructs of an E-R diagram into account. Finally, a recursive algorithm is developed to transform an E-R diagram to a corresponding quality XML Schema.

1 Introduction

XML has emerged as the standard for representing, exchanging and integrating data on the Web. Given that the structure of XML documents is much more flexible than that of a relational database, the design of a quality XML document for an application is non-trivial. By a quality XML document, we mean that it reflects the semantics of the application accurately and can be accessed, updated and integrated efficiently. To guarantee the quality of XML documents, the design of quality XML schemas becomes essentially important.

We reckon that several criteria need to be followed in designing a quality schema. (1) *information preservation* - it is fundamental that the target XML Schema preserves structural and semantic information of the application entirely. (2) *highly nested structure* - nesting is important in XML documents because it allows navigation of the paths in the document tree structures to be processed efficiently. (3) *no redundancy* - there is no data redundancy in the XML documents that conform to the target XML schema, thus no inconsistency will be introduced while updating the XML documents. (4) *consideration of dominant applications* - the structure of XML document should be accommodated such that dominant applications can be guaranteed to be processed efficiently. (5) *reversibility of design* - the original design can be achieved from the target XML schema, which is fundamentally important to data integration.

Kleiner and Lipect [1] proposed a method for generating XML DTD [2] from E-R diagrams. The method preserved as much structural information from E-R diagrams as possible. However, due to the limitation of the DTD, only annotations were used to represent some E-R constructs that have no counterparts in DTD. Many-to-many relationships were translated into top-level elements only so nesting is not maximised. Some advanced features in E-R model such as ISA and aggregation were not considered in their work. Bird et al. [3] proposed an approach to design XML Schemas from the

J.X. Yu, M. Kitsuregawa, and H.V. Leong (Eds.): WAIM 2006, LNCS 4016, pp. 508–519, 2006.
© Springer-Verlag Berlin Heidelberg 2006

Object Role Model (ORM) [4]. The approach considered the dominant applications by analysing the weighting and anchoring of factor types. However, nesting was not discussed in their work. Effort has been put for translating relational database schemas to XML Schemas. An early work in transforming relational schema to XML schema is DB2XML [5]. DB2XML uses a simple algorithm to map flat relational model to flat XML model in almost one-to-one manner. DTD is used for the target XML schema. Based on a flat translation similar to DB2XML, Lee et al. [6] presented two algorithms *NeT* and *CoT*. *NeT* derives nested structures from flat relations by repeatedly applying the nest operator on tuples of each relation. The resulting nested structures may be useless because the derivation is not at the type level. *CoT* considers inclusion dependencies as constraints to generate a more intuitive XML Schema. XViews [7] constructs a graph based on primary key/foreign key relationship and generates candidate views by choosing the node with either maximum in-degree or zero in-degree as the root element. The candidate XML views generated maybe highly nested. DTD is also chosen for target XML schema. This approach does not consider the preservation of integrity constraints. It also suffers considerable level of data redundancy. Liu et al. [8] proposed an approach that ensures the transformed schema in XML Schema [9] is highly nested, redundancy free and preserves all the integrity constraints. However, the dominant applications and the reversibility of transformation were not discussed in their work. Bohannon et al. [10] developed the notion of DTD schema embedding that preserves information by ensuring both effective invertible mapping and efficient XML query translation. Lots of work has been done on mapping from XML to relational databases for storage purpose. Recently, Barbosa et al. [11] proposed a framework for information-preserving XML-to-relational mapping. The framework is extensible and guarantees the target relational schema is equivalent to the original XML Schema.

We aim at designing quality XML Schemas that follows all five criteria we discussed above. Similar to conventional database design, we use E-R model [12] for conceptual modelling, so we assume that E-R diagrams are given when we design XML schema. In this paper, we present our transformation rules and algorithms that automatically generate quality XML Schemas from E-R diagrams by following all five criteria. To preserve information, we choose XML Schema as the target schema language instead of DTD because XML Schema provides far more powerful modelling features than DTD.

The rest of the paper is organised as follows. In Section 2, we briefly introduce the E-R model and XML Schema. Following our design criteria, we design transformation rules that consider all the constructs in the E-R model in Section 3. In Section 4, we propose a recursive algorithm that generates a quality XML schema from a given E-R diagram. Section 5 concludes the paper.

2 E-R Model and XML Schema

Before we discuss the mapping from an E-R diagram to its correspondent schema in XML Schema, we briefly review both the E-R model and XML Schema.

The E-R model employs three basic notions: *entities (entity sets)*, *relationships*, and *attributes*. There are two types of entity sets: *regular* and *weak*. The existence of a weak entity depends on another entity (its parent entity). A relationship has two basic properties: cardinality (*one-to-one, one-to-many, many-to-many*) and participation (*total* and *partial*). Two or more participants may be involved in a relationship. The former is called *binary* while the latter is called *n-ary*. Sometimes, a relationship may have participants that belong to same entity set and play different *roles*. This relationship is called a *recursive* relationship. The relationship from a *parent* entity set to a weak entity set is called *identifying* relationship. An attribute can be *atomic* or *composite* by having its own attributes, and meanwhile can be *single-valued* or *multi-valued*.

The set of attributes that can uniquely identify an entity in a regular entity set is called a *key*. The set of attributes that can identify a weak entity in the context of its parent entity is called a *local key*. A *global key* of a weak entity consists of its local key and the key of its parent entity. A key for a relationship consists of all keys of its participant entity sets.

The E-R model is also extended to support some advanced features. These include *ISA* (*generalisation* and *specialisation*), and *aggregation* where some relationships are treated as *high-level entity sets*.

To incorporate all the constructs introduced above, we give a formal definition in connection to an E-R diagram as follows.

Definition 1. An **E-R diagram** is represented $\delta = (E, R, A, \rho, n_d, s, p, k)$, where

(1) E is the set of entity sets. Each $e \in E$ is defined as (n_e, t) *where* n_e, t are the name and type of e, and $t \in \{regular, weak, high\text{-}level\}$. If $t(e)$ = "*high-level*", e has its own E-R diagram δ_e which includes a single relationship.

(2) R is the set of relationships. Each $r \in R$ is defined as $(n_r, \{(e, card, par, role)\})$ where n_r is the name of the relationship and each tuple $(e, card, par, role)$ in the set is used to describe a participant entity set. The participant entity set, its cardinality, participation and role in the relationship are recorded. Here, $e \in E$, $card \in \{1, n\}$, $par \in \{total, partial\}$.

(3) A is the set of attributes. Each $a \in A$ is defined as (n_a, vt, st) where n_a is the attribute name, $vt \in \{single\text{-}valued, multi\text{-}valued\}$, and $st \in \{atomic, composite\}$.

(4) $\rho : E \cup R \cup A \rightarrow 2^A$ defines the attribute sets of entities, relationships, and composite attributes.

(5) n_d is the name of the diagram.

(6) $s : E \rightarrow E$ defines the *ISA* relationship. For $e \in E$, $s(e)$ is the super entity set of e.

(7) $p : E \rightarrow E$ defines the *identifying* relationship. For a *weak* entity set $e \in E$, $p(e)$ is the *parent* entity set of e.

(8) $k : E \rightarrow 2^A$ defines the key for entity sets. If $t(e)$ = "*weak*", $k(e)$ gives the attribute set for its local key only. The key for a relationship is derived from the keys of all its participant entity sets.

XML Schema is the W3C XML language for describing and constraining the content of XML documents. Compared with DTD, it offers many appealing features. (1) XML Schema provides very powerful data typing. A rich set of built-in data types are provided. Based on that, users are allowed to derive their own simple types by restriction and complex types by both restriction and extension. An ISA construct in an E-R diagram can be mapped to complex type derived by extension. In DTD, only very limited number of built-in types is provided, most for defining attributes only. User cannot define their own types, not to mention complex types. (2) XML Schema provides comprehensive support for representing integrity constraints such as id/idref, key/keyref, unique, fine grained cardinalities, etc. while DTD only provides limited support such as id/idref. The cardinality constraints provided by DTD is mainly based on Kleine closure. (3) Apart from the sequence and selection compositors for grouping elements, XML Schema also provides other compositors such as set. (4) XML Schema has the same syntax as XML. This allows schema itself be processed by the same tools that read the XML documents it describes. In contrast, DTD is in a non-XML syntax. (5) Namespaces are well supported in XML Schema while not in DTD. While DTD is still used for very simple applications, XML Schema is becoming a dominant XML schema language.

For the purpose of information preservation, obviously XML Schema rather than DTD is a better choice for the target schema language.

3 Transformation Rules

To map all constructs of an E-R diagram defined in Section 2 and follow all criteria discussed in Section 1, we design the following set of transformation rules.

Rule 1: E-R diagram - For an E-R diagram δ $(E, R, A, \rho, n_d, \mathcal{S}, \mathcal{P}, \mathcal{K})$, a *root element* named n_d is created as follows.

```
<xsd:element name="n_d">
   <xsd:complexType>
      <xsd: sequence >
         <!-- detail of transformed XML schema goes here -->
      </xsd:sequence>
   </xsd:complexType>
</xsd:element>
```

Rule 2: Regular entity set - For an entity set $e(n_e, t)$ of the E-R diagram δ where $t(e)$ = "*regular*", an element named n_e is created and put under the element for δ. The key of e is specified by a key declaration where $\mathcal{K}(e) = \{k_1, \ldots, k_n\}$.

```
<xsd:element name="n_e">
   <xsd:complexType>
      <xsd: sequence >
         <!-- detail of the entity set goes here -->
      </xsd:sequence>
   </xsd:complexType>
</xsd:element>
<xsd:key name="key_n_e">
      <xsd:selector xpath="path_n_e"/><xsd:field xpath="k_1"/> … <xsd:field xpath="k_n"/>
</xsd:key>
```

Rule 3: Weak entity set - For an entity set $e(n_e, t)$ of the E-R diagram δ where $t(e)$ = "*weak*" and $\mathcal{P}(e) = e'$, an element named n_e is created and put under the element for e'. The key of e is specified by a key declaration where $\mathcal{K}(e') = \{k_{11}, \ldots, k_{1m}\}$, $\mathcal{K}(e) = \{k_{21}, \ldots, k_{2n}\}$.

```
<xsd:key name="key_n_e">
      <xsd:selector xpath="path_n_e"/>
      <xsd:field xpath="../k_11"/> … <xsd:field xpath="../k_1m"/>
      <xsd:field xpath="k_21"/> … <xsd:field xpath="k_2n"/>
</xsd:key>
```

Rule 4: High-level entity set - For an entity set $e(n_e, t)$ of the E-R diagram δ where $t(e)$ = "*high-level*", an element named n_e is created and put under the element for δ. A high-level entity set is used to represent one and only one relationship. As such, the key of e is the key of the relationship which can be achieved while generating the detail of the entity by applying Rule 1 to its own E-R diagram δ_e.

Dominant queries are those queries that are most frequently used. Instead of defining a dominant query, we define the dominant entity set (or role) of a relationship and the dominant relationship of an entity as follows.

Definition 2. Dominant entity set (or role): The dominant entity set e or role l of a relationship $r(n_r, \{(e, card, par, role)\})$ is one of its participant entity sets or roles such that e or l has the highest frequency from which r is visited.

Definition 3. Dominant relationship: The dominant relationship r of an entity set $e(n_e, t)$ is one of its participating relationships such that r has the highest frequency from which e is visited.

Rule 5: One-to-one relationship - For a relationship of the form $r(n_r, \{(e_1, 1, p_1, \_), (e_2, 1, p_2, \_)\})$, an element named n_r is first created, then depending on p_1 and p_2, apply different rules as follows.

(1) both are "*total*" - suppose that e_1 is the dominant entity set, put the element for r under the element for e_2 and change to put the element for e_2 to under the element for e_1.

(2) one of them, say p_1, is "*partial*" - put the element for r under the element for e_2 and change to put the element for e_2 to under the element for e_1.

(3) both are "*partial*" - suppose that e_1 is the dominant entity set, put the element for r under the element for e_1. Foreign key attributes are added in r with a separate keyref declaration where $k(e_2) = \{k_1, \ldots, k_n\}$.

```
<xsd:keyref name="foreignKey_r" refer="key_ne2">
  <xsd:selector xpath="path_r"/><xsd:field xpath="k1"/> … <xsd:field xpath="kn"/>
</xsd:keyref>
```

Rule 6: One-to-many relationship - For a relationship of the form $r(n_r, \{(e_1, 1, p_1, \_), (e_2, n, p_2, \_)\})$, an element named n_r is first created, then depending on p_2, apply different rules as follows.

(1) p_2 is "*total*" - put the element for r under the element for e_2, then change the element for e_2 by adding maxOccurs="*unbounded*" and move it to under the element for e_1.

(2) p_2 is "*partial*" - put the element for r under the element for e_2. Foreign key attributes are added in r with a separate keyref declaration where $k(e_1) = \{k_1, \ldots, k_n\}$.

```
<xsd:keyref name="foreignKey_r" refer="key_ne1">
  <xsd:selector xpath="path_r"/><xsd:field xpath="k1"/> … <xsd:field xpath="kn"/>
</xsd:keyref>
```

Rule 7: Many-to-many relationship - For a relationship of the form $r(n_r, \{(e_1, n, \_, \_), (e_2, n, \_, \_)\})$, an element named n_r is first created with maxOccurs attribute set to "unbounded", then put the element for r under the element for the dominant entity set, say e_1. Foreign key attributes are added in r with a separate keyref declaration where $\mathcal{K}(e_2) = \{k_1, \ldots, k_n\}$.

```
<xsd:keyref name="foreignKey_r" refer="key_n_e2">
    <xsd:selector xpath="path_r"/><xsd:field xpath="k_1"/> … <xsd:field xpath="k_n"/>
</xsd:keyref>
```

Rule 8: Recursive relationship - For a relationship of the form $r(n_r, \{(e_1, c_1, \_, r_1), (e_1, c_2, \_, r_2)\})$, depending on c_1 and c_2, apply different rules as follows.

(1) $c_1 = c_2 =$ "*1*" - suppose that r_1 is the dominant role, an element named $n_r\_r_1$ is created and put under the element for e_1, and foreign key attributes for r_2 are added with a separate keyref declaration.

(2) $c_1 = c_2 =$ "*n*" - suppose that r_1 is the dominant role, an element named $n_r\_r_1$ is created with maxOccurs set to ="*unbounded*" and put under the element for e_1, foreign key attributes for r_2 are added with a separate keyref declaration.

(3) $c_1 \neq c_2$ (suppose $c_1 > c_2$) - an element named $n_r\_r_1$ is created and put under the element for e_1, and foreign key attributes for r_2 are added with a separate keyref declaration.

Rule 9: ISA relationship - For an entity set e_1, if $e_2 = \mathcal{S}(e_1)$ is defined and the complexType defined for the element for e_2 is t_e_2, then an element for e_1 can be created with the t_e_2 as the extension type.

```
<xsd:element name="e_1">
  <xsd:complexType>
    <xsd:extension base="t_e_2">
      <xsd:sequence>
        <!-- transformation of extra attributes of e1 goes here -->
      </xsd:sequence>
    </xsd:extension>
  <xsd:complexType>
</xsd:element>
```

Rule 10: N-ary relationship - For a relationship of the form $r(n_r, \{(e_1, c_1, \_, \_), \ldots, (e_n, c_n, \_, \_)\})$, an element named n_r is created and put under the element for the dominant entity set, say e_1. Foreign key attributes are added in r with n-1 separate keyref declarations where $\mathcal{K}(e_2) = \{k_{21}, \ldots, k_{2m1}\}, \ldots, \mathcal{K}(e_n) = \{k_{n1}, \ldots, k_{nmn}\}$. If exists c_i="*n*", ($2 \leq i \leq n$), maxOccurs="unbounded" is added to the element.

```
<xsd:keyref name="foreignKey_r_e_2" refer="key_n_e2">
    <xsd:selector xpath="path_r"/><xsd:field xpath=" k_21"/> … <xsd:field xpath=" k_2m1"/>
</xsd:keyref>
… …
<xsd:keyref name="foreignKey_r_e_n" refer="key_n_en">
    <xsd:selector xpath="path_r"/><xsd:field xpath=" k_n1"/> … <xsd:field xpath=" k_nmn"/>
</xsd:keyref>
```

Rule 11: Composite attribute - For an attribute $a(n_a, vt, st)$ where $st(a)$= "*composite*", of the entity set e or relationship r or composite attribute a', an element named n_a is created and put under the element for e or r or a'. maxOccurs="unbounded" is added to the element if $vt(a)$= "*multi-valued*".

Rule 12: Atomic attribute - For an attribute $a(n_a, vt, st)$ where $st(a)$= "*atomic*", of the entity set *e* or relationship *r* or composite attribute *a'*, different rules apply depending on *vt*(*a*).

(1) If *vt*(*a*) = "*multi-valued*", an element named n_a is created and put under the element for *e* or *r* or *a'*. maxOccurs="unbounded" is added to the element. The type of *a* is specified in the *type* attribute of the element.
(2) If *vt*(*a*) = "*single-valued*", either an attribute named n_a associated with the element for *e* or *r* or *a'*, or an element named n_a can be created and put under the element for *e* or *r* or *a'*.

From the above transformation rules, it is easy to find that

- Information preservation and design reversibility criteria have been considered in all the transformation rules.
- Highly nested structure criterion has been taken into account in Rules 3, 5, 6 and 7.
- No redundancy criterion has been applied in Rules 3 and 6.
- Dominant applications criterion has been used in Rules 5, 7 and 8.

4 Mapping E-R Diagrams to XML Schemas

Given an E-R diagram δ $(E, R, A, \rho, n_d, s, p, k)$, we design a transformation algorithm called *ERD2XSD* to generate a corresponding XML schema by applying the transformation rules introduced in the previous section. Normally an ISA relationship only applies to regular entity sets. In ERD2XSD, we first generate XML schema elements for *regular* entity sets (Line 4-9) and *ISA* relationships (Line 10-14), then generate elements for all other entity sets (Line 15-26). If an entity set is of type "high-level", the algorithm is called recursively to transform the E-R diagram of the high-level entity set first. The weak entity sets are processed after the regular and high-level entity sets because of the global key derivation caused by the existence dependency. If a weak entity set e_1 depends on another weak entity set e_2, e_1 will also be processed after e_2. After that, relationships are processed (Line 27-49). The order for transforming relationships is considered carefully in the algorithm such that nesting of one entity set under another is done just once. Finally, XML schema elements/attributes are generated for composite or atomic attributes in the diagram δ (Line 50-54).

4.1 Transformation Algorithm

The algorithm *ERD2XSD* is given below.

Algorithm : *ERD2XSD*

Input: an E-R diagram δ $(E, R, A, \rho, n_d, s, p, k)$

Steps:

1. **apply** Rule 1 to create the root element for δ ;
2. E1 = $\{e \mid e \in E \wedge t(e) = \text{"regular"}\}$;

```
E2 = E – E1;
for each e ∈ E1 { /* process "regular" entity sets without supersets
   if s(e) is not defined {
      apply Rule 2 to generate the element for e;
      E1 = E1 – {e};
   }
}
while E1 ≠ ∅ do { /* process ISA relationships
   get e ∈ E1 such that s(e) ∉ E1; /* no dependency on entity sets in E1
   apply Rule 9 to generate the element for e based on its s(e);
   E1 = E1 – {e};
}
while E2 ≠ ∅ do { /* process "high-level" and "weak" entity sets
   get e ∈ E2;
   if t(e) = "high-level" {
      apply Rule 4 to generate the element for e;
      ERD2XSD(δe ) ;   /* recursively processing e
      E2 = E2 – {e};
   }
   else if p(e) ∉ E2 { /* check dependency between weak entity sets
      apply Rule 3 to generate the element for e;
      E2 = E2 – {e};
   }
}
R1 = R; /* process relationships other than 1:1 relationships
for each r ∈ R1 {
   if nary(r) > 2 { /* nary(r) returns the number of participant entity sets
      apply Rule 10 to generate and nest the element for r;
      R1 = R1 – {r};
   }
   else if nary(r) = 1 {
      apply Rule 8 to generate and nest the element for r;
      R1 = R1 – {r};
   }
   else if card(r.e1)="n"∧card(r.e2)="n" {/* card(r.e) returns cardinality of e in r
      apply Rule 7 to generate and nest the element for r;
      R1 = R1 – {r};
   }
   else if card(r.e1)="n"∨ card(r.e2)="n" {
      apply Rule 6 to generate and nest the element for r and to adjust
         the nesting of e1 and e2;
      R1 = R1 – {r};
   }
}
for each r ∈ R1 { /* the remaining relationships are all 1:1
   apply Rule 5 to generate and nest the element for r;
```

```
   R1 = R1 – {r};
}
for each a ∈ A { /* the remaining relationships are all 1:1
   if st(a)= "atomic" apply Rule 12 to generate and nest an ele-
      ment/attribute for a;
   else apply Rule 11 to generate and nest an element for a;
   A = A – {a};
}
```

Output: the root element named n_d for δ in the target XML schema

4.2 Transformation Example

Figure 1 shows an E-R diagram named *company*. The keys and local keys for regular and weak entity sets are underlined with solid and dotted lines, respectively. Given this E-R diagram as input to the ERD2XSD algorithm, the XML schema with the following root element will be generated.

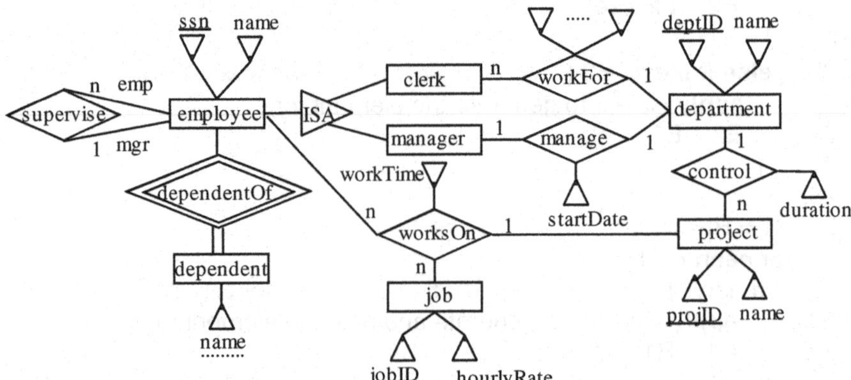

Fig. 1. An example E-R diagram *company*

```
<xsd:element name="company">
  <xsd:complexType>
    <xsd:sequence>
      <xsd:element name="employee" type="t_employee" maxOccurs="unbounded"/>
      <xsd:element name="job" maxOccurs="unbounded">
        <xsd:complexType>
          <xsd:sequence>
            <xsd:element name="worksOn" maxOccurs="unbounded">
              <xsd:complexType>
                <xsd:attribute name="projID" type="xsd:int"/>
                <xsd:attribute name="ssn" type="xsd:int"/>
                <xsd:attribute name="workTime" type="xsd:time"/>
              </xsd:complexType>
              <xsd:keyref name="foreignKey_worksOn_employee" refer="key_employee">
                <xsd:selector xpath="//worksOn"/><xsd:field xpath="@ssn"/>
```

```
        </xsd:keyref>
        <xsd:keyref name="foreignKey_worksOn_project" refer="key_project">
          <xsd:selector xpath="//worksOn"/><xsd:field xpath="@projID"/>
        </xsd:keyref>
      </xsd:element>
    </xsd:sequence>
  </xsd:complexType>
  <xsd:attribute name="jobID" type="xsd:int" use="required"/>
  <xsd:attribute name="hourlyRate" type="xsd:int"/>
  <xsd:key name="key_job">
    <xsd:selector xpath="//job"/><xsd:field xpath="@jobID"/>
  </xsd:key>
</xsd:element>
<xsd:element name="department" maxOccurs="unbounded">
  <xsd:complexType>
    <xsd:sequence>
      <xsd:element name="name" type="xsd:string"/>
      <xsd:element name="clerk" maxOccurs="unbounded">
        <xsd:complexType>
          <xsd:extension base="t_employee">
            <xsd:sequence>
              <xsd:element name="worksFor"> … … </xsd:element>
            </xsd:sequence>
          </xsd:extension>
        </xsd:complexType>
      </xsd:element>
      <xsd:element name="manager">
        <xsd:complexType>
          <xsd:extension base="t_employee">
            <xsd:sequence>
              <xsd:element name="manage">
                <xsd:complexType>
                  <xsd:sequence><xsd:element name="startDate" type="xsd:date"/>
                  </xsd:sequence>
                </xsd:complexType>
              </xsd:element>
            </xsd:sequence>
          </xsd:extension>
        </xsd:complexType>
      </xsd:element>
      <xsd:element name="project" maxOccurs="unbounded">
        <xsd:complexType>
          <xsd:sequence>
            <xsd:element name="control"/>
              <xsd:complexType><xsd:attribute name="duration" type="xsd:duration"/>
              </xsd:complexType>
            </xsd:element>
          </xsd:sequence>
          <xsd:attribute name="projID" type="xsd:int" use="required"/>
          <xsd:attribute name="name" type="xsd:string"/>
        </xsd:complexType>
        <xsd:key name="key_project">
```

```
          <xsd:selector xpath="//project"/><xsd:field xpath="@projID"/>
        </xsd:key>
      </xsd:element>
    </xsd:sequence>
    <xsd:attribute name="deptID" type="xsd:int" use="required"/>
    <xsd:attribute name="name" type="xsd:string"/>
  </xsd:complexType>
  <xsd:key name="key_department">
    <xsd:selector xpath="//department"/><xsd:field xpath="@deptID"/>
  </xsd:key>
 </xsd:element>
 </xsd:sequence>
 </xsd:complexType>
</xsd:element>
<xsd:key name="key_employee">
  <xsd:selector xpath="//employee"/><xsd:field xpath="@ssn"/>
</xsd:key>
<xsd:complexType name="t_employee">
  <xsd:sequence>
    <xsd:element  name="supervise_emp" >
      <xsd:complexType> <xsd:attribute name="mgr" type="xsd:int"/></xsd:complexType>
      <xsd:keyref name="foreignKey_supervise" refer="key_employee">
        <xsd:selector xpath="//supervise_emp"/><xsd:field xpath="@mgr"/>
      </xsd:keyref>
    </xsd:element>
    <xsd:element name="dependent" maxOccurs="unbounded">
      <xsd:complexType>
        <xsd:attribute name="name" type="xsd:string"/>
      </xsd:complexType>
      <xsd:key name="key_dependent"><xsd:selector xpath="//dependent"/>
        <xsd:field xpath="../@ssn"/><xsd:field xpath="@name"/>
      </xsd:key>
    </xsd:element>
  </xsd:sequence>
  <xsd:attribute name="ssn" type="xsd:int"/>
  <xsd:attribute name="name" type="xsd:string"/>
</xsd:complexType>
```

5 Conclusion

In this paper, we first discussed design criteria of a good quality XML schema. Then, we designed transformation rules that translate all the constructs of an E-R model into their counterparts in XML Schema. We claimed that these set of rules follow all five criteria discussed in the paper, i.e., information preservation, highly nested structures, no redundancy, consideration of dominant applications, and design reversibility. Based on the transformation rules, a recursive algorithm called ERD2XSD was proposed that takes an arbitrary E-R diagram as input and generates a correspondent high quality XML schema as output. An illustrative example was given in the end. In the future, we will build a prototype using this algorithm and improve it as a real XML schema design tool.

Acknowledgement

This work was supported by the Australian Research Council Discovery Project under the grant number DP0559202.

Reference

1. C. Kleiner and U. W. Lipeck: Automatic Generation of XML DTDs from Conceptual Database Schemas. GI Jahrestagung (1) 2001. pp. 396-405.
2. C. M. Sperberg-McQueen, E. Maler, T. Bray, J. Paoli and F. Yergeau: Extensible Markup Language (XML) 1.0 (Third Edition). W3C Recommendation, 2004. http://www.w3.org/TR/REC-xml/.
3. L. Bird, A. Goodchild and T. A. Halpin: Object Role Modeling and XML-Schema. ER 2002. pp. 309-322.
4. P. Bernus, K. Mertins and G. Schmidt: Handbook on Architecture of Information Systems. Chapter 4. pp. 81-101. Springer-Verlag, Berlin, 1998.
5. V. Turau: Making Legacy Data Accessible for XML Applications. 2001. http://www.informatik.fh-wiesbaden.de/~turau/DB2XML/.
6. D. Lee, M. Mani, F. Chiu and W. Chu: NeT & CoT: Translating Relational Schemas to XML Schemas using Semantic Constraints. CIKM 2002. pp. 282-291.
7. C. Baru: XViews: XML Views of Relational Schemas. DEXA Workshop. 1999. pp. 700-705.
8. C. Liu, M. W. Vincent and J. Liu: Constraint Preserving Transformation from Relational Schema to XML Schema. World Wide Web Journal, 9(1):93-110, March 2006.
9. D. Beech, N. Mendelsohn, M. Maloney and H. S. Thompson: XML Schema Part 1: Structures Second Edition, W3C Recommendation, http://www.w3.org/TR/xmlschema-1/.
10. P. Bohannon, W. Fan, M. Flaster and P. P. S. Narayan: Information Preserving XML Schema Embedding. VLDB 2005. pp. 85-96.
11. D. Barbosa, J. Freire and A. O. Mendelzon: Designing Information-Preserving Mapping Schemas for XML. VLDB 2005. pp. 109-120.
12. P. Atzeni, S. Ceri, S. Paraboschi and R. Torlone: Database Systems Concepts, Languages & Architectures, part 2. pp. 163-179. McGraw-Hill International (UK) Limited, 1999.

Validating Semistructured Data Using OWL

Yuan Fang Li[1,⋆], Jing Sun[2], Gillian Dobbie[2], Jun Sun[1], and Hai H. Wang[3,⋆⋆]

[1] School of Computing, National University of Singapore, Singapore
{liyf, sunj}@comp.nus.edu.sg
[2] Department of Computer Science, The University of Auckland, New Zealand
{j.sun, gill}@cs.auckland.ac.nz
[3] Department of Computer Science, University of Manchester
hai.wang@cs.manchester.ac.uk

Abstract. Semistructured data has become prevalent in both web applications and database systems. This rapid growth in use makes the design of good semistructured data essential. Formal semantics and automated reasoning tools enable us to reveal the inconsistencies in a semistructured data model and its instances. The Object Relationship Attribute model for Semistructured data (ORA-SS) is a graphical notation for designing and representing semistructured data. This paper presents a methodology of encoding the semantics of ORA-SS in the Web Ontology Language (OWL) and automatically validating the semistructured data design using the OWL reasoning tool - RACER. Our methodology provides automated consistency checking of an ORA-SS data model at both the schema and instance levels.

Keywords: Semistructured Data, Semantic Web, OWL, Formal Verification.

1 Introduction

Semistructured data has become prevalent in both web applications and database systems. It acts as a hinge technology between the data exchanged on the web and the data represented in a database system. This rapid growth in use makes the design of good semistructured data essential. Many data modeling languages [1, 3, 5, 10] for semistructured data have been introduced to capture more detailed semantic information. The Object Relationship Attribute model for Semistructured data (ORA-SS) [4, 9] is a semantic enriched graphical notation for designing and representing semistructured data [8, 9, 11]. The ORA-SS data model not only reflects the nested structure of semistructured data, but also distinguishes between object classes, relationship types and attributes. The main advantages of ORA-SS over other data models is its ability to express the degree of an n-ary relationship type, and distinguish between the attributes of relationship types and the attributes of object classes. This semantic information is

⋆ The author would like to thank Singapore Millennium Foundation (SMF) for the financial support.

⋆⋆ This work was supported in part by the CO-ODE project funded by the UK Joint Information Services Committee, the HyOntUse Project (GR/S44686) funded by the UK Engineering and Physical Science Research Council.

J.X. Yu, M. Kitsuregawa, and H.V. Leong (Eds.): WAIM 2006, LNCS 4016, pp. 520–531, 2006.
© Springer-Verlag Berlin Heidelberg 2006

essential, even crucial for semistructured data representation and management, but it is lacking in other existing semistructured data modeling notations.

A major concern in designing a good semistructured data model using ORA-SS for a particular application is to reveal any possible inconsistencies at both the schema and instance levels. Inconsistencies at the schema level arise if a customized ORA-SS schema model does not conform to the ORA-SS notation. Inconsistencies at the instance level arise if an instance document is not consistent with its ORA-SS schema definition. For example, an inconsistency that might arise at the schema level is the specification of a ternary relationship between only two object classes. An inconsistency that might arise at the instance level is a many to many relationship between elements when a one to many relationship is specified in the schema. These two aspects of validation are essential in the semistructured data design process. Thus, the provision of formal semantics and automated reasoning support for validating ORA-SS semistructured data modeling is very beneficial.

Recent research on the World Wide Web has extended to the semantics of web content. More meaningful information is embedded into the web content, which makes it possible for intelligent agent programs to retrieve relevant semantic as well as structural information based on their requirements. The Semantic Web [2] approach proposed by the World Wide Web Consortium (W3C) attracts the most attention. It is regarded as the next generation of the web. The Ontology Web Language (OWL) is an ontology language for the Semantic Web. OWL can provide not only the structural information of the web content but also meaningful semantics for the information presented. The aim of this paper is to encode the semantics of the ORA-SS notation into the Web Ontology Language (OWL) and automatically verify the semistructured data design using the OWL reasoning tool RACER [6].

The reason that we chose OWL to fulfil our goal is due to the nature of the semistructured data and its strong connections to web technologies. Semistructured data is typically represented using eXtensible Markup Language (XML). XML is a commonly used exchange format in many web and database applications. The introduction of the Semantic Web is to overcome the structure-only information of XML, and to provide deeper semantic meanings to the data. The ORA-SS data model is a semantically enriched data modeling language for describing semistructured data. From the point of capturing more semantic information in semistructured data, OWL and ORA-SS are two approaches that fulfil the same goal, where the former is rooted from the web community and the latter has its basis in the database community. We believe that Semantic Web and its reasoning tools can contribute to the verification phase of the semistructured data design.

In this paper, we propose a methodology to validate semistructured data design using OWL and its reasoner RACER. Firstly, we define an ontology model of the ORA-SS data modeling language in OWL. It provides a rigorous semantic basis for the ORA-SS graphical notation and enable us to represent any ORA-SS data model and its instances in OWL. Furthermore, RACER is used to perform the automated verification of the correctness in a semistructured data design. Our approach is able to provide automatic consistency checking on large semistructured data models and their instances.

The remainder of the paper is organized as follows. Section 2 briefly introduces the background knowledge for the semistructured data modeling language ORA-SS,

Semantic Web ontology language OWL and its reasoning tool RACER. Section 3 presents OWL semantics of the ORA-SS notation and its data models. Section 4 demonstrates a case study on a complete ontology reasoning process for verifying semistructured data design. Examples of both class-level reasoning and instance-level reasoning are presented. Finally, Section 5 concludes the paper.

2 Background

2.1 The ORA-SS Data Modeling Language

The Object Relationship Attribute model for Semistructured data (ORA-SS) data modeling language [4, 9] consists of four basic concepts: object class, relationship type, attribute and reference. It represents these concepts through four diagrams: schema diagram, instance diagram, functional dependency diagram and inheritance diagram. We will focus on the schema and instance diagram in this paper since they are sufficient for our purposes. A full description of the ORA-SS data modeling language can be found in [4, 9].

- An object class is like an entity type in an ER diagram, a class in an object-oriented diagram or an element in an XML document. The object classes are represented as labeled rectangles in an ORA-SS diagram.
- A relationship type represents a nesting relationship among object classes. It is described as a labeled edge by a tuple (`name`, `n`, `p`, `c`), where the `name` denotes the name of relationship type, integer `n` indicates degree of relationship type, `p` represents participation constraint of parent object class in relationship type and `c` represents participation constraint of child object class in relationship type.
- Attributes represent properties and are denoted by labeled circle. An attribute can be a key attribute which has a unique value and represented as a filled circle. Other types of attributes include single valued attribute, multi-valued attribute, required attribute,

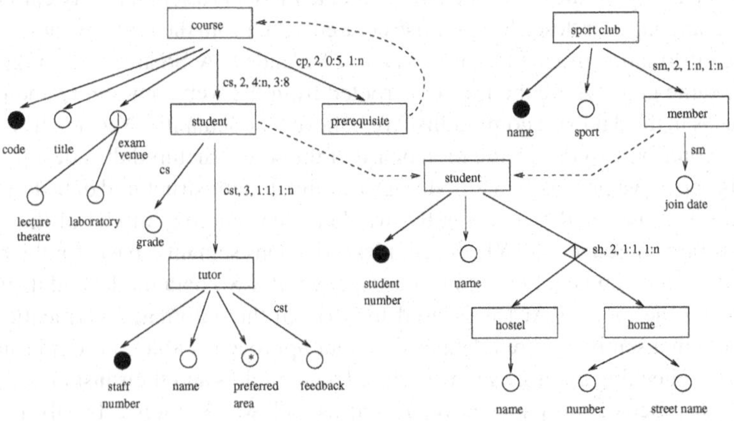

Fig. 1. The ORA-SS Schema Diagram of a Course-Student data model

composite attribute, etc. An attribute can be a property of an object class or a property of a relationship type.
- An object class can reference another object class to model recursive and symmetric relationships, or to reduce redundancy especially for many-to-many relationships. It is represented by a labeled dashed edge.

For the design of semistructured data, an ORA-SS schema diagram constrains the relationships, participations and cardinalities among the instances of the object classes in a semistructured data model. For example, Fig. 1 represents an ORA-SS schema diagram of a `Course-Student` data model. In the diagram, each `course` has `code`, `title`, `exam venue` as its attributes. A relationship type `cs`, which indicates the relationship between a `course` object class and a `student` object class is binary, and each course consists of 4 to many students and each student can select 3 to 8 courses. The `student` object class in the `cs` relationship type has a reference pointing to its complete definition. The `grade` attribute is an attribute belonging to the `cs` relationship type. Based on the above schema definition, two levels of validation can be carried out. Firstly, consistency checking can be performed to determine whether the defined schema model is correct with respect to the ORA-SS language. Secondly, consistency checking can be performed to determine whether a particular instance of semistructured data satisfies the defined ORA-SS schema model. Hence automated tool support for validating the consistency in an ORA-SS data model would be highly desirable.

2.2 Semantic Web – OWL and RACER

Description logics are logical formalisms for representing information about knowledge in a particular domain. It is a subset of first-order predicate logic and is well-known for the trade-off between expressivity and decidability.

The Web Ontology Language (OWL) [7] is the de-facto ontology language for the Semantic Web. It consists of three increasingly expressive sublanguages: OWL Lite, DL and Full. OWL DL is very expressive yet decidable. As a result, core inference problems, namely concept subsumption, consistency and instantiation, can be performed fully automatically. In OWL, conceptual entities are organized as classes in hierarchies. Individual entities are grouped under classes and are called instances of the classes. Classes and individuals can be related by properties. We will be using a synatx similar to that presented in [7].

RACER, the **R**enamed **A**Box and **C**oncept **E**xpression **R**easoner [6], is a reasoning engine for ontologies languages DAML+OIL and OWL. It implements a TBox and ABox reasoner for the description logic $\mathcal{ALCQHI}_{\mathcal{R}^+}(\mathcal{D})^-$ [6]. It is fully automated for reasoning over OWL Lite and DL ontologies.

3 Modeling ORA-SS Data Design Models in OWL

In this section, we show the modeling of ORA-SS schema and instance diagrams as OWL ontologies in three parts. Firstly, we define the ORA-SS ontology in Section 3.1, which contains the OWL definitions of essential ORA-SS concepts. Secondly, in the next 3 subsections, we show how individual schema diagram ontology can be constructed based on the ORA-SS ontology. Finally, in Section 3.5, we show how instance diagrams can be represented in OWL.

Our modeling approach can be regarded as a methodology for creating the OWL representation of ORA-SS diagrams. By strictly following this methodology, a lot of potential modeling errors can be avoided, which will become more evident as we present the approach below. To effectively illustrate the modeling approach, the schema diagram in Fig. 1 is used as a running example.

3.1 The ORA-SS Ontology

The ORA-SS ontology[1] contains the OWL definitions for ORA-SS concepts such as object class, relationship type, attribute, etc. We will model these definitions as OWL classes. The basic assumption here is that all named OWL classes are by default mutually disjoint, which is implied in the ORA-SS diagrams. Essential properties are also defined in the ontology. This ontology, with a namespace of `ora-ss`, can be used later to define ontologies for ORA-SS schema diagrams.

Entities. As each object class and relationship type can be associated with attributes and other object classes or relationship types, we define an OWL class *ENTITY* to represent the super class of both object class and relationship type. The OWL class structure is shown as follows.

$$ENTITY \sqsubseteq \top \qquad ATTRIBUTE \sqsubseteq \top$$

$$OBJECT \sqsubseteq ENTITY \qquad ENTITY \sqcap ATTRIBUTE = \bot$$

$$RELATIONSHIP \sqsubseteq ENTITY \qquad OBJECT \sqcap RELATIONSHIP = \bot$$

It may not seem very intuitive to define relationship types as OWL classes. In ORA-SS, relationship types are used to relate various object classes and relationship types, it might be natural to model relationship types as OWL properties. However, there are two reasons that we decide to model relationship types as OWL classes. Firstly, the domain of ORA-SS relationship types can be relationship types themselves, which describes the relationships of ternary and more. Secondly, classes and properties in OWL DL are disjoint. In our model, a relationship type class consists of instances which are actually pointers to the pairs of object classes or relationship types that this relationship relates.

As ORA-SS is a modeling notation for semistructured data, we need to cater to unstructured data. We define a subclass of *ATTRIBUTE* called *ANY* as a place holder to denote any unstructured data appearing in a model. In ORA-SS, a composite attribute is an attribute composed of other attributes. We also define it as a subclass of *ATTRIBUTE*.

$$ANY \sqsubseteq ATTRIBUTE \qquad CompositeAttribute \sqsubseteq ATTRIBUTE$$

$$ANY \sqcap CompositeAttribute = \bot$$

Properties. A number of essential properties are defined in the `ora-ss` ontology.

Properties Among Entities
In ORA-SS, object classes and relationship types are inter-related to form new relationship types. As mentioned above, since we model relationship types as OWL classes, we need additional properties to connect various object classes and relationship types.

[1] Available at `http://www.comp.nus.edu.sg/~liyf/ora-ss/ora-ss.owl`

Firstly, this is accomplished by introducing two object-properties, *parent* and *child*, which map a *RELATIONSHIP* to its domain and range *ENTITY*s. The following statements define the domain and range of *parent* and *child*. As in ORA-SS, the domain of a relationship (*parent*) can be either an object class or another relationship type, i.e., an *ENTITY*. The range (*child*) must be an *OBJECT*. These two properties are functional as one relationship type has exactly one domain and one range node. Moreover, we assert that only relationship types can have parents and child but object classes cannot.

$$\geq 1\, parent \sqsubseteq RELATIONSHIP \qquad \geq 1\, child \sqsubseteq RELATIONSHIP$$

$$\top \sqsubseteq \forall parent.ENTITY \qquad \top \sqsubseteq \forall child.OBJECT$$

$$\top \sqsubseteq \leq 1\, parent \qquad \top \sqsubseteq \leq 1\, child$$

$$RELATIONSHIP \sqsubseteq \forall parent.ENTITY \qquad RELATIONSHIP \sqsubseteq \forall child.OBJECT$$

Secondly, we define two more object-properties: *p-ENTITY-OBJECT* and *p-OBJECT-ENTITY*. These two properties are inverse of each other and they serve as the super properties of the properties that are to be defined in later ontologies of ORA-SS schema diagrams. Those properties will model the restrictions imposed on the relationship types.

The domain and range of *p-ENTITY-OBJECT* are *ENTITY* and *OBJECT*, respectively. Since the two properties are inverse, the domain and range of *p-OBJECT-ENTITY* can be deduced.

$$p\text{-}OBJECT\text{-}ENTITY = ({}^{-}p\text{-}ENTITY\text{-}OBJECT)$$

$$\geq 1\, p\text{-}ENTITY\text{-}OBJECT \sqsubseteq ENTITY \qquad \geq 1\, p\text{-}OBJECT\text{-}ENTITY \sqsubseteq OBJECT$$

$$\top \sqsubseteq \forall p\text{-}ENTITY\text{-}OBJECT.OBJECT \qquad \top \sqsubseteq \forall p\text{-}OBJECT\text{-}ENTITY.ENTITY$$

$$ENTITY \sqsubseteq \forall p\text{-}ENTITY\text{-}OBJECT.OBJECT \qquad OBJECT \sqsubseteq \forall p\text{-}OBJECT\text{-}ENTITY.ENTITY$$

Properties Between Entities and Attributes

First of all, we define an object-property *has-ATTRIBUTE*, whose domain is *ENTITY* and range is *ATTRIBUTE*. Every *ENTITY* must have *ATTRIBUTE* as the range of *has-ATTRIBUTE*.

$$\geq 1\, has\text{-}ATTRIBUTE \sqsubseteq ENTITY \qquad ENTITY \sqsubseteq \forall has\text{-}ATTRIBUTE.ATTRIBUTE$$

$$\top \sqsubseteq \forall .has\text{-}ATTRIBUTE.ATTRIBUTE$$

For modeling the ORA-SS candidate and primary keys, we define two new object properties that are sub-properties of *has-ATTRIBUTE*. We also make the property *has-primary-key* inverse functional and state that each *ENTITY* must have at most one primary key. Moreover, we restrict the range of *has-candidate-key* to be *ATTRIBUTE*.

$$has\text{-}candidate\text{-}key \sqsubseteq has\text{-}ATTRIBUTE \qquad has\text{-}primary\text{-}key \sqsubseteq has\text{-}candidate\text{-}key$$

$$\top \sqsubseteq \forall has\text{-}candidate\text{-}key.ATTRIBUTE \qquad \top \sqsubseteq \leq 1\, has\text{-}primary\text{-}key^{-}$$

$$ENTITY \sqsubseteq \leq 1\, has\text{-}primary\text{-}key$$

3.2 Object Classes

In this subsection, we present how ORA-SS object classes in a schema diagram are represented in OWL. Moreover, we will discuss how object class referencing is modeled.

Example 1. The schema diagram in Fig. 1 contains a number of object classes [2].

$course \sqsubseteq OBJECT$ $\quad$ $tutor \sqsubseteq OBJECT$

$student \sqsubseteq OBJECT$ $\quad$ $sport\_club \sqsubseteq OBJECT$

$hostel \sqsubseteq OBJECT$ $\quad$ $home \sqsubseteq OBJECT$

... ...

Referencing. In ORA-SS, an object class can reference another object class to refer to its definition, which we say that a *reference* object class references a *referenced* object class. In our model, we model the *reference* object class a sub class of the *referenced* object class. If the two object classes are of the same name, the reference object class is renamed. By doing so, we ensure that all the attributes and relationship types of the referenced object classes are reachable (meaningful). Note that there are no disjointness axioms among the reference and referenced object classes.

Example 2. In Fig. 1, the object class student is referenced by object classes student and member. Hence, we rename the reference student to *student_1* and add the following axioms in to the model.

$student \sqsubseteq OBJECT$ $\quad$ $student\_1 \sqsubseteq student$ $\quad$ $member \sqsubseteq student$

3.3 Relationship Types

In this subsection, we present the details of how ORA-SS relationship types are modeled in OWL. Various kinds of relationship types, such as disjunctive relationship types and recursive relationship types are also modeled. We begin with an example to show the basic modeling of relationship types.

For example, Fig. 1 contains 5 relationship types, namely *cs*, *sh*, *sm*, *cp* and *cst*. The relationship type *cs* is bound by the *parent/child* properties as follows. We use both allValuesFrom and someValuesFrom restriction to make sure that only the intended class can be the parent/child class of *cs*.

$cs \sqsubseteq \forall parent.course$ $\quad$ $cs \sqsubseteq \forall child.student\_1$

$cs \sqsubseteq \exists parent.course$ $\quad$ $cs \sqsubseteq \exists child.student\_1$

Auxiliary Properties. As discussed in Section 3.1, for each ORA-SS relationship type we define two object-properties that are the inverse of each other.

Example 3. Take *cs* as an example, we construct two object-properties: *p-course-student* and *p-student-course*. Their domain and range are also defined.

$p\text{-}student\text{-}course = (^{-}p\text{-}course\text{-}student)$ $\quad$ $p\text{-}student\text{-}course \sqsubseteq p\text{-}OBJECT\text{-}ENTITY$

$p\text{-}course\text{-}student \sqsubseteq p\text{-}ENTITY\text{-}OBJECT$

$\geq 1\, p\text{-}course\text{-}student \sqsubseteq course$ $\quad$ $\geq 1\, p\text{-}student\text{-}course \sqsubseteq student\_1$

$\top \sqsubseteq \forall p\text{-}course\text{-}student.student\_1$ $\quad$ $\top \sqsubseteq \forall p\text{-}student\text{-}course.course$

---

[2] For brevity reasons, the class disjointness statements are not shown from here and onwards.

Participation Constraints. One of the important advantages that ORA-SS has over XML Schema language is the ability to express participation constraints for parent/child nodes of a relationship type. This ability expresses the cardinality restrictions that must be satisfied by ORA-SS instances.

Using the terminology defined previously, ORA-SS parent participation constraints are expressed using cardinality restrictions in OWL on a sub-property of *p-ENTITY-OBJECT* to restrict the parent class *Prt*. Child participation constraints can be similarly modeled, using a sub property of *p-OBJECT-ENTITY*.

Example 4. In Fig. 1, the constraints captured by the relationship type `cs` state that a `course` must have at least 4 students; and a `student` must take at least 3 and at most 8 courses. The following axioms are added to the ontology. The two object-properties defined above capture the relationship type between `course` and `student`.

$course \sqsubseteq \forall\, p\text{-}course\text{-}student.student\_1$ $\quad$ $student\_1 \sqsubseteq \forall\, p\text{-}student\text{-}course.course$

$course \sqsubseteq \geq 4\; p\text{-}course\text{-}student$ $\quad$ $student\_1 \sqsubseteq \geq 3\; p\text{-}student\text{-}course$

$student\_1 \sqsubseteq \leq 8\; p\text{-}student\text{-}course$

Disjunctive Relationship Types. In ORA-SS, a disjunctive relationship type is used to represent disjunctive object classes, where only one object can be selected from a set of object classes. To model this in OWL, we will create a dummy class as the *union* of the disjoint classes and use it as the range of the object-property representing the relationship type. Together with the cardinality constraint that exactly one individual of the range can be selected, the disjunctive relationship type can be precisely modeled.

Example 5. In Fig. 1, *sh* is a disjunctive relationship type where a student must live in exactly one hostel or one home, but not both. We use the following OWL statements to model this situation. Note that *p-student-sh* is an object-property that maps *student* to its range class *home_hostel*, which is the union of *hostel* and *home*.

$hostel \sqsubseteq OBJECT$ $\quad$ $home \sqsubseteq OBJECT$ $\quad$ $hostel \sqcap home = \bot$

$home\_hostel = hostel \sqcup home$ $\quad$ $\top \sqsubseteq \forall\, p\text{-}student\text{-}sh.home\_hostel$ $\quad$ $\geq 1\; p\text{-}student\text{-}sh \sqsubseteq student$

Given the above definitions, the disjunctive relationship type *sh* in the schema diagram can be modeled as follows.

$student \sqsubseteq \forall\, p\text{-}student\text{-}sh.home\_hostel$ $\quad$ $student \sqsubseteq = 1\; p\text{-}student\text{-}sh$

3.4 Attributes

The semantically rich ORA-SS model notation defines many kinds of attributes for object classes and relationship types. These include candidate and primary keys, single-valued and multi-valued attributes, required and optional attributes, etc. In this subsection, we will discuss how these attributes can be modeled.

Example 6. The schema diagram in Fig. 1 includes attributes such as *code*, *title* and *exam_venue*, which are all sub classes of *ATTRIBUTE*.

Modeling of Various Definitions. As OWL adopts the Open World Assumption [7] and an ORA-SS model is closed, we need to find ways to make the OWL model capture the intended meaning of the original diagram. The following are some modeling *tricks*.

- For each *ENTITY*, we use an allValuesFrom restriction on *has-ATTRIBUTE* over the union of all the *ATTRIBUTE* classes this *ENTITY* has in the ORA-SS model to denote the complete set of attributes it holds.

  Example 7. In the running example, the object class *student* has student number and name as its attributes.

  $$student \sqsubseteq \forall\, has\text{-}ATTRIBUTE.(student\_number \sqcup name)$$

- Each entity (object class or relationship type) can have a number of attributes. For each of the entity-attribute pairs in an ORA-SS schema diagram, we define an object-property, whose domain is the entity and range is the attribute.

  Example 8. In Fig. 1, the object class *sport_club* has an attribute *name*. It can be modeled as follows.

  $$\geq 1\; has\text{-}sport\_club\text{-}name \sqsubseteq sport\_club \qquad has\text{-}sport\_club\text{-}name \sqsubseteq has\text{-}ATTRIBUTE$$
  $$\top \sqsubseteq \forall\, has\text{-}sport\_club\text{-}name.name \qquad sport\_club \sqsubseteq \forall\, has\text{-}sport\_club\text{-}name.name$$

Required and Optional Attributes. We use cardinality restrictions of respective object-properties on the owning *ENTITY* to model the attribute cardinality constraints in the ORA-SS model. The default is (0:1). We use a cardinality ≥ 1 restriction to state a required attribute.

Single-Valued vs. Multi-valued Attributes. Single-valued attributes can be modeled by specifying the respective object-property as functional. Multi-valued attributes, on the contrary, are not functional. An attribute is by default single valued.

Primary Key Attributes. For an entity with a primary key attribute, we use an allValuesFrom restriction on the property *has-primary-key* to constrain it. Since we have specified that *has-primary-key* is inverse functional, this suffices to show that two different objects will have different primary keys. Moreover, for every attribute that is the primary key attribute, we assert that the corresponding object property is a sub property of *has-primary-key*.

Disjunctive Attributes. Similar to the treatment of disjunctive relationship types, we create a class as the *union* of a set of disjunctive attribute classes. Together with the cardinality ≤ 1 restriction, disjunctive attributes can be represented in OWL.

3.5 Instance Diagrams in OWL

The representation of ORA-SS instance diagrams in OWL is a straightforward task. As the name suggests, instance diagrams are semistructured data instances of a particular ORA-SS schema diagram. The translation of an instance diagram to an OWL ontology is done by the following 3 steps:

1. Defining individuals and stating the membership of these individuals, by declaring them as instances of the respective OWL classes of object classes, relationship types and attributes defined in the schema diagram ontology.
2. For each OWL class, we state that all its instances are different from each other.
3. By making use of the object-properties defined in the schema diagram ontology, we state the relationships among the individuals.

4 Reasoning About ORA-SS Instance Models

In this section, we demonstrate the validation of ORA-SS schema and instance diagrams using OWL and RACER. We will again use Fig. 1 as the running example.

4.1 Validation of Schema Diagram Ontologies

In order to ensure the correctness of an ORA-SS schema diagram, a number of properties have to be checked, such as:

- The parent of a relationship type should be either a relationship type or an object class, where the child should only be an object class.
- The parent of a higher-degree relationship type (higher than 2) must be a relationship type.
- An object class or relationship type can have at most one primary key, which must be part of the candidate keys.

To manually check the validity of a given schema diagram against these constraints is a highly laborious and error-prone task. By following the methodology presented in this section systematically, a lot of potential violation of the above constraints can be

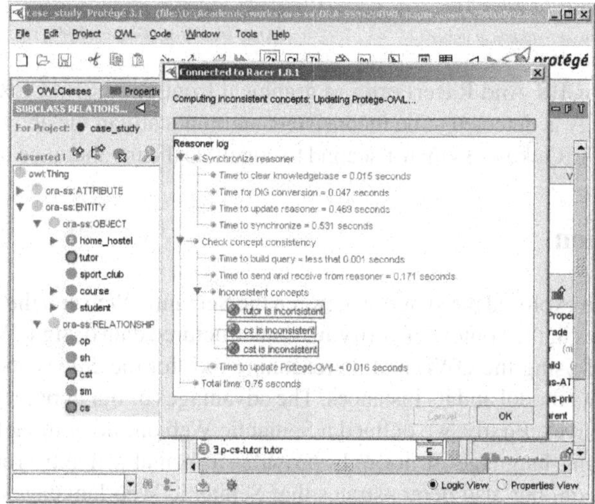

Fig. 2. Schema inconsistency detected by RACER

avoided. Moreover, the highly efficient OWL reasoners such as RACER can check the consistency of ORA-SS schema diagrams in OWL fully automatically. For example, suppose that in the case study, the child of relationship type *cs* is mistakenly put as *cst* instead of *student*_1. Hence, the axiom $\top \sqsubseteq \forall child.OBJECT$ is violated. This error can be picked up by RACER automatically, as shown in Fig. 2. Three classes, *cs*, *cst* and *tutor* are highlighted as inconsistent. Classes *cst* and *tutor* are inconsistent because they are both related to *cs* using existential or cardinality restrictions. Other types of checking can be similarly performed.

It can be seen from Fig. 2 that the detection of inconsistencies in the ORA-SS schema ontology by RACER is quite efficient. On a Pentium IV 2.4GHz machine with 1GB memory, the consistency checking by RACER took only 0.75 second.

4.2 Validation of Instance Diagram Ontologies

After transforming an ORA-SS instance diagram into an OWL ontology. Validation of the consistency of the instance ontology can be done fully automatically by invoking ontology reasoners capable of ABox reasoning. We will use RACER to demonstrate the checking of the above ontology using a few examples.

- Entity/attribute cardinality constraints
  In Fig. 1, each instance of relationship type *cst* has exactly one *tutor*. Suppose that in the instance ontology, *cs*1 is mapped to two tutors, *tutor*1 and *tutor*2 by *cst*.

$$\langle cs1, tutor1\rangle \in p\text{-}cs\text{-}tutor \qquad \langle cs1, tutor2\rangle \in p\text{-}cs\text{-}tutor$$

- Primary key related properties
  Suppose that by accident, two students, *student*4 and *student*5, are both assigned to the same student number.

$$\langle student4, student\_number\_4\rangle \in has\text{-}student\text{-}student\_number \qquad \langle student5, student\_number\_4\rangle \in has\text{-}student\text{-}student\_number$$

By using RACER And RacerPorter (a graphical front-end of RACER) together, the instance ontology is detected to be inconsistent automatically in the above two cases. In each case, RACER takes less than 1 second to conclude the incoherence of the ontology.

5 Conclusion

In this paper, we explored the synergy between the Semantic Web and the database modeling approaches in the context of verifying semistructured data design. We demonstrate the approach of using the OWL and its reasoning tool for the consistency checking of the ORA-SS data model and its instances. The advantages of our approach lie in the following perspectives. Firstly, we defined a Semantic Web ontology model for the ORA-SS data modeling language. It not only provides a formal semantic for the ORA-SS graphical notation, but also demonstrates that Semantic Web languages such as OWL can be used to capture more semantic information of a semistructured data. Furthermore, such a semantics can be adopted by many Semantic Web applications that use the

ORA-SS semistructured data model. Secondly, ontology reasoning tool was adopted to perform automated verification on a semistructured data model. The RACER reasoner was used to check the consistency of an ORA-SS schema model and its instances. We illustrated the various checking tasks through a `Course-Student` example model. In our previous work, we used the Alloy Analyzer for the validation of the ORA-SS data model. The main advantage of our current OWL approach over this is that consistency checking on large ORA-SS models are made feasible, as one of the shortcomings of the current Alloy Analyzer is its limited abilities on verifying large-scale models. Moreover, as Semantic Web reasoners employ highly optimized tableaux-based algorithms, the performance in terms of time is also significantly better than Alloy Analyzer.

References

1. V. Apparao, S. Byrne, M. Champion, S. Isaacs, I. Jacobs, A. L. Hors, G. Nicol, J. Robie, R. Sutor, C. Wilson, and L. Wood. Document Object Model (DOM) Level 1 Specification. `http://www.w3.org/TR/1998/REC-DOM-Level-1-19981001/`.
2. T. Berners-Lee, J. Hendler, and O. Lassila. The Semantic Web. *Scientific American*, 284(5):35–43, 2001.
3. P. Buneman, S. B. Davidson, M. F. Fernandez, and D. Suciu. Adding Structure to Unstructured Data. In *ICDT '97: Proceedings of the 6th International Conference on Database Theory*, pages 336–350. Springer-Verlag, 1997.
4. G. Dobbie, X. Wu, T. Ling, and M. Lee. ORA-SS: Object-Relationship-Attribute Model for Semistructured Data. Technical Report TR 21/00, School of Computing, National University of Singapore, Singapore, 2001.
5. R. Goldman and J. Widom. DataGuides: Enabling Query Formulation and Optimization in Semistructured Databases. In M. Jarke, M. J. Carey, K. R. Dittrich, F. H. Lochovsky, P. Loucopoulos, and M. A. Jeusfeld, editors, *VLDB'97: Proceedings of 23rd International Conference on Very Large Data Bases*, pages 436–445. Morgan Kaufmann, 1997.
6. V. Haarslev and R. Möller. Practical Reasoning in Racer with a Concrete Domain for Linear Inequations. In I. Horrocks and S. Tessaris, editors, *Proceedings of the International Workshop on Description Logics (DL-2002)*, Toulouse, France, Apr. 2002. CEUR-WS.
7. I. Horrocks, P. F. Patel-Schneider, and F. van Harmelen. From $\mathcal{SHIQ}$ and RDF to OWL: The making of a web ontology language. *J. of Web Semantics*, 1(1):7–26, 2003.
8. T. Ling, M. Lee, and G. Dobbie. Applications of ORA-SS: An Object-Relationship-Attribute data model for Semistructured data. In *IIWAS '01: Proceedings of 3rd International Conference on Information Integration and Web-based Applications and Serives*, 2001.
9. T. W. Ling, M. L. Lee, and G. Dobbie. *Semistructured Database Design*. Springer, 2005.
10. J. McHugh, S. Abiteboul, R. Goldman, D. Quass, and J. Widom. Lore: A Database Management System for Semistructured Data. *SIGMOD Record*, 26(3):54–66, 1997.
11. X. Wu, T. W. Ling, M. L. Lee, and G. Dobbie. Designing Semistructured Databases Using the ORA-SS Model. In *WISE '01: Proceedings of 2nd International Conference on Web Information Systems Engineering*, Kyoto, Japan, 2001. IEEE Computer Society.

Dynamic Data Distribution of High Level Architecture Based on Publication and Subscription Tree*

Yintian Liu [1,2], Changjie Tang[1], Chuan Li[1], Minfang Zhu[1,3], and Tao Zeng[1]

[1] School of Computer Science, Sichuan University, Chengdu, 610065, China
[2] Nanjing Army Command College, Nanjing, 210045, China
[3] Dept. of Computer Sci. & Tech., Shaanxi Univ. of Tech., Hanzhong, 723003 China
{liuyintian, tangchangjie, lichuan, zhumingfang, zengtao}@cs.scu.edu.cn

Abstract. To ensure the efficiency of data exchange between simulation members via multicast groups in the simulation system based on High Level Architecture (HLA), this paper proposes a novel method of dynamic data distribution based on publication and subscription tree (PS-Tree). The main contributions of this paper include: (1) Proposing the structure of PS-Tree which can manifest the relationship of data exchange between simulation members. (2) Describing the method of dynamic data distribution based on PS-Tree by mining association rule and (3) Analyzing the performance. Experiment shows that this dynamic data distribution method can implement data distribution efficiently and effectively.

1 Introduction

In the High Level Architecture (HLA), Data Distribution Management (DDM) services [2,3,4,5,6] are used to implement data filtering, which can reduce the amount of irrelevant data being exchanged between simulation members. DDM is based on two methods, i.e. region-based matching and grid-based multicast groups transmission. Through region matching, DDM determines the supply and demand relationship between simulation members, and then the data are exchanged effectively between the members through the multicast groups which are overcast by the matching region's grids. Chunlei Xu [7] proposed a relevant filtering method based on multi-level grid to overcome the shortcoming of even-grid method (difficult to fit all entities in the simulation). Yachong Zhang [8] proposed an algorithm to allocate multicast groups dynamically based on current cells in which there are update and subscription regions matching. These methods can effectively reduce the complexity of region matching and make use of multicast groups to realize the filtering of data belonging to the same object class attributes.

---

* Supported by Grant of National Science Foundation of China (60473071), Specialized Research Fund for Doctoral Program by the Ministry of Education (SRFDP 20020610007) and the Software Innovation Project of Sichuan Youth (AA0807).

J.X. Yu, M. Kitsuregawa, and H.V. Leong (Eds.): WAIM 2006, LNCS 4016, pp. 532–543, 2006.
© Springer-Verlag Berlin Heidelberg 2006

However, by the restriction of multicast groups resource, a region may overcast several multicast groups and various regions binding with various object class attributes or object instance attributes can also overcast the same multicast group. It causes various types of object instance attributes being exchanged via the same multicast group. This phenomenon is especially grievous in a large-scale military simulation system. It is so called the reuse of multicast group address and results in the problem that the subscriber will receive irrelevant data belonging to different object classes although he has not subscribed them via the multicast group he is intercepting. These irrelevant data, i.e. invalid data, worsen the burden of the receiver who will have to consume time and system resource to receive and process every data sent to him to filter for the data he is subscribing. Furthermore, invalid data will make the simulation system unsafely, for the simulation member receives data he should not have received. The traditional methods can not resolve the filtering of invalid data.

To solve the problem of invalid data and to make the simulation system more secure, this paper proposes a dynamic data distribution method based on PS-Tree. The essential idea of this method is: (a) finding the inefficient multicast groups causing invalid data receiving between each pair of publisher and subscriber, (b) constructing a strategy to forward data via other appropriate multicast groups, (c) modifying the strategy along with the advance of system to ensure the efficiency of data exchange by trying to reduce the invalid data receiving.

The rest of the paper is organized as follows: Section 2 introduces the symbols and terms. Section 3 describes the PS-Tree structure. Section 4 gives the association rule mining algorithms of PS-Tree. Section 5 constructs the dynamic data distribution strategy based on PS-Tree. Section 6 analyses the performance of the dynamic data distribution. Section 7 conducts experiments. Section 8 summarizes the paper, and describes future work on PS-Tree.

2 Symbols and Terms

To get the PS-Tree and mine association rules of simulation system based on HLA, it is necessary to transform the publication affairs and subscription affairs of system to publication & subscription records through region matching and region overcastting. The symbols used in this paper are summarized in Table 1.

In a simulation system based on HLA, a number of object instance attributes belonging to the same object class attribute(I_a:count) are transmitted from the publisher(I_p) to the subscriber(I_s) through a multicast group (I_m), which reflects the path and direction of data stream between the simulation members. At the same time, while the simulation system advances forward at the interval of time step, the data stream will change including direction and content. The formal description of the data stream is defined as follows:

Definition 1. In a simulation system based on HLA, the **Data Exchange** between simulation members is a 5-tuple **E=(P,** S, M, A, R), where

(1) $P=\{I_p\}$ is the finite set of simulation members who publish data.
(2) $S=\{I_s\}$ is the finite set of simulation members who subscribe data.
(3) $M=\{I_m\}$is the finite set of multicast groups who transmit data between publisher and subscriber.
(4) $A=\{I_a\}$is the finite set of object class attribute who are transmitted between I_p and I_s through I_m,
(5) $R=\{\delta\}$ is the set of publication & subscription records, and $\delta_i=(I_p, I_s, I_m, I_a:count)$, which describes the action that I_a with quantity of count is transmitted from I_p to I_s through I_m.

During the process of simulation system, the set of publication&subscription records forming during a time step is denoted as **PubsubSet**, and the increase and decrease of publication&subscription records between two time steps are denoted as **PubsubSetNew and PubsubSetDel** respectively.

Table 1. Definition of Symbols

Symbol	Definition
I_{mi}	multicast group item
$\{I_m\}$	multicast group items set of simulation system
I_{ai}	attribute item of object class
$\{I_a\}$	attribute items set of simulation system
I_{pi}	publisher item
$\{I_p\}$	publisher items set of simulation system
I_{si}	subscriber item
$\{I_s\}$	subscriber items set of simulation system
I_{ri}	region item
$\{I_r\}$	region items set of simulation system
$(I_r, \{I_m\})$	region item and multicast group items it overcastting
(I_s, I_r, I_a)	Subscription affair that I_s subscribes I_a with I_r
(I_p, I_r, I_a)	Publication affair that I_p publishes I_a with I_r
(I_s, I_a, I_m)	Subscription record that I_s receives I_a via I_m
(I_p, I_a, I_m)	Publication record that I_p sends I_a through I_m
$(I_p, I_s, I_m, I_a\text{: count})$	record I_p transmits I_a to I_s via I_m with number of count
$\{(I_p,I_s,I_m,I_a\text{:count})\}$	Publication&subscription records set of system at a time

[1] The members who subscribe all data and seldom publish data should not be included in the I_s or I_p set.
[2] In DDM, function SubscribeObjectClassAttributesWithRegion() is based on object class and a region can bind with various object class attributes; the function RegisterObjectInstanceWithRegion() or AssociateRegionForUpdates() is based on object instance and a region can bind with various object instance attributes, but a object instance attribute can only be bound with a region at a time.
[3] A region can only bind with a simulation member.
[4] Subscriber receives an object instance attribute from the publisher via multicast group, if it is valid then form a publication&subscription record $(I_p,I_s,I_m,I_a:1)$, else form a publication&subscrip-tion record $(I_p,I_s,I_m,I_{null}:1)$, I_{null} means the invalid data I_s has not subscribed from I_p through I_m.

Definition 2. A **Forwarding Record** is a 5-tuple $(I_p, I_s, I_m, I_a, I_m')$, where I_p is publisher item; I_s is subscriber item; I_m is the original multicast group item; I_a is the attribute item; I_m' is the forwarding multicast group item. The record describes how to forward I_a from I_p to I_s via I_m' instead of the original I_m. The set of all forwarding records is denoted as **ForwardTable** = $\{(I_p, I_s, I_m, I_a, I_m')\}$.

The dynamic data distribution strategy includes following steps: (1) gaining the PubsubSet according to region matching and region overcastting processes; (2) constructing the PS-Tree according to PubsubSet; (3) mining association rules of PubsubSet via PS-Tree and deciding the role of each path of PS-Tree; (4) creating ForwardTable according to the PS-Tree; (5) gaining the PubsubSetAdd and PubsubSetDel between two time steps, and modifying the PS-Tree according to these record sets and reflecting the modification into ForwardTable.

3 PS-Tree and Related Algorithms

A publication & subscription record (I_p, I_s, I_m, I_a: count) describes the path of data transmission from I_p to I_s, and the PubsubSet reflects the whole data stream (including direction and quantity) of simulation system. The dynamic data distribution uses PS-Tree to describe the data stream in a simulation system.

Definition 3. A **PS-Tree**(publication and subscription tree) is a converse compressed tree with structure as follows:

(1) The depth of PS-Tree is 5 and each layer describes an item set,

(2) The zero-th layer is the root node of tree; the first layer is the node set of publisher item I_p; the second layer is the node set of subscriber item I_s; the third layer is the node set of multicast item I_m; and the fourth layer is the leaf node set of attribute item I_a,

(3) Each record of PubsubSet is reflected to a branch of PS-Tree. The branch begins at root node; the child node of root is node I_p; the child node of I_p is node I_s; the child node of I_s is node I_m; and the child node of I_m is node I_a; the branches can share a common prefix,

(4) Each node of PS-Tree marks its parent link, children links, node-link, count. The node-link is used to link the node-chain with the same item-name which can make the node to find all the nodes with the same item-name. The count reflects the number of data transmitted via this node (marks respectively with valid_count and null_count),

(5) A chain of I_p-I_s-I_m denotes a path which means the link between I_p and I_s through I_m, for each path of PS-Tree, the I_m node marks the role of the path I_p-I_s-I_m, the I_s node marks the node I_m' used to forward the data between I_p and I_s.

For example, given the first five records of PS_Set as follows: (I_{p1}, I_{s2}, I_{m3}, I_{a1}: 1), (I_{p1}, I_{s3}, I_{m3}, I_{a2}: 3), (I_{p1}, I_{s3}, I_{m4}, I_{null}: 7), (I_{p2}, I_{s2}, I_{m4}, I_{a1}: 5), and (I_{p2}, I_{s3}, I_{m5}, I_{a2}: 2). The PS-Tree is then constructed in the following steps: Creating the root node of the tree firstly, and then inserting each record in order of $I_p \rightarrow I_s \rightarrow I_m \rightarrow I_a$ into the tree.

For the first record (I_{p1}, I_{s2}, I_{m3}, I_{a1}: 1), construct the first branch of PS-Tree, where I_{p1} is linked as a child of the root, I_{s2} is linked to I_{p1}, I_{m3} is linked to I_{s2}, I_{a1} is linked to I_{m3}, and increase the valid count of each node by 1. Each node's node-link links to the relevant node-chain with the same item-name and adds to the node-chain. After the

Algorithms of PS-Tree

```
PST-Insert(p, N, m_count, m_nullcount)
Input: node p, parent node N, count of valid/invalid data m_count/m_nullcount
Output: insert node p to his parent node N and increase their related count
if (N has a child node p' such that p'.item-name == p.item-name) then
   increase valid_count/null_count of p' by m_count/m_nullcount
else
   create a new node p' with p'.item-name = p.item-name
   set its valid_count/null_count by m_count/m_nullcount respectively
   set its parent link by N
   set its node-link by the node-chain with same item-name and add to chain
return

PST-Build(PubsubSet)
Input: PubsubSet = {(Ip, Is, Im, Ia:count)}
Output: PS-Tree
create the root node of PS-Tree
for each record (item[4],count) in PubsubSet do
   m_count = (Ia == Inull)? 0 : count
   m_nullcount = (Ia == Inull)? count : 0
   PST-Insert(item[0], root, m_count, m_nullcount)
   for(i=0,i<4,i++) do
      PST-Insert(item[i+1],item[i],m_count,m_nullcount)
return PS-Tree

PST-Delete(item[4], m_count)
Input: publication & subscription record (I_p, I_s, I_m, I_a:count)
Output: modified PS-Tree
find the branch in PS-Tree corresponding to the record
if (I_a == I_null) then
   decrease the null_count of each node in the branch by m_count
else
   decrease the valid_count of each node by m_count
   if (I_a.valid_count == 0) then delete node I_a from branch
   if (I_m.valid_count == 0 and I_m.role == "Forwarding") then
      rebuild PS-Tree
      return
   if (I_m.valid_count == 0 and I_m.role != "Forwarded") then
      decrease the null_count of root,I_p,I_s by I_m's null_count and delete I_m
   if (I_s.valid_count == 0) then
      decrease the null_count of root and I_p by I_s's null_count and delete I_s
   if (I_p.valid_count == 0) then
      decrease the null_count of root by I_p's null_count and delete I_p
   if (root.valid_count == 0) then delete root
return
```

insertion of the record, the first branch of PS-Tree is constructed: root:1,0-I_{p1}:1,0-I_{s2}:1,0-I_{m3}:1,0-I_{a1}:1,0. For the second record (I_{p1}, I_{s3}, I_{m3}, I_{a2}: 3), insert it into PS-Tree like the first record to construct the second branch. Because this branch would share a common prefix root-Ip1 with the first branch and the count of the second branch is valid, we instead increase the valid count of the nodes root and I_{p1} by the count of second branch i.e. 3.

For the third record (I_{p1}, I_{s3}, I_{m4}, I_{null}: 7), insert it into PS-Tree in the order of $I_{p1} \rightarrow I_{s3} \rightarrow I_{m4} \rightarrow I_{null}$ and add the nodes to their node-chains. This branch shares a common prefix root-I_{p1}-I_{s3} with the second branch. Because the data of this record is invalid, each node's invalid count of this branch increases by 7.

The PS-Tree obtained after the insertion of these five records is shown in Figure 1 and the relevant algorithms of PS-Tree are given as follows.

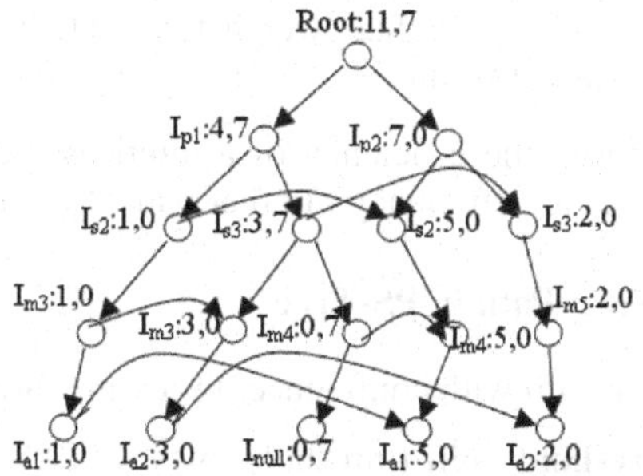

Fig. 1. A PS-Tree

To implement the node insertion algorithm, we store the nodes into a hash table with the item-name as the key. This takes just a step to find whether a node exists and gains its pointer of address. We can gain the PS-Tree via inserting all the records into the tree, and it needs scan the PubsubSet just once, which costs O(n) time.

4 The Association Rule Mining of PS-Tree

4.1 Confidence Calculation of PS-Tree

For a PS-Tree, I_{pi}.valid_count denotes the valid data sent by I_{pi} and its value equals to the node I_{pi}'s valid_count, I_{si}.valid_count denotes the valid data received by I_{si} and its value equals to the sum of all the nodes I_{si}s' valid_count, I_{mi}.valid_count denotes the valid data transformed through I_{mi} and its value equals to the sum of all the nodes I_{mi}s' valid_count, I_{pi}-I_{sj}.valid_count denotes the valid data transmitted from I_{pi} to I_{sj} and its value equals to the node I_{sj}'s valid_count whose father node is I_{pi}, I_{pi}-I_{mj}.valid_count denotes the valid data sent by I_{pi} through I_{mj} and its value equals to the sum of all the nodes I_{mj}s' valid_count whose grandfather node is I_{pi}, I_{si}-I_{mj}.valid_count denotes the valid data received by I_{si} via I_{mj} and its value equals to the sum of all the nodes I_{mj}s' valid_count whose father node is I_{si}, I_{pi}-I_{sj}-I_{mk}.valid_count denotes the valid data transmitted from I_{pi} to I_{sj} through I_{mk} and its value equals to the node I_{mk}'s valid_count of the chain I_{pi}-I_{sj}-I_{mk}. The process of invalid data is similar to valid data.

To mine the association rule of PS-Tree, three types of confidences are proposed.

(1) C_{sm} = confidence($I_m \Rightarrow I_s$)
= support($I_p \cup I_m$)/support(I_m) = I_s-I_m.valid_count/I_m.valid_count.

This confidence describes the ratio of the data I_s receiving from I_m to the data all I_s receiving from I_m.

(2) C_{psm} = confidence(I_p,$I_m \Rightarrow I_s$)=support($I_p \cup I_s \cup I_m$)/support($I_p \cup I_m$)
=I_p-I_s-I_m.valid_count /(I_p-I_s-I_m.valid_count + I_p-I_s-I_m.null_count).

This confidence describes the ratio of the data from I_p to I_s through I_m to the data from I_p to all I_s through I_m.

(3) C_{mix} = C_{sm}*weight1 + C_{psm}*weight2 (weight1,weight2 $\in$ (0, 1.0) and weight1> weight2, weight1 + weight2 = 1).

This confidence describes the efficiency of a multicast item I_m used to sent data form I_p to I_s compared with the efficiency of other paths I_{pj}-I_{sj}-I_m.

4.2 Role Decision of Each Path in PS-Tree

To decide the role of each path with confidence, following thresholds are proposed.

(1) **threshold_max, threshold_min** (threshold_max $\in$ (0.5, 1.0), threshold_min $\in$ (0, (1-threshold_max)).

Thresholds of C_{sm}. If C_{sm}>threshold_max, the I_m can be selected by the I_s to forward data, and all the valid data other I_{sj} receiving from I_m should be forwarded by other I_{mj}. To reduce the invalid data, the threshold_max should be as big as possible. The bigger C_{sm} is, the smaller invalid data receive. On the other hand, it is difficult to find an I_m for an I_s if the value of thredshold_max is too big. So we can properly reduce the value of threshold_max within the permission of network bandwidth to find an I_m for the I_s.

If I_s receive too many invalid data through I_m, i.e. C_{sm}<threshold_min, the I_s needn't intercept this multicast I_m and all the data it receives form I_m should be forwarded through other I_{mj}.

(2) **threshold_tran** $\in$ (0.5, 1.0).

Threshold of C_{psm}. For a path I_p-I_s-I_m, if C_{sm}>threshold_max and C_{psm}> threshold_tran, it means that the most data from I_p to I_s are transmitted through I_m and the most data I_p transmitting through I_m are received only by I_s. The data from I_p to I_s can be forwarded through I_m.

(3) **threshold_min_mix** $\in$ (0, 1.0).

Threshold of C_{mix}. For a path I_p-I_s-I_m that threshold_min<C_{sm}<threshold_max and C_{mix}>threshold_min_mix, it means that whether the path I_p-I_s-I_m is used to forward data or the data under path I_p-I_s-I_m should be forwarded, there are too many repeated data being created and the network data flow will add quickly. So the data from I_p to I_s through I_m are transmitted by its own multicast group and path I_p-I_s-I_m will not forward other path's data.

The path I_p-I_s-I_m of PS-Tree is defined to take one of the roles as follows.

(1) **Forwarded** role. I_a under this path should be forwarded through other I_{mj};
(2) **Retained** role. I_a under this path should be forwarded through its own I_m, including valid data and invalid data;
(3) **Forwarding** role. This path forwards not only its own valid data I_a under this path, but also other valid data I_a between I_p and I_s.

```
Procedure MineAssociation( ) //Association rules Mining of PS-Tree
Input: PS-Tree, threshold_max, threshold_min, threshold_min_mix,
       weight1, weight2
Output: the PS-Tree marked role and transmission path
for each path (Ip-Is-Im) in PS-Tree do
   calculate Csm, Cpsm, Cmix
   if (Csm>thredshold_max) then
      set all the other paths Ip-Is-Im including Im as Forwarded role
      if (Cpsm>0.5) then
         set path as Forwarding role and Ip-Is.forward_channel=Im
      else
         if (Cmix>threshold_min_mix) then set path as Retained role
         else set path as Forwarded role
   else
      if (Csm<threshold_min) then
         mark the role of this path as Forwarded
      else
         if (Cmix>threshold_min_mix) then set path as Retained role
         else set path as Forwarded role
return
```

If there are several paths between I_p and I_s whose role is "Forwarding", then compare their C_{mix}, the largest one is used to forward data.

5 The Dynamic Data Distribution Based on PS-Tree

Based on the association rule mining, the role of each path in PS-Tree is decided. The next step is to deal with this PS-Tree and to achieve the ForwardTable.

The ForwardTable can be built by scanning PS-Tree only once. Each branch forms a forwarding record, and the forwarding I_m' can get just by checking the role of path and the forwarding multicast group between I_p and I_s.

During the time advance of simulation system, when an object instance attribute I_a needs to be transmitted from I_p to I_s through I_m, I_p finds the forwarding record in ForwardTable according to I_p, I_s, I_m, and obtains the forwarding multicast group I_m'.

Along with the time advance of simulation system, some of the records in PubsubSet die and new records occur. It is necessary to reflect the modification of PubsubSet real time and modify the ForwardTable.

Especially, if a node I_m marked as "Forwarding" was deleted, or controlled by simulation system manually, the dynamic distribution strategy should be rebuilt. It needn't reconstruct the structure of PS-Tree because the PS-Tree has been modified real time according to PubsubSetNew and PubsubSetDel. The rebuilding of distribution strategy can be realized by simply re-mining association rules of PS-Tree and gaining the new ForwardTable. The rebuilding of distribution strategy is quick.

The procedure describing the modification of ForwardTable is shown as follows.

```
Procedure StrategyAdjust(PS_SetNew, PS_SetDel)
Input: PubsubSetNew, PubsubSetDel
Output: Adjusted ForwardTable
for each record (I_p, I_s, I_m, I_a:count) in PubsubSetNew do
    Insert record into PS-Tree
    if (new branch occurred) then
      forward_record=(I_p, I_s, I_m, I_a, I_m')
         // I_m' is decided according the original path I_p-I_s-I_m, if the share
         //prefix don't include I_m, the role of new path is "Forwarded"
      ForwardTable.add(forward_record)
for each record (I_p, I_s, I_m, I_a:count) in PubsubSetDel do
    decrease the valid_count or null_count form the relevant branch
    if (there is branch deletion) then
      forward_record = (I_p, I_s, I_m, I_a, I_m') // I_m' = I_s.forward_channel
      ForwardTable.delete(forward_record)
return ForwardTable
```

6 Performance Analysis of Dynamic Data Distribution

Now consider the application of dynamic data distribution. Note that (a) The forwarding of data will result in the repeating transmission of the same data, it will increase the amount of data sent by publishers to some degree, and the whole system's network traffic increases. (b) For the subscribers, the quantity of invalid data they receive can be decreased to the least degree, which can decrease their burden for data filtering and ensure the safety of simulation system too.

Suppose the size of all the object instance attributes is equal and each of them is represented by 1 unit. By the support count calculation of each path of PS-Tree, we can get the performances data of dynamic data distribution, as shown in Table 2.

Table 2 shows that (1) By the association rules mining via PS-Tree, it is easy to gain the relationship of data exchange between publishers and subscribers including direction and size before the push forward of simulation system. (2) We can realize the dynamic data distribution to modify the publication and subscription of members to reduce the receiver of invalid data and the processing burden of subscriber. (3) We can implement the real-time adjustment of distribution strategy according to the network state by modifying the values of the weights and thresholds, which ensure the effective balance between the efficiency of simulation system and the occupation of system resources.

Table 2. Performances Table of Data Distribution

Content	Formula	Comments
Before Strategy Application		
Amount of data I_p sent **Dpub**	$\sum_{I_{mi}}$ (Ip - Im.valid_count + Ip - Im.null_count)	$I_{mi} \in I_m$ nodes set under I_p subtree, and $I_{mi} != I_{mj}$
Amount of data I_s received $\mathbf{D_{sub}}$	$\sum_{I_{pi}}$ (Ip - Is.valid_count + Ip - Is.null_count)	
Amount of data transmitted through network $\mathbf{D_{net}}$	$\sum_{I_{pi}}$ Dpub	
After Strategy Application		
Amount of data I_p sent $\mathbf{D_{pub}}'$	$\sum_{I_{mi}}$ (Ip - Im.valid_count + Ip - Im.null_count)[1] $+ \sum_{I_{si}} \sum_{I_{mi}}$ (Ip - Is - Im.valid_count)[2]	[1] $I_{mi} \in$ Retained I_m nodes set under I_p subtree, $I_{mi} != I_{mj}$ [2] $I_m \in$ Forwarded or forwarding I_m nodes set between I_p and I_s
Amount of data I_s received $\mathbf{D_{sub}}'$	$\sum_{I_{pi}} \sum_{I_{mi}}$ (Ip - Is - Im.valid_count + Ip - Is - Im.null_count)[1] $+ \sum_{I_{pi}} \sum_{I_{mi}}$ (Ip - Is - Im.valid_count)[2]	[1] $I_{mi} \in$ Retained I_m nodes set under I_p subtree [2] $I_m \in$ Forwarded or forwarding I_m nodes set between I_p and I_s
Amount of data transmitted through network $\mathbf{D_{net}}'$	$\sum_{I_{pi}}$ Dpub'	
Performance Affection		
The increment I_p sent $\mathbf{D_{pub\_add}}$	$\sum_{I_{si}} \sum_{I_{mi}}$ Ip - Is - Im.valid_count[1] $- \sum_{I_{si}} \sum_{I_{mi}}$ Ip - Is - Im.null_count[2]	[1] $I_m \in$ Forwarded I_m nodes set between I_p and I_s [2] $I_m \in$ Forwarding I_m nodes set between I_p and I_s
The increment network transmitted $\mathbf{D_{net\_add}}$	$\sum_{I_{pi}}$ Dpub_add	
The decrease Is received $\mathbf{D_{sub\_reduce}}$	$\sum_{I_{pi}} \sum_{I_{mi}}$ Ip - Is - Im.null_count	$I_m \in$ Forwarded or Forwarding I_m nodes set between I_p and I_s
The decrease system received $\mathbf{D_{sys\_reduce}}$	$\sum_{I_{si}}$ Dsub_reduce	

7 Experimental Study

The key steps of experiment include: (a) Integrating the PS-Tree structure and dynamic data distribution technique into UTS-RTI, (b) building a training environment to evaluate the data exchange between simulation members via network by means of recording the data count each member sent and received during every time step, including valid and invalid data, and (c) comparing the amount of data sent and received before and after the application of dynamic data distribution strategy under different scale simulation members and multicast groups.

Figure 2 depicts the change of data during the system propelling process with 50 simulation members and 60 multicast groups. Figure 3 depicts the proportion of the reduction of received data and the increase of published data for the following environments: 50 members and 30 channels, 50 members and 60 channels, 100 members and 30 channels, and 100 members and 60 channels.

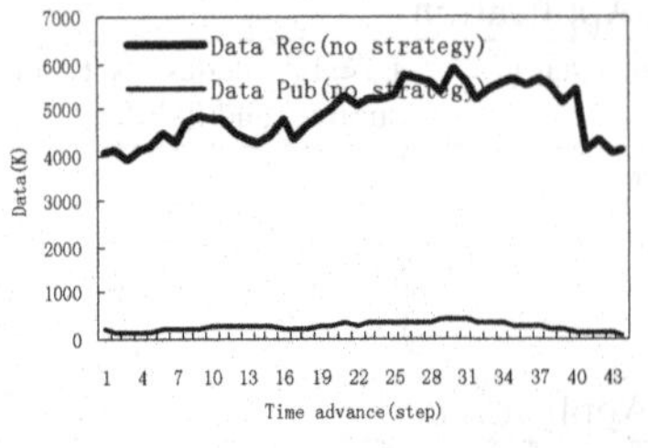

(a) performance before the use of strategy

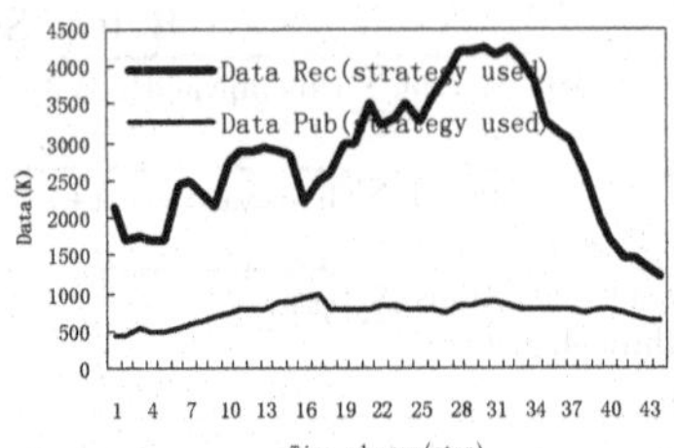

(b) performance after the use of strategy

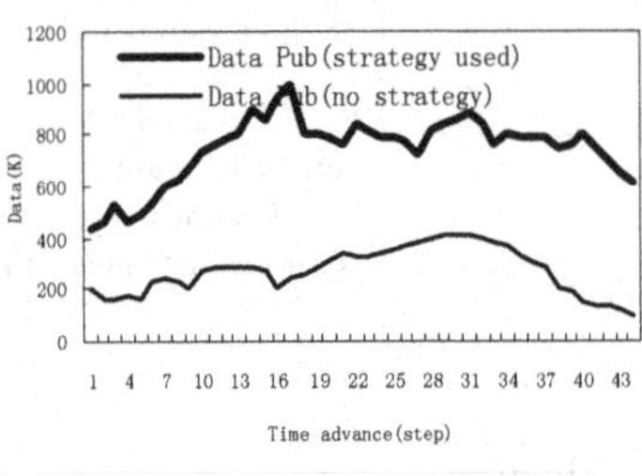

(c) comparison of system publication data

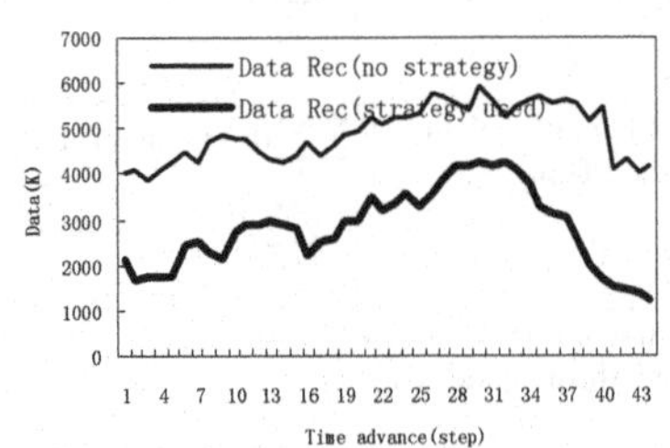

(d) comparison of system receiving data

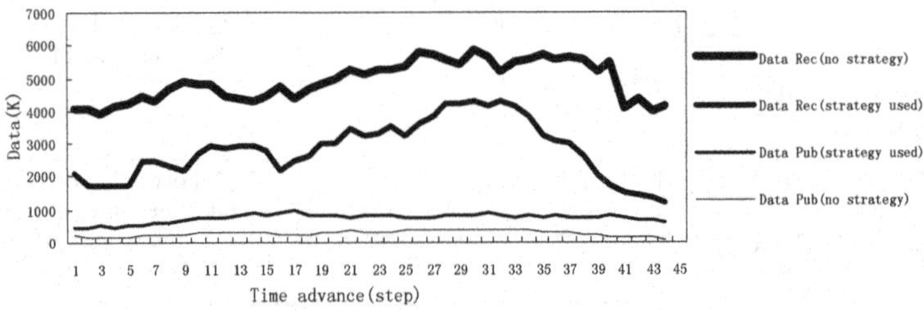

(e) the summary of system performance

Fig. 2. System performance under the environment of 50 members and 60 multicast groups

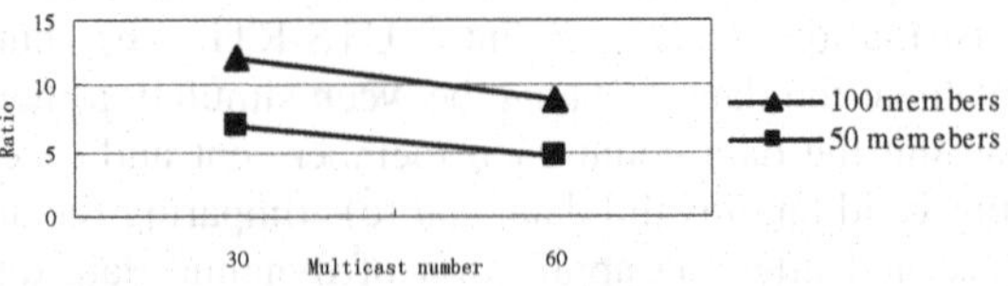

Fig. 3. Ratio variation along with the number of multicast groups

The experiment results show that: (1) The HLA DDM, by multicast technique, greatly reduces the data processing burden of publishers and the quantity of network data flow. (2) The dynamic data distribution greatly reduces the amount of invalid data and release data processing burden of subscribers. (3) Although the dynamic data distribution increases the data publication amount of publishers and the burden of network bandwidth, when compared with the reduction of invalid data, the latter covers larger proportion. Besides, this advantage is more obvious under the condition with numerous participants and insufficient multicast group resources. As a result, within the allowable range of system network bandwidth, the dynamic data distribution can well balance the network bandwidth and the processing burden of members, and enhance the stability and security of simulation system based on HLA.

8 Conclusion and Future Work

Association rule-based dynamic data distribution can well handle the problem of receiving large amount of invalid data in simulation system based on High Level Architecture. This method can balance the relationship of network resources consumption and the efficiency of system real time data exchange.

The PS-Tree can well manifest the data exchange of the whole simulation system, this article only researches on how to mine association rules via PS-Tree in order to implement the optimization of data distribution. Besides, we can also mine the complicated association rules between all kinds of objects, especially in complex military simulation; by analyzing the relationship of data stream between simulation members via PS-Tree, we can provide effective data support for the decision-making of command and control, the evaluation of campaign, etc.

References

[1] Jiawei Han, and Micheline Kambr. Data Mining-Concepts and Tech- niques[M]. Beijing: Higher Education Press, 2001. 225-245.

[2] Department of Defense High Level Architecture Interface Specification, Version 1.3. DMSO [S]. April 1998, available at http://hla.dmso.mil.

[3] High Level Architecture Run-Time Infrastructure Programmer's Guide. DMSO [S]. 1998, available at http://hla.dmso.mil.

[4] Morse, K.L., and J.S. Steinman. Data Distribution Management in the HLA: Multi-dimensional Regions and Physically Correct Filtering [C]. In Proc. the 1997 Spring Simulation Interoperability Workshop (Orlando, FL, March). Spring 1998. 343-352.

[5] Rak, S.J., and D.J. Van Hook. Evaluation of Grid-Based Relevance Filtering for Multicast Group Assignment [C]. In Proc. 14th Workshop on Standards for the interoperability of Distributed Simulations (Orlando, FL, September), March 1996. 739-747.

[6] Katherine L. Morse, Lubomir Bic, and Kevin Tsai. Multicast grouping for dynamic data distribution management [C]. in Proc. 31st Society for Computer Simulation Conference (SCSC '99). 1999.

[7] Xu Chunlei, Zeng Liang, and Li Sikun. An Efficient Multi-level Grids Based Relevance Filtering Method. In Proc. Journal of National University of Defense Technology, Vol. 24 No. 4, Jan 2002.

[8] Zhang Yachong, Sun Guoji, and Yan Hairong. New Algorithm of Data Distribution Management for Distributed Interactive Simulation. In Proc. Journal of System Simulation, Vol. 7 No. 1, Jan 2005.

A Framework for Query Reformulation Between Knowledge Base Peers

Biao Qin, Shan Wang, and Xiaoyong Du

School of Information, Renmin University of China, Beijing 100872, P. R. China
{qinbiao, swang, duyong}@ruc.edu.cn

Abstract. The problem of sharing data in peer-to-peer environment has received considerable attention in recent years. However, knowledge sharing in peer architectures has received very little attention. This paper proposes a framework for query reformulation in peer architectures. We first consider a mapping language based on a particular description logic that includes class connectors. Then a set of rules are proposed for building graphs. Because the axioms in a knowledge base have different properties, our graph generation algorithm classifies the generated graphs into four sets (Ugraph, Bgraph, Cgraph and Dgraph). Furthermore, based on the properties of the unification nodes, our algorithms can reformulate each kind of atom in a special way. Finally we do extensive simulation experiments and simulation results show that the proposed method has better performance than those of Mork's [8].

1 Introduction

The problem of sharing data in peer-to-peer environment has received considerable attention in recent years. Two basic problems in the peer-based integration system are: how to discover, express, and compose the mappings between peers [1, 2, 3], and how to exploit the mappings in order to answer queries posed to one peer [4, 5]. In [6], Tatarinov et al. develop techniques for pruning paths in the reformulation process and for minimizing the reformulated queries as they are created.

However, knowledge sharing in peer architectures has received very little attention. In [7], Calvanese considers the problem of ontology-based query reformulation between knowledge base peers. Based on the peer architecture, he proposes an algorithm, called computeWAT, to answer queries posed to the local peer by relying only on the two query answering services available at the peers. In [8], Mork adopts a description logic formalism to describe the transformations between peers for knowledge sharing. He establishes a set of rules to build a hierarchy H. Based on H, the axiomatic and full reformulation algorithms are proposed. However, if a predicate can be unified with more than one node in H, neither axiomatic nor full reformulation algorithms can deal with it.

Based on the works in [7, 8], we propose a framework for query reformulation between knowledge base peers. We consider a mapping language based on a

J.X. Yu, M. Kitsuregawa, and H.V. Leong (Eds.): WAIM 2006, LNCS 4016, pp. 544–556, 2006.
© Springer-Verlag Berlin Heidelberg 2006

particular description logic that includes class connectors. Then we establish a set of rules to build graphs, which are classified into four sets. Based on them, our algorithms can handle the situation that a predicate is unified with more than one node in the graphs. The main contributions of this paper are as follows.

- This paper establishes a set of rules to build graphs. Based on the rules, this paper proposes a graph generation algorithm, in which the subgraphs are classified into four sets according to different properties of the axioms.
- Based on the graph, this paper proposes the basic and extending reformulation algorithms to reformulate conjunctive queries between knowledge base peers. From our algorithms, a predicate can be unified with more than one node in the graphs.

The paper is organized as follows. Section 2 presents the description logical formalism of knowledge base peers. Section 3 describes our query reformulation algorithms. We do extensive simulation and present the representative experimental results in section 4. Section 5 discusses related work. Section 6 concludes.

2 The Description Logic Between Knowledge Base Peers

Each knowledge-based peer contains a knowledge base K, which comprises two components: a *TBox* and an *ABox* [9]. The peer exports a suitable schema S of K to the agents willing to use the peer, here called *clients*. Clients can ask to the peer only queries that are accepted by the peer. The peer answers such queries by exploiting inference from its knowledge base K. Apart from using its knowledge base K, each peer can be connected with other knowledge-based peers which can answer its queries accepted by them. Suitable mappings between the peers give the means to interpret the answers to queries posed to the remote peer. A knowledge-based peer system is formed by many peers sharing the domain of interpretation and the set of standard names.

Definition 1. A knowledge base peer is a tuple of the form $K_P = < K, S, M >$ where K is a knowledge base written in description logic (we do not consider functions in this paper); S is the schema which is the exported fragment of K, further $S = < C, P, A_T, C_T >$ where C is a set of classes, P is a set of properties, A_T is a set of logical axioms, C_T is a set of class connectors and the set $C \cup P$ is called S's terminology; M is a set of mapping assertions between peers.

Subclass axiom is used to explicitly construct class hierarchy. Components constraints, which include the first component (FCom) and the second component (SCom) axioms, are used in restrict ways in which the class is the first or second component of property. So component axiom includes FCom and SCom axioms. The only number restriction we consider is minimum cardinality (or mandatory participation), which asserts that every instance of a given class has a value for the indicated property. The participation includes the first participation component which is denoted by FPart and the second participation component which is denoted by SPart. So participation axiom includes FPart

Table 1. Axioms place the following restrictions on interpretations

Axiom	Syntax	Semantic Restriction
Subclass	$C_1 \subseteq C_2$	$I(C_1) \subseteq I(C_2)$
FCom	$FCom(P) = C$	$\{x \in R \mid \exists y. < x, y > \in I(P)\} \subseteq I(C)$
SCom	$SCom(P) = C$	$\{y \in R \mid \exists x. < x, y > \in I(P)\} \subseteq I(C)$
FPart	$MinCard_F(C, P) = 1$	$I(C) \subseteq \{x \in R \mid \exists y. < x, y > \in I(P)\}$
SPart	$MinCard_S(C, P) = 1$	$I(C) \subseteq \{y \in R \mid \exists x. < x, y > \in I(P)\}$
Disjoint	$Disjoint(B, C)$	$I(B) \cap I(C) = \emptyset$

Table 2. Connectors define some classes in terms of other classes

Connector	Syntax	Semantic Restriction
Union	$C = C_1 \cup ... \cup C_n$	$I(C) = I(C_1) \cup ... \cup I(C_n)$
Intersection	$C = C_1 \cap ... \cap C_n$	$I(C) = I(C_1) \cap ... \cap I(C_n)$
Complement	$C = \neg B$	$I(C) = R \backslash I(B)$

and SPart axioms. And we support disjoint axioms, which are used to indicate that two classes have no resources in common. We describe the restrictions these axioms place on an interpretation in table 1. In addition to atomic classes, we can define complex classes using class connectors based on set operations. These connectors place additional restrictions on which interpretations are valid as described in table 2.

Definition 2. If $A(x) = B_1(x) \wedge ... \wedge B_n(x)$, we call predicate A a conjunctive predicate. If $A(x) = B_1(x) \vee ... \vee B_n(x)$, we call predicate A a disjunctive predicate.

We coordinate the schemata using mappings that provide additional axioms for logical mediation. In the spirit of Bernstein [10], a mapping is a schema extended to include a set of equivalences that relate the terminologies in S and T to the terminologies in M.

Definition 3. A mapping $M : S \Leftrightarrow T$ that relates S and T is a schema ($< C, P, A_T, C_T >$) augmented with two functions $E_P : (S.P \cup T.P) \rightarrow M.P$ and $E_C : (S.C \cup T.C) \rightarrow M.C$. These functions further restrict the interpretation of $M : \forall < Q, R > \in E_P : I(Q) = I(R)$ and $\forall < A, B > \in E_C : I(A) = I(B)$.

Furthermore, Mork [8] gives the definition of valid and minimal rewritings as follows.

Definition 4. Given $M : S \Leftrightarrow T$, a query Q_T (posed against T) is a valid rewriting of Q_S (posed against S) if and only if the following two conditions hold:

1) $I(Q_T) \subseteq I(Q_S)$ for all valid interpretations of S, T, and M.
2) The predicates appearing in the body of Q_T are all equivalent to some predicate appearing in T's terminology.

Definition 5. A minimal rewriting Q_T is a valid rewriting of Q_S such that whenever any predicate in the body Q_T is removed, the result is not a valid rewriting of Q_S.

3 Reformulation Algorithms Between Peers

3.1 Graph Generation Algorithm

For any two peers S and T, there is a mapping M related to them. Before reformulating any queries between them, our graph generation algorithm (GGA) builds a graph according to the axioms in M, S and T. We call the graph building by the GGA algorithm the GGA graph, in which each node represents an atom. And each atom consists of a predicate (appearing in the mapping's terminology) and an ordered list of arguments. These arguments can include variables (such as x), wildcards (indicated using _), and constants (drawn from the universal resource namespace). We build the GGA graph using the following rules.

Rule 1. If $I(A_1) \subseteq I(A)$ and A is an unary predicate, we have 1) $A(x)$ is the parent node of $A_1(x)$ if A_1 is an unary predicate; 2) $A(x)$ is the parent node of $A_1(x,\_)$ or $A_1(\_,x)$ if A_1 is a binary predicate. If A is a binary predicate, we have 1) $A(x,\_)$ or $A(\_,x)$ is the parent node of $A_1(x)$ if A_1 is an unary predicate; 2) $A(x,\_)$ or $A(\_,x)$ is the parent node of $A_1(x,\_)$ or $A_1(\_,x)$ if A_1 is a binary predicate.

From rule 1, the axioms in table 1 and table 2 can form the following graphs:

1) For each axiom $B \subseteq C$, make $C(x)$ a parent node of $B(x)$;
2) For each axiom $FCom(P) = C$, make $C(x)$ a parent node of $P(x,\_)$;
3) For each axiom $SCom(P) = C$, make $C(x)$ a parent node of $P(\_,x)$;
4) For each axiom $MinCard_F(C,P)$, make $P(x,\_)$ a parent node of $C(x)$;
5) For each axiom $MinCard_S(C,P)$, make $P(\_,x)$ a parent node of $C(x)$;
6) If $C = C_1 \cap C_2 \cap ... \cap C_n$ and for any two predicates C_i and C_j, which have $Disjoint(C_i, C_j)$, make each $C_i(x)$ a parent node of $C(x)$;
7) If $C = C_1 \cup C_2 \cup ... \cup C_n$ and for any two predicates C_i and C_j, which have $Disjoint(C_i, C_j)$, make $C(x)$ a parent node of each $C_i(x)$.

Because the Subclass, FCom and SCom axioms have association, they form a set. And we call them SFS axioms. When we build the graph, we sort the SFS axioms in a topological order. Then those axioms generate the Ugraph, because their parent nodes are unary predicates. The rule for topologically sorting the SFS axioms is as follows.

Rule 2. If a predicate A is in the front of a predicate B, one of the following two cases happens: 1) If they have association, the leaf node of predicate A is the parent node of predicate B; 2) They have no association.

The disjunctive axioms in a knowledge base may have association. When we build the graph, we sort them in a topological order. Then those axioms generate a Dgraph, which come from disjunctive axioms. The rule for topologically sorting disjunctive axioms is as follows.

Rule 3. If a disjunctive predicate A is in the front of a disjunctive predicate B, one of the following two cases happens: 1) If they have association, one of leaf node of disjunctive predicate A is the parent node of disjunctive predicate B; 2) They have no association.

Algorithm 1. GraphGenerationAlg(Axioms A_s, Graph G, Class C, Property P)

```
sorts the SFS axioms of A_s in a topological order;
generates the Ugraph of G;
if (a class C is not unified with any node in the Ugraph) then
    puts an independent node in the Ugraph of G;
end
for (each Spart or FPart axiom A of A_s) do
    puts a subgraph G_s into the Bgraph of G;
end
if (a property P is not unified with any node in the Bgraph) then
    puts an independent node in the Bgraph of G;
end
for (each conjunctive axiom A of A_s) do
    puts a subgraph G_s into the Cgraph of G;
end
sorts the disjunctive axioms of A_s in a topological order;
generates the Dgraph of G;
return G;
```

For each FPart or SPart axiom, the GGA algorithm generates an independent subgraph in Bgraph, whose parent node is binary predicate. For each conjunctive axiom, the GGA algorithm generates an independent subgraph in Cgraph, which comes from conjunctive predicate. For each class $C \in M.C$, if it can not be unified with any node in the Ugraph, an independent node $C(x)$ is added into the Ugraph. For each property $P \in M.P$, if it can not be unified with any node in the Bgraph, an independent node $P(x, y)$ is added into the Bgraph. Our graph generation algorithm is as shown in algorithm 1

3.2 Basic Reformulation Algorithm

From the GGA algorithm, we know $C(x)$ is the parent node of $P(x, \_)$ and $P(\_, x)$ in FCom and SCom axioms respectively. So the binary predicates only appear

---

Algorithm 2. BasicQueryReformulation(Query Q, Graph G, Schema T)

```
Result = {c};
for (each A in Q) do
    Rewritings = BasicAtomReformulation(A, G, T);
    Result = ConjunctionAlgorithm(Rewritings, Result);
end
return Result;
```

Algorithm 3. BasicAtomReformulation(Atom A, Graph G, Schema T)

```
Result = ∅;
if (A is an unary predicate) then G = (Ugraph) G;
else G = (Bgraph) G;
(N,f) = G->unify(A);
for (each n in G->sub(H_N)) do
    if (T->containsPredicate(n)) then Result += f(n);
end
return Result;
```

in the leaf nodes of the Ugraph. And we know $P(x, \_)$ or $P(\_, x)$ is a parent of $C(x)$ in the SPart or FPart axiom, the unary predicates only appear in the leaf nodes of the Bgraph. Because the atom of a leaf node can not be reformulated by the atoms of other nodes, the binary predicate need not unify with any node in the Ugraph. For the same reason, the unary predicate need not unify with any node in the Bgraph.

Given a target schema T and a query Q, we consider each atom of Q in turn. For each atom, we find the corresponding nodes in the graph based on unification. An atom A unifies with a node N if they refer to the same predicate, and there exists a function f from the constants and variables in $A's$ argument list to the variables in $N's$ argument list. We define H_N to be the subgraph in the Ugraph rooted at N; H_N contains N and all of $N's$ descendants. Let n be a node in H_N. If $n's$ predicate is an element of $T's$ terminology, then $f(n)$ is a rewriting of A: replace each variable in $n's$ argument list with the corresponding constant or variable from A.

At this point, we have a collection of partial rewritings, one for each atom. The final result is the cross-product of these partial rewritings, which is the function of ConjunctionAlgorithm(). The basic reformulation algorithm (BRA) is summarized in algorithm 2. The basic rule in the BRA algorithm is as follows.

Rule 4. If a predicate A is conjunctive with a constant c, the result is the predicate. That is, $A \wedge c = A$.

Example 3.1. Consider the schemata in figure 1. Schema S contains three classes and two properties. Moreover, S asserts that the first component of S_D is S_B. Schema T contains one class and one property (and no axioms).

Let M be a mapping that asserts that S_D is equivalent to T_D (i.e., they are both equivalent to M_D) as proposed in [10]. This mapping also asserts that the first participation of M_E, with respect to M_F is 1. So TBox contains axioms $FCom(S\_D) = S\_B$ and $MinCard_F(M\_F, M\_E) = 1$. Thus the GGA algorithm builds the graph as shown in figure 2 and figure 3.

Now, consider the query $Q_S(x) \leftarrow S\_B(x), S\_E(x, \_)$. In figure 2, the unification node of atom $S\_B(x)$ is $M\_B(x)$, whose descendant node is $M\_D(\_, x)$ because of the FCom axiom in TBox. In figure 3, the unification node of atom $S\_E(x, \_)$ is $M\_E(x, \_)$, whose descendant node is $M\_F(x)$ because of the FPart axiom in TBox. From the BRA algorithm, a valid rewriting for Q_S is $Q_T(x) \leftarrow T\_D(\_, x), T\_F(x)$.

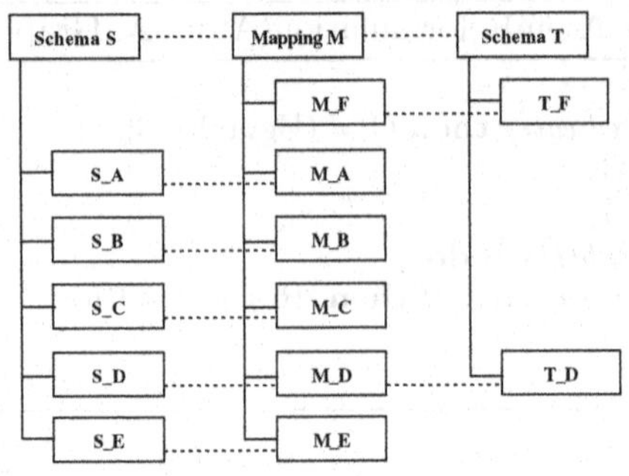

Fig. 1. An example mappings between peers

Fig. 2. The Ugraph of FCom axiom

Fig. 3. The Bgraph of FPart axiom

3.3 Extending Reformulation Algorithm

From the GGA algorithm, we know the conjunctive predicate only appears in the leaf node of the Cgraph. And in the subgraphs of the Dgraph, each leaf node is unified with a basic predicate. The extending reformulation algorithm (ERA) is shown in algorithm 4. Given a target schema T and a query Q, we consider each atom of Q in turn. For each conjunctive predicate, the ERA algorithm unifies it with the leaf node of each subgraph in the Cgraph. If an atom $A(x)$ can unify a node N, the reformulation of $A(x)$ is the cross-product of all elements of N's parent nodes. For each disjunctive predicate, the ERA algorithm unifies it with the non-leaf nodes of each subgraph in the Dgraph. If an atom $B(x)$ can unify a node N, each descendent node is a valid reformulation of the atom $B(x)$. For each basic predicate, the ERA algorithm unifies it with the leaf nodes of each subgraph in the Dgraph. In each subgraph, at most a node can be unified with it. If it can be unified with more than one node, its reformulation results are the cross-product of the predicates in different subgraphs.

Example 3.2. Consider the schemata in figure 4. Schema S contains one concept. Schema T contains two concepts. The TBox includes three axioms: $M\_AC = M\_A \cup M\_C$, $M\_CE = M\_C \cup M\_E$ and $Disjoint(M\_A, M\_E)$. Based on the GGA algorithm, we build the Dgraph as shown in figure 5 and figure 6.

Now, consider the query $Q_S(x) \leftarrow S\_C(x)$, neither T_B nor T_D can be used to answer the original query. However, from ERA algorithm, atom $S\_C(x)$ can unify with two nodes in figure 5 and figure 6. In figure 5 the unification node of atom $S\_C(x)$ is $M\_C(x)$, whose ascendent node is $M\_AC(x)$. In fig-

Algorithm 4. ExtendingQueryReformulation(Query Q, Graph G, Schema T)

```
Result = c;
for (each A in Q) do
    Rewritings = ExtendingAtomReformulation(A, G, T);
    Result = ConjunctionAlgorithm(Rewritings, Result);
end
return Result;
```

ure 6 the unification node of atom $S\_C(x)$ is $M\_C(x)$, whose ascendent node is $M\_CE(x)$. Thus, a valid rewriting for Q_S is $Q_T(x) \leftarrow T\_B(x), T\_D(x)$ by the ERA algorithm.

3.4 Discussion on the Proposed Algorithm

In this paper, we propose a graph generation algorithm. Based on it, we proposes basic and extending reformulation algorithms, which rewrite each atom of Q_S independently. For each atom, the two algorithms search the corresponding subgraphs to find the unification node.

Lemma. The GGA graph generated by the proposed algorithm is acycle.

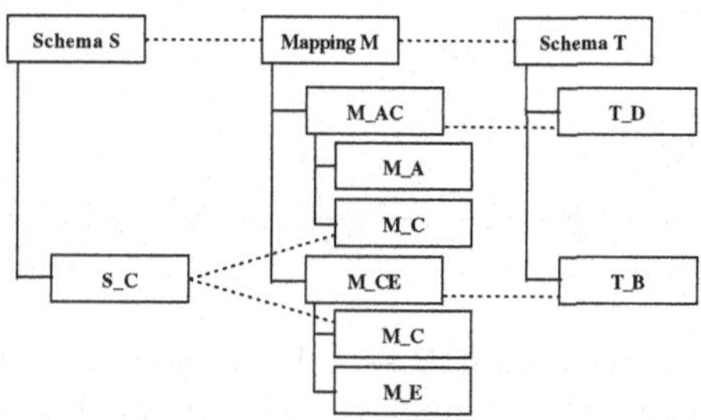

Fig. 4. An example mappings of disjunctive axioms

Proof. From the GGA algorithm, four kinds of subgraphs are generated. They are the Ugraph, Bgraph, Dgraph and Cgraph. Because each subgraph of the Bgraph and Cgraph is built by an axiom, there is no cycle in them.

Because binary predicates only appear in the leaf nodes, FCom and SCom axioms can not cause any cycle in the Ugraph. We assume that Subclass axioms cause a cycle ($A \longrightarrow B$ and $B \longrightarrow A$) in the Ugraph. Because of $A \longrightarrow B$, we have $B \subseteq A$ from the rules. Because of $B \longrightarrow A$, we have $A \subseteq B$. However, because $A \subseteq B$ and $B \subseteq A$, A is the same class as B. So the two nodes in the graph merge. Thus there is no cycle in the Ugraph.

We assume that disjunctive axioms cause a cycle ($A \longrightarrow B$ and $B \longrightarrow A$) in the Dgraph. Because of $A \longrightarrow B$, we have $A = B \cup B_1 ... \cup B_n$ from the rules.

Algorithm 5. ExtendingAtomReformulation(Atom A, Graph G, Schema T)

```
Result = BasicAtomReformation(A, G, T);
if (A is a binary predicate) then return Result;
if (A is a conjunctive predicate) then
    G = (Cgraph) G;
    (N,f) = G->unify(A);
    Result += cross-product of all elements in G->parent(N);
end
if (A is a disjunctive predicate) then
    G = (Dgraph) G;
    (N,f) = G->unify(A);
    for (each n in G->sub(H_N)) do
        if (T->containsPredicate(n)) then Result += f(n);
    end
end
if (A is a basic predicate and unified with more than one nodes in Dgraph) then
    G = (Dgraph) G;
    Rewritings2 = {c};
    for (each subgraph G_d of G) do
        (N,f) = G_d->unify(A);
        if (T->containsPredicate(G_d->parent(N))) then
            Rewritings1 = f(G_d->parent(N));
            Rewritings2 = (Rewritings1 and Rewritings2);
        end
    end
end
Result += Rewritings2;
return Result;
```

Then we have $B \subset A$. Because of $B \longrightarrow A$, we have $B = A \cup A_1 ... \cup A_n$. Then we get $A \subset B$. However, $B \subset A$ and $A \subset B$ is impossible. So there is no cycle in the Dgraph. Thus the theorem follows.

Theorem 1. Let S and T be schemata and let $M : S \Leftrightarrow T$ be a mapping . Let Q_S be a conjunctive query expressed against S. The extending reformulation algorithm terminates.

Proof. First, there are finite axioms in Q_S. Second, each axiom in S has mappings with finite axioms in T. Finally, there are no cycle in the GGA graph. So the extending reformulation algorithm terminates. Thus, the theorem follows.

Theorem 2. Let S and T be schemata and let $M : S \Leftrightarrow T$ be a mapping. Let Q_S be a conjunctive query expressed against S. Let Q_T be a minimal rewriting of Q_S expressed against T. After applying the extending reformulation algorithm to Q_S, the output of the extending reformulation algorithm will contain Q_T.

Proof. Assume that Q_T is a minimal rewriting of Q_S not generated by the extending reformulation algorithm. Because Q_S is a conjunctive query, for each atom $A_S \in Q_S$, there exists some $q_T \subseteq Q_T$ which is satisfied with $q_T \subseteq A_S$. And each atom in Q_T must be unified with a node in the graph. Otherwise Q_T would not be a valid rewriting. We must now show that q_T is generated by the ERA algorithm. There are the following three cases:

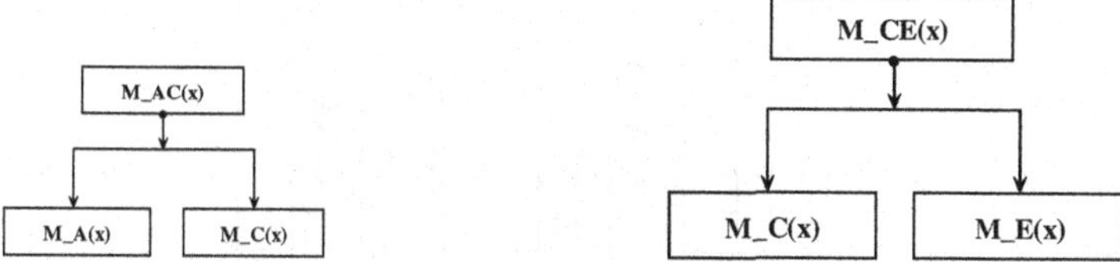

Fig. 5. The Dgraph of $M\_AC = M\_A \cup M\_C$

Fig. 6. The Dgraph of $M\_CE = M\_C \cup M\_E$

First, if q_T is unified with an independent node in the graph, it is identified by the basic reformulation algorithm.

Second, if q_T is unified with a node below A_S in the graph, there are the following two cases: 1) If the graph is built by the axioms in the table 1, q_T is identified by the basic reformulation algorithm. 2) If the graph is built by disjunctive axioms, q_T is identified by the extending reformulation algorithm. In those cases, q_T must only contain a single atom, or the minimal condition is violated.

Finally, if q_T is the conjunctive of some predicates, there are the following two cases: 1) If A_S is a conjunctive predicate, q_T is the cross-product of all elements in $G- > parent(A_S)$. 2) If A_S is a basic predicate and it is unified with more than one node B_i in the Dgraph, q_T is the cross-product of the predicates in $G- > parent(B_i)$ $(i = 1, ..., n)$. So in those cases q_T is identified by the extending reformulation algorithm.

So for any $q_T \subseteq A_S$, the extending reformulation algorithm can generate q_T. The assumption is wrong. Thus the theorem follows.

In [8], Mork gives a set of rules to build a hierarchy H. Based on it, he proposes the axiomatic and full reformulation algorithms to reformulate ontology-based conjunctive queries. And he gives the similar theorem as theorem 2. However, he only proves the first two cases in our theorem 2.

4 Simulation

Our knowledge base architecture is made up of two peers. They are related to university ontology. One is based on [11], the other is ours. Based on the peer architecture, we do extensive simulation experiments comparing the reformulation efficiency of the proposed algorithms with Mork's. The simulation system was tested on a Windows XP Pentium 4 PC running at 2.8 GHz with 1G of memory. During the experiments, we classify our BRA algorithm and Mork's axiomatic reformulation algorithm into the same set, which is called basic set and denoted by BSet. We classify our ERA algorithm and Mork's full reformulation algorithm into the same set, which is called extending set and denoted by ESet.

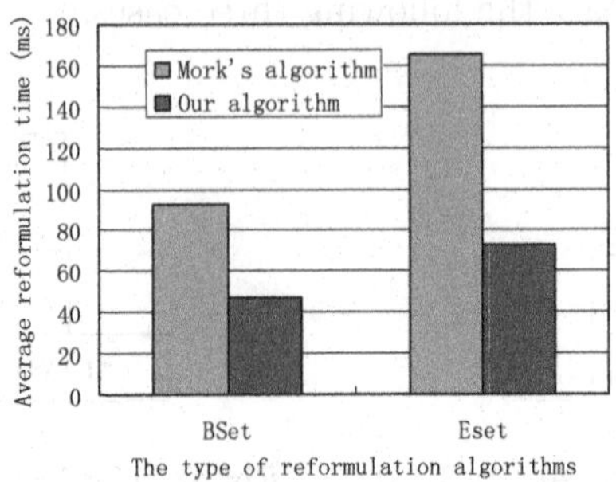

Fig. 7. The reformulation efficiency of our algorithms vs. Mork's

The simulation results are shown in Figure 7, from which we know the proposed algorithms have better performance than those of Mork's for two reasons. First, for any atom $A(x)$ in a conjunctive query, our BRA algorithm does as follows. The binary predicate is only unified with the nodes in the Bgraph, and the unary predicate is only unified with the nodes in the Ugraph. However, for any atom $A(x)$, the axiomatic algorithm searches the whole hierarchy to find the unification node. So our BRA algorithm has better performance than that of axiomatic reformulation algorithm. Second, the algorithms in BSet are based on the algorithms in ESet. For each conjunctive predicate, the ERA algorithm unifies it with the leaf nodes of each subgraph in the Cgraph. For each disjunctive predicate, the ERA algorithm unifies it with the non-leaf nodes of each subgraph in the Dgraph. For each basic predicate, the ERA algorithm unifies it with the leaf nodes of each subgraph in the Dgraph. However, the full reformulation algorithm also searches the whole hierarchy to find the unification node. So our ERA algorithm has better performance than that of full reformulation algorithm.

5 Related Work

In [12], Calvanese addresses the fundamental problem of how to specify the mapping between the global ontology and the local ontologies. He argues that for capturing such mapping in an appropriate way, the notion of query is a crucial one, since it is very likely that a concept in one ontology corresponds to a view over the other ontologies. As a result query processing in ontology integration systems is strongly related to view-based query answering in data integration. In [13], information integration over ontology-based information sources is obtained through a mediator comprising an ontology and a set of articulations to the information sources. Information queries are addressed to the mediator whose task is to analyze each query into sub-queries, translate them into queries to appropriate sources, then merge the results to answer the original query.

Based on the peer-based knowledge system, Calvanese [7] investigates how to solve the so-called "What-To-Ask" problem. And he shows that a solution to this problem exists in the case of peers based on a basic ontology language and provide an algorithm to compute it. In [8], Mork considers a mapping language based on a particular description logic that includes class constructors. Then he proposes a rule system to build hierarchy H. Based on it, he proposes axiomatic and full reformulation algorithms. However, the two algorithms search the whole hierarchy H to find the unification node. Furthermore, his algorithms can not deal with that a predicate can be unified with more than one node in H.

In this paper, we propose a graph generation algorithm, which classifies the graph into four sets. For the conjunctive queries, we propose the basic and extending reformulation algorithms. For each atom, our algorithms only search the corresponding subgraphs to find the unification nodes. And our ERA algorithm can solve the problem that Mork's algorithms meet.

6 Conclusions and Future Work

This paper researches on query reformulation between knowledge base peers. In this paper, we first consider a mapping language based on a particular description logic that includes class connectors. Then we propose a set of rules for building graphs. Because the axioms in a knowledge base have different properties, our graph generation algorithm classifies the generated graphs into four sets. For each kind of atom, our algorithms find the corresponding nodes in the subgraphs based on unification and reformulate it in a special way.

In the future, we will extend our research work to disjunctive queries. Also, we will study query answering in the case where the knowledge bases at the peers are mutually inconsistent, since this is of relevance in real domains.

Acknowledgements. This work is supported by National Natural Science Foundation of China under Grant No. 60503038, 60473069, 60496325 and 60573092.

References

1. J. Madhavan, and A. Y. Halevy. Composing mappings among data sources. VLDB 2003, pp: 572-583.
2. P. A. Bernstein, F. Giunchiglia, A. Kementsietsidis., J. Mylopoulos, L. Serafini, and I. Zaihrayeu. Data management for peer-to-peer computing: A vision. WebDb 2002.
3. R. Fagin, P. G. Kolaitis, L. Popa, and W. -C. Tan. Composing schema mappings: Second-order dependencies to the rescue. PODS 2004, pp: 83-94.
4. A. Y. Halevy. Answering queries using views: A survey. Very Large Database Journal. 2001, 10(4): 270-294.
5. M, Lenzerini. Data integration: A theoretical perspective. PODS 2002, pp: 233-246.
6. I. Tatarinov, A. Halevy. Efficient Query Reformulation in Peer Data Management Systems. SIGMOD 2004.

7. D. Calvanese, G. D. Giacomo, D. Lembo, M. Lenzerini, and R. Rosati. What to Ask to a Peer: Ontology-based Query Reformulation. Proc. of the 9th Int. Conf. on Principles of Knowledge Representation and Reasoning, 2004.
8. P. Mork. Peer Architectures for Knowledge Sharing. PhD thesis, University of Washington, 2005.
9. F. Baader, D. Calvanese, D. Mcguinness, D. Nardi, and P. F. Patel-Schneider. The Description Logic Handbook - Theory, implementation, and applications. Cambridge University Press 2003.
10. P. A. Bernstein. Applying Model Management to Classical Meta-Data Problems. CIDR 2003, pp: 209-220.
11. http://www.cs.umd.edu/projects/plus/SHOE/onts/univ1.0.html.
12. D. Calvanese, G. De Giacomo, M. Lenzerini. A framework for ontology integration. In I. Cruz, S. Decker, J. Euzenat and D. McGuinness, The Emerging Semantic Web - Selected Papers from the First Semantic Web Working Symposium. IOS Press. 2002, pp: 201-214.
13. Y. Tzitizkas, P. Constantopouslos, and N. Spyratos. Mediators over ontology-based information sources. WISE 2001, pp: 31-40.

An Efficient Indexing Technique for Computing High Dimensional Data Cubes*

Fangling Leng, Yubin Bao, Ge Yu, Daling Wang, and Yuntao Liu

School of Information Science & Engineering,
Northeastern University, Shenyang 110004, P.R.China
{baoyb, yuge}@mail.neu.edu.cn

Abstract. The computation of a data cube is one of the most essential but challenging issues in data warehousing and OLAP. Partition based algorithm is one of the efficient methods to compute data cubes on high dimensionality, low cardinality, and moderate size datasets, which exist in real applications like bioinformatics, statistics, and text processing. To deal with such high dimensional data cubes, we propose an efficient indexing technique consisting of a compressed bitmap index and two algorithms for cube constructing and querying. Experimental results show that our method saves at least 25% on storage space and about 30% on computation time compared with the Frag-Cubing algorithm.

1 Introduction

Data warehousing and on-line analytical processing(OLAP) are essential elements of decision support, which has increasingly become a focus of the database industry [1]. Computation of a data cube is a very important problem in the area of data warehousing and OLAP. To fulfill the requirement of fast interactive multidimensional data analysis, database systems have to pre-compute aggregation views on some subsets of dimensions and their corresponding hierarchies. For this task, many efficient cube computation algorithms have been proposed, such as ROLAP-based multi-dimensional aggregate computation [2], multi-way array aggregation [3], Top-k H-Cubing [4], and Star-Cubing [5]. Since computing the whole data cube not only requires a substantial amount of time, but also generates a huge number of cube cells to be stored. Many efficient computation methods have been put forward, such as partial materialization of a data cube [6], Condensed Cube [7], Dwarf [8], Quotient Cube [9], and Object Deputy Model [10]. However, there exist datasets in real applications like bioinformatics, statistics, and text processing that are characterized by high dimensionality, e.g., over 100 dimensions, and moderate size, e.g., around 10^6 tuples that can not be well processed by these algorithms. Since a data cube grows exponentially with the number of dimensions, it is too costly in both computation time and storage space to materialize a full high dimensional data cube. For example, a data cube

* Supported by the National Natural Science Foundation of China under Grant No.60473073, 60503036, 60573090.

J.X. Yu, M. Kitsuregawa, and H.V. Leong (Eds.): WAIM 2006, LNCS 4016, pp. 557–568, 2006.
© Springer-Verlag Berlin Heidelberg 2006

of 100 dimensions each with 10 distinct values may contain as many as 11^{100} aggregate cells. Iceberg Cube [4] used a pruning method to avoid calculating the aggregations below a certain threshold, which is an effective way to derive nontrivial multidimensional aggregations, but the number of the cells in the computing result is still large. For example, an Iceberg cube with 6 million tuples and 60 dimensions will still produce about 2^{60} cells when the threshold is set to be 5. Quotient Cube [9] compresses the data cube through sharing the tuples, but on the same condition the cube size is more than double of the Iceberg Cube [11]. So, it is not suitable for high dimensional datasets. The space complexity of Dwarf [8] was $O(T^{1+1/(\log_d C)})$ [12], where d is the number of dimensions, C is the cardinality, and T is the number of tuples. In a high dimensional dataset above-mentioned where d is large, C is small, $\log_d C$ could become quite small and the cube size still explodes. Frag-Cubing [11] proposed an algorithm based on partitions, but its space cost and time cost are still large.

To solve high dimensional cube computation, we propose a new efficient technique called compressed bitmap index cubing. The cube construction algorithm based on compressed bitmap index vertically partitions a high dimensional dataset into a set of disjoint low dimensional datasets called segments. For each segment, the local data cube is fully computed, and the bitmap index of each attribute value in the segment data cube is constructed. If the value of a bit in a bitmap is equal to 1, it indicates the attribute value is appeared in the corresponding tuple. Then we can re-construct the corresponding cuboid upon request using bit-AND operations. Since the experiments show that there are many continuous 0-bit redundancy in the beginning and the end of the bitmap indices, we can compressed the bitmap indices using two pointers called *start valid pointer* and *end valid pointer*. Because of the fast speed of bit-AND operations and the 0-bit redundancy in the beginning and the end of the bitmap indices, the computation time of data cubes and the storage space spending on compressed bitmap indices are highly reduced.

The method proposed in this paper has excellent performance on computing data cubes with high dimension and low cardinality in both computation time and storage space. The smaller the distinct value is, the better the performance of the method is. In addition, experiments show that the computation time and the storage space of our method are competitive with the Frag-Cubing algorithm either with the dimensions varied from 10 to 80, or with the tuples ranged from 60 thousand to 160 thousand.

The remainder of the paper is organized as follows. Section 2 describes the motivation. We discuss the structure of the compressed bitmap index and two algorithms for cube constructing and querying in Section 3. Section 4 shows the results of experiments and analysis. We gives the conclusion in Section 5.

2 Motivation

To fulfill the requirement of fast interactive multidimensional data analysis, view materialization is very important, especially to the datasets in real applications like bioinformatics, statistics, and text processing that are characterized by high dimensionality, low distinct attribute values, and moderate size. Since a data cube grows exponentially with the number of dimensions, it is too costly in both computation time and storage space to materialize a full high dimensional data cube. We propose an efficient indexing technique, compressed bitmap index, to deal with the computation of such high dimensional data cubes.

2.1 Limitations of Other Cube Computation Algorithms

Most of the traditional cube computation algorithms are focused on partial or fully materializing a data cube. When a cube is partly materialized, if a query can not be answered by the existing materialized views, the re-computation on the whole dataset is necessary. And the speed is sometimes the bottleneck. When a cube is to be fully materialized, the space cost and the time cost are sometimes hardly tolerant. Practices in real applications show that although data analysis tasks may involve a high dimensional space, most OLAP operations are performed only on a small number of dimensions at a time. Most analyses will drill down and pivot a small set of dimensions, and other dimensions are set with a certain value or all values involved, respectively [11]. In [11] the segment cube are fully materialized. The high dimensional dataset is vertically partitioned into a set of disjoint low dimensional datasets. For each partition, the local data cube is fully materialized. If the dimensions involved in a query are in the same partition, the results can be retrieved from the materialized segment cube directly. Otherwise the corresponding attributes in the separate materialized segment cubes are dynamically combined. This might be done efficiently and satisfy the response time of OLAP operations by a partition based method.

2.2 Limitations of Other Partition Based Algorithms

Researchers have proposed a method based on partitions to compute high dimensional data cubes before, e.g., Frag-Cubing algorithm [11]. But it also has its shortcomings. Formally, suppose a database has T tuples, C cardinalities, and D dimensions. In the algorithm Frag-Cubing each tuple ID is associated with D attributes and thus will appear D times in the inverted index. Since there are T tuple IDs in total, the entire inverted index will still need $D \times T$ integers [11]. For example, for a cube with 60-dimensional base cuboids of T tuples, the amount of space to store the fragment of size 3 is on the order of $T(\frac{60}{3})(2^3 - 1) = 140T$. Suppose there are 10^6 tuples in the database and each tuple ID takes 4 bytes. The space needed to store the fragments of size 3 is roughly estimated as $140 \times 10^6 \times 4 = 560$MB.

In the above expression, 140 indicates the number of the cuboids, and the $10^6 \times 4$ is the byte number of the index of each cuboid occupied. If we can reduce the space cost of each cuboid, the total space cost will be reduced. It is well known that bitmap index is suitable for the data with low cardinality, and the bit-AND operation runs faster than the intersecting operation. So we can use bitmap index to compute high dimensional data cubes. Let's see the bitmap index using the same example above-mentioned. Each attribute value takes $\lceil \frac{T}{8} \rceil$ bytes to indicate all the tuples, the space one cuboid needed is between $C \times \lceil \frac{T}{8} \rceil$

and $Min(C^3, T) \times \lceil \frac{T}{8} \rceil$ bytes. So the total space is between $140 \times C \times \lceil \frac{T}{8} \rceil$ bytes and $(\frac{60}{3}) \times (Min(3C, T) + Min(3C^2, T) + Min(C^3, T)) \times \lceil \frac{T}{8} \rceil$ bytes. When T is 10^6, and C is 5, the space is between 87.5MB and 537.5MB. We can see that even on the worst case, the space is smaller than [9].And on the best case the space saving is very excellent. Let C is 10, the result will be between 175MB and 3325MB. With the changing of C from 5 to 10, the space is increasing. The space is very large on the worst case. Thereby if we make good use of bitmap index such as compressing it reasonably, we will get good effects. So we proposed an efficient indexing technique, compressed bitmap index, to compute high dimensional data cubes.

The above observations are very considerable to us. The idea of vertically partitioning the whole data cube into a set of disjoint low dimensional datasets is very good, but the storage of the inverted list and the intersecting operation take a very large amount of resource. If we can find a more effective technique, the performance would be more efficient. By investigating deeply into the bitmap index technique, we find that when we use bitmap index to indicate the ID-lists of a certain attribute value, the continuous 0 bits appeared many times in the beginning, in the end, and in the middle part of the bitmap index. The bitmap index itself is suitable for the low cardinality datasets, and the bit-AND operation is very fast, the rather that we can avoid the storage of the 0-bit redundancies in a bitmap index by recording the start and the end valid positions of the nonzero bits.

3 Compressed Bitmap Index Based Method

Stemming from the above motivation, we propose a new method, called compressed bitmap index, and two algorithms: one for constructing a data cube, and the other one for processing queries. This new method will be able to handle OLAP on datasets with extremely high dimensionality and low cardinality. The general idea is to use a bitmap index compressed by two valid pointers on the divided partitions. The base dataset is projected onto each segment, and the data cube of each segment is fully materialized. With the pre-computed segment cubes, we can dynamically assemble the attributes and answer the queries on-line, which is done efficiently by bit-AND operations on the compressed bitmap indices.

3.1 Compressed Bitmap Index

Many kinds of indices can be used in constructing data cubes, such as B-tree, Hash table. But considering the high dimensional datasets with low cardinality in each dimension, we use the bitmap index in order to storage the data effectively. And it converts the standard comparing, joining and aggregating operations to the bit arithmetic operations and reduces the runtime enormously. Thereby it can improve the performance of the system [13].

To illustrate the algorithm, a tiny dataset (see Table 1) is used as a running example. Let the cube measure be *count*(). Other measures will be discussed later.

The following illustrates the construction and computation of the compressed bitmap index. Firstly, suppose that we divide the 5 dimensions in Table 1 into

Table 1. An example data set

tid	A	B	C	D	E
1	a_1	b_1	c_1	d_1	e_1
2	a_1	b_2	c_1	d_2	e_1
3	a_1	b_2	c_1	d_1	e_2
4	a_2	b_1	c_1	d_1	e_2
5	a_2	b_1	c_1	d_1	e_3

2 independent segments, namely (A, B, C) and (D, E). In the real world applications the attributes in a segment may be determined by the semantics of the data and the query patterns on the data.

Then, it should construct the corresponding bitmap indices (shown in Table 2). Each line in Table 2 records a value of an attribute and the bitmap index, which tells which tuples contain the value. For example, the value a_2 appears in tuple 4 and tuple 5, and then the bitmap index for a_2 contains two 1 bits in the 4th and 5th positions. We use the segment (A, B, C) as an example to illustrate

Table 2. The bitmap index of dimension A, B, C, D and E

Attribute	tid Bitmap Index	Size
a_1	11100	3
a_2	00011	2
b_1	10011	3
b_2	01100	2
c_1	11111	5
d_1	10111	4
d_2	01000	1
e_1	11000	2
e_2	00110	2
e_3	00001	1

the local materialization operation of the method. Use the bit-AND operation in Table 3 on the tid bitmap index of dimension A and dimension B in Table 2, and we can get the Cuboid AB. Similarly we can get the Cuboid ABC using the Cuboid AB and the tid bitmap index corresponding with c_1 in Table 2. Experiments show that the computation time complexity and the storage space complexity are increased linearly with the number of the dimensions when the number of the dimensions in each fragment is less than 4 and more than 2 [11]. Finally, the data cube of each segment is computed. Taking segment (A, B, C) as an example, there are 7 cuboids, namely A, B, C, AB, AC, BC and ABC, to be computed. We can compute the complete data cube by bit-ANDing the bitmap

Table 3. The bitmap index structure of Cuboid AB

Cell	bit-AND	tid Bitmap Index	Size
a_1b_1	11100&10011	10000	1
a_1b_2	11100&01100	01100	2
a_2b_1	00011&10011	00011	2
a_2b_2	00011&01100	00000	0

indices in table 2 in a bottom-up depths-first order in the cuboids lattice. For example, to compute the cell $\{a_1, b_2, *\}$, we may bit-AND the bitmap indices of a_1 and b_2 to get a new bitmap index of {2, 3}. Cuboid AB is shown in Table 3.

After computing Cuboid AB, we can similarly compute Cuboid ABC by bit-ANDing all pair wise combinations between Table 3 and the row c_1 in Table 2. Note that the entry (a_2, b_2) can be effectively discarded because it is all 0 bits. The same process can be applied to computing segment (D, E), which is completely independent from computing (A, B, C). So, it can be computed in parallel.

In this method, we use different approaches to compute different aggregations. For the cube with only the tuple-counting measure, it is unnecessary to access the original dataset for aggregation since the number of the 1 bits in a corresponding index is equivalent to the number of tuples in a group. But for the solution to *average*() or *sum*(), it is necessary to keep an *ID_measure* array instead of the original dataset. For example, for computing *average*(), we just need to keep an array with three elements: (*tid*, *count*, *sum*). The measures of each aggregate cell can be computed by only accessing this *ID_measure* array.

$$\text{a: } \underbrace{0x00 \cdots 0x00}_{n}\ \text{0xA5}\cdots\text{0xE78856724523}$$

$$\text{b: 0xE84445673211}\cdots\text{0xFF } \underbrace{0x00 \cdots 0x00}_{n}$$

$$\text{abc: } \underbrace{0x00 \cdots 0x00}_{n_1}\ \text{0xA5}\cdots\ \text{0xE7 } \underbrace{0x00 \cdots 0x00}_{n_2}$$

Fig. 1. The bitmap index of Cells

Analysis and experiments on the real data distribution show that the bitmap index structure also has great redundancies. Cell a and Cell b (Cell: attribute value, its bitmap index and the corresponding aggregation value) have large amounts of continuous 0 bits in the beginning and the end (see Fig.1). The cases occur frequently in many cells under the combination of multi-dimensional datasets (see Table 3). So it is very necessary to reduce the redundancies.

The compressed bitmap index based algorithm of cube construction registers the start position and the end position of non-zero using two pointers, called *start valid pointer* and *end valid pointer*, in order to compress the storage space of the bitmap index (shown in Fig.2). In this way we only need to store the two pointers and the bitmap index segment between them, but not the whole bitmap index, thereby the 0-bit redundancies in the beginning and the end are reduced, and the storage space is saved.

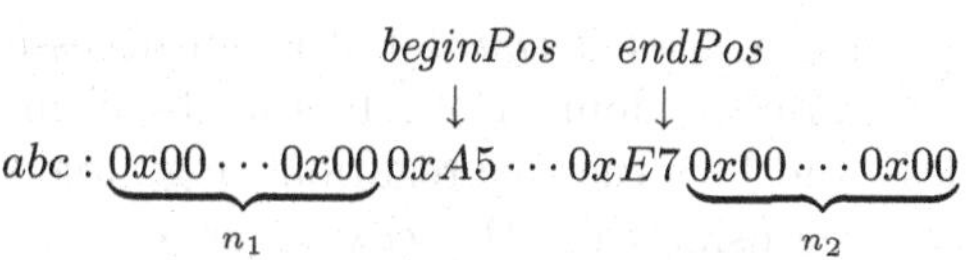

Fig. 2. The compressed bitmap index of Cells

For example, there are two bitmap sequences $Index_1$ and $Index_2$, and the valid pointer of $Index_1$ are $beginPos_1$ and $endPos_1$, the valid pointer of $Index_2$ are $beginPos_2$ and $endPos_2$. To bit-AND such two bitmap sequences only needs to bit-AND the bits between max($beginPos_1$, $beginPos_2$) and min ($endPos_1$, $endPos_2$), but not bit-AND all bits of the sequences. Especially, if the min($endPos_1$, $endPos_2$) is not bigger than max($beginPos_1$, $beginPos_2$), we need do nothing but set all the bits to 0. We only need ($endPos$ − $beginPos$ +1)/8 bytes to store the result instead of (*the total number of the tuples*/8) bytes, so the memory consuming is reduced greatly.

3.2 Cube Construction Algorithm

Based on the above discussion, the algorithm for constructing a data cube using compressed bitmap index can be summarized as follows.

Algorithm 1. Compressed Bitmap index based Algorithm for cube Construction (CBAC).

Input: a fact table D with n dimensions $(A_1, \cdots, A_n)$;

Output: 1) a set of segment partitions $\{P_1, \cdots, P_k\}$ and the corresponding cubes $\{S_1, \cdots, S_k\}$, where P_i indicates a set of dimensions and $P_1 \cup \cdots \cup P_k$ are all the n dimensions; and
2) if the measure is not *count*(), output the $ID\_measure$ array;

1. partition the dimension set $(A_1,\cdots,A_n)$ into a set of k segments $\{P_1,\cdots,P_k\}$;
2. for each tuple t in D do {
3. insert each $\langle tid, measure\rangle$ into $ID\_measure$ array ;
4. construct bitmap index $\langle a_i, BitmapIndex\rangle$ for each element a_i of each dimension A_i; }
5. for each segment partition P_i do {
6. compute the local cube S_i using bit-AND operation;
7. compute the corresponding measures;
8. save S_i and its measure on the disk. }

CBAC algorithm firstly vertically partitions the dataset(line 1), secondly scans the original dataset(line 2) and extracts $\langle tid, measure \rangle$ into the *ID_measure* array if the measure is not *count*()(line 3), at the same time it constructs the bitmap index of each attribute(line 4), thirdly constructs the data cube of each segment(line 5) by the bit-AND operation(line 6), and then computes the aggregations of each segment(line 7), lastly stores the compressed bitmap index on the disk(line 8).

To the line 3, if the aggregation is *count*(), it is not necessary to construct the *ID_measure* array because the number of 1 bits in the bitmap index equals the number of the tuples. And for other aggregations, e.g., *average*(), the aggregations should be computed using the *ID_measure* array.

Because of the limitation of bitmap index itself [14], the algorithm's performance will be affected by the datasets with high cardinalities. With the cardinality increasing the number of 0 bits will increase, and the distribution of attribute values in the tuples will become randomization, so the effect of the compressed algorithm will be weaken.

3.3 Querying Algorithm

The general query for an n-dimensional dataset is in the form of $\langle\, a_1, a_2, \cdots, a_n :$ M $\rangle$. Each a_i has 3 possible values: (a) an instantiated value, (b) aggregate *, (c) inquire ?. The first step is to gather all the instantiated a_i's if there are any. We examine the partitions to check which a_i's are in the same segments. Once that is done, we retrieve the bitmap indices associated with the instantiations at the highest possible aggregation level. For example, suppose a_j and a_k were in the same segment, we would then retrieve the bitmap indices from the (a_j, a_k) cuboid cells. The obtained bitmap indices are to be bit-ANDed to derive the instantiated base table. If all the bits in the bitmap indices are 0s, query processing stops and returns the empty result.

If there are no inquired dimensions, we simply fetch the corresponding measures from the ID_measure array and finish the query. If there is at least one inquired dimension, we continue as follows. For each inquired dimension, we retrieve all its possible values and their associated bitmap indices. If two or more inquired dimensions are in the same segment, we retrieve all their pre-computed combinations and the bitmap indices. Once these bitmap indices are retrieved, they are to be bit-ANDed with the instantiated base table to form the local base cuboid of the inquired and instantiated dimensions.

The above discussion leads our algorithm to processing all the possible queries. Note that function *merge_index*() is implemented by bit-ANDing the corresponding tid bitmap indices of the B_{D_i}'s . Function *compute_cube*() takes the merged instantiated indices and the inquired dimensions as input, derives the relevant base cuboid, and uses the most efficient cubing algorithm to compute the multi-dimensional cubes. The *ID_measure* array will be referenced after the cube is derived in this *compute_cube*() function.

If the dimensions in a query are not in the same segment, we can bit-AND the bitmap indices of the different segments on line, and can get the right answer in time. The computation time complexity and storage space complexity are reduced to linear with the number of the dimensions as well as guaranteeing the response time requirement. So it was suitable for the computation of the above-mentioned high dimensional data cubes.

Algorithm 2. Compressed Bitmap index based Algorithm for Querying(CBAQ).
Input: 1) a set of segment partitions $\{P_1, \cdots, P_k\}$ and the corresponding cubes $\{S_1, \cdots, S_k\}$, where P_i indicates a set of dimensions, and $P_1 \cup \cdots \cup P_k$ are all the n dimensions; and
2) an $ID\_measure$ array if the measure is not $count()$; and
3) a query with the form $\langle a_1, a_2, \cdots, a_n : M\rangle$, where each a_i is either instantiated, aggregated, or inquired for the dimension A_i. M is the measure of the query;
Output: The computed measure(s) if the query contains only instantiated dimensions. Otherwise, the data cube whose dimensions are the inquired dimensions;

for each P_i {//instantiated dimensions
    if $P_i \cap \{a_1, \cdots, a_n\}$includes instantiation(s)
        $D_i \leftarrow P_i \cap \{a_1, \cdots, a_n\}$ with instantiation(s);
        $B_{D_i} \leftarrow$ cells in D_i with associated tid bitmap index; //inquired dimensions
    if $P_i \cap \{a_1, \cdots, a_n\}$ includes inquire(s)
        $Q_i \leftarrow P_i \cap \{a_1, \cdots, a_n\}$ with inquire(s);
        $R_{Q_i} \leftarrow$ cells in Q_i with associated tid bitmap index; }
if there exists at least one not all 0 bits B_{D_i}
    $B_q \leftarrow merge\_index(B_{D_1}, \cdots, B_{D_k})$;
if there exists at least one not all 0 bits R_{Q_i}
    $C_q \leftarrow compute\_cube(B_q, R_{Q_1}, \cdots, R_{Q_k})$.

4 Experimental Evaluation

In this section we will give the performance analysis and comparison of the proposed algorithm on datasets with different sizes, different dimension numbers and different cardinalities. All the experiments are conducted on an Intel Pentium-4, 2.4GHz system with 512MB RAM. The operating system runs Windows 2000 professional. And the dataset is KDD-CUP-99 [15] with 200000 tuples. The experiments in [2] are performed on datasets with 3 to 6 attributes, and obviously it is not to deal with high dimensional datasets. [4] contains only aggregates above certain thresholds, and the information it provides may not satisfy the requirements. Others are similar with them except [11]. So we compare the algorithms with the ones in [11]. To be in step with the Frag-Cubing algorithm and satisfy with the requirement of low cardinality on each dimension, we use 3 as the dimension number of each segment used in the Frag-Cubing algorithm in the following experiments. In the figures, we denote the cardinality as C, Frag-Cubing as FC, and CBAC as CB.

4.1 Computation Time and Storage Space Under Different Dimension Numbers

Figure 3(a) describes the CBAC algorithm and the Frag-Cubing algorithm's computation time changed with the number of dimensions varying from 10 to 80 and the cardinalities are 8 and 15 respectively. It shows that algorithm CBAC is notable on time saving by about 30%. The construction time increases linear with the increasing of the number of the dimensions and the distinct value of each dimension is not affected most to the time complexity. Figure 3(b) describes the CBAC algorithm and the Frag-Cubing algorithm's storage space changed with the number of dimensions varying from 10 to 80 and the cardinalities are 8 and 15 respectively. In the two different cases, the compression ratio of CBAC is very notable, especially when the distinct value is 8, and the compression ratio achieved 80%. However, just as mentioned in Sect.3, it is affected by the limitation of bitmap index itself, when the distinct value increased from 8 to 15, the spatial compression ratio is decreased.

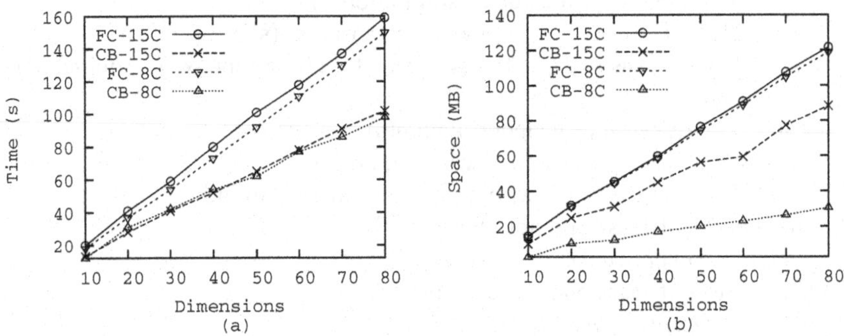

Fig. 3. Computation time(a) and storage space(b) of different dimensions

4.2 Computation Time and Storage Space Under Different Tuple Numbers

Figure 4(a) and (b) respectively show the computation time and the storage space cost of the CBAC algorithm and the Frag-Cubing algorithm with the tuple number varying from 60 thousand to 160 thousand, where the cardinality is 15 and the number of dimensions is 40. From the figures we can see the savings of the computation time and the storage space of algorithm CBAC is very obviously, and it is linear with the increasing of the tuple numbers. Thus, our new algorithm is scalable.

In conclusion, the proposed algorithm CBAC is very suitable for computation of data cubes on the data of bioinformatics, statistics, and text processing that characterized by high dimensionality and low cardinality. And it has more notable compression ratio and faster computing speed than Frag-Cubing. That is very significant for the computation of high dimensional data cubes.

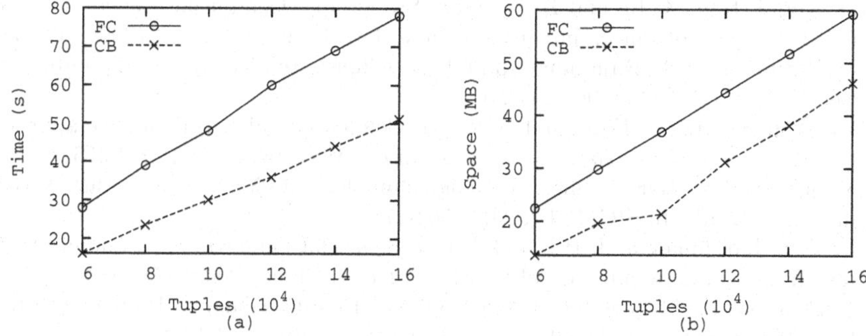

Fig. 4. Computation time(a) and storage space(b) on different tuple numbers

5 Conclusions

In this paper we propose an efficient indexing technique consisting of a bitmap index, and two algorithms for cube computation and querying for high dimensional datasets. The compressed bitmap index structure has the following advantages: (a) a very fast bit-AND operation based on the compressed bitmap index; (b) greatly reduced operations of bit-ANDing and the memory consumption by the introduced *start valid pointer* and *end valid pointer*; (c) effectively savings of the disk space of datacubes. The experimental results show that comparing with the Frag-Cubing algorithm computation time of the algorithm CBAC is saved by 30%, and the storage space is saved by more than 25%, and it is more applicable than the Frag-Cubing algorithm for the datasets with high dimensional and low cardinality.

When the number of the distinct value of each dimension is large, the performance of the CBAC will become worse. We intend to solve this problem to improve our compressing policy for the bitmap index. Not only in the beginning and the end, but also in the middle and other positions there are many continuous 0 bits. So we can compress the bitmap index further to improve the performance. At the same time, the incremental update is important as the computation and storage for an OLAP system, so another future work is to study the issues of on-line incremental update based on compressed bitmap index.

References

1. S. Chaudhuri and U. Dayal. An Overview of Data Warehousing and OLAP Technology. In SIGMOD, September (1997) 26(1):65-74
2. S. Agarwal, R. Agrawal, P. M. Deshpande, et al. On the computation of multidimensional aggregates. In VLDB, Bombay, India (1996) 506-521
3. Y. Zhao, P. M. Deshpande, and J. F. Naughton. An array-based algorithm for simultaneous multidimensional aggregates. In SIGMOD, Tucson, Arizona (1997) 159-170
4. J. Han, J. Pei, G. Dong, and K. Wang. Efficient computation of iceberg cubes with complex measures. In SIGMOD, Santa Barbara, CA, USA (2001) 1-12

5. D. Xin, J. Han, X. Li, and B. W. Wah. Starcubing: Computing iceberg cubes by top-down and bottom-up integration. In VLDB, Berlin, Germany (2003) 476-487
6. V. Harinarayan, A. Rajaraman, and J. D. Ullman. Implementing data cubes efficiently. In SIGMOD (1996) 205-216
7. W. Wang, H. Lu, J. Feng, and J. X. Yu. Condensed cube: An effective approach to reducing data cube size. In ICDE, Madison, Wisconsin (2002) 464-475
8. Y. Sismanis, N. Roussopoulos, A. Deligianannakis, and Y. Kotidis. Dwarf: Shrinking the petacube.In SIGMOD (2002) 564-475
9. L. V. S. Lakshmanan, J. Pei, and J. Han. Quotient cube: How to summarize the semantics of a data cube. In VLDB, Hong Kong, China (2002) 778-789
10. Z. Peng, Q. Li, L. Feng, et al. Using Object Deputy Model to Prepare Data for Data Warehousing. In TKDE, September (2005) 17(9):1274-1288
11. X. L. Li, J. W. Han, and H. Gonzalez. High-Dimensional OLAP:A Minimal Cubing Approach. In VLDB, Toronto, Canada (2004) 528-539
12. Y. Sismanis and N. Roussopoulos. The dwarf data cube eliminates the high dimensionality curse. TR-CS4552, University of Maryland (2003)
13. M. C. Wu and A. P. Buchmann. Encoded bitmap indexing for data warehouses. In ICDE, Orlando, Florida, USA, (1998) 220-230
14. C. Y. Chan and Y. E. Ioannidis. Bitmap index design and evaluation. In SIGMOD, Seattle, Washington, (1998) 355-366
15. KDD CUP 1999 Data http://kdd.ics.uci.edu/databases/kddcup99/kddcup99.html (1999)

A Scientific Workflow Framework Integrated with Object Deputy Model for Data Provenance*

Liwei Wang[1], Zhiyong Peng[1], Min Luo[2], Wenhao Ji[2], and Zeqian Huang[1]

[1] State Key Laboratory of Software Engineering, Wuhan University, Wuhan 430072, China
davilisa@yahoo.com.cn, peng@whu.edu.cn
[2] Computer School, Wuhan University, Wuhan 430072, China

Abstract. There is a critical need to automatically manage large volumes of scientific data and applications in scientific workflows. Database technologies seem to be well suited to handle highly complex data managements. However, most of the workflow management systems (WFMSs) only utilize database technologies to a limited extent. In this paper, we present a DB-integrated scientific workflow framework which adopts the object deputy model to describe the execution of a series of scientific tasks. This framework allows WFMS management operations to be performed in a way analogous to traditional data management operations. Most important of all, data provenance method of this framework can provide much higher performance than other methods. Three kinds of schemas for data provenance are proposed and performance for each schema is analyzed in this paper.

1 Introduction

Today the integration of workflow technology into domains that belong to the natural sciences has recently gained increased interest and become a unifying mechanism for handling scientific data.

Scientific workflows, while sharing commonalities with business workflows, are typically data-centric as opposed to task-centric business workflows [1]. Several scientific WFMSs, such as Kepler [2], ZOO [3], GridDB [4], are architected with a data-centric view of workflows. They can provide a data-centric interactive interface to manipulate workflows more conveniently, and allow users to inspect intermediate results in order to determine the next step of experiments [2], and so on. However, most of current WFMSs do not integrate tightly with data, so they can not satisfy the requirements of data-centric scientific experiments.

Database technologies seem to be well suited to handle highly complex data managements. However, they have been utilized only to a limited extent [5]. To our knowledge, systems advocating a tighter integration of DBMS and WFMS only include ZOO [3], GridDB [4] and [5]. Some technologies such as query optimization,

* This research is supported by National Natural Science Foundation of China (60573095), the Program for New Century Excellent Talents at University of China (NCET-04-0675), Research Fund for the Doctoral Program of Higher Education(20050486024) and State Key Lab of Software Engineering under grant: SKLSE05-01.

J.X. Yu, M. Kitsuregawa, and H.V. Leong (Eds.): WAIM 2006, LNCS 4016, pp. 569 – 580, 2006.
© Springer-Verlag Berlin Heidelberg 2006

fault-tolerance, view, and data provenance should be also applied to workflows in order to enhance the power of large magnitudes of data managements. For example, view mechanism can increase the degree of workflow automation, and combine different experimental results in a view so as to compare them. Data provenance provides derivation histories for terabytes of data products (data in any form, such as files, tables [6]) generated by scientific workflows in order to make sense of and use them. The importance of data provenance has already been recognized in several scientific workflow projects, such as GridDB [4], Chimera [7], myGRID [8], CMCS [9]. As far as we know, the solutions of determining data provenance in the literature usually involve annotations that comprise of the derivation history of a data product and inversion that generates a "reverse" query to find the origins supplied to derive a data product. Annotations may not scale well for fine-grained data as the complete annotations for the data may outsize the storage space required for the data itself. Inversion seems to be more optimal from a storage perspective since an inverse function or query identifies the provenance for an entire class of data. However, it requires a reverse query to be generated and executed to compute provenance every time the provenance of a data product is required.

In this paper, we present a scientific workflow framework integrated with object deputy model [10] which increases automation of scientific workflows by means of update propagation that is similar to view update, and can freely combine different experimental results by means of the object deputy algebra. Moreover, this framework can support incompleteness and uncertainty of workflow specifications. Most important of all, in our framework, it is easy to find sources of data products in terms of bi-directional pointers between the data products and their sources, not only saving a mass of storage space, but also decreasing extra computation cost.

The remainder of this paper is organized as follows: In section 2, a scientific workflow framework integrated with object deputy model is introduced. In section 3 we present provenance method in our framework and propose three kinds of schemas for data provenance. Experimental results and analysis are given in section 4. In section 5 we analyze and compare some related work. Finally, we present a summary of our contributions and our future work.

2 A Scientific Workflow Framework Integrated with Object Deputy Model

Object deputy model [10] can satisfy the requirements stemming from complex, high performance scientific data managements with the concepts of deputy objects and deputy classes. In this section, we adopt the object deputy model to describe the process of scientific workflow executions. Deputy objects and deputy classes are called derived objects and derived classes in our framework.

2.1 Basic Concepts

Scientific workflows consist of scientific data and scientific analysis programs manipulating them. Initial inputs can be described as base scientific objects, intermediate results and outputs can be described as derived scientific objects, and scientific analysis programs can be defined as read methods of object attributes. Scientific classes have no definitions of functions.

Definition 1. Each scientific object has an identifier and some attributes. The schema of scientific objects with the same attributes is defined as a class $C = <O, A>$.

1. O is the extent of C, $o \in O$ is one of instances of C.
2. A is the set of attribute definitions of C, $(T_a : a) \in A$, where T_a and a respectively represent type and name of an attribute. The value of attribute a of scientific object o is expressed by $o.a$. For each attribute, there are two basic methods.
   $read(o, a) \Rightarrow \uparrow o.a$, $write(o, a, v) \Rightarrow o.a := v$.
   Here $\Rightarrow$, $\uparrow$ stand for operation invoking, result returning.

Definition 2. A derived scientific object is derived from object(s) or other derived object(s). The latter is called source object(s) of the former. Source objects and derived objects are linked by bi-directional pointers between them. Derived objects have their own persistent identifiers, and can inherit some attributes from their source objects by switching operations without occupying storage space, and can also add their additional attributes. A derived class defines the schema of derived objects with the same attributes. Let $C^s = <O^s, A^s>$ be a source class, its derived class C^d is defined as $C^d = <O^d, A^d \cup A^d_+>$.

1. Derived object $O^d = \{o^d_i \mid o^d_i \rightarrow o^s_i \mid \cdots \times o^s_i \times \cdots \mid \{o^s_i\}, sp(o^s_i) \mid jp(\cdots \times o^s_i \times \cdots) \mid gp(\{o^s_i\}) == true\}$, is the extent of C^d, where $o^d_i \rightarrow o^s_i \mid \cdots \times o^s_i \times \cdots \mid \{o^s_i\}$ denote o^d_i is a derived object of o^s_i, $\cdots \times o^s_i \times \cdots$, or $\{o^s_i\}$, and sp, jp, gp represent selection, combination, and grouping predicate respectively.
2. $A^d \cup A^d_+$ is the set of attribute definitions of C^d.

   1) $(Ta^d : a^d) \in A^d$ is the attributes inherited from $(Ta^s : a^s) \in A^s$, and attribute values of derived object o^d are computed through switching operations that need to read attribute values of source objects. In scientific computing environments, it is not allowed to update the inherited attributes, so the write method of these attributes is not defined. Switching operation for the read method of these attributes is defined as
   $read(o^d, a^d) \Rightarrow \uparrow fTa^s \rightarrow Ta^d(read(o^s, a^s))$

   2) $(Ta^d_+ : a^d_+) \in A^d_+$ is the additional attributes of C^d, of which basic methods are defined as
   $read(o^d, a^d_+) \Rightarrow \uparrow o^d.a^d_+$, $write(o^d, a^d_+, v^d_+) \Rightarrow o^d.a^d_+ := v^d_+$

According to above definitions, during the course of each query, attribute values of derived scientific objects inherited from source objects are still computed through switching operations that need to communicate with the underlying information source. However, in scientific computing environments, outputs may be generated by long running scientific analysis programs, and information sources may be remote or unavailable for some time, so it might be best to materialize their inherited attribute values instead of re-generating them on each query. The definition of the read method for the inherited attribute of which value is materialized is changed as follows:

$read(o^d, a^d) \Rightarrow \uparrow o^d.a^d$.

That is, the inherited attribute values can be directly read from the derived object.

Definition 3. Update propagation between scientific objects and their derived scientific objects.

1. If a scientific object o is added into class C, then all of derived scientific classes of C are checked. If o satisfies the predicate of some derived class C^d, an object o^d of C^d is created as a derived object of o. Deleting a scientific object causes deletion of all of its derived scientific objects.
2. If a scientific object o in class C is updated, all of its derived scientific objects will be updated automatically. Suppose that there are some derived scientific classes of C, of which predicates might not be satisfied by o before the update and may become satiable after the update, new derived objects of o can be added to these classes. Modification of a scientific object may cause deletion of its derived scientific objects.

Based on the object deputy model, we have implemented a database system called TOTEM and designed an object deputy database language which can create various kinds of deputy classes, including SelectionDeputyClass, JoinDeputyClass, UnionDeputyClass, and GroupDeputyClass.

2.2 A High-Energy Physics Example

In this section, we use the Atlas High-Energy Physics workflow [4] to explain our framework. This workflow consists of three programs: an event generator (*gen*); fast simulation (*atlfast*); and slower simulation (*atlsim*). *Gen* is invoked with inputting an integer parameter *pmas*, and produces an *event* file. The *event* file is then used to feed *atlfase* and *atlsim*, each simulating a detector's reaction to the event, and producing a file which contains an integer value *flmas* or *slmas*. The outputs of two different simulations are compared finally. The Atlas workflow is shown in figure 1(a).

We adopt an object deputy database language [11] to set up the Atlas workflow in the following. Instead of encoding the workflow in a procedural script, we encode it with a schema definition language. Three programs: *gen, atlfast* and *atlsim* are defined as read methods of *event, flmas* and *slmas* respectively.

1. Create Class gC (pmas int);
2. Create SelectionDeputyClass evts as (Select gen(pmas) as (event int) from gC);
3. Create SelectionDeputyClass fC as (Select atlfast(event) as (flmas int) from evts);
4. Create SelectionDeputyClass sC as (Select atlsim(event) as (slmas int) from evts);
5. Create JoinDeputyClass compare as (Select fC.flmas, sC.slmas from fC, sC where fC→evts.event = sC→evts.event);
6. or Select evts→fC.flmas, evts→sC.slmas from evts

Class evts derived from class gC stores *event* files produced by program *gen*, where parameter *event* contains the identifiers of the files. Likewise, fC and sC respectively store outputs of program *altfast* and *atlsim*, where outputs *flmas* and *slmas* are described as integer. We use JoinDeputyClass to compare results of two different simulations, *atfast* and *atlsim*. We can also achieve the same goal by select operation instead of explicitly deriving class compare. Implementation of the function for com

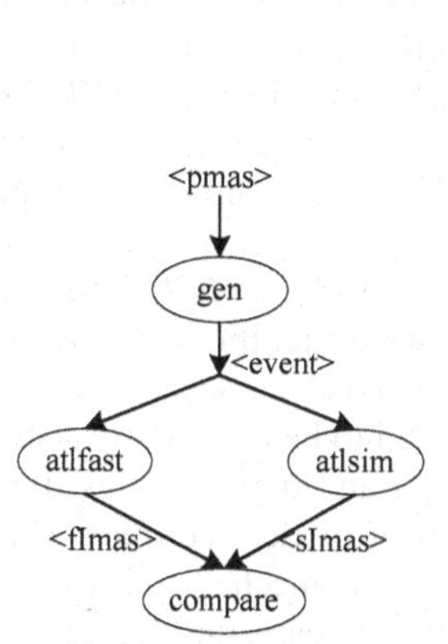

Fig. 1(a). The Atlas workflow

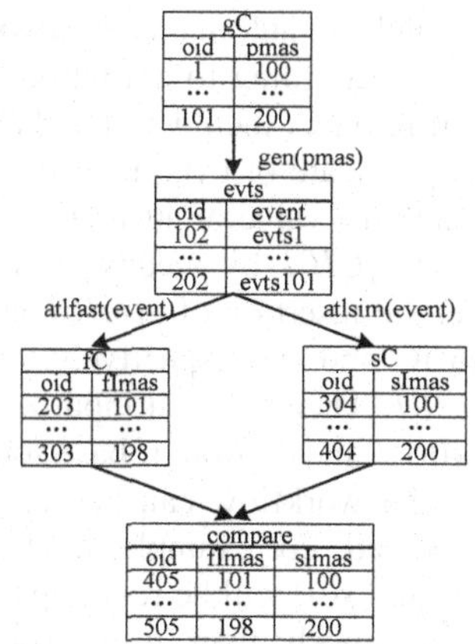

Fig. 1(b). The internal data structures

paring mainly depends on cross-class query ("→")[11]. We can start from an initial object (base object or derived object) to one or more target objects by means of bi-directional pointers between them, and the query path length and the direction are not limited. Therefore workflows are composed by deriving classes in our framework. The internal data structures for Atlas workflows integrated with object deputy model are shown in figure 1(b), in which all *pmas* values change from 100 to 200.

Most scientific data is not relational in nature, but the inputs and outputs to workflows can be still represented as tables. In our framework, they are represented as classes. An example is the output *event* of the program *gen*; it is a file that needs to be stored in file format (such as XML), but it can be also represented as an object. Moreover, most scientific analysis programs are written to deal with data in files. TOTEM allows users to specify a schema for data stored in the file system and query these data using a SQL-like language. It also allows executing external programs that process data in file systems. In TOTEM, files are described as one-attribute objects, which mainly record identifiers of the files. Actual files are stored in *od_largeobject* system table.

Our framework does not need to materialize the intermediate results and outputs, thus reducing storage overhead and maintenance cost. This can optimize workflow executions using database techniques. However, in scientific environments, the derived scientific classes are usually generated by the outputs of possibly long running programs. As we have mentioned above, on each query, inherited attribute values of derived objects are computed through switching operations that need to read attribute values of source objects. In order to avoid re-computing them on each query, it might be best to materialize them. This prevents unnecessary re-execution of programs. The materialized method can be also supported in our framework. We emphasize that final data products must be materialized.

2.3 Workflow Automation and Flexibility

Workflow automation is accomplished by insertion of values into the base classes. For example, the workflow is invoked by the following Insert statements.

Insert into gC values (100)

etc.

Our model can automatically invoke an execution of workflow by means of update propagation according to definition 3. Once a scientific object (for example, *gC101*) is inserted into gC, then derived class evts of gC is checked. Because *gC101* satisfies selection predicate of evts, its derived object *evts101* is automatically added to class evts. In fact, the value of attribute *event* of *evts101* does not occupy storage space, but shares with *gC101* by means of the read method (*gen*) defined in attribute *event*. Likewise, the insertion of *evts101* in evts makes derived objects *fC101* and *sC101* be added to fC and sC respectively, eventually resulting in addition of derived object *compare101*. Thereby each input of class gC corresponds to a separate execution of the workflow. In addition, if base scientific objects need to be revised, then successive stages of the workflow can be automatically invoked and derived scientific objects can be updated. For example, if *gC0* is modified, all of its derived objects including *evt0*, *fC0*, and *sC0* will be re-computed automatically. The mechanism, which is similar to 'push' mechanism in materialized view, would increase the degree of WFMS automation.

Scientific workflows are loosely-defined, that is, the complete structures of workflows are difficult to determine in advance. Our framework allows creating derived classes for partial known experimental steps. By analyzing intermediate results, users are allowed to determine the next step of experiments by defining a new derived class for the new experimental task. For example, we can only define a derived class evts for the first experimental step. After experimental results generated by program *gen* are analyzed, we are allowed to define succeeding experimental steps by deriving class fC, sC and compare. Furthermore, in a scientific environment, a specification may change rapidly as the experimental results are analyzed even while a workflow is being executed. We can also dynamically change specifications of workflows by defining new derived classes instead of the old.

The framework presented above is meant for tight integration with a database. The declaration and definition of workflows are in a SQL-like workflow manipulating language (object deputy database language), and the invocation and query are done in SQL. This will allow most WFMS management operations to be performed in a way analogous to traditional data management operations.

3 Data Provenance

In this section, we first present data provenance method of our framework, and argue that our method has the advantage over annotations and inversion. Then, we propose three kinds of schemas that trace data provenance.

3.1 Tracing Data Provenance

There are two main approaches to representing provenance information, annotations and inversion. From database perspective, we prefer the latter because inversion mainly uses a data-oriented model of provenance. Provenance can be associated not just with data products, but with the processes that enabled the creation of the data products [12], including queries and functions defined by users. According to [2], intermediate data products should be also recorded in a scientific workflow system. We first give a definition about data provenance.

Definition 4. Given an object *o*, the origins from which object *o* evolved, and the transformations of these origins undergo are called provenance of the object *o*. That is,

1. Let *fun* be a scientific analysis program, and let $C^d = fun\ (C_1^s,\ldots, C_m^s)$ be the class that results from applying *fun* to classes $C_1^s,\ldots,C_m^s$. Given a object $o^d \in C^d$, we define o^d's provenance in classes $C_1^s,\ldots,C_m^s$ to be provenance $(o^d)_{(C1^s,\ldots, Cm^s)}$= $\{<\{o_{1j}^s\},\ldots,\{o_{mj}^s\}>,\ fun|m,\ j \geqq 1\}$, where $fun^{-1}(o^d) = \{\{o_{1j}^s\},\ldots,\{o_{mj}^s\}|$ $\{o_{1j}^s\},\ldots,\{o_{mj}^s\}$ are subsets of scientific objects in $C_1^s,\ldots,C_m^s\}$.
2. Likewise, if $C_1^b,\ldots,C_n^b$ are base scientific classes. o^d's provenance in base classes $C_1^b,\ldots,C_n^b$ can be described by using the above definition 4.1 recursively.

In TOTEM, we adopt a system table called *od_collate* to store relationships between source objects and derived objects. Thereby querying the origins of a data product can be directly switched to its source objects. Scientific analysis programs as read methods of object attributes are stored in *od_switching* system table. The internal data structures of *od_collate* and *od_switching* are shown in figure 2.

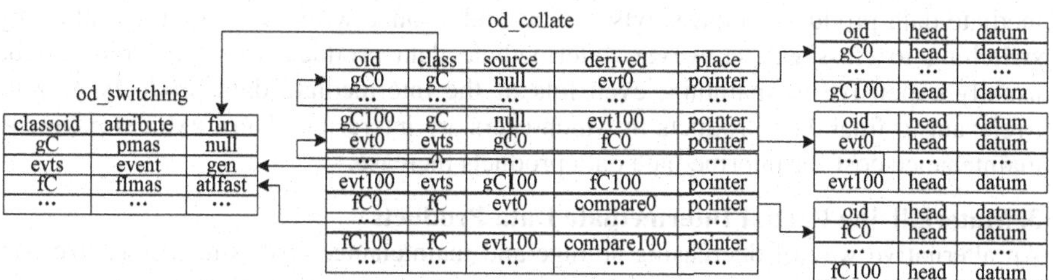

Fig. 2. The internal data structures of *od_collate* and *od_switching*

Considering the example in section 2.2, if we want to compute provenance of object *fC0* in derived class fC, it is easy to find that this object is derived by applying scientific analysis program *atlfast* to the object *evt0* in evts, which is derived by applying *gen* to the object *gC0* in gC. Therefore the provenance of object *<fC0>* = {*<gC0>*, *gen*, *<evt0>*, *atlfast*}.

Compared with either annotations or inversion, our method has the advantage over them. Firstly, annotations are attached to a data product, describing the derivation history of the data product, so annotations can be larger than the data itself even if the data is coarse-grained. In our method, derivation history of a data product can be directly constructed by bi-directional pointers between the data product and its sources, thus saving a mass of storage space. Secondly, our method shares some similarities with inversion, for example, we also require "reverse" query to find the source data supplied to derive the data. However, it is not necessary to compute provenance using inverse queries or inverse functions because we can directly find source data of derived data by bi-directional pointers. This method also effectively avoids some issues about inexistence of inverse functions or inaccuracy of inverse computations. Finally, since source data may be remote or unavailable for some time, the inverse method usually requires storing additional auxiliary information in order to reduce or entirely avoid source accesses. In our method, derived objects can materialize some attribute values from source objects, thus avoiding source accesses.

3.2 Materialize Intermediate Products

During tracing data provenance, intermediate data products also need to be queried, so choosing to materialize intermediate data products can help query intermediate results directly without re-computing them. In this section, we propose three kinds of schemas for materializing intermediate data products.

1. Materializing Nothing
This schema is to materialize no intermediate data products. During tracing data origins, this schema retrieves all necessary information from source data, and then computes intermediate results. It incurs no extra storage or maintenance cost for intermediate data products, but leads to poor tracing performance.

2. Materializing Intermediate Data Products
Compared with the first schema, materializing intermediate data products can improve tracing performance. For example, if we materialize *event* files in class evts. Once users pose tracing provenance of a derived data product in class fC, the intermediate data products in class evts can be find at once without computing values by switching to class gC. However, intermediate data products may be large and be usually expensive to maintain, even lots of the intermediate data products may be irrelevant to final data products in which users are interested. Thus, extra storage and maintenance cost for intermediate data products increase.

3. Materializing Partial Intermediate Data Products
An alternative way of decreasing storage and maintenance cost is to materialize partial intermediate data products, where only contains intermediate data products having derived objects. For example, we assume a part of *event* files are used to feed programs *atlfast* and *atlsim*, and then only these *event* files are required to materialize, which can greatly save storage spaces. Otherwise, in this schema, provenance query for final data products is only related with materialized intermediate data products, hence this schema does not affect tracing query performance.

4 Experiments and Analysis

In this section, we will evaluate performance of the three proposed kinds of schemas for tracing query, maintenance cost and storage cost under the same environmental setting.

4.1 Experimental Model and Design

We design a simple experiment with the architecture in figure 1(b). For simplicity, we assume there is only two-level selection derived class, where the second-level derived class fC has been materialized. The first-level derived class evts stores results of an event generator (*gen*), and completely inherits objects in base scientific class gC; the second-level derived class fC stores results of the fast simulation (*atlfast*), and inherits about 40% of objects in evts. Scientific data analysis programs used in the experiment are some simple mathematic functions. In order to simulate the real environments, we assume that *gen* and *atlfast* consume 3 seconds and 2 seconds respectively. Three kinds of schemas used to materialize class evts respectively are represented by the symbol 1, 2 and 3. The experiment runs on a Celeron machine which has 2.0 GHz CPU, 256MB main memory, and Linux operating system.

In our performance analysis we consider several performance metrics. The first is tracing query, where we use the average object tracing time as the metric. The second metric measures update maintenance cost, including the total time for maintaining the derived classes evts and fC. The third metric measures storage cost, including the storage spaces occupied by evts and fC. We adopt two types of operations, either tracing query or update maintenance, and compute the number of operations having been finished successfully during a given period, about half an hour. We assume that each operation only traces or updates an object.

4.2 Experimental Results and Analysis

Our experiments compare the performance of three proposed kinds of schemas as base class size increases. We vary the size of base class from 100,000 to 500,000 objects. Figure 3(a) shows the average object tracing time of each schema. Figure 3(b) and figure 3(c) show the maintenance cost and the storage cost in each schema respectively. The x-axis represents the number of objects in a base class and the y-axis represents the relevant costs.

From figure 3(a) we can see that the first schema achieves much lower tracing performance than the other two schemas, while the performance is identical for the latter two schemas. The longer the tracing time consumed by the first schema, the more the base class size increases. Because of no materialized intermediate data products in the first schema, in order to get values of the intermediate products, the system has to find their source objects by bi-directional pointers and computes their values, thus consuming a mass of time.

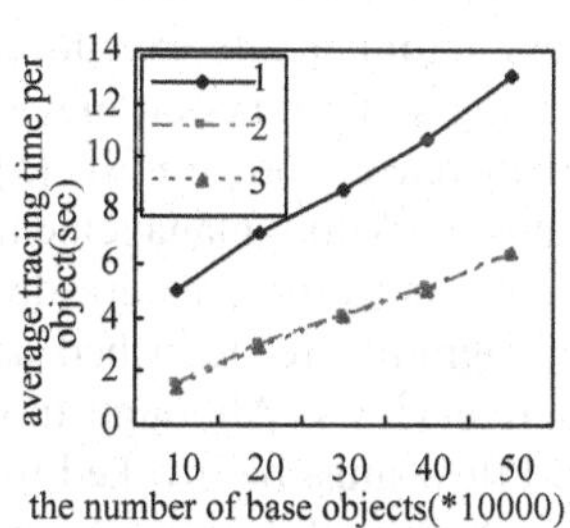

Fig. 3(a). Tracing query

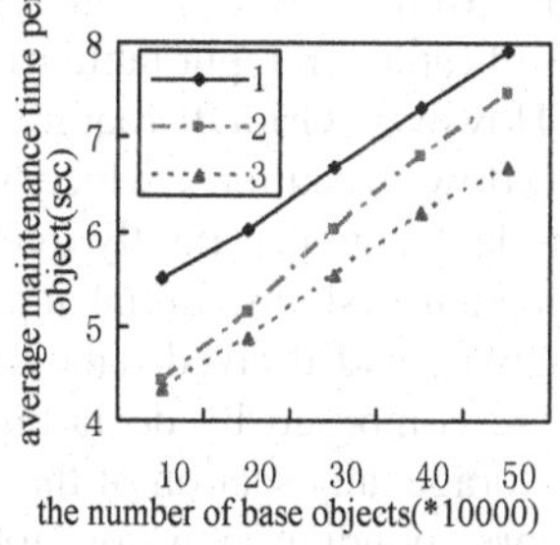

Fig. 3(b). Maintenance cost

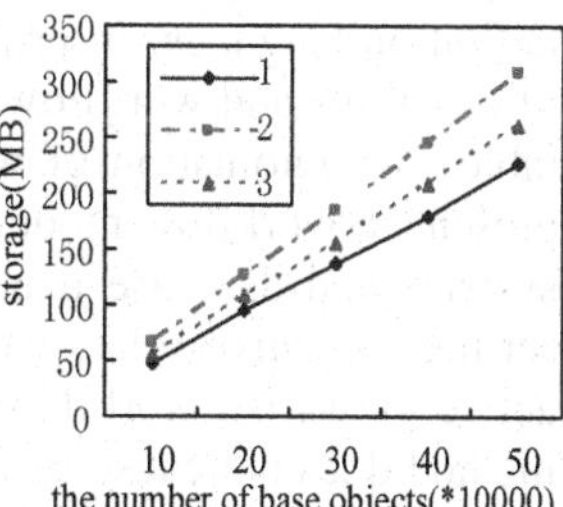

Fig. 3(c). Storage cost

From the results in figure 3(b), we observe the third schema achieves the best main tenance performance, and maintenance cost of the second schema is close to that of the first schema when scaling up source class size. We divide into two cases to analyze the reasons. The first is that updating of objects in gC does not cause updating of derived objects in fC. In this case, the second schema requires consuming extra time (t_1) to maintain class evts completely materialized. The second is that updating of objects in gC will cause updating of derived objects in fC, all the three kinds of sche mas require maintaining the materialized derived class fC, while maintenance time (t_2) of the first schema is higher than that of the other two schemas. It is mainly because the first schema has to find the top-level base objects, and then computes their values, thus consuming a mass of time. At beginning, t_2 is longer than t_1. As the base class size increases, t_2 is gradually close to t_1, thus maintenance cost of the second schema is close to, even exceeds that of the first schema.

It is evident that the storage cost of the second schema is highest, while the storage cost of the first schema is lowest in figure 3(c).

From above analysis, we can know which schema to be adopted mainly depends on the requirements of practical applications. The first schema can be used in applications which store terabytes of scientific data generated by short running programs, while the second schema is fit for managing a small quantity of scientific data. The third schema can be especially useful when a base scientific class has wide objects but the final data products have only a small fraction.

5 Related Work

A few of research efforts have already been made to integrate some database technologies into scientific workflow management systems [2,3,4,5]. The first system in this domain is ZOO [3]. In ZOO, the workflow is fully defined as an object-oriented database schema. The relationships between tasks and data are represented by ordinary object-oriented relationships. Invocation of workflow is triggered by active rules on these relationships. GridDB [4] and [5] share many similarities with ZOO; for example, workflows in these systems are architected with a data model. However, both [4] and [5] use the simpler relational model, and are mainly focused on the grid environment. In GridDB, the inputs and outputs of programs are modeled as relational tables. Programs and workflows can be represented as typed functions. So users can define programs and the relationships between their inputs and outputs in a schema definition language. Insertion of tuples in input table triggers automatically execution of programs and workflows. However, GridDB requires storing some function memo tables for automation of workflow executions, which will increase storage cost. [5] presents a workflow modeling language that tightly integrates workflow management systems and database management systems. Initial input data and programs are described as active relational tables, and derived data and programs are described as active views, so workflows are composed by declaring active views. Although this method does not cause extra storage, any section of the workflow must be invoked by issuing a SQL query on the corresponding views or tables, which will decrease automation of workflow executions.

As a critical component, data provenance has been studied by a lot of scientific workflows and database communities. To our knowledge, annotations and inversion are two main approaches to representing provenance information. At present, most of the workflow management systems more depend on annotations [7,8,9]; Chimera [7] analyzes the virtual data catalog and comes up with an abstract DAG representing the sequence of operations that produce that data. Some provenance systems [8,9] also provide semantic information using RDF and OWL in order to realize interaction of scientific workflows in collaborative environments. However, annotations may occupy a mass of storage spaces and even outsize the storage spaces required for the data itself, even if some systems such as Chimera [7] only record the immediately previous source data and transformation step that creates the data product in order to reduce storage cost. Inversion seems to be more optimal from a storage perspective especially for a large number of fine-grained data since an inverse function or query identifies the provenance for an entire class of data. Many database communities adopting this method such as [13,14,15,16] provide data-oriented provenance services to users. Any scientific workflow systems that use database queries and functions to model workflows can apply such techniques. Trio [14] just uses the inverse method [16] to automatically determine the source data for tuples created by view queries or user defined functions. However, inversion used in these systems may not be the best way for not all functions has inverse functions [6]. [15] presents a framework for computing the approximate provenance based on weak inversion. The paper does not, however, provide a mechanism for generating the weak inversion. Computing provenance using inverse methods usually requires accessing sources which are inaccessible or time consuming. By storing additional auxiliary information in the warehouse, [16] can reduce or entirely avoid source accesses. [17] indicates that it is not a good choice to compute provenance if a large amount of provenance information are required.

6 Conclusions and Future Work

In this paper, we have presented a DB-integrated scientific workflow framework which adopts the object deputy model to describe execution of a series of scientific tasks. In particular, the deputy objects, which are similar to view, improve workflow automation greatly and incur no extra storage or maintenance cost. The object deputy approach is superior in resolving automatic update maintenance and supporting dynamic or incomplete specification of workflows. Most important of all, data provenance method of this framework can provide much higher performance than annotations or inversion. At present, web services, as a standard for inter-operability, have widely used in distributed grid applications and workflows, and grid has also become the platform for the creation, processing, and management of experimental data. Hence, scientific experimental environments tuned to an increasingly distributed and service-oriented grid infrastructure. How to seamlessly integrate our framework into the infrastructure is one of our future works.

References

1. Bertram Lud ascher, Carole Goble: Guest Editors' Introduction to the Special Section on Scientific Workflows. SIGMOD Record, Vol. 34, No. 3. 2005
2. B. Lud¨ascher, I. Altintas, C. Berkley, D. Higgins, E. Jaeger-Frank, M. Jones, E. Lee, J. Tao, and Y. Zhao: Scientific workflow management and the Kepler system. Concurrency and Computation: Practice & Experience, Special Issue on Scientific Workflows, 2005

3. Anastassia Ailamaki, Yannis E. Ioannidisz, Miron Livny: Scientific Workflow Management by Database Management. In 10th conference on scientific and statistical database management (SSDBM).1998
4. David T. Liu Michael J. Franklin. GridDB: A Data-Centric Overlay for Scientific Grids. Proceedings of the 30th VLDB Conference, Toronto, Canada, 2004
5. Srinath Shankar Ameet Kini David J DeWitt Jeffrey Naughton: Integrating databases and workflow systems. SIGMOD Record, Vol. 34, No. 3. 2005
6. Y. L. Simmhan, B. Plale, and D. Gannon: A Survey of Data Provenance Techniques. In Technical Report TR-618: Computer Science Department, Indiana University, 2005
7. I. Foster, J. Vöckler, M. Wilde, Y. Zhao: Chimera: A Virtual Data System for Representing, Querying, and Automating Data Derivation. In 14th conference on scientific and statistical database management (SSDBM). 2002, 37-46.
8. J. Zhao, C. A. Goble, R. Stevens, S. Bechhofer: Semantically Linking and Browsing Provenance Logs for E-science. In ICSNW, 2004, 158-176
9. C. Pancerella, J. Hewson, W. Koegler, D. Leahy, edc: Metadata in the collaboratory for multi-scale chemical science. In Dublin Core Conference, 2003
10. Zhiyong Peng, Qing Li, Ling Feng, etc: Using Object Deputy Model to Prepare Data for Data Warehousing. IEEE Transaction on Knowledge and Data Engineering. Vol. 17, No. 9. 2005
11. Boxuan Zhai, Zhiyong Peng: object-deputy database language. The Fourth International Conference on Creating, Connecting and Collaborating through Computing, 2006, to be appear.
12. M. Greenwood, C. Goble, R. Stevens, J. Zhao, M. Addis, D. Marvin, L. Moreau, and T. Oinn: Provenance of e-Science Experiments - experience from Bioinformatics. In Proceedings of the UK OST e-Science 2nd AHM, 2003
13. P. Buneman, S. Khanna, and W. C. Tan: Why and Where: A Characterization of Data Provenance. In ICDT, 2001, 316-330
14. J. Widom: Trio: A System for Integrated Management of Data, Accuracy, and Lineage. In CIDR, 2005
15. A. Woodruff and M. Stonebraker: Supporting Fine-grained Data Lineage in a Database Visualization Environment. In ICDE, 1997, 91-102
16. Y. Cui and J. Widom: Practical Lineage Tracing in Data Warehouses. In ICDE, 2000
17. Deepavali Bhagwat, Laura Chiticariu, Wang-Chiew Tan, Gaurav Vijayvargiya: An Annotation Management System for Relational Databases. In Proceedings of the 30th VLDB Conference, Toronto, Canada, 2004

On the Development of a Multiple-Compensation Mechanism for Business Transactions

Zaihan Yang and Chengfei Liu

Faculty of Information and Communication Technologies
Swinburne University of Technology
Melbourne, VIC 3122, Australia
{zyang, cliu}@ict.swin.edu.au

Abstract. Compensation is a widely used concept for maintaining atomicity in both the advanced transaction models and transactional workflow systems. Some Web service protocols also adopt the compensation mechanism for failure recovery when providing transaction management. However, the compensation mechanisms used in these models or protocols are too fixed and cannot satisfy the various requirements of different applications. In this paper, a multiple-compensation mechanism is proposed and defined explicitly in a business process model. An algorithm on how to implement this multiple-compensation mechanism for backward recovery is designed and its computation complexity is analysed.

1 Introduction

These years have seen the widespread use of transaction management in non-traditional applications. The transactions in these applications are different from traditional transactions [1,2] for their long-time running and for that they may access data held in heterogeneous, autonomous and distributed systems. The ACID properties will be too strict for them to follow. To overcome the limitations of traditional transactions, some advanced transaction models (ATMs) [3] have been proposed, such as Sagas [4], closed/open nested transactions [5, 6], multi-level transactions [6], flexible transactions [7] and Contracts [8].

The mechanism of compensation is originally proposed by Gray in [9], and then widely used in ATMs to maintain atomicity when the isolation property has been relaxed [9, 10]. For a transaction T, its compensating transaction C is a transaction that can semantically eliminate the effects of the transaction T after T has been successfully committed. For example, for a DEPOSIT transaction, its compensating transaction can be a WITHDRAW. We take the Sagas model as an example to clarify how the compensation mechanism is used. In Sagas, the long transaction is divided into several short subtransactions each of which strictly follows the ACID properties. The isolation for the global transaction is relaxed, since subtransactions can release the resources they hold and publicise their effect to other subtransactions before the global transaction commits. For each subtransaction (except for the very last one), there exists a corresponding compensating transaction. When a subtransaction fails, it

J.X. Yu, M. Kitsuregawa, and H.V. Leong (Eds.): WAIM 2006, LNCS 4016, pp. 581 – 592, 2006.
© Springer-Verlag Berlin Heidelberg 2006

will firstly be rollbacked by a transaction manager and all its preceding subtransactions will be compensated by executing their corresponding compensating transactions in a reverse order.

A compensating transaction has some special characteristics besides the fundamental properties of a transaction. First of all, a compensating transaction eliminates a transaction's effect in a semantic manner, rather than by physically restoring to a prior state. Secondly, a compensating transaction is retriable, namely, once the compensating transaction is invoked to execute, it will ultimately commit successfully. Thirdly, a compensating transaction is always regarded as being associated with a compensated-for transaction. In most situations, it is the programmer's responsibility to predefine a compensating transaction.

Compensation mechanism is not only widely used in ATMs but also adopted by transactional workflows to maintain reliability and consistency of business processes. It is assumed that users can define for each task in a business process one compensating task [11, 12]. When some committed tasks which are called compensated-for tasks need to be undone, their corresponding compensating tasks will be invoked.

The loosely coupled property of Web services offers a good environment for business process collaborations. Some existing Web service protocols, such as WSCI [13], BPEL4WS [14] and WS-CDL [15] also provide some transaction management by supporting the open nested transaction model and compensation mechanism.

Currently, each task can only have one compensating task. This compensation mechanism is too fixed and not flexible enough to adjust to different application requirements. For example, when penalty has to be considered for carrying out compensation, different penalty polices will result in different compensation strategies. As a result, a multiple-compensation mechanism is necessary. This paper proposes a concept of multiple-compensation and describes how to incorporate it in workflow systems. The rest of the article is organised as follows. Section 2 gives a motivating example to clarify the importance of multiple-compensation. Section 3 defines a business process model with the multiple-compensation feature. Section 4 introduces an algorithm on how to implement the multiple-compensation mechanism and analyse its complexity. Section 5 discusses the related work on compensation. Section 6 concludes the paper and indicates the future work.

2 Motivating Example for Multiple-Compensation

Consider a travel reservation process shown in Figure 1 as an example. The whole business process has ten tasks. Travellers will send their trip requests to a travel agent (SR). After receiving the request and sending back acknowledgment (SA), the travel agent will invoke two concurrent activities at the same time: to reserve proper tickets for the traveller via the airline company (BAT) and to book a hotel for the traveller to reside in the destination place (BH). Whether to rent a car in the visiting place is an optional task determined upon the traveller's requirements (RC). During the booking process, travellers should provide their credit card information for identity validation. After all the necessary reservations have been completed, the travel agent will send an itinerary describing the reservation information and an invoice to the traveller (SBS). The traveller can send acknowledgment to confirm his or her bookings (ACK). Before the airplane departure, the traveller can still choose to cancel the booking (TC) or confirm the booking by paying the money (TP). After the traveller finishes purchasing, the travel agent will send airplane ticket and confirmation letter for hotel booking and for car rental to the traveller. If the traveller cancels the booking or does not complete purchasing after departure, a penalty will apply.

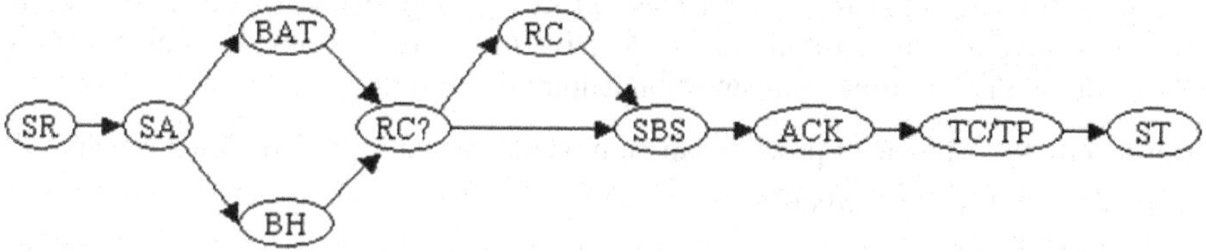

Fig. 1. A travel reservation business process example

There exists compensation dependency among tasks. For example, since BAT and BH are concurrent tasks, and only when both of them successfully complete can the succeeding task be executed, consequently, either BAT or BH fails, the other committed task should be compensated.

Consider the situation for the traveller to cancel the booking after having sent out the acknowledgment information. Some corresponding compensation tasks should be carried out due to the cancelling behaviour. Associated with these cancellations, the companies such as the airline company will normally take actions based on some penalty policies for the sake of their own interests. The following table illustrated the penalty policies taken by an airline company.

Table 1. An example of the penalty policy of an airline company

Penalty / Time / Users	2 weeks	5 days	2 days	0 days
VIP Users	None	None	None	None
Members	None	10%	20%	50%
Non-Members	None	20%	50%	100%

Time column indicates when the traveller cancels his booking, 2 weeks before departure, 5 days, 2 days or right before departure (0 days); User column indicates the different status of the users and correspondingly they have different privileges. Penalty column indicates the different charges the company will ask for due to the time to cancel and the user status.

A penalty policy is associated with a compensation task and can be regarded as part of the compensation task. Different penalty policies will be adopted in different cases, leading to different compensation tasks. Our multi-compensation mechanism is motivated to deal with this situation.

3 Business Processes with Multiple-Compensation Mechanism

From the motivating example described in the previous section, we can see that the multiple compensations are common phenomena in real applications. Consequently, a corresponding multiple-compensation mechanism should be considered and reflected in the business process models. In this section, we introduce the multiple-compensation mechanism in a business process environment which associates for each task several compensating tasks. We give formal definitions of a business process model with a multiple-compensation feature in the following.

Definition 1. A business process can be modelled as an acyclic directed graph in the form of $G(N, E, t, n_S)$, where

(1) N is a set of nodes. Each node corresponds to a task in the business process. Namely, $N = \{n_1, n_2, ..., n_m\}$, $n_i \in N (1 \le i \le m)$ represents a task.

(2) E is a set of directed edges. Each edge $e = (n_1, n_2) \in E$ corresponds to the control dependency between n_1 and n_2, where $n_1, n_2 \in N$.

(3) For each $n \in N$, *Ind(n)* and *Outd(n)* define the number of edges which take *n* as the terminating node and starting node, respectively.

(4) *t: N→ Type* is a mapping function, where *Type={normal, And-Join, And-Split, Or-join, Or-Split}*. It is easy to see that:
If *t(n) = "normal"* then *ind(n) = outd(n) = 1.*
If *t(n) = "And-Split"* or *"Or-Split"* then *ind(n) = 1, outd(n) > 1.*
If *t(n) = "And-Join"* or *"Or-Join"* then *ind(n) > 1, outd(n) = 1.*

(5) n_s is the starting task of the business process, which satisfies that $n_s \in N$ and $Ind(n_s) = 0$.

Tasks are the main components of a business process. A task can be modelled as a combination of a normal part (of operations), which is used for forward execution and a compensation part (of operations), which is used for backward recovery. In order to introduce the mechanism of multiple-compensation, we define for the compensation part of each task not only one, but a set of compensating tasks. We can model a task as follows.

Definition 2. A task n is defined as (tf, tb, C) where,

(1) *tf* defines the forward execution part (normal part) of *n*. The set of input and output parameters of *tf* is denoted as *Par.* When *tf* is invoked, *Par* will be recorded in a system log.

(2) *tb* defines the backward execution part (compensation part) of *n*. When *tb* is invoked, the *Par*, which is stored in a system log, will be adopted.

(3) *C* is a set which consists of a set of compensating tasks defined for the task *n*. When a task needs to be compensated, its backward execution part *tb* will be invoked. Then the *tb* will select from the set *C* one appropriate compensating task for execution according to some decision criteria.

More details on the process of selecting will be explained in Section 4.

Definition 3. An instance of a business process graph $G(N,E,t,n_s)$ is defined as an acyclic graph $\overline{G}(\overline{N},\overline{E},t,st,et,s,\overline{n}_s)$, where

(1) $\overline{N} \subseteq N$ Each $\overline{n}_i \in \overline{N}$ corresponds to a task instance in the business process instance.

(2) $\overline{E} \subseteq E$. Each edge $\overline{e} = (\overline{n}_1, \overline{n}_2) \in \overline{E}$ corresponds to the control dependency between task instances $\overline{n}_1$ and $\overline{n}_2$, where $\overline{n}_1, \overline{n}_2 \in \overline{N}$.

(3) $t : \overline{N} \rightarrow Type$ is the same mapping function as that defined in the business process model G.

(4) $st, et : \overline{N} \rightarrow Time$ are functions which map a $\overline{n}_i \in \overline{N}$ to a specific system time, where $st(\overline{n}_i)$ indicates the starting time of $\overline{n}_i$ and $et(\overline{n}_i)$ indicates the terminating time of $\overline{n}_i$.

(5) $s : \overline{N} \rightarrow States$ is a function which maps each task instance in set $\overline{N}$ to a certain kind of states in set $States$, where $States = \{$*initial, active, complete, ended, selecting, compensating, faulting*$\}$.

(6) $\overline{n}_s$ indicates the starting task instance.

(7) $prec, succ : \overline{N} \rightarrow 2^{\overline{N}}$ are functions which define for each task instance $\overline{n}_i \in \overline{N}$ its preceding task instances and succeeding task instances respectively. $\overline{n}_j$ is said to be the preceding task instance of $\overline{n}_i$ when it exists that $(\overline{n}_j, \overline{n}_i) \in \overline{E}$. $\overline{n}_j$ is said to be the succeeding task instance of $\overline{n}_i$ when it exists that $(\overline{n}_i, \overline{n}_j) \in \overline{E}$.

Definition 4. The executed part of $\overline{G}(\overline{N},\overline{E},t,st,et,s,\overline{n}_s)$ is denoted as $\overline{G}_E(\overline{N}_E,\overline{E}_E,t,st,et,s,\overline{n}_s)$, where $\overline{N}_E$, $\overline{E}_E$ are subsets of $\overline{N}$ and $\overline{E}$ respectively and for each $\overline{n}_i \in \overline{N}_E$, $s(\overline{n}_i) \neq "initial"$.

4 Implementing Multiple-Compensation

Upon the definitions given in Section 3, we present an algorithm on how to implement the multiple-compensation mechanism in this section. Before the presentation of the algorithm, the main ideas of it will be firstly introduced. The analysis for the computational complexity of the algorithm will be given in the end.

4.1 Algorithm Introduction

The algorithm describes what should be done with the multiple-compensation mechanism to maintain atomicity and consistency of the whole business process in the presence of tasks' failures. The algorithm is invoked by the input of the executed part of a business process instance $\overline{G}_E$ with one or more failed task instances. A system log will play an important role in the algorithm. For each executed task instance $\overline{n} \in \overline{G}_E$, the input/output parameters *Par* of $\overline{n}.tf$, the starting time $st(\overline{n})$, the terminating time $et(\overline{n})$ and the current state $s(\overline{n})$ will all be kept in a system log.

Due to the compensation dependencies among tasks, the abortion or compensation of some tasks will lead to the abortion or compensation of other tasks. For example, when a "*normal*" task is aborted or compensated, its only one preceding task should be compensated. When an "*And-Join*" task is aborted or compensated, all of its multiple preceding tasks should be compensated. When a task that is one of the succeeding tasks of an "*And-Split*" task is aborted or compensated, not only the "*And-Split*" task itself but all the tasks on its succeeding branches should also been compensated for. The abortion or compensation of tasks should be executed in a reverse order with the business process control flow.

The main principle of the algorithm is to traverse the graph $\overline{G}_E$ twice in opposite directions. One is backward traversing (recovery), which keeps processing and removing nodes from set *NP* (*Nodes-to-be-Processed*) as well as repetitively adds new traced preceding tasks into set *NP* for processing. The other is forward traversing (tracing), which keeps tracing succeeding tasks until some certain tasks are reached.

The algorithm starts from a failed task in graph $\overline{G}_E$ and invokes the backward traversing first. During the process of backward traversing, the preceding tasks except those *And-Split* tasks of the currently processed task will be put into set *NP* in order for processing. The order of adding tasks into set *NP* indicates the corresponding compensation order. The tasks in *NP*, which have not been completed successfully, will be aborted by system. Other tasks in *NP*, which have already successfully committed will be compensated for. When a task is going to be compensated, its backward part *tb* will be invoked. The backward part *tb* will then select from the set of compensating tasks one appropriate compensating task to execute according to those system-logged information of the task.

When the preceding task of the currently processed task is an *And-Split* task, a forward traversing process will be needed. The forward traversing process will traverse all the succeeding branches of the *And-Split* task until a certain task of each branch which has no further succeeding task or which has already been in set *NP* is reached. The whole algorithm will be terminated when the starting task instance in graph $\overline{G}_E$ is reached.

Please note that we only consider the execution part of the business process instance. So for those *Or-Join* and *Or-Split* tasks, their proceding tasks and succeeding tasks will be specific. We can treat them as normal tasks.

4.2 Algorithm Description

We now describe the algorithm for implementing the multiple-compensation mechanism in a more formal way as follows.

Algorithm 1. backward-recovery

Input

The executed part of a business process instance $\overline{G}_E(\overline{N},\overline{E},t,st,et,s,\overline{n}_s)$, where $\exists \overline{n}_i(\overline{n}_i \in \overline{N} \wedge s(\overline{n}_i) = "faulting")$.

Output

The updated executed part of a business process instance $\overline{G}_E(\overline{N},\overline{E},t,st,et,s,\overline{n}_s)$, where $\forall \overline{n}_i(\overline{n}_i \in \overline{N} \rightarrow s(\overline{n}_i) = "ended")$.

Steps:

1. **for** ***each*** $\overline{n}_i \in \overline{N}$, **if** $s(\overline{n}_i) = "faulting"$ **then** {*NP*={ $\overline{n}_i$ }; Skip} /* put one faulting task in *NP* */
2. *ASMarded* = ϕ /* used for marking tasks of the type "*And-Split*" */
3. **for** ***each*** $\overline{n}_i \in NP$ {

/* ***Processing Part*** */

4.   **if** $s(\overline{n}_i) = "active"$ **then** $s(\overline{n}_i) = "ended"$;
5.   **if** $s(\overline{n}_i) = "faulting"$ **then** $s(\overline{n}_i) = "ended"$;
6.   **if** $s(\overline{n}_i) = "complete"$ **then** { $s(\overline{n}_i) = "selecting"$; *multiple-compensate(* $\overline{n}_i$ *);*} /* invoke algorithm 3 of *multiple-compensate* */
7. $NP = NP - \{\overline{n}_i\}$;
8.   **if** $\overline{n}_i = \overline{n}_s$ **then return** updated $\overline{G}_E$.

/* ***Generating Part*** */

9.   **if** $t(\overline{n}_i) = "normal"$ or $t(\overline{n}_i) = "And-Split"$ **then** {
10. $\overline{n}_p = getone(prec(\overline{n}_i))$; /* getone(s) take one element from set s */
11.   **if** $t(\overline{n}_p) \neq "And-Split"$ **then** $NP = NP \cup \{\overline{n}_p\}$;
12.   **else if** $\overline{n}_p \notin ASMarked$ **then** { /* *the And-Split node has not been marked* */
13.   *forward-tracing* ($\overline{G}_E, NP, ASMarked, succ(\overline{n}_p) - \{\overline{n}_i\}$)); /* invoke algorithm 2 of *forwardtracing* */
14. $ASMarked = ASMarked \cup \{\overline{n}_p\}$;
15.   }
16.   **else** { /* *the And-Split node has been marked* */
17. $Asucc = succ(\overline{n}_p)$;
18.   **for each** $\overline{n}_j \in Asucc$ **if** $s(\overline{n}_j) = "ended"$ **then** $Asucc = Asucc - \{\overline{n}_j\}$;
19.   **if** $Asucc = \phi$ **then** { $NP = NP \cup \{\overline{n}_p\}$; $ASMarked = ASMarked - \{\overline{n}_p\}$;}
20.   }
21.   }
22.   **else if** $t(\overline{n}_i) = "And-Join"$ **then** $NP = NP \cup prec(\overline{n}_i)$;
23. }

Algorithm 1 describes the backward traversing process. It takes the executed part of a business process instance graph $\overline{G}_E$ as an input and starts from an arbitrary faulting task in the graph. After the execution of the algorithm, all the current states of tasks in $\overline{G}_E$ will be set into "ended". The main body of the algorithm consists of two parts, processing part and generating part. During the processing part, tasks in set *NP* will be processed differently. For those tasks with current states of "active" or faulting", they will be undone by the transaction manager, while if their states are "complete", they will be compensated for. Algorithm 3 will be invoked to compensate these compensated-for tasks. During the generating part, the preceding tasks of the currently processed task will be traced. For a *normal* task or *And-Split* task, its preceding task that is not an *And-Split* task will be added into set *NP*. For an *And-Join* task, all its preceding tasks will be added into set *NP*. The process happens repetitively until at last the starting task is reached. When an *And-Split* task is first reached, a forward tracing process is associated, which will be described explicitly in algorithm 2. In order to avoid reduplicate traversing, a set *ASMarked* is constructed. The *And-Split* tasks, which have once been processed, will be added into set *ASMarked.* They will not be forward traced again even though they will be reached later during the traversing.

Algorithm 2. forward-tracing
Input: $\overline{G}_E, NP, ASMarked, Asucc$
Output: *NP*
Steps:

$AJMarked = \phi$
for each $\overline{n}_i \in Asucc$ {
  $Asucc = Asucc - \{\overline{n}_i\}$;
  if $\overline{n}_i \notin NP$ and $succ(\overline{n}_i) = \phi$ **then** $NP = NP \cup \{\overline{n}_i\}$
  else if $succ(\overline{n}_i) \neq \phi$ **then** {
    $Asucc = Asucc \cup (succ(\overline{n}_i) - AJMarked)$;
    if $t(\overline{n}_i) = "And-Split"$ **then** $ASMarked = ASMarked \cup \{\overline{n}_i\}$
    else if $t(\overline{n}_i) = "And-Join"$ **then** $AJMarked = AJMarked \cup \{\overline{n}_i\}$
  }
}
return *NP.*

Algorithm 2 describes a forward tracing process invoked when an *And-Split* task is first reached. For those *And-Split* tasks, all of its succeeding branches except those that have been processed will be traversed until the task of each branch that has

---

Algorithm 3. multiple-compensate
Input: $\overline{n}_i$
Steps:

invoke $\overline{n}_i.tb$;
$tb(par, st(\overline{n}_i), et(\overline{n}_i)) \rightarrow c_j : c_j \in C$; /* select from set *C* one appreciate compensating task based on some system-logged information*/
$s(\overline{n}_i) = "compensating"$;
execute c_j;
$s(\overline{n}_i) = "ended"$;
return.

---

already been in set *NP* or has no succeeding task is reached. In the latter situation, the task that has no succeeding tasks will be put into set *NP*. To avoid reduplicate traversing, two sets *ASMarked* and *AJMarked* are used to contain those *And-Split* tasks and *And-Join* tasks that have once been traversed.

Algorithm 3 describes the multiple-compensation process. When a task in set *NP* is going to be compensated, its *tb* part will be invoked. Then it will choose from the set of its compensating tasks one appropriate task for executing.

4.3 Computational Complexity Analysis

Algorithms 1, 2 and 3 describe the whole process of backward recovery using the multiple-compensation mechanism. The main principle is to traverse the graph $\overline{G}_E$ for two times, one for backward traversing, and the other for forward traversing.

For algorithm 1, we can see that it traverses backward through edges in the graph $\overline{G}_E$ from a faulting node to the starting node and repetitively adds preceding nodes into set *NP*. Set *NP* grows dynamically during the process of traversing. Consequently, the complexity of algorithm 1 should be equal to $O(|E|)$.

For algorithm 2, it describes a forward traversing process from any *And-Split* node in the graph to the node of each of its branch paths that is in set *NP* or has no succeeding nodes. New found succeeding nodes during traversing are added into set *Asucc* thus makes it grow gradually. Its complexity should also be equal to $O(|E|)$. However, extra cost comes from step 6, which contains two set computation between $succ(n_i)$ (through traced edges) and *Asucc* and *AJMarked,* respectively. We consider the worst situation when *Asucc* and *AJMarked* are proportional to $|N|$, so the complexity for $Asucc = Asucc \bigcup (succ(\overline{n}_i) - AJMarked)$ will be equal to $O(|E|\log|N|)$ (we may use indices for both *Asucc* and *AJMarked*). As a result, the complexity of algorithm 2 should be $O(|E|\log|N|)$.

For algorithm 3, it will be invoked for all nodes that have been completed successfully. The complexity for selecting one appropriate compensating task among several compensating tasks would be a constant. So, the complexity for algorithm 3 would be $O(|N|)$, which is less than $O(|E|)$.

We can conclude that the total complexity for algorithms 1, 2 and 3 is $O(|E|\log|N|)$.

5 Related Work

Compensation mechanism is firstly proposed in ATMs. It is then widely adopted by transactional workflows and Web service transaction protocols to maintain atomicity when isolation property is relaxed.

For transactional workflow systems, the notion of compensation is of great importance, since most workflow instances tend to be long running and the processing entities of some tasks do not support transaction management (such as file systems or legacy systems). The backward recovery based on compensation is well supported in some workflow systems, the most typical of which are the FlowMark workflow systems and the Virtual Transaction Model.

In FlowMark [16] workflow systems, the notion of sphere of joint compensation, which is proposed by Frank Leymann [17] for providing partial backward recovery, is well supported. A sphere is a collection of tasks in a workflow. It should be satisfied that either all the tasks in the sphere successfully complete or all of them should be compensated. Each sphere and each task enclosed in the sphere is defined to be associated with a compensating task. The sphere can be aborted by compensating its composed tasks individually or by invoking the compensation task for the sphere as a whole. Spheres can overlap and be nested. If a task fails, the sphere that immediately encloses it is compensated. Optionally, other spheres that enclose this sphere can be compensated and this can go on recursively.

The Virtual transaction model [18] specifies Virtual Transaction (VT) regions on top of a workflow graph. Upon a failure during the execution of a task enclosed in a VT region, all tasks in the region are compensated in the reverse order of their forward execution, until a compensation end point is reached.

Confirmation is a new mechanism proposed in [19]. It is able to modify some non-compensatable tasks to make them compensatable. While compensation is to semantically eliminate the effects of some completed tasks, confirmation is to semantically commit them. With confirmation mechanism, a task in a business process will not only be associated with a compensating task but also a confirmation task. Once a workflow process instance is executed successfully, the confirmation tasks of all the executed tasks will be executed automatically.

The technology of Web service is developing rapidly. It offers a good environment for business process execution since the Web service components are loosely coupled with each other. Some Web service protocols include transactional support mechanism. For example, the WSCI, WSBPEL and WS-CDL all support open nested transaction model and compensation mechanism. The Web service business activity transaction protocol (WS-BA) [20] is also compensation-based.

Compared with our multiple-compensation mechanism, those compensation mechanisms proposed in ATMs, transactional workflows are not flexible enough. They associate for each task only one compensating task. The compensation mechanism adopted in some Web service protocols is targeted at a scope (or context) level. Scopes and contexts can be nested, which will lead to redundant definition of compensation tasks and cannot be executed automatically. Our multiple-compensation mechanism defines for each task several compensating tasks, thus can satisfy various application demands. The compensating task can be invoked and executed automatically once its corresponding task needs to be compensated for.

6 Conclusion

Compensation is an important mechanism for backward recovery in long running business processes. Its main principle is to semantically eliminate the effects of some successfully committed tasks in the business process. System developers or users can define for each task in the business process a corresponding compensating task. When a certain task needs to be compensated, its compensating task will be invoked.

In the previous studies, only one compensating task is defined to be associated with a task, which cannot satisfy the different requirements in real applications when some other conditions should be considered, such as penalty, time limits, different user privilege, etc. In this paper, we took into account this problem and proposed a new mechanism of multiple-compensation, which associates for each task several compensating tasks. When a task should be undone, one appropriate compensating task will be selected to invoke under some pre-fixed conditions.

We incorporated the multiple compensation mechanism into a business process model by giving some formal definitions. We then introduced and described in detail an algorithm on how to decide which tasks should be compensated, in which order they should be compensated and which one specific compensating task should be selected to compensate them. The algorithm is efficient, which basically traverses the executed part of a business process graph twice. In most cases, the complexity of the algorithm is $O(|E|)$, with the worst case to be $O(|E|\log|N|)$.

For future work, we would like to take into account the concept of sphere of the joint compensation to see how the multiple compensation mechanism can be applied to it. We also would like to incorporate the mechanism of multiple-compensation into a Web service environment to see what benefits it will bring to improve the existing Web service protocols on Web service transactions.

Acknowledgement

This work is supported by the Australian Research Council Discovery Project under the grant number DP0557572.

References

1. J. Gray and A.Reuter. Transaction Processing: Concepts and Techniques, Morgan Kaufmann,1993.
2. N.Lynch, M.Merritt, W.Weihl and A. Fekete. Atomic Transactions. Morgan Kaufmann, 1993.
3. A. Elmagarmid (Ed.). Database Transaction Models for Advanced Applications, Morgan Kaufmann, 1992.
4. H. Garcia-Molina, K. Salem. Sagas. In the Proceedings of the ACM Conference on Management of Data, 1987, pp.249-259.
5. J.Moss. Nested Transactions and Reliable Distributed Computing. In Proceeding of the 2nd Symposium on Reliability in Distributed Software and Database Systems, 1982, pp. 33-39, Pittsburgh, PA. IEEE CS Press.
6. G.Weikum and H. Schek. Concepts and applications of multiple transactions and open-nested transactions. A.Elmagarmid(Ed.), Morgan Kaufmann, chapter 13, 1992.
7. A. Zhang, M. Nodine, B. Bhargava and Bukhres,O. Ensuring Rlaxed Atomicity for Flexible Transactions in Multidatabase Systems. In Proceedings of 1994 SIGMOD International Conference on Management of Data, 1994, pp. 67-78.
8. H. Wachter and A. Reuter. "The Contract Model", Database Transaction Models for Advanced Applications, A.Elmagarmid (Ed.) Morgan Kaufmann, San Francisco, CA, 1992.
9. J. Gray. The transaction concept: Virtues and Limitations. In Proceeding of the International Conference on Very Large Data Bases, Cannes, France, 1981, pp. 144-154.

10. H.F. Korth, E. Levy and A. Silberschatz. A formal approach to recovery by compensating transactions. In the Proceedings of the 16th VLDB Conference, 1990, pp. 139-146.
11. B. Kiepuszewski, R. Muhlberger and M. Orlowska. Flowback: Providing backward recovery for workflow systems. In the Proceedings of the ACM SIGMOD International Conference on Management of Data, 1998, pp. 555-557.
12. D.Kuo, M. Lawley, C. Liu and M. Orlowska. A model for transactional workflows. R. Topor (Ed.). In the Seventh Australasian Databases Conference Proceedings, vol. 18, Melbourne, Australia, 1996, Australian Computer Science Communications, pp. 139-146.
13. A.Arkin, et al. Web Service Choreography Interface (WSCI) 1.0, August 2002, http://www.w3.org/TR/wsci/.
14. T.Andrews, et al. Business Process Execution Language for Web Services (BPEL4WS) 1.1, May 2003, http://www.ibm.com/developerworks/library/ws-bpel.
15. N.Kavantzas. et al. Web Services Choreography Description Language (WS-CDL) 1.0. 2004. http://www.w3.org/TR/2004/WD-ws-cdl-10-20040427.
16. F.Leymann and D.Roller. Business process management with FlowMark. In the Proceedings of IEEE CompCon (San Francisco, CA, 1994) (Los Alamitos), CA: IEEE Computer Society Press), pp 230-234.
17. F.Leymann. Supporting business transactions via partial backward recovery in workflow management systems. In the Proceedings of BTW'95, 1995, pp. 51-70.
18. V.Krishnamoorthy and M.Shan. Virtual Transaction Model to support Workflow Applications. SAC (2), 2000, pp. 876-881
19. C. Liu, X. Lin, M. E. Orlowska and X. Zhou. Confirmation: increasing resource availability for transactional workflows. Inf. Sci. 153, 2003, pp. 37-53.
20. L. F. Cabrera et al. Web Services Business Activity Framework (WS-BusinessActivity). 2005. http://ftpna2.bea.com/pub/downloads/webservices/WS-BusinessActivity.pdf.

OS-DRAM: A Delegation Administration Model in a Decentralized Enterprise Environment

Changwoo Byun[1], Seog Park[1], and Sejong Oh[2]

[1] Department of Computer Science, Sogang University,
Seoul, 121-742, South Korea
{chang, spark}@dblab.sogang.ac.kr

[2] Department of Computer Science, Dankook University,
Cheonan,330-714, South Korea
sejongoh@dankook.ac.kr

Abstract. In this paper, we propose an effective delegation administration model using the organizational structure. From a user-level delegation point of view, previous delegation models built on the (Administrative) Role-Based Access Control model cannot present the best solution to security problems such as the leakage of information and the abuse of delegation in a decentralized enterprise environment. Thus, we propose a new integrated management model of administration role-based access control model and delegation policy, which is called the OS-DRAM. This defines the authority range in an organizational structure that is separated from role hierarchy and supports a clear criterion for user-level delegation administration. Consequently, the OS-DRAM supports a decentralized user-level delegation policy in which a regular user can freely delegate his/her authority to other users within a security officer's authority range with-out the security officer's intervention.

1 Introduction

In recent years, access control has been monitored as an important security area. The Role-Based Access Control (RBAC) model is well known among enterprise organizations because its main concept is based on an enterprise environment [1-3]. The RBAC model is guided by its central aim of preventing users from discretionally accessing the organization's information. As such, access rights are associated with roles, and users are assigned to appropriate roles.

In a large organization, security administration is a critical issue because a single security officer cannot manage the whole access control system. Therefore, the Administrative RBAC (ARBAC) model was proposed for a decentralized RBAC administration [4,6,7,9,10].

It is important for administrative RBAC to support the efficient execution of business activity such as the delegation of duties, which should be considered in access control. The basic idea behind delegation is that some active entities (users) in an organization can delegate authority to another active entity (user) to carry out some functions on behalf of the former [13]. Since delegation can cause unexpected information flow, delegation should be dealt with carefully.

J.X. Yu, M. Kitsuregawa, and H.V. Leong (Eds.): WAIM 2006, LNCS 4016, pp. 593–604, 2006.
© Springer-Verlag Berlin Heidelberg 2006

In general, granting/revoking access rights is part of the security officer's rights. In user-level delegation, however, an individual user grants (revokes) own access rights to (from) others. Fig. 1(a) shows this situation. Therefore, the abuse of delegation authority power leads to exclusion from the security officer's authority range. Fig. 1(b) depicts a wrong delegation of authority. The objective of our work is to control user-level delegation authority power within the security officer's authority range as shown in Fig. 1(c).

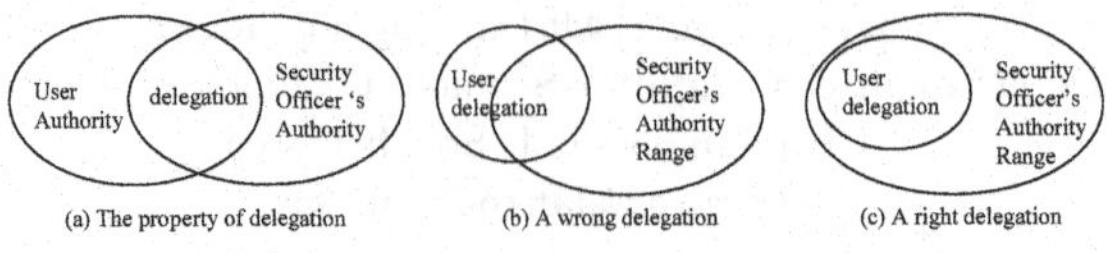

Fig. 1. The quality of delegation

Our proposed delegation methodology is similar to that of the Permission-Based Delegation Model (PBDM) [13] which is built on the ARBAC model for managing administrative activities. However, the ARBAC model induces various administration problems by role hierarchy for basis of the security officer's authority range. These problems affect the PBDM. We describe the detailed shortcomings of the ARBAC model and PBDM in Section 2. We also try to develop an effective and practical model for decentralized delegation administration. Delegation administration implies managing users' delegation authority range, restricting delegation role creation, user-delegation role assignment, and permission-delegation role assignment, managing can-delegate constraints, and so on. We refer to the OS-RBAC model for the administrative RBAC model [10], which modifies the ARBAC model and adds new components in the organizational structure.

Our proposed model is called the 'Organizational Structure and Delegation Role Administration Model' (OS-DRAM).

The rest of this paper is organized as follows: In Section 1, we briefly review the ARBAC model and related models, and describe their weaknesses. Then we explain the reason in choosing PBDM's delegation methodology in Section 2. Section 3 introduces the motivation of this work and some problems involved in the PBDM which is built in the ARBAC97 model. In Section 4, we introduce an integrated management model, the OS-DRAM, which integrates delegation policy into the OS-RBAC model. In addition, we suggest integrity rules of delegation for preventing security threats in this new model. Example scenarios are discussed in Section 5, followed by the conclusion which summarizes our contributions and discusses future research directions in Section 6.

2 Related Works

The ARBAC Model. In the ARBAC97 model [4] which is based on the RBAC model [3], administrative roles and administrative role hierarchy are added for

RBAC administration. Security officers are assigned to proper administrative roles. The ARBAC97 model has three components: (1) URA97 which is concerned with user-role assignment, (2) PRA97 with permission-role assignment, and (3) RRA97 with role-role assignment. The purpose of these components is to assign administrative authority to security officers and to prevent any illegal activity from them [4,5]. However, the ARBAC97 model has a lot of shortcomings [6,7]. Its main shortcoming is its authority range for security officers in the role hierarchy. As a result, unexpected outcomes may take place when a security officer modifies the role hierarchy. To prevent this, ARBAC97 puts strict integrity rules into RRA97, thereby restricting flexible administration.

The ARBAC02 model moves user/permission pool from role hierarchy to organizational structure [7]. It adopts two separated organizational structures for user pool and permission pool. However, it does not solve the RRA97 problem. Furthermore, there is no information on how to manage administrative role hierarchy.

The Administrative Organization-Based Access Control (AdOr-BAC) model [9] suggests using the organization for access control. The AdOr-BAC model adds administrative function to the Or-BAC model [8] which adopts contextual rules for access control. In spite of AdOr-BAC's advantages, it does not fully use the ARBAC feature. Furthermore, there is no clear principle for making contextual rules and administrative functions in AdOr-BAC. If the chief security officer fails to make safe rules, there can be no safe access control.

Delegation Methods on the RBAC Model. Barka and Sandhu [11] discussed some advanced features of the Role-Based Delegation Model (RBDM). The delegation method used in RBDM is the URA method. Role Delegation Model 2000 (RDM2000) [12] proposed a rule-based framework and specification language for role-based delegation. The RDM2000 model also uses the URA method and additionally, the PRA method for partial delegation. To illustrate, Fig. 2(a) shows Bob assigning a role PL to Tom. This URA method results in two disadvantages. One is that Bob cannot delegate a piece of role. The other is that Tom can inherit the sub-role(s) of the role PL through the inheritance property of role hierarchy. Fig. 2(b) shows Bob partially assigning the 'confirm_program' of role PL to role PE1 which is assigned to Tom. In this PRA method, another user U1 assigned to role PE1 can access the 'confirm_program'. Consequently, both URA and PRA methods result in the violation of the 'least privilege principle'.

The Permission-Based Delegation Model (PBDM) [13] solved these role-level delegation problems in a role- and permission-level delegation way through the

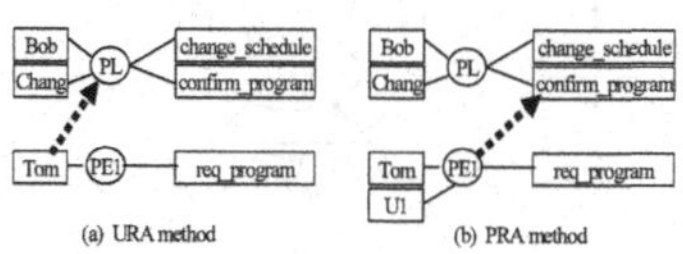

Fig. 2. Simple delegation method in RBAC

creation of new delegation roles. However, the PBDM was built on the ARBAC97 model for delegation role administration in which delegation role(s) would be included in the role hierarchy. In this case, invalid permission inheritance and user-delegation role assignment may also happen. In Section 3, we will further elaborate on this problem.

The OS-RBAC Model. The main issue in decentralized security administration is the determination of each security officer's authority range. The OS-RBAC model is designed for decentralized security administration [10]. It follows the basic features of the RBAC model and the administrative role/hierarchy of ARBAC97. The main idea of OS-RBAC is injecting organizational structure to RBAC for security administration. An organizational structure is a hierarchy of organizational units. Meanwhile, an organizational unit pertains to a department such as the sales department, the accounting department, or a project team. Each organizational unit involves workers and authority to achieve its mission. In the OS-RBAC model, workers are identified as users and authority as permission.

The OS-RBAC model has two sub-models. The Organizational Structure Administration Model guides a company to build and modify its organizational structure. If a security officer *SO1* belongs to an organizational unit *OU1*, *SO1* can create a new organizational unit *OU2* under *OU1*, and link *OU1* to *OU2* by adding an edge between them. Edge *OU1* → *OU2* denotes that *OU1* is a parent organizational unit of *OU2*. *SO1* can also move users/permissions from *OU1* to *OU2* (or from *OU2* to *OU1*). Finally, *SO1* can delete *OU2*. This model involves administration rules for the above administration activities. These rules are grouped into three–UOA (user-organization assignment), POA (permission-organization assignment), and OOA (organization-organization assignment) as shown in Fig. 3.

Meanwhile, the Role Administration Model states that administration activities such as creating/deleting a role, assigning users/permissions to the role, and composing a part of role hierarchy are related to the roles of each security officer. This model is also composed of administration rules for these administration activities. These rules are categorized into three groups: URA (user-role

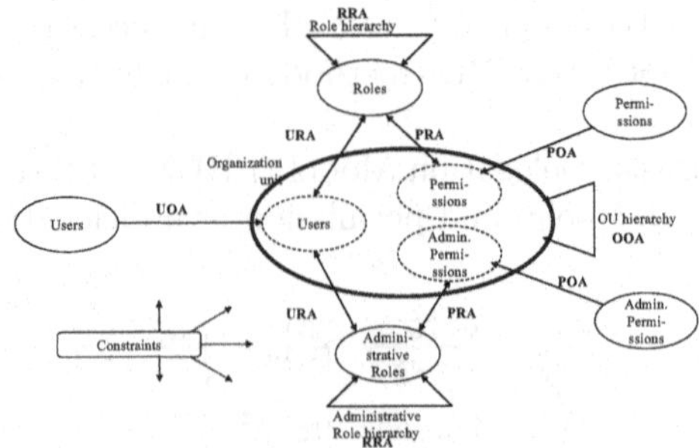

Fig. 3. The OS-RBAC model combining the Organizational Structure Administration Model and the Role Administration Model

assignment), PRA (permission-role assignment), and RRA (role-role assignment) as shown in Fig. 3.

3 Motivation

If the PBDM is supported in the ARBAC97 model, there are two resulting problems from the fact that a basic security officer's authority range is a role hierarchy. One is the position problem of a delegation role in role hierarchy. The other is the invalid inheritance problem through role hierarchy, which results in a wrong delegation as shown in Fig. 1(b). We further discuss these problems in the following paragraphs.

3.1 Position Problem of a Delegation Role in Role Hierarchy

The PBDM has three integrity rules which prevent users from discretionally accessing the organization's information. One of them is as follows [13]:

[Integrity rule of PBDM] For each delegation role, there is no senior regular role: $\{x \in \mathbf{RR} \mid x\ is\ a\ parent\ role\ of\ y \in\ set\ of\ Delegation\ Role\ \} = \emptyset$

Since the PBDM is supported in the ARBAC97 model and since the base of the security officer's authority range is a role hierarchy, delegation role(s) is included in the security officer's authority range.

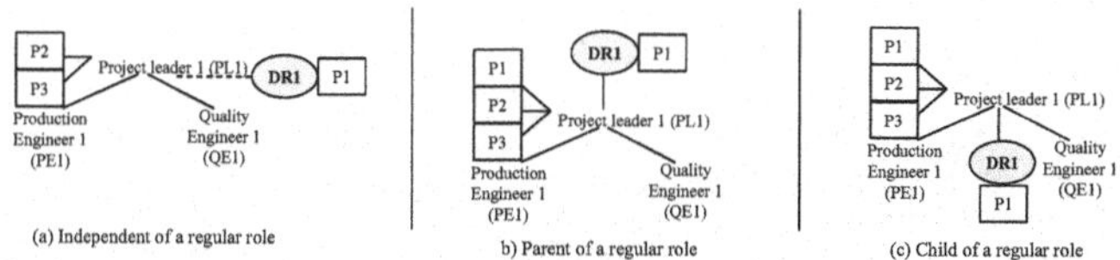

Fig. 4. Relationship between delegation role and regular role

Fig. 4 shows three cases with respect to the position of a delegation role in role hierarchy. Fig. 4(b) shows that a delegation role DR1 is the parent role of a regular role PL1. In this case, a delegatee assigned to DR1 can get invalid permissions assigned to PL1 and sub-roles PE1 and QE1 by the inheritance property of role hierarchy. Thus, this approach is not reasonable. Fig. 4(c) shows DR1 as a child role of PL1. This case prevents DR1 from getting invalid permissions. However, this approach leads to an administrative problem. Others who are assigned to PL1 get the authority of DR1. Fig. 4(a) shows that DR1 is separated from the role hierarchy. This case does not lead to the invalid inheritance of Fig. 4(b) and the invalid user-delegation role assignment of Fig. 4(c). However, the insertion of a delegation role which has no parent/child is not permitted in the RRA97 sub-model of the ARBAC97 model because this case makes the delegation role not to belong to any authority ranges.

3.2 Deviation of Delegation from the Authority Range

The ARBAC97 and ARBAC02 models need administrative data. Data-based administration involves at least three problems. First, there may be integrity problems in the administrative data. If there are wrong administrative data stored, some security officers can do illegal administration. A more serious problem is that there is no criterion to find wrong administrative data. Data integrity is wholly the responsibility of the senior security officer. Second, there may be inconsistency among the administrative data. Third, there can be an illegal modification of the administrative data. In general, administrative data are separately stored from the access control module. A malicious security officer may modify administrative data if the system is vulnerable. These problems directly affect the *can-delegate* constraint because this constraint is closely related to *can-assign* and *can-assignp* administrative data. The PBDM defines the *can-delegate* constraint as follows: $(r1,\ cr,\ s,\ n) \in$ *can-delegate.*

This means that a user assigned to a role *r1* (or a role senior to the *r1*) can delegate a set of permissions (delegation range) *s* through the inheritance property of role hierarchy.

Users assigned to the role PE1 or a role senior to PE1 (e.g., PL1 and DIR) may be a delegator. Users assigned to the role ED or a role senior to ED (e.g., E1, PE1, QE1, PL1, E2, PE2, QE2, PL2, and DIR) may be a delegatee. Thus, this *can-delegate* constraint allows bottom-up and top-down delegations. However, bottom-up delegation leads to illegal information flow.

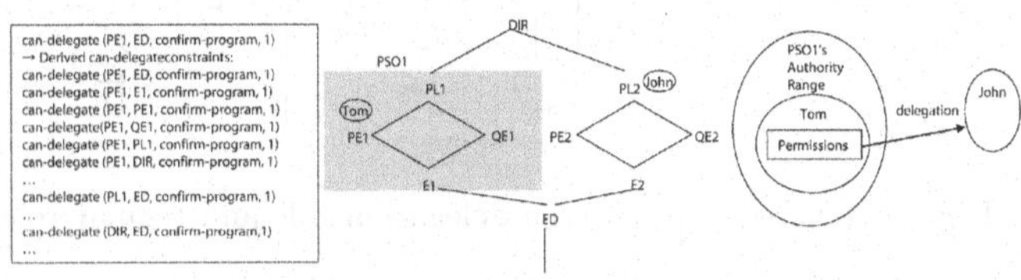

Fig. 5. The *can-delegate* constraint and an example of deviation of delegation

There exists another problem in the *can-delegate* constraint. For example, suppose that Tom delegates 'req_program' to John who is assigned to a role PE2. This delegation is permitted because PE2 is senior to ED, and John is assigned to PE2. In this case, John may not properly use Tom's authority because Tom's administration role is PSO1, but John is beyond PSO1's authority range. The right side of Fig. 5 depicts this case. If the type of Tom's delegation is 'backup of role,' it is not reasonable. However, if the type of Tom's delegation is 'collaboration of work', it may be permitted. Therefore, different delegation policies are required for 'backup of role' delegation and 'collaboration of work' delegation.

4 An Integrated Management Model of OS-RBAC and Delegation Policy

Our delegation policy is as follows: First, if a user who is not a security administrator wants to delegate his/her task, he/she can create a delegation role and specify the initial value of the 'DR.org_unit' which is capable of including delegating permissions. Second, the user who created the delegation role in the previous step assigns his/her permissions to the delegation role. Finally, the user de-escalates the 'org_unit' of the delegation role and the permissions in the delegation role, and assigns the delegation role to other users. Fig. 6 shows the OS-DRAM to support this user-level delegation policy.

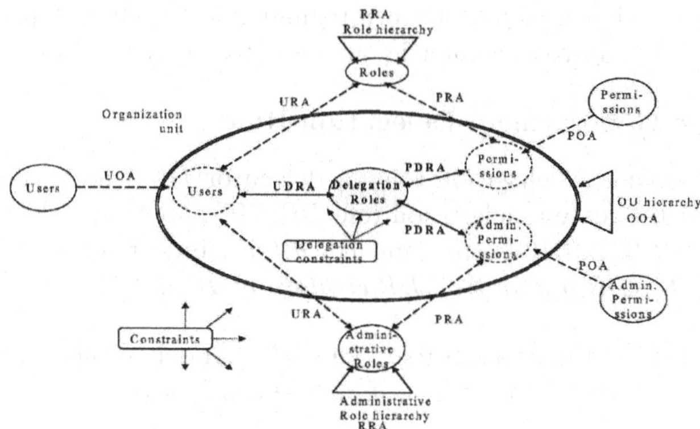

Fig. 6. The OS-DRAM

Before we describe the delegation policy, we first define common terms in the OS-DRAM.

- OT: set of organizational unit *ot*.
- U: set of user *u*.
- - *u.org_unit*: attribute that contains an organizational unit.
- P: set of permission *p*.
- - *p.org_unit*: attribute that contains an organizational unit.
- - *p.type*: attribute that contains one of the 'GPs'(general permissions or 'APs'(administrative permissions).
- R: set of role *r*.
- - *r.org_unit*: attribute that contains an organizational unit.
- - *r.type*: attribute that contains one of the 'GRs'(general roles) or 'ARs'(administrative roles).
- - *r.group*: attribute that contains one of the 'DRs'(department roles) or 'JRs'(job roles).
- DR: set of delegation role *dr*.
- - *dr.org_unit*:attribute that contains a delegatee's organizational unit.
- - *dr.type*: attribute that contains one of the 'GRs'(general roles) or 'ARs'(administrative roles).

- *dr.creator*: attribute that contains a tuple(user's ID, regular role).
- *dr.d_type*: attribute that contains one of the delegation type 'C'(Collaboration of work) or 'B'(Backup of role).

• $R = RR \cup DR$: RR means regular roles in the OS-RBAC model.
• $RR \cap DR = \emptyset$.
• *Permission(r)*: $R \rightarrow 2^P$, a function mapping a role (regular role or delegation role) to a set of permissions.
• Set:$\mathcal{U}(user\ data\ set), \mathcal{R}(\ role\ data\ set), \mathcal{P}(permission\ data\ set), \mathcal{URA}$ $(user - role\ data\ set), \mathcal{PRA}(permission - role\ data\ set)$.

- $\exists dr \in DR, (dr.creator = (du,\ rr)) \wedge ((du,\ rr) \in \mathcal{URA}) \rightarrow Permissions(dr) \in Permission(rr)$.
- If a delegator *du* generates a delegation role *dr*, *du* can only delegate permissions assigned to his/her own regular role *rr*. That is, permissions inherited from sub-roles cannot be assigned to any delegation role.

4.1 Rules in Generating a Delegation Role

[D-Rule 1] (Create a delegation role) A delegator DU who is a member of a regular role r can create a delegation role DR. DU should specify the values of $DR.org\_unit$, $DR.type$, $DR.creator$, and $DR.d\_type$ subject to:
$(DU.org\_unit \geq DR.org\_unit) \wedge (DR.creator = (DU,\ r))$

[D-Rule 2] (Delete a delegation role) The DU can delete the DR subject to:
$(DR.creator = (DU,\ r)) \wedge (DU.org\_unit \geq DR.org\_unit)$

4.2 PDRA (Permission-Delegation Role Assignment) Rules

[D-Rule 3] (Assign a delegating permission) A delegator DU can assign a permission p to DR subject to:
$(DR.creator = (DU,\ r)) \wedge ((DU,\ r) \in \mathcal{URA}) \wedge ((p,\ r) \in \mathcal{PRA}) \wedge (DU.org\_unit \geq DR.org\_unit) \wedge (DR.org\_unit \geq p.org\_unit) \wedge (DR.type = p.type)$

[D-Rule 4] (Revoke a delegated permission) DU can revoke a permission p from DR subject to:
$(DR.creator = (DU,\ r)) \wedge (DU.org\_unit \geq DR.org\_unit)$

4.3 UDRA (User-Delegation Role Assignment) Rules

If a delegator wants to assign a delegatee to a delegation role, He/she should de-escalate the initial organizational units of both the delegation role and the permissions in the delegation role.

[D-Rule 5] (De-escalate a delegation role and permissions in the delegation role) A delegator DU can de-escalate an organizational unit of a delegation role DR and a permission p in DR in order to assign a delegatee DDU to DR subject to:
$(DR.creator = (DU,\ r)) \wedge (DU.org\_unit \geq DR.org\_unit) \wedge (DDU.org\_unit \geq DR.org\_unit) \wedge (DU.org\_unit \geq p.org\_unit) \wedge (DDU.org\_unit \geq p.org\_unit)$

[D-Rule 6] (Assign a delegatee) DU can assign DDU to DR subject to:
$(DR.creator = (DU,\ r)) \wedge (DU.org\_unit \geq DDU.org\_unit) \wedge (DDU.org\_unit \geq DR.org\_unit)$

[D-Rule 7] (Revoke a delegatee) DU can revoke DDU from DR subject to:
$(DR.creator = (DU,\ r)) \wedge (DU.org\_unit \geq DDU.org\_unit) \wedge (DU.org\_unit \geq DR.org\_unit)$

4.4 Delegation Authorization and Additional Integrity Rule

In delegation authorization, the goal of the *can-delegate* constraint is to restrict the range of delegation activity. In the OS-DRAM, a security officer should select who and what belongs to his/her own organizational unit or its child organizational units. We call it the '**integrity rule of generating can-delegate constraints**'.

- Extension to the *can-delegate* constraint :$(rr,\ pc,\ s,\ n) \in can\text{-}delegate$
A user assigned to a role rr (or a role senior to rr) can delegate a set of permissions (delegation range) s to others who satisfy the pre-requisite condition pc. In addition, re-delegation is permitted within the maximum depth of delegation n. **This generation of the *can-delegate* constraint can be run within the same security officer's authority range.**

[D-Rule 8] (Generate the can-delegate constraint)
$(SO.org\_unit \geq rr.org\_unit) \wedge (SO.org\_unit \geq max\{pc.org\_unit\}) \wedge ((\exists u1, u2 \in \mathcal{U}, (u1,\ rr), (u2,\ pc) \in \mathcal{URA} \rightarrow (u1.org\_unit \geq max\{pc.org\_unit\})) \wedge (u1.org\_unit \geq u2.org\_unit)) \wedge (\exists \{s\} \subseteq \mathcal{P}, rr.org\_unit \geq max\{s.org\_unit\}) \wedge (\{s\} \subseteq Permission(rr))$

Another additional rule is a delegation type [13]. The 'backup of role' delegation type should be dealt with in a security officer's authority range. However, the 'collaboration of work' delegation type may be dealt with beyond a security officer's authority range. A senior security officer manages this delegation.

[D-Rule 9] (Two types of delegation policy) If the delegation type is 'backup of role', the delegation is managed by a delegating user. If the delegation type is 'collaboration of work', the delegation is managed by a security officer who can be responsible for the delegation. In addition, [D-Rule 8] is disregarded.

- $(DR.d\_type =' B') \wedge (DR.creator = (DU,\ r))$
- $(DR.d\_type='C') \wedge (DR.creator = (SO(security\ officer), administrativerole) \wedge ([D - Rule8]isdisregarded)$

5 Scenarios Forbidding Illegal Delegation Role Administration

The purpose of each delegation rule is to prevent individual users from performing unauthorized activities, and to keep the integrity of the *can-delegate*

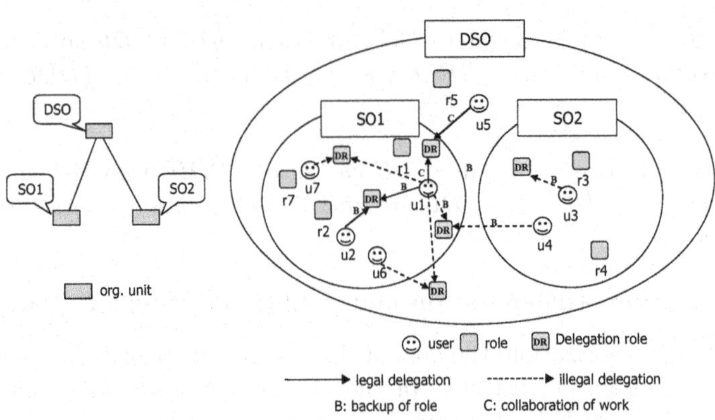

Fig. 7. The OS-DRAM

constraint. Fig. 7 shows an example of legal and illegal delegation. If a user *U1* delegates parts of his/her own permissions to a user *U2*, and the *can-delegate* constraint allows this delegation process, it is a legal delegation. If the delegation type is 'collaboration of work', *U1* can delegate parts of his/her own permissions to a user *U5*, within the organizational unit, DSO. However, the delegating entity is a security officer DSO and not *U1*.

We assume that there exist $\mathcal{URA}$ *and* $\mathcal{PRA}$ as follows:

$(U1,\ r1), (U7,\ r7) \in \mathcal{URA}, (p1,\ r1) \in \mathcal{PRA}$.

Suppose that *U1* tries to illegally delegate some tasks. There exist some examples of illegal delegation as follows:

1) *U1* tries to delegate his/her own permissions, which belong to SO1's authority range, to user *U4* who does not belong to SO1's authority range.
2) *U1* tries to delegate permissions, which do not belong to SO1's authority range, to a user *U6* who belongs to SO1's authority range.
3) *U1* tries to delegate permissions, which do not belong to SO1's authority range, to a user *U3* who does not belong to SO1's authority range.

The first case is prevented by $U1.org\_unit \geq U2.org\_unit$ in [D-Rule 6], while the second case is prevented by $U1.org\_unit \geq DR.org\_unit$ in [D-Rule 3]. The third case is also prevented by $U1.org\_unit \geq DR.org\_unit$ in [D-Rule 1], $DR.org\_unit \geq target\_permission.org\_unit$ in [D-Rule 3], and $U1.org\_unit \geq U3.org\_unit$ in [D-Rule 1]. Similarly, we can detect the delegation activities which are able to get out of the security officer's authority range from [D-Rule 1] to [D-Rule 7]. However, we cannot detect disallowed delegation activities in the same security officer's authority range. Nevertheless, these delegation activities are detected by the *can-delegate* constraints.

We assume that there exists a *can-delegate* constraint which is as follows:

$(r1,\ r2,\ p1,\ 1) \in$ *can-delegate*.

Suppose that *U1* tries to delegate parts of his/her own permissions, which belongs to SO1's authority range, to a user *U7* who belongs to SO1's authority range. This delegation process is trivially illegal because this can-delegate constraint explains that a delegatee should be assigned to a role *r2*. Now we observe the integrity problem of generating the *can-delegate* constraint.

4) Security officer SO1 tries to add the *can-delegate* constraint, (*r3, r1, p3, 1*)
5) Security officer SO1 tries to add the *can-delegate* constraint, (*r1, r4, p1, 1*)
6) Security officer SO1 tries to add the *can-delegate* constraint (*r1, r6, p4, 1*)

The fourth to sixth cases are prevented by [D-Rule 8], respectively.

Case 4: *SO1.org_unit* $\geq$ *r3.org_unit* (*r3* is not a regular role of SO1),
Case 5: *SO1.org_unit* $\geq$ *r4.org_unit* (*r4* is not included in SO1's authority range),
Case 6: $\{p4\} \subseteq \{p1\}$ (*p1* is a unique permission of the regular role *r1*).

However, if the type of delegation is 'collaboration of work' [13], the delegation can be performed not by U1 but by a responsible senior security officer, DSO. We can review other delegation administration rules in a similar way, but for brevity's sake, we have omitted their reviews.

6 Conclusion

In this paper, we presented a new integrated management model, the OS-DRAM which satisfies the needs of delegation role administration and delegation policy in large decentralized organizations or information systems. Although delegation raises the degree of availability of individual users' access rights, it violates confidentiality and integrity in a distributed environment. Therefore, if the decentralized administrative access control model has no suitable way to control delegation, it may excessively restrict availability, or infringe upon confidentiality and integrity.

The main reasons why the OS-DRAM can support efficient decentralized access control management and available delegation policy are the separation of authority range and role hierarchy. Organizational structure plays on the boundary of delegation activity.

As a result, the OS-DRAM supports a decentralized user-level delegation in which individual users can freely delegate their authorities to other users within a security officer's authority range and without the security officer's intervention. This paper followed the multi-step delegation method of the PBDM. However, multi-step delegation is very difficult to perform. We will probe further as to what constitutes a secure multi-step delegation. In addition, we will add the 'Separation of Duty' constraint when a delegation role has two or more regular roles.

Acknowledgements

This research was supported by the MIC(Ministry of Information and Communication), Korea, under the ITRC(Information Technology Research Center) support program supervised by the IITA(Institute of Information Technology Assessment).

References

1. D. Ferraio, J. Cugini, and R. Kuhn, "Role-based Access Control (RBAC): Features and motivations", Proc. of 11th Annual Computer Security Application Conference, pp. 241-248, Dec. 1995.
2. R.Sandhu, E. J. Coyne, H. L. Feinstein, and C. E. Youman, "Role-Based Access Control Method", IEEE Computer, vol.29, pp. 38-47, Feb. 1996.
3. R. Sandhu, D. Ferraiolo, and D. Kuhn, "The NIST model for role-based access control: towards a unified standard", Proc. of Fifth ACM Workshop on Role-Based Access Control, pp. 47-63.
4. R. Sandhu, V. Bhamidipati, and Q. Munawer, "The ARBAC97 model for role-based admini-stration of roles", ACM Trans. Inf. And Syst. Sec. 1, 2, pp. 105-135.
5. S. I. Gavrila and J. F. Barkley, "Formal Specification for Role Based Access Control User/Role and Role/Role Relationship Management", Proc. of the 3rd ACM workshop on Role-Based Access Control, pp. 81-90, 1998.
6. R. Sandu, Q. Munawer, "The ARBAC99 Model for Administrative Roles", 15th Annual Conputer Security Applications Conference, pp. 229-240, Dec. 1999.
7. S. Oh and R. Sandhu, "A Model for Role Administration Using Organization Structure", Proc. of the 7th ACM Symposium on Access Control Models and Technologies (SACMAT 2002), pp. 155-162, June 2002.
8. F. Cuppens, P. Balbiani, S. Benferhat, Y. Deswarte, A. Abou El Kalam, R. El-baida, A. Mige, C. Saurel, and G. Trouessin, "Organization Based Access Control", Proc. of IEEE 4th Inter-national Workshop on Policies for Distributed Systems and Networks (POLICY 2003), pp. 120-130, Jun. 2003.
9. F. Cuppens and A. Mige, "Administration Model for Or-BAC", Workshop on Meta-data for Security, International Federated Conference (OTM'03), pp. 754-768, Nov. 2003.
10. S. Oh, C. Byun, and S. Park, "An Organizational Structure-Based Administration Model for Decentralized Access Control", Journal of Information Science and Engineering, 2005(submitted).
11. E. Barka and R. Sandhu, "A Role-Based Delegation Model and Some Extensions", Proc. Of 23rd National Information Systems Security Conference (NISSC) 2000.
12. Longhua Zhang, Gail-Joon Ahn, Bei-Tseng Chu, "A Rule-Based Framework for Role-Based Delegation and Revocation", ACM Transactions on Information and System Security, Vol.6, No.3, pp.404-441, Aug. 2004.
13. Xinwen Zhang, Sejong Oh and Ravi Sandhu, "PBDM: A Flexible Delegation Model in RBAC", Proc. 8th ACM Symposium on Access Control Models and Technologies (SACMAT), pp.149-157, 2003.

Author Index

Lecture Notes in Computer Science

For information about Vols. 1–3956

please contact your bookseller or Springer

Vol. 4060: K. Futatsugi, J.-P. Jouannaud, J. Meseguer (Eds.), Algebra, Meaning and Computation. XXXVIII, 643 pages. 2006.

Vol. 4058: L.M. Batten, R. Safavi-Naini (Eds.), Information Security and Privacy. XII, 446 pages. 2006.

Vol. 4055: J. Lee, J. Shim, S.-g. Lee, C. Bussler, S. Shim (Eds.), Data Engineering Issues in E-Commerce and Services. IX, 290 pages. 2006.

Vol. 4054: A. Horváth, M. Telek (Eds.), Formal Methods and Stochastic Models for Performance Evaluation. VIII, 239 pages. 2006.

Vol. 4053: M. Ikeda, K.D. Ashley, T.-W. Chan (Eds.), Intelligent Tutoring Systems. XXVI, 821 pages. 2006.

Vol. 4044: P. Abrahamsson, M. Marchesi, G. Succi (Eds.), Extreme Programming and Agile Processes in Software Engineering. XII, 230 pages. 2006.

Vol. 4043: A.S. Atzeni, A. Lioy (Eds.), Public Key Infrastructure. XI, 261 pages. 2006.

Vol. 4041: S.-W. Cheng, C.K. Poon (Eds.), Algorithmic Aspects in Information and Management. XI, 395 pages. 2006.

Vol. 4040: R. Reulke, U. Eckardt, B. Flach, U. Knauer, K. Polthier (Eds.), Combinatorial Image Analysis. XII, 482 pages. 2006.

Vol. 4039: M. Morisio (Ed.), Reuse of Off-the-Shelf Components. XIII, 444 pages. 2006.

Vol. 4038: P. Ciancarini, H. Wiklicky (Eds.), Coordination Models and Languages. VIII, 299 pages. 2006.

Vol. 4037: R. Gorrieri, H. Wehrheim (Eds.), Formal Methods for Open Object-Based Distributed Systems. XVII, 474 pages. 2006.

Vol. 4036: O. H. Ibarra, Z. Dang (Eds.), Developments in Language Theory. XII, 456 pages. 2006.

Vol. 4034: J. Münch, M. Vierimaa (Eds.), Product-Focused Software Process Improvement. XVII, 474 pages. 2006.

Vol. 4033: B. Stiller, P. Reichl, B. Tuffin (Eds.), Performability Has its Price. X, 103 pages. 2006.

Vol. 4031: M. Ali, R. Dapoigny (Eds.), Innovations in Applied Artificial Intelligence. XXIII, 1353 pages. 2006. (Sublibrary LNAI).

Vol. 4027: H.L. Larsen, G. Pasi, D. Ortiz-Arroyo, T. Andreasen, H. Christiansen (Eds.), Flexible Query Answering Systems. XVIII, 714 pages. 2006. (Sublibrary LNAI).

Vol. 4026: P. Gibbons, T. Abdelzaher, J. Aspnes, R. Rao (Eds.), Distributed Computing in Sensor Systems. XIV, 566 pages. 2006.

Vol. 4025: F. Eliassen, A. Montresor (Eds.), Distributed Applications and Interoperable Systems. XI, 355 pages. 2006.

Vol. 4024: S. Donatelli, P. S. Thiagarajan (Eds.), Petri Nets and Other Models of Concurrency - ICATPN 2006. XI, 441 pages. 2006.

Vol. 4021: E. André, L. Dybkjær, W. Minker, H. Neumann, M. Weber (Eds.), Perception and Interactive Technologies. XI, 217 pages. 2006. (Sublibrary LNAI).

Vol. 4020: A. Bredenfeld, A. Jacoff, I. Noda, Y. Takahashi, RoboCup 2005: Robot Soccer World Cup IX. XVII, 727 pages. 2006. (Sublibrary LNAI).

Vol. 4018: V. Wade, H. Ashman, B. Smyth (Eds.), Adaptive Hypermedia and Adaptive Web-Based Systems. XVI, 474 pages. 2006.

Vol. 4016: J.X. Yu, M. Kitsuregawa, H.V. Leong (Eds.), Advances in Web-Age Information Management. XVII, 606 pages. 2006.

Vol. 4013: L. Lamontagne, M. Marchand (Eds.), Advances in Artificial Intelligence. XIII, 564 pages. 2006. (Sublibrary LNAI).

Vol. 4012: T. Washio, A. Sakurai, K. Nakashima, H. Takeda, S. Tojo, M. Yokoo (Eds.), New Frontiers in Artificial Intelligence. XIII, 484 pages. 2006. (Sublibrary LNAI).

Vol. 4011: Y. Sure, J. Domingue (Eds.), The Semantic Web: Research and Applications. XIX, 726 pages. 2006.

Vol. 4010: S. Dunne, B. Stoddart (Eds.), Unifying Theories of Programming. VIII, 257 pages. 2006.

Vol. 4009: M. Lewenstein, G. Valiente (Eds.), Combinatorial Pattern Matching. XII, 414 pages. 2006.

Vol. 4007: C. Àlvarez, M. Serna (Eds.), Experimental Algorithms. XI, 329 pages. 2006.

Vol. 4006: L.M. Pinho, M. González Harbour (Eds.), Reliable Software Technologies – Ada-Europe 2006. XII, 241 pages. 2006.

Vol. 4005: G. Lugosi, H.U. Simon (Eds.), Learning Theory. XI, 656 pages. 2006. (Sublibrary LNAI).

Vol. 4004: S. Vaudenay (Ed.), Advances in Cryptology - EUROCRYPT 2006. XIV, 613 pages. 2006.

Vol. 4003: Y. Koucheryavy, J. Harju, V.B. Iversen (Eds.), Next Generation Teletraffic and Wired/Wireless Advanced Networking. XVI, 582 pages. 2006.

Vol. 4001: E. Dubois, K. Pohl (Eds.), Advanced Information Systems Engineering. XVI, 560 pages. 2006.

Vol. 3999: C. Kop, G. Fliedl, H.C. Mayr, E. Métais (Eds.), Natural Language Processing and Information Systems. XIII, 227 pages. 2006.

Vol. 3998: T. Calamoneri, I. Finocchi, G.F. Italiano (Eds.), Algorithms and Complexity. XII, 394 pages. 2006.

Vol. 3997: W. Grieskamp, C. Weise (Eds.), Formal Approaches to Software Testing. XII, 219 pages. 2006.

Vol. 3996: A. Keller, J.-P. Martin-Flatin (Eds.), Self-Managed Networks, Systems, and Services. X, 185 pages. 2006.

Vol. 3995: G. Müller (Ed.), Emerging Trends in Information and Communication Security. XX, 524 pages. 2006.

Vol. 3994: V.N. Alexandrov, G.D. van Albada, P.M.A. Sloot, J. Dongarra (Eds.), Computational Science – ICCS 2006, Part IV. XXXV, 1096 pages. 2006.

Vol. 3993: V.N. Alexandrov, G.D. van Albada, P.M.A. Sloot, J. Dongarra (Eds.), Computational Science – ICCS 2006, Part III. XXXVI, 1136 pages. 2006.

Vol. 3992: V.N. Alexandrov, G.D. van Albada, P.M.A. Sloot, J. Dongarra (Eds.), Computational Science – ICCS 2006, Part II. XXXV, 1122 pages. 2006.

Vol. 3991: V.N. Alexandrov, G.D. van Albada, P.M.A. Sloot, J. Dongarra (Eds.), Computational Science – ICCS 2006, Part I. LXXXI, 1096 pages. 2006.

Vol. 3990: J. C. Beck, B.M. Smith (Eds.), Integration of AI and OR Techniques in Constraint Programming for Combinatorial Optimization Problems. X, 301 pages. 2006.

Vol. 3989: J. Zhou, M. Yung, F. Bao, Applied Cryptography and Network Security. XIV, 488 pages. 2006.

Vol. 3987: M. Hazas, J. Krumm, T. Strang (Eds.), Location- and Context-Awareness. X, 289 pages. 2006.

Vol. 3986: K. Stølen, W.H. Winsborough, F. Martinelli, F. Massacci (Eds.), Trust Management. XIV, 474 pages. 2006.

Vol. 3984: M. Gavrilova, O. Gervasi, V. Kumar, C.J. K. Tan, D. Taniar, A. Laganà, Y. Mun, H. Choo (Eds.), Computational Science and Its Applications - ICCSA 2006, Part V. XXV, 1045 pages. 2006.

Vol. 3983: M. Gavrilova, O. Gervasi, V. Kumar, C.J. K. Tan, D. Taniar, A. Laganà, Y. Mun, H. Choo (Eds.), Computational Science and Its Applications - ICCSA 2006, Part IV. XXVI, 1191 pages. 2006.

Vol. 3982: M. Gavrilova, O. Gervasi, V. Kumar, C.J. K. Tan, D. Taniar, A. Laganà, Y. Mun, H. Choo (Eds.), Computational Science and Its Applications - ICCSA 2006, Part III. XXV, 1243 pages. 2006.

Vol. 3981: M. Gavrilova, O. Gervasi, V. Kumar, C.J. K. Tan, D. Taniar, A. Laganà, Y. Mun, H. Choo (Eds.), Computational Science and Its Applications - ICCSA 2006, Part II. XXVI, 1255 pages. 2006.

Vol. 3980: M. Gavrilova, O. Gervasi, V. Kumar, C.J. K. Tan, D. Taniar, A. Laganà, Y. Mun, H. Choo (Eds.), Computational Science and Its Applications - ICCSA 2006, Part I. LXXV, 1199 pages. 2006.

Vol. 3979: T.S. Huang, N. Sebe, M.S. Lew, V. Pavlović, M. Kölsch, A. Galata, B. Kisačanin (Eds.), Computer Vision in Human-Computer Interaction. XII, 121 pages. 2006.

Vol. 3978: B. Hnich, M. Carlsson, F. Fages, F. Rossi (Eds.), Recent Advances in Constraints. VIII, 179 pages. 2006. (Sublibrary LNAI).

Vol. 3977: N. Fuhr, M. Lalmas, S. Malik, G. Kazai (Eds.), Advances in XML Information Retrieval and Evaluation. XII, 556 pages. 2006.

Vol. 3976: F. Boavida, T. Plagemann, B. Stiller, C. Westphal, E. Monteiro (Eds.), Networking 2006. Networking Technologies, Services, and Protocols; Performance of Computer and Communication Networks; Mobile and Wireless Communications Systems. XXVI, 1276 pages. 2006.

Vol. 3975: S. Mehrotra, D.D. Zeng, H. Chen, B.M. Thuraisingham, F.-Y. Wang (Eds.), Intelligence and Security Informatics. XXII, 772 pages. 2006.

Vol. 3973: J. Wang, Z. Yi, J.M. Zurada, B.-L. Lu, H. Yin (Eds.), Advances in Neural Networks - ISNN 2006, Part III. XXIX, 1402 pages. 2006.

Vol. 3972: J. Wang, Z. Yi, J.M. Zurada, B.-L. Lu, H. Yin (Eds.), Advances in Neural Networks - ISNN 2006, Part II. XXVII, 1444 pages. 2006.

Vol. 3971: J. Wang, Z. Yi, J.M. Zurada, B.-L. Lu, H. Yin (Eds.), Advances in Neural Networks - ISNN 2006, Part I. LXVII, 1442 pages. 2006.

Vol. 3970: T. Braun, G. Carle, S. Fahmy, Y. Koucheryavy (Eds.), Wired/Wireless Internet Communications. XIV, 350 pages. 2006.

Vol. 3969: Ø. Ytrehus (Ed.), Coding and Cryptography. XI, 443 pages. 2006.

Vol. 3968: K.P. Fishkin, B. Schiele, P. Nixon, A. Quigley (Eds.), Pervasive Computing. XV, 402 pages. 2006.

Vol. 3967: D. Grigoriev, J. Harrison, E.A. Hirsch (Eds.), Computer Science – Theory and Applications. XVI, 684 pages. 2006.

Vol. 3966: Q. Wang, D. Pfahl, D.M. Raffo, P. Wernick (Eds.), Software Process Change. XIV, 356 pages. 2006.

Vol. 3965: M. Bernardo, A. Cimatti (Eds.), Formal Methods for Hardware Verification. VII, 243 pages. 2006.

Vol. 3964: M. Ü. Uyar, A.Y. Duale, M.A. Fecko (Eds.), Testing of Communicating Systems. XI, 373 pages. 2006.

Vol. 3963: O. Dikenelli, M.-P. Gleizes, A. Ricci (Eds.), Engineering Societies in the Agents World VI. XII, 303 pages. 2006. (Sublibrary LNAI).

Vol. 3962: W. IJsselsteijn, Y. de Kort, C. Midden, B. Eggen, E. van den Hoven (Eds.), Persuasive Technology. XII, 216 pages. 2006.

Vol. 3960: R. Vieira, P. Quaresma, M.d.G.V. Nunes, N.J. Mamede, C. Oliveira, M.C. Dias (Eds.), Computational Processing of the Portuguese Language. XII, 274 pages. 2006. (Sublibrary LNAI).

Vol. 3959: J.-Y. Cai, S. B. Cooper, A. Li (Eds.), Theory and Applications of Models of Computation. XV, 794 pages. 2006.

Vol. 3958: M. Yung, Y. Dodis, A. Kiayias, T. Malkin (Eds.), Public Key Cryptography - PKC 2006. XIV, 543 pages. 2006.